D1747340

ATĪŚA AND TIBET

ATĪŚA AND TIBET

Life and Works of Dīpaṃkara Śrījñāna
in relation to the
History and Religion of Tibet
With Tibetan Sources
translated under
PROFESSOR LAMA CHIMPA

ALAKA CHATTOPADHYAYA

MOTILAL BANARSIDASS PUBLISHERS
PRIVATE LIMITED • DELHI

First Edition: Calcutta, 1967
Reprint: Delhi, 1981, 1996

ISBN: 81-208-0928-9

Also available at:

MOTILAL BANARSIDASS

41 U.A. Bungalow Road, Jawahar Nagar, Delhi 110 007
120 Royapettah High Road, Mylapore, Madras 600 004
16 St. Mark's Road, Bangalore 560 001
Ashok Rajpath, Patna 800 004
Chowk, Varanasi 221 001

PRINTED IN INDIA
BY JAINENDRA PRAKASH JAIN AT SHRI JAINENDRA PRESS,
A-45 NARAINA, PHASE I, NEW DELHI 110 028
AND PUBLISHED BY NARENDRA PRAKASH JAIN FOR
MOTILAL BANARSIDASS PUBLISHERS PRIVATE LIMITED,
BUNGALOW ROAD, DELHI 110 007

Author's Preface

But for the initial encouragement and general guidance of Dr. Niharranjan Ray, now Director, Indian Institute of Advanced Study, Simla, I could not have started the work at all and without the ungrudging help of Professor Lama Chimpa of the Visvabharati University I could never have completed it. As a matter of fact, while sponsoring the research, the first step taken by Dr. Niharranjan Ray was to create for me the scope for learning the Tibetan language and studying the Tibetan texts under Professor Lama Chimpa. Dr. Ray wrote to authorities of the Visvabharati University requesting them to grant me the facilities for studying there under Professor Lama Chimpa and he also made a personal request to Professor Lama Chimpa to help me. I am extremely grateful to the authorities of the Visvabharati University for granting me all the facilities I required and my indebtedness to Professor Lama Chimpa is certainly much more than I can adequately express. The views soemtimes expressed in this work are mine, and so of course are its errors. Without the patient help of Professor Lama Chimpa, however, these views would have been inadequately substantiated and the errors would have been too many.

In the matter of editing the manuscript and brushing up its language, the most arduous task has been that of Sri Radhamohan Bhattacharyya, who has kindly corrected the entire manuscript excepting only the *Appendices*. If I hesitate to be explicit about the extent of my real indebtedness to him, it is only because with his characteristic modesty he is likely to be annoyed by it.

The manuscript of *Appendix C* (and partly of *Appendix A*) is kindly revised by Professor Benoyendra Mohan Choudhuri, Department of Humanities, Indian Institute of Technology,

Kharagpur, on whose kind help I have also relied in many other ways.

To Dr. D. C. Sircar, Carmichael Professor of Ancient Indian History, Calcutta University, I am grateful for not only allowing me to quote from his manuscript on *Indian Paleography* but also for revising my chapter on the origin of the Tibetan script (Section 22).

Dr. R. N. Bhattacharya of the Department of Mathematics, Jadavpur University, helped me by evolving simpler methods of tackling the Tibetan calendar. The calculations forming the basis of *Appendix D* are entirely his.

To my colleague Professor Sunil Munshi, Department of Geography, Vidyasagar College, Calcutta, I am indebted for clarifications of many a problem concerning medieval Asian geography and most particularly for helping me to trace the possible route of Dīpaṃkara to western Tibet.

While I was working under Professor Lama Chimpa for the translation of Dīpaṃkara's *Bodhi-patha-pradīpa*, another colleague of mine, Professor Mrinalkanti Gangopadhyaya, Department of Sanskrit, Vidyasagar College, Calcutta, joined us and, depending on strict Sanskrit equivalents of Tibetan words, attempted a restoration of the original text. I am thankful to him for allowing me to incorporate it into my *Appendix C.*

To Principal Keshaveswar Bose of Sibnath Sastri College, Calcutta, I am grateful for helping me to get many rare books which I needed for the work.

The Librarians and their assistants of the Calcutta University Library, the Cheena-bhavana Library of the Visvabharati University, the Asiatic Society Library and the National Library, Calcutta, have always extended their help and cooperation to me. I cannot indeed thank them enough.

To my husband Debiprasad I am indebted for discussions on Buddhist philosophy and very much else besides.

●

For using more or less long extracts, I want to express full gratitude to the following in particular : The Asiatic Society,

Calcutta (for extracts from the *Blue Annals*), the publishers of the *Indian Historical Quaterly* (for extracts from Petech), of the *Journal of the Buddhist Text Society* (for extracts from S. C. Das), W. Heffer & Sons Ltd., Cambridge (for extracts from Waddell's *Lamaism*), Oxford University Press (for extracts from Richardson's *Tibet and its History*), the Archaeological Survey of India (for extracts from Francke's *Antiquities of Indian Tibet*), etc. etc. Quotations from other works are acknowledged in the notes.

Vidyasagar College for Women,
Calcutta.
January 10, 1967

Alaka Chattopadhaya

Transliteration, Notes and References

1. Tibetan words are given according to their spellings and not according to their pronunciations. (Words occurring even within quotations are usually changed to follow this uniform principle).
2. Transliteration of Tibetan words is broadly based on the principles followed by S. C. Das in his *Tibetan-English Dictionary*, only with this difference that apostrophe-sign (') instead of *h* is used for the Tibetan letter འ
3. In cases of Tibetan proper names, only the first letter actually pronounced is given in capital, lower case types being used for silent prefixes.
4. In cases of there being a single work by an author in the Bibliography, the notes mention only his name (which is followed by the volume-number and page-number without the usual abbreviations "Vol." and "P."). In cases, however, of there being more than one work by the same author included in the Bibliography, the notes mention the author's name followed by the initials of the particular work referred to.
5. When the notes refer to the contribution by an author to a Journal or to a Reference Work, the word "in" is put between the name of the contributor and the initials of the Journal, etc.
6. Texts of the bsTan-'gyur are mentioned in the notes according to their numbers in Cordier's *Catalogue.*

CONTENTS

Part III

Atiśa in Tibet

APPENDICES

Appendix A

Biographical Materials : Tibetan Sources rendered into English

Appendix B

The Works of Dīpaṃkara

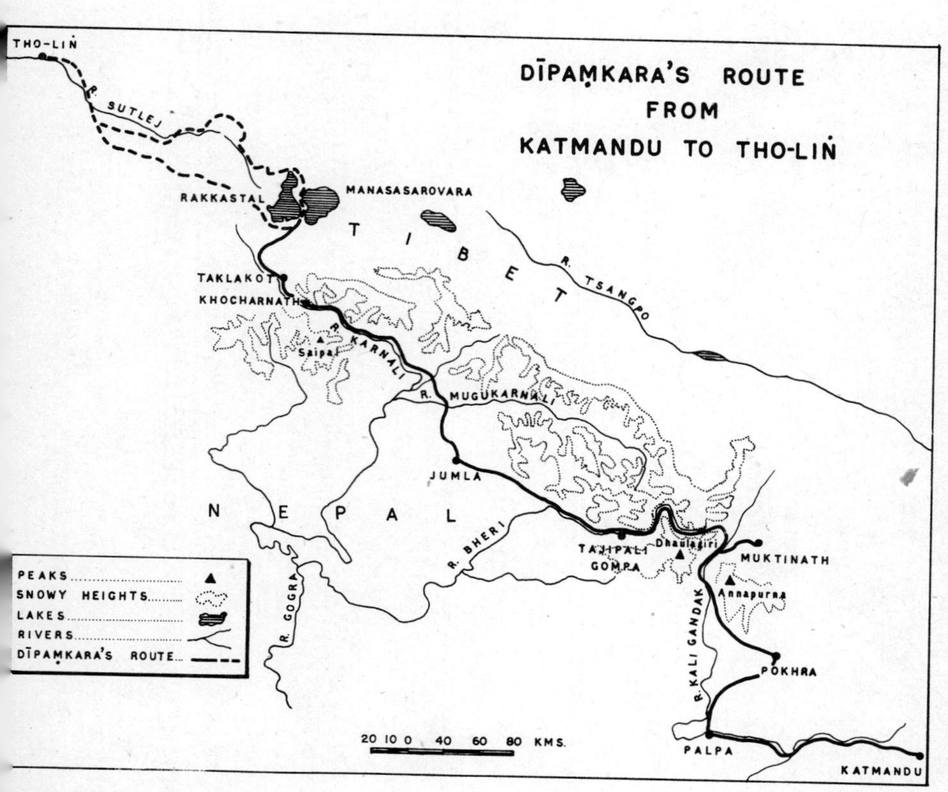

ap kindly prepared by
ail Munshi, Professor of Geography,
tre for Studies in Social Sciences, Calcutta.

PART I
INTRODUCTORY AND EARLY CAREER

ཇོ་བོ་ཆེན་པོ་དཔལ་ལྡན་ཨ་ཏི་ཤ་ལ་ན་མོ།

1. Dipamkara in the Religious History of India and Tibet

Notwithstanding the uncertainties about our knowledge of some of the details of the life and activities of Dīpaṃkara Śrījñāna —*alias* Atīśa—his importance in the religious history of India and Tibet is, on the whole, clear and unmistakable. He was in fact a landmark in both,—being about the last of the great Buddhist *ācārya*-s in India and, though not the first, he is remembered in Tibetan tradition itself as by far the greatest of the teacher-reformers of Tibet. From this follows also his stature in the world-history of Buddhism. For Tibet, as is well-known, is one of the important centres to have kept the flame of Buddhism alive after it had been almost[1] completely extinguished in the land where it kindled first.

Our historians have already explained the circumstances in which, after Dīpaṃkara, there could hardly be any Buddhist teacher of great eminence in India. By the middle of the eleventh century, the time of Dīpaṃkara's departure for Tibet, Buddhism in India—or, more specifically, in Eastern India, its last Indian stronghold—was already facing a serious crisis. The crisis was both external and internal. Externally, the Pāla rulers, on whose active support Buddhism vitally depended for the last phase of its history in India,[2] were then themselves facing impending breakdown of their kingdom.[3] Only about a century after Dīpaṃkara left India, the Pālas, too, driven out of their last refuge by the Senas, "passed out of

1. For survival of Buddhism in Bengal after A.D. 1200, see P. C. Bagchi in HB i. 418n ; Waddell L 16n. 2. R C. Majumdar in HB i. 101 : "for nearly four hundred years their court proved to be the last stronghold of that dying faith in India" ; cf. P. C. Bagchi in HB i.416.
3. HB i. 144ff.

history."[4] "The Sena kings do not seem to have had any special leaning towards Buddhism, and Buddhism does not seem to have had any patronage from them. The Buddhist institutions soon disappeared for want of royal support, and those which lingered on did not appear to have long survived the invasion of Muhammad Bakhtyār."[5]

Bakhtyār's attack on the Buddhist monasteries, attested to by both the Muslim[6] and Buddhist[7] sources, is generally considered responsible for the final extinction of Buddhism in India : "The Muhammadan invasion swept over India in the latter end of the twelfth century A. D. and effectually stamped Buddhism out of the country. The fanatical idol-hating Afghan soldiery especially attacked the Buddhist monasteries, with their teeming idols, and they massacred the monks wholesale ; and as the Buddhist religion, unlike the more domestic Brahmanism, is dependent on its priests and monks for its vitality, it soon disappeared in the absence of these latter."[8]

But the persecution of Buddhism in India or abroad was not entirely unprecedented[9] and it is difficult to believe that external aggression alone could root out a religion from a country in the way in which Buddhism was virtually rooted out of India by the middle of the thirteenth century. For a fuller explanation of this, therefore, we have also to take note of the internal decay of Buddhism, to which eminent scholars rightly draw our attention.

"Buddhism under the Pālas," says P. C. Bagchi,[10]

4. *Ib*. i. 171. 5. P. C. Bagchi in HB i. 418. 6. *Tabaqāt-i-Nāsirī* quoted in HB i.242 ; cf. Elliot ii. 306 ; Sankalia 212. 7. Sum-pa 112. 8. Waddell L 16 ; cf. Waddell in JASB lxvi. 20ff. 9. Sogen, 16, depending on Hiuen Tsang, says, "Too well-known to mention here is the royal mandate of Śaśāṅka, king of Karṇasuvarṇa, commanding the utter extermination of Buddhists from the face of India with the unwholesome alternative of the penalty of death to be inflicted on the executioners themselves in case they neglected to carry out the inhuman order of the king and master." P. C. Bagchi in HB i. 416 suspects exaggeration in this account. The persecution of Buddhism in Tibet by gLaṅ Dar-ma will be discussed later. 10. P. C. Bagchi in HB i. 419.

"appears to have been completely different from the Buddhism which even Hiuen Tsang describes in the middle of the seventh century A. D. The ancient schools, like Sarvāstivāda, Sammatīya etc., are no longer spoken of in Eastern India, and the trace of pure Mahāyāna that we discover in the invocations used by kings in their inscriptions does not give a correct picture of the Buddhism of the period. The Mahāyāna had developed forms of mysticism which are known as Vajrayāna and Tantrayāna." "The ancient Vinaya schools like Sarvāstivāda, Mahāsāṅghika, etc., had only a limited scope for giving initiation to the novices ; but the more complicated domain of Mahāyāna practices was reserved for those who had special initiation in Vajrayāna, Sahajayāna and Kālacakrayāna."[11] As a result, "Buddhism was soon unhinged. As time passed on, less and less importance was attached to the ceremonial aspect which still retained a faint stamp of Buddhism. The ceremonial being once completely eliminated, it was not long before what remained of Buddhism was absorbed in the Brahmanical Tāntric system of Bengal."[12]

That by the time of Dīpaṃkara's departure for Tibet Buddhism in India was clearly on its decline is attested to by the Tibetan sources. 'Brom-ston-pa, the chief Tibetan disciple of Atīśa, said that "at the time the Master left India, Buddhism was, as it were, at its lowest ebb."[13] The Tibetan scholar Tshul-khrims-rgyal-ba (Jayaśīla) of Nag-tsho, who came to India and stayed at the Vikramaśīla *vihāra* for inviting Atīśa to Tibet, said that during Dīpaṃkara's time

At Odantapurī,
There were 53 monks.
At Vikramaśīla,
There were about a hundred monks.[14]

There being so few monks in these *vihāra*-s, as Roerich[15] rightly points out, "shows that at the beginning of the 11th century A. D. the monastic colleges of Odantapurī and Vikramaśīla were already falling into decay."

11. *Ib.* i. 420. 12. *Ib.* i. 421-2. 13. Quoted by Rahula in *2500 Years* 236. 14. Quted by Roerich in BA i. 243n. 15. *Ib.*

This process of decay, aided by the impact of the Muslim conquest of Eastern India, left, within a period of about two hundred years, the famous centres of Buddhism like Vajrāsana (Buddhagayā) and Nālandā almost completely desolate and deserted. Here is an interesting Tibetan evidence of the condition of these Buddhist centres by the first half of the thirteenth century A. D. 'Gos lo-tsā-ba, one of the most respected of the Tibetan historians, describes as follows the Indian adventure of a Tibetan scholar called Chag Chos-rje-dpal, who was born in A. D. 1197[16] and who came to India shortly after A.D. 1216[17] : "After that he proceeded to India. He visited Vaiśālī *via* Tirhut. In a dream he had a clear vision of Vajrāsana. On reaching Vajrāsana, he found that there was no one there, all having fled from fear of Turuṣka troops. For a long time he was unable to see the Mahābodhi image (for the doors of the *vihāra* were blocked with bricks). Later he saw the image, made offerings to the Mahābodhi, and examined the sacred place. At Nālandā he met the *paṇḍita* Rāhula Śrībhadra and obtained from him many doctrines. The Gar-log troops (Qarluq : here the name designates Muhammedan troops) arrived there, all the natives and their king fled away. Rāhula said to Chag : 'I, being ninety years old, am unable to flee away. But you, fool, why don't you go away ?' Chag replied : 'Even if murdered, I could not separate from my Teacher !' Rāhula having found him to be a trustworthy person, became pleased from the bottom of his heart. Having taken his Teacher on his back, he carried him to a temple of Mahākāla, which was feared by the Gar-log troops, and the latter did not harm them. In Magadha he caught fever, and when the fever left him, (his body) became covered with sores. He again caught fever in Tirhut. Slowly he journeyed to Tibet."[18] According to the same historian, Dīpaṃkara left India for Tibet in A.D. 1040.[19]

16. BA ii. 1057. 17. *Ib.* ii. 1056-7. 18. *Ib.* ii. 1058.
19. *Ib.* i. 247.

Thus Buddhagayā and Nālandā were ruined within a period of hardly two hundred years after that.[20]

Our knowledge of Buddhism for the period intervening between Dīpaṃkara's departure for Tibet and the fall of these Buddhist *vihāra*-s in Eastern India is necessarily obscure and uncertain. We have today to depend for this mainly on the Tibetans, who, in their turn, had to depend largely on rumours floating from India to Tibet,—rumours that were interested mainly in the miraculous. In this confused heap of Tibetan legends, certain names of Indian *ācārya*-s after Dīpaṃkara are found to occur, of course. But we have hardly anything about any of them that can be considered as positive evidence of great eminence. Thus, e.g. Bu-ston,[21] after describing the coming of Atīśa to Tibet, mentions a long list of Indian *paṇḍita*-s, like Kashmirian Jñānaśrī, Candrarāhula, Parahitabhadra, Bhavyarāja, Sajjana, Amaragomin, Sthirapāla, Atulyadāsa, Sumatikīrti, Amaracandra, Kumārakalaśa, Kanakavarman, Gayadhara, etc., etc. But the historian has nothing to say about them beyond this that they were invited to Tibet and took part in the Tibetan translation of one or two Buddhist works. It is true that 'Gos lo-tsā-ba has a great deal to say about the Kashmirian *paṇḍita* Śākyaśrībhadra, who came to Tibet in A.D. 1204 at the age of seventyeight, spent ten years in Tibet, went back to Kashmir in A.D. 1214 and died there in A.D. 1225.[22] However, apart from Sum-pa's[23] statement that he was the last abbot of the Vikramaśīla *vihāra*, which he left just before its fall, we know practically nothing about his Indian career. 'Gos lo-tsā-ba describes the great influence he had in Tibet and his name remains associated in the bsTan-'gyur with a considerable amount of literary output.[24] But neither from the point of view of his success in

20. Samaddar, 161, gives the date of the destruction of Nālandā, Vikramaśīla and Odantapurī as A. D. 1199 ; Sankalia, 213f, suggests A. D. 1205-6 as the date of the destruction of Nālandā. But these dates do not agree with the Tibetan evidence just quoted, according to which Chag came to India after A. D. 1216 (BA ii. 1056). 21. Bu-ston ii. 215f. 22. BA ii. 1063ff. 23. Sum-pa 121. 24. The bsTan-'gyur contains

Tibet nor from that of his literary activities, Śākyaśrībhadra stands even any remote comparison with Dīpaṃkara-śrī-jñāna. The other Indian *ācārya* after Dīpaṃkara specially glorified by 'Gos lo-tsā-ba was Vanaratna, who reached Tibet in A. D. 1426[25] and is often called "The Last Paṇḍita." He preached Kālacakra Tantrism, took part in literary activity of some significance[26] and, according to 'Gos lo-tsā-ba, "seems to have been the most popular among the *paṇḍita*-s who visited Tibet in later times."[27] But, again, any comparison of his stature with that of Dīpaṃkara in the religious history of India or Tibet is inconceivable.

Thus, in short, the conditions in India after Dīpaṃkara were not favourable for the appearance of great Buddhist teachers and there was surely none of Dīpaṃkara's eminence. Other considerations apart, his sheer literary output verges almost on the fabulous. Yet Dīpaṃkara is remembered primarily because of the last phase of his career, namely his activities in Tibet, in the religious history of which his position is, in an important sense, without parallel.

There is no doubt that among his Indian predecessors[28] who had been to Tibet, Śāntarakṣita and Kamalaśīla in particular, judging them by their extant works, were great philosophers dialectically defending the Mahāyāna views. Compared to them, Dīpaṃkara himself was perhaps temparamentally more inclined to moral precepts and practices conducive to meditation, though of course not at the cost of logical and philosophical discussions. And though the Tibetan tradition has no dearth of miraculous legends about Dīpaṃkara ,the same tradition remembers Padmasambhava, the Tāntrika contemporary of Śāntarakṣita, as a far greater wielder of magical spells and charms. Besides, the founding of the bSam-yas monastery, with which the names of Śāntarakṣita and

25 works attributed to Śākyaśrī, one to Śākyaśrījñāna and 34 to Śākyaśrībhadra. 25. BA ii. 799ff. 26. The bsTan-'gyur contains 24 works attributed to Vanaratna. Also one attributed to Vanaratnapāda. 27. BA ii. 802. 28. For Śāntarakṣita, Padmasambhava and Kamalaśīla, See Sections 25-6.

Padmasambhava are so persistently connected by the Tibetan tradition, had undoubtedly been an event of great significance for the spread of Buddhism in Tibet, and, incidentally, also for the preservation of a large number of Buddhist texts lost and forgotten in India. Further, the defeat of the Chinese *ho-shang* Mahāyāna by Kamalaśīla, according to the Tibetan historians themselves, was an event of great significance for the spread of the Doctrine in Tibet.

Still, not to speak of the other Indian *ācārya*-s who preached Buddhism in Tibet—and according to a list prepared by S. C. Das[29] there were no less than eightynine of them—the influence even of Śāntarakṣita and others in the development of Buddhism in Tibet was neither as profound nor as enduring as that of Dīpaṃkara. It will perhaps be argued that the memory of Padmasambhava has a greater halo in Tibetan history. He is "now deified and as celebrated in Lāmaism as Buddha himself, than whom, indeed, he receives among several sects more worship."[30] But his memory is cherished in certain circles of Tibet not so much for the preaching of the Buddhist doctrine there as for the performance of certain grotesque miracles by which he subdued the equally grotesque devils of the land and recruited them to his following. From this point of view, Padmasambhava perhaps helped the perpetuation of the older faith of Tibet against which Buddhism had to fight for centuries before being finally victorious. In Tibet, as H. P. Sastri says, "Dīpaṃkara is worshipped as a god by thousands of people even today."[31] But this is essentially different from the awe which Padmasambhava, the great sorcerer, inspires today in certain quarters of Tibet. As Waddell puts it, "Atiśa is held to be an incarnation of Mañjuśrī, the Bodhisat of Wisdom : which is merely a way of stating that he was the greatest embodiment of Buddhist Wisdom that ever visited Tibet."[32] This is fully confirmed by the way in which the Tibetan historians and scholars repeatedly assert that Tibet remains ever-grateful to

29. S. C. Das in JBTS I. i. 1-2. 30. Waddell L 24. 31. H. P. Sastri, *Prācīn Bāṅglār Gaurava* (Bengali) 25. 32. Waddell L 62.

him for the purity of the Doctrine he preached. In the *stotra* to Dīpaṃkara, 'Brom-ston-pa says,

> Though Buddhism could exist in Tibet even without the arrival there of a great scholar like thee, yet many people (in Tibet) were mistaken about its deeper significance and thou gave them the right teaching ; to thy feet I offer prayer.[33]

Thus, in short, Dīpaṃkara's success in the history of Tibetan Buddhism is quite unique and this in spite of the intrinsic greatness of some of his predecessors. How are we to account for this ?

It will perhaps be suggested that the terrible persecution of Buddhism by gLaṅ Dar-ma, which intervened between the activities of Śāntarakṣita and the arrival of Dīpaṃkara in Tibet, largely accounts for the difference in their historical success. For, though Waddell[34] thinks that "gLaṅ Dar-ma's persecution was very mild for a religious one, and very short-lived", that is not the way in which the Tibetan historians of Tibet want us to look back at it. According to the account usually given by them, gLaṅ Dar-ma virtually annihilated Buddhism in Tibet, or, as they put it, because of this persecution, "the Doctrine was rooted out"[35], or, "the Doctrine ceased to exist."[36] Tibet witnessed "the second beginning of Buddhism" or "Later spread of the Doctrine"[37] only some years before the arrival of Dīpaṃkara there. Thus the edifice built by Śāntarakṣita and others was violently demolished while Dīpaṃkara had the advantage of working when an influential section of the Tibetans including the ruling family of Western Tibet showed new enthusiasm for rebuilding it.

Practically the same suggestion may be put forth in a different way. The tenacity of the priests and priestesses of the Bon religion,[38] with which they clung to the older faith of Tibet and with which the persecution of Buddhism by gLaṅ Dar-ma

33. Appendix A, Section 2, *śloka* 11. The Tibetan historians, generally speaking, assert that Atīśa purified Buddhism in Tibet. See Appendix A Sections 3 and 5. 34. Waddell L 34. 35. Bu-ston ii. 199. 36. BA i. 53. 37. *Ib.* i. 63ff ; Bu-ston ii. 201ff. 38. For Bon religion, see Section 19

was not unconnected after all, had to recede before Buddhism could gain solid ground in Tibet. Besides, it was necessary for the Tibetans to achieve sufficient cultural progress—including progress in literacy—before being able to receive and retain the influence of the Buddhist scriptures preached to them. During the time of the great predecessors of Dīpaṃkara, these conditions were far from being fulfilled. Śāntarakṣita and others had to work against very stiff resistance and under the most adverse conditions, trying as they did to teach abstruse Buddhist philosophy in a country where the first introduction of literacy was then barely a century old—not to speak of the organised force with which the effects of their teachings were eventually sought to be wiped out. However, by the time of Dīpaṃkara's arrival in Tibet, the representatives of the Bon religion were clearly on the defensive, having little or no active support of the royal families behind them. Moreover, by this time Tibet made sufficient cultural progress and was ready to receive Buddhism properly. As Waddell,[39] referring to the reforms of Dīpaṃkara, says, "Perhaps the time was now ripe for the reform, as the Lāmas had become a large and influential body, and possessed a fairly full and scholarly translation of the bulky Mahāyāna Canon and its Commentaries, which taught a doctrine very different from that then practised in Tibet."

The main point of all these is that Dīpaṃkara's success in Tibet is largely to be accounted for by the external circumstances that favoured him. The obvious truth in this need not, of course, be doubted. But the risk of taking this as the whole truth is equally obvious. That compared to his predecessors Dīpaṃkara was favoured much by the external circumstances is quite clear. But can we expect the full explanation of his success from the mere fact of the external circumstances favouring him ? The answer is in the negative. For there is the evidence of another Indian *ācārya* who went to Tibet and

39. Waddell L 54.

worked there under the same or similar circumstances, but whose success, compared to that of Dīpaṃkara, was only negligible.

He was *ācārya* Dharmapāla[40] of Eastern India, a senior contemporary of Dīpaṃkara, who went to Tibet being invited by the Tibetan king Lha-rgyal bLa-ma Ye-śes-'od (Devarāja Guru Jñānaprabha). This ruler of Western Tibet was an ardent Buddhist, whose great fame in Tibetan history was primarily because of the way he sacrificed his life to the cause of bringing some great Indian *paṇḍita* to Tibet for purifying the corrupt form of religious practices then prevalent there.[41] Dīpaṃkara went to Tibet shortly after his death, depending mainly on the patronage of his family. However, *ācārya* Dharmapāla was invited to Tibet by the king Ye-śes-'od himself and was evidently very highly respected. In a poem quoted by 'Gos lo-tsā-ba we read,

Lha-rgyal bLa-ma Ye-śes-'od,
Known as a manifestation of Mañjuśrī,
as prophesised in the great Mūla Tantra[41a]
built the incomparable and miraculous *vihāra*
of Tho-liṅ.
From Eastern India, a learned monk, endowed with the
thunder of Fame,
the lofty banner of glory,
apparent to all, named Dharmapāla,
was invited by Ye-śes-'od.
He, whose mind was exhorted by the Sun of Mercy,
in order to promulgate the Precious Doctrine,
acted as *upādhyāya*, and spread the Meditative Lineage.[42]

Thus Dharmapāla went to Tibet when the organised resistance to Buddhism there was already on its decline and when at least parts of Tibet were being swept by the wave of Buddhist renaissance which shortly afterwards brought Dīpaṃkara there. Still his success in Tibet cannot stand even any remote comparison to that of Dīpaṃkara.

40. S. C. Das in JASB, 1881. 236; cf. BA i. 69 & 83f.
41. See section 29.
41a. The *Mañjuśrī-mūla-tantra*.
42. BA i. 84.

Bu-ston[43] refers to him only cursorily as one under whom rGyal-ba'i Śes-rab of Shaṅ-shuṅ "took order." What Sum-pa[44] has to say about him is summed up by S. C. Das as follows : "The great Buddhist sage Dharmapāla of Prācya (modern Darbhanga or Bihar), while sojourning in Nepal, on pilgrimage, was invited by king Ye-śes-'od to Tibet. He accepted the tutorship of the king. Dharmapāla had ordained three Tibetans into the Holy Order and given them Indian religious names, all ending in Pāla. From one of them, named Prajñāpāla, rGyal-ba'i Śes-rab of Shaṅ-shuṅ took the holy vow and proceeded to Nepal, where he learnt the practices of Vinaya." 'Gos lo-tsā-ba, being more encyclopædic, has some little details to add to the Tibetan career of Dharmapāla, from which the only significant information that we have is that from Dharmapāla began one of the following three Lineages of the monastic community of Tibet, viz, "the so-called 'Lower' Lineage of the *mahā-upādhyāya* Śāntarakṣita...the so-called 'Upper' Lineage of the East Indian *paṇḍita* Dharmapāla, ...and the Lineage handed down by the Kashmirian *paṇḍita* Śākyaśrī(-bhadra)'"[45]

Though 'Gos lo-tsā-ba calls it the "so-called Upper Lineage," its importance in the religious history of Tibet must not be exaggerated. In his enormous work, 'Gos lo-tsā-ba mentions almost countless "Lineages" (*brgyud-pa*) like this,—which, incidentally, are not to be confused with the sects of Buddhism,—and there is nothing to indicate that the particular "Lineage" of Dharmapāla ever acquired any momentous significance. By contrast, Dīpaṃkara's work did in an important sense shape the religious destiny of Tibet and continued to do so for about a thousand years.

The first sect of Tibetan Buddhism and the one directly associated with the name of Dīpaṃkara is called the bKa'-gdams-pa. In modern Tibet, however, the most important and influential sect of Buddhism is known as the dGe-lugs-pa.

43. Bu-ston ii. 213. 44. Sum-pa, *Contents* xvii-xviii. 45. BA ii. 1062. It is curious to see that the authors of *An Advanced History of India*, 168, freely bracket the names of Dharmapāla and Dīpaṃkara.

Next in importance are the two sects called the bKa'-rgyud-pa and Sa-skya-pa. Of these, the dGe-lugs-pa was the direct outcome of Atīśa's teachings, to which the last two were also greatly, though somewhat indirectly, indebted. Thu-bkan-blo-bzaṅ-chos-kyi-ñi-ma, the learned 18th century historian of the religious sects of Tibet,[46] clearly shows how much these sects of Tibetan Buddhism owe to Dīpaṃkara.[47] With regard to Tsoṅ-kha-pa, the founder of the dGe-lugs-pa sect, the historian observes, "(he) was in fact the same (i.e. the incarnation of) Jo-bo-rje (Atīśa). Only in the eyes of the common people he appeared to receive the *upadeśa* of *Mārga-krama* (i.e. the main work of Tsoṅ-kha-pa directly based on Dīpaṃkara's *Bodhi-patha-pradīpa*) of the bKa'-gdams from *mahā-upādhyāya* Nam-mkha'-rgyal-mtshan and Chos-skyabs-bzaṅ-po. He removed the dirt of doubt and distortions and whatever other changes occurred in Jo-bo's *upadeśa* in the course of time... So it is nothing but the bKa-'gdams-pa doctrine. Some of the *chos-'byuṅ*-s even call the dGe-ldan-pa (dGe-lugs-pa) as but the new bKa'-gdams-pa." The historian also shows how the sects called the bKa'-rgyud-pa and Sa-skya-pa are fundamentally based on Dīpaṃkara's teachings. Mar-pa lo-tsā-ba, the grand-founder of the bKa'-rgyud-pa sect, when he went to India for the second time, met Atīśa and received his *upadeśa*. Other great exponents of this sect were disciples of Atīśa's personal disciples and the basic tenets of the bKa-'rgyud-pa are based on Atīśa's teachings. Similarly Sa-skya *paṇḍita*, the founder of the Sa-skya-pa sect, was a disciple of a grand-disciple of Atīśa and the fundamental doctrines of this sect were the out-come of Atīśa's doctrines.

Following is Waddell's account of the relation of the dominant sects of Tibetan Buddhism to Dīpaṃkara's teachings :

"No sects appear to have existed prior to gLaṅ Dar-ma's persecution, nor till more than a century and a half later. The sectarial movement seems to date from the Reformation started by the Indian Buddhist monk Atīśa... The first of the

46. See S. C. Das in JASB, 1881, 187f on this historian. 47. Appendix A, Section 5.

reformed sects and the one with which Atiśa most intimately identified himself was called the bKa'-gdams-pa...and it ultimately, three and a half centuries later, in Tsoṅ-kha-pa's hands, became less ascetic and more highly ritualistic under the title of...dGe-lugs-pa, now the dominant sect in Tibet, and the Established Church of Lāmaism...The rise of the bKa'-gdams-pa (dGe-lugs-pa) sect was soon followed by the semi-reformed movements of bKa'-rgyud-pa and Sa-skya-pa, which were directly based in great measure on Atiśa's teaching. The founders of those two sects had been his pupils, and their new sects may be regarded as semi-reformations adapted for those individuals who found his high standard too irksome, and too free from their familiar demonolatry."[48]

It is no wonder, therefore, that in the history of Tibet as told by its own historians, Dīpaṃkara's stature should have been so great. To the Tibetans themselves the history of Tibet is above all the history of the spread of Buddhism there and this history is generally told as a series of events which culminated in the coming of Atiśa to Tibet and the propagation by him of the Doctrine there. That he was largely helped by the external circumstances is obvious. But it is idle to expect full explanation of his success from these alone.

To sum up : For understanding the Tibetan career of Dīpaṃkara, it is as important to consider the historical setting under which he worked as it is to have a clear idea of the nature of his personality and activities, and, above all, of his actual teachings. Yet all these, as is evident from the writings of Sir Charles Bell, have the risk of being grossly misunderstood because of the want of proper care in handling the Tibetan source-materials.

48. Waddell L 55-6.

2. *Misunderstanding Dipamkara and his Message*

Sir Charles Bell, the late British Political Representative in Tibet, is naturally struck by the great veneration of the Tibetans for Dīpaṃkara : "in the historical books as well as in the conversation of today, Atīśa is habitually termed 'Lord' or 'Noble Lord' and few are more highly venerated."[1] Again, "Among all the Paṇḍits who *flocked to Tibet* none exercised so great an influence as Atīśa."[2] The expression "flocked to Tibet" is peculiar. Waddell would not endorse it. "There seems no evidence," says he, "to support the assertion that this Lāmaist revival was determined by any great influx of Indian monks fleeing from persecution in India, as there is no record of any such influx about the time of the Muhammadan invasion of India."[3] As for the Tibetan authorities, on whom we are to depend almost exclusively for our knowledge of Atīśa, such an expression would hardly make any sense at all. The story of Dīpaṃkara's coming to Tibet, as persistently told by them, is the story of an ardous and prolonged undertaking on the part of the Tibetan rulers and scholars for inviting him to Tibet. But let us for the present skip over such points of comparatively minor importance. Sir Charles has greater surprises for us,—surprises, in fact, even for the Tibetan authorities on whom he claims to depend.

Dīpaṃkara's personality, according to the picture drawn by Sir Charles, was full of conceit and vanity. Here is how, according to him, Dīpaṃkara compared his own scholarly achievements with those of his predecessors to Tibet : "Atīśa travelled through Tibet from the West and eventullay arrived in Lhasa. The learned teachers of Tibet asked him regarding the qualification and attainments of those Paṇḍits who were in Western Tibet. He replied that a certain Paṇḍit had so much knowledge and another had so much. When questioned regarding his own

1. Bell, R.T. 59. 2. *Ib.* 53. emphasis added. 3. Waddell L 37.

attainments, he looked into the sky, saying *Tak tak* a sound betokening surprise, and adding, 'His accomplishments ! Oh, his accomplishments !' Thus, *says the history* he silenced them."[4]

This gives us the picture of one, who, with a great deal of demonstration of his own vanity, made the Tibetan scholars somewhat dumbfounded. But what is the "history" which, according to Bell, says the above ? It is the famous history of the Doctrine or the *chos-'byuṅ* by 'Gos lo-tsā-ba, usually referred to by its abbreviated title *Deb-sṅon* and translated by Roerich as *The Blue Annals.* In Roerich's English rendering, the actual passage in this history which forms the basis of Sir Charles' observation runs as follows :

"Later, when the Master was residing in Central Tibet (dBus), Lha-bla-ma came to meet him. About that time, Tibetan teachers inquired from him about the knowledge of different *paṇḍita*-s who had come to mÑa'-ris, he replied : 'This teacher possesses this (knowledge), that one—that, etc.' When they inquired about the Master's knowledge, he (Lha-bla-ma) raised his eyes towards the sky, and emitting a smacking sound with his tongue, uttered : 'O ! His knowledge ! O ! His knowledge !' By this he expressed that the Master's knowledge was surpassing words."[5]

There is thus no difficulty about the actual passage itself. It was intended to show the great veneration that the Tibetan ruler had for Atīśa. For Sir Charles, however, the whole thing is an evidence of Atīśa's personal vanity. That is hardly the way of drawing upon Tibetan history.

Besides, a simple acquaintance with Atīśa's works makes it quite clear that it must have been palpably absurd for him to have compared his own accomplishments with those of his predecessors in the way in which Sir Charles describes him to have done it. Much of the time and energy of his mature years was devoted to the Tibetan translation of Indian works, including works by his predecessors like Śāntarakṣita,[6] Kamala-

4. Bell, R.T. 54. emphasis added. 5. BA i. 247-8. 6. *Tattva-siddhi-nāma-prakaraṇa* (rG. lxxii. 4).

śīla[7] and Padmasambhava.[8] One who publicly declared himself so much superior to them would not surely take such pains to translate their works.

Still this distorted understanding of Tibetan "history" by Sir Charles is not entirely accidental. It is prompted by the peculiarly contemptuous notion of Dīpaṃkara's personality and his teachings which is repeatedly shown by Sir Charles. He is aware no doubt that Dīpaṃkara's name was intimately connected with the sect of reformed Buddhism known as the bKa'-gdams-pa. To him, however, this was not of much significance. "There was not much difficulty", he says,[9] "in forming a new sect at that time, for Buddhism was at a low ebb in consequence of the anti-Buddhist movement that had only recently lost force." But, apart from any real assessment of the role of the bKa'-gdams-pa sect in Tibetan history—and even assuming that it was quite easy to found a sect in Tibet at that time,—the question remains : How are we to explain the great success which this sect had in the religious history of Tibet ? With Sir Charles the explanation of this success is too easy. With a great deal of shrewdness, he argues, Dīpaṃkara knew well how to cater to the debased Tibetans with a suitably debased doctrine of his own. "Atīśa's teaching," he says,[10] "was largely based on the Kala Cakra system, one of the most debased forms of Buddhist Tantrism. But it evidently met the needs of Tibet, and in him they had a man who had studied hard and gained a wide outlook." "There was," continues Sir Charles,[11] "evidently a strong feeling in Tibet against this Indian importation, and Atīśa, though largely brought up in the Kala Cakra tenents, was distinguished by a wide erudition, and, having come late to the priesthood, seems to have been a man of the world. So, whatever his own views may have been, he bowed to Tibetan opinion."

It may be a little difficult to see full consistency between the two observations quoted above. If the most debased form

7. *Kṛṣṇa-yamāri-sādhana* (rG. xliii.10.) 8. *Bhikṣu-varṣāgra-pṛcchā* (mDo xc 21). See BA i. 30-1. 9. Bell, R.T. 59. 10. *Ib*. 53-4. 11. *Ib*. 54-5.

of Buddhist Tāntrism, which Dīpaṃkara is alleged to have represented, did meet the needs of Tibet, it is not clear why there was in Tibet a strong feeling against this Indian importation and why, further, Atīśa had to use his worldly wisdom to bow to the Tibetan opinion apparently concealing his own. But let us concentrate on the main thesis of Sir Charles, namely, that Dīpaṃkara's own teachings were largely based on the most debased form of Tāntrism known as the Kālacakra.

What can be the basis of such a remarkable assertion ?

'Gos lo-tsā-ba, for whose work Sir Charles himself[12] shows great admiration, devotes a long chapter[13] to the discussion of the Kālacakra. In this he mentions many "Lineages," both Indian and Tibetan, of this system of Tāntrism. Throughout the whole discussion, however, Dīpaṃkara's name is conspicuously absent. It is inconceivable that Dīpaṃkara was a real representative of the Kālacakra and yet 'Gos lo-tsā-ba, perhaps the greatest encyclopædist of Buddhist Tāntrism, was entirely unware of this.

But we need not depend upon such a negative evidence alone. There are direct ways of ascertaining the actual nature of Atīśa's teachings. We may have some idea of these from the theory and practice of the bKa'-gdams-pa sect. Besides, the actual writings of Atīśa, particularly of his mature years, are there to tell us whether he represented any form of debased Tāntrism, be it the Kālacakra or anything else.

We shall later have the occasion to discuss the bKa'-gdams-pa sect in greater details. For the present, however, we may mention only one point about it. The Tibetan authorities[14] frequently mention "The Six Basic Texts" of the bKa'-gdams-pa sect. These are : The *Mahāyānasūtrālaṃkāra*, *Bodhisattvabhūmi*, *Śikṣāsamuccaya*, *Bodhisattvacaryāvatāra*, *Jātakamālā* and *Udānavarga*. These are well-known texts of the classical Mahāyānists and it is not necessary to

12. Bell, R.T. 33: 'Gos lo-tsā-ba's work is characterised as "perhaps the most trustworthy of all Tibetan histories". 13. BA ii. 753-837

14. BA i. 268 ; ii. 810. See also Section 5 of Appendix A.

argue in detail that these have hardly anything to do with any particularly debased form of Tāntrism. It would therefore be most remarkable had Dīpaṃkara been himself a representative of such Tāntrism and yet the study of the texts he introduced among his followers are completely free from it.

That Bell's view of Dīpaṃkara's teachings has little or no relation with the teachings themselves becomes more obvious when we proceed to consider the actual writings of Dīpaṃkara. In his *Bodhi-patha-pradīpa*, far from subscribing to any form of debased Tāntrism, Dīpaṃkara clearly warns the Buddhist monk against certain forms of Tāntrika practices. "The *brahmacārī*," says Dīpaṃkara, "cannot receive *guhya-jñāna-abhiṣeka*, for it is strongly prohibited in the *Ādi-buddha-mahā-tantra*. For the *brahmacārī* receiving this form of initiation means the violation of the prohibitions and hence a fall from the *tapaḥ-saṃvara*. Such a *vratī* will suffer great sin (*mahā-pātaka*) and will certainly fall among the low-born. He will never attain *siddhi*."[15]

We shall later have the occasion to see how the Tibetan historians of Tibet express their greatest reverence for Dīpaṃkara, not because he catered the debased Tibetans with an equally debased doctrine of his own but above all for reforming the Tibetan religion which, particularly in the name of Tantra, became awfully corrupted before the arrival of Dīpaṃkara in Tibet. There is no doubt that he did not preach an outright rejection of Tāntrism. But the real sense in which he retained an affiliation to the Tāntrika modes of propitiation and meditation is in need of separate discussion. However, for the purpose of understanding whether his teachings were actually debased or not, we may have here only a few extracts from his writings that have special bearing on his ethical attitude. Here is a short religious song by him[16] :

> If you know *vikalpa*, the dangerous thief, to be a danger, then guard against it the great treasure of *śīla* and keep it safe. Oh, do not be a fool and remain sunk in a sleep of

15. *Bodhi-patha-pradīpa*, *śloka*-s 63-5. See Appendix C. 16. *Dīpaṃkara-śrī-jñāna-dharma-gītikā*. See Appendix C.

delusion (*moha*) throughout the long night which is *saṃsāra*. Keep close watch on your mind. If you remain asleep, the thief will enter your room and your treasure of *śīla* will be stolen. Without the wealth of *śīla*, there will be no *samādhi*. And without *samādhi* there will be no sun-rise. Therefore, save your *samādhi*. For a single moment do not imagine that the wealth of *śīla* is an ordinary wealth. Then will emerge absolute knowledge like the rising sun. Thus there will be the dawn and the end of *saṃsāra*. Oh, do not be a fool. Guard your *citta*.

We have in this song a favourite theme of Dīpaṃkara. He repeats it almost *in toto* elsewhere.[17] It is decidedly useless to search for anything debased or banal in this.

Dīpaṃkara had the rare honour of being the spiritual guide of at least two[18] kings of his time. One of them was Nayapāla of Bengal and the other was Byaṅ-chub-'od of Western Tibet. To the former he wrote a moving letter from Nepal and, in response to the special request of the latter, he wrote the *Bodhi-patha-pradīpa*, his *magnum opus*. We may have here two extracts from these.

To Nayapāla he wrote[19] :

Behave like (one with) eyes with regard to your own faults but as the blind with regard to the faults of others. Avoid arrogance and egoism and always meditate on the void. Give publicity to your own faults ; do not find faults of others. Give publicity to the virtues of others ; keep your own virtues hidden.

Do not accept gain and gifts. Always avoid profit and fame. Meditate on *maitrī* and *karuṇā*. Strengthen the *bodhicitta*. The ten *akuśala-karma*-s are to be avoided. Reverence is to be always strengthened. Remember to curb the desires, to remain self-content and to act in the virtuous way.

And so on. The entire letter is in fact nothing but a collection

17. *Caryā-gīti*. See Appendix C. 18. King of Nepal and others are often mentioned among the royal disciples of Atīśa. 19. *Vimala-ratna-lekha-nāma, śloka*-s 6-9. See Appendix C.

of moral precepts like these. A strong emphasis on moral purity, again, forms an important theme of the *Bodhi-patha-pradīpa.* This will be obvious from the following extract :

> By the adherence to *brahmacarya* and the avoidance of sin and lust and by remaining content with the *śīla-saṃvara* one follows the precepts of the Buddha.
>
> Do not be anxious to attain enlightenment quickly. Live up to the end (of the *saṃsāra*) for the sake of even a single living being.
>
> Purify the boundless and unthinkable (number of) *kṣetra*-s and live for (the emancipation of) each individual by name that exists in all the ten directions.
>
> Purify all actions—physical, oral and mental—and never indulge in any sinful act.[20]

To the nobles and the common people, to the scholars and the crowd, to the monks and the householders, in short, to the whole people of Tibet, Dīpaṃkara had always the message of moral purity and of selfless sacrifice for others, of the virtuous life and of the adherence to the pure Mahāyāna teachings. His writings apart, this is evident from the floating oral tradition about him, which has become almost a part of the cultural heritage of Tibet and from which the Tibetan historians frequently draw their materials.

A nun once made a precious gift to Dīpaṃkara and she received from him the following *upadeśa* : "Serve those that are sick and those that are tired. Serve the parents and the old. This is true religion. By thus serving, you will acquire all the *puṇya*-s that one acquires by meditating on the *bodhicitta* and *śūnyatā*"[21]

When Dīpaṃkara went to Tibet, the great Tibetan scholar Rin-chen-bzaṅ-po was eighty-five years old and was proud of his own learning. Dīpaṃkara easily dispelled his pride and said, "O Great lo-tsā-ba ! The sufferings of this Phenomenal World are difficult to bear. One should labour for the benifit

20. *Bodhi-patha-paradīpa, śloka*-s 27-30. See Appendix C. 21. BA i. 256. The *upadeśa* quoted is from Nagwang Nima's biography of Dīpaṃkara. See Section 6, Appendix A.

of all living beings. Now, pray practise meditation !"[22] This we are told, proved a decisive turning point in the life of the scholar.

A young monk once approached Dīpaṃkara for some special *upadeśa* and here is an extract of what he received :

> Do not say, 'I am a *bhikṣu*', so long as you care for material wealth and livelihood, with which the householder is concerned. You may be living in the monastery, but do not say, 'I am a *bhikṣu*, I live in the monastery', etc.. so long as you are affected by the worldly affairs. Do not say, 'I am a *bhikṣu*, I live in the monastery', etc., so long as you harbour worldly wishes or any thought of injuring others...[23]

Many more examples like these may be mentioned. But that is not necessary. We shall later have the occasion to discuss Dīpaṃkara's teachings more fully.

22. BA i. 250. 23. Sayings of Atīśa. See Section 8, Appenpix C.

3. The Sources

It follows from the above that for a proper understanding of the life and activities of Dīpaṃkara it is necessary to be very careful of the sources of our information about him. What, then, are these sources ?

To begin with, these sources are exclusively Tibetan. That his activities in Tibet should be known from the Tibetan sources is, of course, not unusual. What is peculiar, however, is that though Dīpaṃkara went to Tibet at an advanced age, his earlier or Indian career, too, so far as it can be known at all, is known not from any Indian source, but only from what the Tibetans have to say about it.

Apart perhaps from a mound in the Vajrayoginī village, Vikramapura, Dacca, to which people conventionally bow down as the residence of Atīśa ("*atīśer bhiṭā*" in Bengali), nothing concrete survives in the country of his birth to commemorate him. The archæologists are yet to identify definitely the site of the Vikramaśīla *vihāra*, which, as we know from the Tibetan sources, was the principal centre of his later activities as a Buddhist monk in India. As for the literary sources, not to speak of anything that may enlighten us about the personal life of Dīpaṃkara, even the very scriptural works of the religion he professed and preached were largely lost to India, some of these being only recently recovered from other countries and sometimes only in translations. Dīpaṃkara's own works would have perished but for the care with which the Tibetans preserved these in Tibetan translation.[1]

What, then, are the Tibetan sources ? Apart from the rich oral tradition about Dīpaṃkara current in Tibet, and apart from the archæological materials to which Francke has recently drawn our attention, the main Tibetan sources of our information about Dīpaṃkara may be classed under four broad heads :

1. The Mongolian translations are mostly based on the Tibetan translations.

1) Historical and semi-historical literature, called *chos-'byuṅ* or The Histories of the Doctrine and the *rgyal-rabs* or The Royal Chronicles,
2) Extensive biographical literature or *rnam-thar*,
3) Certain *stotra-s* or *bstod-pa* i.e, eulogies to Dīpaṃkara, and
4) The vast collection called the bsTan-'gyur, containing the Tibetan translations of mainly Indian works.

A great deal of critical care is needed to handle the mate rials contained in the first three of the above. The reasons are obvious. In the historical and semi-historical literatures of Tibet, the demarcating line between fact and fiction is not always clear. In the biographies and eulogies, again, the authors are generally more eager to express their reverence for Dīpaṃkara and to describe the Master's supernatural powers than to give real facts about his life. Moreover, there are considerable differences of opinion among the Tibetan authorities themselves about both the Indian and Tibetan careers of Dīpaṃkara. We may mention here only one example.

Sum-pa[2] says, "(His) total stay in Nepal and Tibet (was for) 15 years. In Tibet itself (his stay was for) 13 years...What is said above about the number of years he spent in Tibet is just according to the general account. But the *Mārga-krama* says that he was in mÑa'-ris for three years, in sÑe-thaṅ for nine years, in dBus, gTsaṅ and other places for five years—which means seventeen years (in all). This is said according to the *rNam-thar-chen-mo*, etc., which counted the first and last years of the middle years twice and counted two years more for his travels between sÑe-thaṅ, dBus, and other places. Thus it is a rough account. Nag-tsho said, 'I had been under him for nineteen years.' (Further), 'In Vikramaśīla at the time of his departure for Tibet (Atīśa said) :—I shall leave my mortal body after eighteen years.' The *Lam-yig-gsaṅ-'khor-ma* says, 'Born in India in the Fire-Male-Horse year, till the age of 60, he protected India by the Doctrine.' The *rNam-thar-yi-ge* says' 'Jo-bo (Atīśa) was born in the Iron-Horse year after 3047 years of the Buddha's *nirvāṇa* ; in the Fire-Tiger year he left

2. Sum-pa 186. Translation ours.

India for Tibet, in the Wood-Pig year he was in bSam-yas, in the Fire-Hare year he reached sÑe-thaṅ, on the 18th day of dBo-zla of the Water-Horse year he passed away at sÑe-thaṅ.' Such calculations are very difficult. But most of the scholars agree that he was born in the Water-Horse year. So the Fire-Horse year, as mentioned in the *Lam-yig*, seems to be a verbal error. Jo-bo's *rNam-thar-rgyas-pa*, like the *Lam-yig-chen-mo*, is not very reliable. Some of these (mistakes) are pointed out in the *rNam-thar-brgya-rtsa-brgyad*. But what is said in the *Mārga-krama* of rJe (Tsoṅ-kha-pa) is very good. Also, what is described in Nag-tsho's *bsTod-pa-brgyad-cu-pa* and Gro-luṅ's (?) *bsTod-pa-sum-cu-pa* is mostly correct."

In view of so much differences among the Tibetan authorities themselves, it will be obviously risky for us to depend upon any single *rnam-thar* or any single *chos-'byuṅ* for reconstructing the life-history of Atīśa. But this does not mean that all the Tibetan biographical and historical sources are equally unrealiable. As for the historical literature, there are at least two that command great prestige, not only among the Tibetan and Mongolian learned Lāmas but also among the modern Tibetologists outside Tibet. These are :—

1). The History of Buddhism in India and Tibet by Bu-ston Rin-po-che, the full Tibetan title of which is *bDe-bar gśegs-pa'i bstan-pa'i gsal-byed chos-kyi 'byuṅ-gnas gsuṅ-rab rin-po-che'i mdzod*. Bu-ston (A.D. 1290-1364) had undoubtedly been one of the greatest of the Tibetan scholars of Buddhism. He composed this history in A.D. 1322.[3] "This work," says Roerich, "is especially important for the history of Buddhist canonical literature in Tibet."[4] Its first part, says Stcherbatsky,[5] "is of an overwhelming scientific value. It represents a synthesis of everything which directly or remotely bears the stamp of Buddhism...The whole of its literature, sacred or profane, is here reviewed as divided in periods, schools and subject-matter. No one was better qualified for such a task than Bu-ston, for he was one of the redactors of the

3. BA Intro. viii. 4: *Ib.* 5. Bu-ston i., Intro. 3.

bKa'-'gyur and bsTan-'gyur great collections in their final form." The chapters of this work on Buddhist canonical literature as well as its part dealing with the propagation of Buddhism in India and Tibet are already made available for us in excellent English translation by Obermiller. Since the Tibetan career of Dīpaṃkara can be followed only in the general background of the history of Buddhism in Tibet, Bu-ston's work is of immense importance for any study of the life and activities of Dīpaṃkara.

2). The *chos-'byuṅ* by 'Gos lo-tsā-ba gShon-nu-dpal, the full Tibetan title of which is *Bod-kyi-yul-du-chos-daṅ-chos-smra-ba-ji-ltar-byuṅ-ba'i-rim-pa-deb-ther-sṅon-po* or "The Blue Annals, the Stages of the Appearance of the Doctrine and Preachers in the Land of Tibet." The work is usually referred to by the abbreviated form *Deb-sṅon* (Blue Annals) or *'Gos-lo'i Deb-ther* (The Annals of 'Gos lo-tsā-ba). 'Gos was born in A.D. 1392 and died in A. D. 1481. He composed this enormous work between A. D. 1476-78. "The work", says Roerich, "is invaluable for its attempt to establish a firm chronology of events of Tibetan history. All dates are given in the Sexagenary Cycle of the Tibetans, and the author takes great pains to calculate the various dates backwards and forwards linking them to the year A.D. 1476 (Fire-Ape), during which he wrote his work, or calculating dates from some well-known dates, such as for example the date of the death of king Sroṅ-btsan-sgam-po in 650 A.D. Sometimes he states the number of years which had elapsed between two dates. Page after page of the chronicle contain lists of names of famous religious teachers, and their Spiritual Lineages, mentioning sometimes their birth-places, and the names of their monasteries, sometimes giving the years of their births and deaths. The work...is divided into *fifteen chapters or books,*...each dedicated to the history of one particular school or sect of Tibetan Buddhism."[6] It is translated in full into English by Roerich and the special importance of his translation consists

6. BA Intro. iii.

in the care with which he has throughout calculated the years of the Tibetan Sexagenary Cycle in terms of the standard European calendar.

In the 18th and first half of the 19th centuries a number of large historical compilations were prepared by the Tibetan scholars. But the main sources of their information happen to be the two *chos-'byuṅ*-s just mentioned.[7] Of the 18th century works, our modern historians frequently draw upon one called the *dPag-bsam-ljon-bzaṅ* (literally, The Wish-yielding Tree) by Sum-pa-mkhan-po-ye-śes-dpal-'byor (A.D. 1702-75), usually referred to simply as Sum-pa. This work was composed in A.D. 1748 and, as edited with a list of contents and an analytical index in English by S. C. Das, was published from Calcutta in 1908. The contents and index are extremely valuable ; yet important details of the life and works of Atīśa as discussed by Sum-pa are often missing in these. We have prepared a literal translation of the part of this work devoted to Dīpaṃkara. It is to be found in our *Appendix A*, along with certain other Tibetan source-materials rendered into English.

Another small extract of Sum-pa's work discussing the ruling family of Western Tibet is rendered into English by Francke and incorporated into the second part of his *Antiquities of Indian Tibet*. This extract is of special importance for our study of Dīpaṃkara, because Dīpaṃkara's Tibetan career was intimately related to the rulers of Western Tibet. But Francke's own contribution to our knowledge of the history of Western Tibet and of Dīpaṃkara's Tibetan career is much more important than merely this translation. First, his archaeological work in Western Tibet helped the modern scholars to prove the historicity of many events of the life of Dīpaṃkara and of his royal patrons, which otherwise would have remained somewhat fabulous or legendary. Secondly, in the second part of the same work, he makes available for us certain extremely important Tibetan chronicles—along

7. *Ib*. Intro. i.

with extensive notes on these—dealing with the history of Western Tibet, the extract from Sum-pa being only a minor one among these.

However, in view of the strong differences of opinion often expressed even by the foremost of the Tibetan authorities, we have to seek for corroborative evidence, as far as possible, before accepting the statement of any. Such evidence is often to be found in the bsTan-'gyur collection, particularly in the colophons of the works of which Dīpaṃkara was the author or translator. These colophons are extremely important. Apart from mentioning the names of the authors or translators of the texts, they often contain certain additional historical information about them and there are grounds to think that these are on the whole authentic. For though the bsTan-'gyur received its present form in the 14th century A.D., the Tibetan colophons of Dīpaṃkara's works included in it were presumably written and "fixed" at a much earlier time. Though not all, at least some of these could have been composed during the life-time of Dīpaṃkara himself, and therefore, with his personal approval. A few of these colophons appear to have been written by Dīpaṃkara himself.[8] Thus the importance of the bsTan-'gyur for our study of Dīpaṃkara is two-fold. First, preserving as it does all the works of which Dīpaṃkara was the author or translator, it gives us a direct knowledge of his enormous literary activity. Secondly, we have in the colophons of these works also some additional historical information of obvious importance about Dīpaṃkara.

Our survey of these source-materials cannot be complete without a few words on the *Life of Atīśa* by Sarat Chandra Das. Though Koppen[9] was the first Tibetologist outside Tibet to have taken serious notice of Dīpaṃkara, yet there is no doubt that the curiosity of the modern scholars about him was

8. In the Peking edition, the colophon of *Ārya-avalokita-lokeśvara-sādhana* (rG. xl. 21), e.g., reads : "I, Dīpaṃkara-śrī-jñāna, have written it on the basis of the collection of *upadeśa*-s. Written by *mahā-ācārya* Śrī-dīpaṃkara-jñāna."

9. C. F. Koppen, *Lamaische Hierarchie und Kirche*, (Berlin 1857-59), ii. 78, 117, 127, 285.

first fully aroused by the long biography of Atīśa prepared by Das and that this biography remained for a considerable period the main work on which the modern scholars relied for their knowledge of Dīpaṃkara.

What, then, is the source of this biography and how much authenticity can we credit it with ?

There is some confusion about Das' own source. Francke[10] gives us the impression that it is at least largely based on Sum-pa's work. But Das himself left nothing vague about his own source. His life of Atīśa was first published in 1893 in the *Journal of the Buddhist Text Society* and it contained the following note[11] :

"Kalyāṇamitra Phyag-sor-pa being anxious to write an account of Atīśa went to see Nag-tsho, who still alive, was residing at his native place of Guṅ-thaṅ. Having attended the great Indian Paṇḍit for a period of nineteen years, he was peculiarly qualified to furnish a faithful account of Atīśa's life. He met the old lo-tsā-ba at Yaṅ-thog-lha-khaṅ and spent two years in his company. ...He furnished Phyag-sor-pa with a mass of information regarding Atīśa's religious career and performances. mKhan-po-mchim-thams-cad-mkhyen-pa got fragments of them which he arranged into a book at the monastery of sNar-thaṅ and shaped them into a memoir with the healing reed of faith. This book was printed (at sNar-thaṅ) in the country of Gaṅs-chen (Tibet) in the year called Dog", i.e. about A.D. 1250.

Thus the work was composed by mKhan-po-mchim-thams-cad-mkhyen-pa earlier than A.D. 1250 and it claims to be based on the direct communication of Nag-tsho to Phyag-sor-pa. When this biography was later reprinted as incorporated in Das' *Indian Pandits in the Land of Snow*, the editor inadvertently chose to omit the above note, thereby creating the possibility of confusion about its source. Yet the note is important, for the bKa'-gdams-pa tradition, as recorded by 'Gos lo-tsā-ba, corroborates that Nag-tsho did communicate the life of Atīśa

10. Francke AIT i. 19, 50n.

11. S. C. Das in JBTS I. i. 7n.

to Phyag-sor-pa. "The one known as Roṅ-pa Phyag-sor-pa... was of the opinion, that because of the excellence of the Master's precepts, there must have existed an account of the Master's invitation to Tibet, (but) he was unable to find it anywhere. He visited Nag-tsho lo-tsā-ba who was residing at Khab-guṅ-thaṅ. Nag-tsho bestowed on him numerous secret precepts of the Mantrayāna and he spent three years (with him). Next year he requested Nag-tsho to relate to him *the story of the Master's invitation to Tibet.* The lo-tsā-ba said : 'I attended for 19 years on the Master and have invited him to Tibet', and he gladly related to him the story."[12] Incidentally, the life of Atīśa translated by S. C. Das is in fact *mainly the story of the Master's invitation to Tibet* and not a full-fledged biography of Atīśa, his Tibetan career in particular is discussed in this in a desultory manner. Further, certain interesting details of this biography indicate that it must have originally been communicated by someone who came to India and had personal knowledge of the Indian conditions and Nag-tsho, we are told, came twice to India and, on the second occasion, stayed at the Vikramaśīla *vihāra* a few years for the purpose of inviting Atīśa to Tibet. Thus Das' life of Atīśa[13] has a special importance, though this does not mean that we can rely outright on all the details contained in it.

We have also a few short life-sketches of Atīśa by modern scholars, though the sources on which these are based are not always clearly given.

12. BA, i. 321. emphasis added. 13. Waddell, L. 35n, claims to have consulted the Tibetan original of the biography, though, curiously enough, he adds that it was written by 'Brom-ston-pa.

4. *The Name*

For the purpose of discussing the different names of Dīpaṃkara, or, more properly, the different ways in which he is referred to, we may begin with a historical parallel with which we are more familiar, namely that of Caitanya or Śrī-caitanya, another great preacher-reformer of Bengal born about five centuries after the birth of Dīpaṃkara.

Caitanya was not his original name. From his biographers we learn that the name he received from his parents was Viśvambhara.[1] His *guru* Keśavabhāratī gave him the name Śrī-kṛṣṇa-caitanya, abbreviated as Śrī-caitanya or simply Caitanya, at the time of his initiation.[2] To the large majority of his followers, the name Viśvambhara is practically forgotten, who would moreover refer to him generally as *prabhu* (The Lord) or still more frequently as *mahā-prabhu* (The Great Lord). Though not a proper name, only one person in Bengal is understood by the reverential title *mahā-prabhu*, and he is Caitanya.

The name which Dīpaṃkara originally received from his parents was Candragarbha. The Tibetan sources are unanimous about it. According to some of these sources, the first initiated name which he received was Guhya-jñāna-vajra. This name is patently Tāntric, and as such is indicative of an early Tāntrika initiation, which is often mentioned by the Tibetan sources to have characterised his early spiritual career. Nevertheless, this name Guhya-jñāna-vajra, like the original one Candragarbha, is no more than mere curiosity for us. Dīpaṃkara himself in his mature years is never known to have used this name. We shall later see the significance of this.

1. *Caitanya-bhāgavata* (Bengali), Ādi-khaṇḍa, chapter 2; *Śrī-caitanya-caritāmṛta* (Bengali), Ādi-līlā, chapter 3. 2. *Śrī-caitanya-bhāgavata* (Bengali), Madhya-khaṇḍa, chapter 26.

The name Dīpaṃkara was conferred on him during his Buddhist ordination and became firmly fixed throughout his subsequent career. Thus, much in the manner in which Viśvambhara acquired the name Śrī-kṛṣṇa-caitanya, Candragarbha came to be known as Dīpaṃkara. According to the biographers of Caitanya, this particular name was chosen by his *guru* because of a special reason. By preaching through his devotional songs the name of Śrī-kṛṣṇa, he brought consciousness (*caitanya*) among the people ; hence, it is said, he was given the name Śrī-kṛṣṇa-caitanya.[3] However, the Tibetan sources, generally speaking, do not mention any such special reason for the choice of the name Dīpaṃkara for him, beyond the general one that this was the name of one of the Buddhas[4] of the past and, as such, a holy name to the Buddhists. The choice of this particular name, in other words, could have been merely conventional. There were other Buddhist monks who bore the name Dīpaṃkara.[5]

However, Rahula Sankrityayan proposes to attach some special significance to the ordained name of Dīpaṃkara. "In Buddhist lore," says he, "Dīpaṃkara is a highly revered name, because it was the name of a Buddha who came long before Śākyamuni, the historical Buddha. Śrījñāna was added to his name as he was expected to become a scholar."[6]

We may go into this more fully. Though his ordained name is usually mentioned as Dīpaṃkara-śrī-jñāna, yet we do not come across in the Tibetan sources the special significance which Rahula reads in the Śrījñāna-part of the name. Besides, there are certain considerations that make us hesitate to assert categorically that Śrījñāna did form a necessary part of his ordained name.

'Brom-ston, in his *stotra*, generally mentions the name as Dīpaṃkara-śrī. The addition of the "śrī" is clearly conventional, inasmuch as while enumerating the different names of the Master he says that in India (*ārya-deśa*) he was honoured under the name Dīpaṃkara.[7] If Śirjñāna actually formed a

3. *Ib.* 4. Winternitz ii. 160n, 186f. 5. See next section.
6. Rahula in *2500 Years*, 228. 7. See Section 2, Appendix A, *śloka* 25.

necessary part of the name, 'Brom would not have uniformly dropped it in the *stotra,*—not even for metrical consideration.

Further, in the bsTan-'gyur we find the name recorded in various forms. These are : simply Dīpaṃkara, Śrī-dīpaṃkara, Dīpaṃkara-jñāna, Dīpaṃkara-jñāna-pāda, Śrī-dīpaṃkara-jñāna, Dīpaṃkara-śrī-jñāna, etc., though surely the last two forms are most frequent. Here are a few examples.

As author of the *Kāya-vāk-citta-supratiṣṭhā-nāma,*[8] we have the name Śrī-dīpaṃkara-jñāna. Its translators, however, are "*upādhyāya* Dīpaṃkara and lo-tsā-ba Vīryasiṃha of rGya." It is also mentioned that the translation was done at the Vikramaśila *vihāra*. That the author Śrī-Dīpaṃkara-jñāna could be none else than the translator *upādhyāya* Dīpaṃkara is evident from the consideration that it is inconceivable for Vīryasiṃha to have worked under any other Dīpaṃkara at the Vīkramaśila *vihāra.*[9]

Of the *Caryā-gīti-vṛtti,* which is but Dīpaṃkara's auto-commentary on the *Caryā-gīti,* the author is mentioned as *paṇḍita* Dīpaṃkara and the translators as "author and lo-tsā-ba Jayaśīla (Nag-tsho)." That this author could be none else than our Dīpaṃkara is again evident from the inconceivability of Nag-tsho working under any other Dīpaṃkara.

The work *Dharma-dhātu-darśana-gīti* occurs twice in the bsTan-'gyur, the second version being only a literal reproduction of the first. As the author of the first, however, we have the name simply Dīpaṃkara, while that of the second Dīpaṃkara-śrī-jñāna.

The colophon of the *Vajra-yoginī-stotra* reads, "Written by *paṇḍita* Dīpaṃkara, translated by the same *paṇḍita* and lo-tsā-ba Ratnabhadra (Rin-chen-bzaṅ-po)." Ratnabhadra, as we shall see, worked under many Indian *paṇḍita*-s but there was only one Dīpaṃkara among them and he was Atīśa.

Many other examples from the bsTan-'gyur may be

8. For this and other texts mentioned in this connection, see Appendix B.
9. For Vīryasiṃha and Jayaśīla see section 31. Incidentally, the mode of Tibetan translation presupposes personal contact between the Indian *paṇḍita* and the Tibetan lo-tsā-ba.

mentioned where Atiśa's name occurs simply as Dīpaṃkara. Again, the name is often found to occur as Śrī-dīpaṃkara. The name occurring in the form of Dīpaṃkara-jñāna, too, is not rare. Thus, the *Ārya-acala-krodha-rāja-stotra* occurs twice in the bsTan-'gyur, the second version being a literal reproduction of the first. However, the author of the first is Dīpaṃkara-jñāna, while that of the second Śrī-dīpaṃkara-jñāna. We have the name Dīpaṃkara-jñāna also as the author of *Āyuḥ-sādhana*, *Deva-pūjā-krama*, *Peyotkṣepa-vidhi*, *Mṛtyu-vañcana*, *Mumūrṣu-śāstra*, etc.

But more interesting is the evidence of the colophon of Dīpaṃkara's auto-commentary on his *magnum opus*, the *Bodhi-patha-pradīpa*. This auto-commentary is called *Bodhi-mārga-pradīpa-pañjikā-nāma*. In the Peking edition its colophon, after first mentioning the name of the author as Dīpaṃkara-śrī-jñāna, goes on saying, "Representing the Buddha this time, Dīpaṃkara-śrī-pāda was born in Bengal"...and adds, "translated and revised by the Indian *mahā-paṇḍita guru bodhisattva* the Bengalee Śrī-dīpaṃkara-jñāna-pāda and lo-tsā-ba *bhikṣu* Jayaśīla." In Cordier's *Catalogue*, also, we come across the names of the translators as Śrī-dīpaṃkara-jñāna-pāda and Jayaśīla of Nag-tsho.

More examples are not necessary. However, since the name is often given simply as Dīpaṃkara and since, moreover, the additions to it are very irregular, it will not be safe to assert categorically that Śrī-jñāna formed an indispensable part of the full ordained name of Dīpaṃkara.

Before we pass on to discuss the other—and characteristically Tibetan—ways in which he is referred to, it may be of interest to note how exactly his Indian name is preserved in the bsTan-'gyur. We find it being retained in mainly two ways. First, there are exact transliterations of the name in Tibetan scripts. Secondly, there are exact translations of the name in Tibetan language.

Thus we have the name as

དཱི་པཾ་ཀ་ར

ཤྲཱི་དཱི་པཾ་ཀ་ར་ཛྙཱ་ན

དཱི་པཾ་ཀ་ར་ཤྲཱི་ཛྙཱ་ན

དཱི་པཾ་ཀ་ར་ཛྙཱ་ན

i.e. the Tibetan transliterations respectively of

Dīpaṃkara
Śrī-dīpaṃkara-jñāna
Dīpaṃkara-śrī-jñāna
Dīpaṃkara-jñāna.

In Tibetan translation again,

dīpa = mar-me
kara = mdzad
śrī = dpal
jñāna = ye-śes.

Thus, in Tibetan translation, the name occurs in various forms like—

Mar-me-mdzad=Dīpaṃkara,
dPal-mar-me-mdzad=Śrī-dīpaṃkara,
Mar-me-mdzad-ye-śes=Dīpaṃkara-jñāna,
dPal-mar-me-mdzad-ye-śes=Śrī-dīpaṃkara-jñāna,
Mar-me-mdzad-dpal-ye-śes=Dīpaṃkara-śrī-jñāna,

and so on.

But apart from thus retaining Dīpaṃkara's Indian name both in transliteration and translation, the characteristically Tibetan way in which he is referred to is as Jo-bo, Jo-bo-rje, Jo-bo-chen-po, and also, of course, as Atīśa. Jo-bo means, "Lord, Master, Noble, Venerable." Chen-po means "The great." Jo-bo-chen-po thus means "The Great Lord." Practically the same idea is conveyed by Jo-bo-rje, "The Noble Lord." These are, in other words, the Tibetan equivalents of the Indian words *prabhu* and *mahā-prabhu*. Obviously enough, these are not proper names. Nevertheless, just as the Vaiṣṇavas of Bengal refer to only one person by the word *prabhu*,—or, more particularly, *mahā-prabhu*,—only one person is referred to by the Tibetan Buddhists when they use the words Jo-bo-rje or Jo-bo-chen-po,—or sometimes simply Jo-bo,—and he is none but Dīpaṃkara.[10] This is of material importance for identifying the works of Dīpaṃkara in the bsTan-'gyur.

The other word by which he is freely referred to by the Tibetans and the Mongolians is *atīśa*. Already, at the time of 'Brom-ston-pa,—and, therefore, during the life-time of Dīpaṃkara himself,—this word acquired the status of practically a proper name. It is evident from 'Brom's *stotra*, in which is said,[11]

> I offer prayer to his feet, who is honoured everywhere,—in the Tuṣita heaven by the name Vimala-ākāśa, in India (*ārya-deśa*) by the name Dīpaṃkara, and in the Land of Snow (Himavant) by the name Śrīmat Atīśa.

Yet nowhere do we come across any reference to Dīpaṃkara having ever acquired this as his proper name, either before or after his ordination. The word is certainly Indian. Jaschke says that it is Sanskrit.[12] As such, it can only mean *ati*+*īśa*, 'the super lord' or 'the great lord',—something very near *mahā-prabhu* or Jo-bo-rje.

A Tibetan translation of the word is in circulation. It is Phul-byuṅ or Phul-tu-byuṅ-ba, meaning the accomplished or the perfect. According to both Das[13] and Jaschke,[14] this Tibetan word invariably stands for Atīśa. Francke,[15] coming across the word in a Tibetan inscription, readily concludes that the inscription contains the name of Dīpaṃkara.

But how could the word *atīśa* acquire the status of practically a proper name in Tibet and Mongolia? An exact answer may not be possible. But since the word is clearly Indian and since, as an Indian word, it was presumably used

10. The epithet Jo-bo-chen-po for any other person is clearly exceptional and perhaps also the result of immitation. 11. *śloka* 25. See Section 2, Appendix A. 12. J-TED 603. 13. D-TED 826. 14. J-TED 344. 15. Francke AIT i. 41.

originally as a reverential epithet, we may perhaps conjecture that this reverential epithet for Dīpaṃkara was already current in India and that the Tibetans, apart from using an equivalent for it, namely Phul-byuṅ, or, more frequently, a near-equivalent for it, namely Jo-bo-rje, respected the original Indian epithet so much that to them it became as good as a proper name.

There are at least two distinct indications that the reverential epithet Atīśa was current in India. In Das' life of Atīśa, we find a beggar-boy near the Vikramaśīla *vihāra* addressing him as "*bābā Atīśa*" or "father Atiśa."[16] Again, in the Vajrayoginī village, Vikramapura, there remains a mound to which people still bow reverentially as "*atīśer bhiṭā*" or the residence of Atīśa.

If it is difficult to determine how the word *atīśa* became so prevalent in Tibet, it is all the more perplexing why among the Mongolians the practice of referring to Dīpaṃkara as Atīśa became even more firmly fixed. The Mongolians, too, have an exact translation of the name Dīpaṃkara which is Jol-uile-degechi (*Jol* meaning *dīpa* or 'the lamp', *Uiledegechi* meaning *kara* or 'one who does').[17] But the use of this form is sparse and, in Mongolia, Atīśa became practically an equivalent of the Tibetan Jo-bo-rje. In the Mongolian translations of Dīpaṃkara's works, his name almost invariably occurs as Atīśa. This is extremely important for identifying some of the works of Dīpaṃkara. If we find the Tibetan colophon of a work in the bsTan-'gyur is silent about its author or translator, or, if we find in it the name of Dīpaṃkara mentioned in a somewhat irregular manner, but if, at the same time, we find that the Mongolian version of the same work mentions Atīśa as its author or translator, then we should have little hesitation in attributing it to our Dīpaṃkara. For only one person in Mongolia is referred to as Atīśa and he is none but Dīpaṃkara.

16. S. C. Das in JBTS I. i. 19.

17. I am indebted for this information to Professor Lama Chimpa.

5. How Many Dipamkaras ?

Dīpaṃkara being the holy name of a past Buddha, it was but natural for many Buddhist monks to have received this as the ordained name. How many of them are we aware of ?

H. P. Sastri,[1] depending mainly on an analysis of Cordier's *Catalogue* of the bsTan-'gyur, cautiously suggests the possibility of there being two different Dīpaṃkaras whose works are to be found in this collection. In the bsTan-'gyur, Dīpaṃkara is sometimes mentioned as a Bengalee, sometimes as an Indian. To such occurrences of the name are attached adjectives like *mahā-ācārya, paiṇḍapātika*, etc. In many other cases, however, the name Dīpaṃkara is found to occur with simple adjectives like *ācārya, paṇḍita, upādhyāya.* In these cases, moreover, it is not mentioned that he came from India or Bengal. Therefore, thinks H. P. Sastri, it is reasonable to assume that the works of two different Dīpamkaras are to be found in the bsTan-'gyur. Of them, one was a great *paṇḍita* or a great *ācārya*, who went to Tibet from Bengal and the other was a scholar of comparatively lesser eminence.

The basic assumption of such a suggestion is that some special care was taken in the use of the adjectives—like *ācārya*, *paṇḍita* and *upādhyāya*, or *mahā-ācārya*. *mahā-paṇḍita* and *mahā-upādhyāya*—for the authors or translators mentioned in the bsTan-'gyur, or that some uniform method was followed while offering additional information about them. But a closer scrutiny of the bsTan-'gyur shows that such an assumption is untenable. No principle whatsoever was followed in the colophons for the use of the adjectives and it is difficult, if not impossible, to determine why in the colophons of certain texts some additional information about the author or translator is given while in the colophons of certain others no such

1. *Bauddha Gān O Dohā* (Bengali), 22.

information is to be found. We may have here only a few examples of the irregularities in the bsTan-'gyur colophons.

The *Madhyamaka-upadeśa-nāma*[2] occurs thrice in the bsTan-'gyur, the latter two of these versions being but literal reproductions of the first. As the author of the first version, however. we find the name of *mahā-ācārya* Śrī-dīpaṃkara-jñāna, of the second, *ācārya* Śrī-dīpaṃkara-jñāna. The *Ārya-acala-krodha-rāja-stotra* occurs twice in the bsTan-'gyur, the second version being only the literal reproduction of the first. As author of the first, however, we have the name of *paṇḍita* Dīpaṃkara-jñāna, while as that of the second *mahā-ācārya* Śrī-dīpaṃkara-jñāna.

Besides, we frequently find that when Dīpaṃkara is both author and translator of a work, one adjective is used for him when he is mentioned as the author while another adjective is used when he is mentioned as the translator—and this, in spite of the clear statement that the author is the same as the translator. Thus the colophon of the *Garbha-saṃgraha-nāma* mentions "*mahā-ācārya* Śrī-dīpaṃkara-jñāna" as the author ; but the translator is said to be "the same *paṇḍita* and lo-tsā-ba *bhikṣu* Śīlākaraśānti." The *Cittotpāda-saṃvara-vidhi-krama* has the following colophon : "Written by *mahā-ācārya* Śrī-dīpaṃkara-jñāna ; translated by the same Indian *paṇḍita* and lo-tsā-ba *bhikṣu* Śubhamati. And again, revised by the same *paṇḍita* and lo-tsā-ba Jayaśīla." The colophon of *Dharma-dhātu-darśana-gīti* says, "Written by *mahā-ācārya* Dīpaṃkara-śrī-jñāna and translated by the same Indian *upādhyāya* and Tibetan lo-tsā-ba Jayaśīla." There are many more examples like these.

From the evidences just cited, one may have the impression that the colophons of the works in the bsTan-'gyur mention more honourable adjectives for the author and some shorter and apparently lesser ones for the same person when he is himself the translator. Such a principle again is not uniformly followed. Thus, e.g., the colophon of *Ārya-gaṇapati-rāga-vajra-stotra-nāma* says, "Written by *paṇḍita*

2. For this as well as other texts mentioned in the present Section, see Appendix B.

Dīpaṃkara-śrī-jñāna ; translated by the same *mahā-paṇḍita* and lo-tsā-ba Jayaśīla". Moreover, how obviously risky it is to attribute special significance to the use of the adjectives in these Tibetan colophons becomes clearer when we see that sometimes extremely highflown adjectives are used for the Tibetan lo-tsā-ba who worked under Dīpaṃkara, while to the name of Dīpaṃkara himself, mentioned as both author and translator, is attached a minor adjective or none at all. Thus the colophon of the *Prajñāpāramitā-piṇḍārtha-pradīpa* is, "Written by Śrī-dīpaṃkara-jñāna and translated by the same *paṇḍita* and lo-tsā-ba *mahā-mahā-paṇḍita* Jayaśīla".

We shall presently take up the other argument of H. P. Sastri, namely that some of the colophons in the bsTan-'gyur mention Dīpaṃkara as coming from Bengal or India while some others do not do so. But in view of the extreme irregularity of the mode in which the names of the authors and translators are mentioned in these, it may be worthwhile to try to determine first some of the basic principles according to which it is reasonable to identify our Dīpaṃkara in the bsTan-'gyur. We have, while discussing the various names of Dīpaṃkara, or more properly, the various ways in which he is referred to, already distinct indications of two such principles. There is only one person referred to by the Tibetan epithet Jo-bo-rje and that is our Dīpaṃkara. Again, only one person is referred to by the Tibetans—and more particularly by the Mongolians—by the word Atīśa, and that is our Dīpaṃkara. Cordier's *Catalogue* of the bsTan-'gyur provides us, for most of the works, with the names of the authors and translators as given in the *Index Tibetan* and *Index Mongolian.* As is to be expected, these indexes generally mention Dīpaṃkara as Jo-bo-rje and Atīśa respectively. Thus we have two distinct principles for identifying our Dīpaṃkara in the bsTan-'gyur. *First, when the Index Tibetan mentions one as Jo-bo-rje we may be certain that he is none but our Dīpaṃkara, whatever may be the form in which his Indian name is given and whatever may be the nature of the adjectives added to this Indian name. Secondly, when the Index Mongolian mentions one as Atīśa, we may be certain that he is our Dīpaṃkara, notwithstanding the variations in his Indian name.* Pending the discussion of the other principles of identifying our Dīpaṃkara in the bsTan-'gyur, we may have here some idea of the implications of these two. In the *Index Tibetan* and *Index Mongolian* the name of the author of all the following works occurs as Jo-bo-rje and Atīśa respectively, but his Indian name is mentioned in various ways with various adjectives in the colophons of the same works. Thus :

Ārya-tārā-stotra etc. : (simply) Dīpaṃkara-śrī-jñāna
Kāya-vāk-citta-supratiṣṭhā-nāma etc. : (simply) Śrī-dīpaṃkara-jñāna
Ārya-acala-krodha-rāja-stotra : *paṇḍita* Dīpaṃkara-jñāna
Caryā-gīti-vṛtti : *paṇḍita* Dīpaṃkara
Akṣobhya-sādhana-nāma : etc. *ācārya* Dīpaṃkara-śrī-jñāna
Pañca-caitya-nirvapaṇa-vidhi : *upādhyāya* Dīpaṃkara-śrī-jñāna of India
Aṣṭa-bhaya-trāṇa : *ācārya paṇḍita* Śrī-dīpaṃkara-jñāna
Abhisamaya-vibhaṅga-nāma etc. : *mahā-paṇḍita* Dīpaṃkara-śrī-jñāna
Vajrāsana-vajra-gīti : *mahā-paṇḍita* Śrī-dīpaṃkara-jñāna
Bodhi-patha-pradīpa : *mahā-ācārya* Śrī-dīpaṃkara-jñāna
Caryā-saṃgraha-pradīpa etc. : *ācārya mahā-paṇḍita* Śrī-dīpaṃkara-jñāna
Vimala-ratna-lekha-nāma : *sthavira mahā-paṇḍita* Dīpaṃkara-śrī-jñāna.

These are only a few examples chosen at random from our *Appendix B.*

There are also other ways of identifying our Dīpaṃkara in the bsTan-'gyur. One of these is to consider *the evidence of the lo-tsā-ba-s who worked directly under him.* It is important to note that the names of some of them are quite familiar to us and from the *chos-'byuṅ*-s and other sources we know that they could not conceivably have worked under any other Indian *paṇḍita* bearing the name Dīpaṃkara. Thus the names of Jayaśīla (Tshul-khrims-rgyal-ba of Nag-tsho) and Vīryasiṃha (brTson-'grus-seṅ-ge of rGya) are known to us primarily because of their association with Atīśa and the possibility of their working under any other Dīpaṃkara is inconceivable. Again, though the great lo-tsā-ba Ratnabhadra (Rin-chen-bzaṅ-po) worked under many Indian *paṇḍita*-s, there could be none other among them bearing the name

Dīpaṃkara. Therefore if we find in the bsTan-'gyur that a work was translated by Dīpaṃkara along with any one of such well-known lo-tsā-ba-s, we can safely assert that this Dīpaṃkara is none else than Atīśa, regardless of the irregularities of mentioning his name or of adding titles to it like *paṇḍita*, *mahā-paṇḍita*, etc.

We may have here a few instances of the varied ways in which Dīpaṃkara's name occurs in the bsTan-'gyur as associated with such well-known lo-tsā-ba-s :

Abhisamaya-alaṃkāra-nāma-prajñā-pāramitā-upadeśa-śāstra-vṛtti-durbodha-āloka-nāma-ṭikā : translated by *upādhyāya paṇḍita* Dīpaṃkara-śrī-jñāna of India and the grand lo-tsā-ba *bhikṣu* Ratnabhadra,

Ārya-sahasra-bhuja-avalokiteśvara-sādhana : translated by *upādhyāya mahā-paṇḍita* Dīpaṃkara-śrī-jñāna of India and lo-tsā-ba *bhikṣu* Ratnabhadra,

Ekavīra-sādhana-nāma : translated by *ārya* Dīpaṃkara and lo-tsā-ba Jayaśīla of Nag-tsho,

Kalaśa-sādhana-nāma : translated by *paṇḍita* Dīpaṃkara-śrī-jñāna of India and lo-tsā-ba Vīryasiṃha of rGya,

Kṛṣṇa-yamāri-sādhana : translated by *upādhyāya mahā-paṇḍita* Dīpaṃkara-śrī-jñāna of India and lo-tsā-ba *bhikṣu* Jayaśīla of Nag-tsho,

Cakra-upadeśa-nāma : *paṇḍita* Dīpaṃkara-śrī-jñāna of India and lo-tsā-ba Vīryasiṃha of rGya,

Tri-śaraṇa-(gamana)-saptati : translated by *upādhyāya mahā-paṇḍita* Dīpaṃkara-śrī-jñāna of India and lo-tsā-ba *bhikṣu* Ratnabhadra.

More examples are not necessary. It is already obvious that the grounds on which H. P. Sastri suggests the possibility of there being the works of two different Dīpaṃkaras in the bsTan-'gyur are not tenable.

But this by no means implies that the bsTan-'gyur contains the works of only one Dīpaṃkara or that we come across only one Dīpaṃkara in the Tibetan sources. There are other considerations which deserve serious note and some of these indicate the clear possibility of there being more than one Indian Buddhist bearing the name Dīpaṃkara.

How many of them do we know of ?

"Besides Dīpaṃkara Śrī-jñāna", observes S. K. De,[3] "the bsTan-'gyur has preserved numerous works under the names Dīpaṃkara, Dīpaṃkara-candra, Dīpaṃkara-bhadra and Dīpaṃkara-rakṣita, who were probably not all identical". S. K. De apparently overlooks the existence in the bsTan-'gyur of other names like Dīpaṃkara-rāja, Dīpaṃkara-kīrti and Śrī-dīpaṃkara-jñāna-pāda, which, therefore, are to be added to his list. But how are we to determine whether all these names refer to the same person or which of these are indicative of different Dīpaṃkaras ? The question is a complex one and it can be answered on the basis of an examination of the evidences both internal and external to the bsTan-'gyur.

Let us begin with the name given as mere Dīpaṃkara. From 'Gos lo-tsā-ba[4] we learn that there was a Buddhist Tāntrika called Dīpaṃkara, who "possessed supernatural power", belonged to the Śūdra caste, was a disciple of *ācārya* Rakṣitapāda of a forest in Koṃ-ko-na (of the Guntur district) and had for his spiritual associates the Brāhmaṇa Guhyaparta, Mañjuśrī of the Kṣatriya caste, Pūrṇabhadra of the Vaiśya caste, Karṇaputra of the Śūdra caste and the harlots Ālokī and Duḥśīlā. Evidently, this Dīpaṃkara was not the same as Atiśa, with whom none of the above information agrees.

There is nothing to indicate that this Dīpaṃkara of the Śūdra caste ever wrote or translated any work which is included in the bsTan-'gyur. Yet the evidence of this Dīpaṃkara is important, for it shows that when we come across in the bsTan-'gyur a name given merely as Dīpaṃkara we cannot take him as identical with our Dīpaṃkara-śrī-jñāna unless there is some positive collateral evidence indicating it.

The bsTan-'gyur contains a considerable number of works the author or translator of which is mentioned simply as

3. S. K. De in HB i. 334n   4. BA i. 368.

Dīpaṃkara. Are we to attribute these to Atīśa ? A simple answer is not possible. For though in certain cases there are clear grounds to judge that the person mentioned could be none else than Atīśa, in certain other cases there are clear grounds to doubt this. In short, the bsTan-'gyur appears to contain the works of more than one person mentioned merely as Dīpaṃkara and only one of them could definitely be Atīśa. Here are some of the evidences of the bsTan-'gyur.

The author of the *Caryā-gīti-vṛtti* is mentioned as *paṇḍita* Dīpaṃkara. That this Dīpaṃkara could be none else than Atīśa is evident from the following. The *Index Tibetan* mentions him as Jo-bo-rje, the *Index Mongolian* mentions him as Atīśa and lo-tsā-ba Jayaśīla worked under him in translating this. On exactly the same grounds we are to consider the author of *Dharma-dhātu-darśana-gīti*, though mentioned as *mahā-ācārya* Dīpaṃkara, or the translator of *Eka-vīra-sādhana-nāma*, though mentioned as *ārya* Dīpaṃkara, as identical with Atīśa, Similarly the *upādhyāya* Dīpaṃkara, mentioned as translator of *Bodhisattva-caryāvatāra-piṇḍārtha*, or *paṇḍita* Dīpaṃkara, mentioned as the translator of the *Bodhisattva-caryāvatāra-ṣattriṃśat-piṇḍārtha*, could be none else than our Dīpaṃkara, because he is also mentioned as Jo-bo-rje and Atīśa in the *Index Tibetan* and the *Index Mongolian* respectively and because Jayaśīla worked under him for these translations.

Further, the author of the *Vajra-yoginī-stotra* is mentioned as *paṇḍita* Dīpaṃkara. But since the *Index Tibetan* calls him as Jo-bo-rje and the *Index Mongolian* Atīśa, and since, the great lo-tsā-ba Ratnabhadra worked under him for the translation of this work, he could be none else than Dīpaṃkara-śrī-jñāna. On exactly the same grounds, the author of the *Sarva-karma-āvaraṇa-viśodhana-vidhi*, though mentioned simply as *ācārya* Dīpaṃkara, is to be considered the same as Dīpaṃkara-śrī-jñāna.

Thus it was not against the convention of the writers of the bsTan-'gyur colophons to mention the same person alternatively as Dīpaṃkara and Dīpaṃkara-śrī-jñāna. That the same was not against the convention of the Tibetan historians is clear from the work of 'Gos lo-tsā-ba. In certain places of the work—e.g., in connection with the translation of the *Bhikṣu-varṣāgra-pṛcchā*—he speaks of Dīpaṃkara-śrī-jñāna.[5] Elsewhere, however, he refers to Atiśa simply as Dīpaṃkara.[6]

But the question is : Wherever in the bsTan-'gyur we come across the name simply as Dīpaṃkara, are we justified in assuming that he is the same as Dīpaṃkara-śrī-jñāna ? That we are not justified to do this will be obvious from the following cases, where the assumption would at best be doubtful.

In Cordier's *Catalogue*, as translators of Lalitavajra's *Kṛṣṇa-yamāri-cakra-nāma*[7] are mentioned *paṇḍita* Dīpaṃkara and lo-tsā-ba Vajrakīrti. Cordier himself does not mention any equivalent of *paṇḍita* Dīpaṃkara from *Index Tibetan* or *Index Mongolian*. In the Peking edition of the bsTan-'gyur, the colophon of the work is silent about its author or translator. Thus we have nothing direct on the strength of which we may take this *paṇḍita* Dīpaṃkara as Atiśa. The only clue we can work on is the name of the Tibetan lo-tsā-ba. Who, then, was this Vajrakīrti ? 'Gos lo-tsā-ba[8] mentions a famous Tibetan scholar called Vajrakīrti of Rwa. He was better known as the lo-tsā-ba of Rwa or the Rwa lo-tsā-ba.[9] This Rwa lo-tsā-ba could have worked directly under Dīpaṃkara. Yet there is nothing to prove that the translator of the *Kṛṣṇa-yamāri-cakra-nāma* was the same person. We hear of another Tibetan scholar called Vajrakīrti or rDo-rje-grags, also referred to as Master Ras-chuṅ-pa, and who was born, according to 'Gos lo-tsā-ba[10] in A.D. 1083, i.e. much later than the death of Atiśa. In view of the fact that the bsTan-'gyur[11] contains a number of translations by this Ras-chuṅ-pa or rDo-rje-grags there is nothing to disprove decisively the possibility of his working on the translation of the *Kṛṣṇa-yamāri-cakra-nāma*.

5. *Ib.* i. 30-1. 6. *Ib.* i. 44 ; ii. 732, 852. 7. rG. lxxxi. 11. 8. BA i. 374ff ; ii. 789. 9. *Ib.* i. 293, 325, 328 ; ii. 407, 442, 756, 765--the Tibetan translator is mentioned as Rwa-lo. i. 71, 296, 377, 379, 396 ; ii. 659, 755, 862--he is mentioned as Rwa lo-tsā-ba. 10. *Ib.* ii. 436. 11. rG. lxxiii. 8 ; lxxxii. 21, 60, 69. Lalou 190 brackets his name with rDo-rje-grags, the translator of the *Kṛṣṇa-yamāri-cakra-nāma*.

And if this was so, then the *paṇḍita* Dīpaṃkara under whom he worked could not be the same as our Dīpaṃkara. Incidentally, Vajrakīrti is mentioned to have worked under *paṇḍita upādhyāya* Dīpaṃkara of India for the translation of the *Cakra-nāma*,[12] and according to *Index Tibetan*, under *paṇḍita* Dīpaṃkara for the translation of the *Samayāmṛta-khāda-nāma*,[13] both written by Lalitavajra. Assuming this Vajrakīrti to be the same as the Rwa lo-tsā-ba, the *paṇḍita* Dīpaṃkara under whom he worked could be the same as our Dīpaṃkara ; assuming, however, that he was the same as Ras-chuṅ-pa, the Indian *paṇḍita* called Dīpaṃkara must have been a different one.

If the identity of Dīpaṃkara under whom the above Vajrakīrti worked is at best doubtful, there is clear evidence that in the bsTan-'gyur another Indian author is often mentioned simply as Dīpaṃkara though his full name was Dīpaṃkara-bhadra and that he must have been quite different from Dīpaṃkara-śrī-jñāna.

In Tibetan translation, the name of Dīpaṃkara-bhadra stands as Mar-me-mdzad-bzaṅ-po. The bsTan-'gyur contains thirtynine Tāntrika treatises of which he was the author. These are : rGyud-'grel xxxix. 13 ; xl. 18 ; xliii. 6 ; lxix. 7-13, 16-20, 31-40, 59-61, 68, 85, 92, 94-8, 100, 102, 107-9 ; lxxi. 385 and lxxxii. 45.

Interestingly, the colophons of only 30 out of these 39 works directly mention the author as Dīpaṃkara-bhadra (or, Śrī-dīpaṃkara-bhadra), adding occasionally to his name titles like *ācārya* and *mahā-ācārya*. The colophons of the remaining 9 works mention the author simply as Dīpaṃkara or Śrī-dīpaṃkara.[14] That the author of these nine works was in fact Dīpaṃkara-bhadra is known to us from the *Index Tibetan*. But since this Dīpaṃkara-bhadra was clearly different from our Dīpaṃkara-śrī-jñāna, we have in these nine works distinct warning against too readily concluding that when the

12. rG. lxxi. 13. 13. rG. lxxxi. 12. 14. rG. lxix. 7, 9, 10, 12-5, 18-9.

bsTan-'gyur mentions a name only as Dīpaṃkara he must have been the same as Atiśa.[15]

But what are the grounds for considering that this Dīpaṃkara-bhadra must have been quite different from Dīpaṃkara-śrī-jñāna ? The decisive evidences in support are external to the bsTan-'gyur. Still it is worthwhile to review first the information we have about Dīpaṃkara-bhadra in the bsTan-'gyur itself.

Of the 39 works attributed to Dīpaṃkara-bhadra, the bsTan-'gyur mentions the translators of only three.[16] Among the translators of these three works, again, the name of Dīpaṃkara-bhadra himself as the Indian *paṇḍita* is conspicuously absent. Besides, there is nothing to indicate in the bsTan-'gyur that this Dīpaṃkara-bhadra ever took any part in the Tibetan translation of any other Indian text. In other words, the possibility of Dīpaṃkara-bhadra having any personal contact with a Tibetan lo-tsā-ba is quite remote. Though not a decisive proof, it strongly suggests the possibility of Dīpaṃkara-bhadra never going to Tibet.

But let us pass on to consider the other and clearer evidences about Dīpaṃkara-bhadra. Considering that he was the author of at least 39 Tāntrika treatises,—and it is quite conceivable that some of his works were never translated into Tibetan and are thus not preserved in the bsTan-'gyur,—we are to admit that he must have had considerable reputation as a Tāntrika. Therefore it is only to be expected that the Tibetan historians of Buddhism, who considered Tāntrism as a very important form of Buddhism, should take note of such an eminent Tāntrika. As a matter of fact, we find 'Gos lo-tsā-ba, Tāranātha and Sum-pa referring to him and from the information we have about Dīpaṃkara-bhadra from these historians we can clearly see that he must have been quite different from and much earlier than Atiśa.

15. rG. lxix. 78, 79, 101, and 103 mention the author simply as Dīpaṃkara. But since these Tāntrika treatises are found in the bunch of the works of Dīpaṃkara-bhadra, we have hesitated to include these in our *Appendix B* containing the list of Atiśa's works. 16. rG. xxix. 13 ; lxxi. 385 ; lxxxii 45.

'Gos lo-tsā-ba refers to Dīpaṃkara-bhadra thrice.

While discussing Buddhaśrījñāna, a great adept in the Guhya-samāja-tantra, he says,[17] "He (Buddhaśrījñāna) had eighteen excellent disciples. Among them Dīpaṃkara-bhadra, Praśāntamitra, Rāhulabhadra and Mahāsukhatā-vajra....The names of the remaining fourteen disciples cannot be ascertained with certitude."

The second reference by 'Gos lo-tsā-ba to Dīpaṃkara-bhadra is as follows : "His (Balin *ācārya*'s) previous Lineage : 'Jam-pa'i-rdo-rje, the *ācārya* Buddhajñānapāda, Mar-me-mdzad-bzaṅ-po (Dīpaṃkara-bhadra), Mañjuśrīkīrtimitra, the keeper of horses dPal-bde-ba-chen-po, also known by the name of Kamalakuliśa and Anaṅgavajra and the *ācārya* Yi-ge-pa. He was a clerk of the king Śrī Dharmapāla. Besides receiving the blessing of Śar-ba-pa, he also attained excellent realisation (Buddhahood). He was the spiritual teacher of the former king."[18]

Again, in connection with the tradition of the same Guhya-samāja-tantra, 'Gos lo-tsā-ba says, "The other Lineage of this initiation is as follows : Mañjuśrī, Jñānapāda (Buddhajñāna), Dīpaṃkara-bhadra, Ānandagarbha, Tha-ga-na, Śānti-pā, Śraddhākara, Padmākara."[19]

Tāranātha gives a fairly long account of Buddhaśrījñāna and his disciple Dīpaṃkara-bhadra. "In Madhya-deśa", says Tāranātha, "in the district of Khabi was the city of Takṣaśilā (Tavila). There was a Brāhmaṇa *ācārya* who became a monk in Nālandā of Mahāsāṅghika school and received the name of Buddhaśrījñāna. Some say he was of Kṣatriya caste and reader to the king...As Buddhaśrījñāna went to the west towards Udayāna he discussed with *ācārya* Līlāvajra and *yoginī* Guṇeru about many heterodox and Buddhist Dhāraṇī-learnings. In the north of Udayāna there was a Caṇḍāla girl by the name of Jaṭijālā. With this holy queen for eight months he gave himself up to some Tantras and as he had received a prophecy from Jambala he got Vidyātantra

17. BA i. 371. 18. *Ib*. i. 372. 19. *Ib*. i. 373.

immediately with it. As regards the history of offerings at Vajrāsana, it is thus : As once the *ācārya* sat in his hut which he had built near Vajrāsana, there came king Dharmapāla to give alms to Vajrāsana. All the Bauddha *ācārya*-s came to the gift. As he saw the *ācārya* not taking part in it, the king thought that he wanted to humiliate him. Now as he entered the hut of the *ācārya*, he saw that the *ācārya* was not there, but a statue of Mañjuśrī. Then he looked around and asked his companions. With their answer : 'But he is here' he re-entered and the *ācārya* became visible. (Then followed a miracle). The king became a believer and prayed for *abhiṣeka* and as he had no more gift to give, bound himself and his wife to be his servants ; in the meantime he brought gold from his palace as high as his stature and that of his wife as ransom money..."[20]

Much of this is, of course, transparent fiction. But the whole thing cannot be rejected like that. Some of the details given by Tāranātha about Buddhaśrījñāna—like that of his going to the country of Oḍḍiyāna, his meeting with Lalitavajra and Gu-ṇe-ru, his Tāntrika practices for eight months with the 16 year old Caṇḍāla girl Jaṭijālā (Dza-thig-dza-la), etc.—substantially agree with those of the account given by 'Gos lo-tsā-ba.[21] Evidently the two historians were drawing upon the same tradition and there is nothing to prove that the entire tradition was baseless. That Buddhaśrījñāna was a contemporary of Dharmapāla appears to have formed part of the same tradition, because it was distinctly hinted at by 'Gos lo-tsā-ba as well. Therefore, if Dharmapāla ruled during A.D. 770-810,[22] Dīpaṃkara-bhadra, the direct disciple of Buddhaśrījñāna, must have been much earlier than Dīpaṃkara-śrī-jñāna.

Tāranātha has the following account of Dīpaṃkara-bhadra himself. "Dīpaṃkara-bhadra was born in western India. After learning the Vedas, he became later either a monk of a temple-monastery (!) or the president of Mahāsāṅghika Saṅgha. He met the great *ācārya* Buddhaśrījñāna in Nālandā. He was

20. B. N. Datta, *Mystic Tales*, 51-2. 21. BA i. 367-8. 22. HB i. 176

killed by a Tīrthika king in Sindhu, who always used to harm the disciples of the *ācārya.* Some historians mention him as the Turuska king Bhūṣaṇa, but there were no Turuskas in Madhyadeśa at that time."[23]

Sum-pa[24] mentions Dīpaṃkara-bhadra while giving a list of the successive *sthavira*-s of the Vikramaśīla *vihāra.* It is not easy to follow the exact chronological order of these *sthavira*-s from the way in which Sum-pa mentions them. This much seems to be clear, however, that long before Atīśa became the *upādhyāya* of the *vihāra*, Dīpaṃkara-bhadra, who, "by attaining *siddhi* subdued the Tīrthika king", succeeḍed Buddhajñāna as the *sthavira* of Vikramaśīla.

One point definitely emerges from all these. According to the tradition on which the Tibetan historians depend, Dīpaṃkara-bhadra was much earlier than Dīpaṃkara-śrī-jñāna. Therefore the works in the bsTan-'gyur attributed to Dīpaṃkara-bhadra must have been composed by another Tāntrika Buddhist.

We may now take the case of Dīpaṃkara-candra. The bsTan-'gyur mentions him only once—as the Indian *paṇḍita* who participated in the translation of Bodhigarbha's *Śrī-hevajra-sādhana-nāma.*[25] In the *Index Tibetan* the name occurs as Dīpaṃkara-rāja. From the internal evidence of the bsTan-'gyur itself it appears that he could not have been the same as Atīśa. The Tibetan lo-tsā-ba who worked under him for the above translation is, according to Cordier's *Catalogue*, "Muni-rāja, the powerful sovereign", or, according to the colophon of the Peking edition, Lha-btsan-po Mu-ne-rāja. This "mighty sovereign" was presumably the Tibetan king Mu-ne-btsan-po, who, according to 'Gos lo-tsā-ba[26] ruled for seventeen years and died in A.D. 797, i.e. long before the birth of Atīśa. He was the eldest son of king Khri-sroṅ-lde-btsan, who, according to 'Gos lo-tsā-ba, ruled during the years A.D. 755-780 and under whose patronage the translation activity of Indian

23. B. N. Datta, *Mystic Tales*, 54. 24. Sum-pa 121f. 25. rG. xxi. 9.
26. BA i. 52. Bu-ston ii. 196f.

texts into Tibetan received its first great incentive.[27] Up to A.D. 836,—the time of Ral-pa-can's death,—the Tibetan kings took a great deal of interest in the Tibetan translation of Buddhist works and some of them took direct part in these translations. Therefore, it is quite conceivable that though a king Mu-ne-btsan-po acted also as a lo-tsā-ba. And if this was so, the Indian *paṇḍita* Dīpaṃkara-candra or Dīpaṃkara-rāja under whom he worked must have lived a few centuries earlier than Dīpaṃkara-śrī-jñāna. Since there is nothing to indicate in the colophon under discussion that this Tibetan king ever came to India, we are left to presume further that Dīpaṃkara-candra must have visited Tibet to be able to work with Mu-ne-btsan-po, though beyond this we know practically nothing about him. The *sBa-bshed*[28] or "Affirmation of Faith", which contains the history of the reigns of Khri-sroṅ-lde-btsan and Mu-ne-btsan-po, may perhaps be searched for some further information of Dīpaṃkara-candra.

We are now left to consider the names of Śrī-dīpaṃkara-jñāna-pāda, Dīpaṃkara-rakṣita and Dīpaṃkara-kīrti, whose works are preserved in the bsTan-'gyur and our main question is : Are we to consider them as different from Dīpaṃkara-śrī-jñāna ? The internal evidences of the bsTan-'gyur lead us to the view that though the case of Dīpaṃkara-kīrti may be somewhat doubtful the names Dīpaṃkara-jñāna-pāda and Dīpaṃkara-rakṣita are but variations of the name of Dīpaṃkara-śrī-jñāna.

The name of Śrī-dīpaṃkara-jñāna-pāda occurs only once in the bsTan-'gyur—as the translator of the work *Bodhi-mārga-pradīpa-pañjikā-nāma.*[29] The work itself, as its Tibetan subtitle in the Peking edition clearly says, is "the auto-commentary on the *Bodhi-patha-pradīpa* done by Jo-bo-rje." Its colophon

27. See Sections 25 and 26. N. Dutt in *Prajñā,* Foreword vii, attributes to Khri-sroṅ-lde-btsan the credit of finally revising the rules for Tibetan translation, which, according to Bu-ston, ii. 197, was really due to Ral-pa-can, or, according to the colophon of the *Mahāvyutpatti* (mDo cxxiii. 44), was due to king Khri-lde-sroṅ-btsan. 28. BA i. Intro. v. 29. mDo xxxi. 10. See Appendix B for the long colophon.

is long and interesting. From it we gather that the translator mentioned as Śrī-dīpaṃkara-jñāna-pāda was but the same as the author mentioned alternatively as Dīpaṃkara-śrī-jñāna and Dīpaṃkara-śrī-pāda of Bengal. Besides, the lo-tsā-ba who worked under him for the translation was none but the author's faithful disciple Jayaśīla of Nag-tsho. These evidences are decisive. Śrī-dīpaṃkara-jñāna-pāda or Dīpaṃkara-śrī-pāda could be none else than Atīśa.

The name Dīpaṃkara-kīrti occurs only once in the bsTan-'gyur and this as the translator of the *Samaya-tārā-stava.*[30] In the Peking edition, its colophon is : "Written by Vāgīśvara-kīrti, the immortal and the resident of Ratnagiri of Kośala ; translated by the Indian *upādhyāya* Dīpaṃkara-kīrti and lo-tsā-ba Prabhākara of Tshur." We may mention here only a few points regarding the possible identity of Dīpaṃkara-kīrti with Atīśa, though none of these can perhaps be regarded as conclusive.

First, the *Index Tibetan* mentions him as *mahā-ācārya* Dīpaṃkara-jñāna of India. Though the most typical form in which the *Index Tibetan* mentions Atīśa is Jo-bo-rje, '*mahā-ācārya* Dīpaṃkara-jñāna of India' is also a form in which Atīśa is frequently mentioned by the Tibetan sources. Secondly, Atīśa is clearly known to be a translator of many other works by the same Vāgīśvarakīrti. Thus, e.g., two different works by Vāgīśvarakīrti bearing the same title *Mṛtyu-vañcana-upadeśa*[31] and the work called *Mṛtyu-vañcana-piṇḍārtha*[32] by Vagīśvarakīrti were translated by Dīpaṃkara-śrī-jñāna and lo-tsā-ba *bhikṣu* Ratnabhadra. Besides, Dīpaṃkara-śrī-jñāna participated in the translation of many other works of Suvāgīśvarakīrti,[33] who could have been the same as Vāgīśvarakīrti, because 'Gos lo-tsā-ba mentions only one Vāgīśvarakīrti, who was a great adept in Tantrism and was a gate-keeper scholar of the Vikramaśīla *vihāra* sometime before the time of Atīśa[34]

30. rG. lxxxii. 48. 31. rG. xxvi. 68 & lxxxi. 21. 32. rG. lxxxi. 19.
33. See Section 4, Appendix B : nine such works are mentioned. 34. BA i. 206 ; ii. 758.

Thirdly, Dīpaṃkara-kīrti in the colophon above could have only meant "Dīpaṃkara, the famous", the actual Tibetan form in which this name is given being "Dīpaṃkara-grags-pa" and *grags-pa* means "the famous or the well-known." Prabhākara of Tshur, however, who worked under Dīpaṃkara-kīrti for the translation of this work must have been a scholar of minor importance, for his name does not occur either in 'Gos lo-tsā-ba's encyclopaedic work or in the bsTan-'gyur as working under Atīśa for the translation of any other work.

None of these grounds can perhaps be taken as decisive for the identification of Dīpaṃkara-kīrti with Atīśa. Still, since the bsTan-'gyur shows considerable variation in mentioning the name of Dīpaṃkara-śrī-jñāna, the possibility of Dīpaṃkara-kīrti being one of such variants is perhaps not to be entirely ruled out.

The grounds for considering Dīpaṃkara-rakṣita of the bsTan-'gyur as identical with Dīpaṃkara-śrī-jñāna are comparatively clear.

In the bsTan-'gyur, the name Dīpaṃkara-rakṣita occurs five times. Thus—

1). According to Cordier's *Catalogue*, the work *Vajrasattva-sādhana-nāma*[35] was "corrected by *upādhyāya mahāpaṇḍita* Dīpaṃkara-rakṣita of India and lo-tsā-ba (Ratnakīrti) of Bari of Kham origin. The correction was executed at the Śrī-Anupama-nirābhoga Vihāra". The colophon of its Peking edition also says, "And again, Indian *upādhyāya* Dīpaṃkara-rakṣita and the Kham-pa *bhikṣu* lo-tsā-ba Bari revised it, and commented on it at the 'incomparable and miraculous *vihāra*' (dpe-med-lhun-grub-gtsug-lag-khaṅ)". This description, viz. the incomparable and miraculous *vihāra,* is typical of the Tho-liṅ monastery, which means that the correction of the above text was executed by Dīpaṃkara-rakṣita in Tibet.

2). In the Peking edition of the bsTan-'gyur, the *Pramāṇa-vārttika-alaṃkāra-ṭīkā*[36] contains the following colophon : "Written by *ācārya* Jaya. Translated very carefully by

35. rG. xxxiii. 18. 36. mDo ci and cii.

mahā-paṇḍita Srī-dīpaṃkara-rakṣita, the Indian *upādhyāya* of Vikramaśīla, and the great lo-tsā-ba 'Or Ban-de Byaṅ-chub-śes-rab (Bodhiprajña) of Shaṅ-shuṅ at the incomparable and miraculous temple of Tho-liṅ, under the request of Tibet's *bodhisattva-vaṃśadhara-narottama*, created by the *devatā*-s, the Lha-btsan-po Śākya-bhikṣu Lha-bla-ma Shi-ba-'od (Devaguru Śāntiprabha) and Lha-btsan-po dBaṅ-phyug-btsan-pa'i mṄa'-bdag-chen-po Khri-bkra-śis-rtse-lde-btsan.".

3). As the translators of the *Vajra-bhairava-gaṇacakra-nāma*,[37] we have "*upādhyāya* Dīpaṃkara-rakṣita of India and lo-tsā-ba *bhikṣu* Vajrakīrti of Rwa."

4). The colophon of the *Vajra-sattva-sādhana-bhāṣya*[38] says, "Written by *ācārya* Tathāgatarakṣita ; translated by Indian *upādhyāya mahā-paṇḍita* Dīpaṃkara-rakṣita and lo-tsā-ba Bari of Kham at the incomparable and miraculous temple of Tho-liṅ."

5). The translators of the *Śrī-cakra-samvara-sahaja-tattva-āloka*[39] are *paṇḍita* Dīpaṃkara-rakṣita of India and lo-tsā-ba Dharmeśvara of Mar-pa."

Let us consider the information we have about Dīpaṃkara-rakṣita in the above colophons. First, this Dīpaṃkara-rakṣita originally belonged to the Vikramaśīla *vihāra* of India. Secondly, he worked in Tibet at the Tho-liṅ *vihāra* as an Indian *paṇḍita*. Thirdly, the use of titles like *upādhyāya, mahā-paṇḍita* apart, the subject-matter as well as the bulk of the *Pramāṇa-vārttika-alaṃkāra-ṭīkā* translated by him are enough to covince us of the great stature of this Indian scholar.

But when did such a great scholar bearing the name Dīpaṃkara come from the Vikramaśīla *vihāra* to Tibet ? We have definite evidence for this in the colophon of the *Pramāṇa-vārttika-alaṃkāra-ṭīkā*, which states that one of the Tibtean rulers at whose request this translation was carried out was Lha-btsan-po *śākya-bhikṣu deva-guru* Śāntiprabha. This evidence is decisive. For the fame of king Śāntiprabha in Tibetan history rests, above all, on one fact and that is being

37. rG. xliii. 67. 38. rG. xxxiv. 9. 39. rG. xiii, 53.

the royal patron of Dīpaṃkara-śrī-jñāna. The long name of the other Tibetan king mentioned in the same colophon is that of Śāntiprabha's nephew.[40] Therefore, to think that Dīpaṃkara-rakṣita of the bsTan-'gyur was different from Dīpaṃkara-śrī-jñāna, it is necessary to imagine that another scholar of great eminence bearing the name Dīpaṃkara came from the Vikramaśila *vihāra* to Tibet round about the same time as Dīpaṃkara-śrī-jñāna and worked there translating and correcting extremely important Indian texts, though no other Tibetan source cares to take any note of him. Such an assumption, to say the least, would be untenable.

The possible identity of Dīpaṃkara-rakṣita with Dīpaṃkara-śrī-jñāna is further suggested by the evidences of the lo-tsā-ba-s said to have worked under Dīpaṃkara-rakṣita. They are lo-tsā-ba Ratnakīrti of Bari, generally referred to as Bari lo-tsā-ba, lo-tsā-ba Bodhiprajña (Byaṅ-chub-śes-rab) of Shaṅ-shuṅ, lo-tsā-ba Vajrakīrti of Rwa and lo-tsā-ba Dharmeśvara of Mar-pa.

Lo-tsā-ba Ratnakīrti of Bari worked directly under Dīpaṃkara-śrī-jñāna. As translators of the *Seka-prakriyā*,[41] the bsTan-'gyur mentions "*mahā-paṇḍita* Dīpaṃkara-śrī-jñāna and Ratnakīrti, the lo-tsā-ba of Bari."

The evidence of lo-tsā-ba Byaṅ-chub-śes-rab or Bodhiprajña working in Tibet while Atīśa was there is as follows. The same lo-tsā-ba is mentioned[42] to have worked under *upādhyāya* Kumārakalaśa of India for the translation of *Śrī-hevajra-stotra* and *upādhyāya* Kumārakalaśa translated the *Mañjuśrī-mūla-tantra* at the Tho-liṅ *vihāra* under the request[43] of king Bodhiprabha (Byaṅ-chub-'od), the royal disciple of Atīśa.

Lo-tsā-ba Vajrakīrti of Rwa is not to be confused with the other Tibetan scholar Vajrakīrti or Ras-chuṅ-pa who, as we have seen, was later than Atīśa. Rwa lo-tsā-ba, we learn from the work of 'Gos lo-tsā-ba, attended the Council of the

40. *Deb-ther-dmar-po* (Tr. Tucci, Rome 1959), 27. 41. rG. xl. 15.
42. rG. xxii. 16. 43. BA i. Intro. x.

Fire-Dragon year, i.e., of A.D. 1076.[44] It is, therefore, not improbable for him to have worked under Atīśa.

Lo-tsā-ba Dharmeśvara of Mar-pa (Mar-Pa Chos-kyi-dbaṅ-phyug), we are told by 'Gos lo-tsā-ba,[45] "attended the classes" of a contemporary of Atīśa.[46] Therefore it is quite conceivable for lo-tsā-ba Dharmeśvara of Mar-pa to have worked directly under Atīśa.

To sum up : Though Atīśa's name often occurs simply as Dīpaṃkara, he is to be distinguished from the Tāntrika writer Dīpaṃkara-bhadra, whose name also is found in the bsTan-'gyur sometimes as simply Dīpaṃkara. Dīpaṃkara-candra or Dīpaṃkara-rāja of the bsTan-'gyur is clearly different from Atīśa, though Dīpaṃkara-kīrti was possibly the same as Atīśa. Atīśa's name occurs in the bsTan-'gyur in various forms, inclusive of Dīpaṃkara-pāda, Dīpaṃkara-jñāna-pāda and Dīpaṃkara-rakṣita.

44. *Ib*. i. 70 - date of the council. i. 328 - Rwa attending it. 45. *Ib* i. 163. 46. *Ib*. i. 163.

6. *Birth and Lineage*

"There has been", says Rahula Sankrityayan, "useless controversy as to whether Dīpaṃkara was born in Bengal or in Bihar. Authoritative Tibetan sources leave us in no doubt that he was born in Bhagalpur".[1] One cannot, without hesitation, question the authority of a Tibetologist of Rahula's stature. Nevertheless, since Rahula himself does not mention any Tibetan source on which this statement is based, and since, moreover, such a statement goes against the unanimous view of practically all the other reputed scholars, it is necessary for us, before subscribing too readily to this statement, to review the actual information we have about Dīpaṃkara's birth-place in the 'authoritative Tibetan sources'.

Of the *bsTod-pa*-s or *stotra*-s to Dīpaṃkara, two are considered to be specially authentic by the Tibetan historians. One of these is by 'Brom-ston-pa, the foremost disciple of Dīpaṃkara. The other is by Jayaśīla of Nag-tsho, who, "attended for nineteen years on the Master",[2] inclusive of his few years' stay at the Vikramaśīla *vihāra*.

Says 'Brom-ston-pa in his *stotra*, "I offer prayer to the feet of Dīpaṃkara-śrī, who was born in the noble Jīva family of the kings of *za-hor* of the *tri-sampanna* Bengal in the same line to which Śāntijīva (Śāntarakṣita) belonged".[3]

Says Nag-tsho[4] in his *stotra*,

In the east, in the marvellous country of *za-hor*,
There has been a great city
Called Vikramapura.
In its centre (stood) a royal residence,
A very spacious palace it was,
Called 'Golden Bannered'.

1. Rahula in *2500 Years*, 227. 2. BA i. 216. 3. *śloka* 1, See Section 2, Appendix A. 4. Quoted by Roerich BA i. 241-2.

In wealth, subjects and revenue,
(The king) was the equal of the king sToṅ-khun of China.
The kingdom's ruler Kalyāṇaśrī
And his queen Prabhāvatī
Had three sons :
Padmagarbha and Candragarbha,
And Śrīgarbha...
The middle son, Candragarbha
Is at present the Venerable Teacher (bLa-ma rJe-btsun,
i.e. Atīśa).

Of the Tibetan histories of Buddhism, two in particular are very highly respected. One of these is by Bu-ston and the other by 'Gos lo-tsā-ba. Bu-ston says that Dīpaṃkara-śrī-jñāna "was the son of Kalyāṇaśrī, the king of Bengal."[5] Says 'Gos lo-tsā-ba, "This great teacher : King Kalyāṇaśrī of the great kingdom called Sa-hor by the Indians and Za-hor by the Tibetans, whose might was equal to that of the king sToṅ-khun of China, dwelling in a palace called 'Golden Banner', and his queen named Śrīprabhā had three sons : the eldest son was Padmagarbha, the second son was Candra-garbha, and the youngest son was Śrīgarbha. The Venerable Master was the second son Candragarbha."[6]

Another history of Buddhism which enjoys considerable prestige among the modern scholars is by Sum-pa, in which is said, "At the time the Buddha came to the world, he (Atīśa) was born as a householder called Jinaputra-bhadracaryā in Rājagṛha. One thousand eight hundred and fifteen years after the Fire-Hare year of the Buddha's *nirvāṇa*, towards the end of the Fire-Sky-Ocean period, he (Atīśa) acted as if being reborn in the Water-Horse year in *za-hor* in Bengal in Eastern India in the central palace with golden banners of the city of Vikramapura in the noble family which had the greatest *paṇḍita* Śāntijīva in its line of descent, having for his father

5. Bu-ston ii.213. 6. BA i.241.

Kalyāṇaśrī and mother Padmaprabhā and as the middle of the three sons with the name Candragarbha. It is said that in his youth he had five queens and nine princes called Puṇyaśrī, etc., were born of him."[7]

In the *Life of Atīśa* by mKhan-po-mchim-thams-cad mkhyen-pa translated by S. C. Das we read, "Dīpaṃkara was born A.D. 980 in the royal family of Gaur at Vikrama-(ni)pur in Bāṅgālā, a country lying to the east of Vajrāsana."[8]

Waddell[9] says that Dīpaṃkara was born "of the royal family of Gaur at Vikramanipur (?) in Bengal". Jaschke,[10] Cordier,[11] and other scholars[12] take this for granted.

Among the modern scholars who emphatically assert that Dīpaṃkara was a Bengalee, special mention may be made of H.P. Sastri[13] and S. K. De,[14] the decisive evidence for both being the colophons of two works in the bsTan-'gyur, viz. the *Ekavīra-sādhana* and the *Bali-vidhi*. But it is possible to find in the bsTan-'gyur more evidences to support the claim.

In the Peking edition of the bsTan-'gyur, the colophon of the *Prajñā-pāramitā-piṇḍārtha-pradīpa*[15] reads, "This alone contains the Buddha's doctrines. The Bengal-born *bhikṣu* Dīpaṃkara-śrī-jñāna wrote it according to the *śāstra*-s and *guru-vacana*-s." The colophon of the *Bodhi-mārga-pradīpa-pañjikā-nāma* contains the following : "...Dīpaṃkara-śrī-jñāna, a descendant of the Bengalee king ...Representing the Buddha this time, Dīpaṃkara-śrī-jñāna was born in Bengal." As the author of the *Ekavīra-sādhana* is mentioned "*ārya paiṇḍapātika* Śrī-dīpaṃkara-jñāna of Bengal." Again, in the Peking edition, the colophon of the *Caṇḍa-mahāroṣaṇa-sādhana-paramārtha-nāma* says, "Written by Dīpaṃkara-śrī-jñāna, the

7. Sum-pa 183. 8. S. C. Das in JBTS I.i.7. 9. Waddell L 35n. 10. J-TED 603. 11. See Cordier's understanding of the colophons of mDo x.2 ; xxxi. 10 ; cxxviii. 10, etc. 12. Bell 53. 13. *Bauddha Gān O Dohā* (Bengali) 22. cf. *Prācīna Bāṃlār Gaurava* (Bengali) 33ff 14. S. K. De in HB i. 335. 15. For this and other texts mentioned in this connection, see Appendix B.

mahā-ācārya paṇḍita of Bengal" ; the colophon of the *Bali-vidhi* says, "*bhikṣu* Dīpaṃkara-śrī-jñāna, who was born in Bengal, wrote this *Bali-vidhi* under the blessings of his *guru*". The colophon of the *Nikāya-bheda-vibhaṅga-vyākhyāna* says, "translated and revised by *ācārya paṇḍita* called *mahā-paṇḍita* Dīpaṃkara-śrī-jñāna of Bengal (Baṃgāl).

That Dīpaṃkara was actually born in Bengal clearly follows from the Tibetan sources mentioned above, assuming, of course, that the English rendering of these sources is correct. But it is necessary to have some clarification on the Tiebtan word which is rendered in these as "Bengal". Generally speaking, this word is Bhaṅgala, uniformly rendered as "Bengal" by Cordier and others. What, then, is their justification ?

First, as Jaschke[16] points out, the letter "*bha* is sometimes written for *ba*, either from ignorance or in order to appear as learned." Thus, Baṅgala could have easily assumed the form Bhaṅgala in the Tibetan writings. That this actually happened is attested to by the *Tibetan-English Dictionary*[17] of S. C. Das, where Bhaṅ-ga-la is rendered as Baṅgala (modern Eastern Bengal). As an illustration of the use of the word, Das quotes the following line : *bhaṅ-ga-la-pa-thams-cad-dmag-tu-spran-nas* and renders it as "(king Deva Pāla) summoning all the Baṅgala-pa into war". Thus, the word Bhaṅgala in the Tibetan sources appears to be but a variation of the word Baṃgala or Baṅgala, as it is actually written in the colophon of the *Nikāya-bheda-vibhaṅga-vyākhyāna* of the Peking edition of the bsTan-'gyur.

Secondly, the word Bhaṅgala frequently occurs in Tāranātha's *chos-'byuṅ* and R. C. Majumdar[18] has made a detailed survey of all these occurrences for determining the location of the original kingdom of the Pālas, which, according to Tāranātha, was Bhaṅgala. From this he concludes that the

16. J-TED 386. 17. D-TED 861-2 18. Majumdar in HB i. 182ff, 336f ; in IHQ xvi. 219f.

Bhaṅgala of Tāranātha "may be taken to denote, in a general way, southern and eastern Bengal."

That Dīpaṃkara was born in the eastern rather than the southern part of Bengal is evident from the clear mention of Vikramapura in connection with the birth-place of Dīpaṃkara. Nag-tsho and Sum-pa, as quoted above, give a transliteration of the name Vikramapura in Tibetan characters[19] and we are aware of only one Vikramapura in eastern India and that is in Dacca. This, as corroborated by the popular tradition which connects the residence of Atīśa with the village Vajrayoginī of Vikramapura, Dacca, leads us to accept the older view of Sashibhusana Vidyalamkara and others,[20] namely that Atīśa was born in the Vajrayoginī village of Vikramapura, Dacca.

It may incidentally be mentioned here that whatever may be the present condition of the Vajrayoginī village of Vikramapura, there are grounds to think that this was once a prosperous centre of eastern India. "Vajrayoginī (in E. Bengal)", says S. C. Sarkar,[21] "which exists even now as a well-known village was the capital of Baṅgala on the eve of Gopāla's accession. The place was therefore a flourishing one three centuries before Atīśa's time." The Vajrayoginī copper-plate of Sāmalavarman also indicates the past glory of Vajrayoginī and Vikramapura.[22]

In connection with the question whether Dīpaṃkara was actually born in Bengal, or whether he was a Bengalee, we may mention here one extremely interesting evidence preserved in a Tibetan source which indicates that he himself spoke the Bengali language, though perhaps outside the academic discussions.

The *Life of Atīśa* translated by S. C. Das, while describing Atīśa's journey to Tho-liṅ, says, "His demeanour, personal beauty, though sixty years old, and his pleasant appearance made him worthy of divine honour. A smile was ever present

19. Sometimes in its corrupted form as Vikramaṇipura. 20. *Jīvanī-koṣa* (Bengali), *Bhāratīya Aitihāsika*, i.26. 21. S. C. Sarkar in JBORS xxvii.567. 22. R. C. Majumdar in HB i. 200-2.

on his face, and Sanskrit *mantra*-s were always on his lips. His voice was distinct, loud and impressive. At the end of a sentence, he often said, *Ati Bhāla ! Ati Bhāla ! Ati Maṅgala. Ati Bhāla haé.*"[23]

This is the only extant record of words actually spoken by Atīśa, and as the word *bhāla* suggests, the language was old Bengalī. mKhan-po-mchim-thams-cad-mkhyen-pa, the author of this biography, could not have produced these words from his own imagination. These could only be based on some actual observation. According to the Tibetan tradition, this biography is based on the communication by Nag-tsho to Phyag-sor-pa,—a tradition which we have no ground to reject as baseless.[24] Nag-tsho, of all the Tibetan scholars, had the best opportunity of observing how Atīśa himself spoke in his moments of ecstasy during the journey to Tho-liṅ.

There remains another important point to be considered in connection with the birth-place of Atīśa. There is some controversy over the word *za-hor*, which, as we have seen, frequently occurs in the Tibetan sources in this context. "This place Zahor", says S. K. De,[25] "is conjectured in turns to be Lahore and Jessore in South Bengal (Waddell and Sarat Chandra Das) and Sabhar in East Bengal (H. P. Sastri)... A. H. Francke would with great probability identify it with Mandi in North-Western India." But we failed to find any substantial evidence offered by Francke in support of his own conjecture. In two places of his work, he simply puts the word Mandi within brackets after mentioning the word Zahor.[26] Of course, Jaschke,[27] on the basis of his understanding of 'The Collection of Legends of Padmasambhava', proposes to locate Zahor in north-west India, and adds "by the statements of Lamas, the present Mandi, a small principality under British protection, in the Punjab, between the rivers Byas and Ravi, where there is a sacred lake, celebrated as a

23. S. C. Das in JBTS I. i. 29.
24. See Note 12, Section 3.
25. S. K. De in HB i. 331n.
26. Francke AIT ii. 65, 89.
27. J-TED 485.

place of pilgrimage, from which the Brahmins residing there derive a considerable income".

That it is palpably absurd to take such a geographical location of *za-hor* in connection at least with the birth-place of Dīpaṃkara is clear from the circumstances that the Tibetan sources, while mentioning the birth-place of Dīpaṃkara, over and above the use of the word *za-hor*, say that Dīpaṃkara was born in Bhaṅgala in Eastern India and in a palace at Vikramapura. None of these details fits in with Mandi of the Punjab. What, then, can the word *za-hor* mean in connection with the birth-place of Dīpaṃkara ?

A way out of this difficulty is perhaps suggested by the understanding of the word *za-hor* by Csoma de Coros[28] and Sarat Chandra Das.[29] According to Csoma de Coros, the word *za-hor* is but an equivalent of the word *sahor*, the common name for a city. Sarat Chandra Das also points out that the Tibetan word *za-hor* is only a corrupt form of the word *sahor*. This is fully confirmed by 'Gos lo-tsā-ba,[30] who says that Thon-mi Sambhoṭa, while first devising the Tibetan alphabets, "added the sounds of *sha*, *za* and ('), which he thought necessary in Tibetan, though absent in the Indian alphabet. Of these three the sound *sha* has the same sound as *śa* of the Indian alphabet, because of this (similarity) a certain *paṇḍita* from Nepal, when addressing a letter to the Dharmasvāmin Bu-ston called him : 'Śa-lu *paṇḍita*' (instead of Sha-lu paṇḍita). Because the sound *za* is similar to *sa* the Indians pronounce Sa-hor, while the Tibetans call (this country) Za-hor".

There is thus the possibility of taking the word *za-hor* not as a proper name but as the Tibetan equivalent of the Indian word pronounced as *sahor* (or *śahor*), meaning city. And this may resolve some of the difficulties of the modern scholars,

28. *Tibetan English Dictionary*. Quoted by S. C. Das in JBTS I. i 8n. cf. J-TED 485. 29. D-TED 1089. In JBTS I i. 8n S. C. Das suggests that the word could have been derived from Urdu. 30. BA i. 39. Incidentally, Atīśa is said to have had the same line of descent to which Śāntarakṣita belonged and Sum-pa 112 asserts that Śāntarakṣita was born in the royal family of za-hor of Eastern Bengal.

inasmuch as the mention of *za-hor*, meaning *sa-hor*, does not necessarily connect the place with the Punjab alone.

The word *sahor* is Persian in origin. S. K. Chatterji[31] remarks that Persian words were current in Eastern India already in the 7th century A. D. It is, therefore, quite conceivable that the Tibetans were acquainted with the word *sahor* long before the birth of Dīpaṃkara.

As for the lineage of Dīpaṃkara, the Tibetan sources repeatedly assert that he was born in a royal family. Nag-tsho, as we have seen, says that his father Kalyāṇaśrī was as wealthy and powerful a king as sToṅ-khun of China (Indo-China ?) and that the palace in which Dīpaṃkara was born had golden flags flying on it. The same or similar accounts occur in the statements of Bu-ston, 'Gos lo-tsā-ba and Sum-pa. Further, the colophons of some of Atīśa's works[32] assert that *bhikṣu* Dīpaṃkara was originally the son of a king.

S. C. Das, however, quotes certain statements alleged to have been made by Dīpaṃkara himself. "During my time", runs one such statement, "the king called Bhū Indra Chandra reigned in Bāṅgāla. The extent of his *rāj* was what could be traversed by a she-elephant in seven days. A she-elephant is very swift. She walks a great distance, only taking a short respite at mid-day."[33] We have, unfortunately, no means ascertaining whether this statement was actually ever made by Atīśa. The name Bhū-indra-candra cannot be traced in the *History of Bengal*, though it mentions "the traditions of the long line of Chandra kings ruling in Bhaṅgala", having their capital "probably near Comilla."[34] "At all events, the six Chandra kings, known from inscriptions, may be regarded as having ruled in Eastern or Southern Bengal (and some over both) during the period between 900 and 1050 A.D."[35] Since the date of Dīpaṃkara's birth falls within this period and since, moreover, he was born in Eastern Bengal, the possibility

31. S. K. Chatterji ODBL i 192ff. In ODBL i. 465 he says that Tibet was linguistically influenced by Bengal from the 7th century A.D. 32. e g., *Bodhi-mārga-pradīpa-pañjikā-nāma*, mDo xxi. 10. 33. S. C. Das in JBTS I. i. 7n. 34. HB i. 194. 35. *Ib*. i. 196.

of some Candra king reigning in Bhaṅgala during his time cannot perhaps be entirely discarded. P. C. Bagchi even conjectures that Dīpaṃkara himself could have been actually related to the Candra rulers of Bengal. "The Tíbetan sources", says he,[36] "tell us that Tāntric Buddhism flourished in Vaṅgāla under the Chandras, and that king Gopīchandra, who is associated by tradition with a particular form of mysticism, belonged to this dynasty. The famous Buddhist scholar of Vikramapura, Atiśa Dīpaṃkara, is said to have been born in the royal house of that place.".

Again, rNal-'byor-pa-chen-po is alleged by some to have related the following as said by Atiśa himself: "In our (country) India, there are Royalty and Royal race. The former owns kingdom. The latter, though royalty in blood, has no *Rāj.* I belong to the Royal race. My father called 'The Lord of Heaven' was a householder *upāsaka* (lay devotee). He was a great Bodhisattva."[37] rNal-'byor-pa-chen-po[38] was a close Tibetan disciple of Dīpaṃkara and, as 'Gos lo-tsā-ba says, after 'Brom's death, he acted as abbot of the Rwa-sgren monastery. "He used to be groom and domestic attendant of the Master. He had...thoroughly studied the Doctrine under him". As such, it would be difficult to reject his report outright, had there been any certainty that he actually made it. But S. C. Das says that the Tibetan authorities themselves "have not accepted these accounts on the authority of Nag-tsho and 'Brom-ston-pa".[39] Still the exaggeration particularly in Nag-tsho's own account of Dīpaṃkara's ancestry is obvious: had Kalyāṇaśrī been actually as wealthy and powerful a king as Nag-tsho wants us to believe, he would not have been remembered in the history of Bengal by the sole circumstance of being Dīpaṃkara's father. At the same time, since most of the Tibetan sources persistently attribute a royal birth to Dīpaṃkara, we have at least to admit that he was born in a highly noble family and that his father was possibly a ruling chief of his locality.

36. P. C. Bagchi in HB i. 418. 37. JBTS I. i. 7n. 38. BA i. 264-5.
39. S. C. Das in JBTS I. i. 7n.

If this was actually so, then the inflated accounts of the wealth and power of king Kalyāṇaśrī are perhaps to be taken as but ways of describing the glory of the Master. S. C. Das quotes two other passages, which show the same tendency to exaggerate the greatness of Dīpaṃkara's lineage. "To the East of Vajrāsana," runs one of these,[40] "lies the great country of Bāṅgāla in which there was the place called Dsa-hor containing twenty hundred thousand habitations. At its centre was situated the capital which was prosperous, opulent, spacious, filled with a large population, well-swept and kept clean. The king's palace stood at the middle of the city, lofty and furnished with many golden *dhvaja*." "He was born", according to another passage,[41] "in the central palace called the Suvarṇadhvaja of the city of Vikramapurī in Bāṅgālā, as the son of Rājā Kalyāṇaśrī by his wife Padmaprabhā. He was the second of the three brothers and given the name of Candragarbha. At an early age he was married to five wives. He was courageous and possessed of the nine talents which are the requisites of a great man." We do not know if the mention of having five wives at an early age—which we come across also in Sum-pa[42]—was meant to be a mark of the prosperity of his family, though the birth of Dīpaṃkara in a noble family need not be doubted.

Incidentally, according to Rahula Sankrityayan,[43] this noble lineage of Dīpaṃkara created special problems for his early education. When the young prince Candragarbha first met Jeṭāri (Jitāri) and Jeṭāri asked him who he was, Candragarbha replied that he was the son of the master of the land. "Jiṭāri thought that this answer showed pride. 'We neither have any master nor any slave. If you are the ruler of the land,

40. *Ib.* 8n. 41. *Ib.* 42. Sum-pa 183. Sum-pa himself does not attach much importance to this, as is evident from his use of the words "it is said". Nag-tsho, in his *stotra* (See BA i. 241), says that the elder brother Padmagarbha had five queens and nine sons.

43. Rahula in *2500 Years*, 227-8

then go away', he answered. Very humbly he (Candragarbha) told him that he wanted to renounce the world. At this, Jitāri advised him to go to Nālandā, as he thought that if the prince was ordained too close to his father's capital, it would be difficult for him to overcome pride."

S. C. Das, as we have seen, mentions A.D. 980 as the year of Dīpaṃkara's birth. Francke[44] and Waddell[45] concur. According to Rahula,[46] however, it was A.D. 982, a Water-Male-Horse year. That there is considerable confusion among the Tibetan authorities with regard to the date of Dīpaṃkara's birth is obvious from Sum-pa,[47] who mentions different years as given by the different biographers. According to Sum-pa himself, Dīpaṃkara was born in the Water-Horse year, which is evidently to be taken as the Water-Male-Horse year, i. e. A. D. 982. We are inclined to take this as the correct view for this is the year mentioned also by 'Gos lo-tsā-ba,[48] the special merit of whose work consists in the great care he takes to determine the chronological considerations. Another argument in favour of accepting this date is that it corresponds better with the recorded dates of later incidents of Dīpaṃkara's life.

To sum up: Prince Candragarbha, later called Dīpaṃkara, was born in A.D. 982 in Vikramapura of Bengal; his father Kalyāṇaśrī was presumably a ruler of some status and the name of his mother was Prabhāvatī or Śrīprabhā. According to the Tibetan tradition, it was the same family in which Śāntarakṣita was born a few centuries earlier.

44. Francke AIT ii. 170. 45. Waddell L 35n. 46. Rahula in *2500 Years* 227. 47. Sum-pa 186. 48. BA i. 247.

7. *Early Career*

It is difficult for us today to be exact about the early educational and spiritual career of Dīpaṃkara. The Tibetan sources on which we are exclusively to depend for its reconstruction are, at least in matters of details, extremely muddled and even mutually contradictory. We have frequently in these altogether different versions of the same event, frequently again versions of different events altogether. Here are only a few examples.

Depending on the biography of Atiśa alleged to have come down from Nag-tsho, S. C. Das is led to assert that Dīpaṃkara's parents sent him at a very young age "to the sage Jetāri, an Avadhūta adept, for his education. Under Jetāri he studied the five kinds of minor sciences, and thereby paved his way for the study of philosophy and religion."[1]

But Rahula Sankrityayan,[2] on the basis of some other Tibetan source (he does not mention), asserts that the prince, at about the age of eleven, "while roaming one day went by chance to a nearby jungle. There he met Ācārya Jitāri, who lived in a cottage...Jitāri advised him to go to Nālandā." According to this version, Jitāri had little to do directly with the early education of Dīpaṃkara.

By trying to combine the two versions above, we may perhaps be led to assert that Dīpaṃkara met Jetāri very early in life and that Jetāri either directly instructed him in the five sciences or at least directed him to go to the proper educational centre. However, all the Tibetan sources do not agree even on such a compromise assertion. Thus, e. g., Sum-pa's account of the early career of Dīpaṃkara does not mention his coming in contact with Jetāri at all. The instructors of Dīpaṃkara, according to Sum-pa, were Rāhulagupta, Śīlarakṣita, Dharmarakṣita, Dharmakīrti, Śānti-pā, Nāro-pā, the junior Kusali-pā, Avadhūti-pā and Dombi-pā.

1. S. C. Das in JBTS I. i. 7-8. 2. Rahula in *2500 Years*, 227-8.

In the list of the major preceptors of Dīpaṃkara given by 'Gos lo-tsā-ba,[3] the name of Jetāri is conspicuously absent. They are: Rāhulaguhyavajra, Avadhūti-pā, Śīlarakṣita, Dharmarakṣita, Ratnākaraśānti and Dharmakīrti, under each of whom Dīpaṃkara is said to have spent a consiberable period of time studying various subjects. But 'Gos lo-tsā-ba also mentions a list of fourteen "other teachers" of Dīpaṃkara, where alone the name of Jetāri occurs. Apparently, the education Dīpaṃkara received under these "other teachers" was somewhat secondary in importance, for, contrasted with the cases of Rāhulaguhyavajra and others, the historian does not mention any specific form of instruction that Dīpaṃkara received from any of them. Besides, this list of the fourteen "other teachers" appears to have an interest of its own. It seems to include practically all the eminent representatives of the later phase of Indian Buddhism whose fame reached the Land of Snow. The names are: Jñānaśrīmati, the younger Kuśali, Jetāri, Kṛṣṇapāda also known as Ballācārya, the younger Avadhūti-pā, Dombi-pā, Vidyākokila, Matijñānabodhi, Nāro, Paṇḍita Mahājana, Bhūtakoṭipā, the great scholar Dānaśrī, Prajñābhadra and Bodhibhadra. It is extremely difficult for us today to gather much of real historical information about them all and though Nāro-pā and a few others like Jetāri are known to have been the senior contemporaries of Dīpaṃkara, it is not easy to be sure that all those mentioned in the list were actually so and as such historically could have been Dīpaṃkara's preceptors. Besides, we know little of the nature of the doctrines they preached,—that of Nāro-pā being about the only important exception to this,—whose doctrine, again, did not have any decisive influence on the mature views of Dīpaṃkara. The doctrine preached by Nāro-pā[4] was some form of Tāntrism while Dīpaṃkara, as the learned Tibetan historian Thu-bkan-blo-bzaṅ-chos-kyi-

3. BA i. 242-4. 4. H. V. Guenther, *The Life and Teaching of Nāropa*, Oxford 1963. The dates given in the book appear to be peculiar.

ñi-ma pointedly asserts,[5] fully subscribed to the Prāsaṅgika Mādhyamika philosophy—associated particularly with the names of Nāgārjuna, Candrakīrti and others.

Are we, then, to take 'Gos lo-tsā-ba's long list of the teachers of Dīpaṃkara, covering as it tries to do all the eminent spiritual leaders of the age, as a piece of actual historical information, or merely as indicative of the historian's anxiety to show how complete and exhaustive Dīpaṃkara's early education was ? A categorical answer may not be possible. Still there is nothing definite to rule out the second alternative.

To mention only another example of the difficulty of reconstructing Dīpaṃkara's early career from the Tibetan sources :

We have in these at least four versions, substantially differing from one another, of Dīpaṃkara's Buddhist ordination. "At the age of nineteen," says S. C. Das,[6] "he took the sacred vows from Śīlarakṣita the Mahāsāṅghika *ācārya* of Odantapurī, who gave him the name of Dīpaṃkara Śrī-jñāna." According to Rahula Sankrityayan,[7] however, at the age of eleven he was sent by Jetāri to *ācārya* Bodhibhadra of Nālandā. "As one could be initiated as a *bhikṣu* only at the age of twenty, the prince had perforce to wait for nearly nine years. Meanwhile, however. *ācārya* Bodhibhadra initiated him into the life of a *śramaṇa* (novice), made him wear saffron-coloured clothes and called him Dīpaṃkara Śri-jñāna." But 'Gos lo-tsā-ba says, "in his 29th year he accepted ordination from Śīlarakṣita who was established on the path of Practice, and was the Elder (*sthavira*) of the Mahāsāṅghika school, belonging to the Lineage of Buddhajñānapāda at the Mativihāra at Vajrāsana."[8] Sum-pa's[9] account partially agrees but partially also differs from that of 'Gos lo-tsā-ba. "At (the age of) twenty-nine" says he, "by the instructions of his *guru*-s and tutelar

5. See Section 5, Appendix A, pp 63-4 of the work quoted. 6. S. C. Das in JBTS I. i. 8. 7. Rahula in *2500 Years*, 228. 8. BA i. 242-3. 9. Sum-pa 183-4.

deity, he received the *pravrajyā* ordination at Odantapurī under Śīlarakṣita, a Mahāsāṅghika *ācārya*." Thus these four accounts of Dīpaṃkara's ordination differ as to the age when he received it, the preceptor under whom and the monastery where he received it.

Many more examples of such discrepancies may easily be mentioned. The discrepancies are perhaps inevitable. The Tibetan authorities had to depend on the accounts floating from India to Tibet and since the historians on whom we are to depend lived several centuries after Atīśa, they had inevitably to depend on the oral transmission of these accounts through generations. In such circumstances, it is idle to expect all the accounts of Dīpaṃkara's early career preserved in the Tibetan sources to agree on all points of details.

Nevertheless, from the medley of assorted information we have in these sources, it may be possible for us to divide, with reasonable certainty, his early educational and spiritual career into three broad phases, howevermuch uncertain we may be about their details. These are :

First, his early Tāntrika career.

Secondly, his Buddhist ordination and the study of the Buddhist scriptures, both the so-called Hīnayāna and Mahāyāna.

Thirdly, his travels abroad and his studies particularly under Dharmakīrti, the *guru* of Suvarṇadvīpa.

8, The Tantrika Initiation

There is nothing to wonder at the earliest career of Dīpaṃkara being that of a full-fledged Tāntrika. Rather it would have been most remarkable had he actually been free from any Tāntrika background. He grew up in an age in which the spiritual atmosphere of the country was saturated with Tāntrism. Māhāyana Buddhism, under various names, was becoming then more and more indistinguishable from Tāntrism and the Tāntrika Buddhists, under the title of the Siddhācāryas, were enjoying the highest spiritual prestige. In short, there was then in Eastern India no wisdom that was not essentially spiritualistic and Tāntrism represented spiritua-ism *par excellence.*

The question why Tāntrism assumed such an overwhelming importance in that age[1] and why, further, Buddhism itself was getting transformed into some kind of Tāntrism, may remain to be fully answered by further sociological enquiries. Meanwhile, what is important for our immediate purpose is to note that it must have been quite inevitable for Dīpaṃkara to aspire, at least to begin with, after a thorough proficiency in the theory and practices of the Tantras. As is only to be expected, the Tibetan sources inevitably indicate that the earliest phase of Dīpaṃkara's spiritual career was that of a Tāntrika. At the same time, it will be wrong to expect all these sources to be unanimous in matters of details concerning this.

rNal-'byor-pa-chen-po or Mahā-yogī, one of the earliest of the Tibetan disciples of Atīśa,[2] quotes a statement alleged to have been made by Atīśa himself, according to which the first Tāntrika initiation he received was from his own father.

1. H. P. Sastri (*Bauddha-dharma,* Bengali, 78ff), P. C. Bagchi (*Bauddha-dharma O Sāhitya,* Bengali, 88f), S. B. Dasgupta (ORC 13ff; ITB 5ff), Valle-Poussin (in ERE xii. 193ff), Waddell (L 141ff), and others have discussed the question. 2. D-TED 763 ; BA i. 262.

"He (i.e. my father)", Atīśa is reported to have said, "practised the Tantra of the Mātṛ class. I obtained an *abhiṣeka* of one (of the Tantras) from him."[3] However, since according to the same statement or similar ones, Atīśa's mother was a Brāhmaṇī from whom he received also the knowledge of the Vedas, the later Tibetan authorities have not accepted this as authentic. "These anecdotes," according to them, "may have been connected with Atīśa's previous births or may be interpolations connected with the life of any other *ācārya*".[4]

But this does not at all imply that the Tibetan authorities are in any way hesitant to admit that a Tāntrika initiation formed the beginning of Atīśa's spiritual career. From their repeated assertions it appears that he actually received this initiation from a Tāntrika *yogī* called Rāhulagupta or Rāhulaguhyavajra who lived in the "Black Mountain" and that during this initiation the young prince Candragarbha received the Tāntrika name Jñāna-guhya-vajra.

"In his childhood", says 'Gos lo-tsâ-ba,[5] "he had a vision of Ārya-Tārā, the tutelary deity of his lives. Under her influence, he did not get attached to royal power, but proceeded to another country in search of a teacher. He requested Rāhulaguhyavajra (sGra-gcan-gsaṅ-ba'i-rdo-rje), a *yogī* of the 'Black Mountain' (to bestow on him) the initiation into the cycle of Hevajra, and listened to the exposition of the Tantra and precepts".

In the Life of Atīśa translated by S. C. Das[6] we read, "he went to the *vihāra* of Kṛṣṇagiri to receive his lessons from Rāhulagupta. Here he was given the secret name of Guhya-jñāna-vajra, and initiated into the mysteries of esoteric Buddhism".

"Thus", says Sum-pa,[7] "without caring for the kingdom and in search of the *dharma*, he went to the temple of the Black Mountain, received the *abhiṣeka* from guru Rāhulagupta, acquired the esoteric name Jñāna-guhya-vajra and became a profound adept in *mantra* (*sṅags*)".

3. JBTS I. i. 7n 4. *Ib.* 5. BA i. 241-2. 6. JBTS I. i. 8.
7. Sum-pa 183.

The Black Mountain or Kṛṣṇagiri (Ri-nag-po) is considered by R. C. Majumdar[8] to be the same as modern Kanheri in the Bombay Presidency. But this is without any sound evidence. B. C. Law,[9] on the other hand, identifies it with Kālaśilā, one of the famous seven hills near Rājagṛha. Thus, it could not have been too far for the young prince to go in search of spiritual wisdom. The name of Rāhulaguhya of the Black Mountain occurs in the Tibetan sources[10] as that of a famous Tāntrika *yogī* of Atīśa's time. Therefore, the account of Atīśa meeting him and receiving from him a Tāntrika *abhiṣeka* need not be considered a fable and there is nothing to discard the possibility of his receiving the first initiated name Jñāna-guhya-vajra.

'Gos lo-tsā-ba, however, has more details to add to the early Tāntrika career of Atīśa. "After being established in the degrees of *utpannakrama* and *sampannakrama*, he (Dīpaṃ-kara-jñāna) proceeded to foreign countries. For seven years he became an attendant of Avadhūti-pā, who had attained the highest realisation. For three years he practised rigorous mental training, took part in Tāntric feasts (*gaṇacakra*) in the company of *ḍākiṇī*-s in the country of Oḍḍiyāna, and listened to numerous secret (*vajra*) songs."[11]

That Atīśa had several years of spiritual apprenticeship under Avadhūti-pā is also indicated by the sources of Rahula Sankrityayan. "The twelve-year old Dīpaṃkara", says Rahula,[12] "stayed with him (i. e. Avadhūti-pā) until he was eighteen". However, it is difficult to see why 'Gos lo-tsā-ba says that Atīśa "proceeded to foreign countries" for this purpose. The only account of Avadhūti-pā we have in 'Gos-lo-tsā-ba's[13] own history is as follows :

"The great Avadhūti-pā or Paiṇḍapātika, the Great" received the "exposition and meditative practice of the system known as Phag-mo-gshuṅ-drug (the six Dhāraṇīs of Varāhī)"

8. Majumdar in HB. i. 674. 9. B.C. Law IDETBJ 39, 237. 10. BA ii. 732. 11. *Ib.* i. 242. 12. Rahula in *2500 Years*, 229. 13. BA i. 390.

from the venerable Virū-pā, who, in his turn, received it from Indrabhūti's sister Lakṣmīṅkarā. He (Avadhūti-pā) was a native of Eastern Bengal and a Kṣatriya by caste. He was ordained in the Mahāsāṅghika sect and practised meditation on Guhyasamāja-Mañjuvajra. After he had seen a distressing dream that he had swallowed the Sun and Moon, he went to see Virū-pā, and obtained from him the initiation into the Cycle of the Yoginī (i.e. Vajravarāhī) and at the same time saw a vision of the goddess. He listened to the exposition of the Tantra and its mystic precepts, and practised them. Then Virū-pā introduced him to the practice (*caryā*). When he began his mystic practice on the banks of the Ganges, there was a trident which could not be moved by men, and on which heretics used to jump, believing that death would give them emancipation. He seized it and threw it into the Ganges. The heretics begged him to restore the trident, and having taken it out (from the river), he handed it to them, saying : 'On this path there is no emancipation'.

'Gos lo-tsā ba, as we have just said, does not mention any other Avadhūti-pā and it is obviously difficult to recover much of strict historical truth from the legends he relates. According to Rahula Sankrityayan,[14] he was also called Advayavajra and was the same as Maitri-pā, the *guru* of Bodhibhadra of the Nālandā *vihāra*. Following H. P. Sastri,[15] P. C. Bagchi[16] and S. K. De[17] also think that Avadhūti-pā was the same as Advayavajra. From the bsTan-'gyur.[18] however, it appears that there could have been more than one Avadhūti-pā, whose writings are preserved in this collection. From all these and certain other conjectures about him we may assert that he was one of the famous Siddhācāryas and was a senior contemporary of Dīpaṃkara.

The other important thing said by 'Gos lo-tsā-ba about the early Tāntrika career of Dīpaṃkara is that he spent three years in the country of Oḍḍiyāna, participating at the Tāntrika

14. Rahula *op. cit.* 228-29. 15. H. P. Sastri in *Advayavajrasaṃgraha*, p. vi. 16. P. C. Bagchi in HB i. 423. 17. S. K. De in HB i. 341n. 18. See Lalou 138 & 129.

feasts in the company of the *ḍākinī*-s. The modern scholars like P. C. Bagchi,[19] N. Dasgupta,[20] Sylvain Lévi,[21] F. W. Thomas[22] and others have discussed the possible identity of the place referred to by the Tibetan sources as Oḍḍiyāna, or alternatively as, Uḍḍiyāna, Uḍyāna, O-rGyan and U-rgyan. "B. Bhattacharyya, following H. P. Sastri, would identify it with Orissa and draw far-reaching conclusions about Buddhist Tantric centres in Orissa... There is great probability in the identification proposed by Sylvain Lévi with the Swat valley in North-western India, the people of which, even in Hiuen Tsang's time, made 'the acquaintance of magical formulas their occupation'."[23] That some of the Tibetan authorities would not favour the identification of Oḍḍiyāna with Orissa is clear from 'Gos lo-tsā-ba,[24] who says that it "was situated 230 *yojana*-s to the north of Magadha", though it is a different question altogether whether it can be definitely identified with the Swat valley or not. In any case, there is no doubt that the Tibetans knew this to be a great centre of Tantrism. It was from this place, according to 'Gos lo-tsā-ba, that the Guhyasamāja Tantra (with which the names of king Indrabhūti of Oḍḍiyāna and his sister Lakṣmiṅkarā were particularly associated) was introduced to Āryāvarta.[25] Therefore, 'Gos lo-tsā-ba's statement that Dīpaṃkara went there and spent three years in the company of the *ḍākinī*-s participating at the Tāntrika feasts, even if not taken as a piece of exact historical record, goes at least to show that the

19. P. C. Bagchi in IHQ vi. 580-3. 20. N. Dasgupta in IHQ xi. 142-44.
21. Levi in JA 1915. 105f. 22. Thomas in JRAS 1906 461n.
23. S. K. De in HB i. 333n. 24. BA i. 367. But 'Gos lo-tsā-ba's geographical location of Indian places is not always reliable (See note 42, Section 13). The following note by R. C. Majumdar and D. C. Ganguly (HB i. 673n) appears to be extremely significant: "According to *dPag-bsam-ljon-bzaṅ*, the first Siddhācārya Lui-pā belonged to the fisherman caste of Uḍḍiyāna, and was in the service of the king of Uḍḍiyāna as a writer. He is referred to in the bsTan-'gyur as a Bengali (Cordier - *Cat.* ii. 33). He composed some Bengali songs (*Bauddha-Gān-O-Dohā* 21). On this and other grounds it has been suggested that Uḍḍiyāna might have been situated in Bengal (IHQ xi. 142-4)" 25. BA. i. 361f.

Tibetan historian is extremely anxious to prove how complete was Dīpaṃkara's early Tāntrika career.

We have unfortunately nothing to corroborate 'Gos lo-tsā-ba's statement that Dīpaṃkara actually went to Oḍḍiyāna and practised the Tantras in the company of the *ḍākinī*-s. Nevertheless, from the persistent assertions of the Tibetan authorities we are to admit that, in accordance with the general spirit of his age, Dīpaṃkara must have shown a great deal of enthusiasm in his early youth for mastering the theories and practices of the Tantras. Further, whatever might have been his later attitude to Tantrism, or more specifically, to certain forms of the Tāntrika theories and practices, that his knowledge of the Tantras must have been actually stupendous is attested to by the story told by the Tibetan historians of how he easily humbled the pride of Rin-chen-bzaṅ-po (Ratnabhadra), the greatest Tibetan scholar of Tantrism trained by a large number of eminent Indian Tāntrikas. But more of this later.

9. The Buddhist Ordination

It is not necessary for us to compile here more details of Dīpaṃkara's early Tāntrika carrer. What is important, instead, is to note that the Buddhist ordination which he eventually received meant some kind of a decisive turning point in his spiritual career.

We have already seen that the accounts of his Buddhist ordination preserved for us in the Tibetan sources vary in matters of detail. He received this ordination, according to some, at the age of nineteen, while, according to others, at the age of twentynine. Again, the monastery where he was ordained is variously mentioned as Nālandā, Odantapurī and Mativihāra of Vajrāsana (Buddha-gayā). There is, moreover, some confusion as to the name of the *ācārya* under whom he received this ordination. According to Rahula Sankrityayan, Dīpaṃkara was first ordained as a *śramaṇa* (novice) by *ācārya* Bodhibhadra of Nālandā and that much later he became a disciple of Śīlarakṣita. But according to 'Gos lo-tsā-ba, Sum-pa and the biographer translated by S. C. Das, it was under Śīlarakṣita himself that Dīpaṃkara received his ordination. This seems to be the suggestion of 'Brom-ston-pa, too, for though 'Brom does not in his *stotra* mention the name of the *ācārya* under whom Dīpaṃkara was ordained, he says, "He (Dīpaṃkara) was ordained as a *bhikṣu* by the Mahāsāṅghika" and from 'Gos lo-tsā-ba, Sum-pa and others we learn that Śīlarakṣita was then a famous *ācārya* of the Mahāsāṅghika school.

We do not have much knowledge of Śīlarakṣita himself. The bsTan-'gyur collection does not contain any work by him and the only thing 'Gos lo-tsā-ba has to say about him is that "he was established on the Path of Practice and was the Elder (*sthavira*) of the Mahāsāṅghika school, belonging to the lineage of Buddhajñānapāda". Sum-pa and others have nothing to add to this and it is not possible for us to form any idea of Śīlarakṣita's stature as a Buddhist teacher from scanty bits of information like these. Yet there seems to be no doubt that the ordination Dīpaṃkara received under him was quite different from the Tāntrika form of initiation. It was, in other words, distinctly *prabrajyā* rather than an *abhiṣeka*, which Dīpaṃkara previously had under Rāhulagupta of the Black Mountain.

Why did Dīpaṃkara go in for the purer form of the Buddhist ordination in spite of his early Tāntrika initiation ? We may not find today an exact answer to this. This much is sure, however, that the Buddhist ordination meant for him a clear break from his earlier Tāntrika career, or at least from that form of Tantrism to which he was devoting himself so long with great enthusiasm. This is evident from a number of circumstances.

First, the name Dīpaṃkara or Dīpaṃkara-śrī-jñāna, which he received at his Buddhist ordination, became firmly fixed for the rest of his career *to the exclusion of the name Jñāna-guhya-vajra or Guhya-jñāna-vajra*, which he received earlier during his Tāntrika initiation. Even none of the Tāntrika works attributed to him in the bsTan-'gyur mentions the name Jñāna-guhya-vajra. The bsTan-'gyur contains fifteen works attributed to a certain Jñāna-guhya as the translator.[1] But this Jñāna-guhya was evidently a different person altogether—probably the same person who is mentioned by 'Gos lo-tsā-ba[2] as a Kashmirian Tāntrika. Thus, if the Tibetan sources remember Dīpaṃkara's earlier Tāntrika name, it is no more for them than a mere historical curiosity, like his childhood name Candragarbha. And if, after the Buddhist ordination, Atīśa's earlier Tāntrika name became but a historical curiosity, the significance can only be that the Buddhist ordination meant for him a serious break with the earlier Tāntrika career.

Secondly, 'Gos lo-tsā-ba has something significant to say about Atīśa's decision in favour of the Buddhist ordination.

1. rG. xlvii. 48-62.
2. BA ii. 871-2.

"While he (Atiśa)", says 'Gos lo-tsā-ba,[3] "was being established in the excellent method of the Vajrayāna, he heard in his dream the Blessed One Śākyamuni, surrounded by a retinue of numerous monks, saying : 'Why are you attached to this life ? Why did you not take up ordination ?' He thought that if he were to take up ordination, great benefit would arise for the Doctrine". So it was under the direct inspiration of the Blessed One that Atiśa decided in favour of the Buddhist ordination. If it is a myth, it could have grown much later than the event. But the question is : Why was there such a myth ? Do we find anything in the subsequent career of Dīpaṃkara which gives us a clue to its need ? The answer is not a difficult one. Unlike the Siddhācaryas, under some of whom he received his early spiritual training, Dīpaṃkara himself, as is evident from his mature writings like the *Bodhi-patha-pradīpa*, did not consider Vajrayāna (or for that matter, any form of the so-called later Tāntrika Buddhism) as representing the true spirit of the Buddha. Far from remaining an exclusive follower of Tantrism, Dīpaṃkara grew into a strong critic of some of its theories and practices and took his own philosophical and ethical stand on the classical works of the earlier *ācarya*-s, i.e. on Buddhism in its pre-Tāntrika phase. It is true that even later in his life he did not propose an outright rejection of Tantrism. He even composed, commented on and translated a number of Tāntrika treatises. But whatever might have been the sense in which Dīpaṃkara later retained a formal allegiance to the Tantras, the philosophical view and the codes of ethical conduct he eventually championed were really far form the theory and practices of Vajrayāna of the Siddhācaryas. We shall later have occasion to discuss this in greater detail. For the present, however, it is important to note that the Buddhist ordination meant for him a distinct departure from his earlier Tāntrika career. It is no wonder that the Tibetan historians and biographers of Dīpaṃkara wanted to find a convincing explanation of such a departure, and hence the myth

3. *Ib*. i. 242.

concerning the divine inspiration leading Dīpaṃkara to the Buddhist ordination. Significantly, in this myth Śākyamuni told Dīpaṃkara to renounce the life of Vajrayāna, in which he was already well-established, and to become a Buddhist monk in the older sense of the term.

Thirdly, the Tibetan historians and biographers of Atīśa presistently assert that after this ordination Dīpaṃkara devoted himself fully to the arduous study of the canonical and classical texts of Buddhism. We hear no longer of Dīpaṃkara participating at the Tāntrika feasts in the company of the *ḍākinī*-s or of his running after any great adept in Tantra with the hope of obtaining from him any secret or miraculous power. On the contrary, from his ordination onwards, we hear only of his great eagerness to learn the three Piṭakas, the *Mahāvibhāṣā* and other Buddhist texts, which had little or nothing to do with the Tāntrika beliefs and practices. "After that (i.e. his ordination)", says 'Gos lo-tsā-ba,[4] "till the age of thirtyone, Dīpaṃkara-śrī-jñāna studied most of the Three Piṭakas of the four schools (sDe-pa bshi : Mahāsāṅghikas, Sarvāstivādins, Sammitīyas and Sthaviravādins) and became proficient in the practice (of the Vinaya), as well as mastered the problems of all schools. For two years at the monastic college of Odantapurī, he heard the *Mahāvibhāṣā* from the teacher Dharmarakṣita, who being a *śrāvaka*, the Master had to change his residence every seven days (for according to the vows of the Bodhisattva-śīla, a Bodhisattva was not permitted to spend more than seven days in the company of a Hīnayāna *śrāvaka*)". "At the age of thirtyone", says S. C. Das,[5] "he was ordained in the highest order of Bhikṣus and also given the vows of a Bodhisattva by Dharma Rakṣita. He received lessons in metaphysics from several eminent Buddhist philosophers of Magadha. Lastly, reflecting on the theory of 'the evolution of matter from voidity' he acquired what is called the 'far-seeing wisdom' ". According to Sum-pa,[6] again, after receiving the ordination at the age of twentynine, Dīpaṃkara spent two years under Dharmarakṣita and others for studying

4. *Ib*. i. 243. 5. S. C. Das in JBTS I. i. 8. 6. Sum-pa 183.

the *Mahāvibhāṣā* and for fully mastering philosophy and logic (*lakṣaṇa-śāstra*). "Dīpaṃkara", says Rahula Sankrityayan,[7] "went to the Mativihāra in Vajrāsana and became the disciple of Mahāvinayadhara Śīlarakṣita, the great Vinaya-piṭaka scholar. He studied the Vinaya-piṭaka with him for two years. Thus, by the time he reached the age of thirty-one, Dīpaṃkara Śrījñāna had already become a master of the Three Piṭakas and the Tantras, and an all-round scholar".

We have quoted above four accounts of the post-ordained period of Dīpaṃkara's educational career. Three things appear to be quite striking about these.

First, Dīpaṃkara is said to have mastered during this period certain texts and all these are either canonical or classical works of Buddhism, like the Three Piṭakas and the *Mahāvibhāṣā*. These Three Piṭakas may or may not have been the Pali ones. But there is no doubt about the *Mahāvibhāṣā*, alternatively known as the *Abhidharma-vibhāṣā* or simply the *Vibhāṣā*. It is the commentary on Kātyāyaniputra's *Jñānaprasthāna* supposed to have been composed at the Fourth Buddhist Council under the patronage of king Kaniṣka. Though preserved in Chinese translation, the Sanskrit original of this text is lost to us, but it was once considered so supremely important by the Sarvāstivādins that an adherence to the *Vibhāṣā* gave them also the name Vaibhāṣikas. In any case, this work which Dīpaṃkara is said to have studied most earnestly during the post-ordained period of his educational career had little to do with Tantrism of the later days and we are doubtful if any Siddhācārya or any of the later Tāntrika seriously devoted himself to its study.

Secondly, in spite of the obvious zeal of the Tibetan writers to show how complete Dīpaṃkara's Buddhist education was, they do not really have many names of the Buddhist *ācārya*-s under whom Dīpaṃkara could pursue his Buddhistic studies. The name Śīlarakṣita, as mentioned by Rahula Sankrityayan, could have been the same as Dharmarakṣita mentioned by

7. Rahula in *2500 Years*, 229.

'Gos lo-tsā-ba, Sum-pa and S. C. Das. We have, thus, only one name of an important Buddhist teacher under whom Dīpaṃkara could study the canonical and classical works of Buddhism. Not that the Tibetans did not know of many wise men of India—or more specifically, of Eastern India—living in those days. But they were mostly Tāntrikas, with only a formal allegiance to Buddhism. This shows that there could hardly be much scope for advanced study of classical Buddhism in India then.

That during Dīpaṃkara's time India was hardly left with outstanding exponents of the canonical and classical works of Buddhism is further evidenced by the *chos-'byuṅ* of Bu-ston. In this history,[8] the story of the great Indian exponents of Buddhism—or, more properly, of Mahāyāna Buddhism—practically ends with Śāntideva, "who probably lived in the seventh century A.D."[9] After giving an account of Śāntideva, Bu-ston describes a very brief 'History'[10], mainly legendary, of the Indian grammatical literature and then passes on to discuss the canonical texts lost to India.[11] This is followed by the prophecies of an apocalyptic character foretelling the disappearance of the Buddhist Doctrine in India.[12] His next chapter is on the history of Buddhism in Tibet, Dīpaṃkara's life being incorporated into it. Apparently, the historian knows of no great master of genuine Mahāyāna after the seventh century A. D. and it is no wonder that during the first quarter of the eleventh century A.D., when Tantrism practically eclipsed the older form of Buddhism, the newly ordained Dīpaṃkara could not find many *ācārya*-s in India to teach him the older works on Buddhism.

The third significant thing we hear from the Tibetan historians and biographers of Atīśa is that at the age of thirty-one, he acquired full mastery not only of the Three Piṭakas and the *Mahāvibhāṣā* but also of all the philosophical and logical works. Since nobody says that Dīpaṃkara devoted himself seriously to the study of such works before his ordi-

8. Bu-ston ii. 166f
9. Winternitz ii. 365.
10. Bu-ston ii. 166-9.
11. *Ib.* ii. 169-71.
12. *Ib.* ii. 171-80.
13. *Ib.* ii. 181ff.

nation and assuming that 'Gos lo-tsā-ba and Sum-pa are right in claiming that he was ordained at the age of twentynine, the alleged proficiency acquired at the age of thirty-one is to be taken as an exaggeration. In two years' time, nobody could study such texts, particularly during an age when the study of these was on its decline. Nevertheless, judging Dīpaṃkara by his own writings preserved in the bsTan-'gyur, we are obliged to admit that he must have acquired a real mastery of Buddhist scriptures and philosophical works, though, as we have just seen, it could hardly be by the time he reached the age of thirty-one. Why, then, do the Tibetan sources particularly mention this age? The answer seems to be that the age of thirty-one was really crucial for the educational career of Dīpaṃkara, for it was at this age that he left India for higher studies abroad. This leads us to see the third important phase of his educational career, namely, his studies under *ācārya* Dharmakīrti of Suvarṇadvīpa.

10. *Suvarnadvipa and Dharmakirti*

Let us first note what the Tibetan authorities have to say about Dīpaṃkara's studies under *ācārya* Dharmakīrti of Suvarṇadvīpa. We shall next try to answer the following questions :

First, what was this place referred to as Suvarṇadvīpa and how did Dīpaṃkara go there ?

Secondly, what do we know of it as a centre of Buddhist learning ?

Thirdly, what do we know of *ācārya* Dharmakīrti, whose fame as a Buddhist teacher attracted Dīpaṃkara in such a manner that he decided to spend several years studying under him ?

'Brom-ston-pa's *stotra* and Thu-bkan-blo-bzaṅ-chos-kyi-ñi-ma's history of the bKa'-gdams-pa sect simply mention that Atīśa received the *upadeśa* of *bodhicitta* from the *guru* of Suvarṇadvīpa. 'Gos lo-tsā-ba does not have much more to add to this : "Later (i.e. after finishing his studies under the Indian *ācārya*-s)", says 'Gos lo-tsā-ba,[1] "Dīpaṃkaraśrījñāna visited the teacher gSer-gliṅ-pa. From him he obtained numerous secret precepts, placing foremost the Mental Creative Effort towards enlightenment (i.e. *bodhicitta-utpādana*)."

gSer-gliṅ-pa literally means Suvarṇadvīpī, i.e. one belonging to Suvarṇadvīpa. This is the form in which Dīpaṃkara's preceptor of Suvarṇadvīpa is frequently referred to by the Tibetan sources. His real name was Dharmakīrti, translated into Tibetan as Chos-kyi-grags-pa, though as we shall presently see, in a colophon of his work preserved in the bsTan-'gyur, the name occurs as Dharmapāla. This Dharmapāla must not be confused either with the earlier Vijñānavādī writer who[2] commented on Vasubandhu's

1. BA i. 244. 2. Winternitz ii. 362-3.

Vijñaptimātratā-siddhi or with the Indian *ācārya* bearing the same name who visited Tibet shortly before Dīpaṃkara, just as Dharmakīrti of Suvarṇadvīpa must not be confused with the famous and much earlier Buddhist logician bearing the same name.[3]

By the age of thirty-one, says Sum-pa,[4] Dīpaṃkara went to Suvarṇadvīpa and met Dharmakīrti and learnt from him for twelve years the practice of *bodhicitta*, both *praṇidhāna* and *avatāra*. Dīpaṃkara, says Rahula Sankrityayan,[5] started his voyage for Suvarṇadvīpa in 1013 A.D., ten years before the last invasion by Mahmud Ghaznavi in A.D. 1023. This calculation is presumably based on the assumption that Dīpaṃkara went to Suvarṇadvīpa at the age of thirty-one. However, accepting the date of his birth to be A. D. 982—and Rahula himself accepts this date—it must have been A.D. 1012 when Dīpaṃkara was thirty-one according to the Tibetan way of reckoning years.[6] It may, therefore, be desirable to modify Rahula's statement and assume that Dīpaṃkara actually started his voyage for Suvarṇadvīpa in A. D. 1012. He travelled, according to Rahula, for fourteen months before reaching Suvarṇadvīpa. At that time, continues Rahula, *ācārya* Dharmapāla (Dharmakīrti) of Suvarṇadvīpa was famous for his scholarship throughout the Buddhist world.

In the *Life of Atīśa* translated by S. C. Das we read, "On account of these diverse attainments which moved his mind variously in different directions, he resolved to go to *ācārya* Dharmakīrti, the High Priest of Suvarṇadvīpa. Accordingly, in the company of some merchants he embarked for Suvarṇadvīpa in a large vessel. The voyage was long and tedious, extending over several months, during which the travellers were overtaken by terrible storms. At this time Suvarṇadvīpa was the headquarters of Buddhism in the East, and its High Priest was considered the greatest scholar of his age. Dīpaṃkara resided there for a period of twelve years in order to completely

3. Though in JBTS Das gives the name as Dharmakīrti, the same work, when later edited as the *Indian Pandits*, changes the name into Candrakīrti - an error repeated in HB i. 674. 4. Sum-pa 183. 5. Rahula in *2500 Years*, 230-1. 6. BA i. Intro. p. xiii.

master the pure teachings of Buddha of which the key was possessed by the High Priest alone".[7]

What exactly is the place referred to as Suvarṇadvīpa and what do we know of this *guru* ?

S. C. Das[8] translates a Tibetan passage which gives us a palpably legendary account of both. "There is a country", according to it, "filled with precious minerals and stones called Suvarṇadvīpa in the neighbourhood of Jambu-dvīpa. It is not included in the eight *dvīpa*-s or continents mentioned in the sacred books. Lama gSer-gliṅ-pa was born in the royal family of that country. As soon as he was born it is said that he cried *sina*, *sina*, expressive of the name of the three Holies. Though the people of that country were all Tīrthikas, they had not, owing to the prince's moral merits, the power of disobeying the king's commands. The prince once obtained a cast image of Buddha Śākya Muni in a mountain cave. On account of his paying reverence and worshipping it, the people reaped an abundant harvest and enjoyed immunity from visitation of epidemics. He caused all the people of Suvarṇadvīpa to imbibe faith in the religion of Buddha. Then with a view to acquire a thorough knowledge of the Dharma he obtained leave from his father to go to Jambudvīpa, for a pilgrimage to Vajrāsana, the place of attaining to the state of perfect Buddhahood. At the time he arrived there the Rākṣasas (probably the Simhalese) had also come to reverence the Mahābodhi. There also simultaneously congregated all the learned and talented men of the Buddhist world. The great *ācārya* Mahā Śrī Ratna, who had acquired the power of attaining to extraordinary longivity, was also present on the occasion. The prince became faihfully attached to him and except him he trusted in no other holy man. He reverenced him, and during the seven days that he was in his company he became more and more devoted to him. On the sage having suddenly vanished from his sight the prince in vain called him and searched for him everywhere. He visited the Lumbini grove at Kapilāvāstu, the sites on the banks of

7. Das in JBTS I. i. 8-9. 8. *Ib*. 8-9n.

Nairañjanā and Vārāṇasī to trace him out. But nowhere was the sage to be found. He resided in India for seven years during which time he studied the law and the sciences under several learned *guru*-s and sages.Once in a dream, he was told by his *guru* that the position of a king being not holy was not to be envied. He was thrice asked by him if he could aspire to the kingdom of Dharma. The prince thrice answered,—yes, he could. Then when his dream was over he found his teacher seated near him. By his teacher's blessings he learned the Law and the sacred literature of the Buddhists. He was initiated in the secrets of attaining to the saintly path. In this manner the prince gained knowledge from various masters, having attended to them one after another. His *guru* had given him the name of Dharma Kīrti of Suvarṇadvīpa. On account of the preponderance of *maitrī* (friendly feeling) in him, he was called Maitra. Then returning to Suvarṇadvīpa he converted all who had been devoted to the Tīrthika religion to Buddhism. So his name Dharmakīrti of Suvarṇadvīpa became practically significant. His fame, being based on Dharma, also spread over Jambudvīpa. Though he resided in Suvarṇadvīpa his name became known everywhere abroad."

All these are practically useless for the purpose of identifying the place Dīpaṃkara went to or for having any historical information of *ācārya* Dharmakīrti. Fortunately we are not obliged to remain satisfied only with such legendary accounts of Suvarṇadvīpa and Suvarṇadvīpī.

Let us begin with the question of Suvarṇadvīpa.

R. C. Majumdar's extensive work bearing the title *Suvarṇadvīpa* shows that it was the general name for Sumatra, Java and the islands of Eastern Archipelago.[9] "There can be... hardly any doubt", says Majumdar,[10] "in view of the statements of Arab and Chinese writers, and the inscription found in Sumatra itself, that that island was also known as Suvarṇabhūmi and Suvarṇadvīpa. Ferrand points out that even now Sumatra is designated by the Malays as Pūlaw Emaś or the

9. S. C. Das' conjecture (D-TED 1310) that gSer-gliṅ probably mean the ancient Pegu is baseless. 10. R. C. Majumbar AICFE II. i. 47.

island of gold. But the Arab writers definitely imply that Suvarṇadvīpa included a number of islands. Alberuni is quite clear on this point. 'The islands of the Zābaj', says he, 'are called by the Hindus Suvarṇadvīpa, i.e. the gold islands'. Ibn Said (13th century A.D.) definitely asserts that Zābag is an archipelago consisting of a large number of islands which produce excellent gold."

But this, again, is much too general to give us the specific idea of the place Dīpaṃkara went to for his advanced studies. Fortunately, an extremely significant clue to it is retained for us in the form of a colophon of one of the works of Dharmakīrti himself preserved in the bsTan-'gyur. The work is called *Abhisamaya - alaṃkāra - nāma-prajñāpāramitā-upadeśa - śāstra - vṛtti - durbodha - āloka-nāma-ṭīkā.*[11] In the Peking edition of the bsTan-'gyur, the colophon reads as follows : "Written by Dharmakīrti on the request of king Śrī Cūḍāmaṇivarman, during the tenth year of the reign of king Cūḍāmaṇivarman, in Vijayanagara of Suvarṇadvīpa." In Cordier's *Catalogue*, the author of the text is mentioned as *ācārya* Dharmakīrti-śrī of Suvarṇadvīpa and it is added : "The work was composed during the reign of Deva-śrī-varmarāja, the Cūḍāmaṇi, *alias* Cūḍāmaṇimaṇḍapa, in Malayagiri in Vijayanagara of Suvarṇadvīpa".

Where, then, was Vijayanagara of Suvarṇadvīpa ? What do we know of Malayagiri there ? Who, moreover, was king Cuḍāmaṇivarman or Cuḍāmaṇimaṇḍapa, also known as Cuḍāmaṇi or Deva-śrī-varmarāja.

Śrī-vijaya of Suvarṇadvīpa was the name of a "rich and powerful state. The territory under its rule had shifting boundaries, but between the 8th and 12th centuries extended, temporarily at least, not only over Minagkabu and Batak districts of Sumatra, but also went far beyond the island to reach Cambodia, Siam and Ceylon, to cover the greater part of Java and the coastal districts of Borneo, and thence to strech out through Banjermasin and Brunei to the Philippines."[12] The capital of the state of Śrī-vijaya—also men-

11. mDo viii. 3. 12. Robequain 66f.

tioned as Śrī-vijaya and presumably the same as our Vijaya-nagara of Suvarṇadvīpa—is usually located by the modern scholars near the modern Palembang[13] of Sumatra : it was the most important port of Sumatra[14] as well as the old name of the capital city in Sumatra.[15] Four inscriptions found in old Malay language "prove incontestably that Śrī-vijaya was already a powerful kingdom before 683 A.D.,...that the king of Śrī-vijaya as well as the rulers of neighbouring states favoured Buddhism, and that Śrī-vijaya was a centre of Buddhist learning in the islands of the Southern Sea"[16]

As R. C. Majumdar points out, it is possible for us to have some idea of the importance of Śrī-vijaya as a centre of Buddhist learning from the following : "I-Tsing has left some details of his own journey which throw interesting light on the culture and civilization in Malayasia. On his way to India, the pilgrim halted in Śrī-vijaya for six months, and learnt the Śabdavidyā (Sanskrit grammar). During his return journey also he stopped at Śrī-vijaya, and, after a short stay in China, he again returned to the same place. Here he was engaged in copying and translating the voluminous Buddhist texts which he had brought with him from India. Why he chose this place for his work is best explained in his own words : 'Many kings and chieftains in the islands of the Southern Ocean admire and believe (Buddhism), and their hearts are set on accumulating good actions. In the fortified city of Bhoja (i.e. Śrī-vijaya) Buddhist priests number more than 1000, whose minds are bent on learning and good practices. They investigate and study all the subjects that exist just as in the Middle Kingdom (Madhya-Deśa, India) ; the rules and ceremonies are not at all different. If a Chinese priest wishes to go to the West in order to hear (lectures) and read (the original), he had better stay here one or two years and practise the proper rules and then proceed to Central India'."[17]

13. *Ib.* 145. 14. R. C. Majumdar AICFE II. i. 7-8. 15. *Ib.* II. i. 45.
16. *Ib.* II. i. 123. 17. *Ib.* II. i. 142.

Thus already in the seventh century A.D. Śrī-vijaya became an important centre of Buddhist culture. "The importance of Śrī-vijaya...", continues R. C. Majumdar, "deserves, however, more than a passing notice. Apart from its position as a great centre of Buddhism, it merits distinction as the earliest seat of that Mahāyāna sect which was destined ultimately to play such a leading part in the whole of Malayasia".[18] This, as Majumdar shows, is proved not only by the statement of I-Tsing but also by the inscriptions of the kings of Śrī-vijaya.

In the 10th-11th century A.D., the period that interests us most, "Śrī-vijaya formed an important and an integral part of" the Śailendra Empire,—"a mighty empire, comprising a large part of the Malay Archipelago and Malay Peninsula".[19] "In the eleventh century A.D.", says Majumdar, "the one outstanding fact in the history of the Śailendras, known to us, is a long-drawn struggle with the powerful Cola rulers of South India. At first there existed friendly relations between the Cola kings and the Śailendra rulers. This is proved by an inscription, which is engraved on twentyone plates, and is now preserved in the Leiden Museum along with another of three plates. The two records are known respectively as the Larger Leiden Grant and Smaller Leidan Grant. ...The Larger Leiden Grant is written partly in Sanskrit and partly in Tamil. The Tamil portion tells us that the Cola king Rājarāja, the great, granted, in the twenty-first year of his reign, the revenues of a village for the upkeep of the shrine of Buddha in the Cūlāmaṇivarma-vihāra which was being constructed by Cūlāmaṇivarman, king of Kaḍāram, at Nāgapaṭṭana. The Sanskrit portion tells us that Rājarāja gave, in the twenty-first year of his reign, a village to the Buddha residing in the Cūlāmaṇivarma-vihāra which was built at Nāgīpattana by Śrī-Māra-Vijayottuṅgavarman in the name of his father Cūlāmaṇivarman. It further informs us that Māra-Vijayottuṅgavarman was born in the Śailendra family,

18. *Ib.* II. i. 143. 19. *Ib.* II. i. 164.

was the lord of Śrī-vijaya, had extended the suzerainty of Kaṭāha and had '*makara* as the emblem of his banner'... This interesting record naturally recalls the Nālandā copper-plate of the time of Devapāla. In both cases an Indian king grants villages to a Buddhist sanctuary, erected in India by a Śailendra king".[20]

R. C. Majumdar adds in a note that the "name Cūlāmaṇivarman written in Tamil character is equivalent to Cūḍāmaṇivarman". We can thus see that the Suvarṇadvīpa king Cūḍāmaṇivarman, in the tenth year of whose reign *ācārya* Dharmakīrti wrote his *Abhisamaya-alaṃkāra-nāma-prajñāpāramitā-upadeśa-śāstra-vṛtti-durbodha-āloka-nāma-ṭikā*, was a Śailendra king and that his son Māra-Vijayottuṅgavarman built a monastery in southern India in the name of his father. We have no clear knowledge of the date of the accession of Cūḍāmaṇivarman, though, on the basis of Chinese and Indian sources, R. C. Majumdar[21] puts the date of his death and that of the accession of his son between A.D. 1005 and 1008., i.e. only a few years before Atiśa went to Suvarṇadvīpa. Dharmakīrti's work under consideration, therefore, must have been written some years earlier than this.

Atīśa, as we have seen, started his voyage for Suvarṇadvīpa in A.D. 1012. The voyage must have been a long one, extending over several months. There is, therefore, some ground to presume that he reached Sumatra in A.D. 1013. The Tibetan sources repeatedly assert that he spent twelve years in Suvarṇadvīpa, studying under *ācārya* Dharmakīrti. That is, he might have started his return voyage to India sometime in A.D. 1025. This, again, roughly coincides with another important date of the history of Suvarṇadvīpa. viz, that of the fall of the Śailendra empire. "The oversea conquests of Rājendra Cola", says R. C. Majumdar,[22] "took place in the 13th year of his reign, i. e. A.D. 1024-25, possibly during its latter part. We may, therefore, provisionally accept A.D. 1025 as the date of the great catastrophe which befell the Śailendra empire". Atīśa, thus, left Sumatra shortly after

20. *Ib.* II. i. 167-9. 21. *Ib.* II. i. 169-70. 22. *Ib.* II. i. 179.

the fall of the Śailendras. Was it because of the disturbed conditions of Śrī-vijaya, which, in all probability, followed the political catastrophe ?

We do not know what happened after this to *ācārya* Dharmakīrti or to the monastery of Śrī-vijaya of which he was the High Priest. Sum-pa[23] tells us that he lived up to the age of 150 and that he was living in Suvarṇadvīpa when Atīśa was appointed the High Priest of the Vikramaśīla monastery in India. Nevertheless, it was not unlikely for the political catastrophe to have affected Dharmakīrti. The Śailendra kings were not only his patrons but moreover could have been his actual relations, because the Tibetans repeatedly assert that *guru* Dharmakīrti was born in the royal family of Suvarṇadvīpa.

In his *stotra* to Dīpaṃkara, 'Brom says that the *guru* of Suvarṇadvīpa was of royal descent.[24] We have already seen the legendary account of Dharmakīrti quoted by S. C. Das, according to which, he was born in the royal family of Suvarṇadvīpa. Sum-pa[25] asserts that gSer-gliṅ-pa was a son of the king of Suvarṇadvīpa. The sources on which Nagwang Nima and Lama Chimpa base their Life of Atīśa make the same assertion.[26]

To all these are to be added the following evidences of the bsTan-'gyur. As the author of *Śikṣā-samuccaya-abhisamaya-nāma*[27] is mentioned gSer-gliṅ-rgyal-po dPal-ldan-chos-skyoṅ, meaning Śrī Dharmapāla, the king of Suvarṇadvīpa (Suvarṇadvīpa-rāja Śrī-dharmapāla). In the colophon of the *Satya-dvaya-avatāra*[28] by Dīpaṃkara are mentioned the names of certain Mahāyāna teachers, in the list of which occurs "*guru* Dharmapāla, king of Suvarṇadvīpa".

Are we to reject all these as mere fables or as the Tibetan ways of glorifying the teacher ? Were the Tibetans, in other words, trying to exalt the *ācārya* according to the image of Śākyamuni, who renounced the kingdom in favour of the life of a monk ? We have no direct evidence in the history

23. Sum-pa 118. 24. *śloka* 7. 25. Sum-pa, *Index* cxxxii. 26. See Appendix A, Section 6. 27. mDo xxxi. 4. 28. mDo xxxix. 9.

of Suvarṇadvīpa to confirm the royal birth of Dharmakīrti. But let us not conjecture. The fact is that the history of Suvarṇadvīpa is not yet known to us in all details and our knowledge of the personal life of Dharmakīrti is extremely meagre. Sum-pa[29] asserts that he studied for 12 years at the Vikramaśila monastery. There is, unfortunately, nothing definite either to corroborate or to reject it. What is definitely known of him is his stature as a teacher and exponent of Buddhism.

Dharmakīrti had presumably some other notable Indian students besides Dīpaṃkara. Rahula[30] mentions the names of certain illustrious Indian scholars having been students of Dharmakīrti and this perhaps on the basis of Sum-pa's account. We positively know, however, of another important student of Dharmakīrti, namely Kamala or Kamalarakṣita, who was a contemporary of Dīpaṃkara. In the colophons of three of the works[31] of Dharmakīrti in the bsTan-'gyur, it is said that the texts were exposed by the request of his disciples Kamalarakṣita (or Kamala) and Dīpaṃkara-śrī-jñāna. We do not have, in the Tibetan sources, much account of the life of Kamalarakṣita. Nevertheless, that he was a significant Buddhist writer can be judged from the fact that about nine of his works[32] are preserved in the bsTan-'gyur. It is, therefore, remarkable that in the list of the outstanding students of Dharmakīrti or gSer-gliṅ-pa, Sum-pa[33] does not mention Kamalarakṣita at all. Sum-pa mentions four eminent students of gSer-gliṅ-pa and they were Śānti, Jo-bo, Jñānaśrī-mitra and Ratnakīrti.

We are left to judge the stature of Dharmakīrti or Dharmapāla of Suvarṇadvīpa as a Buddhist writer mainly from his works that are preserved in Tibetan translation in the bsTan-'gyur, though of course there is nothing to presume that all his works were translated into Tibetan.

29. Sum-pa 118. 30. Rahula in *2500 Years*, 230 31. mDo xxvii. 6 ; mDo xxvii. 7 ; mDo xxxi. 4. 32. mDo xxvii. 6, 7 ; xxxi. 4 ; xxxiii. 87 ; rG. xliii. 10, 12, 27, 32 ; rG. lxxxi. 15. Possibly also mDo cxxviii. 3. 33. Sum-Pa 118.

Six works in the bsTan-'gyur[34] are definitely to be attributed to him. These are: (1) *Abhisamaya-alaṃkāra-nāma-prajñāpāramitā-upadeśa - śāstra-vṛtti-durbodha-āloka-nāma-ṭikā*, (2) *Bodhisattva-caryāvatāra-piṇḍārtha*, (3) *Bodhisattva-caryāvatāra-ṣaṭtriṃśat-piṇḍārtha*, (4) *Śikṣā-samuccaya-abhisamaya-nāma*, (5) *Ārya-acala-sādhana-nāma* and (6) *Krodha-gaṇapati-sādhana*. Dīpaṃkara took part in the Tibetan translation of all these, except the last one. In the Peking edition, the colophon of the *Ārya-acala-sādhana-nāma* even mentions that the work was translated by Dīpaṃkara himself, i.e. without the help of any Tibetan lo-tsā-ba.

The first of the above-mentioned works appears to be the *magnum opus* of Dharmakīrti. Rin-chen-bzaṅ-po or Ratnabhadra, perhaps the greatest of the Tibetan translators, worked under Dīpaṃkara for its translation. It is a stupendous work on Mahāyāna philosophy, devoted mainly to the clear exposition of the highest *pāramitā* conceived by the Mahāyānists, namely the *prajñāpāramitā*. In bulk the work is about forty times that of Dīpaṃkara's *Bodhi-patha-pradīpa* : in the Peking edition of the bsTan-'gyur, while the latter occupies only 53 lines the former occupies about 2044 lines.

From this work alone, we could have perhaps considered him as one of the most outstanding representatives of the Mahāyāna philosophy of the 10th-11th century A.D. But there is another way of assessing his stature as a Mahāyāna philosopher and it is to review the subsequent career of Dīpaṃkara himself. From the works of Dīpaṃkara it is quite clear that he acquired a great proficiency in Mahāyāna philosophy and logic. But where and when did he acquire this ? We have already seen that it is difficult to think that Dīpaṃkara acquired this in India : he spent about two years in India after his Buddhist ordination and there is no evidence to indicate that before his ordination he made any serious effort at studying the Buddhist canonical and classical works. He next spent twelve years in Suvarṇadvīpa studying under Dharmakīrti. Apparently it was during this period that he became a

34. See Appendix B, Section 4.

master of the Mahāyāna philosophy and logic. Thus Dharmakīrti, who made Dīpaṃkara a master in the Mahāyāna philosophy, must have been a great scholar himself. It is no wonder that the colophons of at least two of the important philosophical works of Dīpaṃkara, the *Satya-dvaya-avatāra*[35] and the *Bodhicaryā-avatāra-bhāṣya*,[36] express direct inspiration to the teachings of Dharmakīrti, and this as the continuer of the tradition of the Mahāyāna philosophy represented by Nāgārjuna, Maitreyanātha and Candrakīrti.

35. mDo xxix. 9. 36. mDo cxxviii. 9.

11. Back to India : Peace Mission

At the age of about fortyfour Dīpaṃkara returned to India from Suvarṇadvīpa. He had about fifteen years to stay in India before he left for Tibet. Two events of outstanding importance are mentioned by the Tibetan sources as connected with his life during this period. These are : 1) his mission of peace in the war between Nayapāla, the king of Magadha, and the heretical (*tīrthika*) king Karṇa of the west, and 2) his appointment as the High Priest of the Vikramaśīla *vihāra*, where he spent most of his mature years in India.

Before we proceed to discuss these, it may be useful to recapitulate certain dates.

Atīśa was born in A.D. 982. At the age of thirtyone (according to the Tibetan way of reckoning) i.e. presumably in A.D. 1012, he sailed for Suvarṇadvīpa, reaching it very likely in A.D. 1013. After spending twelve years there, i.e. about A. D. 1025, he sailed back for India. According to the Tibetan way of reckoning years, again, in A.D. 1025 Atīśa was forty-four, the age actually mentioned by some of the Tibetan sources when he returned. Atīśa finally left India for Tibet in the Iron-Male-Dragon year, i. e. A.D. 1040, notwithstanding the controversies about this date. Further, though there are controversies about the Pāla chronology, the date of the accession of Nayapāla is generally accepted as A. D. 1038.[1] On this calculation Atīśa stayed for only two years in India after the accession of king Nayapāla of Magadha.

With these dates in mind, we may now proceed to consider the peace mission of Atīśa.

According to the *Life of Atīśa* translated by S. C. Das, after returning from Suvarṇadvīpa Atīśa spent some time at the "*vihāra* of Mahā Bodhi at Vajrāsana", where "he thrice defeated

1. HB. i. 177.

the Tīrthika heretics in religious controversy and thereby maintained the superiority of Buddhism over all other religions of Magadha".[2] After this, continues the biography, "At the request of king Naya Pāla he accepted the post of High Priest of Vikrama Śīlā. At this time Magadha was invaded by the king of Kārṇya (probably Kānauj). Naya Pāla's armies first suffered a defeat at the hands of the enemy who had advanced up to the capital. The king of Magadha was victorious at last when his enemy sued for peace, and a treaty was signed by which friendship was established between the two kingdoms. In this treaty Dīpaṃkara took an active part. It was he who brought about a reconciliation between the king of Kārṇya and Naya Pāla".[3]

In his notes,[4] S. C. Das translates another Tibetan passage glorifying the role of Dīpaṃkara in bringing about this peace : "During Atiśa's residence at Vajrāsana a dispute having arisen between the two, Naya Pāla, king of Magadha, and the Tīrthika king of Kārṇya of the west ; the latter made war upon Magadha. Failing to capture the city his troops sacked some of the sacred Buddhist institutions and killed altogether five (men), out of whom four were ordained monks and one *upāsaka*. When a good deal of church furniture was carried away as booty (from the possession of the clergy) Atiśa did not shew any kind of concern or anger at it, but remained quiet, meditating on the *bodhicitta*, love for humanity and compassion. Afterwards when victory turned towards (Nayapāla) and the troops of Kārṇya were being slaughtered by the armies of Magadha, he took the king of Kārṇya and his men under his protection and sent them away. The king of Kārṇya reverenced Atiśa and became devoted to him. He invited him to his country which was in Western India and did him honour. Atiśa also caused a treaty to be concluded between the two kings. With the exception of the articles of food that were destroyed at the time of war, all other things which had fallen

2. S. C. Das in JBTS I. i. 9. 3. *Ib.* 9-10. 4. *Ib.* 9n.

in the hands of the parties were either restored or compensated for. Unmindful of his health, even at the risk of his life, Atīśa again and again crossed the rivers that lay between the two kingdoms and thereby brought peace to all living beings".

The historians of Bengal find it necessary to examine critically this Tibetan account of the role of Atīśa in his contemporary political history.

There can be no doubt about the intimate relation Atīśa had with king Nayapāla. The letter he wrote to Nayapāla from Nepal (on his way to Tibet), which is preserved in the bsTan-'gyur under the title *Vimala-ratna-lekha-nāma*,[5] could in fact be written only by a spiritual preceptor to his dear disciple. If, therefore, Nayapāla was actually in war with some king and Atīśa wanted to effect a peace, he could have easily influenced Nayapāla in favour of it. Historically, however, the more important questions are : Who was this king of Kārṇya of the West and did his war against Nayapāla occur at a time when Atīśa was in India to be able to conduct the peace mission ?

R. C. Majumdar[6] identifies this hostile king as "the Kalachuri king Karṇa or Lakṣhmīkarṇa", a long-drawn struggle with whom formed the most important event during the reign of king Nayapāla. The generally accepted view is that the Kalachuri king Karṇa succeeded his father king Gāṅgeyadeva in A.D. 1041,[7] though J. C. Ghosh[8] suggests that it was in A.D. 1039. Thus, assuming the latter date to be correct, there is no difficulty in accepting to plausibility of Dīpaṃkara mediating in the war between Karṇa and Nayapāla. Accepting, however, A.D. 1041 as the correct date of the accession of king Karṇa, the difficulty in admitting the Tibetan account of Dīpaṃkara's peace mission becomes obvious, the date of his departure for Tibet being A.D. 1040.

Following R.C. Majumdar, two ways of solving the difficulty may be suggested. First, there are grounds to think that the hostility between the Pāla rulers and the Kalachuri kings broke

5. See Appendix C, Section 5. 6. Majumdar in HB i. 144.
7. *Ib.* i. 145. 8. Ghose in IC i. 289.

out a number of years before the accession of Karṇa. It is "likely that the war, referred to in the Tibetan texts, is only a phase of the long-drawn struggle between the Pālas and the Kalachuris, which had been going on since the time of Gāṅgeyadeva".[9] Secondly, the actual date of Atīśa's departure for Tibet could have been later than A.D. 1040, or more specifically, A.D. 1042, as is sometimes suggested by S. C. Das.[10] "The initial success of the Kalachuris", says R. C. Majumdar,[11] "is testified to by the Tibetan tradition, the claim in Kalachuri records that Gāṅgeyadeva defeated the ruler of Aṅga, and the occupation of Benares by the latter. The discomfiture of the Kalachuris towards the end, and their treaty with the Pālas, may have been due, to a great extent, to the death of the great king Gāṅgeyadeva. This theory fits in well with the date of departure of Dīpaṃkara as given in the Tibetan texts, if we take the latest date proposed, viz. 1042 A.D.".

It is not for us to suggest here any definite view, though we shall see later that A. D. 1042 cannot be taken as the date of Dīpaṃkara's departure for Tibet. At the same time, the difficulty about the first solution above is obvious : if the war mentioned took place before the accession of Karṇa, why do the Tibetan sources refer to it as between Karṇa and Nayapāla ? Could it be that Karṇa was then leading his army not as the king but as the prince and heir-apparent ?

9. Majumdar in HB i. 145. 10. Das in JASB 1881. 237. In his different contributions, however, S. C. Das himself suggests different dates for this. See section 31. 11. Majumdar in HB i. 145.

12. The Indian Monasteries

As is only to be expected, Atīśa's activities in India for about fifteen years intervening between his return from Suvarṇa-dvīpa and the departure for Tibet were centered in some of the monasteries of the time. Of these the monastery known to the Tibetans by the name of Vikramaśīla must have been the foremost. According to the persistent assertions of the Tibetans, it was the main centre of Atīśa's mature Indian career and it was at this monastery that he received the invitation to Tibet. However, Vikramaśīla was by no means the only monastery to which his activities were confined. Apart from Nālandā, where Atīśa executed a literar work,[1] and apart of course from Vajrāsana, where like any other devout Buddhist Atīśa must have made a number of pilgrimages, the Tibetan sources distinctly mention two other monasteris, called Odantapurī and Somapurī, as connected with his career.

Thus as seats of Atīśa's mature Indian career the names of three monasteries interest us most. These are Vikramaśīla, Odantapurī and Somapurī. Before, however, we proceed to discuss the nature of Atīśa's connections with these, it may be worthwhile to try to have some idea of the monasteries.

All the three monasteries came to prominence during the last phase of Buddhism in India, or more specifically, during the Pāla rule in Eastern India. So we do not expect the earlier Chinese travellers to leave for us any record of these. Neither I-Tsing nor Hiuen Tsang, from whom we know so much about the earlier monasteries like Nālandā and others, have anything to say about Vikramaśīla, Odantapurī and

1. In the Peking edition, the colophon of rG. lxvi. 6, reads "... translated by the Indian *paṇḍita* Dīpaṃkara-śrī-jñāna and the Tibetan lo-tsā-ba Vīryasiṃha of rGya at the corridor of Śrī Nālandā".

Somapurī. Further, and this is somewhat strange, though our knowledge of the earlier Buddhist monasteries like Nālandā are definitely authenticated by the archaeological recrods, we have to depend mainly on the Tibetan accounts for these later monasteries, Somapurī being the only exception to this. The monastery excavated at Paharpur in Rajsahi district, according to our archaeologists, is the same as Somapurī. Judging it by its ruins, we are led to the view that it must once have been an extremely imposing *vihāra* of the Pāla times. This, again, is a little strange. For in the Tibetan accounts of the Buddhist monasteries of the Pāla period Somapurī does not figure so prominently compared to Vikramaśila and Odantapurī. This by itself indicates that the Tibetan accounts of the Buddhist *vihāra*-s of Dipaṃkara's time are to be viewed with considerable critical caution and since the same legends are sometimes mentioned in connection with both Odantapurī and Somapurī, even the possibility of some cunfusion of the names of these monasteries in the Tibetan sources connot be entirely ruled out. However, since our knowledge of these *vihāra*-s, particularly as centres of Dīpaṃkara's activities, is based primarily on the Tibetan sources, it is only reasonable for us to begin by compiling here what we hear of these from the Tibetans.

13. The Vikramasila Vihara

To begin with, there is some confusion about the actual name of this monastery. Though throughout the *History of Bengal* the name occurs as Vikramaśila, modern scholars like H. D. Sankalia,[1] Nundolal De,[2] S. Dutt[3] and others[4] spell it as Vikramaśīlā. This is perhaps because throughout the *Indian Pandits* by S. C. Das, upon which these scholars largely depend for the knowledge of the monastery, its name occurs as Vikrama Śīlā, though S. C. Das himself, in his English Index and Contents of Sum-pa's work[5] gives the spelling as Vikrama Śīla and in his *Tibetan-English Dictionary*[6] mentions it as Vikramaśīla. This is quite curious. It is curious, again, that though S. C. Vidyabhusana[7] prefers to spell the name as Vikramaśīlā, in his notes he quotes two Sanskrit passages in which the name of the monastery is clearly given as Vikramaśila in Devanāgarī script. Thus, the colophon of the *Srag-dharā-stotra-tīkā* contains the words : *śrīmad-vikramaśīla-deva-mahāvihārīya* etc. In the *Vṛhat-svayambhu-purāṇa*, again, occur the words : *tadā vikramaśilasi vihāre* etc.

S. Dutt[8] even goes to the extent of suggesting that the fact of the monastery being situated on "a bluff hill", "is taken to be a justification of the spelling" Vikramaśīlā. What is overlooked, however, is the more important fact that the Indian word for stone or rock is *śilā* and not *śīlā*. As such, even if the monastery was actually called Vikramaśīlā its possible significance is to the sought somewhere else than the "bluff hill" on which it was supposed to have been situated. But where else can such a significance be sought ? This is a difficult question. Assuming it to have been an Indian

1. Sankalia 179ff. 2. N. De JASB 1919. 1ff. 3. Dutt in *2500 Years*, 190f. 4. P. N. Bose 33. 5. Sum-pa, *Index* xlvii ; *Contents* xv. 6. D-TED 869. 7. Vidyabhusana HMSIL 150. 8. Dutt in *2500 Years*, 190.

(Sanskrit) word, it is really hard, if not impossible to make any coherent meaning of *vikramaśīlā*.

But there is really no reason to think that the actual name of the monastery was Vikramaśīlā rather than Vikramaśīla. It is necessary to remember that the monastery is known to us mainly from the Tibetan sources and the actual Indian evidence to corroborate these is extrelemy slender. So the main question is : How do the Tibetans themselves mention the name ?

Like the name of Dīpaṃkara, the name of this monastery occurs in the Tibetan sources in two forms. First, in the form of an exact transliteration of the Indian word in Tibetan characters. Secondly, in the form of what the Tibetans intend to be an exact translation of the Indian word into their own language. Of these the first form is more common and we read it as

བི་ཀྲ་མ་ཤཱི་ལ

i. e. Vikramaśīla, notwithstanding the occasional and obviously corrupt form as Vikramalaśīla or Vri-ka-ma-la-śi-la. Vikramaśīla, e.g , is the form in which Tāranātha[9] uses the name and it is also found to occur in the colophons of a number of works in the bsTan-'gyur.[10] Further, judging from the fact that Roerich, in his translation of the *Blue Annals*, throughout uses the spelling in Roman script as Vikramaśīla, we are left to presume that 'Gos lo-tsā-ba, too, uses the same spelling in Tibetan characters.

But this, it will be argued, cannot be a decisive evidence for the name being actually Vikramaśīla rather than Vikramaśīlā. The reason is simple. Ordinarily speaking, there is no provision in Tibetan script to differentiate between the sounds *a* and *ā*, as between *i* and *ī*. Only when the Tibetans feel the need of an absolutely accurate transliteration of an Indian word—as they sometimes do in the cases of the Tāntrika spells (*dhāraṇī*-s), where the exact sound of a word is supposed to be of great

9. Tāranātha, Benares ed., 201. 10. See Appendix B.

significance—they indicate the long sound by adding the special sign of *dīrgha*[11] under a letter. But there is no ground to think that they feel the need of being so scrupulous while giving the name of the monastery in their own script and, therefore, even if this name were actually Vikramaśīlā they can as well transliterate it simply as Vikramaśīla, i. e. without adding the sign of *dīrgha* under the last *a*.

However, the force of this argument is only apparent. It needs to be noted that while transliterating the name of the *vihāra,* the Tibetans do use the special sign of *dīrgha* for *śī* of Vikramaśīla, though no sign is added to the ending *a* for the purpose of making it a long one. This indicates that the Tibetan transliteration of the name Vikramaśīla cannot be taken as a casual one : if special care is taken to indicate that the *ī* in the name is a long one and no such care is seen in the case of the last *a*, the presumption is that they know the monastery as Vikramaśīla rather than Vikramaśīlā. There is another and more convincing argument in favour of this assumption. It is to be found in what the Tibetans intend to be an exact translation of the name into their own language.

In Tibetan translation, the name of the monastery occurs as rNam-gnon-ṅaṅ-tshul.[12] Ṅaṅ-tshul literally means "natural disposition, temperament, etc."[13] That is, it is the Tibetan equivalent of the Indian word *śīla* in the broader sense. *gNon* means 'to press, to force down, to suppress, etc.'[14] *rNam* is the Tibetan equivalent of the Sanskrit prefix *vi,* meaning strongly or well. So, *rnam-gnon* means to press or suppress firmly. Thus, rNam-gnon-ṅaṅ-tshul may roughly be rendered as 'one who strongly subdues natural disposition' or 'one with strong moral conduct'. Such a sense is quite near the literal meaning of the Sanskrit word *vikramaśīla*. In any case, the evidence of the word *ṅaṅ-tshul* is decisive. The obvious Sanskrit equivalent that it suggests is *śīla* and it is quite far from conveying any idea of *śilā*, i,e. stone, rock or hill. The Tibetan

11. namely

2. e. g., Sum-pa 73. 13. D-TED 348. 14. *Ib.* 754.

word for stone is *rdo*, for hill *ri* and for rock *brag*. The absence of any such word in the Tibetan translation of the name Vikramaśīla proves that the name, as the Tibetans understood it, had nothing to suggest the idea of a rock or hill. On the other hand, what is positively conveyed by the Tibetan translation of the name of the *vihāra* is the idea of strong moral conduct or of what is being conveyed by the Sanskrit word *śīla*.

It may be tempting to conjecture from all these that such a name was chosen for the monastery for glorifying it is a centre of strong moral discipline. As a matter of fact, in the *Life of Atīśa* translated by S. C. Das it is suggested that "according to some writers" the monastery owed this name "to the high moral character of its monks."[15] Though Sankalia[16] is inclined to take this suggestion seriously, it is quite evident that the biographer of Atīśa himself does not agree to do so, for an expression like "according to some" etc. is the usual Tibetan way of differing from a suggestion under consideration or of expressing doubt about it. Besides, notwithstanding the effort at constructing an honorific sense of the name Nālandā,[17] the names of the Buddhist *vihāra*-s known to us, like Somapurī, Odantapurī, Jagaddala, etc., do not usually have any honorific significance.

On the other hand, R. C. Majumdar suggests another consideration from which the Vikramaśīla monastery could have received this name. As we shall presently see, the founder-patron of this monastery was king Dharmapāla, though it is sometimes conjectured that his successor Devapāla could have founded it. "The reference", says R. C. Majumdar, "to the *vihāra* as *Śrīmad-vikramaśīla-deva-mahāvihāra* (Mitra—*Nepal*,, 229) shows that Vikramaśīla was another name or *biruda* of Dharmapāla (or Devapāla) who founded it".[18] This,

15. JBTS I. i. 11. 16. Sankalia 81. 17. *Ib*. 35f. 18. Majumdar in HB i. 115n.

Majumdar thinks, is corroborated by the following evidence of the *Rāmacarita* : "Yuvarāja Hāravarsha belonged to the Pāla family of Bengal....It has been suggested that Vikramaśīla, the father of Yuvarāja, was another name of Dharmapāla, who founded the Vikramaśīla monastery and Hāravarsha is identical with Devapāla."[19]

Thus, like the Cūḍāmaṇivarman *vihāra* of south India, which owed its name to its founder-patron the Śailendra king Cūḍāmaṇivarman, the Vikramaśīla *vihāra*, too, could have owed its name to its founder-patron king Vikramaśīla who was none else than Dharmapāla. However, as we have already said, the Vikramaśīla *vihāra* is known to us mainly from the Tibetan sources and though the Tibetans repeatedly assert that the monastery was founded by Dharmapāla, they appear to be totally unaware of the possibility of it being named after Dharmapāla, *alias,* Vikramaśīla.

What, then, the Tibetans have to say about this name ? We have, in their writings, certain explanations of the name which are but transparent fictions. Thus, e.g., it is suggested that "because of its being the site where a Yakṣa...of the name of Vikrama was suppressed, it was called the Vikrama Śīlā."[20] At the same time, we have in the same Tibetan work a suggestion about the name of the monastery which, historically speaking, may be extremely significant. "The Vihāra", according to it,[21] "became known by four names in the four quarters. In Tibet it was famed under the name of Vikrama Śīlā." In his note, S. C. Das adds, "it is probable that the great religious establishment which rose by the side of the little Vihāra of Vikrama Śīlā and afterwards incorporated with it was anciently called by *the above-mentioned three* names. Hence it may be that Vikrama Śīlā had four names of which the most famous was Vikrama Śīlā, by which it was well-known to the people of Himavat, i.e. Tibet".[22] Astonishingly, "the above-mentioned three names" are nowhere to be traced in the writings of S. C.

19. *Ib.* i. 123. 20. JBTS I. i. 11. 21. *Ib.* 22. *Ib.* 10n. Italics added.

Das himself—an omission that appears to be absolutely unaccounted for—though the obvious presumption is that S. C. Das himself came across in some of the Tibetan sources the alternative names by which the *vihāra* was better known in India. But for his forgetfulness to mention these alternative names, we could have perhaps been better equipped today to answer certain questions concerning this monastery which remain for us quite confounding.

Let us, however, begin with what the Tibetan historians have to say about this monastery and its founder-patron.

"After it", says Tāranātha,[23] "that king's son Dharmapāla became king. His reign was for sixty-four years. He ruled over Kāmarūpa, Tirahuti, Gauḍa, etc., in the east up to the sea, in the west up to Delhi, in the north up to Jalandhar, in the south up to Vindhya. Then Siṃhabhadra and Jñānapāda were his *guru*-s. He collected *paṇḍita*-s of *prajñāpāramitā* and *guhyasamāja* from ten directions. At that time, the *paṇḍita*-s of *guhyasamāja* and *prajñāpāramitā* could fill whole areas. When he became king, in Bengal the *siddha ācārya* Kukuri-pa (Kukkuri-pā) was working for the welfare of every living being. The history of this can be known elsewhere. In fact, he (Dharmapāla) started, since the time of his ascending the throne, to invite *paṇḍitas*-s of *prajñāpāramitā*, including *ācārya* Siṃhabhadra, etc. The king built about fifty Buddhist centres in all, among which thirtyfive were centres for the study of *prajñāpāramitā*. Śrī Vikramaśila *vihāra* (was built) on the bank of the Gaṅgā in the north of Magadha on top of a hill. At its centre was built a shrine with a life-size image of Mahābodhi. Around this (were built) fiftythree small shrines for the study of *guhyatantra* and another fiftyfour common temples. Thus the number of temples was one hundred and eight and also the outer wall. He (Dharmapāla) provided for the livelihood of one hundred and eight *paṇḍita*-s."

"After that", says Sum-pa,[24] "the king's son Dharmapāla,

23. Tāranātha, Benares ed , 200-1. Free Translation. 24. Sum-pa 112-3. Free Translation.

who had a great devotion to *prajñāpāramitā* ruled up to Kāmarūpa, Tirahuti, Gauḍa, etc., up to the coast of the sea on the east, in the west up to Delhi, in the north up to Jalandhar, and in the south up to Vindhya. He reigned for sixty-four years. During his reign, he became a disciple of both Haribhadra and his student Buddhajñānapāda. On the first month of the calendar year, he attained great bliss. On the north of Magadha, on the bank of the Gaṅgā and on top of a hill was built (by Dharmapāla) the Vikramaśīla *vihāra,* which had one hundred and seven shrines around the Central Hall and an outer wall. It was supported by fifty endowments for the religious centre and provided the livelihood for one hundred and eight *paṇḍita*-s. At that time, *prajñāpāramitā* and *samāja* were widely spread. That was the time when in the west king Cakrāyudha (!) and in the north in Tibet Khri-sroṅ-lde-btsan were ruling. This is a rough account."

The surprising similarity between the two accounts is obvious, as obvious perhaps are the exaggerations in the descriptions of the extent and duration of Dharmapāla's rule, for an actual historical assessment of which we are to look elsewhere.[25] The names Siṃhabhadra and Haribhadra occurring in the passages quoted from Sum-pa and Tāranātha[26] are but two ways of retranslating the Tibetan version of the name, which is Seṅ-ge-bzaṅ-po. The two authorities mention the two names as the preceptor of *ācārya* Jñānapāda, variously mentioned as Buddhajñāna,[27] Buddhaśrījñāna[28] or Buddhajñānapāda.[29] From the Tibetan accounts it appears that Haribhadra and Jñānapāda belonged to Dharmapāla's time and enjoyed his patronage.[30]

What particularly interests us here is that of all the religious centres sponsored by Dharmapāla, both Tāranātha and Sum-pa choose to mention only one by name, and it is Vikramaśīla. Apparently both the historians feel that this *vihāra* was of most outstanding importance. Further, the location of the monastery as mentioned by both is identical. In other words, both Tāranātha and Sum-pa depend here on a tradition according

25. HB i. 108ff. 26. See also B. N. Datta, *Mystic Tales* 51. 27. BA i. 353, 367f 28. *Ib.* 29. Bu-ston ii. 159f. 30. For Dharmapāla's patronage of Haribhadra, see Bu-ston ii. 158.

to which the most important religious establishment sponsored by Dharmapāla was situated on top of a hill, on the bank of the Gaṅgā, somewhere to the north of Magadha and that the Tibetans knew this as the Vikramaśīla *vihāra*.

The biographer of Atīśa translated by S. C. Das seems to depend substantially on the same tradition, though he adds obvious legends to it. "Ācārya Kampala", says he,[31] "a learned professor of the school of Buddhist Tantras at Śrī Nālandā, who had obtained the *siddhi* or perfection in the *mahāmudrā* mysticism, was once struck with the features of a bluff rocky hillock which stood in the bank of the Ganges. Observing its peculiar fitness for the site of a Vihāra he remarked that under royal auspicious it could be turned into a great place for the use of the *saṃgha*,...By dint of fore-knowledge he also knew that one time there on that hill a great Vihāra would be built. It is said that in course of time Kampala was born as Dharmapāla, the renowned king of Magadha. He built the monastery of Vikrama Śīlā on that hill...the king furnished the Vihāra with four establishments, each consisting of twentyseven monks belonging to the four principal sects of the Buddhists."

There is some confusion over the question whether Dharmapāla or Devapāla was actually the founder of the monastery. "According to other traditions, however", says R. C. Majumdar,[32] "Devapāla is regarded as its founder." The only evidence given by Majumdar for such a remark is the reading by Cordier of a colophon of one of Dīpaṃkara's works in the bsTan-'gyur,[33] called the *Ratna-karaṇḍodghāṭa-nāma-madhyamaka-upadeśa*. According to this colophon, the text was written by Dīpaṃkara on the request of *śākya bhikṣu* Jayaśīla (Nag-tsho), the good disciple, at the Vikramaśīla temple. There is no difficulty about the colophon so far. But while mentioning the name of the Vikramaśīla temple, the colophon also mentions the name of Devapāla and, peculiarly

31. JBTS I. i. 10-11. 32. HB i. 115n. cf Das in JBTS 1. i. 10n.
33. mDo xxx. 24.

enough, uses the Tibetan word *thugs-dam* along with the name of Devapāla. Cordier, apparently with the hope of making a coherent meaning of the colophon, renders the Tibetan word as "foundation de Devapāla".[34] That Cordier himself has some hesitation about this rendering is evident from his giving the original Tibetan word *thugs-dam* within brackets, which occurs also in the Peking edition of the bsTan-'gyur. But the literal meaning of the word does not suggest any idea of founding any *vihāra* or temple. It means "holy opinion, advice, oath, vow, solemn promise."[35] Can it be that the word is used in the colophon just to suggest that the Vikramaśīla *vihāra* enjoyed the patronage of Devapāla or perhaps was the place where Devapāla took some solemn oath ? Historically there is nothing to rule out any such possibility, or the possibility in particular of Devapāla devoting himself to the development of the great monastery founded or started by Dharmapāla. In any case, Cordier's reading of the colophon, if taken to mean that Devapāla was the original founder of the monastery, can at best be doubtful, and thus it cannot by itself cast doubt on the possibility of Dharmapāla being the actual founder of the monastery. It should be noted, however, that Tibetan historians sometimes do confuse the names of Dharmapāla and Devapāla, inasmuch as identical legends are attributed by them to the birth of these two Pāla kings.

The exact site of the Vikramaśīla *vihāra* is still a matter for conjecture. Cunningham's[36] view that it could be the modern village Silao about three miles from Baragaon (the ancient Nālandā) and six miles to the north of Rajgir, the ancient capital of Magadha, in the subdivision of Bihar in the district of Patna, is not seriously taken by other modern scholars. S. C. Das cautiously suggests that it could have been modern Sultangunj near Bhagalpur. "Just as the Brāhmaṇas", says he,[37] "had their city on the holy land of the Uttara Vāhinī Gaṅgā, the Buddhists whose veneration for the sacred stream

34. Cordier iii. 321-2. 35. D-TED 579. 36. Cunningham in ASR viii. 83. 37. S. C. Das in JBTS I. i. 10n.

was no less than that of their adversaries, the Brāhmaṇas, had built Vikrama Śīlā on a rival spot situated on the northern reach of the Ganges. These circumstances, and the account of its being originally built on a rocky hill on the right bank of the Ganges, and the similarity of the names Vaishkaran with the name Vikrama, may tempt one to risk the identification of Vikrama Śīlā with Vaishkaran Śīlā of modern Sultan Gung near Bhagalpur".

S. C. Vidyabhusana[38] substantially agrees with this and the modern Tibetan scholar dGe-'dun-chos-'phel[39] locates Vikramaśīla somewhere in the same area. "On the route from Gaya to Calcutta", says the latter, "one reaches a (railway) station called Sultangunj. Near this town, on the middle of the Gaṅgā, there is a small rock with a temple on it. This side of the Gaṅgā (i.e. on the side of Sultangunj), there is a small rocky mound. There lie the ruins of the Vikramaśīla monastery. But the exact site is not known, because it is not excavated."

But Nundalal De[40] criticises Vidyabhusana and complains that "the learned professor has assigned no reason for this identification". Nundalal De himself wants to identify the site of Vikramaśīla as modern Patharghata of Bhagalpur district. "A day's sail below Sultanganj", says he, "is situated a projecting steep hill called Patharghata, which is a spur of the Coloong range. It is about six miles to the north of Coloong, twentyfour miles to the east of Bhagalpur and twenty-eight miles to the east of Champânagar, the ancient Champa, the capital of Aṅga." And, "there can be no reasonable doubt that Patharghata near Coloong in the district of Bhagalpur was the ancient Vikramaśīlā and that the ruins upon it are the remains of the celebrated monastery which existed for about four centuries from the middle of the eighth century to the later end of the twelfth century A. D." Though Samaddar[41] fully subscribes to it and calls it "the best

38. S. C. Vidyabhusana in *Bhāratī* (Bengali), Vaiśākha 1315; *Sāhitya* (Bengali), Śrāvaṇa 1314. 39. Guide 26. 40. N. De in JASB (NS) 1901. 1ff. 41. Samaddar 157.

identification" of the site of Vikramaśīla, Banerji-Sastri[42] rejects it altogether on the ground that excepting for the hill the site does not answer any other description given by the Tibetans. As a plausible site of Vikramaśīla, Banerji-Sastri himself mentions modern Keur, three miles south-east of Hulasganj and just behind the south-west corner of the Hilsa police station.

All these conjectures are basically determined by the Tibetan accounts of the geographical location of Vikramaśīla. But it is not necessarily safe to depend literally on the geographical accounts of the Indian *vihāra*-s given by the Tibetan historians. Thus, e.g., according to even such a reputed Tibetan historian like 'Gos lo-tsā-ba,[43] Somapurī was "in the country of Kośala (*dakṣiṇa-kośala*) in southern India", though we know its real site to have been Rajshahi of north Bengal (Paharpur) Obviously, 'Gos lo-tsā-ba's error of the geographical location of Somapurī cannot prove that the site of Vikramaśīla as mentioned by Tāranātha, Sum-pa and, more particularly by the author of the *Life of Atīśa*, which claims to be based on the direct communication of Jayaśīla of Nag-tsho, is wrong. Nevertheless, in default of positive archaeological evidence, any identification of the actual site of Vikramaśīla based exclusively on the Tibetan descriptions of the site has the risk of being more or less conjectural and therefore it is desirable to leave the question as still an open one.

42. Banerji-Sastri in JBORS xv. 276. 43. BA ii. 844.

14. Odantapuri and Somapuri

We have just seen that according to Tāranātha and Sum-pa, Vikramaśīla was by far the most important monastery sponsored by Dharmapāla. But there is some difficulty in accepting this suggestion. Bu-ston mentions the founding of only one monastery by Dharmapāla and he calls it the Odantapurī *vihāra*, though the account given by him of the founding of this monastery is as legendary as that of the birth of Dharmapāla. "Gopāla's queen", says Bu-ston,[1] "who had no power over the king, resolved to bring him under her influence and asked a Brāhmaṇa to give her magical power in order to accomplish this. The Brāhmaṇa brought from the Himālaya an enchanted drug, sealed it and handed it over to (the queen's) slave-girl. The latter, whilst crossing a bridge, fell down, and (the drug) was carried away by the stream, gradually reached the ocean, and was seized by the Nāga king who swallowed it up. Thus, by the force of the drug, the Nāga king, the sovereign of the ocean, became subjected to the power of the queen, united with her, and from this union a son named Śrīmad Dharmapāla was born. ...When the latter grew up, he became possessed of the desire of building a temple more magnificent than all the others, and inquired the sooth-sayers (on this subject). The sooth-sayers said that it was necessary to make a wick out of the cotton belonging to ascetics and Brāhmaṇas, to get oil from the houses of kings and merchants, to fetch an oil-burner from a place of penance, and to place the burning lamp before the tutelary deity : —If thou shalt address an entreaty, the incarnation of the watch-god will throw the lamp away, and at the place (where it falls) the

1. Bu-ston ii. 156-7.

temple must be built. This was done, but there suddenly appeared a raven, that threw the lamp into a lake. (The youth) was distressed, but in the night the king of the Nāgas with 5 serpent-heads came to him and said :—I am thy father, and I will cause this lake to dry up. Thou shalt build thy temple in the place of it. (In order to bring this about) thou must perform sacrifices for 7 weeks. This was accordingly done. On the 21st day the lake was dried up and (in its place) the monastery of Odantapurī was built".

It is interesting that both Tāranātha and Sum-pa, without themselves subscribing to it, relate the same legend current among the Tibetans about the birth of Devapāla and the building by him of the monastery called Somapurī. Says Tāranātha[2] : "And king Devapāla. It is even said by some that he was a son of the Nāgas. But (I) think he was born as a descendant of Gopāla...However, the tradition is like this : 'The youngest queen of Gopāla requested a Brāhmaṇa, who was a master of magical charm (*mantravidyādhara*) for something with which to charm the king and keep him under control (*vaśīkaraṇa*). The Brāhmaṇa secured some medical herb from the Himālaya, charmed it with magical spell, and said : Mix this with food, seal the food and send it to the king. She sent it through her maid. After reaching the bank of a river, (the maid) dropped it into the water. It was carried by the water to the Nāga-loka. The Nāga king Sāgarapāla swallowed it and thereby came under the magical charm (of Gopāla's queen). He came in the guise of the king (Gopāla) and united with the queen. When the queen conceived, the king (Gopāla) wanted to punish her. (The queen) told the king that the king himself (i.e. Gopāla) had gone to her on such and such time. Well, said the king, I shall then think over it. When the queen gave birth to a son, the son was found to have the head of a snake and also a ring on his finger. On examination, the ring was found to have a letter in Nāga script. So the king came to know that it was the son of the Nāga king. After Gopāla's death, he was made the king, became more

2. Tāranātha, Benares ed., 194-5. Free Translation.

powerful than the previous kings and brought Varendra under his rule. He wanted to build a special temple and built Somapurī. About it (i.e. the building of Somapurī) most of the Tibetan legends say (the following) :

"The astrologer (*lakṣaṇajña*) told (the king) : Prepare a wick with the clothes of *śramaṇa*-s and *brāhmaṇa*-s, obtain oil from the house of kings and merchants, get a lamp from the hermitage, light it, put it before the tutelar deity (*kula-devatā*) and pray,—the incarnation of Dharmapāla will then drop it at some place and you build the temple there. By doing this, the king was to be powerful, famed everywhere and would be beneficent to all. All these were done. Then a crow came, took the lamp and threw it into a lake. This made the king extremely worried. At night the five-headed Nāga king appeared before him and said : I am your father. So I shall dry up the lake and you build the temple. Remember to do offerings in big scale for twentyone days.

"This was done and within twentyone days the lake dried up and the temple was built.

"That is what occurs (in the Tibetan legends). In the history of the building of the Samudragupta temple of Kashmir, a black man said in a dream, 'Do offerings to Mahākāla and the Yakṣas will dry up the lake'. Excepting this, other details (in both the legends of the building of Somapurī and Samudra-gupta temple) are the same. So it is better not to connect this legend with Somapurī.

"Similarly, the account of the birth of Devapāla and of Sahajalīla are the same. So one must be careful about this also."

The distrust expressed by Tāranātha in the legends about the birth of Devapāla and the construction of Somapurī by him is quite unambiguous. But the point is, he cannot ignore the legends altogether. The same is true of Sum-pa.[3] He relates identical legends in almost the same language about the birth of Devapāla and the foundation by him of Somapurī and he also expresses the same distrust in the legends. Evidently the

3. Sum-pa 111.

legends were much too deep-rooted in the Tibetan tradition to be simply ignored by the historians. Bu-ston mentions the same legends about the birth of Dharmapāla and the building by him of Odantapurī, without giving any hint as to the incredulity of these legends. And this leads us to an interesting point. Tāranātha and Sum-pa express their doubts about these legends not because these are patently miraculous nor because these closely resemble those told by Bu-ston about Dharmapāla and Odantapurī. What they clearly say instead is that in the understanding of Indian history by the Tibetans, the legend about Sahajalīla somehow got mixed up with Devapāla and that of the Kashmerian temple Samudragupta with the legend of Somapurī. It may thus be permissible to conjecture that Bu-ston could have himself confused these with the history of Dharmapāla and Odantapurī.

One point is already evident from the above. It is precarious to depend on the Tibetan accounts alone for the knowledge of the Buddhist monasteries with which Dīpaṃkara was connected. This becomes all the more obvious when we take note of the accounts given by both Tāranātha and Sum-pa about the building of Odantapurī. Here is Tāranātha's account[4] :

"Between Gopāla and Devapāla, Śrī Odantapurī temple was built. A *tīrthika yogī*, with purity of character, obtained miraculous power somewhere near Magadha. His name was Narada. He wanted to perform the ritual with a corpse (*śava-sādhanā*). For this purpose, he needed a companion who was to be physically strong, without any disease, possessing the nine signs of bravery, truthful, intellectually sharp, honest and versed in all crafts and branches of knowledge. He could not find any other person like that excepting a Buddhist *upāsaka*. He requested the *upāsaka* to assist him in the ritual with the corpse. (The *upāsaka*) replied, 'I cannot be an assistant of a *tīrthika*.' He (Narada) said, 'You need not be a *tīrthika*. (Besides, by assisting me) you will find inexhaustible wealth. With that you can spread your own religion.' So he

4. Tāranātha, Benares ed , 192-4. Free Translation.

(the *upāsaka*) said, 'Then I shall go and ask my *guru*'. He went to his *guru*, told him everything and received the *guru*'s permission and became Narada's assistant. As the ritual was nearing its fulfilment, he (Narada) said, 'When the corpse sticks out its tongue you must catch it. If you can catch the tongue the first time it is stuck out, you will attain supreme success (*mahā-siddhi*). Being able to catch it on the second occasion will bring you intermediate success; being able to catch it for the last (third) time will bring small success. If you fail to catch it even on the third occasion, he (the dead) will first devour the two of us and will next make the whole world empty'. The *upāsaka* failed to catch the tongue for the first and the second time. Then he sat with his own mouth near that of the corpse, ready to catch its tongue with his own teeth. And the third time (the corpse stretched out its tongue), he caught it with his teeth. Then the tongue became a sword and the corpse itself turned into gold.

"The *upāsaka* took hold of the sword and went round the corpse. With the sword in hand, he began to fly in the sky. The *tīrthika* said, 'I have done this for the sake of the sword. Therefore, give me the sword'. The *upāsaka* said, 'Yes. I will give you the sword after I have had some sight-seeing'. So he flew to the top of Sumeru, circled it along with its four *dvīpa*-s and their *upa-dvīpa*-s. Within a moment he came back and gave the sword to the *tīrthika*. He (the *tīrthika*) said, 'You take the golden body. You can have gold from it so long as you do not touch its bones. But do not spend the gold on evil purposes like wine and women. You can spend it for your own use and for holy undertakings. If you do that, any part of the body that you may slice off during the day will be replaced during night'. After saying this, he (Narada) flew to heaven with the sword. And the *upāsaka*, with the *vetāla*'s gold built the colossal temple of Odantapurī. *Odanta* means 'flying over' (*'phur-byed*) ; for the *upāsaka* flew in the sky over Sumeru along with its four *dvīpa*-s and saw these with his own eyes. That is why, he built the temple (Odantapurī) in its model (i.e. in the model of Sumeru along with its four *dvīpa*-s). And the *upāsaka*'s name became Unna Upāsaka.

"This temple was not built by any king or minister. The craftsmen and artists that worked for building the temple and its images were paid and fed from the gold of the *vetāla*'s body. Only from this gold were maintained 500 *bhikṣu*-s and 500 *upāsaka*-s. Till his own death, that *upāsaka* (Unna) acted according to his own religion. He knew that the gold could not be used by others after his death. So he buried it under the earth with the prayer that it may benefit all living beings in future. And he gave his temple (Odantapurī) to Devapāla."

Sum-pa's account of the building of Odantapurī, though very brief, depends substantially on the same legend. "At that time (i.e. between Gopāla and Devapāla)", says Sum-pa,[5] "a Tāntrika called Narada wanted to perform the ritual with a corpse to attain *siddhi* of the sword, met Unna, discussed with him and arranged for the ritual performance. They could convert the corpse into gold. With that gold, he (Unna) built Odantapurī near Nālandā, having for its model Sumeru with its four *dvīpa*-s".

However quaint it may be, the legend contains an important suggestion and it is pointedly emphasised by Tāranātha. *Odantapurī was not built by any king or minister.* The gold needed for it was obtained, miraculously though by a Buddhist *upāsaka*, who, only at the time of his death, handed over the monastery to king Devapāla. This, again, is in flat contradiction to Bu-ston, according to whom Odantapurī was built by Dharmapāla.

Remarkably, none of the Tibetan historians quoted above mentions the name of king Dharmapāla in connection with the foundation of the Somapurī *vihāra*. Bu-ston himself is evidently unaware of the name of this monastery, while both Tāranātha and Sum-pa quote a legend strongly current in Tibet according to which Somapurī was founded by Devapāla. Yet Somapurī is about the only *vihāra* of the Pāla period the historicity of which is authenticated by the archaeologist's spade and, on the basis of archaeological evidence, our historians conclude that it was founded by Dharmapāla.

5. Sum-pa 111. Free Translatoin.

Somapurī is identified with the *vihāra* excavated at modern Paharpur in Rajshahi district. The decisive ground for this identification is an antiquity found among the ruins of Paharpur. It is a clay sealing[6] (1·9" in diameter) with the following inscription in lower register: *śrī-somapure-śrī-dharmapāla-deva-mahā-vihārīya-ārya-bhikṣu-saṅghasya*—i. e. issued by the "community of the venerable monks belonging to the great *vihāra* of Somapura founded by Dharmapāla". Besides, a village about a mile from the Paharpur ruins still bears the name Ompur, which is taken to be reminiscent of Somapura. As R. C. Majumdar[7] sums up, "the recent archaeological excavations carried out at Paharpur, in Rajshahi district, leave no doubt that its ruins represent the famous Somapura *vihāra*, and the name of the place is still preserved in the neighbouring village called Ompur. According to the short inscriptions on some clay seals found in Paharpur, the Somapura-*vihāra* was founded by Dharmapāla".

Like that of Vikramaśīla, the exact site of Odantapurī remains yet to be definitely identified by our archaeologists and historians. Depending on Sum-pa's descriptions, S. C. Das[8] conjectures that it was "erected on a hill near the town of modern Behar." The Tibetan scholar dGe-'dun-chos-'phel[9] very cautiously suggests, "On the railway line from Patna to Rajgir, there is a station called Bihar-Sharif. If one looks to the west after reaching the station, one will see a low mound. This is said to contain the ruins of Odantapurī *vihāra*. On this place was a famous monastery of India and our bSam-yas was modelled on it. There is nothing to prove that this was the spot except the saying that it was so. Anyway, this mound is a place where Na-ro-pa stayed and its name was Phullahari. There can be no doubt about that. In his *rNam-thar*, Chag lo-tsā-ba says that there is a hill at a distance of half day's journey by foot (*tsha-'bog*) to the north of Nālandā (where

6. Dikshit 90. 7. Majumdar in HB i. 115; cf. HB i. 129, 199n; H. C. Raychaudhuri in HB. i. 30; P. C. Bagchi in HB i. 417; S. K. Sarasvati in HB i. 489f. 8. S. C. Das in Sum-pa, *Index* cxlii. 9. *Guide* 9.

Phullahari was). In the north of Nālandā there is no other hill except this. Besides, the shape of the hill is stooping towards Tibet and this agrees with the description given by Mi-la-ras-pa". However, in default of actual archaeological work, the site of Odantapurī remains yet to be definitely ascertained.

Thus, of the three monasteries connected with the mature Indian career of Dīpaṃkara, namely, Vikramaśīla, Odantapurī, and Somapurī, we have definite knowledge only of the last. Though the Tibetans want us to believe that of these three Vikramaśīla was the biggest and most important, the magnificence of the ruins of Paharpur leads the archaeologist K. N. Dikshit to conclude that of all the monasteries built during the Pāla period, Somapurī was the grandest. "The second and the third kings of the dynasty", says he,[10] "Dharmapāla and Devapāla, built up at the end of the 8th and beginnings of the 9th centuries A.D. a large empire... It was during this period that many new Buddhist temples and *vihāra*-s must have been established in Bengal under royal patronage. The biggest and most important of these must have been the establishment at Paharpur which received royal patronage from the kings of the early Pāla empire."

What is no less surprising, however, is that the history of the rise and fall of Somapurī, as told by the archaeologist, corresponds, at least roughly, to the history of the rise and fall of Vikramaśīla as told by the Tibetans. Thus, e.g., according to the Tibetans, Vikramaśīla enjoyed, after Dharmapāla and Devapāla, another phase of affluence under Mahīpāla I and Nayapāla, both of whom are mentioned as appointing Atiśa as the High Priest of the *vihāra* and that the monastery was finally ruined by the Muhammadan conquest towards the end of the 12th century A.D. Referring to the Paharpur (Somapurī) monastery, again, Dikshit[11] observes, "Prosperity seems to have returned at the end of the tenth century when Mahīpāla I founded the second Pāla empire... About the end of the 10th century or beginning of the 11th century, the prosperity of the

10. Dikshit 5. 11. *Ib.* 5-6.

establishment was reflected in a wholesale renovation in the Main Temple and in the monastic cells where a number of ornamental pedestals seem to have been installed and at the shrine of Tārā in the Satyapīr Bhiṭā numerous votive *stūpa*-s were constructed. After Mahīpāla and his son Nayapāla, the fortunes of the Pāla dynasty again suffered a reverse and Bengal was overrun in turn by the Chedi king Karṇa (Central India), the Chola king Rājendra and a local Kaivarta chief named Divya...In the 12th century the sovereignty of Bengal passed over to the Senas...In the beginning of the 13th century came the onslaught of the Muhammadans who before long overran the whole of north Bengal and it is not improbable that the Paharpur temple with its conspicuous height must have been one of the first places to attract the attention and stimulate the iconoclastic zeal of the invaders. Thereafter the temple and monastery seem to have fallen into desolation".

This could as well be the outline of the history of the Vikramaśila *vihāra* as told by the Tibetans. Perhaps all the *vihāra*-s of Eastern India sponsored by the Pālas and dependent on their patronage had similar fate. Nevertheless, the archaeological evidence of the "wholesale renovation" of the Somapurī *vihāra* during the end of the 10th and beginning of the 11th century A.D. under the patronage of Mahīpāla I and Nayapāla cannot be without interest for us. The period roughly coincides with that of the mature Indian career of Atīśa, who, as we have already seen, returned from Suvarṇadvīpa roughly in A.D. 1025, and, according to the Tibetan accounts, shortly afterwards became the High Priest of Vikramaśīla.

Is it this surprising similarity between the histories of Somapurī and Vikramaśīla that leads the archaeologist K. N. Dikshit to attribute certain events to Somapurī which, according to repeated assertions of the Tibetans, happened only at Vikramaśīla ? "In the Tibetan life of Dīpaṃkara Śrījñāna Atīśa, the well-known Buddhist monk from Bengal", says Dikshit,[12] "it is stated that he lived for years in the Somapura

12. *Ib.* 74.

monastery and that his spiritual preceptor, Ratnākara-śānti, was the *sthavira* of the *vihāra*". What can be the basis of such a remarkable assertion ? Dikshit himself does not mention any, and no standard Tibetan source says in so many words that Dīpaṃkara spent a considerable number of years at the Somapurī *vihāra* with Ratnākara as the *sthavira* of the monastery. On the contrary, according to the Tibetans this happened only at theVikramaśīla *vihāra*. Perhaps the only way in which Dikshit can substantiate his assertion is by claiming that the Vikramaśīla *vihāra* mentioned by the Tibetan sources was the same as the Somapurī *vihāra* of Paharpur. But the difficulty of such a claim is obvious. The Tibetans mention the two as names of two distinct *vihāra*-s. Besides, the site of Vikramaśīla usually given by them is quite different from Somapurī, Paharpur being quite far from the old course of the Gaṅgā. At the same time there are certain considerations that cannot be entirely overlooked. First, there are grounds to believe that the same monastery famed in Tibet as Vikramaśīla was perhaps better known in India by some other name. Secondly, the exact site of Vikramaśīla is yet to be definitely identified and it is risky to try to do it exclusively on the basis of the Tibetan descriptions. Thirdly, there are considerable confusions in the Tibetan sources about the names of the Indian monasteries. In view of all these, and, moreover, since the archaeologists consider Samapurī to have been the biggest and most important of all the *vihāra*-s sponsored by the Pālas while according to the Tibetans Vikramaśīla was actually so, it may be tempting to compare the Tibetan description of Vikramaśīla with what the archaeologists reconstruct of Somapurī, though even if the two descriptions substantially correspond the possibility will not be ruled out that the Pālas followed the same plan for the construction of two separate *vihāra*-s.

But let us not conjecture. Let us rather keep ourselves confined to the actual evidences we have. The standard Tibetan sources, as we have just said, do not mention Somapurī as an important centre of Dīpaṃkara's activities. But that does not really mean that Dīpaṃkara did not and could not have any connection with Somapurī. On the other hand, our evidences of Dīpaṃkara's activities at Somapurī, though indirect, are nonetheless definite. These are :

i) the colophon of a work in bsTan-'gyur, and

ii) a statement by Jayaśīla of Nag-tsho in his *stotra* to Dīpaṃkara. The latter clearly substantiates the former.

According to Cordier's *Catalague*,[13] it was at Somapurī *vihāra* that the two Tibetan translators, Vīryasiṃha of rGya and Jayaśīla of Nag-tsho, worked under Dīpaṃkara-śrī-jñāna for preparing the Tibetan version of the *Madhyamaka-ratna-pradīpa-nāma* by Bhavya or Bhāvaviveka. In the Peking edition of the bsTan-'gyur, the colophon of the work reads : "Written by *mahā-paṇḍita* Bhavya, according to the words of *ārya ācārya* Nāgārjuna. Later, Vīryasiṃha and Jayaśīla of Nag-tsho translated it by revising it over and over again at the Somapurī temple under the oral communication (!) of *mahā-paṇḍita* Dīpaṃkara-śrī-jñāna to *guru bhaṭṭāraka* Tāmradvīpī *upāsaka* Nātha."[14]

We have already discussed the special importance of the bsTan-'gyur colophons. From the evidence of the colophon just quoted we may, therefore, assert with reasonable certainty that Dīpaṃkara explained or expounded the *Madhyamaka-ratna-pradīpa-nāma* of Bhavya at the Somapurī *vihāra* and that his two faithful Tibetan disciples, Vīryasiṃha and Jayaśīla, prepared the Tibetan version of the work based on this exposition. From this evidence it will be legitimate to infer further that Dīpaṃkara's connection with the Somapurī *vihāra* could not have been just casual. The *Madhyamaka-ratna-pradīpa-nama* is not only an extremely difficult and abstruse work on Buddhist philosophy and logic ; it is moreover quite substantial in bulk. Dīpaṃkara presumably took a considerable period of time to expound the text in such a manner as to make it possible for Vīryasiṃha and Jayaśīla to prepare its Tibetan version.

We may have here a few words about the nature and volume of the text itself. Bhavya or Bhāvaviveka[15] was the

13. Cordier iii. 299. 14. See Section 3, Appendix B. 15. Winternitz ii. 362.

founder of the Svatantra school of the Mādhyamikas, the main purpose of this school being to prove by independent arguments the correctness of the Madhyamaka philosophy and this, as contrasted with the Prāsaṅgika school of the Mādhyamikas founded by Buddhapālita, the main effort of which is to substantiate negatively the Madhyamaka philosophy by leading all opponents to utter absurdities. The *Madhyamaka-ratna-pradīpa-nāma*, being a basic work of Bhavya, is highly technical and abstruse. In the Tibetan version in which alone it survives for us, its volume, also, is quite substantial. It occupies about 627 lines in the Peking edition of the bsTan-'gyur,—i.e. is roughly twelve times that of Dīpaṃkara's own *Badhi-patha-pradīpa*.

That Dīpaṃkara actually expounded Bhavya's work at Somapurī is corroborated by Jayaśīla's *stotra* to Dīpaṃkara. "When", says Jayaśīla in this *stotra*, "you were at the Somapurī *vihāra* expounding (*gsuṅ*) the *Tarka-jvālā* (*rTog-ge-'bar-ba*), you said that twenty years from then on you will leave your mortal body in Tibet. Two years after that, when you were to leave Vikramaśīla for Tibet, you repeated that eighteen years hence you will leave your mortal body in Tibet".[16] As Jayaśīla spent a number of years in India before taking Dīpaṃkara to Tibet, his account is to be looked at as based on personal acquaintance rather than mere heresay. Of course, the prediction of leaving the mortal body in Tibet was obviously for glorifying Dīpaṃkara. Still the mention of the work and particularly the monastery where it was expounded by Dīpaṃkara cannot be dismissed as mere fables. But what is this work *Tarka-jvālā* which Jayaśīla says, Dīpaṃkara was expounding at Somapurī about two years before his departure for Tibet? Its full title is *Madhyamaka-hṛdaya-vṛtti-tarka-jvālā* and it is an enormous auto-commentary—occupying about 5385 lines in the Peking edition of the bsTan-'gyur—by Bhavya on his *Madhyamaka-hṛdaya-kārikā*. Incidentally, it is difficult to imagine that Jayaśīla himself can make any mistake about the name of this text. Like the other works of Bhavya,

16. Quoted by Nagwang Nima and Lama Chimpa. See Appendix A, Section 6.

the *Tarka-jvālā* too is preserved for us only in Tibetan translation and this translation was executed by Jayaśīla himself under Dīpaṃkara, though much later, i.e. when Dīpaṃkara reached Lhasa. "Indian *upādhyāya* Dīpaṃkara-śrī-jñāna", says the colophon of the *Tarka-jvālā* in the Peking edition,[17] "and lo-tsā-ba *bhikṣu* Jayaśīla translated and revised it at Rasa (ancient name of Lhasa) temple." Thus, the evidence of the bsTan-'gyur, corroborated by Jayaśīla's *stotra*, indicates that about two years before his departure for Tibet, Dīpaṃkara, along with Vīryasiṃha and Jayaśīla, spent a considerable period of time at Somapurī, expounding Bhavya's works. These evidences are extremely important. At the same time the peculiar difficulties about these must not be overlooked. According to the usual account we have, Jayaśīla came to Vikramaśīla to invite Atīśa to Tibet and Vīryasiṃha was already there as a student and that the two Tibetans studied and remained at the same *vihāra* up to the time of Atīśa's departure for Tibet. In other words, the usual Tibetan accounts of Jayaśīla and Vīryasiṃha in India leave hardly any scope to imagine that during the time they spent in India they were in some *vihāra* other than Vikramaśīla, listening to the Master's exposition of Bhavya's works and actually translating one of these works based on the Master's exposition. Yet the evidences of bsTan-'gyur and Jayaśīla's *stotra* cannot be lightly looked at. Thus we have either to assume some important gap in the usual accounts of Jayaśīla and Vīryasiṃha in India, or,—the possibility of which is more remote,—we have to imagine that by Somapurī in the bsTan-'gyur colophon and the *stotra* is somehow or other meant Vikramaśīla itself or some temple of this monastery. Both these alternatives are highly conjectural. But conjecture here is in a way forced on us by the peculiar nature of the evidences themselves.

Regarding the exact connection of Odantapurī with Dīpaṃkara's mature Indian career, there is again some confusion. In his English *Index* to Sum-pa's work, S. C. Das[18] says "the

17. mDo xix. 2. See Section 3, Appendix B. 18. Sum-pa *Index* xlvii.

celebrated Atiśa of Tibet... was High Priest both at Vikramaśīla and Odantapurī". But this seems to be based on a somewhat overgeneralised understanding of Sum-pa himself. What Sum-pa[19] exactly says is, "When Bheyapāla reigned for thirty-two years, the six gate-keepers (*dvārapāla*-s) passed away. After them, Jo-bo-rje Dīpaṃkara-śrī-jñāna, whose biography will be briefly mentioned later, was *upādhyāya* (*mkhan-po*) of Vikramaśīla. He also nourished (*bskyans*) Odantapurī". We shall presently discuss the exact nature of the monastic post held by Dīpaṃkara at Vikramaśīla. For the present the point is that Sum-pa uses two different words altogether to indicate Dīpaṃkara's connection with Vikramaśīla and Odantapurī. He was the *upādhyāya* of the former and he "nourished" the latter. Incidentally, Tāranātha[20] says practically the same thing. He even uses identical words to indicate Dīpaṃkara's connection with the two *vihāra*-s. "After that", says he, "king Bheyapāla... And during the reign of this king, after the six gate-keepers, Dīpaṃkara-śrī-jñāna, famed as (*grags-pa*) Jo-bo-rje Śrī Atiśa, was invited as the *upādhyāya* (*mkhan-po*) (of Vikramaśīla). By him was also nourished (*bskyans*) Odantapurī".

What do the two historians mean when they say that Atiśa also "nourished" Odantapurī ? It is difficult to say. From the use of the words *mkhan-po* and *bskyans*, however, it is quite evident that according to them Dīpaṃkara did not occupy the same monastic post in the two *vihāra*-s.

19. Sum-pa 118.

20. Tāranātha, Benares ed, 223.

15. Dipamkara at Vikramasila

But whatever might have been the exact nature of Dīpaṃkara's connection with Odantapurī and Somapurī, one point is quite clear. Of all the monasteries with which he was connected, the Tibetans knew Vikramaśīla to have been the foremost. This monastery was the main centre of his activities after he returned from Suvarṇadvīpa.

In the *Life of Atīśa* translated by S. C. Das we come across the names of both Mahīpāla and Nayapāla appointing him as the "High Priest" of Vikramaśīla. "At the request of king Nayapāla", says the biographer, "he accepted the post of High Priest of Vikrama Śīlā".[1] Again, "At the time when Atīśa was appointed the chief High Priest by king Mahīpāla there were 57 Paṇḍits of great learning at Vikrama Śīlā"[2] Which of the two accounts, then, is to be looked at as historically more plausible ? Secondly, what is meant here by the "High Priest" or "chief High Priest" ?

In spite of much controversy about Pāla chronology, our historians[3] are now inclined to view A.D. 988 as the approximate date of the accession of Mahīpāla I and A.D. 1038 as that of Nayapāla. The former is known to have reigned for about 48 years and the latter 15 years. We have already seen that the approximate date of Dīpaṃkara's return from Suvarṇadvīpa is A.D. 1025 and, as we are going to see, the actual date of his final departure for Tibet is A.D. 1040. Accepting these dates, the presumption is that Atīśa had hardly two years to spend in India after the accession of Nayapāla. On the other hand, according to the Tibetan accounts, by the time the Tibetan team headed by Jayaśīla of Nag-tsho reached India to invite Atīśa to Tibet, the latter was already occupying his position of high honour at Vikramaśīla and the Tibetans had to spend more than two years at that monastery

1. JBTS I. i. 9. 2. *Ib.* I. i. 11. 3. HB i. 177.

waiting for the Master to prepare himself for the departure for Tibet. Besides, the assumption that Atīśa became the High Priest of Vikramaśīla during the reign of Nayapāla leaves about thirteen years of Dīpaṃkara's mature Indian career largely unaccounted for. Thus, in all likelihood, Atīśa became the High Priest of Vikramaśīla during the reign of Mahīpāla I, when Nayapāla himself was presumably very young—a presumption which, again, accounts for the peculiarly affectionate tone of the *Vimala-ratna-lekha-nāma*, the letter Dīpaṃkara wrote to Nayapāla from Nepal *en route* to Western Tibet.

But what exactly is meant by the biographer when he says that Atīśa became the "High Priest" or the "chief High Priest" of Vikramaśīla ? What, in other words, was the nature of the monastic post he held at Vikramaśīla ? We may note here only what we hear from the Tibetans.

'Gos lo-tsā-ba says in one place that Atīśa "spent most of his time as Elder of the monastic college of Vikramaśīla"[4] The Tibetan word rendered here as "Elder", as is evident from Roerich's mention of it within brackets, is *gnas-brtan-chen-po*. The Sanskrit equivalent of *gnas-brtan* being *sthavira* and of *chen-po* being *mahā*, Roerich gives the Sanskrit equivalent of this as *mahā-sthavira*. But there are clear grounds to doubt that Atīśa ever held this post at Vikramaśīla. 'Gos lo-tsā-ba[5] himself mentions another *ācārya* called Śīlākara who was the Elder of Vikramaśīla during the time of Atīśa's departure for Tibet. This leads Roerich to add the following just after 'Gos lo-tsā-ba's mention of Elder Śīlākara : "Abbot of Vikramaśīla. At that time Atīśa acted as Steward (*shal-ta-ba*) of the monastic college." *Shal-ta-ba* means a monastic post that does not appear to be very important[6] and it is difficult to trace the source from which Roerich gets the information that Atīśa actually held such a post at Vikramaśīla on the eve of his diparture for Tibet. In any case, the mention by 'Gos lo-tsā-ba of Śīlākara as the actual Elder of Vikramaśīla at that time clearly indicates that Atīśa never attained the post of the

4. BA i. 244. 5. *Ib.* i. 247. 6. J-TED 473 ; D-TED 1069.

Elder of the Vikramaśīla *vihāra*. What post, then, did he held at Vikramaśīla ?

Sum-pa[7] uses two expressions in one and the same paragraph of his work to indicate the nature of this post. These are : *mkhan-po* and *dge-skyos*. According to S. C. Das,[8] *mkhan-po* means "*upādhyāya* ; a professor employed to teach ; the head of a monastery. In Tibet the head of a particular college attached to a monastery, high priests who give vows to the junior or inferior Lamas, and professors of sacred literature, are called *mkhan-po* ; also learned men, who as such are endowed with the *mkhan-rgyud* or spiritual gifts or descended heritage from their spiritual ancestors, are called *mkhan-po*." Jaschke[9] gives the following meaning of *mkhan-po* : "*upādhāya, paṇḍita*. A clerical teacher, professor, doctor of divinity, principal of great monastery ; abbot, who as such is endowed with the *mkhan-rgyud* or spiritual gifts handed down from Buddha himself by transmission ; ... next to him comes the *slob-dpon*, or professor in ordinary."

All these seem to suggest that Atīśa was some kind of academic head of Vikramaśīla, without being its Elder or *sthavira*, though it is quite conceivable that *upādhyāya* (*mkhan-po*) and *sthavira* (*gnas-brtan*) were chiefs in their respective spheres and that the *mkhan-po* was even superior to the *sthavira* in certain respects. We shall presently see that the actual administrative head of the monastery during Atīśa's time was somebody else, and this in spite of the great academic prestige enjoyed by Atīśa himself. At the same time it is difficult to conceive that Atīśa himself was entirely free from the administrative responsibilities of the monastery. The other expression used by Sum-pa to indicate his post at Vikramaśīla is *dge-skyos*, which means "*upadhivārika*, a superior or director of monks in a monastery. A sort of provost-sergeant in the larger monasteries who keeps strict order and punishes transgressors. He is also called *chos-'khrims-pa* in some monas-

7. Sum-pa 118. 8. D-TED 179. 9. J-TED 53.

teries."[10] Sum-pa's use of this expression in connection with Atiśa's post at Vikramaśīla could not have been just casual. According to the Tibetan accounts, an important event which took place at Vikramaśīla during Atiśa's time was the expulsion by Atiśa of another monk from the monastery on the ground of his violation of the codes of monastic conduct.

Let us go into some details of both these aspects of the Tibetan accounts, viz. i) there being another administrative head of the monastery during Atiśa's time, and ii) Atiśa being also in some way responsible for the maintenance of the monastic discipline of the *vihāra*. The first of these is best discussed by reviewing the usual accounts of Atiśa's acceptance of the invitation to Tibet and the second by considering the account of the expulsion by Atiśa of a certain Tāntrika from the *vihāra*.

Following is 'Gos lo-tsā-ba's brief account[11] of Atiśa's acceptance of the invitation to Tibet. Jayaśīla of Nag-tsho was sent by the Tibetan ruler to Vikramaśīla for inviting Atiśa. When he reached Vikramaśīla, Vīryasiṃha of rGya was already there as a student. Along with Vīryasiṃha, Jayaśīla earnestly entreated the Master to come to Tibet. Thus entreated, Atiśa said, "You are right! The Tibetan king has spent much gold for my sake! Several people who had come with the invitation, had been smitten by fever. I feel ashamed before the Tibetan king, and having considered the matter, I have decided to proceed in any case to Tibet, if I can be of help. *But it is difficult for the Elder* (sthavira) *of Vikramaśīla to let us go, and one must find a way out of the difficulty.*" Turning to Nag-tsho, continues 'Gos lo-tsā-ba, Atiśa said, "Do not say to any one that you had come to invite me! Say that you have come for study. Begin your studies!" Accordingly, the lo-tsā-ba (Nag-tsho) took up study (at Vikramaśīla).

Thus Atiśa wanted to maintain strict secrecy about his decision of going to Tibet and this primarily because he apprehended that the Elder of the monastery was going to refuse the required permission. This is corroborated by 'Gos lo-tsā-ba's

10. D-TED 269. 11. BA i. 245-6 ; emphasis added.

account of how Śīlākara, then the Elder of Vikramaśīla, reacted to Atīśa's plan to go to Tibet when this was discovered practically on the eve of his final departure. "Both the lo-tsā-ba-s (i.e. Vīryasiṃha and Jayaśīla)", says 'Gos lo-tsā-ba, "were attending on the Master, and at the time of his departure the Elder Śīlākara said to Nag-tsho : 'I was thinking, O Long-lived One ! you had come here for study, but you are stealing away our Paṇḍita ! And the Paṇḍita himself seems to be happy at going away ! I shall not hinder his departure, but do not remain in Tibet for more than three years. After that, the Paṇḍita should be escorted back (to India).' Nag-tsho promised it."[12]

The clear suggestion of all these is that howevermuch Atīśa might have been respected at Vikramaśīla, the actual *sthavira* of the *vihāra* was somebody else, who evidently enjoyed greater authority in the administration of the monastery and who referred to Atīśa as the *paṇḍita.*

In the *Life of Atīśa* translated by S. C. Das, we have a much more detailed account of the Tibetan invitation, which basically agrees with that of 'Gos lo-tsā-ba, only with this difference that in the former the name of the *sthavira* occurs as Ratnākara.

According to this biographer, when Jayaśīla met Vīryasiṃha at Vikramaśīla, the latter told him, "There are many eminent Paṇḍits under Atīśa, who are like the stars of heaven :—namely, Ratnakīrti, Vairocana Rakṣita, Kanakaśrī of Nepal, and others. Though there are so many Paṇḍits, they would not be of any service to Tibet. Atīśa being possessed of an extraordinary intellect and moral excellence would be of real service to our country, should we succeed to take him there. *It would not be wise to give out that you have come here to invite him*".[13] He also advised Nag-tsho to be a resident pupil of *sthavira* Ratnākara. "*Here in this monastery, Sthavira Ratnākara is most influential.* Besides being the superior of the monastery, *he is also the chief of Atīśa.* You should study under him and gain his confidence by your good

12. *Ib.* i. 247. 13. JBTS I. i. 17; emphasis added.

behaviour and assiduity in study. You must not in any way displease him. Now, you go to him with half an ounce of gold and presenting it to him solicit for admission into the monastery as his pupil. Then when Atiśa comes to our place, we shall offer our prayer to him to visit our country".[14] According to the same biography, when Atiśa finally made up his mind to go to Tibet he advised Jayaśīla and Vīryasiṃha : "Keep this matter secret, do not talk of my intended visit to Tibet". Looking at Nag-tsho he added, "You had better continue to study Buddhist authors under Sthavira Ratnākara."[15] And here is the biographer's account of the final phase of Atiśa's departure from Vikramaśīla : "After three days, preparations were made to entertain Atiśa reverentially at the residence of rGya-brtson (Vīryasiṃha). On this occasion further prayers were made, and Atiśa allowed his things to be carried to the Mitra Vihāra. In the meantime, he made over the charge of the various offices to the monastic authorities. Everything was now placed in readiness for him to set out for Tibet. But still being afraid of incurring Ratnākara's displeasure they were careful not to make any noise in equipping themselves and in packing up their travelling appurtenances. Nag-tsho busied himself in packing sixty loads which were placed on thirty bullocks...To avoid suspicion and confusion, the caravan set out at midnight and crossed the Ganges. Atiśa having completed his unfinished works now prepared himself to proceed to Tiebt. With a view that others may not know of his intention of leaving India, he made up his mind to make pilgrimage to the eight sacred places of Buddhist sanctity. One morning he went to the residence of Sthavira Ratnākara and addressed him : 'Most venerable sir, it is necessary to show all the great places of pilgrimage to these Āyuṣmats of Tibet...' The Sthavira said : 'That is very good, if you go I shall accompany you to those places, and after visiting every one of them we shall come back together'. A young monk of Vikrama Śīlā having perceived the plans of Nag-tsho about Atiśa's mission, said : 'This Master (Aiśa) is like an eye unto

14. *Ib* I. i. 17-8; emphasis added. 15. *Ib*. I. .. 21.

us—the Indians. In his absence we should indeed be blind. If I communicated your plans to the king, there would be danger to your life, but I must not tell him anything about it. Proceed with our Master to your country and take care that he does not meet with accidents and suffer privations on the way. When the object for which you have come is fulfilled bring him back to our midst'. Atīśa secretly said to Nag-tsho : 'Now that we were about to start for Tibet, we should first go to Vajrāsana...' Having finished religious service at Vajrāsana and other places Atīśa returned to Vikrama Śīlā. His companions about sixty including Sthavira Ratnākara also returned with him. Atīśa then expressed to him his intention of going on a pilgrimage to the Caitya of Svayambhu in Nepal... The Sthavira now clearly perceived that by going there Atīśa meant to proceed to Tibet. Then pointing to Nag-tsho he said : This Āyuṣmat has not really come here for the sake of study. The king of Tibet has sent him to steal away my man. On a former occasion he sent an invitation to him but *I did not let Atīśa go. This time I can resort to means to prevent his going there, but Atīśa out of his own good-will and purity of heart, likes to secretly visit Tibet.* Besides, if I do not let him go, it would be putting obstructions in his way in doing good to others.' Then addressing Nag-tsho he continued : 'Āyuṣmat, as you have been a pupil of mine, to displease you would be to shake your confidence in my kindness. Out of compassion for you and your countrymen, many of whom have died for taking Atīśa to Tibet, *I lend his services to your country for three years, and after that you must bring him back here.* Āyuṣmat, you should also accompany him back so far as this side of Nepal, otherwise it would be a breach of promise.' ...Atīśa as the High Priest of the monastery now made over charge of all that was with him to Sthavira Ratnākara".[16]

Sum-pa,[17] also gives the name of the *sthavira* as Ratnākara, to whom Jayaśīla promised to bring back Dīpaṃkara after three years.

We do not know much about the *sthavira* called Śīlākara

16. *Ib.* I. i. 22-3. 17. Sum-pa 185.

or Ratnākara and it is no use speculating whether he was the same as Ratnākara-śānti or Śānti-pa, one of Dīpṃkara's teachers. What concerns us rather is the clear account that the actual *sthavira* of Vikramaśīla during Dīpaṃkara's time was somebody else and that Dīpaṃkara wanted to maintain strict secrecy about his plan to go to Tibet particularly because of his apprehension of the *sthavira's* possible reaction to it. In face of all these accounts it is quite amazing to see Sankalia saying, "*With great persuasion of Sthavira Ratnākara*, and entreaties of the Tibetan ambassador...he (Atīśa) visited Tibet".[18]

But though the above accounts suggest that Atīśa, with all his academic prestige, was not the administrative head of the monastery, the distinct suggestion of another account repeated in the Tibetan sources is that he was not entirely free from the administrative responsibilities of the monastery. Thus, e.g., Sum-pa gives the following account of a certain Tāntrika, called 'Śavareśvara, the latter' (Ri-khrod-dban-phyug-phyi-ma), *alias* Maitrīgupta, expelled by Atīśa from Vikramaśīla. "At that time", says Sum-pa, "one Brāhmaṇa *paṇḍita* met Naro-pā and became a Buddhist, accepted the Buddhist ordination, studied under Ratnākara-śānti and became learned. At Vikramaśīla he studied both *sūtra* and *tantra*. While studying, he turned milk into wine and drank it. He drank wine in the form of milk and was expelled by Jo-bo-rje (Atīśa), who at that time was the provost-sergeant (*dge-skyos*) of the monastery. Then he showed many signs of the *siddha*, like crossing the Gaṅgā while sitting on a skin, etc. He had four great students,—Naṭekana, Devākaracandra, Rāmapāla and Vajrapāṇi. Then seven (students of) medium (stature) and ten (of) junior (stature). This man is also known as Maitrīgupta, and also as Śavareśvara the latter. His influence was widely spread. He went to Śrīparvata, met the rain-bow body of Śavarī and come back. It was the time shortly after the passing of the six gate-keepers".[19]

18. Sankalia 184 ; emphasis added. 19. Sum-pa 118. Free translation.

In the *Life of Atīśa* translated by S. C. Das, we have a more elaborate account of the same expulsion[20] : "There was in the monastery a class of Tāntriks called by the name of Kiṃsukhā, who once brought much trouble on him. One Maitrī who belonged to that class was charged of certain irregularities in matters connected with doctrinal, ritual and other collateral matters, on account of which, something condemnatory was written on the wall at the entrance of the Vihāra by a monk called Śānti. On another occasion a quantity of wine was detected in the possession of Maitrī, which he had kept secretly in his place and which he alleged to have brought for presenting to a Buddhist 'Yoginī whom he intended to consult on certain matters. The fact being brought to the notice of the Saṅgha, they expressed their indignation at his conduct and decided to expel him from the monastery, but Maitrī was unwilling to abide by their decision. At this there arose a difference in the opinions of the members of the Saṅgha, some taking his side, others opposing him vehemently. The majority of the monks insisted on his being turned out of the monastery. Some one of the monks observed : If his stay in our midst does not affect me or you individually, it may injure others (less guarded). So at last his expulsion was decided upon. His offence being considered a serious one he was not permitted to be expelled by the main entrance. He was sent out across the wall of the monastery. Atīśa, though as the head of the Saṅgha, he had acquiesced in their decision about Maitrī, yet personally he entertained doubts as to its propriety and equity. Accordingly he consulted the goddess Tārā, his tutelary deity, offering his prayers to her in the usual manner at night. The goddess appearing in a dream thrice said to him : 'Son, it has not been good'. He suddenly awoke and came out of his room, but did not find anybody. Again he prayed to the gods and Bodhisattvas, for further enlightenment on the subject. He heard a voice which said, 'Maitrī has been innocent of the offence. As he has had acquired the true conception of the Bodhi life, you have committed a serious sin in

20. JBTS I. i. 11-2.

permitting his expulsion from the monastery'. It was also said that in consequence of it Atīśa was destined to be born as a huge bird of Sumeru that in making three rounds around the peak of Sumeru would kill numerous living beings. The only means by which he could get out of the difficulty was to proceed in the northern direction towards Tibet, to preach the Mahāyāna Dharma there... Again Atīśa inquired of his Lama (*guru*) Gagapāla as to the best remedy against this sin. He assured him that as the step was taken with a good motive, there could not be any sin in it. If any such thing had accrued, he should go to Tibet to be free from it by becoming the spiritual instructor of a certain king, who in his former life had bestowed alms consisting of a pound of rice (to a *pratyeka* Buddha)."

From Sum-pa's account quoted above, it appears that the Tāntrika monk expelled by Atīśa enjoyed considerable reputation of spiritual power. If the story of his expulsion is true, the presumption would be that Atīśa had to face some trouble about this. Probably that explains the legends given by the biographer. Besides, we hear nowhere else of Atīśa having any *guru* called Gagapāla on whose advice he could depend on moments of grave crisis during his career at Vikramaśīla and whose advice, moreover, flatly contradicted even the prediction of Tārā Devī ! But the Tibetan biographer does not bother. He is interested above all in telling his Tibetan readers that the coming of Atīśa to Tibet, which proved such a great fortune for the Tibetan people, was somehow or other divinely engineered.

Still, granting some basis for this account of the expulsion of Śavareśvara or Maitrīgupta, two significant points emerge for us from it. First, though Atīśa was not the administrative head of the *vihāra*, he was somehow or other not fully free from the administrative responsibility of Vikramaśīla. The same is indicated by the following alleged to have been said by *sthavira* Ratnākara to Vīryasiṃha and Jayaśīla when they first approached him for sounding his possible reaction to the proposal of Atīśa's going to Tibet. "Āyuṣman", said Ratnākara, "in the absence of Atīśa no other Paṇḍit would be able to preserve the moral discipline of the monks here... He holds the keys of many a monastery of Magadha. For these reasons we can ill-afford to lose his valuable presence."[21]

Secondly, the account of Atīśa expelling Maitrīgupta from Vikramaśīla also suggests his mature attitude to certain forms of Tāntrika practices current in these days. The spiritual leaders in India during Atīśa's time were above all Tāntrikas and would not have perhaps objected to the alleged practices of Maitrīgupta for which he was expelled by Dīpaṃkara from the monastery. From Sum-pa's account it appears that even after being expelled from Vikramaśīla, he went on gaining the reputation of spiritual powers and gathered substantial followings for himself. People these days were readily inclined to believe in such practices as shortcuts to miraculous powers. Under the influence of the prevailing ideas of his time, Atīśa himself began his spiritual career as a full-fledged Tāntrika. He, too, sat in the company of the *ḍākinī*-s and participated at their Tāntrika feasts. However, the Buddhist ordination meant a decisive turning point for his spiritual career and it is quite conceivable that as a result of this he developed strong support for the traditional codes of monastic conduct with which such Tāntrika practices did not agree. In his *Bodhi-patha-pradīpa*,[22] he clearly said that such practices were not compatible with the monastic life. Thus, judging Dīpaṃkara by his attitude to religion from the time of his ordination onwards, we find no incongruity in the story of his expelling Maitrīgupta from Vikramaśīla, though like most of the accounts of Dīpaṃkara at Vikramaśīla this story also is somewhat legendary.

There is, however, one interesting passage preserved in the *Life of Atīśa* translated by S. C. Das which claims to give a more authentic account of Dīpaṃkara at Vikramaśīla than most others. This biography is said to be based on the direct communication of Jayaśīla of Nag-tsho and we have seen that the claim may not be entirely baseless. In this, the biographer,

21. *Ib*. I. 1. 22. 22. See Note 15, Section 2.

after describing how Jayaśīla met Vīryasiṃha at the Vikramaśīla *vihāra,* quotes somewhat abruptly a long passage from Jayaśīla's *own narrative* : "At this Nag-tsho (Jayaśīla) begged him to show Jo-bo Atīśa. rGya (Vīryasiṃha of rGya) observed, 'We Tibetans have no influence here, but still I am well-known to Atīśa. He likes me. Tomorrow there will be a grand congregation of all classes of monks at Vikrama when 8,000 Bhikṣus will assemble together. In their midst he who will appear very bright, venerable, exalted, majestic in appearance should be recognised as Atīśa'. Nag-tsho *in his own narrative* wrote :

"Then accompanied by rGya-brtson-'grus-seṅ-ge (Vīryasiṃha of rGya), I went to Sthavira Ratnākara, made profound salutation, presented him with half an ounce of gold, and made prayers to him as advised by the lo-tsā-ba.... In the morning when the monks congregated together, being conducted by the Sthavira, I was given a seat in the rank of the learners.... When all the rows of seats were filled up, there came Jo-bo Atīśa, the venerable of all venerables, at whose sight the eyes felt no satiety. His graceful appearance and smiling face struck every one of the assembly. From his waist hung down a bundle of keys. The Indians, Nepalese and Tibetans all looked at him and took him for a countryman of their own. Even the gods would own him for their own. There was brightness mixed with simplicity of expression in his face which acted as a magic spell upon those who beheld him.

In the following morning I went to the door of a Vihāra. While I was reciting the Prajñā Sāra, a venerable Ācārya with bright looks and smiles in his face entered the Vihāra. Observing the simple, unostentatious demeanour which marked him I resolved within myself : If we fail to take Atīśa to our country, this Paṇḍit might as well serve our purpose. Next morning I happened to be at the place where that venerable Ācārya was distributing alms and food to the poor and making offerings to spirits. A beggar boy who failed to get his share of alms ran after him and exclaimed : *Bhālā ho O, Nāth Atīśa, Bhāt-ona Bhāt-ona.* Blest be thou O patron Atīśa ! Give me rice. Hearing this I became delighted. Tears of joy flowed from my eyes. I followed him as he walked towards his place, and was about to fall from a bridge while walking over it, my attention being wholly engrossed upon Atīśa. He recognised me as a Tibetan and said, 'Ah Tibetan Āyuṣmat ! You are earnest men, do not shed tears. I have much regard for the Tibetan people,—your king and ministers. You have again come for me without losing heart, offer your prayers to the three Holies'. As soon as these words dropped from his lips, I became hopeful and cheerful".[23]

Authentic or not, this is about the only description we have of Atīśa at Vikramaśīla which claims to come down from one of his closest associates. By contrast, some other accounts of Atīśa at Vikramaśīla are clearly less reliable, because the historicity of these are doubted by the Tibetan authorities themselves. Thus, e.g., the same work contains an impressive description of how the venerable Nāro-pā came to Vikramaśīla and appointed Atīśa as the head of the Buddhist religion. "At this time", says the biographer, "the venerable Nāropānta came on a visit to the Vihāra of Vikrama Śīlā. All the ordained monks of the monastery gave him a warm reception. In getting down from the *dooly,* he leaned on the right arm of Atīśa while Jñāna-śrī-mitra helped him with his left arm. In course of conversa-

23. JBTS I. i. 18-9.

tion Nāro said : 'Prabhu Dīpaṃkara, now you should be the minister of the religion of Buddha'. So saying he made over to him the ministry of the Dharma. Atīśa meekly replied : 'In the presence of your venerable self, who may be likened to the sun and moon, I am but a fire-fly. How can I illumine the world ?' The venerable Nāro replied : 'As I shall not live long, you must necessarily be the minister of the religion of Buddha'. During the twenty days he stayed at Vikrama Śīlā, Nāro did not enter into any religious discussion with Atīśa. Thereafter Nāro proceeded towards the south and after a few days he breathed his last. Some relics of his remains were brought to Tibet by Atīśa. They are said still to exist, being preserved in the sacred *stūpa* of 'Or at sÑe-thaṅ".[24] But 'Gos lo-tsā-ba clearly doubts the entire account. "In the Book containing the story of Atīśa", says he, "it is said that the Master Nārotapa had entrusted the Doctrine to Atīśa, and then proceeded towards the South, etc. Though there exist many similar accounts, I was unable to write them down".[25]

We have, however, the feeling of moving on securer grounds when we pass on to consider the evidences of Dīpaṃkara's activities at Vikramaśīla preserved in the bsTan-'gyur. The colophons of a number of works in this collection definitely mention Vikramaśīla as the monastery where these were either written by Dīpaṃkara or rendered into Tibetan under him.

In the Peking edition, the colophon of *Kāya-vāc-citta-supratiṣṭhā-nāma*[26] reads, "Written by Śrī-dīpaṃkara-jñāna ; translated and revised very nicely by the Indian *upādhyāya* Dīpaṃkara and lo-tsā-ba Vīryasiṃha of rGya at Vikramaśīla". Cordier's *Catalogue*, too, mentions Vikramaśīla as the place of its translation.

We have already seen that there is some confusion in the colophon of the *Ratna-karaṇḍa-udghāṭa-nāma-madhyamaka-upadeśa*[27] concerning the connection of this monastery with Devapāla. However, that this work was written by Dīpaṃkara at Vikramaśīla is quite clear. Its colophon leads us to presume

24. *Ib.* I. i. 21. 25. BA i. 25. 26. rG. xlviii. 154.
27 mDo xxx 24.

further that it was translated at the same *vihāra* by his two faithful Tibetan disciples working under him. "Written", says the colophon, "by Dīpaṃkara-śrī-jñāna on the request of the good disciple *śākya bhikṣu* Jayaśīla at Vikramaśīla temple connected with the solemn vow (*thugs-dam*) of Devapāla. Dīpaṃkara executed it on the basis of his *guru*'s sayings and not with any financial motive. It should be given to those who are without strict observances. One not devoted to *ārya* Nāgārjuna's *śāstra* has abandoned the real doctrine and is destined to go to hell. Here ends the precious jewel of the *madhyamaka-upadeśa* of Mahāyāna called the Karaṇḍodghāṭa written by *mahā-paṇḍita* Dīpaṃkara-śrī-jñāna. Translated and revised by the same Indian *upādhyāya* Dīpaṃkara-śrī-jñāna and lo-tsā-ba *mahā-upāsaka* Vīryasiṃha of rGya and *bhikṣu* Jayaśīla".

We have an interesting colophon of the *Sūtra-samuccaya-sañcayārtha,*[28] which, among other points, suggests Vikramaśīla as the place where it was written (or compiled) by Dīpaṃkara and translated by Vīryasiṃha under him. "The Tibetan *bhikṣu* Jayaśīla", says the colophon in the Peking edition, "offering 14 *pala*-s of gold with flowers to *ācārya* Dīpaṃkara-śrī-jñāna, requested him to come to Tibet. For completing his meditational practice, he could enter his way (to Tibet) after sixteen months. At the time of his departure for Tibet, the beloved students requested him for the final *upadeśa* (*bka'-chems*, literally 'testament'). He delivered this, which is the essence of the *sūtra*-s, as his *upadeśa* to them. At that time, Vīryasiṃha asked for his permission and did the translation. Wanting to propagate this, *bhikṣu* Jayaśīla said, 'The Tibetan masters are very proud and jealous. Let their ego (*ahaṃkāra*) be washed away by this precious water'. Being requested by the pupils (*ban-de*-s) of the Keru temple in the same way, he (Dīpaṃkara) gave this to them along with other *upadeśa*-s. Jo-bo's *guru* Avadhūti-pā gave him three *upadeśa*-s together, namely *a-pratiṣṭhita-siddhānta, karmānta-cittotpādana-vidhi* and *sūtra-samuccaya-artha-upadeśa.*"

28. mDo xxx. 32.

Vikramaśīla is mentioned as the monastery where Vīryasiṃha translated under Dīpaṃkara the *Saṃsāra-manoniryāṇīkāra-nāma-saṅgīti*[29] by Dīpaṃkara, Jayaśīla translated under Dīpaṃkara the *Ārya-tārādevī-stotra-muktikā-mālā-nāma*[30] by Candragomin and the short anonymous work called *Tri-ratna-tārā-stotra.*[31]

At least one point clearly emerges from these evidences of the bsTan-'gyur. It is impossible to doubt the basic historicity of the Tibetan accounts of Vīryasiṃha spending a considerable period of time at Vikramaśīla, where he was joined by Jayaśīla, who came evidently as the leader of the team sent from Tibet to invite an eminent Buddhist scholar from India. We shall see more of these two Tibetans in connection with the account of Atīśa's departure for Tibet.

However, in the Tibetan histories the account of Atīśa's coming to Tibet is generally told as the culmination of a long series of events connected with the spread of Buddhism there. Therefore, for a proper understanding of Atīśa's image in the minds of the Tibetan historians, it is necessary to begin with a brief review of the Tibetan history as told by its own historians.

29. rG. xlvii. 46 and mDo xxxiii. 9.
30. rG. lxxxii. 40.
31. rG. xxvi. 14.

PART II
THE TIBETAN BACKGROUND

16. *How the Tibetans tell their own History*

For the purpose of understanding what Stcherbatsky[1] calls 'Tibetan historiography' it is necessary to anticipate a few facts of general interest, the history of which would be discussed later.

Literacy began in Tibet with the beginning there of the spread of Buddhism and as inseparably related to it. The pioneers of Tibetan education had their own education in India, presumably at some Buddhist *vihāra*. The Tibetan script was modelled on Indian script, the Tibetan grammar on Indian grammar. Throughout the subsequent history of Tibet education remained primarily Buddhist.[2] Knowledge of Buddhism was the highest mark of Tibetan learning and, at least up to the 14th century,[3] the translation of an Indian text under an Indian *paṇḍita* was the peak of academic ambition for a Tibetan scholar.

It is therefore idle to expect the Tibetan historians, who are among the foremost of the learned men of Tibet, to have any sense of history independent of the Buddhist faith or to attach to the political or economic events any importance independent of the religious. Events relating to Buddhism have in fact for them incomparably greater importance than those taking place in the political sphere. Thus Bu-ston takes hardly any notice of the Tibetan expeditions to China and Central Asia—expeditions which in the 8th century A.D. made

1. Bu-ston i. Intro. p. iii. 2. Lama Chimpa in ISPP vi. 90ff; cf. Richardson 13-4. 3. i.e., the date of the redaction of the bKa'-'gyur and bsTan-'gyur in their present form.

Tibet one of the chief military powers of Asia[4]—though he devotes pages[5] to describe how the Indian Buddhist Kamalaśīla defeated in a philosophical controversy the Buddhist priest (*ho-shang*) from China. Similarly, 'Gos lo-tsā-ba speaks of the meeting of Dīpaṃkara with the Tibetan scholar Rin-chen-bzaṅ-po (Ratnabhadra) as if it were an event of momentous historical significance and describes with great enthusiasm how the Master humbled the pride of the latter,[6] though he takes only a cursory notice of the victorious campaigns of the Tibetans to China[7] and hardly any notice at all of the subjugation of Turkistan[8] by them or of their campaigns to India.[9] And Bu-ston and 'Gos lo-tsā-ba are surely the greatest of the Tibetan historians.

In other words, Tibetan history as told by its own historians is not a secular history. It is religious history *par excellance.* The usual Tibetan word for it is *chos-'byuṅ*, 'the history of the Doctrine.' Even what is called a *rgyal-rabs* or 'royal chronicle' is not mere dynastic history ; it also puts great emphasis on the history of Buddhism. The foremost of the Tibetan historians are but historians of Buddhism. Political events have for them only an incidental importance, i.e. importance in so far as these enable them to explain what helped or hindered the progress of Buddhism. An inevitable consequence of this tendency is the marked importance attached to the struggle between their newly acquired faith and their ancient creed called Bon : the political history of Tibet from Sroṅ-btsan-sgam-po to gLaṅ Dar-ma, i.e. of the period of Tibetan monarchy proper, is generally told as if for the purpose of providing us with a suitable background for understanding the progress of Buddhism in Tibet and the strong resistance offered to it by the representatives of the Bon religion.

This tendency of the Tibetan historians earns for them

4. Petech 66-9 ; Bell 37. 5. Bu-ston ii. 191ff. 6. BA i. 249ff. 7. *Ib.* i. 49. See Bushell in JRAS 1880. 435ff. for the Chinese version of the same. 8. Bell 53. 9. See Section 21 for Lévi's account of gNam-ri-sroṅ-btsan's victorious campaign to central India. Cf. Petech 68 for the Tibetan campaign to India during the reign of Khri-sroṅ-lde-btsan.

extremely disparaging remarks from some of the modern scholars. "The historians so-called of Tibet", comments Waddell,[10] "wrote mostly inflated bombast, almost valueless for historical purposes." "In the Lamaist chronicles", says Petech,[11] "the history of Tibetan monarchy is nothing but a pretext for edifying tales, or, at the most, the framework in which the life and work of the great apostles of Buddhism are bound together. A little more than the skeleton of the history of the dynasty and almost nothing of the history of the nation has been saved from the general shipwreck".

What Tibetan history inevitably loses as a result of the religious zeal of its own historians need not be under-estimated. At the same time any sweeping rejection of Tibetan historiography entails the risk of over-simplification and sometimes even of utter confusion. It is true that even the best of the Tibetan historians are not particularly interested in describing the political and military strength of Tibet during the 7th-9th centuries. Mainly from Chinese records[12] we learn how spectacular all these were. But this is not without some compensation. The religious zeal of the Tibetan historians that makes them somewhat indifferent to political history also makes them keenly interested in religious history and this, paradoxical though it may sound, helps us afterall to understand Tibet's political destiny itself. For the fact is that religion did play an overtly important role in the making of Tibetan history[13] and even real political struggles were often carried on under religious pretexts. It is important no doubt to try to trace the political and economic undercurrents of the religious strifes described in the Tibetan histories. But such an attempt presupposes an analysis of Tibetan history as told by its own historians, which, therefore, cannot be summarily

10. Waddell L 19n. 11. Petech 60-1. 12. Our main source is the *T'ang-shu*. The *rGyal-rabs-gsal-ba'i-me-loṅ* also describes these, though partly : See Petech 36. 13. Richardson 11 : "The one aspect of the national character that has most influenced their past and their present is the devotion to religion which dominates the thoughts and actions of every Tibetan".

brushed aside. Besides, at least historians like Bu-ston and 'Gos lo-tsā-ba are really not as naive as Waddell wants us to believe all Tibetan historians to be. Without the encyclopaedic work of 'Gos lo-tsā-ba, Tibetan chronology, particularly after the tenth century, would have been a hopeless mess for the modern scholar. Without the writing of Bu-ston, on whom the later Tibetan historians like Tāranātha and Sum-pa so vitally depend, our knowledge of the history of Indian Buddhism, particularly of its so-called Mahāyāna phase, would have remained largely incomplete. If the religious zeal of the Tibetan historians causes a general shipwreck in the political history of Tibet the same religious zeal saves the history of Mahāyāna Buddhism from the general shipwreck it suffered in India itself.

This leads us to consider another peculiarity of the Tibetan histories which is likely to appear strange to the modern readers outside Tibet. The typical way in which these histories open is with a peculiar cosmogony and cosmology, an account of the different aeons in which the Buddhas do or do not appear, some lengthy details of a fanciful genealogy of the Śākyas, etc., etc,.—the only relevance of all these in Tibetan history being that the Tibetan historians conceive their own history to be but a continuation of the history of Indian Buddhism.

Two points in particular need to be noted about this tendency.

First, like the Indian Purāṇas, Tibetan history, particularly in its earlier part, is saturated with mythology. Secondly, it is not confined to events supposed to have taken place in Tibet proper. Tibetan events are rather described as but continuations of Indian events, primarily concerned of course with the rise and progress of Buddhism.

For the purpose of understanding the tremendous impact of Dipaṃkara on the minds of the Tibetan historians the second of these two points interests us most. But it will not be out of place to have a few words here on the first as well.

The mythological elements found in the earlier parts of Tibetan histories and the enthusiasm shown by the historians for ascertaining the accuracy of their details certainly look peculiar to us. The modern scholar[14] is sometimes led to presume that much of this is incorporated into Tibetan histories from the ancient Bon beliefs. However, apart from the difficulties of having a clear idea of the Bon beliefs before these got mixed up with Indian mythologies[15] and even granting the possibility of their survival in Tibetan Buddhism,[16] it is necessary not to overlook the more important fact that the cosmogony and cosmology, the account of the different aeons, the fabulous genealogy of the Śākyas, etc., though usually found in the Tibetan histories, are really not of Tibetan origin. On the contrary, these formed part of Indian Buddhism itself,[17] or more properly, of that form of later Indian Buddhism which is generally referred to as the Mahāyāna, and it was Buddhism in this form that found its way to Tibet. In other words, Buddhism in its later or Mahāyāna form itself developed elaborate mythologies and these were recorded by the Indian Buddhists in scriptural or semi-scriptural form. The Tibetan historians naturally relied on these.

It is not necessary for our present purpose to reiterate the history of the rise of Mahāyāna Buddhism in India. Still it is necessary for us to remember that its departure from the older form of Buddhism was a radical one. Here is how Stcherbatsky[18] describes this departure: "When we see an atheistic soul-denying philosophic teaching of a path to personal final deliverance, consisting in an absolute extinction of life and a simple worship of the memory of its human founder —when we see it superseded by a magnificent High Church with a Supreme God, surrounded by a numerous pantheon

14. Francke AIT ii. 9. 15. *Ib.* ii.79f. See Section 19. 16. Waddell in ERE xii. 333f. 17. Petech 9 comments that the *La-dvags-rgyal-rabs* (translated by Francke AIT ii) "seems to be the only Tibetan chronicle of which the cosmology is not purely Buddhistic. It has preserved for us some of the Bon-po legends on the creation of the world and of the gods."
18. Stcherbatsky CNB 33.

and a host of saints, a religion highly devotional, highly ceremonious and clerical, with an ideal of Universal Salvation of all living creatures, a Salvation by the divine grace of the Buddhas and the Bodhisattvas, a Salvation not in annihilation, but in eternal life—we are fully justified in maintaining that the history of religions has scarcely witnessed such a break between the new and the old within the pale of what nevertheless continues to claim common descent from the same religious founder."

As is only to be expected, to explain and defend this new form of the faith there came into being an extensive literature which in general is referred to as the Mahāyāna-sūtras or Vaipulya-sūtras, including the miraculous biography of the Buddha called the *Lalita-vistara.* These Mahāyāna texts have a spirit "very similar to that of the Purāṇas"[19] and, as Winternitz observes, show a "preference for phantasmagorias."[20] Another important characteristic of the Mahāyāna-sūtras is the glorification of the texts themselves, "the enumeration of the merits and advantages which one gains by propagating and honouring"[21] these. This "bibliotary...conspicuous in the texts themselves" accounts for the ceremonial worship of the books in Nepal and Tibet.[22]

Thus it was Buddhism in its new form and as embodied in these highly mythological texts with bibliotary inherent in them that really reached Tibet. The Tibetan historians, being above all ardent Buddhists, take everything about this new religion with utmost seriousness. The cosmology etc. with which they usually open the history of Tibet, far from being manufactured by the Tibetans themselves or being borrowed from Bon mythology, are only evidences of how much Tibetan historiography is saturated with a veneration for Mahāyāna Buddhism.

It is basically the same veneration that leads the Tibetan historians to view the Tibetan events proper as, in some way

19. Winternitz ii. 245. 20. *Ib.* 21. *Ib.* ii. 252. 22. *Ib.* ii. 295n.

or other, continuations of Indian events, i.e. of events related to Buddhism. The tendency of seeing in Tibetan history a continuation of Indian history leads the Tibetan historians to imagine that the first king of Tibet—even the very people of Tibet[23]—came originally from India. Surprisingly, the Tibetan historians try to substantiate even these claims by scriptural evidences, by which are meant the evidences of the Mahāyāna texts.

23. Rockhill NET 670 comments that Tibetan historical works, as guides to the question of their national origin, are of little, if any, assistance. Nevertheless, these are interesting documents of the Tibetan way of traditional thinking.

17. Tibetans and their First King

Bu-ston,[1] on the authority of the commentary on the *Devātiśaya-stotra*,[2] says, "At the time when the five Pāṇḍavas were fighting with the twelve armies of the Kauravas, the king Rūpati with 1,000 warriors, in the disguise of women, fled into the rocky district of the Himalaya. Of these (the Tibetans) are considered to be the offspring". S. C. Das,[3] however, says that after migrating to Tibet Rūpati "found the country Pu-rgyal (sPur-rgyal[4] : for such was the ancient name of Tibet, which in later times was converted into Bod) widely peopled by a race of men still in a primitive state. They welcomed him as their king. By his mild and peaceful behaviour he won their affection and ruled over them for many years". This seems to be based on some confusion. The Tibetans generally consider Rūpati and his associates as the progenitors of the Tibetan people and the first King of Tibet is invariably mentioned as gÑa'-khri-btsan-po.

Bu-ston[5] is aware of another tradition according to which the Tibetans are the descendants of a monkey. But the authority of the commentary on the *Devātiśaya-stotra* has apparently stronger force for him and he does not discuss the question further.

According to Sum-pa[6] this monkey to whom the Tibetans trace their descent was Avalokiteśvara incarnate. Following Rockhill,[7] Waddell[8] says that the name given to this monkey ancestor is Hilumandju, "evidently intended for Hanumānji, the Hindu monkey-god". Thus, even admitting Francke's view[9] that the early legendary accounts of Tibet are presumbly

1. Bu-ston ii. 181. 2. bsTod i. 4 ; mDo xxxiii. 100. 3. S. C. Das in JASB 1881. 212. 4. on sPur-rgyal, see D-TED 800. 5. Bu-ston ii. 181. 6. Sum-pa 148. 7. Rockhill LL 355. 8. Waddell L 19n. 9. Francke AIT ii. 9 ; 40.

of Bon origin, it is interesting to note how the Bon mythology already leaned on Indian mythology.

'Gos lo-tsā-ba proposes to take a more credible view of the origin of the Tibetans. "Without contradicting scriptures and reason", says he, "one may safely state that the country of Tibet was similar to that of India with regard to country and people, etc., and that its origin goes back to the beginning of the present Cosmic Period (*kalpa*)".[10] This remarkable statement earns for him high compliments from S. C. Das, who says that the historian is "less influenced by the love of the marvellous, or the appetite for wonders, which marks all early oriental writings".[11] But this should by no means lead us to overlook that the decisive authority even for 'Gos lo-tsā-ba is some Indian scripture or an Indian scholar. "In the beginning of the Kali-yuga", says he,[12] "before the appearance of the teacher Muni, when the five Pāṇḍava brothers led to battle a host consisting of 12 or 13 divisions, a king named Rūpati, who fought at the head of his army, suffered a defeat and fled to the region situated inside the snowy mountains disguised as a woman. His descendants settled there. 'Nowadays his line is called Bod', so said the *ācārya* Prajñāvarman (Śes-rab-go-cha). In the old chronicles of the past (it is said): 'The ancient name of this country was sPur-rgyal. Later it was called Bod'. This agrees with the account of Prajñāvarman. Specially in the *Vinayavibhaṅga* it is said : 'It was called Bod in the life-time of the Muni'. also it is said in the *Kālacakra* : 'To Āryāvarta, Bod (Tibet), etc'."

Prajñāvarman or Śes-rab-go-cha, as Sum-pa[13] tells us, was a Buddhist sage of Kashmir and from the bsTan-'gyur[14] it appears that he was an author of some eminence. It is, therefore, interesting to note that even a historian like 'Gos lo-tsā-ba, mainly on the authority of Prajñāvarman and a few scrappy

10. BA i. 36. 11. S. C. Das in JASB 1881. 212. 12. BA. i. 36.
13. Sum-pa 110. 14. See Lalou 154, 214.

20

words of Indian texts, argues that the Tibetans were afterall the descendants of migrating Indians.

It is not important for our present purpose to go into the question of the actual origin of the Tibetan people.[15] What is important instead is to note that the tendency of the Tibetan historians to connect Tibetan history with Indian history leads them to the further assumption that the first king of Tibet came from India and was an Indian.

"As regards the genealogy of the Tibetan kings", says Bu-ston,[16] "some say that (their ancestor) was the fifth descendant of Prasenajit, king of Kośala ; according to some it was the fifth descendant of the youngest, feeble son of Bimbisāra. Still others say that at the time when the Tibetans were oppressed by 12 petty chiefs of the demons and Yakṣas, the king of Vatsa, Udayana, had a son born to him, whose eyelids were overhanging and whose fingers were connected with a web. As the child with such distinctive marks appeared, (the king) was frightened and ordered him to be put into a leaden box and thrown into the Ganges. (The boy) was however found by a peasant who brought him up. When he grew older, and the story (how he was found) was related to him, he became full of grief and fled to the Himalayas. Gradually he passed by the Lha-ri-yol-ba and came out into the plain of bTsan-thaṅ-sgo-bshi. The Bon priests who came from the dMu-thag and dMu-skas declared that he was a god...After they had asked him who he was and he replied : I am a 'mighty one' (*btsan-po*),—they inquired from where he came and he pointed with his finger to the sky. After their efforts to comprehend the language of each other turned to be unsuccessful, (the Bons) placed him on a wooden throne which they loaded on the necks of four men and said : We shall make him our lord. —Thereupon he derived his name gÑa'-khri-btsan-po, 'the neck-chaired Mighty One'. It was he who became the first king of Tibet".

The Tibetan historians are in fact unanimous in considering

15. See Richardson 5f. 16. Bu-ston ii. 181-2.

gÑa'-khri-btsan-po to be the first king of Tibet, and gÑa'-khri-btsan-po is usually considered to be a descendant of Prasenajit, the king of Kośala.

'Gos lo-tsā-ba[17] asserts that this king came from the Licchavi race, his main argument being that his later descendants are clearly mentioned in the *Mañjuśrī-mūla-tantra* to have Licchavi origin : "Thus it is correct to state that the kings (of Tibet) belong to the Licchavi race." Some of the modern scholars propose to take this suggestion seriously. The ancient Buddhist and Jaina sources mention the migration of the Licchavis towards Nepal and, on the basis of this, S. C. Das[18] conjectures that the Tibetan account of the first king of Tibet being of Licchavi origin may not be unfounded afterall. V. A. Smith[19] comments, "Several facts indicate a close connection between Tibet and the Licchavis, and give probability to the theory that the Licchavis were really a Tibetan tribe which settled in the plains during pre-historic times... Much more significant are the undoubted similarities between the customs of the Tibetans and those of the Licchavis which are reported in the important matters of sepulture and judicial procedure." But Roerich[20] argues that 'Gos lo-tsā-ba thoroughly misunderstands the passage of the *Mañjuśrī-mūla-tantra* on the evidence of which he attributes Licchavi origin to the Tibetan kings.

The *Chronicle of Ladakh*[21] translated by Francke gives a lengthy account of the first king of Tibet. According to it, the original Indian name of gÑa'-khri-btsan-po was Buddhaśrī and, though he was one of the five sons of Prasenajit, the king of Kośala, he was "certainly a Śākya of Gohutama" !

Even the Bon tradition shows unmistakable signs of Indian influence in the legend concerning the first king of Tibet. The *rGyal-rabs-bon-gyi-'byuṅ-gnas*, considered to be a Bon chronicle, gives many *Mahābhārata* tales in this connection and considers the first king of Tibet to be the son of Pāṇḍu and Krasnā ![22]

17. BA i. 36. 18. D-TED 802. 19. V. A. Smith in IA xxxii. 233f.
20. Roerich BA i. Intro. p. x f. 21. Francke AIT ii. 76f. 22. *Ib.* ii. 78n. Francke's interpretation of Krasnā as Kṛṣṇā or Draupadī is no less absurd.

Francke[23] comes across the name of gÑa'-khri-btsan-po as an ancestor of the Ladakhi kings in 9 inscriptions of his collection, though, according to him, like all other kings before Sroṅ-btsan-sgam-po, this first king of Tibet has "nothing to do with history. They belong to the Bon-po mythology."[24] But some of the modern scholars try to determine the date[25] of gÑa'-khri-btsan-po : according to I. J. Schmidt it was 314 B.C., according to Csoma de Koros it was 250 B.C., according to Schlagintweit and S. C. Das it was 50 B.C.

But the more important question is : why do the Tibetan historians invariably begin with an account of gÑa'-khri-btsan-po as their first king ? 'Gos lo-tsā-ba[26] gives a remarkable answer to this question : "It is said that there were twelve small feudal principalities in Tibet. These were merely small states, and there does not exist an account of the fostering of the Doctrine by their descendants. For this reason, Tibetan scholars wrote the story of the Tibetan kings, beginning with king gÑa'-khri-btsan-po only. I shall do likewise." In other words, gÑa'-khri-btsan-po is considered the first king of Tibet because his supposed descendants favoured Buddhism. Here is, thus, a frank admission by one of the leading Tibetan historians that the real reason for conceiving gÑa'-khri-btsan-po as the first king of Tibet is nothing but the veneration for Buddhism on the part of the later Tibetan historians.

We may follow this suggestion a little further. Prasenajit was an intimate associate of the Buddha himself. Therefore, to conceive the first king of Tibet as a descendant of Prasenajit means also a sanctification of the line of the Tibetan kings. As Rockhill[27] suggests, "Another consideration, however, exercised great influence with Tibetan historians when, in the reign of Ral-pa-can, they commenced writing their national history, and that was to make the genealogy of their monarchs ascend, if not to the Buddha himself, at least to one of his friends and protectors. And as we have in Europe families

23. *Ib.* ii. 77n. 24. *Ib.* ii. 11. 25. *Ib.* ii. 78n. 26. BA i. 35.
27. Rockhill LB 203.

who are proud to claim descent from the Virgin Mary or from the Wise Men of the East, so likewise the first Tibetan monarch claims descent from Prasenajit, king of Kośala, one of the early converts and the life-long friend of the Buddha Gautama".

King Ral-pa-can,[28] from the time of whose reign this mode of writing Tibetan history became prominent, was himself one of the most pious and enlightened Buddhist to have ruled Tibet. Therefore, there is nothing to wonder at the Buddhist bias given to Tibetan history from his time. In this connection Petech draws our attention to certain extremely interesting evidences that give us a glimpse of the pre-Buddhistic Tibetan tradition according to which the first Tibetan king was somebody else, though all the Buddhist chronicles of Tibet consider gÑa'-khri-btsan-po as the founder of the Tibetan dynasty.

As Petech[29] puts it, "there are traces of another and more ancient account. One of the Lhasa Pillar edicts published by Waddell[30] mentions the 'divine magic king' 'O-lde-spur-rgyal. The same name is to be found in one of the documents discovered by Sir Aurel Stein in Central Asia and published by Thomas.[31] The *T'ang-shu* speaks as well of this king, whose name is transcribed with the characters Hu-t'i-po-si-yeh...There is also a shorter form : Su-po-yeh... corresponding perfectly to sPur-rgyal ; it is an additional name of Fan-ni, the first king of Tibet according to the Chinese sources".

The inscriptions bearing the name of gÑa'-khri-btsan-po are of much later date. They belong to 16-18th centuries. But no document earlier than that of the 9th century bears his name. At the same time the name of 'O-lde-spur-rgyal disappears from later chronicles. "But before it disappeared, it was so widely known that it gave a nickname to Tibet : sPur-rgyal Bod (sPur-rgyal's Tibet)."[33]

28. See Section 26. 29. Petech 19f. 30. Waddell in JRAS 1909. 923ff. 31. Thomas in JRAS 1928. 71, 77. 32. *T'ang-shu* Ch. 216A, folio 1A. the reference is from Petech 20. 33. Petech 20. cf. D-TED 800.

Thus it seems that the later historians, in their zeal to trace the descent of the Tibetan kings to a near-associate of Gautama Buddha, discard the earlier tradition according to which 'O-lde-spur-rgyal rather than gÑa'-khri-btsan-po was the first king of Tibet. This creates a peculiar difficulty for the later historians. Historically speaking, the first real king of Tibet was Sroṅ-btsan-sgam-po or his father and Sroṅ-btsan belonged to the 7th century A.D. The Tibetan historians are aware of this and they are too well-read in the Buddhist lore to be unaware of the long time-gap between Prasenajit and Sroṅ-btsan. How, then, are they to account for it ? The only way of doing it is to give a long list of successive kings between gÑa'-khri-btsan-po, the descendant of Prasenajit, and Sroṅ-btsan-sgam-po or his father. But the Tibetan historians do not have to fabricate such a list from their own imagination. They find themselves provided with a ready-made one by the Bon mythology. The later Tibetan historians simply graft the list obtained from the Bon mythology in between gÑa'-khri-btsan-po and Sroṅ-btsan-sgam-po. This leads us to see the list of the early legendary kings of the Bon period usually found in the Tibetan Buddhist chronicles.

18. *Early Legendary Kings*

Beginning with gÑa'-khri-btsan-po, says Petech,[1] we have "five groups of kings, or (we may better say) of gods : seven heavenly Khri-s (thrones), two upper sTeṅ-s (high ones), six middle Legs-s (good ones), eight earthly lDe-s, three lower bTsan-s (mighty ones). This system is essentially the same in all chronicles, although some difference may be noticed and although it has been fully developed in the *rGyal-rabs-gsal-ba'i-me-loṅ* only. The series of the 27 gods is undoubtedly of Bon-po origin... Evidently, the Tibetan historians built their royal genealogies on the same lines as followed by the Bon-po in the classification of the elements in their cosmology. This explains the purely mythological character of these genealogies."

But there are certain interesting features of this mythology itself. Thus, according to the list prepared by S. C. Das,[2] the names of the first seven kings (Khri-s), *along with their queens*, are :

1. gÑa'-khri-btsan-po, who married Nam-*mu*(*g*)-mu(g)
2. *Mu*(*g*)-khri-btsan-po, who married Sa-*diṅ*-diṅ
3. *Diṅ*-khri-btsan-po, who married *So*-than-than
4. *So*-khri-btsan-po, who married Dog-*mer*-mer
5. *Mer*-khri-btsan-po, who married *gDags*-lha-mo-dkar-mo
6. *gDags*-khri-btsan-po, who married *Sribs*-lha-mo
7. *Sribs*-khri-btsan-po, who married Sa-btsan-luṅ-rje.

Bu-ston[3] says that up to the time of Sribs-khri-btsan-po "the worship called rDol-bon was spread." rDol-bon, as we shall see,[4] is supposed to be the first or earliest stage of the Bon religion.

These kings, referred to as a group under the general title

1. Petech 21-2.
2. S. C. Das in JASB 1881. 213ff and 231ff.
3. Bu-ston ii. 182.
4. See Section 19.

"The Heavenly Thrones" (*gnam-gyi-khri*), "are said to have ascended to the skies, being carried there by their queens, *who were celestial beings*, in consequence of which their mortal relics were not left below."[5] The mention of the queens as celestial beings is not without an interest. Could it be that this was the way in which the memory of the ancient Tibetan matriarchy lingered in later times ? The names of the kings suggest an answer in the affirmative. "The names of all these kings, it is worthy of remark, were formed by a combination of the names of their parents, *the mother's name generally preceding that of the father*."[6] Thus the name of Mu(g)-khri-btsan-po begins with the name of his mother Nam-mu(g)-mu(g), of Diṅ-khri-btsan-po begins with the name of his mother Sa-diṅ-diṅ, and so on. This peculiarity, as Herbert Müller[7] rightly argues, is reminiscent of ancient Tibetan matriarchate. It remains for us to see if the ancient form of the Bon religion, which Bu-ston says flourished during these kings, contained any hint of the same.

Incidentally, from the Chinese historians we learn that matriarchate—even gynaecocratic government—was actually prevalent over an extensive area of ancient Tibet : "The Chinese annals of the Sui and of the T'ang dynasties (A.D. 581-905) contain accounts of the Kingdom of Su-pi, or as it was called by the Chinese, Nu-kuo, that is, the Kingdom of Women, which *comprised the whole of northern Tibet*. The accounts in the *Sui-shu* and *T'ang-shu* run as follows : 'The Kingdom of Women is south of the Tsung-ling mountains, and is a division of the Ch'iang. From east to west it is nine days' journey, from north to south twenty days' journey. It has eighty towns, and there are over 40,000 families and 10,000 soldiers. In this country the sovereign is a woman... The queen's husband...has nothing to do with the government of the State. There is also a "little queen", the two together ruling the kingdom. As to their customs, the women hold in light esteem their husbands, nor are they jealous... *The*

5. S. C. Das in JASB 1881. 215. Emphasis added. 6. *Ib.* Emphasis added. 7. See Francke AIT ii. 78n.

sons take the family name of their mother... The sovereign has near her person several hundred women, and once every five days there is a council of state. They depute men to perform all outside duties, and these are thence known as "women's deputies". From the interior of the palace the men receive and transmit the orders. When the sovereign dies the people pay several myriad of gold coins, and select from the royal clan two clever women, one to reign, the other as assistant sovereign to succeed her in case of death... The *sovereign wears a black (or blue) plaited skirt* of a rough texture..."[8] Briffault comments, "There is no ground to doubt the substantial accuracy of those accounts. The gynaecocratic organisation of the kingdom of Su-pi merely represents on a somewhat larger scale the matriarchal tribal organisation which is found in Assam."[9] In his archaeological work in Leh, Francke[10] comes across a grave which "calls to mind at once the description of the form of burial practised in the 'Empire of the Eastern Women' of the Chinese historians." "Hiuen Tsiang", adds Francke, "also heard of this empire, and a little after his time, we read that the last queen died and was replaced by a king." About this remarkable people of Eastern Tibet, Bushell[11] says, "They are first mentioned in the Northern History, and are more fully described in the Sui History, after they had sent envoys to the founder of that dynasty in the year 588 (A.D.)... In the period 618-626 the queen named T'angp-'ang first sent envoys with tribute (to the Chinese Emperor)... Since the year 742 they have elected a man to be their ruler."

But let us return to the list of the early legendary kings.

There is a clear break in the list after the mention of the first seven kings. We no longer find the names of the subse-

8. Briffault iii. 23-4. Emphasis added. 9. *Ib.* iii. 24.
10. Francke AIT i. 73-4. 11. Bushell in JRAS 1880. 531-2.

quent kings being derived from the family name of their mothers. The next two kings in the list are :

Gri-gum-btsan-po

Bya-khri-rgyal (or sPu-de-guṅ-rgyal).

The group formed by these two kings is called "soaring in the middle regions" (*bar-gyi-ldiṅ*). S. C. Das[12] says that Gri-gum-btsan-po "had three sons. His minister was a very ambitious man, who rebelled against him. An internecine war followed in which the king was killed... The victorious minister, having married one of the widows of the late king, usurped the throne and obliged the three princes to fly... He reigned for several years. The widow of the late king and mother of the three princes, by invoking the goblin...got a son, who eventually rising to the post of minister killed the usurper. He now invited three exiled princes...the eldest of whom named Bya-khri-rgyal quietly ascended the ancestral throne."

Petech,[13] however, has an interesting observation on this group. It contains the names of only two kings, of whom the place of the first in the group is somewhat doubtful. "Sanang Setsen makes Gri-gum-btsan-po the last member of Khri series and Bu-ston omits him altogether." This leaves us with the name of only one king, namely Bya-khri, who, according to the *Chronicle of Ladakh*, "received the name of sPu-de-guṅ-rgyal".[14] Petech draws our attention to the similarity between the names sPu-de-guṅ-rgyal and 'O-lde-spu-rgyal of the Lhasa edict and of the *T'ang-shu*. The two names have in common three components out of four. 'O-lde-spu-rgyal was the name of the first king of Tibet according to the older or pre-Buddhist tradition. "It is in fact certain", says Petech,[15]

12. S. C. Das in JASB 1881. 214. 13. Petech 23f. 14. Francke AIT ii. 79. Bu-ston ii. 182 spells the name as sPu-lde-guṅ-rgyal, Sum-pa 150 as sPu-de-kuṅ-rgyal. The spelling adopted by Francke, Roerich and Petech is followed here. 15. Petech 24; but Petech's reliance on the similarity of the two names leading him to assume the identity of the two as one person is precarious.

"that we first come across sPu-rgyal, interested herein by the later historians who contented themselves with placing him in the background, as they could not possibly omit him altogether, since he was too deeply rooted in the tradition. But the break in the list of the kings has remained clearly visible." Further, adds Petech, the chronicles attribute to sPu-de-guṅ-rgyal activities that are characteristic of the founder of a nation : he discovered the principal metals, introduced agriculture and irrigation, built the first capital of Tibet, i.e. the great castle of Yar-luṅ, and, most important of all, helped the rise of the Bon religion.

The list next mentions a group of six kings called "excellent (*legs*) of the land (*sa*)". Next comes a group of eight kings, collectively called *lde*, "which means the commander and corresponds to the Sanskrit word *sena*."[16] The list ends with the names of five more, who also, as Francke observes, "form a group according to *dPag-bsam-ljon-bzaṅ*, where they are called 'the five lower majesties' (*smad-kyi-btsan-lṅa*)."[17]

"This", observes Francke,[18] "is the last group of kings who are furnished with a group name. After this the kings show more individuality and may be historical personages. Looking at their various groups it occurs to me that through their group names they are connected with the three realms of the world, according to pre-Buddhist ideas. According to the *gLiṅ-chos*, the world consists of *steṅ-lha*, heaven of gods, *bar-btsan*, the earth, and *gyog-klu*, the realm of the Nāgas. The first group of kings, the Seven Heavenly Thrones, are evidently connected with *steṅ-lha* ; the second, third and fourth groups... belong to the earth ; and the last group... belongs to the realm of the Nāgas." Petech[19] substantially agrees with this. The historians of Tibet, however, maintain the attitude that these early kings do not deserve much discussion because theirs was the period of the prosperity of the Bon religion. "It was", as S. C. Das[20] sums up their attitude, "in the 27th generation

16. S. C. Das in JASB 1881. 232. 17. Francke AIT ii. 81n.
18. *Ib.* 19. Petech 22. 20. S. C. Das in JASB 1881. 216.

of the royal succession that the Bon religion rose to the zenith of its power and when the sun of Buddhism was shinning in its meridian lustre all over Jambudvīpa, snow-girdled Tibet remained buried in the impenetrable darkness of Bon mysticism."

19. The Bon Religion

But what was the nature of this ancient religion of Tibet called Bon—pronounced as Pon[1]—and the follower of which is called a Bon-po ?[2] In spite of all that the Tibetan historians tell us about the great resistance it offered to the introduction of Buddhism into Tibet, our actual knowledge of the nature of the Bon religion is at best vague and fragmentary. This is all the more surprising because the modern investigators do not consider it as a dead and forgotten creed only of the past. On the contrary, as Rockhill[3] says, "this creed is still followed by part of the Tibetans and the barbarous tribes of the Himalayas". He even goes to the extent of estimating that almost two-third of the population of Tibet are Bon-pos.[4] Though the religion is "strictly forbidden by the Lamaist hierarchy which holds the temporal rule in Central and Western Tibet", adds Waddell,[5] "it is still largely and openly professed over the greater part of Eastern and South-Eastern Tibet, the most populous part of the country". In Eastern Tibet, the Bon priests live in large monasteries,[6] with all sorts of images of gods, saints and demons. They have also a considerable bulk of their "scriptural literature", discussed not only by the learned Tibetan Buddhists but also actually examined by modern scholars.

Still our knowledge of the real nature of the Bon religion is extremely poor. Following Cunningham, Rockhill[7] claims that the "word Bon-pa is unquestionably derived from *Puṇya*, one of the names of the *Svastikas* or worshippers of the mystic

1. Waddell in ERE xii. 333. 2. D-TED 879. Sometimes wrongly written as Bon-pa, which means "to express, to mutter". 3. Rockhill LB 206. 4. Rockhill DJMT 68, 86f. 5. Waddell *op. cit.* 6. S. C. Das JL 205ff describes a Bon-po monastery. 7. Rockhill LB 206. On *gyuṅ-druṅ* see D-TED 1153.

cross *swasti,* which in Tibetan is called *gyuṅ-druṅ.*" But Waddell[8] seems to be frankly sceptical about it. The real meaning of the word Bon, according to him, remains unknown. S. C. Das and Jaschke, instead of giving any meaning of the word Bon, sum up the vague descriptions of the religion usually given. Bon, says S. C. Das,[9] is "the ancient religion of Tibet which was fetishism, demon-worship and propitiation by means of incantations. The word *chos,* which ordinarily means religion, is used as the antithesis to Bon. Bon now signifies the kind of shamanism which was followed by Tibetans before the introduction of Buddhism and in certain parts still extant". Jaschke[10] says that Bon is the "name of the early religion of Tibet, concerning which but very imperfect accounts are existing ; so mnch is certain that sorcery was the principal feature of it. When Buddhism became the religion of state, the former was considered heretical and condemnable, and *lha-chos* and *bon-chos,* or shorter, *chos* and *bon,* were placed in opposition, as with us Christianity and Paganism ; at the present time, both of them seem to exist peaceably side by side, and the primitive religion has not only numerous adherents and convents in central (northern ?) Tibet, but manifold traces of it may be found still in the creed of the Tibetans of today".

Hodgson[11] says, "in the Himalayas even the Bon-po priests themselves can tell nothing of the origin of their beliefs". "As yet", says Schlagintweit,[12] "little is known about the Bon religion. Judging from the way in which Tibetan books speak of the followers of this sect, it is probable that the name Bon-pa was restricted to those who neglected to embrace Buddhism upon its first introduction".

But how is it that in spite of Bon being still a living creed in Tibet and in spite, moreover, of the availability of a considerable bulkof Bon "scriptures", our knowledge of the real nature of the religion should be so vague and mainly negative ? The answer is suggested by Schlagintweit[13] when he says,

8. Waddell *op. cit.* 9. D-TED 879. 10. J-TED 372.
11. Hodgson in JRAS xvii. 396-9. 12. Schlagintweit 74. 13. *Ib.*

"By degrees they (Bon-pos) have, however, adopted Buddhist principles, still rigorously preserving as far as we are able to infer from the meagre information hitherto known about them, the ancient superstitious ideas and rites of the primitive inhabitants of Tibet".

A number of pictures of the Bon deities is published by Hodgson.[14] But they look surprisingly similar to the Buddhist deities of modern Tibet. In *A Brief Sketch of the Bon Religion of Tibet*, S. C. Das[15] gives an account of gŚen-rabs of Shaṅ-shuṅ (Guge), the legendary founder of the Bon religion. But the legend related about him is clearly modelled on that of the Buddha. The Tibetan scholar Chos-kyi-ñi-ma, in his work entitled *Explanation of the Origin and Theories of all Schools*, devotes a longish chapter to the nature and history of the Bon religion.[16] He mentions a large number of the "scriptural works of the Bon-pos". These discuss theology, philosophy, rituals and meditative practices. But these books are useless for understanding the real nature of Bon, because these are nothing but "wholesale plagiarism of Buddhist canonical works." The history of this literature is given as follows : "During the reign of king Khri-sroṅ-lde-btsan, an edict was issued requiring all the Bon-pos to renounce their faith and embrace Buddhism. The minister rGyal-ba'i-byaṅ-chub requested the Bon priest named Rin-chen-mchog to adopt Buddhism, which he declined to do. Having been punished by the king for his obstinacy he became greatly enraged, and, in company of some other Bon-pos, secretly composed Bon scriptures by means of wholesale plagiarism from Buddhist canonical works. The king hearing that the excellent sayings of the Tathāgata had been converted into Bon scriptures, ordered the priests to be beheaded. Many of the Bon-pos were thus killed ; the rest secretly multiplied their works and, through fear, concealed them under rocks. Afterwards they brought out their religious books from the various hiding

14. Hodgson in JRAS 1861. 15. S. C. Das in JBTS I. i. Appendix, 1-7.
16. Translated by S. C. Das in JASB 1881. 195ff.

places, in consequence of which these books are called Bon-gter-ma or 'The Hidden Treasures of the Bon-po'. Subsequent to the overthrow of Buddhism by gLaṅ Dar-ma, two Bon priests...sitting in a solitary cavern in dBus, consecrated as a place of Bon religion, altered many Buddhist works by using an orthography and terminology different from those of the Buddhists. These they concealed under the rock...Afterwards they brought the hidden books to light as if they were accidental discoveries. Afterwards...other Bon priests, in the same manner, converted other Buddhist works into Bon scriptures".[17]

The obvious Buddhist bias of this account need not be doubted. Equally indubitable, however, is the fact that the Bon "scriptures", as actually available, are nothing but plagiarisms of Buddhist works. The doctrines expounded in these are clearly Buddhist, though presented with a thin varnish of terminological innovation. Thus, e.g., in these "scriptures" are taught the unsteadiness of all things, *karma, phalam,* love and compassion, the *bodhisattva* feeling, the six *pāramitā*-s, the five ways of emancipation, etc., etc., though in these works are to be found peculiar words substituting Sambhogakāya, Dharmakāya, Buddha, etc.[18]

It is, therefore, idle to expect any idea of the real nature of the Bon religion from this mass of forged scriptures. This is confirmed by the experience of the modern investigators. "They (the Bon-pos) have", says Waddell,[19] "bulky printed and manuscript books of ritual, which Rockhill found to consist of a Sanskritic jargon for the most part interspersed with other meaningless words. The present writer observed that the words in some of their MSS, which are written in the Tibetan script, were the Lamaist Sanskritic words spelt backwards : the lotus-jewel formula of the Lamas was spelt '*Muh-em-pad-ni-mo*'."

17. *Ib.* 199. 18. *Ib.* 201f. Cf. Rockhill LB 207 for the patently Buddhist doctrine found in the *gTsaṅ-ma-klu-'bum-dkar-po,* a Bon work (see D-TED 46) translated by A. Schiefner. 19. Waddell in ERE xii. 333.

At the same time it is interesting to note that the Tibetan scholar Chos-kyi-ñi-ma, because of the Buddhistic contents of these works, finds the Bon religion as represented by these as acceptable to a certain extent, or at least as less objectionable than the religion in its earlier stages. He divides the history of the Bon religion into three stages, of which the final or "reformed" stage (*bsgyur-bon*) is represented by these works. The two earlier stages of the religion are characterised by him as "corrupted" (*'khyar-bon*) and "wild" (*rdol-bon*).

For the purpose of understanding why the newly introduced Buddhism came to a long-drawn conflict with the Bon religion, the earlier stages of Bon interest us most. But even the so-called "corrupted" or second stage of the religion has little clue to its original nature. At this stage, the religion seems to have borrowed freely from Hindu ideas, particularly of Śaivism and Śaktism. Chos-kyi-ñi-ma tells us that the religion assumed this peculiar form long ago, i. e. when the early legendary king Gri-gum-btsan was assassinated. At that time, "the Bon priests, not knowing how to conduct the funeral rites (so as to prevent his spirit from doing mischief to the living), invited three Bon priests, one from Kashmir, a second from the Dusha country and a third from the country of Shaṅ-shuṅ, to perform the 'funeral of the stabbed'. One of these priests propitiated...the god of fire and thereby was enabled to travel in the sky, mounted on a tambourin, and to discover mines. He could perform miraculous feats such as cutting iron with the quills of birds, etc. Another priest was skilled in delivering oracles and telling fortunes...The third priest was famed for his skill in conducting the funeral ceremonies of the dead, especially of those murdered with knives, etc...Previous to the appearance of these Bon priests there existed no Bon religious theories. Since their time the Bon doctrines have come into existence. This stage of the Bon religion, called 'erroneous' ('corrupted') Bon was mixed up with the Śaiva doctrine of the Tīrthikas".[20]

20. Chos-kyi-ñi-ma translated by Das in JASB 1881. 198.

Whatever may be the historicity of such an account, the fact is that patent Hindu ideas somehow or other did creep into the Bon religion, though it may be difficult for us to determine when exactly this happened. Thus, e.g.. the Bon chronicle called *rGyal-rabs-bon-gyi-'byuṅ-gnas*[21] is full of Hindu ideas.

The "second" or "corrupted" stage of the Bon religion, therefore, like its still later "reformed" stage, does not give us much idea about its original nature. What, then, was the nature of the religion in its "first" or "wild" stage ? Chos--kyi-ñi-ma himself does not help us much in answering this question. The mythology he narrates about this first stage has little bearing on the nature of the creed itself. As for the nature of the creed, he simply says, "The Bon-pos of that age were skilled in witchcraft, the performance of mystical rites for suppressing evil spirits and cannibal hobgoblins of the nether regions, the invocation of the venerable gods above, and the domestic ceremonies to appease the wrath of malignant spirits of the middle region (earth) caused by the 'pollution of the hearth'. Besides these, there did not then exist any other theories or works concerning the Bon religion."[22]

Such an account, like the description of the ancient Bon as "an animistic and devil-dancing or Shamanist religion",[23] is too vague to be of use for understanding the actual nature of primitive pre-Buddhist creed of Tibet.

The work called *Sa-bdag-klu-gñan-gyi-srog-'khrol*, translated by Laufer, is said to contain Bon songs of exorcism "untouched by Hindu or Buddhist ideas."[24] The *gLiṅ-chos*, containing Bon mythology and folklore, is discussed by Francke.[25] These, with a few scattered studies of the Bon religion,[26] remain to

21. Edited by S. C. Das, 1915. Francke AIT ii. 80n says that the chronicle was compiled later than A.D. 1328. 22. Translated by S. C. Das in JASB 1881. 196-7. 23. Waddell L 19. 24. See Francke AIT ii. 80n. 25. Francke in ERE viii. 75ff. 26. e.g. Li An-Che in *South Western Journal of Anthropology* iv. 32-42 ; Francke in IA xxx. 131ff, 359 ; Jaschke refers to the *Report of the Royal Bavarian Academy of Sciences*, 13th Jan. 1886.

be critically utilised for a fuller understanding of the ancient creed. Only on the basis of such an understanding, we can judge the value of the older view[27] concerning the relation between Taoism of ancient China and Bon of ancient Tibet.

The Chinese annals compiled in the 10th-11th centuries retain for us a vivid description of a primitive Tibetan ritual, which presumably formed part of the ancient Bon. In Bushell's[28] translation, the ritual was as follows : "The officers are assembled once every year for the lesser oath of fealty. They sacrifice sheep, dogs and monkeys, first breaking their legs and then killing them, afterwards exposing their intestines and cutting them into pieces. The sorcerers having been summoned, they call on the gods of heaven and earth, of the mountains and rivers, of the sun, moon, stars, and planets, saying : 'Should your hearts become changed, and your thoughts disloyal, the gods will see clearly and make you like these sheep and dogs.' Every three years there is a grand ceremony, during which all are assembled in the middle of the night and on a raised altar, on which are spread savoury meat. The victims sacrificed are men, horses, oxen and asses, and prayers are offered in this form : 'Do you all with one heart and united strength cherish our native country. The god of heaven, and the spirit of the earth, will both know your thoughts, and if you break this oath they will cause your bodies to be cut into pieces like unto these victims'." To this may be added S. C. Das' remark : "Animal sacrifices form an important part in the religious observances of the Bon-po."[29]

Rituals like these are known to characterise other primitive creeds of the world. From two more features of the Bon religion, we have perhaps the further glimpse of its originally being a form of the mother-cult, which so many primitive religions of the world are known to have been.[30] First, in the Bon pantheon "the goddesses take precedence over the

27. Klaproth 97, 148 ; Waddell L 19 ; S. C. Das in JASB 1882. 112.
28. Bushell in JRAS 1880. 441.
29. Das in JASB 1881. 198n.
30. See e.g. E.O. James.

gods."[31] Secondly, the female priests in this religion have superiority over the male.[32] Both these are said to be well-known marks of the mother-cult,[33] and since the mother-cult is usually connected with matriarchate,[34] the ancient matriarchate of northern Tibet was not perhaps entirely unconnected with the ancient religion which still remains strongly entrenched in northern Tibet. It is tempting to add one more point in this connection. Francke[35] refers to his "discovery of an ancient Bon-po temple at Lamayuru with frescoes of Bon-po priests represented in *blue and black dress.*" S. C. Das[36] also speaks of the blue and black dress of the Bon priests. This is reminiscent of the practice of wearing blue and black robes by the queens of Nu-kuo, the Kingdom of Women, which, according to the Chinese annals, comprised the whole of northern Tibet.

All these are, however, conjectural. What is not conjectural is that though the Tibetan historians give us extremely meagre idea of the actual nature of the Bon religion, they are most eager to tell us how the Tibetans were eventually emancipated from the darkness of the Bon beliefs as a result of the coming of Buddhism toTibet. This leads us to see the story usually told by them of the first coming to Tibet of Buddhist scriptures and Buddhist objects of worship.

31. S. C. Das in JBTS I. iii. Appendix 1, p.1. 32. S. C. Das in JASB 1881. 197n. 33. See Briffault. 34. Starbuck in ERE v. 828; R. P. Chanda IAR 148ff; Paton in ERE ii. 115, etc. 35. Francke AIT ii. 80n. 36. S. C. Das in JASB 1881. 198 & 211.

20. *The Mysterious Helper*

After a cursory mention of the early legendary kings of the Bon period, the Tibetan historians pass on to describe—usually with a great deal of enthusiasm—the miracle of miracles that eventually took place in the Land of Snow. It was the first appearance of certain Buddhist texts and objects of worship. At that time, literacy was unknown to Tibet and the Buddhist scriptures, being totally inaccessible, were nothing more than curiosities. Nor did the Tibetans then have even a faint idea of what these objects of worship actually were. The Tibetan historians are clearly aware of all these. But they do not bother. For them the event itself was of the most momentous significance. It was the first touch of the Holy Doctrine that Tibet had.[1] The darkness of Bon mysticism was going to be dispelled, it did not matter though that the Tibetans had to wait for several more generations for a real idea of the Holy Doctrine.

It happened, according to the usual account, during the reign of Lha-tho-tho-ri-gñan-btsan, the king mentioned either at the end of the list of the twentyseven early legendary kings[2] or immediately after it.[3] When this king, says Bu-ston,[4] "attained the age of 16 years and was abiding on the summit of the palace Yam-bu-lha-khaṅ, a casket fell from the skies, and when its lid was opened, the *Kāraṇḍa-vyūha-sūtra*, the *100 Precepts*

1. On the authority of Lassen, Schlagintweit 63 mentions a much earlier attempt to introduce Buddhism into Tibet : "The first attempts apparently led to very unsatisfactory results ; at least the monastery which is reported to have been erected in the year 137 B.C. on the slopes of the Kailāsa range seems to have been soon abandoned and to have fallen into ruins." But Waddell L 19n comments that the alleged erection on Mount Kailāsa in 137 B.C. of a Buddhist monastery could have "nothing to do with Tibet"; it might have belonged to Kashmir Buddhism. 2. Bu-ston ii 182.
3. S. C. Das in JASB 1881. 233. 4. Bu-ston ii. 182-3.

Concerning Worship and a golden Caitya were found within. The casket received the name of the 'Mysterious Helper' and was worshipped (by the king). The latter came to live 120 years and came to witness the dawn of the Highest Doctrine ; up to that time the kingdom had been ruled by the Bon. In a dream (which this king had) it was prophesied to him that on the 5th generation one would come to know the meaning of these (sacred texts which he had miraculously obtained)."

'Gos lo-tsā-ba[5] says, "In the reign of Lha-tho-tho-ri-gñan-btsan the *Cintāmaṇi-dhāraṇī* and the *sPaṅ-skoṅ-phyag-rgya-ma*[6] fell from Heaven, and were worshipped. Because of this, the life-span of the king and that of the kingdom increased. This became known as the Beginning of the Holy Doctrine."

Sum-pa's[7] account of the Mysterious Helper is substantially the same as given by Bu-ston. The *Chronicle of Ladakh*,[8] however, not only inflates the list of objects contained in it but moreover makes the account of their coming to Tibet much more spectacular : "He (Lha-tho-tho-ri) reigned for sixty-two years. At the time when he dwelt at the great palace of 'Um-bu-rdzans-mkhar, which had come into existence of itself without being built, a basket came down from heaven, as a premonition of the spread of Buddha's teaching in Tibet. Sliding down together by a ray of light, there came down to the king's palace the book *Za-ma-tog* (*Kāraṇḍa-vyūha-sūtra*) ; the *sPaṅ-skoṅ-phyag-rgya-pa* ; the essence (of religion) namely the six syllables (*om-maṇi-padme-hum*) ; a golden *mchod-rten* (*caitya*) a yard high ; a *tshindhamaṇi* (*cintāmaṇi*) *tsha-tsha* (a terra-cotta Buddha's image) ; and all the *mudrā* positions of the fingers. Not knowing whether these were Bon or Buddhist, they honoured them with beer and turquoise offerings. Blessing resulted from it, and (the king) attained to 120 years of age. Thus, during the life-time of this king the beginning of the Holy Religion took place."

According to the account quoted by Rockhill[9] also, the

5. BA i. 38. 6. The *100 Precepts* etc. 7. Sum-pa 167.
8. Francke AIT ii. 81. 9. Rockhill LB 210.

mysterious casket contained the six essential syllables, namely, *om-maṇi-padme-hum.* Much is written by the modern scholars about this *mantra* so favourite among the Tibetan Buddhists. Though Vallée-Poussin[10] is inclined to consider it to be quite old, Waddell[11] asserts that it was not invented till many hundred years—probably a thousand—after the time of Lha-tho-tho-ri. Petech[12] says that even the two Buddhist works, namely the *Za-ma-tog* (*Kāraṇḍa-vyūha-sūtra*) and *sPaṅ-skoṅ-phyag-rgya* (100 *Precepts* etc.) "belong to a much later period" and the Tibetan account of their antiquity is purely legendary. But it is difficult to be exact about their dates, particularly of the former, which occupies an extremely important place in Nepalese and Tibetan Buddhism and which, therefore, needs some discussion here.

The *Kāraṇḍa-vyūha* is a long Mahāyāna-sūtra, having for its full title *Avalokiteśvara-guṇa-kāraṇḍa-vyūha,* i.e. "the detailed description of the basket of the qualities of Avalokiteśvara."[13] Its main theme is the glorification of the Bodhisattva Avalokiteśvara. There are two versions of this work, an earlier one in prose and a later one in *śloka*-s. The existing Tibetan translation of it in the bKa'-'gyur (which bears the title *Ārya-kāraṇḍa-vyūha-nāma-mahāyāna-sūtra*)[14] is based upon the prose version. Winternitz thinks that it is possible that the metrical *Kāraṇḍa-vyūha* was in existence even prior to the fourth century A.D. The clear implication of this is that the prose version of the work, which went to Tibet, was even earlier. But Winternitz himself hesitates to assert this in view of Vallée-Poussin's[15] dating of its Tibetan translation as A.D. 616. But this dating itself is questionable. Though literacy was introduced into Tibet in the earlier half of the seventh century[16] and though, according to a number of Tibetan historians,[17] the *Kāraṇḍa-vyūha-sūtra* was translated shortly after that, the Tibetan translation of the

10. Vallée-Poussin in ERE ii. 259n. 11. Waddell L 19n. 12. Petech 33n. 13. Winternitz ii. 305ff. 14. bKa'-'gyur No. 784, Vol. 30, Peking edition. 15. Vallée-Poussin in ERE ii. 259n. 16. See Section 22. 17. Bu-ston ii. 184.

work as actually preserved in the bKa'-'gyur bears the following names as these of its translators : Jinamitra, Dānaśīla and Ye-śes-sde. They are definitely known to belong to the 9th century A.D.[18] Thus the actual date of the Tibetan translation of the *Kāraṇḍa-vyūha-sūtra* could be much later than that considered by Vallée-Poussin. But this proves nothing about the date of the text itself, just as the dates of the Tibetan translation of the other Mahāyāna-sūtra-s do not prove anything about the dates of the *sūtra*-s themselves. In short, the *Kāraṇḍa-vyūha* could have been one of the early works of Mahāyāna Buddhism and so the Tibetan account of its coming to Tibet at an early period is not at least *prima facie* absurd. Still the question remains : how actually it could have reached Tibet ?

Francke[19] says that, according to the *Bodhimor*, "a few years after the supposed descent of the Buddhist books several strangers arrived in Tibet to make known their importance". This gives us a hint of some sort of early missionary activity of the Buddhists, a hint further strengthened by a statement made by 'Gos lo-tsā-ba[20] on the authority of Nel-pa *paṇḍita* : "Nel-pa *paṇḍita* said, 'Because the Bon-pos adored Heaven, it was said that (these books) had fallen from Heaven'. Instead of this Bon-po tradition, it is said that (these) books had been brought (to Tibet) by the *paṇḍita* Buddhirakṣita (bLo-sems-'tsho) and the translator Li-the-se. Since the (Tibetan) king could not read, and did not understand the meaning (of the books) the *paṇḍita* and the translator returned. This (account) seems to me to be true".

There is some speculation among the modern scholars about these early missionaries. "In the year 371 A.D.", says Schlagintweit,[21] "there suddenly appeared five foreigners before the king Tho-tho-ri-gñan-btsan, who instructed him how he might use for the general welfare of Tibet four objects, which, in the year 331 A.D., had fallen from heaven". "It is not

18. See Section 26. 19. Francke AIT ii. 8ln. 20. BA i. 38.
21. Schlagintweit 63-4.

stated", adds he,[22] "whence these five men proceeded, but I believe them, for reasons which will hereafter become apparent, to have been Chinese Buddhist priests." The reason eventually offered[23] by the author is nothing but the story of the famous philosophical debate that took place in Tibet many centuries later between the Chinese Buddhist priest (*ho-shang*) and the Indian scholar Kamalaśīla. This hardly justifies the conjecture that the first Buddhist missionaries to Tibet came from China, particularly when 'Gos lo-tsā-ba mentions an obviously Indian name—Buddhirakṣita—and possibly the name of a Nepalese interpreter (Li-the-se)[24] as the earliest missionaries to Tibet. Rockhill's[25] conjecture concerning these Buddhist missionaries to Tibet seems to be based on sounder grounds. "It is remarkable", says he, "that the *Kāraṇḍa-vyūha-sūtra*, which does not appear to be specially venerated in China or in India, was one of the favourite books of the Nepalese, and an object of great veneration in their country. This is one of the reasons which has led me to suggest that Buddhism first came to Tibet from Nepal."

For our understanding of Tibetan history the more interesting question is concerning the great veneration shown by the Tibetan historians to Lha-tho-tho-ri. This is somewhat puzzling, for traditionally the fact seems to be that during his reign the Bon religion reached the zenith of its glory.[26] Still Lha-tho-tho-ri is considered to be an incarnation[27] of Kun-tu-bzaṅ-po or Samantabhadra, the first *dhyānī* Bodhisattva, good to all and everywhere at all times.[28] Only two other Tibetan kings receive such a great honour from the Tibetan historians. As Petech[29] says, "He appears in the chronicles as the first of

22. *Ib*. 64n. 23. *Ib*. 68. 24. *Li* in Tibetan probably means Nepal. See Section 22, Notes 35-6. 25. Rockhill LB 210. 26. S. C. Das in JASB 1881. 216. 27. Francke AIT ii. 81n, S. C. Das in JASB 1881. 216. 28. D-TED 25 ; J-TED 4. Interestingly, Kun-bzaṅ is a sage and teacher even in the Bon religion - D-TED 28 ; JASB 1881. 216n. 29. Petech 32.

the three incarnated kings. With this title the Tibetans honoured the greatest rulers of the dynasty ; they are : Lha-tho-tho-ri, incarnation of Samantabhadra, Sroṅ-btsan-sgam-po, incarnation of Avalokiteśvara, Khri-sroṅ-lde-btsan, incarnation of Mañjuśrī. No doubt the last two fully deserve the honour, ...for they were undoubtedly the two greatest kings of Tibet. But it is difficult to make out why for this high honour was selected just Lha-tho-tho-ri."

The Tibetan historians want us to believe that this was simply because during the reign of this king Tibet first received the Holy Doctrine. But Petech proposes to explain this in a different way altogether. Sroṅ-btsan-sgam-po's father gNam-ri-sroṅ-btsan was the first Tibetan ruler "who is known with certainty to have really existed."[30] The Tibetan historians, however, give us a long list of kings preceding him. This list, as we have seen, was drawn from mythology rather than history. After the list comes the name of Lha-tho-tho-ri, supposed to be the fifth ancestor of Sroṅ-btsan-sgam-po. In all probability, argues Petech, the names of these ancestors of Sroṅ-btsan-sgam-po beginning with Lha-tho-tho-ri "apply to something real."[31] "Tibetan literature began with the introduction of alphabet during the reign of Sroṅ-btsan-sgam-po ; at this time probably the first attempts were made at writing history, and it is impossible that the names of the immediate predecessors of the ruling king were no longer remembered."[32] Thus, continues Petech,[33] "at the time of the first compilation of the chronicles, the consciousness was not yet lost of Lha-tho-tho-ri being the most remote ancestor of Sroṅ-btsan-sgam-po, the memory of whose real existence still survived. Being thus the historical founder of the dynasty...he was from the earliest times an object of devotion. This position of his was subjected to a revision with the advent of Buddhism, and in the light of the new teachings he was given the rank of an incarnation, while formerly he was worshipped as a god or demi-god (*Lha*=god)."

Petech's assumption that Lha-tho-tho-ri could have been

30. *Ib*. 30. 31. *Ib*. 32. *Ib*. 33. *Ib*. 33.

the first real ancestor of Sroṅ-btsan-sgam-po remembered by the Tibetan historians need not be discarded, though, assuming this, the problem of determining his actual date remains a difficult one. According to S. C. Das[34] it was A.D. 441. According to Rockhill[35] he was born in A.D. 347. According to Schlagintweit[36] and Waddell[37] the Mysterious Helper came to Tibet in A.D. 331. It is perhaps no use trying to be precise. This much alone can be asserted that Lha-tho-tho-ri is mentioned as the fifth ancestor of Sroṅ-btsan-sgam-po, who died in A.D. 650.

34. S. C. Das in JASB 1881. 233.
35. Rockhill LB 209.
36. Schlagintweit 63.
37. Waddell L 19n.

21. *Sroṅ-btsan-sgam-po*

"In the beginning of the Doctrine", says 'Gos lo-tsā-ba,[1] "in the reign of Tho-tho-ri-gñan-btsan, though religious books had become available (in Tibet), there was no one to write, read or explain (their meaning)." From the point of view of the propagation of the Doctrine, the next important landmark in Tibetan history is the introduction of literacy into Tibet, as a result of which the Tibetans could have, for the first time, real access to the Buddhist scriptures. According to the usual Tibetan accounts, this took place during the reign of king Sroṅ-btsan-sgam-po and under his direct initiative. Because of this alone, the Tibetan historians have their justification in glorifying Sroṅ-btsan as an incarnation of Avalokiteśvara.[2] Sroṅ-btsan-sgam-po, however, was really one of the greatest kings of Tibet under whose leadership the Tibetans moved from barbarism to civilization.

His descent is usually given as follows :

Lha-tho-tho-ri-gñan-btsan
Khri-gñan-gzuṅs-btsan
'Bro-gñan-lde'u
sTag-ri-gñan-gzigs
gNam-ri-sroṅ-btsan
Sroṅ-btsan-sgam-po.

Though Francke[3] is sceptical about the historicity of all the kings before Sroṅ-btsan-sgam-po and Petech[4] is inclined to view his ancestors up to Tho-tho-ri as belonging to real history, there is at least no doubt about the historicity of gNam-ri-sroṅ-btsan, the actual founder of Tibetan monarchy.

1. BA i. 39. 2. Bu-ston ii. 185 ; Sum-pa 167. See also Waddell L 22 and Petech 32. Richardson *plate V* facing p. 86 gives a photograph of an image supposed to be of the king as actually worshipped in Tibet.
3. Francke AIT ii. 11. 4. Petech 33.

"According to Ma Tuan-lin", says Petech,[5] "the founder of the Tibetan kingdom and at the same time of the Tibetan nation was Lun-tsan-so-lung-tsan." In part this name corresponds "perfectly to btsan-sroṅ-btsan. The only Tibetan king before Sroṅ-btsan-sgam-po whose name ends in sron-btsan is gNam-ri-sroṅ-btsan. Thus Lun-tsan-so-lung-tsan is a transcription, either inexact or based on an original different from the normal one, of the name of Sroṅ-btsan-sgam-po's father."

According to the account compiled by Lévi,[6] sometime between A.D. 581-600 gNam-ri-sroṅ-btsan united the scattered hill-tribes of Tibet, formed a powerful kingdom, raised an army of 100,000 soldiers and led a victorious campaign to central India. Lévi even suggests that the era *san* current in Bengal and Assam is equivalent to the last part of the name of this Tibetan king and its epoch, namely 593-4, "commemorates this forgotten foreign invasion of Bengal."[7]

But what could have been the nature of the "administrative system" introduced by gNam-ri-sroṅ-btsan? Petech[8] answers that though we have no particulars about it, "it follows clearly from all we know about the history of Tibetan monarchy that it had no centralised character... gNam-ri-sroṅ-btsan himself was probably little more than the head of a tribal confederation. The former independent princes and their descendants maintained a great deal of their power and constituted that strong and war-like Tibetan nobility that fashioned so many generals and ministers to the state, but that, like the European nobility, was very turbulent and not seldom revolting against the royal authority." "The landlords constituted the real power in the state and in fact it follows from a careful study of the *T'ang-shu* that the Chinese mostly were concerned with them. The kings, with two or three exceptions, seem to have been left somewhat in the background as nominal rulers more or less respected."[9]

5. *Ib.* 35. 6. Lévi N ii. 147, 153-4. Summarised in HB i. 91.
7. Jayaswal in JBORS xxii. 172 proposes to reject this view of the origin of the *san* era. 8. Petech 36-7. 9. *Ib.* 37.

Sroṅ-btsan-sgam-po was undoubtedly one of these exceptions and so was possibly his father, under whom the political unification of Tibet made its first substantial progress. "The Chinese sources, always well-informed about the neighbouring peoples, explicitly affirm that up to the end of the sixth century Tibet was divided into a large number of petty states without any connection among themselves... During their six centuries of acquaintance with the Tibetans, they never became aware of the existence of a Tibetan kingdom, but were concerned with single tribes, more or less big and powerful, but always without any political organisation. The two historians of the T'ang are very definite on this point."[10]

Such a state of affairs came to an end when gNam-ri-sroṅ-btsan unified Tibet and established the first monarchy there. "The place from which this work of unification started is called by all the Tibetan sources by the name Yar-luṅ... There is no doubt that the Yar-luṅ of the historians refers to the fertile valley of the same name, watered by a tributary of the Brahmaputra, to the south-east of Lhasa."[11] Hence Petech[12] proposes that the ancestors of gNam-ri-sroṅ-btsan, beginning with Lha-tho-tho-ri, should better be called the chiefs of Yar-luṅ rather than the kings of Tibet. There was no "king" of Tibet before gNam-ri-sroṅ-btsan.

But the figure of Sroṅ-btsan-sgam-po in Tibetan history is much more imposing than that of his father. Under him the work of political unification of Tibet became fully consolidated. "Thirteen years of age", says Bu-ston,[13] "he (Sroṅ-btsan) ascended the throne and brought under his power all the petty chieftains of the borderland who offered him presents and sent their messages of submission." "During the life-time of this king", repeats the *Chronicle of Ladakh*,[14] "all the kingdoms of the frontier were united under his rule, and every one of the little kings sent presents and letters."

Bu-ston gives us the interesting information of how the king

10. *Ib*. 30-1. 11. *Ib*. 31. 12. *Ib*. 32. 13. Bu-ston ii. 183.
14. Francke AIT ii. 82.

received the name Sroṅ-btsan-sgam-po : "He was born in the year of the Fire-Cow and received the name of Khri-lde-sroṅ-btsan... At that time the Tibetan subjects were disregarding the royal power, (the king) introduced laws harmonising with the 10 virtues and converted the Tibetans to Buddhism. Owing to this he is known by the name of Sroṅ-btsan-sgam-po."[15] Petech shows that the original name of the king is preserved also in the *Padma-dkar-po* and is corroborated by the Chinese sources. "No Tibetan source other than Bu-ston and *Padma-dkar-po* has preserved the real name of the king. But this is not surprising at all, because it is a fact which occurs very often in the history of Tibetan monarchy that the real name of a king is nearly forgotten, being substituted in common use by a title or a nickname."[16]

Thus, in short, the original name of the king was Khri-lde-sroṅ-btsan. This Khri-lde-sroṅ-btsan must not be confused with another later king bearing the same name about whose identity, we shall see,[17] there is some confusion. But this original name of the king is practically forgotten in Tibetan history and his honorific name Sroṅ-btsan-sgam-po is firmly fixed.

He was the first to have introduced legal codes into Tibet. "The king", says 'Gos lo-tsā-ba,[18] "introduced a legal code and established punishments for murder, robbery and adultery." S. C. Das[19] gives a list of his 16 ethico-legal codes. The king brought from China silk-worms, mulberry trees, barley-beer, water-mills, paper, ink and calendar.[20] The technological innovations introduced by him are commemorated in a popular song of Ladakh :

Pots from clay ;
Mills turned by water ;
Weaving with looms
And many mechanical arts.[21]

15. Bu-ston ii 183-4. 16. Petech 48. 17. Section 26.
18. BA i. 40 ; cf Bu-ston ii. 184. 19. S. C. Das in JASB 1881. 219.
20. *Badhimor* quoted by Francke AIT ii. 84n. 21. Francke AIT ii. 83.

But the Tibetan historians are above all anxious to tell us what the king did for the spread of Buddhism in Tibet. According to them, he was inspired to work for Buddhism by his two wives,—a Nepalese princess and a Chinese princess,—about whom the Tibetan historians give us lengthy accounts.[22]

The Nepalese princess was the daughter of king Aṃśuvarman[23] and Sroṅ-btsan's marriage with her, which took place a few years before his marriage with the Chinese princess, was the result of successful negotiations carried on by the talented minister Thon-mi Sambhoṭa.[24] There are many romantic fables[25] in Tibet about the king's marriage with the Chinese princess and particularly about the role played by another—politically more powerful—minister called 'Gar-ston-btsan in effecting it. From the Chinese annals, however, it is clear that this marriage was not the result of any peaceful negotiation. In A.D. 634, according to the Chinese annals,[26] the Emperor of China exchanged presents with the Tibetan king and made a treaty of friendship. The Tibetans requested that a Chinese Imperial Princess may be sent as spouse for the king. But this was refused. As a result, the Tibetans invaded China with an army of 200,000 men and waged war for about eight years. Eventually, in A.D. 641 the Chinese Emperor was forced to bow to the Tibetan demand and princess Wen-ch'eng-kung-chu, daughter of T'ai-tsung, was sent to Tibet.

According to the Tibetan historians, both these princesses were devout Buddhists and it was because of their influence that Sroṅ-btsan-sgam-po became a convert to Buddhism. One of the Tibetan histories "puts in the mouth of Sroṅ-btsan-sgam-po, when he sues for the hand of his first wife, the Nepalese

22. Lévi N ii. 149 suggests that the king's marriage with these two princesses was designed to consolidate the political power of Tibet.

23. Bu-ston ii. 184 ; Das in JASB 1881. 220 gives the name as Yativarman, correcting it in D-TED 1161. For Aṃśuvarman, see Lévi N ii. 149 and Regmi 70ff, though the latter does not attach much importance to the Tibetan account of the marriage of Aṃśuvarman's daughter to Sroṅ-btsan-sgam-po - see Regmi 59.

24. Francke AIT ii. 82.

25. See S. C. Das in JASB 1881. 220.

26, Bushell in JRAS 1880. 443f ; BA i. 49.

princess, the following words : 'I, the King of barbarous Tibet, do not practise the ten virtues, but should you be pleased to bestow on me your daughter, and wish me to have the Law, I shall practise the ten virtues with a five-thousand-fold body..., though I have not the arts...if you so desire... I shall build five thousand temples."[27]

The Chinese historians tell us that the king developed a great admiration for Chinese culture as a result of his marriage with the Chinese princess : "From this time, he (Sroṅ-btsan-sgam-po, transcribed as Lung-tsan by the Chinese) praised the costume of the great empire, and the perfection of their manners, and was ashamed of the barbarism of his own people. ...As the princess disliked their custom of painting their faces red, Lung-tsan ordered his people to put a stop to the practice, and it was no longer done. He also discarded his felt and skins, put on brocade and silk, and gradually copied Chinese civilization. He also *sent the children of his chiefs and rich men to request admittance into the national schools to be taught the classics, and invited learned scholars from China to compose his official reports to the Emperor.*"[28] Though Rockhill[29] appears to take such an account seriously, no Tibetan historian recognises its credibility, particularly with regard to education. Sroṅ-btsan-sgam-po's zeal for introducing literacy into Tibet, according to the Tibetan historians, led him to send a team of chosen Tibetans headed by Thon-mi Sambhoṭa to India, from where literacy was brought to Tibet.[30] That the Tibetan version is nearer actual facts than the Chinese one is corroborated by the close resemblance of the Tibetan script and Tibetan grammar to Indian script and Indian grammar. At the same time, the Tibetan historians themselves are extremely eager to say how, under the influence of both the Nepalese and Chinese wives, Sroṅ-bstan-sgam-po started to work for Buddhism.

27. Waddell L 21.
28. Bushell in JRAS 1880. 445 ; emphasis added.
29. Rockhill NET 672.
30. See Section 22.

Because of his alleged work for Buddhism in Tibet, Sroṅ-btsan-sgam-po himself, as already said, is considered by the Tibetan historians as an incarnation of Avalokiteśvara and it is no wonder that, in the Tibetan tradition, his two foreign wives, who converted him to Buddhism, "were canonized as incarnations of Avalokita's consort, Tārā,...and the fact that they bore him no children (his issue proceeded from two or four Tibetan wives) is pointed to as evidence of their divine nature. The Chinese princess...was deified as the *white* Tārā...while the Nepalese princess...was apotheosised as the *green* Bhṛkuṭi Tārā."[31]

The Nepalese princess, we are told, brought with her the images of Akṣobhya-vajra, Maitreya and Tārā, while the Chinese princess brought with her an image of Śākyamuni as a young prince.[32] These were the images of Buddhist deities first brought to Tibet and the Tibetan historians attach great importance to these. The first Buddhist temples built in Tibet by Sroṅ-btsan-sgam-po were called the Ra-mo-che and Ra-sa, in which were enshrined the images of Akṣobhya-vajra and Śākyamuni respectively.[33] According to S. C. Das,[34] Ra-mo-che is the "name of the sanctuary built on a plain in the north quarter of Lhasa by the Chinese wife of king Sroṅ-btsan-sgam-po...and containing the image of Akṣobhya-buddha which was carried from Nepal under the orders of Sroṅ-btsan-sgam-po's Nepalese wife." Though Francke[35] comments, "I do not believe that anybody has seen traces of it," S. C. Das[36] claims to have seen it personally. Ra-sa is the old name of Lhasa or "God's place" and the temple built there is said to have been due to the initiative of the Nepalese princess to enshrine the image of Śākyamuni brought by the Chinese princess.[37] The sweet relation between the two princesses suggested by the above accounts is slightly damaged by Waddell's comment

31. Waddell L 22-3. 32. This image "is said to have been taken from Magadha by the Chinese about the first century B.C." : D-TED 1161.
33. Francke AIT ii.83 ; Waddell L 23n. 34. D-TED 1160-1 ; cf Bu-ston ii. 185. 35. Francke AIT ii. 83n. 36. S. C. Das JL 155.
37. D-TED 1161.

that the Nepalese princess had a fiery temper and was "the cause of frequent brawls on account of the precedence given to the Chinese princess."[38]

Though the construction of the Potala palace of Lhasa perhaps began during the reign of Sroṅ-btsan-sgam-po,[39] the account given by the Tibetan historians of the number of monasteries built by him is clearly exaggerated.[40] Even the personal piety of the king is sometimes questioned. As Waddell says, the glimpse we have of him from the Chinese sources "shows him actively engaged throughout his life in the very un-Buddhist pursuit of bloody wars with neighbouring states."[41] "But he was not the saintly person the grateful Lamas picture, for he is seen from reliable Chinese history to have been engaged all his life in bloody wars, and more at home in the battle-field than the temple. And he certainly did little in the way of Buddhist propaganda, beyond perhaps translating a few tracts into Tibetan, and building a few temples to shrine the images received by him in dower, and others which he constructed. He built no monasteries."[42] However, if the Tibetan historians exaggerate his personal piety, the possibility of the Chinese historians underestimating it cannot be entirely ruled out. Petech[43] proposes to take on the whole a common-sense view of the possible religious attitude of Sroṅ-btsan-sgam-po: "Although the Tibetans have made a *chos-rgyal* ('king of the Law') of Sroṅ-btsan-sgam-po, the introduction of Buddhism with which he is credited does not appear to make him deserve the name. He respected the religion of his two foreign wives and welcomed their images and other sacred objects with that mixed feeling of veneration and fear, with

38. Waddell L 23n. 39. Francke AIT ii. 83. According to the *Chronicle of Ladakh*, "palaces were built (by Sroṅ-btsan-sgam-po) on the dMar-po-ri and on the lCag-po-ri and these two mountains were connected with an iron-chain bridge." dMar-po-ri or the Red Hill is today better known as Po-ta-la of Lhasa, lCag-po-ri or the Iron Hill is situated in the close vicinity of the former and is still known by its old name.
40. Bu-ston ii. 184; cf Francke ii. 83. 41. Waddell L 21.
42. *Ib*. 23. 43. Petech 50.

which all sacred objects are accepted in Tibet, from whatever part they might be forthcoming, for fear of offending the gods (or demons) that dwell in them."

The date of Sroṅ-btsan-sgam-po is crucial for the early history of Tibet. But it is a much debated one and the available data for it are confusing. Before proceeding to discuss the date of the king, it may be useful to remember a few points of general interest about the mode of Tibetan dating.

"The well-known sexagenary system," says Petech,[44] "resulting from the combination of five elements (wood, fire, earth, iron, water) with the cycle of twelve animals has an origin not very ancient so far as Tibet is concerned. The cycle of the twelve animals, dating back to a remote past and familiar to several peoples of Central and Eastern Asia, was the only system used during the period of monarchy and even later on...Much later, at the time of the second introduction of Buddhism (11th century), the necessity of greater precision was felt by the Tibetan scholars and the sexagenary cycle was adopted, introduced (as it was) from India together with the Kālacakra Tantric system." Laufer[45] even considers Kālacakra to be "nothing but a designation of the sexagenary cycle," which was introduced into Tibet by Ñi-ma-'khor-gyi-jo-bo in A.D. 1027,[46] the first year of the first cycle of the sexagenary system. Thus, prior to A.D. 1027, the Tibetan dates were mentioned in terms of only one of the twelve animals, while from this year onwards the Tibetans learnt the advantage of prefixing the animal name with one of the five elements for purpose of dating —e. g., instead of mentioning a date simply as the Dog year, the Tibetans eventually adopted the method of specifying it as Wood-Dog or Fire-Dog etc. year.[47]

The advantage once realised, the Tibetan chroniclers started

44. *Ib.* 41. 45. Laufer in *T'oung-Pao* xiv. 589. 46. Laufer *Ib.* argues that the earlier view of Csoma de Koros that this happened in 1026 needs certainly to be corrected. 47. See also Roerich BA i. Intro. p. viii-ix.

re-stating or re-constructing the dates of the earlier events in the new way, i.e. by putting the name of an element before the name of the animal. But this created fresh problems for Tibetan chronology of the early period. While adopting the new method, the later chroniclers sometimes committed the error of putting the name of a wrong element before that of the right animal traditionally known to them. Petech,[48] therefore, rightly comments, "It is necessary to be very cautious in accepting the Tibetan dates as they are; the second component in them is usually reliable, but the first is always a later deduction, which may sometimes be exact, but very often is wrong. In fact, a great deal of the differences between the various dates of the same event as recorded in diverse sources consists only in the different name of the elements, the name of the animal remaining the same."

But how is one to exercise such a caution ? The modern European scholars are generally inclined to think that the most important way to do it is to seek corroborative evidence, as far as possible, in the official history of the T'ang dynasty of China founded in A.D. 618.[49] It is available for us in two redactions,[50] both containing special chapters on Tibet,[51] and these, so far as they provide us with any date about the earlier history of Tibet, are usually considered extremely trustworthy.[52] Various reasons are given for this. First, the Chinese historians were keenly chronology-conscious. Secondly, they had to be well-informed about the political history of Tibet because of prolonged warfare between China and Tibet. Thirdly, they were themselves nearer the events of the

48 Petech 42. 49. Bushell in JRAS 1880. 436. 50. The first is called *Kiu T'ang-shu* or the old history of the T'ang compiled in the first half of the 10th century A.D. and the second is called *Sin T'ang-shu* or simply *T'ang-shu*. See also Rockhill in JRAS 1891. 1-291 for Tibetan history from Chinese sources. 51. Petech 88. 52. Petech 39-40 : "The two *T'ang-shu* give us the most important dates of the history of Tibet from 634 to 879 ; without them, Tibetan chronology would have remained a matter of pure guess, specially on account of the discrepancies in the native sources and the uncertainty of the Tibetan sexagenary cycle."

early history of Tibet than the best of the Tibetan historians: the two T'ang annals were compiled in the 10th-11th centuries whereas "the golden epoch of Tibetan historiography" belongs to the 14th-15th centuries.[53]

With these preliminary remarks, we may proceed to consider the complicated question of the date of Sroṅ-btsan-sgam-po.

According to a chronicle written in 1662 by the Mongol prince Sanang-Setsen,[54] Sroṅ-btsan-sgam-po died in the Earth-Dog year.[55] This corresponds to either A.D. 638 or 698. Schmidt, the translator of the Mongolian chronicle, accepts the latter as the actual date of the king's death—a view endorsed by Schlagintweit[56] and others. But, as Petech shows, this dating is really absurd. Though the king died in a Dog year, the Mongol chronicler wrongly put the element Earth before it. There is no doubt that the king actually died in an Iron-Dog year, which in this case could be only A.D. 650. As Petech asserts, "the year of death 650 is fixed beyond any shadow of doubt by the concurring authority of the two *T'ang-shu*, of the *Deb-ther-sṅon-po* (of 'Gos lo-tsā-ba) and of the *Chronicle of the Fifth Dalai Lama*."[57] Roerich[58] fully agrees with this view.

But the Chinese chronicles do not help us in determining the date of the king's birth, about which the leading Tibetan authorities differ widely. Bu-ston[59] mentions it as a Fire-Ox year, which, as preceding A.D. 650, is either A.D. 557 or A.D. 617. 'Gos lo-tsā-ba[60] gives the date as an Earth-Ox year, which, in this case, is either A.D. 569 or 629. Thus, there is agreement on the Ox year, though either Bu-ston's addition of the element Fire to it is wrong or so is the addition of the element Earth to it by 'Gos lo-tsā-ba. Roerich[61] argues in defence of Bu-ston's dating and says that the king was born

53. Petech 88. 54. *Ib.* 40. 55. *Ib.* 41. 56. Schlagintweit 65. S.C. Das says that Sroṅ-btsan was a contemporary of Śilāditya, Muhemmed and Hiuen Tsang : D-TED 1297. This is roughly true. 57. Petech 43. 58. BA i. Intro, p. ix f. 59. Bu-ston ii. 183. 60. BA i. Intro. p. ix f. 61. *Ib.*

in A.D. 617. Petech[62] argues in defence of 'Gos lo-tsā-ba and asserts that the king was born in A.D. 569.

Let us first review the case as argued by Roerich. In view of the evidence of the Chinese annals, he finds it impossible to deny that the king actually died in A.D. 650. Therefore, the main difficulty he faces in accepting A.D. 617 as the date of Sroṅ-btsan's birth is created by the Tibetan tradition according to which the king died at the age of 82. Both Bu-ston[63] and 'Gos lo-tsā-ba [64] accept this tradition. Roerich is constrained to argue that the tradition itself is baseless. For this purpose, he takes upon himself a two-fold responsibility. He tries, on the one hand, to prove that the real source of this tradition is to be traced to a mistaken understanding by the Tibetan scholars of an Indian text called *Mañjuśrī-mūla-tantra*. On the other hand, he tries to prove that as a matter of fact the king died early, namely at the age of 33.

What, asks Roerich, could be the basis of the assertion of both Bu-ston and 'Gos lo-tsā-ba that the king died at the age of 82 ? It is, he[65] answers, a "prophecy" contained in the *Mañjuśrī-mūla-tantra*, which 'Gos lo-tsā-ba quotes in so many words and which is also fully known to Bu-ston. But both 'Gos lo-tsā-ba and Bu-ston thoroughly misunderstand the "prophecy". From the Sanskrit original of the text now available it is evident that the "prophecy" refers neither to Tibet nor to the Tibetan king Sroṅ-btsan-sgam-po. It refers instead to Nepal and to a king called Mānavendra. Yet 'Gos lo-tsā-ba thinks that the "prophecy" refers to Sroṅ-btsan-sgam-po and since, according to the "prophecy" the king in question ruled for 80 years, 'Gos lo-tsā-ba is misled to believe that Sroṅ-btsan-sgam-po lived up to the age of 82.

That 'Gos lo-tsā-ba misunderstands the "prophecy" need not be doubted. Roerich shows this quite clearly. But Roerich's further contention, namely that this mistaken understanding of the "prophecy" is the real source of the assertion

62. Petech 44. 63. Bu-ston ii. 185. 64. BA i. 46.
65. BA i. Intro. p. x ff.

of both Bu-ston and 'Gos lo-tsā-ba that the king died at the age of 82, can hardly be substantiated. 'Gos lo-tsā-ba's own writing[66] gives rather the impression that he is already aware of the tradition that the king died at the age of 82 and, since the plain meaning of the "prophecy" does not agree with this, 'Gos lo-tsā-ba tries his best to twist the meaning of the "prophecy" to make it agree with the tradition that came down to him independently of the "prophecy". Thus, the "prophecy" as 'Gos lo-tsā-ba understands it, plainly means, "He will *rule for 80 years*." In order to make it agree with the Tibetan tradition, 'Gos lo-tsā-ba interprets it as meaning : "*lived for 82 years*." "(Because)", adds 'Gos lo-tsā-ba, "during this period Guṅ-sroṅ-guṅ-btsan (i.e. Sroṅ-btsan's son, who died before the father) also ruled for a short time." If 'Gos lo-tsā-ba is basically influenced by the "prophecy" itself, as Roerich argues, why should he at all try to twist the "*80 years*" of the "prophecy" to mean "*82 years*" and interpret the word "*ruled*" to mean "*lived*" ?

Roerich's other argument, namely that the king actually died rather early in age, leads him to the unfortunate position of emphasising comparatively inferior evidences at the cost of superior ones. The only Tibetan source he cites in favour of such a view is of doubtful authenticity : "According to the *rGyal-rabs-bon-gyi-'byuṅ-gnas*, 'The king was short-lived and is said to have died at the age of thirty-six'."[67] The text mentioned is the Bon chronicle and its evidence cannot outweigh the unanimous assertion[68] of *rGyal-rabs-gsal-ba'i-me-loṅ*, *Padma-dkar-po* and the two famous chronicles by Bu-ston and 'Gos lo-tsā-ba that the king died at the age of 82.

Further, Roerich's idea that the king died at the age of thirtythree leads him to overlook many other important considerations.

First, Sroṅ-btsan-sgam-po's son died before him, as a result of which he was succeeded by his grandson. It is impossible

66. *Ib.* i. 46. 67. *Ib.* i. Intro. p. xii. 68. See Petech 44. Cf. also Sum-pa 150 : the king died at the age of 82.

to ignore this succession. In addition to 'Gos lo-tsā-ba,[69] the *rGyal-rabs-gsal-ba'i-me-loṅ*[70] and *Chronicle of the Fifth Dalai Lama*,[71] the Chinese chronicle *T'ang-shu*[72] is quite categorical about it. If Sroṅ-btsan was succeeded by his grandson, he could not have died at the age of thirty-three.[73]

Secondly, according to the *rGyal-rabs-gsal-ba'i-me-loṅ* the king married the Nepalese princess at the age of sixty-six and according to the *T'ang-shu* he married the Chinese princess at the age of 72.[74] These assertions appear to be compatible with the fact that these foreign wives bore him no child but these are absolutely incompatible with the theory that the king died at the age of 33.

Thirdly, 'Gos lo-tsā-ba correlates the following dates of the Chinese and Tibetan history : "T'ang Kao-tsung occupied the throne in the Earth-Male-Tiger year (A. D. 618), which is the fiftieth year of king Sroṅ-btsan-sgam-po. Having added the 49 years which preceded this year, one gets 271 years which have passed since the birth of Sroṅ-btsan till the year Earth-Female-Sheep (A.D. 839)."[75]

This evidence, says Petech, is decisive. The Earth-Female-Sheep year of the passage quoted refers to the year of the persecution of the Doctrine by gLaṅ Dar-ma, who ruled, according to the *T'ang-shu*, from 839-842.[76] Therefore, argues Petech, "The passage contains two known chronological elemets: 1) The Earth-Tiger year 618 in which Kao-tsu founded the T'ang dynasty ; the fiftieth year preceding 618 is 569. 2) The Earth-Sheep year, which, falling in the reign of gLaṅ Dar-ma, must be 839 ; 271st year preceding 839 is 569. Thus the date of the king's birth is well ascertained by this double element of proof."[77]

This date of the king's birth, namely A. D. 569, has the

69. BA i. 49. 70. See Petech 54. 71. *Ib.* 72. Bushell in JRAS 1880. 446. 73. Incidentally, according to 'Gos lo-tsā-ba, this grandson succeeded him at the age of 13 : See BA i. 49. 74. Petech 53. 75. BA i. 53. 76. BA i. Intro. p. xix. 77. Petech 43-4.

advantage of reconciling the Chinese date of the king's death with the Tibetan tradition that he lived up to the age of 82: if the king was born in 569 then, according to the Tibetan way of reckoning years, he must have been 82 in 650. Further, the succession of Sroṅ-btsan-sgam-po by his grandson is easily explained by this dating.

Though satisfactory in many respects, the acceptance of this date of Sroṅ-btsan-sgam-po (A. D. 569-650), does not really solve certain fundamental problems concerning Tibetan chronology. The problems are best illustrated by the writings of 'Gos lo-tsā-ba, who, of all the Tibetan historians, shows the greatest interest as well as competence in matters of dating. The method he frequently follows for establishing a firm chronology for Tibetan history is to calculate the various dates backwards and forwards linking them to certain well-known events in Tibetan history. Peculiarly enough, when he depends mainly on the Chinese chronology for determining the dates of the earlier period, we have from him one version of these. But when he calculates back from certain other events that took place after A. D. 1027 (i.e. the date of the introduction of the Kālacakra system) he appears to give us a different version of the same dates, or, more specifically, advances these by a complete cycle of 60 years (*rab-byuṅ*). We may illustrate this with a passage from 'Gos lo-tsā-ba where he relates the date of Sroṅ-btsan-sgam-po with a number of other important events of Tibetan history, both of the early and later periods. For the purpose of following the complicated calculations contained in this passage, we add our analytical comments within square brackets. Says 'Gos lo-tsā-ba :[78]

"In general, in the year Iron-Female-Ox, 252 years having passed since the birth of Sroṅ-btsan-sgam-po, king Ral-pa-can concluded the treaty with China. In the next Water-Male-Tiger year, the Pillar of Lhasa was erected.

78. BA i. 71-2. The passage contains references to certain other events of Tibetan history. Of these, events relating to Ral-pa-can are discussed in Section 26 and those relating to gLaṅ Dar-ma in Section 27.

[a) The Iron-Female-Ox year of two successive cycles of sixty years are A.D. 821 and 881. Since the date of Ral-pa-can's reign was 817-839 according to the Chinese annals and 814-836 according to 'Gos lo-tsā-ba himself, the Iron-Female-Ox year can here be taken only as A.D. 821.

b) Deducting 252 years from this, we get A.D. 569 as the year of Sroṅ-btsan's birth.

c) The "next Water-Male-Tiger year" is to be taken here to mean "the next year which was a Water-Male-Tiger year" in order to concur with the usually accepted date of the famous Lhasa Pillar as A.D. 822, a Water-Male-Tiger year.

d) Thus, the chronology so far can be summed up as follows :

Sroṅ-btsan, born A.D. 569
Ral-pa-can's peace-treaty with China, A.D. 821
Lhasa Pillar, A.D. 822.]

'In the fifteenth year after this Water-Tiger-year, in the Fire-Male-Dragon year, king Ral-pa-can died.

[Assuming this Water-Tiger year to be A. D. 822, the fifteenth year after this is A.D. 836, which is a Fire-Male-Dragon year. This agrees with 'Gos lo-tsā-ba's date of Ral-pa-can's death as A.D. 836.]

"From that year to the year Iron-Female-Hen, Dar-ma ruled. The Doctrine of Ordination disappeared. This Fire-Male-Ox year (? Fire-Female-Ox year,—an Ox year in Tibetan calendar is always Female) is the 77th year since the year Iron-Hen, when the Doctrine disappeared.

[The Iron-Hen year is to be taken here as A.D. 841 in order to concur with both the Chinese dating of gLaṅ Dar-ma's rule (A.D. 839-842) and 'Gos lo-tsā-ba's dating of it (836-841). The 77th year after this Iron-Hen year (841) is A.D. 917, which is a Fire-Ox year.]

"Sixty-four years have passed between the next Earth-Male-Tiger and the Iron-Serpent year which precedes Atīśa's coming to Tibet in the year Water-Male-Horse.

[a) The Water-Male-Horse year of Atīśa's coming to Tibet can be taken only as A.D. 1042, for it is absurd to imagine it to be A.D. 982, i.e. the Water-Horse year of the previous *rab-byuṅ*.

b) The Iron-Serpent year preceding it can only be taken as A.D. 1041.

c) Therefore, though according to the Tibetan calendar a Fire-Ox year is followed by an Earth-Tiger year, "the next Earth-Male-Tiger year" of the present passage can only mean "the Earth-Tiger year of the next cycle (*rab-byuṅ*)", i.e. as A.D. 978 and not as A.D. 918, (i.e. not the Earth-Tiger year immediately following the Fire-Ox year or A.D. 917 of the previous sentence). Otherwise the calculations of the present sentence connecting Atīśa's coming to Tibet with the Earth-Tiger year cannot be accepted: according to the Tibetan mode of calculation, 64 years can pass between the Earth-Tiger year or A.D. 978 and the Iron-Serpent year, which in this case can be only A.D. 1041. Thus, to concur with the chronology of the previous sentences, "the next Earth-Male-Tiger year" of the present sentence can only be taken to mean "the Earth-Tiger year of the next *rab-byuṅ*." But we have here a hint of the difficulties 'Gos lo-tsā-ba is getting involved in—difficulties that become overt in his statement that follows.]

"...Thus from the birth of Sroṅ-btsan-sgam-po 413 years have passed. The year Water-Male-Horse of the coming of Atīśa to Tibet, is the 141st year since the disappearance of the Doctrine. At that time Lord Mar-pa was in his thirty-first year."

[This introduces us to the most serious difficulty of Tibetan chronology. 'Gos lo-tsā-ba connects here the date of Atīśa's coming to Tibet with two other crucial dates of Tibetan history of the earlier period and another important date of Tibetan history of the later period. In the previous case, however, he is clearly advancing both the dates by 60 years, i.e. by a complete cycle or *rab-byuṅ*, though in the latter case he is not constrained to do it :

a) Assuming 1042 to be the Water-Horse year of Atīśa's coming to Tibet and assuming 413 years to have passed between this and the birth of Sroṅ-btsan-sgam-po, the date of the latter becomes A.D. 629 instead of A.D. 569, as previously assumed.

b) Similarly, assuming A.D. 1042 as the Water-Horse year of Atīśa's coming to Tibet, and assuming it to be the 141st year of the destruction of the Doctrine, the date of the latter becomes A.D. 901 and not A.D. 841, as previously assumed.

c) Both A.D. 569 and 629 are Earth-Ox years while both A.D. 841 and 901 are Iron-Hen years ; i.e. in both cases 'Gos lo-tsā-ba advances the dates by an entire *rab-byuṅ*.

d) However, to connect the date of Atīśa's coming to Tibet with the date of Mar-pa's birth (another important event of later Tibetan history), he is not constrained to do it. According to him Mar-pa was born in a Water-Male-Mouse year, i.e. A.D. 1012.[79] Thus Mar-pa was in his 31st year in A.D. 1042.]

To sum up : 'Gos lo-tsā-ba depends in the above passage on two different traditions for dating two cardinal events of early Tibetan history. According to one tradition, Sroṅ-btsan was born in A.D. 569, while according to the other, in A.D. 629. Similarly, according to the two traditions, the persecution of the Doctrine took place either in A.D. 841 or 901. A *simple explanation* of all these is that 'Gos lo-tsā-ba somehow or other makes a mistake in his calculations. But even assuming this, the exact cause of his "mistake" needs to be determined and that can be done only on the basis of a more intense research in Tibetan chronology. But more of this in connection with the date of the persecution of Buddhism by gLaṅ Dar-ma.

79. BA i. 123.

22. Thon-mi Sambhota

The Tibetans believe that literacy was introduced into their country during the reign of Sroṅ-btsan-sgam-po and the person to whose genius the first script and the first grammar of Tibet owe their origin was Sroṅ-btsan's minister Thon-mi Sambhoṭa. But the modern scholars often show a tendency of treating this tradition rather lightly.

"The Tibetan script itself," says S. Dutt,[1] "was fashioned by Dīpaṃkara out of the old Indian script." It is indeed a wonder to come across such an absurdity in a book sponsored by one of our responsible Ministries. The fact, on the contrary, is that by the time Dīpaṃkara reached Tibet, the Tibetans already possessed an extensive body of Indian literature in Tibetan translation and, though Dīpaṃkara's own activities greatly enriched the cultural heritage of Tibet,[2] these had nothing to do with the "fashioning" of the Tibetan script, the history of which is quite different.

If Dutt tends to make the history of Tibetan script younger by several centuries, Francke's tendency is to make it appear much older than it actually is. He suggests that the Tibetan script "was invented not many centuries before Sroṅ-btsan-sgam-po, possibly one or two centuries before him."[3] This implies that already in the fifth or sixth century A.D. the Tibetans knew the art of reading and writing, an assumption for which there is no evidence either in or outside the Tibetan tradition. Equally unfounded is Diringer's[4] statement that the

1. S. Dutt in *2500 Years* 192. 2. The Tibetan historians would fully endorse 'Brom-ston-pa's eulogy to Dīpaṃkara : "I offer prayer to thy feet, who, by translating the *śāstra*-s, by correcting the previous translations, by commenting on the *śāstra*-s and by composing *śātra*-s himself, led the disciples along the correct path and helped the Doctrine to flourish" - *śloka* 12. See Section 2, Appendix A. 3. Francke in JASB 1910. 98.
4. Diringer 453. Emphasis added.

"Tibetan character is however *not an invention but a revision of an older script already in use in Tibet at an earlier period.*" The Chinese historians, evidently better informed about their neighbours, tell us that in the earlier period,—i.e. before Sroṅ-btsan-sgam-po,—"They (Tibetans) have no written characters. Notched pieces of wood and knotted strings are used in convents."[5] From the paleographic point of view also there is evidence neither of any older script already prevalent in Tibet nor of any radical revision[6] of it taking place at any time.

The "oldest monument extant in Tibetan language"[7] is the inscription of the Lhasa Pillar recording the treaty between China and Tibet in A. D. 821-22.[8] Waddell[9] is the first European Tibetologist who studied it carefully and, though his dating of the inscription itself is now usually questioned,[10] his general observation on the light thrown by the inscription on the antiquity of the Tibetan script remains worth quoting. "In the light shed by the edict on many subjects," says he,[11] "illumination is also thrown on a question which has recently been raised as to whether the accepted date of the introduction of writing into Tibet should not be put back several hundreds of years at least. This suggestion is based solely on the orthographical ground...We have seen, however, from the positive evidence of the edict that this may be easily explained. And, to my mind, there is in the...semi-classic inscriptlon of the edict, nothing incompatible with our accepting 640-7 A. D. as approximately the date for the introduction of writing into Tibet."

5. Bushell in JRAS 1880. 440. Cf. Waddell in JRAS 1909. 946 : "Chinese sources . . . testify to the fact that until Sroṅ-btsan-sgam-po's reign Tibet was without a written language." 6. Richardson 6 : "The form of letters and orthography are virtually unchanged since their introduction. The oldest surviving inscriptions . . . can be read easily by present-day Tibetans." 7. Rockhill in JRAS 1891. 5. 8. Richardson 244-5. 9. Waddell in JRAS 1909. 923ff. 10. Waddell thinks that the inscription records the treaty of A.D. 783, but the usually accepted view today is that it records the treaty of A D. 821-2. See Petech 67.
11. Waddell *op. cit.* 945.

To this Waddell adds the argument that the "forms of the alphabetical letters themselves declare their origin from the developing Indian Devanāgarī characters at the stage to which they had attained in mid-India in the seventh century A.D., and, it would appear, *not any earlier*, as a reference to the fine photographic illustrations of Indian inscriptions of that period in Mr. Fleet's *Corpus Inscriptionum Indicarum*, III, will show. These help to make it clear that the so-called 'Tibetan' letters bear a strong family resemblance to those of the somewhat florid style which Mr. Fleet has called 'the Kuṭila variety of the Magadha alphabet of the seventh century A.D.' Many of the letters are identical in shape...so close is the general resemblance that the Tibetans can, as I have personally ascertained, read a considerable portion of these early Kuṭila inscriptions from Magadha, such as the Aphsaḍ inscription of Ādityasena of Magadha (Pl. xxviii of Mr. Fleet's *Corp. Ins. Ind.*)."[12]

Fleet's proposal to call the acute-angled alphabet "the Kuṭila variety of the Magadha alphabet of the 7th century" is not accepted by other scholars. "I feel disinclined", comments Bühler,[13] "to adopt the term Kuṭila, which was first used by Prinsep, and since has been employed by many other writers, because it is based on an erroneous rendering of the expression *kuṭila akṣara* in the Deval Praśasti." Bühler himself suggests that it is "advisible to class the characters of the whole group as those of the 'acute-angled alphabet'."[14] On the evidence of Al Birūnī, however, he adds[15] that possibly its Indian name was Siddhamātṛkā (*-lipi*), a name which is adopted by the later authorities on the subject. The Tibetan historians themselves,[16] however, tell us that of their two forms of script the one called dBu-can (i.e. those furnished with heads or *mātrā*) was derived from the Indian script called Lantsha (or Lan-dsa) and the other called dBu-med (i.e. those without heads or *mātrā*) was fashioned in the likeness of War-tu-la or Vartula. Of these, the former is nothing but an adaptation of the Indian Siddhamātṛkā while the latter was modelled[17] on

12. *Ib.* 946-7. 13. Bühler 69. 14. *Ib.* 68. 15. *Ib.* 69.
16. Sum-pa 167. 17. Perhaps adopted by the Tibetans at a later period.

the roundish script used in Bengal etc. for purposes of commercial and other records.

"The modern Tibetan alphabet", says D. C. Sircar,[18] "is practically the same as the North Indian Siddhamātṛkā script introduced in that country in the seventh century. To indicate some peculiar Tibetan sounds, diacritical marks were added or the letters were turned from right to left. The fact that modification of the alphabet has been negligible in Tibet is probably the result of the practice of printing from wooden blocks prevalent in that country since the medieval age. In China and Japan, Buddhist Dhāraṇīs in Sanskrit are written in the same Siddhamātṛkā alphabet even now, and its stationary character throughout the centuries may be ascribed to the religious importance attached to it. The Rañjā or Rañjanā alphabet used by the Buddhists of Tibet and Nepal was a derivative of Siddhamātṛkā... The Rañjanā or Rañjā (Lan-ja in Tibetan) script is a somewhat ornamental alphabet developed out of Siddhamātṛkā and its characters exhibit the influence of both Nāgarī and Gauḍī. Besides Rañjā, two regional varieties of the Gauḍī alphabet in Nepal are known as Vartula or Bhuñji-mol and Nepālī, Newārī or Pācu-mol. The characters of the Vartula and Nepālī alphabets are similar, the main point of difference between the two being the hook-like sign used in the place of the top *mātrā* of the letters in the former. The name *Vartula* meaning 'round' is based on the roundish appearance of the characters owing to the said top curve. The same hook-sign was also a characteristic of the Gauḍī alphabet as prevalent in Orissa and is often noticed in the epigraphic and manuscript records of Bengal, Assam and Bihar."

It seems, therefore, that there is little to justify the conjecture that the Tibetan script, instead of being adopted from an Indian script, was but a revision of an older script already current in Tibet. In other words, there is nothing definite on

18. D. C. Sircar, *Indian Paleography* (in press). Quoted by kind permission of the author.

the strength of which we can discard the Tibetan tradition about the introduction of literacy into Tibet. At the same time, it follows from what we have considered to be the characteristic peculiarity of Tibetan historiography, that the version of the event we have from the Tibetan historians themselves is inevitably influenced by their overriding anxiety to discuss everything in the perspective of the propagation of the Doctrine. Thus they are eager to tell us that the urge to translate the Buddhist scriptures into their own language led the Tibetans to devise a suitable script for themselves and that the greatest benefit they derived from it was the ability to put in their own language the Holy or Buddhist teachings.

With these preliminary remarks, we may quote some typical statements of the Tibetan historians concerning the history of Tibetan literacy.

At the time of Sroṅ-btsan-sgam-po, says Bu-ston,[19] "no writing existed in Tibet, the son of Anu of the Thon-mi tribe was sent with 16 companions (to India) in order to study the art of writing. After having studied with the *paṇḍita* Deva-vidyā-siṃha (Lha'i-rig-pa-seṅ-ge), they shaped, in conformity with the Tibetan language, (the alphabet) consisting of 30 consonants and 4 vowels. The form (of these letters) was given a resemblance with the Kashmirian characters. After (this alphabet) had been definitely formed at the Ma-ru temple of Lhasa, (Thon-mi) composed 8 works on writing and grammar, and the king studied them 4 years abiding in seclusion. The *Kāraṇḍa-vyūha-sūtra*, the *100 Precepts*, the *Ratna-megha-sūtra* and others were then translated (into Tibetan)."

"In the reign of Sroṅ-btsan-sgam-po," says 'Gos lo-tsā-ba,[20] "Thon-mi Sambhoṭa was sent to India. He thoroughly studied the alphabet and the (Sanskrit) language with the *ācārya* Devavitsiṃha (Lha'i-rig-pa-seṅ-ge). On his return to

19. Bu-ston ii. 183-4. It needs to be noted, however, that the translations of the texts mentioned in this connection, as actually preserved in the bKa'-'gyur and bsTan-'gyur, belong to a later period. But the possibility of earlier Tibetan translations, eventually replaced, need not be rejected - See Bu-ston ii. 196-7. 20. BA i. 39-40.

Tibet, he created the 30 letters [i.e. consonants] of the Tibetan alphabet from the 50 letters of the Indian (alphabet). He selected the signs for *a, i, e, o, u* from the 16 vowel sounds[21] of the (Indian alphabet), and omitted the rest. He added the sound *a* to the consonants [i.e. he shifted the vowel *a* to the Tibetan consonant group], but omitted the *ṭ*-class among the consonants. On finding that the fourth sounds of the four remaining classes [i.e. *gha, jha, dha* and *bha*], and the letter *ṣ* were unnecessary (in Tibetan), he omitted them. The sounds *tsa, tsha* and *dza* are pronounced as *ca, cha* and *ja* by some East Indians. He kept them. He also added the sounds of *sha, za* and (')[22] which he thought necessary in Tibetan, though absent in the Indian alphabet...After the completion of the work, the king pretended to study the alphabet for a long time (the king being an incarnation of the All-knowing Avalokiteśvara pretended to study the alphabet). Thon-mi translated the *Ratna-megha-sūtra.* Further the king, in his capacity of Protector of the Doctrine, preached many religious texts, such as the *sPyan-ras-gzigs-yi-ge-drug-ma*[23], the *Ārya-yamantaka,* the *Dharma-pāla-nātha,* the *Devī* and others."

"At the time," says Sum-pa,[24] "as Tibet itself had no script, Sambhoṭa, the son of Anu of Thon-mi, blessed by Mañjughoṣa, was sent to India with 16 attendants to learn the script. After learning the script from the *brāhmaṇa* Li-byin and grammar from *paṇḍita* Lha'i-rig-pa-seṅ-ge, he returned to Tibet and the king also practised (the art of writing). In the palace of Ma-ru at Lhasa was framed by Thon-mi the Tibetan script dBu-can, furnished with heads, (*mātrā*) in the likeness of Lan-tsa and the script of Kashmir, and also (the script called) dBu-med, in the likeness of War-tu-la." Adds S. C. Das[25] on the basis of Sum-pa, "According to the legendary will of king Sroṅ-btsan-sgam-po called the

21. The Sanskrit *ṃ* and *ḥ*, considered by the Indian grammarians as *ayoga-vāha-varṇa*-s, are taken by the Tibetans as Indian vowels. Hence is their version of 16 Indian vowels.
22. i.e. the Tibetan letter
23. bsTan-'gyur rG. lxxi. 27.
24. Sum-pa 167. Free translation.
25. *Ib. Contents* p. ix.

bKa'-chems-ka-khol-ma,[26] Thon-mi translated the works called the *sPan-skon*[27] (*sPan-skon-phyag-rgya'i*), the *Za-ma-tog* (the *Kāraṇḍa-vyūha-sūtra*), the *dKon-mchog-sprin* (the *Ratna-megha-sūtra*) and several other Buddhist scriptures with the help of *ācārya* Kusara, *brāhmaṇa* Śaṃkara, the Nepalese *ācārya* Śīla-mañju and the Chinese *ho-shang*, the Senior Mahāyāna, and others."

The *Chronicle of Ladakh*[28] gives us the following account of the introduction of literacy into Tibet : "Although this king issued innumerable documents signed with his seal, there were no characters in Tibet to send replies to the letters from (various) quarters. And, as (the books of) the famous sanctuary of his ancestor Tho-tho-ri-sñen-bsal remained a mystery, (since they were written) in Indian characters, he thought, 'We must translate them so as to be in Tibetan writing.' Therefore he sent Thon-mi, the son of Anu, with a *'bre* (a measure) of gold, and sixteen fellow-students to Kashmir to learn the characters. They learnt the characters from the *brāhmaṇa* Li-byin; *paṇḍita* Seṅ-ge-sgra (Siṃhanāda) taught them (the language). Bringing them into agreement with the Tibetan language, they made 24 *gsal-byed* (consonants) and 6 *riṅs*, (altogether) thirty (characters).[29] Besides, they made them to agree in form with the Nāgara characters of Kashmir. Then, when Thon-mi arrived in Tibet, he met with the king, who was in the garden of his wife 'U-ru. The king said : 'Have you learnt the letters and the language ? Then you may offer praise to sPyan-ras-gzigs (Avalokita) !' Thereupon Thon-mi wrote down the *śo-lo-ka* (*śloka*) :—

26. *Ka-khol-ma* is the "name of a historical pillar in the grand temple of Buddha at Lhasa. inside of which the earliest known manuscript of Tibet, called *bKa'-chems-ka-khol-ma*, and said to be the will of king Sroṅ-btsan-sgam-po, was alleged to have been found in the middle of the 11th century A.D." : D-TED 6. According to the Tibetan tradition, it was discovered by Dīpaṃkar-See BA ii. 984; cf. 'Brom's *stotra*, śloka 20, Sec 2, Appendix A.

27. *100 Precepts*, etc.

28. Francke AIT ii. 82-3.

29. As a matter of fact, however, the Tibetans have 30 consonants and 4 vowels, altogether 34 characters. This by itself shows that the account of the *Chronicle of Ladakh* is comparatively undependable.

gshal-ras-gsal-la-ṅad-mdaṅs-gaṅ-ba-bzaṅ,

'A good and full (offering of) fresh scent to Avalokita,' and presented it to the king. The king was much pleased, and erected the temple of Byin-gyi-khod-mar-rdo; and before the image of Avalokita these letters (the *śloka*) were carved on stone. These are the earliest inscription (in Tibet) and the oldest temple....In his time the Indian teacher Kumāra, the Nepalese teacher Śila-mañju, the Kashmiri teachers Tabuta and Ganuta, the *brāhmaṇa* Li-byin, and the Chinese teacher *ho-shang* Mahādeva were invited. The translators Thon-mi, Dharma-gośa [? *Dharmaghoṣa*] and dPal-gyi-rdo-rje of Lha-luṅ translated religious books in every possible manner and edited them."

Petech thinks that the verse quoted in the passage as illustrating the first literary composition of Thon-mi Sambhoṭa is misread and misunderstood by Francke. "The verse", says Petech, "does not form a part of the chronicle. It is of an erudite origin and is the first verse of a poem which in its entirety is given in the *rGyal-rabs-gsal-ba'i-me-loṅ*. It is a sort of grammatical joke and...is rather obscure. It is beyond our knowledge why Francke takes *gshal-ras-gsal* as a name of sPyan-ras-gzigs (Avalokiteśvara); this is completely groundless. Comparing the various readings, I propose to reconstruct the verse as follows: *shal-ras-gsal-ba-daṅ-mdaṅs-gaṅ-ba-bzaṅ*, and to translate it : 'The face (of Avalokiteśvara) is completely luminous and the colour is altogether auspicious.'"[30]

Much more serious, however, is the doubtful corollary Francke draws concerning the history of Tibetan literacy from a slender evidence mainly of the *Chronicle of Ladakh*, (though

30. Petech 93-4. Assuming this reconstruction of the verse, however, its simple significance appears to be some kind of respectful greeting by Thon-mi Sambhoṭa to the king. The verse roughly means, "Well (art thou), (for thy) face is beaming and full of brightness." The suggestion of Avalokiteśvara, if it is there at all, may afterall be nothing but an indication of the Tibetan belief that the king thus addressed was an incarnation of Avalokiteśvara.

it is to found also in Sum-pa's work). It mentions two names of the teachers of Thon-mi Sambhoṭa, namely the *brāhmaṇa* Li-byin and the *paṇḍita* Seṅ-ge-sgra (Siṃhanāda). Of these, the second is a palpable corruption of the name of Lha'i-rig-pa-seṅ-ge, mentioned by both Bu-ston and 'Gos lo-tsā-ba, which is a perfect translation of the Indian name Deva-vidyā-siṃha. "It might be remarked", Petech[31] rightly says, "that the name of the *paṇḍita* who taught Sanskrit to Thon-mi Sambhoṭa is not Seṅ-ge-sgra (Siṃhanāda) but, by agreement of all the other sources, Lha'i-rig-seṅ-ge." If this chronicle gives a corrupt form of the second name, the first name it mentions—namely of the *brāhmaṇa* Li-byin—needs to be taken with some critical caution, particularly when the most authentic of the Tibetan historians like Bu-ston and 'Gos lo-tsā-ba are totally unaware of any such name. Thus the name Li-byin by itself hardly provides us with any secure foundation for building a hypothesis concerning the history of Tibetan literacy. Yet Francke argues that this name itself proves that the Tibetan language was first reduced to writing in Turkestan or Khotan. Let us see how he argues his case.

"This name (Li-byin)," says Francke,[32] "has always been wrongly translated. It has to be translated as Glory (or Blessing) of the land Li...The land Li is either a country near Nepal or Turkestan. I am convinced that it here signifies Turkestan...In the Turkestan monasteries Tibetan was first reduced to writing." "My own view," repeats Francke,[33] "is that the Tibetan alphabet was quietly worked out in the ancient monasteries of Turkestan, the Tibetan Li-yul, and that Sroṅ-btsan-sgam-po's minister Thon-mi Sambhoṭa reaped the fruit of such learning. My reasons are the following: The script used for Sanskrit in Turkestan, the so-called Central Asian Brāhmī, is another descendant of Indian Gupta and closely related to the Tibetan script...Then the man who taught Thon-mi in Kashmir is called Li-byin, which name doubtless means

31. *Ib.* 49. 32. Francke in JASB 1910. 97. 33. Francke in EI xi. 267f.

'Blessing of the Land of Li' (Blessing of Khotan). This name may be compared with such names as Khri-bdun-yul-byin, 'Blessing of the Land of Khri-bdun.' Thus the man who taught Thon-mi may have been a native of Turkestan."

The evidences for the theory of the Tibetans deriving their script from India *via* Khotan[34] do not appear to be sufficiently strong to reject the firm tradition of the Tibetans themselves, according to which they derived their script directly from India. We may try to examine here Francke's view in so far as it is based on the evidence of the name Li-byin. The two components of this name—namely Li and byin—, argues Francke, mean Turkestan and Glory respectively. But such an interpretation is not beyond the scope of any doubt. The Tibetan word *byin*[35] has various meanings, of which only one is 'glory,' etc. What Francke completely ignores, however, is that, as derived from the verb *sbyin-pa*, it means 'bestowing or presenting,' i.e. roughly suggests an equivalent of the Sanskrit word *datta* or giver. Accepting this meaning of the word and depending on the Tibetan tradition that *li* in *li-byin* is but an abbreviated form of the Sanskrit *lipi* (script), earlier Tibetologists like S. C. Das[36] and Waddell[37] preferred to translate the name Li-byin as Lipi-datta. But Francke completely rejects the suggestion that *li* has anything to suggest *lipi* or script. It can only be a place-name and, as a place-name, Francke feels convinced that it means here Turkestan. However, apart from the question whether the word *li* in Tibetan can by itself be a place-name and even granting that it means Li-yul, the exact identification of the Tibetan Li-yul is doubtful. As Jaschke[38] says, Li-yul means "according to Wasiljew,

34. Following Hoernle, Diringer 354 comments, "The Tibetan alphabet can be called Indian only in the sense that its direct source the Khotanese alphabet, is ultimately an Indian alphabet." It is for the paleographists to discuss the question more fully. 35. D-TED 888 : "pomp, splendour, magnificence ; *byin-rlabs* - blessing, a bestowing of blessings ; *byin-bab* - received blessings," (cf J-TED 376). D-TED 939 - *byin* is perfect and imperative form of the verb *sbyin-pa*, meaning 'to give, bestow, make a present of,' (cf. J-TED 405). 36. Sum-pa, *Contents* p. viii. 37. Waddell L 22. 38. J-TED 546.

Buddhist countries in northern Tibet, especially Khoten; according to others in nothern India or Nepal." "Li-yul," says S. C. Das,[39] "is identified with Nepal by the translators of bKa'-'gyur. I have been able to ascertain that the ancient name of Nepal in Tibetan is Li-yul...Alexander Csoma identifies Li-yul with S. E. Mongolia."

Thus, even assuming that Li in Li-byin means Li-yul, the identification of this place with Turkestan or Khotan is not unanimously accepted. Besides, the word *byin* does not necessarily mean 'glory', as Francke wants us to accept. In other words, Francke's theory that Li-byin means 'the Glory of Turkestan' is itself in need of stronger substantiation and, therefore, fails to provide a secure basis for his theory of the Tibetan script being derived *via* Turkestan. Further, as we have already said, he completely ignores the fact that Li-byin, as a name of Thon-mi Sambhoṭa's teacher, occurs only in the much later Tibetan chronicles and is absent in the most authentic of these, viz. those, e.g., of 'Gos lo-tsā-ba and Bu-ston.

On the other hand, if there is any indication of historical value in the names concerned, it is perhaps to be sought in that of Thon-mi Sambhoṭa. Sambhoṭa could not have formed part of his original name. The word is Indian,[40] meaning "the accomplished (*sam*) Tibetan (*bhoṭa*)." It needs to be noted in this connection that both the letters *bha* and *ṭa* are absent in Tibetan. For the special purpose of transliterating Indian words, an equivalent of *bha* is made by adding *ha* under *va* and the Tibetan *ta* is inverted to make an equivalent of the Indian *ṭa*. Both the devices are found in the Tibetan transliteration of the word Sambhoṭa. We can, therefore, argue that Sambhoṭa was but a title, Indian in origin, acquired by Anu or Thon-mi. Anu appears to be his family name, for he is generally mentioned as "the son of Anu." Thon-mi means "the man (*mi*) of Thon" and Thon is the "name of a village at the foot of the Khambala ridge on the south side of Ya-ru gTsan-po",[41] a village still honoured as the

39. S. C. Das in JASB 1881. 223n.
40. Waddell L 21n.
41. D-TED 592.

birth-place of Thon-mi Sambhoṭa, the father of Tibetan literacy. His Indian title Sambhoṭa perfectly agrees with the Tibetan tradition concerning his educational career in India.

Thon-mi must have been a person of remarkable abilities. Apart from devising the suitable script for the Tibetan language—a work, if true, indicating an extraordinary intellectual gift—Thon-mi also played a significant role in the contemporary politics of Tibet. He was an important minister of Sroṅ-btsan-sgam-po and is credited with the successful negotiation of the king's marriage with the Nepalese princess. Francke even asserts that during the period immediately after Sroṅ-btsan-sgam-po, Thon-mi ruled the country for some time and was succeeded by his own son : "At first Lutung-tsan (Thon-mi Sambhoṭa) governs the country ; later on Thon-mi Sambhoṭa's son (Majordomo)."[42] But this is, unfortunately, a serious mistake. Lu-tung-tsan is nothing but the Chinese transcription of the name of Sroṅ-btsan-sgam-po's other minister called 'Gar. The Chinese annals do speak of the regency, after the death of Sroṅ-btsan-sgam-po, of Lu-tung-tsan or 'Gar and of his son mentioned by the Chinese as K'in-ling.[43] Francke misunderstands the name Lu-tung-tsan as that of Thon-mi Sambhoṭa and ignores the Chinese version of the name of 'Gar's son.[44]

Notwithstanding Francke's confusion, however, it will be wrong to overlook the political role actually played by Thon-mi even after the death of Sroṅ-btsan-sgam-po. As Petech[45] points out, during the regency of K'in-ling, when the Tibetans were engaged in a long-drawn struggle with the Chinese, Thon-mi "seems to have assisted him (K'in-ling) chiefly through his skill of diplomacy." Further, according to the *T'ang-shu*, in A.D. 675, Thon-mi was sent with the proposal of peace to the Chinese court.[46]

42. Francke AIT ii. 84n. 43. See Section 23. 44. In spite of Francke's use of capital for Majordomo it appears to be the simple word *majordomo*. See Petech 55. 45. Petech 55. 46. *Ib*. 55n.

But the cultural achievements of Thon-mi far outweighed his political ones. The fashioning of the Tibetan script apart, he composed the first Tibetan grammar modelled on the Indian one. Two grammatical works of Thon-mi are preserved in the bsTan-'gyur. One of these is called *Luṅ-du-ston-pa-rtsa-ba-sum-cu-pa-shes-bya-ba*, the Sanskrit title of which is given as *Vyākaraṇa-mūla-triṃśaka-nāma.*[47] It is usually referred to by its abbreviated title *Sum-cu-pa*, i.e. as consisting of thirty *śloka*-s, and is still widely used.[48] The other grammatical work attributed to him bears the title *Luṅ-du-ston-pa-rtags-kyi-'jug-pa-shes-bya-ba* or *Vyākaraṇa-liṅgāvataraṇa-nāma.*[49]

The Tibetan historians, with their pronounced Buddhist bias, tell us that with this newly acquired script and grammar the Tibetans immediately set themselves to the holy task of translating Buddhist scriptures. They mention the names of certain scholars brought to Tibet from India, Nepal and China to help the first group of Tibetan translators. It may be difficult to have exact historical information of these first scholars invited to Tibet and the literary output of the first Tibetan translators might not have been really as much as these historians tell us. But there is no doubt that the work of Thon-mi Sambhoṭa gave the first great impetus to Tibetan literary activity, which, to begin with, was mainly the translation of Indian works. Jaschke, in his brief but brilliant summary of the history of Tibetan literature, divides it into two periods. The first was the period of translations, the second of independent compositions. We are concerned here particularly with the first. "This period", observes Jaschke,[50] "begins in the first half of the seventh century, when Thon-mi Sambhoṭa, the minister of king Sroṅ-btsan-sgam-po, was sent to India to learn Sanskrit. His invention of the Tibetan alphabet gave a two-fold impulse : for several centuries the wisdom of India and the ingenuity of Tibet laboured in unison and with the greatest industry and

47. bsTan-'gyur mDo cxxiv. 3. 48. Francke AIT ii. 84n.
49. mDo cxxiv. 4. 50. J-TED Intro. p. iv.

enthusiasm at the work of translation. The tribute due to real genius must be awarded to these early pioneers of Tibetan grammar. They had to grapple with the infinite wealth and refinement of Sanskrit, they had to save the independence of their own tongue, while they strove to subject it to the rule of scientific principles, and it is most remarkable, how they managed to produce translations at once literal and faithful to the spirit of the original. The first masters had made for their later disciples a comparatively easy road."

23. *Khri-sron-lde-btsan*

Tibetan history, as told by its own historians, is somewhat uncertain and obscure for a period of over fifty years after the death of Sroṅ-btsan-sgam-po. The next kings about whom they show distinct interest were Khri-lde-gtsug-brtan[1] and more particularly his son Khri-sroṅ-lde-btsan. The apathy of the Tibetan historians for the intervening period is easily explained. During it nothing worth reporting about the spread of the Doctrine took place in Tibet and the Tibetan rulers took no interest in Buddhism. The interest reappeared with Khri-lde-gtsug-brtan and became extremely pronounced with Khri-sroṅ-lde-btsan. It was during the reign of the latter that the great Indian *ācārya*-s Śāntarakṣita, Padmasambhava and Kamalaśīla were brought to Tibet, the bSam-yas monastery was built, the Bon religion aggressively suppressed and the translation of the Buddhist works began in a grand scale. As is remembered in a Tibetan song,[2]

> Then the deputy of the conqueror (Buddha), the holy
> Shi-ba-'tsho (Śāntirakṣita),
> And the superior master of incantations, the ascetic
> Padma-'byuṅ (Padmasambhava),
> Kamalaśīla, the crest-ornament of the wise,
> And Khri-sroṅ-lde-btsan, of surpassing thoughts;
> Through these four, like sunrise in the dark country
> of Tibet,
> The light of the holy religion spread as far as the
> frontiers;
> The holy men of unchanging kindness
> All Tibetans will for ever reverentially salute.

1. This is the spelling given in BA i. 50 and Bu-ston ii. 185. Petech 62 prefers to spell the last part as *btsan*. The Chinese annals preserve the name as Khi-li-so-tsan : see Petech 62n. 2. Francke AIT ii. 87.

Khri-sroṅ-lde-btsan was undoubtedly one of the greatest rulers of Tibet and also one of the greatest patrons of Buddhism. These two attributes were perhaps not entirely unconnected. The political history of Tibet after Sroṅ-btsan-sgam-po, for which we are to depend mainly on the Chinese sources, has some light to throw on his support of Buddhism.[3]

'Gos lo-tsā-ba[4] says, "His (Sroṅ-btsan's) son Guṅ-sroṅ-guṅ-btsan having died before (in the life-time of his father) Maṅ-sroṅ-maṅ-btsan mounted the throne at the age of thirteen. He befriended the minister 'Gar, who ruled for fifteen years." Roerich takes the last sentence to mean, "the king ruled the country for fifteen years assisted by the minister 'Gar." It remains for us to see, however, the real meaning of it as is indicated by the Chinese annals.

As for Guṅ-sroṅ-guṅ-btsan and Maṅ-sroṅ-maṅ-btsan, S. C. Das[5] says that these two were the names of the two sons of Sroṅ-btsan-sgam-po. But this is frankly misleading. The Tibetan sources[6] generally state that Sroṅ-btsan's son died at an early age, as a result of which the king was succeeded by his grandson. This is fully confirmed by the Chinese annals.[7] Thus the statement of 'Gos lo-tsā-ba should be taken to imply that Guṅ-sroṅ-guṅ-btsan was the name of Sroṅ-btsan's son and Maṅ-sroṅ-maṅ-btsan that of his grandson. Unfortunately, the historians of Tibet are not agreed on this. According to the *Chronicle of Ladakh*,[8] Maṅ-sroṅ-maṅ-btsan was the son of Sroṅ-btsan and the name of his grandson was Guṅ-sroṅ-guṅ-btsan. According to Sum-pa[9] and the *Bodhimor*,[10] the opposite was the case. But the later chroniclers alone are not to be accused of this confusion. It is to be traced to the foremost of the Tibetan historians themselves. Thus, as against 'Gos lo-tsā-ba, Bu-ston[11] says, "The son of this king (Sroṅ-btsan) was Maṅ-sroṅ-maṅ-btsan, his son—Guṅ-sroṅ-guṅ-btsan."[12]

3. See Section 24, Note 16. 4. BA i. 49. 5. S. C. Das in JASB 1881. 221. 6. See Petech 53. 7. Bushell in JRAS 1880. 446. 8. Francke AIT ii. 84. 9. Sum-pa 150. 10. Quoted by Francke AIT ii. 84n. 11. Bu-ston ii. 185. 12. Petech 53-4 attributes to

The confusion itself is interesting. The real reason of the name of Sroṅ-btsan's grandson being indifferently remembered is that he hardly mattered in the history of Tibet. This is known mainly from the Chinese annals.[13]

After the death of Sroṅ-btsan-sgam-po, his powerful minister 'Gar—mentioned by the Chinese annals as Lu-tung-tsan —usurped the political power and Sroṅ-btsan's grandson was allowed to maintain a merely titular position. This is what 'Gos lo-tsā-ba means when he says, "He befriended the minister 'Gar, who ruled for fifteen years." 'Gar was succeeded by his own son, called K'in-ling[14] in the Chinese annals "in the management of the state."[15] Thus, according to the Chinese sources, the period after the death of Sroṅ-btsan-sgam-po "is characterised by the brilliant and happy regency of Lu-tung-tsan first, and of his son K'in-ling next. The latter was for about thirty years the most powerful man in Central Asia ; to him is due the increase of Tibetan power in such enormous proportions as to become a serious danger not only to the external possessions but also to the interior territories of China and even to the very existence of the Empire."[16] During this regency, Sroṅ-btsan's grandson remained king merely in name. The only information that the Tibetan chronicles have to add about him is that he married a princess of Gilgit and died in A.D. 679.[17]

The Tibetan chronicles ignore the regency and tell us that in A.D. 679 Sroṅ-btsan's grandson (Maṅ-sroṅ or Guṅ-sroṅ) was succeeded by his own son 'Du-sroṅ-maṅ-po-rje, whose real name, as Petech argues, was Khri-'du-sroṅ-btsan.[18] He

Bu-ston and 'Gos lo-tsā-ba views that are opposite of what they actually maintain. But he draws our attention to the fact that the Chinese sources are not of any help in this matter. Ma Tuan-lin mentions the gradson and successor of Sroṅ-btsan-sgam-po as Khi-li-phi-phu, from which it is not possible to reconstruct the Tibetan original. Bushell in JRAS 1880. 430 gives the Chinese version of the name as Ch'ilipapu.

13. See Petech 54ff. 14. *Ib.* 57. It is difficult to find the real Tibetan equivalent of the name. 15. Bushell *op.cit.* 447 : the name is transcribed as Ch'inling. 16. Petech 54. 17. *Ib.* 58 ; cf. BA i. 49. 18. Petech 58n : "Maṅ-po-rje constitutes nothing but a laudative surname."

ascended the throne during the regency of K'in-ling. On growing up, however, he became tired of the minister's tutelage and refused to remain in the political background. In a passage of an ancient Tibetan manuscript,[19] "the king Khri-'du-sroṅ-btsan, singing during a banquet, makes the following allusions to the minister-regent K'in-ling... : 'The subject hopes to become the sovereign. The sons of the minister hope to become king. The toad hopes to fly and pretends to scale the sky'."[20]

The *T'ang-shu* describes how the king actually succeeded in overthrowing K'in-ling and how the latter, driven by despair, committed suicide. That marked the end of the regency and the re-establishment of Tibetan monarchy. 'Du-sroṅ-maṅ-po-rje or Khri-'du-sroṅ-btsan was himselft a powerful king. The *Chronicle of Ladakh*[21] gives us a list of his conquests and describes how the political horizon of Tibet expanded during his rule. In 702, says Petech, "the king himself for the first time since Sroṅ-btsan-sgam-po took the field personally against the Chinese, although with little success. A little later he died during a campaign against Nepal and the peoples of the Indian frontier that had rebelled against him."[22]

It is a pity, comments Petech, that the chronicles of Central Tibet do not pay sufficient tribute to the political glory of this king. 'Gos lo-tsā-ba[23] simply says that he ruled for 26 years and died in 704. But the desultory interest taken by the Buddhist historians in this king is perhaps because of the fact that he did hardly anything in the cause of Buddhism. It was different, however, with his son and successor, about whom the Tibetan historians show a renewed interest.

'Gos lo-tsā-ba[24] says that the year after the death of 'Du-sroṅ-maṅ-po-rje, i.e. in A.D. 705, his son Khri-lde-gtsug-brtan, better known by his surname Mes-ag-tshoms, was installed on the throne. He died in A.D. 755. The same

19. The MS is preserved in the Fond Pelliot of the Bibliotheque Nationale of Paris : see Petech 38. 20. Petech 38. 21. Francke AIT ii. 85. 22. Petech 59. 23. BA i. 50. 24. *Ib.* i. 50 1.

year, his son Khri-sroṅ-lde-btsan became the king, who died in 780, though the Chinese annals give the date of his death as 797, which is considered to be much more dependable.[25]

We may sum up here the political history of Tibet up to Khri-sroṅ-lde-btsan :

A.D. 650—Sroṅ-btsan-sgam-po died.

He was succeeded by his grandson, called either Guṅ-sroṅ-guṅ-btsan or Maṅ-sroṅ-maṅ-btsan. This king was but a puppet, the real political power being usurped by the minister 'Gar, who died about fifteen years after Sroṅ-btsan and was succeeded by his own son called by the Chinese K'in-ling.

A.D. 679—Sroṅ-btsan's great-grandson Khri-'du-sroṅ-btsan *alias* 'Du-sroṅ-maṅ-po-rje, ascended the throne and eventually overthrew the regency of K'in-ling.

A.D. 704—Khri-'du-sroṅ-btsan died.

A.D. 705—His son Khri-lde-gtsug-brtan (or Mes-ag-tshoms) ascended the throne. (This name is not to be confused with that of Khri-gtsug-lde-btsan, which occurs later in Tibetan history).

A. D. 755—He died and was succeeded by his son Khri-sroṅ-lde-btsan (not to be confused with the later king called Khri-lde-sroṅ-btsan).

A.D. 797—(though, according to 'Gos lo-tsā-ba, A.D. 780) Khri-sroṅ-lde-btsan died.

The Tibetan historians are quite frank about their renewed interest in Tibetan kings from Khri-lde-gtsug-brtan onwards. "In a later period," says 'Gos lo-tsā-ba,[26] "a minister of Khri-lde-gtsug-brtan discovered an inscribed copper-plate in a rocky ravine at 'Chims-phu, on which were inscribed the words

25. Petech 70 : "The date of the king's death is according to the *T'ang-shu*, 797. Tibetan sources widely disagree on this point. The *rGyal-rabs-gsal-ba'i-me-loṅ* gives the Wood-Ox year 785 ; the *Chronicle of the Fifth Dalai Lama* the Iron-Dragon year 800 ; Bu-ston (ii. 196) the Water-Tiger year 762 or 822 ; the *Deb-ther-sṅon-po* the Iron-Monkey year 780 . . . All this bewildering cluster of dates has no weight against the authority of the *T'ang-shu*, so much nearer in time to the events concerned."

26. BA i. 40.

of king Sroṅ-btsan : 'My nephew (!) bearing my name with the addition of the word *lde* will spread the Doctrine of the Buddha.' Khri-lde-gtsug-brtan thinking that 'this *lde* must be me,' built several *vihāra*-s...He invited (Buddhist) priests who had been expelled from Li-yul, and many Buddhist monks (*ho-shang*) from China." It was during his reign, says Bu-ston,[27] that the literary activity of the Tibetans received a new impetus : "Mūlakoṣa of bLaṅ-ka and Jñānakumāra of gÑags translated the *sūtra*-s *Karma-śataka* and *Suvarṇa-prabhāsottama*, as well as works on Mathematics and Medicine and furthered the spread of the Doctrine."

From the point of view of the propagation of the Doctrine, however, the reign of his son Khri-sroṅ-lde-btsan was immensely more important and the Tibetan historians glorify him in the highest way they can conceive of, namely by declaring him as an incarnation of Boddhisattva Mañjuśrī.[28] And it is one of the rare instances in which the modern scholars do not complain of a lop-sided emphasis by the Tibetan historians on the religious history of the country. "His reign", as Petech[29] observes, "is doubly important because it marks the zenith of Tibetan power and the affirmation of Buddhism as the chief religion of the state."

The year of Khri-sroṅ-lde-btsan's birth is difficult to determine. According to the old tradition it appears to have been a Horse year, but some of the later chroniclers add to it the element Iron while others the element Water.[30] In the former case (Iron-Horse) it is A.D. 730 while in the latter case (Water-Horse) it is 742. The second date agrees better with Bu-ston's assertion that the king ascended the throne at the age of thirteen,[31] though, assuming the Chinese date of his death (797), the former date agrees better with the other assertion of Bu-ston that the king died at the age of 69.[32]

27. Bu-ston ii. 186. Cf. Francke AIT ii. 85. 28. Bu-ston ii. 196. 29. Petech 65. 30. *Ib.* 31. Bu-ston ii. 186. The age 13, however, appears to be merely conventional. 32. Bu-ston ii. 196.

The king was born of a Chinese princess called Chin-ch'eng-kung-chu. S. C. Das[33] gives us a romantic account of how this princess, though originally sent to be married to a son of Khri-lde-gtsug-brtan called 'Jaṅ-tsha-lha-dbaṅ, actually got married to Khri-lde-gtsug-brtan instead: "Prince 'Jaṅ-tsha-lha-dbaṅ was famous for the extraordinary beauty of his person. His father sent ambassadors all over Tibet to find a match for him, but they all returned without success. At last he sent an ambassador to China to propose a marriage between his son and the accomplished princess Chin-ch'eng-kung-chu... The princess hearing the account of the extraordinary beauty of the Tibetan prince, prayed to her father to consent to the marriage, to which he at last acceded; and the princess started for Tibet. In the meantime one of the Tibetan chiefs... being offended with the king for not selecting his daughter for the prince's wife, treacherously murdered the prince. King Ag-tshom (Khri-lde-gtsug-brtan), therefore, at once despatched messengers to convey the melancholy news to the princess who was on her way to Tibet. The princess, deeply disappointed, did not like to return to China, but taking a fancy to see the snowy country of Tibet, continued her journey to Tibet, where she was warmly welcomed by king Ag-tshom... Her beauty so much charmed the king that he at once proposed to marry her... and to the great wonder and joy of the people the betrothed daughter-in-law became the bride of the father. She gave birth to the famous monarch Khri-sroṅ-lde-btsan."

But Bu-ston[34] has a different story to tell about the birth of Khri-sroṅ-lde-btsan: "(The king Khri-lde-gtsug-brtan) had a son called 'Jaṅ-tsha-lha-dbaṅ, who married the daughter of the Chinese Emperor... The son of these died. (The princess) united with the grandfather [? father-in-law] and worshipped the statue of Śākyamuni. Thereafter, a boy endowed with special marks of beauty was born."

33. S. C. Das in JASB 1881. 223f. This is evidently based on *rGyal-rabs-gsal-ba'i-me-loṅ*: see Petech 63.

34. Bu-ston ii. 186.

For the Chinese historians, however, all these are nothing but useless gossip. According to them, this marriage was concluded in 710, when king Khri-lde-gtsug-brtan was very young. 'Gos lo-tsā-ba[35] seems to depend on the Chinese version, though he gives the date of the marriage as 712. Petech proposes a summary rejection of the Tibetan version in favour of the Chinese. "The *T'ang-shu*," says he,[36] "explicitly states that the king at the time of his wedding was a mere youth. Whenever there is a contrast between the Chinese and Tibetan sources, it is always preferable to rely on the Chinese version, not only because it is much nearer to the events, but above all for the infinitely greater historical sense that distinguishes the Chinese chroniclers." From the Chinese sources it further appears that the marriage, far from being any romantic affair, was really due to the political and military pressure put by the Tibetans on the Chinese. As Petech[37] puts it, "the wars continued uninterruptedly, but for the moment there was no decision. An attempt was made by the Chinese for arriving at an agreement, giving in marriage to the Tibetan king an Imperial Chinese Princess, but the result of this policy was nil."

Though born of the Chinese princess, Khri-sroṅ-lde-btsan showed little interest in eassing Tibet's military tension with China. On the contrary, his reign was characterised by the definite superiority won by the Tibetan arms against the Chinese. "In the years between 760 and 766 the Tibetans conquered almost the whole of Kansu, thus cutting off the Chinese army of Turkestan...While the northern army was fighting in Kansu and Turkestan, the eastern army obtained in 763 its greatest success in two centuries of struggle, entering victoriously in the very capital of the T'ang's, Ch'ang-an."[38] The Chinese Emperor Tai-tsung "fled to Shang-chou. The Tibetans installed on the throne the Chinese minister Kao-hun."[39] The reign of this puppet ruler lasted for only 15 days, after which he was

35. BA i. 50-1. 36. Petech 64. 37. *Ib*. 63. 38. *Ib*. 66.
39. BA i. 51 2.

killed by the Chinese Emperor who reoccupied his capital. But the war between the two countries went on, until in 783 an "eternal" treaty of peace was signed, only to be broken soon after its conclusion.[40]

The king made an alliance with the Arabs and extended his conquests in all directions, including India where the Pāla rulers, it is said,were forced to pay tribute to Tibet.[41] But the Tibetan historians are not much interested in describing all these. They are keen instead in telling us how the king favoured the spread of Buddhism. "When," says Bu-ston,[42] "the biography of this father and grandfather was related to him, the Doctrine was likewise mentioned (in the narrative). (The king)... became full of faith."

An inevitable consequence of his patronage of Buddhism was a clash with the representatives of the Bon religion, openly for the first time in Tibetan history, during the reign of Khri-sroṅ-lde-btsan. The Tibetan historians glorify him for the way in which he suppressed the Bon religion. "During the life-time of this king", says the *Chronicle of Ladakh*,[43] "the Bon religion was suppressed, and the Holy religion was made to spread and flourish." "The king", says S. C. Das,[44] "put down the Bon religion and persecuted all unbelievers in Buddhism." The Bon chronicle called *rGyal-rabs-bon-gyi-'byuṅ-gnas* describes in some length the fall of the Bon religion under king Khri-sroṅ-lde-btsan.[45] But, as the Tibetan historians want us to believe, the supporters of the Bon religion did not yield without offering active resistance. Such a resistance, according to the typical Tibetan account, was particularly strong during the earlier part of the king's rule, though, thanks to the great abilities of some Indian Buddhists brought to Tibet, the king could eventually overcome it.

40. Petech 66-7. 41. *Ib.* 68. 42. Bu-ston ii. 187.
43. Francke AIT ii. 87. 44. S. C. Das in JASB 1881. 226.
45. See Francke AIT ii. 80n.

24. The Ministerial Intrigues

The military expeditions apart, Khri-sroṅ-lde-btsan's reign also exercised "a great indirect influence on the ultimate destiny of Central Asia, through the elevation of Buddhism to the state religion of Tibet."[1] His patronage of Buddhism is historically indisputable, however difficult it may be for us to reconcile this with his extensive and unceasing military campaigns or even to find an adequate explanation for his adoption of the Buddhist faith.

Waddell[2] suggests that he "inherited through his mother a strong prejudice in favour of Buddhism." But neither the Chinese nor the Tibetan historian is aware of his mother being a zealous Buddhist. If she actually had anything to do with the spread of Buddhism in Tibet, at least the Tibetan historians would have greatly glorified her, as they have done the Chinese queen of Sroṅ-btsan-sgam-po. The glimpse of her nature we have from the Tibetan historians is, on the contrary, quite different from that of a fervent Buddhist. They[3] describe a plot of another queen[4] of Khri-lde-gtsug-brtan, who stole the new-born prince Khri-sroṅ-lde-btsan and claimed him as being born of her. This enraged the Chinese queen, who, "burning with a spirit of revenge tried to bring damnation on Tibet by means of her incantations, and wrote treatises construing astrology in a perverse way." When this plot was discovered and the prince returned to her, she "exerted herself to avert some of the evils she had brought on Tibet by her incantations ; but as she did not fully succeed in correcting astrology, it is alleged by several native historians that the Tibetans cannot make correct calculations."[5]

1. Petech 69. 2. Waddell L 24. 3. Bu-ston ii. 186 ; BA i. 41 ; S. C. Das in JASB 1881. 224f. 4. Bu-ston ii. 186 gives her name as sNa-nan-za and Petech 64 conjectures that she could have been a princess of Samarkand. 5. S. C. Das in JASB 1881. 225.

From the Tibetan histories it further appears that Khri-sroṅ-lde-btsan himself had, at least to begin with, hardly any positive affiliation to Buddhism. Even his idea of the new religion was vague. He was only a child when his father died and he ascended the throne at a very early age. At this tender age, he had apparently little control over the affairs of the state, which were left to the ministers. These ministers were divided into two groups, fighting against each other. The Tibetan historians give a religious colouring to the story of this ministerial intrigue and assert that it was a fight between the supporters of Bon and of Buddhism.

The leader of the group opposing Buddhism was Ma-shaṅ. Important among the ministers supporting Buddhism were Saṅ-śi, gSal-snaṅ, 'Gos-rgan and others. To begin with, the latter received much support from the Chinese Buddhists, though their final victory was due to the Indian *ācārya*-s brought to Tibet.

"When he (Khri-sroṅ-lde-btsan)", says Bu-ston,[6] "was still a child, Saṅ-śi and others, altogether four in number, were sent to China in search of kanonical works. At that time a Chinese *ho-shang* who was endowed with the supernatural faculties spread the rumour that the Tibetan messengers were incarnations of Bodhisattva Saints and recommended to treat them as such. (The messengers) came, were honoured by the Chinese Emperor and sent back in the company of a *ho-shang*. When they returned to Tibet, the king (Khri-lde-gtsug-brtan) had died, and, as the prince was still a child, the ministers violated the laws and customs, banished those who were acting according to the Doctrine, and made arrangements to send the statue of Śākyamuni back to China...and made of the temple a slaughter-house... Khri-sroṅ-lde-btsan, having attained the age of thirteen, ascended the throne... The Chinese Me and Go, and the *paṇḍita* Ananta, these three were appointed to translate (the texts). The translation was accordingly begun, but the minister Ma-shaṅ-grom-pa-skyes and others caused

6. Bu-ston ii. 186-7.

impediments to this. The ministers who were devoted to the Doctrine, sent Saṅ-śi to Maṅ-yul. gSal-snaṅ did not remain at Maṅ-yul, but went to India and presented his sacrificial offerings at Mahābodhi and Śrī Nālandā."

"After the death of the king (Khri-lde-gtsug-brtan)," says 'Gos lo-tsā-ba,[7] "Khri-sroṅ-lde-btsan mounted the throne. There was a powerful minister called Ma-shaṅ, who was an enemy of the Doctrine. He ordered the deportation of Buddhist monks to another country, and carried the Image of Buddha of Lhasa away to sKyi-roṅ (on the border of Nepal). He transformed *vihāra*-s into butchers' shops, and though the king had faith in the Doctrine, he was unable (to stop the persecution). When the Chinese Buddhist priests (*ho-shang*), residents at Ra-mo-che, were returning to China, the eldest (of them) accidentally left behind one of his shoes, and said : 'The Doctrine will again return to Tibet.' According to these words, the Doctrine returned...The king was assisted by friends of the Doctrine, such as 'Gos-rgan, dBa' Saṅ-śi, dBa' gSal-snaṅ and others. Saṅ-śi and gSal-snaṅ proceeded to the Imperial Court of China. On presenting their request to the Emperor, they met a *ho-shang*, who was an adept of mystic concentration (*dhyāna*), and obtained from him instruction in mystic concentration...They brought with them from China about 1,000 metrical compositions, but being afraid of Ma-shaṅ's persecution, they buried them."

Bu-ston, however, adds that one of these ministers, gSal-snaṅ, after visiting Nepal and Buddhagayā, became an ardent Buddhist and acquired the name Jñānendra (Ye-śes-dbaṅ-po).[8] 'Gos lo-tsā-ba adds that he met Śāntarakṣita in Nepal, and, after returning to Tibet, advised the king on the desirability of inviting the Indian *ācārya* to Tibet. The king said, "You might be punished by Ma-shaṅ ! Go away quickly ! I shall secretly confer with 'Gos-rgan and others, and shall send an invitation to the *upādhyāya*."[9]

Apparently Ma-shaṅ was too powerful for the king.

7. BA i. 40-1.

8. Bu-ston ii. 187.

9. BA i. 42.

He had, therefore, to be eliminated before the ministers favouring Buddhism could make any real progress. The Tibetan historians tell us how Ma-shaṅ was tricked to death. 'Gos lo-tsā-ba[10] says, "Then 'Gos-rgan began an intrigue against (Ma-shaṅ) and the latter was buried alive in a tomb at sTod-luṅs." Bu-ston[11] says that the minister 'Gos-rgan cast Ma-shaṅ "alive into a grave and covered the aperture with a block of stone." S. C. Das,[12] on the basis of the popular Tibetan tradition,[13] describes the murder of Ma-shaṅ in greater detail : "The Buddhist party now, with the king's connivance, entered into a conspiracy against the life of Ma-shaṅ the prime-minister. They bribed the sooth-sayers and astrologers to declare that some great calamity was imminent over the king which could be only averted by two of the high officers of state entering grave-like cells and remaining there for a period of three months. The king, therefore, offered large presents to those who would undergo this self-sacrifice. The minister Ma-shaṅ volunteered to do so, and was followed by 'Gos, the Buddhist minister. They both entered the cell, the depth of which was three times a man's length. At midnight, 'Gos's friends threw a rope into the grave, by means of which he climbed up and escaped. The unfortunate Ma-shaṅ was left alone there, to realise the horrors of the grave. His mortal enemies, the 'Buddhist Ministers' blocked the mouth of the grave with a huge rock and buried him alive."

For the Tibetan historians, perhaps the end justifies the means. They describe how with the elimination of Ma-shaṅ the greatest obstacle to Buddhism was removed and the king gathered courage to invite Śāntarakṣita, who, in his turn, persuaded the king to bring Padmasambhava and Kamalaśīla to Tibet and the activities of these three proved to be the most important land-mark of the earlier period of the spread of Buddhism in Tibet.

10. *Ib.* 11. Bu-ston ii. 188. 12. S. C. Das in JASB 1881. 225-6.
13. BA i. 42.

Petech raises a serious doubt concerning the historicity of this account of ministerial intrigues. Could it be that the later Tibetan historians thoroughly misunderstood the actual sequence of events and misplaced in the earlier part of Khri-sroṅ-lde-btsan's reign a distorted version of the regency of 'Gar and his son, the history of which is actually to be traced to the time of Sroṅ-btsan's successor ? Petech is inclined to take the possibility seriously. "The Tibetan sources," says he,[14] "not confirmed by the Chinese, tell us of a regency of ministers hostile to Buddhism, who were overthrown and killed when the king reached majority. As we see, it is merely the same story as the *T'ang-shu* relates about K'in-ling and 'Du-sroṅ-maṅ-po-rje sixty years before. But there are no evidences as to whether these facts are historical or are the result of a bad mistake of the chroniclers, who transferred events of Sroṅ-btsan-sgam-po's successors to the reign of Khri-sroṅ-lde-btsan."

But the difficulty of sharing this scepticism is obvious. It is based on *the assumption that the Tibetan evidences, unless corroborated by the Chinese ones, are no evidences at all.* But such an assumption leads to the absurd position that the majority of the names of the Tibetan kings—because only a few of these are actually mentioned in the *T'ang-shu*—are fictitious. It is true that the Chinese historians, because of their primary interest in the political relation between Tibet and China, emphasise certain facts of Tibetan history, which the Tibetan historians themselves, because of their primary interest in the spread of Buddhism in Tibet, ignore or under-estimate. For the same difference in basic approach, the Tibetan historians are likely to take a keener interest in certain events considered superfluous by the Chinese historians. Thus the Chinese annals speak so much of the regency of 'Gar and his son since it affected the political destiny of China, whereas,

14. Petech 68.

as this regency had nothing to do with the assertion of Buddhism in Tibet, the Tibetan historians simply ignore it. Similarly, it is quite conceivable that the Chinese historians are silent about the ministerial intrigues of Khri-sroṅ-lde-btsan's reign, because it little affected Chinese politics, whereas the Tibetan historians are so much concerned with this, for, according to their understanding, it was of great significance for the progress of Buddhism in Tibet. On the other hand, it is too much to assume that historians like Bu-ston and 'Gos lo-tsā-ba simply commit the "bad mistake" of transferring a sixty-year old event to Khri-sroṅ-lde-btsan's reign, particularly when there is not much of real similarity between the Chinese account of the overthrow of K'in-ling and the Tibetan account of the overthrow of Ma-shaṅ. Besides, some of the names as occurring in the latter—like that of gSal-snaṅ or Jñānendra for example—reoccur too prominently in the subsequent period to be easily removed from the reality of Tibetan history.[15]

It may further be observed here that Petech's own theory concerning Khri-sroṅ-lde-btsan's support of Buddhism presupposes the reality of the ministerial intrigue which, Petech argues, the king wanted to overcome by elevating Buddhism to the status of the state religion. The Tibetan ministers usually came from the strong and war-like nobility, which, like the European nobility, was extremely turbulent and constantly trying to grab the state-power and Petech conjectures that Khri-sroṅ-lde-btsan's support of Buddhism could have been designed to crush the power of this nobility. "It is also very likely," says he,[16] "that political considerations largely influenced his activities in favour of the new faith, because its introduction largely helped to the destruction of *power of numerous noble*

15. See Section 25, particularly the account of the great debate. It may incidentally be mentioned here that even the Tibetan sources are not without any indication of ministerial intrigues during the reign of Khri-lde-gtsug-brtan and Khri-sroṅ-lde-btsan : See the inscription on the southern face of the stone pillar below the Potala translated by C. Bell, *Tibet Past & Present* 273. 16. Petech 69. Emphasis added.

families which had hereditary Bon-po priesthood and took advantage of the religion for increasing their political fortunes." This hypothesis agrees well not only with the account of the aggressive suppression of the Bon religion by Khri-sroṅ-lde-btsan but also with the fact that he was about the only ruler other than Sroṅ-btsan-sgam-po who fully succeeded in imposing his authority upon the nobility, holding with an iron hand the reins of the state. At the same time, whatever might have been the real motive of his support of Buddhism, the fact is that Buddhism made stupendous progress in Tibet during his reign.

25. Santaraksita, Padmasambhava and Kamalasila

Khri-sroṅ-lde-btsan's success in making Buddhism the state religion of Tibet was primarily due to the help he received from Śāntarakṣita, Padmasambhava and Kamalaśīla. Let us begin with a brief account of them we have from the Tibetan historians. Śāntarakṣita was invited to Tibet by one of the ministers of the king. But his preaching of Buddhism there stirred up great resistance: the devils and demi-gods of the country, say the historians, were in revolt. He had, thus, to be sent back. On his advice, however, the great *guru* Padmasambhava was brought to Tibet, who, with his magical power, subdued all the local devils and demi-gods and even recruited a large number of them to his own following. This created conditions for the return of Śāntarakṣita to Tibet and the king, with the help of the two Indian Buddhists, built the monastery of bSam-yas. After this, Buddhism made steady progress in Tibet. But sometime later, a great controversy arose over the interpretation of the Buddhist ideas between the followers of Śāntarakṣita and the Chinese Buddhist (*ho-shang*).[1] The king invited Kamalaśīla, a disciple of Śāntarakṣita, to defend the Indian interpretation of the Buddhist ideas and, in an open debate, Kamalaśīla silenced his opponents.

It is suggested[2] that there could have been two Buddhist authors, both bearing the name Śāntarakṣita. One of them wrote the stupendous *Tattva-saṃgraha*, which, along with the commentary of Kamalaśīla, survives both in Sanskrit original[3] and Tibetan translation.[4] It gives us the impression of the

1. Rockhill LB 220n : "A Chinese expression for Buddhist monk The word was transferred from the language of Khoten to Chinese. It corresponds to the Sanskrit *upādhyāya* or Master." Cf. D-TED 1326.
2. S K. De in HB i. 333.
3. GOS xxx-xxxi, Baroda 1926.
4. mDo cxiii. 1. Kamalaśīla's Pañjikā mDo cxiii. 28, cxiv.

author's extraordinary gift for logical analyses and philosophical polemics. He refutes in this work, from the philosophical standpoint of the Svātantrika Yogācāra[5] school, all the rival philosophies of his time—both non-Buddhist and Buddhist. It is presumed that the same philosopher wrote the *Vāda-nyāya-vṛtti-vipañcitārtha*[6] and the *Madhyamaka-alaṃkāra-kārikā*,[7] the latter with an auto-commentary,[8]—works that survive only in Tibetan translation. At the same time the bsTan-'gyur contains a number of patently Tāntrika works[9] attributed to Śāntarakṣita and the modern scholar is reluctant to think that a remarkable logician like the author of the *Tattva-saṃgraha* could compose Tāntrika treatises like these. Hence is the theory of two Śāntarakṣitas.

The Tibetan historians, however, seem to be aware of only one Śāntarakṣita, the *guru* of Kamalaśīla, and they seem to find no incongruity between one being a keen logician and at the same time an ardent Tāntrika. It needs to be noted here that, like the life of many other eminent Buddhists of the later period, that of Śāntarakṣita is known to us mainly from the Tibetan sources. Thus, even if the modern scholar fails to favour the idea of a logical bend of mind also indulging in Tāntrika beliefs, he has no positive evidence to prove the existence of two Śāntarakṣitas, unless it is definitely ascertained that the type of Tantrism represented by the Tāntrika treatises attributed to Śāntarakṣita in the bsTan-'gyur historically developed at a later time than that of Khri-sroṅ-lde-btsan when the *guru* of Kamalaśīla—and therefore the author of the *Tattva-saṃgraha*—went to Tibet. However, the evidence of Padmasambhava, who was a great Tāntrika Buddhist and a contemporary of Kamalaśīla's *guru*, cannot rule out the possibility of Mahāyāna Buddhism developing into Tantrayāna at that age.[10] But even assuming that the logician Śāntarakṣita

5. Winternitz ii 374. 6. mDo cviii. 2 : cxii. 4. 7. mDo xxviii. 4.
8. mDo xxviii. 5. 9. rG lxxii. 4, xxii. 29, bsTod i. 55.
10. P. C Bagchi *Bauddhadharma-O-Sāhitya* (Bengali) 44 traces the beginnings of Tantrayāna to the 8th century A D.

wrote also the Tântrika treatises, there are hints in the Tibetan sources that he maintained a remarkably rational attitude even in his Tibetan career and that he was the first to preach in Tibet the essentials of Buddhist ethics and metaphysics in their classical or pre-Tāntrika sense.

At least one point is quite clear. The most important phase in the propagation of Buddhism in Tibet before Dīpaṃkara was initiated by Śāntarakṣita. It is, therefore, interesting to note that, according to the Tibetan tradition, Dīpaṃkara had the same line of descent to which Śāntarakṣita belonged.[11] This, by itself, favours the view that Śāntarakṣita was born in Bengal,—a view maintained by S. C. Das[12] and supported by the statement of Sum-pa,[13] according to which Śāntarakṣita was born "as the son of a king of *sahor* (*zahor*) of Eastern Bengal" : *śar-baṅg-la'i-za-hor-rgyal-po'i-sras-su-'khruṅs.*

Sum-pa[14] further asserts that Śāntarakṣita must have lived from the time of king Gopāla to that of king Dharmapāla : *rgyal-po-go-pa-la-nas-dharma-pa-la'i-bar-bshugs-ṅes-la.* According to the usually accepted Pāla chronology,[15] the approximate year of Gopāla's accession was A.D. 750, of Dharmapāla A.D. 770 and the latter ruled for about 32 years. Accepting this chronology, Sum-pa's statement amounts to the assertion that Śāntarakṣita must have lived between A.D. 750 and 802. Though too broad to give us an exact date of Śāntarakṣita, this agrees with the Tibetan chronology according to which Khri-sroṅ-lde-btsan ruled during the period A.D. 755-797. Thus the assertion of Csoma de Koros[16] that Śāntarakṣita was invited to Tibet in A.D. 747 seems to be in need of correction. Equally so appears to be the view subscribed to by B. Bhattacharya[17] and P. N. Bose[18] that Śāntarakṣita visited Tibet in A.D. 743 and built the bSam-yas monastery in A.D. 749.

The Tibetans usually give the name of Śāntarakṣita as

11. See Section 6, Note 3.
12. S. C. Das in JBTS I. i. 1.
13. Sum-pa 112.
14. *Ib.*
15. HB i. 176.
16. Csoma de Koros G 183.
17. Intro. to the *Tattva-saṃgraha* p. xivf.
18. P. N. Bose 124.

Shi-ba-'tsho,[19] literally Śānti-jīva, though Bu-ston[20] and Sum-pa[21] also mention him as Bodhisattva and Francke[22] says that his name "occurs in the Alci monastery inscription in the form of Śāntipā."

In India, according to Sum-pa,[23] Śāntarakṣita acted as the *upādhyāya* of Nālandā : *mkhan-po-bodhisattva-'am-shi-'tsho-shes-pa-na-len-dra'i-mkhan-po-mdsad*—"*upādhyāya* called Bodhisattva or Śāntijīva was acting as the *upādhyāya* of Nālandā." We do not know what brought him from Nālandā to Nepal, where Khri-sroṅ-lde-btsan's minister gSal-snaṅ first met him. "In Nepal," says Bu-ston,[24] "he met with the preceptor Bodhisattva and invited him to Maṅ-yul." "He (gSal-snaṅ)," says 'Gos lo-tsā-ba,[25] "then visited Nepal and met there with Śāntarakṣita. They held lengthy consultations and agreed, saying : 'We should establish the Doctrine of the Buddha in Tibet'."

But Ma-shaṅ was then still alive and gSal-snaṅ could not dare take the Indian *upādhyāya* straight to Tibet. With the elimination of Ma-shaṅ things became easier for the ministers favouring Buddhism. "Thereupon (i.e. after the death of Ma-shaṅ)," says Bu-ston,[26] "Jñānendra (gSal-snaṅ) was sent to invite the *ācārya* Bodhisattva." According to 'Gos lo-tsā-ba,[27] "Then gSal-snaṅ sent an invitation to the *upādhyāya*, who settled in Lhasa."

The king, however, felt uncertain about the real views of the *upādhyāya* and about the desirability of accepting him. Accordingly, says Bu-ston,[28] three Tibetans "were sent (to get information on the subject), but they did not understand the language (of the *ācārya*). They then prayed the Kashmirian

19. e.g. BA i. 39 Sum-pa 112 gives the abbreviated form as Shi-'tsho.
20. Bu-ston ii. 187. 21. Sum-pa 112. 22. Francke AIT ii. 88n.
23. Sum-pa 112. 24. Bu-ston ii. 187. Schlagintweit 67 says, the king "induced the learned *paṇḍita* Śāntarakṣita . . . to leave Bengal and settle in Tibet." This is groundless. 25. BA i. 42 ; cf i. 38. Sum-pa 170 says that gSal-snaṅ came to India from Maṅ-yul, made offerings to Mahābodhi, Nālandā and invited Bodhisattva (Śāntarakṣita) from Nepal to Maṅ-yul. 26. Bu-ston ii. 188. 27. BA i.42. 28. Bu-ston ii. 188.

Ananta to be interprete, and inquired of what kind the *ācārya* was. And, as it was said that he was virtuous and had no obscene thoughts, he was invited to the palace."

'Gos lo-tsā-ba's[29] account of this shows an interesting variation : "The king ordered his ministers to examine the doctrine and the character of the teacher, saying that should he prove virtuous, he, the king, would also extend an invitation to him. The ministers then visited the *upādhāya*, and inquired : 'What was his doctrine ?' The *upādhyāya* replied : '*My doctrine is to follow whatever was proved correct after examining it by reason, and to avoid all that does not agree with reason*'." This answer is remarkable in its rational spirit and something like this is perhaps only to be expected of the author of the *Tattva-saṃgraha*, though how far such an answer could historically satisfy the miracle-minded Tibetans of the time is a different question altogether.

The enquiry having been proved satisfactory for the Tibetan ruler, Śāntarakṣita was allowed to preach his doctrine. But what could he after all preach in Tibet at that time ? It could not be anything like the sharp philosophical polemics with which, in the *Tattva-saṃgraha,* he seems to sweep away all the rival philosophical standpoints. There was then in Tibet none to understand all these even remotely. Tibet received the initiation in literacy only a little more than a century before and was yet to make any appreciable cultural progress.[30] Though the Tibetan historians say so much about the translation of the Buddhist works during the time of Sroṅ-btsan-sgam-po and Khri-lde-gtsug-brtan, these were after all only sporadic activities confind to a limited few and even assuming that the texts like the *Kāraṇḍa-vyūha-sūtra* and *Ratna-megha-sūtra* were really understood by the Tibetan elite at an earlier period, they could have at best derived from these some idea of the later Mahāyāna mythology but not much of the fundamentals of Buddhist ethics and metaphysics in their classical sense.

29. BA i. 42. Emphasis added. 30. Waddell L 24n suggests that during the reign of Khri-sroṅ-lde-btsan Tibet was hardly recognised as a Buddhist country. But this cannot be true at least of the latter part of his reign.

Śāntarakṣita must have himself realised all these. He, therefore, concentrated in his preachings on the essentials of Buddhism, the *daśa-kuśala*-s and the *dvādaśa-nidāna*-s, i.e. the ten basic codes of the virtuous life and the chain of the twelve causes explaining the misery of earthly existence. He preached perhaps also the doctrine of the eighteen component elements of the individual.

Bu-ston[31] says that with the Kashmirean Ananta as the interpretor, "he expounded in the palace Luṅ-tshug for 4 months the teaching of the 10 virtues, of the 18 component elements of the individual, and of the 12 membered causal chain." "Then," says 'Gos lo-tsā-ba,[32] "the *upādhyāya* expounded to the king many doctrines, including that of the ten virtues and that of the eighteen *dhātu*-s." According to the *Chronicle of Ladakh*,[33] "This king invited the teacher Bodhisattva from India (!). Ananta of Kashmir became translator, and preached on the ten virtues, the eighteen regions (or elements), and the twelve causes of existence." "In the fifth generation from Sroṅ-btsan," says S. C. Das,[34] "the illustrious king Khri-sroṅ invited the great Indian *paṇḍita* Śāntarakṣita who introduced the observance of the 'ten virtues' and Dharma which teaches the real state of the eighteen physical and corporeal regions with the eight prohibitions such as killing, the taking of what is not given, the commission of foul actions, lying, drinking, dancing and singing, and sitting on lofty seats."

We have thus the impression that Śāntarakṣita was the first to preach in Tibet the real message of Śākyamuni whose image was brought there about a century before. As is, therefore, only to be expected, his teachings came in sharp clash with the theory and practices of the ancient Bon religion. There is no

31. Bu-ston ii. 188. 32. BA i. 43. 33. Francke AIT ii. 86.
34. S. C. Das in JASB 1882. 7.

record of the resistance to Buddhism during the time of Sroṅ-btsan-sgam-po, because there was very little of the nature of real Buddhism preached during his time. The resistance to Buddhism led by Ma-shaṅ during the earlier part of Khri-sroṅ-lde-btsan's reign appears to us to be more of the nature of ministerial intrigues, only with a thin varnish of ideological issues—the groups of ministers both favouring and opposing Buddhism during this time being almost equally innocent of the basic teachings of the Buddha.[35] But Śāntarakṣita's teachings must have provoked the first real resistance to Buddhism in Tibet, particularly because the new codes of moral conduct preached by him were directly opposed to the age-old practices of the Bon religion.

The typical Tibetan way of describing this resistance is to say that the malignant deities and devils of Tibet conspired against Śāntarakṣita, as a result of which Tibet was visited by all sorts of evil omens. His teachings, says Bu-ston,[36] "brought the malignant deities of Tibet into a fury. 'Phaṅ-thaṅ was carried away by a flood, lightning struck dMar-po-ri, and diseases befalling men and cattle broke out. The Tibetan subjects declared that this was a consequence of the propagation of a false doctrine, and the *ācārya* was sent back to Nepal." "But," says 'Gos lo-tsā-ba,[37] "the great gods and demons of Tibet became wrathful. Lightning struck the palace on the dMar-po-ri, and the royal palace of 'Phaṅ-thaṅ was carried away by water. Harvest was damaged, and a great epidemic took place. This encouraged the ministers, who were looking for mischief, and they used to say : 'This was done by the Doctrine ! This Indian ascetic should be expelled !' The king then offered a large quantity of gold to the *upādhyāya* and told him about the situation. The *upādhyāya* then said : 'I shall go to Nepal ! The Tibetan *asura*-s are displeased ! There is in Jambudvīpa a great and learned *mantrin* called Padmasambhava. I shall invite him, and you, king, should yourself send an invitation to him'."

35. Only later the minister gSal-snaṅ became a Buddhist monk.

36. Bu-ston ii. 188.

37. BA i. 43.

Śāntarakṣita, thus, had to leave Tibet. But the king, on his advice,[38] agreed to invite the great Tāntrika Padmasambhava to tackle the Tibetan devils and demi-gods. Waddell[39] says that Padmasambhava came to Tibet in A.D. 747. But this seems to be unlikely in view of the date of Khri-sroṅ-lde-btsan's reign.[40]

What Padmasambhava actually did in Tibet and how he brought the situation under control are at best matters for conjecture. Everything we are told about him by the Tibetans is fabulous, fantastic and grotesque. "Numerous biographies of him are extant, all of which give different accounts of his life."[41] Waddell[42] compiles from a number of Tibetan sources[43] a legendary history of Padmasambhava according to which he was a son of king Indrabhūti (Indrabodhi) of Udyāna (or Urgyan), though born in a miraculous way. Amitābha, the great Buddha of Boundless Light, sent like a lightning flash a miraculous incarnation of himself in the form of a red ray of light to the sacred lake of that country and the king found on the pure bosom of the lake a lotus-flower of matchless beauty, on whose petals sat a lovely boy eight years old, sceptred and shining like a god. Hence was his name 'The Lotus-born.' He had many wives,[44] one of whom is said to have been Śāntarkṣita's sister Mandaravā,[45] who accompanied him during his Tibetan expedition. From his early infancy he exhibited all sorts of miraculous feats, the descriptions of some of which have even a humourous element. "Athirst one day," runs one of these,[46] "he seeks a wine-shop,

38. Cf. Bu-ston ii. 189. 39. Waddell L 27. 40 A.D. 755-797 : See Section 23. 41. S. C. Das in JASB 1882. 9. 42. Waddell L 380f. 43. Waddell L. 379n mentions the following Tibetan works on which he depends : *Padma-bka'-than*, *Than-yig-gser-'phren*, etc. According to him none of these is six or seven hundred years old. Petech 88 thinks that the *Padma-bka'-than* dates back to the first period of Tibetan historical literature covering roughly 7th (!) - 13th centuries A.D., though "in its present form it is certainly of much later period." 44. Petech 71n says that king Khri-sroṅ-lde-btsan gave his daughter Khrom-pa-rgyan to Padmasambhava in marriage. 45. See Grünwedel in ZDMG 1898. 447ff. 46. Waddell L 382.

and, with companions, drinks deeply, till, recollecting that he has no money wherewith to pay his bill, he asks the merchant to delay settlement till sunset, to which the merchant agrees, and states that he and his comrades meanwhile may drink their fill. But the *guru* arrests the sun's career, and plagues the country with full day-light for seven days. The wine-seller, now in despair, wipes off their debt, when welcome night revisits the sleepy world."

There appears, indeed, no limit to the imagination of the Tibetans when they relate the miraculous feats of *guru* Padmasambhava. Specially grotesque are the stories of the way in which he subdued the devils and demi-gods of Tibet.[47] A female deity tried to destroy him by squeezing him between two mountains, but he overcame her by his *ṛddhi*-power of soaring in the sky. He then received her submission and her promise to become a guardian of his religion. Another fiendess showered thunderbolts upon him. He retaliated by melting her snow-dwelling into a lake and by causing the lake to boil. "But though her flesh boiled off her bones, still she did not emerge, so the *guru* threw in his thunderbolt, piercing her right eye. Then came she forth and offered up to him her life-essence, and was thereon named The Snow-white, Fleshless, One-eyed Ogress of the Vajra."[48]

The Tibetans tell us of numerous feats like these. Significantly in these legends Padmasambhava did not annihilate the devils and demi-gods. On the contrary, after subduing them, he recruited them to the Buddhist camp with some sort of subordinate status for them. As 'Gos lo-tsā-ba[49] puts it, "On his way (to Tibet), the twelve guardian-goddesses at first made an attempt to harm him, but he subdued them, and *then after initiating them, he entrusted to them the guardianship of the Doctrine.*"

The modern way of putting it would perhaps be that instead of an outright rejection of the ancient faith of Tibet, Padmasambhava somehow or other managed to absorb it within the

47. *Ib.* 382n. 48. *Ib.* 49. BA i. 43. Emphasis added.

structure of the Buddhist religion. It is in this aspect of the legends that Waddell finds the clue to Padmasambhava's success in Tibet. The Buddhists, says he,[50] for the purpose of extending their doctrines throughout Asia, "pandered to the popular taste by admitting within the pale of Buddhism the pantheon of those new nations they sought to convert." Arguing on this line, Waddell proceeds to show that the primitive Lamaism[51] founded by Padmasambhava in Tibet was but a blend of the Bon religion and Mahāyāna Buddhism, particularly in its Tāntrika phase. This primitive Lamaism was later reformed by various teachers in various ways, among whom Dīpaṃkara was about the most outstanding. However, there still lingered in Tibet an element of the unreformed Lamaism of Padmasambhava's brand and, even much later, its adherents sought support specially in the authority of Padmasambhava and they worshipped this *guru* as much as they worshipped the Buddha. This residual element of primitive Lamaism, according to Waddell, forms the rÑiṅ-ma-pa sect of modern Tibet. "The residue who remained wholly unreformed," says he[52] "and weakened by the loss of their best members, were now called the rÑiṅ-ma-pa or 'the old ones', as they adhered to the old practices. And now, to legitimize many of their unorthodox practices which had crept into use, and to admit of further laxity, the rÑiṅ-ma-pa resorted to the fiction of *gTer-ma* or hidden revelations...rÑiṅ-ma Lamas now began to discover new gospels, in caves and elsewhere, which they alleged were hidden gospels of the *guru,* Saint Padma." The follower of the rÑiṅ-ma-pa sect "worships the *guru* Padmasambhava, the founder of Lamaism, in a variety of forms, both divine and demoniacal, expressive of his different moods at different times."[53]

How far such an explanation of Padmasambhava's success in Tibet is to be accepted as historically adequate ? This is a difficult question. The orthodox Tibetans even outside the

50. Waddell L 26-7. 51. *Ib.* 30; 55. 52. *Ib.* 56-7.
53. *Ib.* 72-3.

rÑiṅ-ma-pa sect will not accept it. Padmasambhava commands a tremendous respect in the general religious history of Tibet. Besides, there is at least one point which shows that it is inadequate to consider that Padmasambhava's contribution consisted merely in a tactful absorption of the primitive faith of Tibet within Buddhism or in effecting some kind of synthesis of primitive Bon with Mahāyāna Tantrism. The Tibetan historians tell us not merely the weird legends of how Padmasambhava subdued the Tibetan devils, they also tell us that he took a leading role in founding the bSam-yas monastery in Tibet.

Petech[54] thinks that the importance of the bSam-yas monastery is "undoubtedly exaggerated" by the Tibetans, his main argument being that this importance is to be found specially in the *rGyal-rabs-gsal-ba'i-me-loṅ* written by bSod-nam-rgyal-btsan who was himself a monk of the bSam-yas and, therefore, "was naturally inclined to exalt his own monastery." But this argument is hardly convincing. Practically all the important historians of Tibet glorify this monastery and there are clear reasons to think that it became a great centre of Buddhist studies in Tibet. Numerous Buddhist texts were collected in this monastery, some of which were lost in India even during the time of Atīśa. While describing the Tibetan career of Atīśa, 'Gos lo-tsā-ba[55] says, "After that the Master proceeded to bSam-yas...The master also saw there many Indian manuscripts, and when he noticed many manuscripts which were not to be found in India, he said : 'It seems the Doctrine had first spread in Tibet, even more than in India.'... On the whole, the Master was very pleased with the monastery and intended to stay there for a considerable time."

There is no doubt that the building of this monastery owed much to the initiative of Padmasambhava. According to the usual Tibetan accounts, after the local devils and demi-gods were subdued by Padmasambhava, he, along with Śāntarakṣita, laid the foundation of the bSam-yas monastery, which, king

54. Petech 70. 55. BA i. 257; cf i. 44.

Khri-sroṅ-lde-btsan got constructed. This means that Śāntarakṣita was brought back to Tibet before the work on the bSam-yas monastery started. From 'Gos lo-tsā-ba's account (in Roerich's translation), however, it is not clear whether Śāntarakṣita returned to Tibet before the first initiative was taken towards the building of the monastery. "On his (Padmasambhava's) arrival at bSam-yas," says 'Gos lo-tsā-ba,[56] "a god belonging to the retinue of the four Guardian Kings" started a new round of anti-propaganda against Padmasambhava. "All these (attempts)were mastered by the *ācārya.* They (?) laid the foundation of the great *vihāra* of bSam-yas. The *upādhyāya* (Śāntarakṣita) was then again invited (to Tibet)." This seems to imply that after being expelled from Tibet by the wave of anti-Buddhist feelings provoked by his first attempt to preach Buddhism, Śāntarakṣita returned to Tibet after Padmasambhava took the initial steps to establish the great monastery. According to Bu-ston,[57] however, after Padmasambhava subdued the Tibetan demons, Śāntarakṣita was invited to bSam-yas and established his residence there. "The *ācārya* Bodhisattva in his turn, examined the ground, took the monastery of Odantapurī as a model and made a plan containing the forms of the mount Sumeru, the 12 continents, both the sun and the moon, all these surrouned by a circumference of iron." bSam-yas was built according to this plan. From Bu-ston's account, therefore, it appears that the first real initiative of the building of bSam-yas was taken by Śāntarakṣita, though only after the great exploits of Padmasambhava.

Waddell[58] asserts that the monastery was built in A.D. 749. This date is accepted by both P. N. Bose and B. Bhattacharya,[59] though, curiously enough, on the authority of S. C. Das,[60] who actually says that the "monastery was completed in the year called *she-fire-hare.*" The two Fire-Hare years proximate to Khri-sroṅ-lde-btsan's reign were A.D. 727 and 787. In the present case it means the latter, for, according to the concurrent

56. *Ib.* i. 43-4. 57. Bu-ston ii. 189. 58. Waddell L 28.
59. See HB i. 333n. 60. S. C. Das in JBTS I. i. 4.

authority of 'Gos lo-tsā-ba and the Chinese annals, Khri-sroṅ-lde-btsan ascended the throne in A.D. 755.

'Gos lo-tsā-ba's own dating of the bSam-yas is interesting. According to him, "From the Hare year till the Sheep year the king built the *vihāra*."[61] It is to be noted first that this is one of the exceptional cases in which 'Gos lo-tsā-ba gives the dates only in terms of the animals and this indicates that he is possibly quoting here some ancient text, for the earlier authorities alone mention dates only in terms of the animals. The Hare year in which, according to the older tradition, the foundation of the monastery was laid is not difficult to reconstruct. Depending presumably on the same tradition, Bu-ston[62] says that in the Female-Fire-Hare year the foundation of the monastery was laid. Thus the Fire year of 'Gos lo-tsā-ba is to be understood as a Fire-Hare year. According to the Tibetan sexagenary cycle, three successive Fire-Hare years are A.D. 727, 787 and 847. Of these, neither 727 nor 847 can be accepted as the year in which the work on the monastery began, because both these fall outside the reign of Khri-sroṅ-lde-btsan. Thus, the Hare year of 'Gos lo-tsā-ba can be taken only as A.D. 787. But how are we to understand the Sheep year of the same passage ? According to the Tibetan sexagenary cycle, the first Sheep year after a Fire-Hare year is an Iron-Sheep year and the next Sheep year is a Water-Sheep year. Following A.D. 787, the first Iron-Sheep year is A.D. 791 and the Water-Sheep year A.D. 803. The latter date is unacceptable, because bSam-yas was completed during the life-time of Khri-sroṅ-lde-btsan. Thus, in short, 'Gos lo-tsā-ba's dating of the monastery is to be taken as A.D. 787-791. But this flatly contradicts his own dating of the death of Khri-sroṅ-lde-btsan as A.D. 780. This is one of the important considerations for the acceptance of the Chinese date of the king's death as A. D. 797—a date that

61. BA i. 44. 62. Bu-ston ii. 189. The *Padma-dkar-po* also gives the same date - See Petech 70. Bu-ston ii. 189 says that in the Female-Earth-Hare year the work was accomplished. Two successive Earth-Hare years are A.D. 739 and 799, none of which agrees with the date of Khri-sroṅ-lde-btsan's reign.

agrees well with Bu-ston's statement that the king "died 69 years of age."

The bSam-yas monastery, it is generally said, was modelled on the Odantapurī *vihāra* of India. But the history of Odantapurī is itself uncertain.[63] Bu-ston says that it was built during the reign of Gopāla, while, according to Sum-pa and Tāranātha, it was built sometime between Gopāla and Devapāla. Further, Sum-pa is quite categorical that Śāntarakṣita lived from the time of Gopāla to that of Dharmapāla. Thus Odantapurī could have been the latest of the Indian *vihāra*-s with which Śāntarakṣita was acquainted and he could have persuaded the Tibetan king to imitate its model. According to S. C. Das,[64] however, at least from the architectural point of view bSam-yas was not a copy of Odantapurī. "The top of the monastic temple (of bSam-yas)," says he, "was constructed in Chinese style, the middle part in Indian style, and the lowest part in Tibetan style."

The full Tibetan name of the monastery is bSam-yas-mi-'gyur-lhun-gyis-grub-pa'i-gtsug-lag-khaṅ,[65]—"The academy for obtaining the heap of unchanging meditation." "The explorer Nain Singh resided in this monastery in 1874 and has given a good account of it. It is situated about thirty miles to the S. E. of Lhasa, near the north bank of the gTsaṅ-po river amidst hillocks of deep sand, clothed with scanty herbage. Part of the original building yet remains. The monastery, which contains a large temple, four large colleges, and several other buildings, is enclosed by a lofty circular wall about a mile and half in circumference, with gates facing the cardinal points, and along the top of the wall are many votive brick *caitya*-s, of which the explorer, Nain Singh, counted 1,030, and they seem to be covered with inscriptions in ancient Indian characters. In the centre of the enclosure stands the assembly hall, with radiating

63. See Section 14. 64. S. C. Das in JASB 1882. 9n. For a modern photograph of the monastery, see Richardson *Plate 15* facing p. 230.
65. Waddell L 266.

cloisters leading to four chapels, facing at equal distances the four sides of the larger temple. This explorer notes that 'the idols and images contained in these temples are of pure gold, richly ornamented with valuable cloths and jewels. The candle-sticks and vessels are nearly all made of gold and silver.' And on the temple walls are many large inscriptions in Chinese and ancient Indian characters... The library contains many Indian manuscripts, but a great number of these were destroyed at the great fire about A.D. 1810."[66]

Much more important than the imposing physical description of the monastery is its significance as a centre of Buddhist learning in Tibet. The initiative for this could be taken only by somebody with considerable academic background and Śāntarakṣita alone was such a person in Tibet at that time.[67] The Tibetan histories contain the accounts of all sorts of miraculous feats performed by Padmasambhava during and after the construction of this monastery and these also contain hints that he became eventually somewhat unpopular in Tibet.[68] In any case, there is no ground to think that he remained in Tibet long after the building of the bSam-yas.[69] The Tibetans usually say that he went to quell the demons elsewhere.[70] But Śāntarakṣita remained back. He became the first *upādhyāya* of the bSam-yas monastery and continued to work there for 13 more years.[71]

The bSam-yas was in fact the first Buddhist monastery in Tibet in the real sense of the term. We are told no doubt of many Buddhist *vihāra*-s and temples built in Tibet from the time of Sroṅ-btsan-sgam-po. However, like the sporadic translations of a few Buddhist texts carried out in the earlier period, these so-called early *vihāra*-s made little or no impact on the Tibetans from the point of view of the propagation of

66. *Ib*. 266-7. 67. Petech 50 asserts that "the work of translation in a large scale" started in Tibet "under the supervision of Padmasambhava"; but this is not corroborated either by the Tibetan histories or by the evidences of the bKa'-'gyur and bsTan-'gyur.

68. Bu-ston ii. 190. Francke AIT ii. 87. 69. Waddell L 32n.

70. Francke AIT ii. 87; Waddell L 32n. 71. Waddell L 29.

genuine Buddhism. By contrast, the bSam-yas was the first full-fledged Buddhist monastery in Tibet with regular provisions for resident monks and for their teaching.[72] With a scholar like Śāntarakṣita to guide it, the monastery soon became an important centre of Buddhist learning, for Śāntarakṣita was the first Buddhist *ācārya* in the classical sense of the term who worked effectively for the propagation of Buddhism in Tibet.

We have an interesting passage in 'Gos lo-tsā-ba[73] in which is frankly admitted that during the centuries that intervened between the first miraculous appearance of Buddhist scriptures in Tibet and the reign of Khri-sroṅ-lde-btsan, Śāntarakṣita was about the only scholar in Tibet who cared above all for "ordination" and "Vinaya", while the others—including Sroṅ-btsan-sgam-po himself—were concerned mainly with weird religious beliefs and practices described under the vague epithet "Tantra". The passage deserves to be quoted in full, for it contains a brief but realistic account of the history of Tibetan religion up to the time of Khri-sroṅ-lde-btsan.

"The Holy Doctrine originated during the time of Tho-tho-ri-gñan-btsan, which preceded that of gNam-ri-sroṅ-btsan. Nothing else is known, except that the royal family worshipped the gÑan-po-gsaṅ-ba (the books that were said to have fallen from Heaven). Sroṅ-btsan-sgam-po adhered to the Tantric Sādhanas of various benign and wrathful deities, and it seems that there have been many people propitiating these deities. Before (king) Me Ag-tshom (Khri-lde-gtsug-brtan) Tantric Sādhanas existed in secret... The book containing the conjuration of Bhairava, composed by Sroṅ-btsan, exists even nowadays... Then Khri-sroṅ-lde-btsan invited the *mahā-upādhyāya* Śāntarakṣita. Many Tibetans took up ordination, and propagated the doctrine of the Vinaya. Therefore his fame of having propagated widely the Doctrine is well founded. Further, Padmasambhava having come (to Tibet) during that time, he propagated the Tantras. Padma himself bestowed on the king (the initiation) of Vajrakīla and Hayagrīva. The king

72. BA i. 44. 73. *Ib*. i. 105-6.

especially propitiated Hayagrīva. On three occasions the neighing of a horse was heard, and many people heard it. The Vajrakīla : Padma bestowed it on the queen (Ye-śes-tshogs-rgyal) and on A-tsar Sa-le. Later it spread widely through its Lineage and various schools. *'Jam-dpal-sku* (one of the eight rÑiṅ-ma Tantras) : the *ācārya* Śāntigarbha having come to Tibet, propagated (this Tantra). He is known to have performed the consecration ceremony of bSam-yas."

Because of 'the destruction of the Doctrine' by gLaṅ Darma followed by the dark period of Tibetan history, much of the details of Śāntarakṣita's work at bSam-yas are evidently lost to us. From the few hints we are left with, we may infer that as the *upādhyāya* of the monastery he took two extremely important steps for the propagation of Buddhism in Tibet. On the one hand, he created the first genuine team of Tibetan monk-scholars, which could soon devote itself in right earnest to the work of translating Buddhist works into the Tibetan language. On the other hand, he caused to be brought from India a number of Indian scholars under whom the Tibetans could study and translate. As a result, Tibetan translation of Buddhist works received such a stimulus that within a few years[74] the majority of works contained in the bKa'-'gyur and bsTan-'gyur, totalling over four thousand and five hundred, were rendered into the Tibetan language.

"At first," says 'Gos lo-tsā-ba,[75] "the 'Seven Men on probation' (*sad-mi mi-bdun*) took up ordination." S. C. Das[76] explains *sad-mi mi-bdun* as "the seven most distinguished and talented among the young Tibetans who were selected by king Khri-sroṅ-lde-btsan to be trained as monks by *ācārya* Śāntirakṣita, and thoroughly instructed in religion and sacred sciences. The three elder ones among them were : Mañjuśrī of dPa', Devendra of rTsaṅs, Kumudika of Bran ; while the three junior ones were : Nāgendra of 'Khon, Vairocanarakṣita of Pagor and *ācārya* Rin-chen-chog of rMa and an intermediate one was Katana of gLaṅ."

74. i.e., by the time of Ral-pa-can's death. See Section 26.
75. BA i. 44. 76. D-TED 1266.

From Bu-ston's account it appears that there is some difference of opinion among the Tibetan authorities about the names of the Seven Selected Ones as well as of their actual Preceptor, though Bu-ston himself argues that they were the pupils of Śāntarakṣita. After the consecration of the bSam-yas monastery, says Bu-ston,[77] "12 monks of the sect of the Sarvāstivādins were invited, and it was put to the test, whether the Tibetans could become monks or not. For this purpose 7 men were selected and ordained as monks...These are spoken of as 'the 7 selected ones.' If we examine the ends of their names and take in consideration that the name of Bodhisattva was Śāntarakṣita, it will be clear that they were the pupils of the latter."

Quite a few Indian scholars were brought to Tibet, under whom this group of newly initiated Tibetans worked for the translation of Buddhist texts, for the first time in Tibetan history, in a really systematic manner. "Furthermore," continues Bu-ston,[78] "the Indian teachers Vimalamitra, Buddhaguhya, Śāntigarbha, Viśuddhasiṃha with the Tibetan translators, viz. the 7 selected ones, Dharmāloka, the Ban-de Nam-mkha', Ratnasena of sGro, rNam-par-mi-rtog-pa, Śākyaprabha and others interpreted and translated numerous kanonical works...By these and other similar works the Doctrine was fully and thoroughly introduced. In the year of the Dragon the teachers residing in the palace of lDan-dkar, the translators Ban-de dPal-brtsegs, the Ban-de Nāgendra and others made a list of the titles of the sacred texts that were translated in Tibet, as well as the number of divisions and *śloka*-s contained in them, and wrote all this down in the form of a catalogue."

All these took place during the lifetime of Śāntarakṣita. But his life came to an abrupt end because of an accident: "having been kicked by a horse, he went to his rest."[79]

The last thing attributed by Bu-ston to Śāntarakṣita was a prophecy according to which the Tibetan Buddhists were soon to be divided into two sects and Śāntarakṣita's student

77. Bu-ston ii. 190. 78. *Ib.* ii. 190-1. 79. *Ib.* ii. 191.

Kamalaśīla was to be brought to Tibet 'to pacify all strife and establish the true form of the teaching.'

The story of the split in the Buddhist camp in Tibet is best told by Bu-ston.

During the ministerial intrigues of the earlier part of Khri-sroṅ-lde-btsan's reign, the Chinese priests substantially helped the Tibetan ministers favouring Buddhism. Their activity continued to persist even after the foundation of the bSam-yas monastery, when, according to Bu-ston,[80] they "underwent the practice of meditation in the Mi-gyo-bsam-gtan-gliṅ." After the death of Śāntarakṣita, when Śrīghoṣa (dPal-dbyaṅs) was acting as the teacher at the bSam-yas[81] and Jñānendra (formerly minister gSal-snaṅ) gave himself up to meditation, the number of the pupils of the Chinese *ho-shang* Mahāyāna increased. These favoured nihilistic views and did not exert themselves in the practice of virtue, saying : 'By acting according to the Doctrine, by virtuous acts of body and speech, one cannot become a Buddha. One attains the state of the latter by abiding in perfect inactivity.'—The Tibetans, for the greater part, found pleasure (in such a conception of the Doctrine) and studied the system (of the *ho-shang*). Śrīghoṣa, Ratna of Ba and a few others who adhered to the system of the *ācārya* Bodhisattva did not agree (with the *ho-shang*) neither in the theory nor in the practice, and there was strife (between the two parties). When the king gave the order that one should follow theoretically and practically the system of the *ācārya* Bodhisattva, the sTon-mun-pa (the Chinese party) were enraged, *armed themselves with sharp knives and threatened to kill all the Tsen-min-pa* (the adherents of Bodhisattva)."[82] They interpreted the *Śata-sāhasrikā* and other *sūtra*-s according to their own views and fabricated works like *Dhyāna-svapna-cakra*, etc. in which "was demonstrated that the action according to the Doctrine was unnecessary, and that it was sufficient to abide in a state of sleep."[83]

Khri-sroṅ-lde-btsan, feeling highly disturbed, brought back

80. *Ib.* 81. *Ib.* 82. *Ib.* ii. 191-2. Emphasis added. 83. *Ib.* ii. 192.

Jñānendra from the solitude of his meditation. On his advice, the king invited Kamalaśīla from India to defend Śāntarakṣita's views against the Chinese *ho-shang*. After Kamalaśīla came to Tibet, a grand philosophical debate was organised between the Chinese priests and the followers of Śāntarakṣita, with the king as the judge. Bu-ston gives us some details of the debate which are not without interest for the understanding of the Mahāyāna ethics and philosophy. The main points of the Chinese *ho-shang* and of Kamalaśīla are summed up by him as follows :[84]

"Then the *ho-shang* spoke : 'If one commits virtuous or sinful deeds, one comes to blissful or to evil births (respectively). In such a way the deliverance from the *saṃsāra* is impossible, and there will be always impediments to the attainment of Buddhahood. (The virtuous and the sinful deeds) are just like white and black clouds which alike obscure the sky. But he who has no thoughts and inclinations at all, can be fully delivered from Phenomenal Life. The absence of any thought, search, or investigation brings about the non-perception of the reality of separate entities. In such a manner one can attain (Buddhahood) at once, like (a Bodhisattva) who has attained the 10th Stage.'

"To this Kamalaśīla himself answered as follows : 'Thou sayest thus that one ought not to think about anything whatever. But this means the negation (or rejection) of the Highest Analytic Wisdom likewise. Now as the latter represents the foundation of the Divine Wisdom of a Saint, the rejection of it necessarily leads to the negation of this sublime Transcendental Wisdom. If Analytic Wisdom is absent, what meditator can come to abide in a state where there is no constructive thought ? If one has no thought concerning any of the elements of existence and does not direct the mind upon them, this does not mean that one can cease to remember all that one has experienced and to think of it. If I think : I must not recall in my mind any element of existence, such a thought

84. *Ib.* ii. 193-4.

will itself be an intense recollection and activity of the mind. If the mere absence of (consciousness and) recollection is regarded as sufficient, it follows that in a swoon or at the time of intoxication one comes to the state where there is no constructive thought. Now, (in reality) without correct analysis there is no means of attaining the liberation from constructive thought. If we merely cease to reflect and have no discrimination, how can we come to the cognition of the non-substantiality of all the elements ? And, without the cognition of Non-substantiality, it is impossible to remove the Obscurations. Therefore, the incorrect representation can be cast away only by means of the correct Analytic Wisdom. For this reason it is not proper to say, that one does not reflect, when in reality it is the reverse. Without recollection and correct activity of the mind, how can one come to remember the place of former residence and attain Omniscience ? And how will it be possible to extirpate the passions ?—But the Yogin who reflects over an object by means of correct Analytic Wisdom, cognizes all the external and internal elements in the present, past, and future as non-substantial, has all thought-construction pacified within him, and rejects all the evil doctrines. On this foundation he becomes skilful in expedients and in the manifestation of Highest Wisdom. And, having through this cleared all the Obscurations, he can attain the state of a Buddha."

Bu-ston says that after Kamalaśīla's speech, Śrīghoṣa and Jñānendra offered more arguments against the Chinese priests, as a result of which "Co-rma-rma and other (adherents of the *ho-shang*) were distressed and having smitten their bodies with stones, died, as runs the tradition."[85]

There is same speculation among the modern scholars on the real issue of this famous controversy. Schlagintweit[86] is inclined to see at its basis a clash between the Mādhyamika an Yogācāra interpretations of the Mahāyāna outlook. The Chinese priests, says he, "seem to have taught the principles of Nāgārjuna with the modification established by the Yogācāra school... Padmasambhava and subsequent Indian priests,

85. *Ib.* ii 195. 86. Schlagintweit 67-8.

however, explain the Law in the sense of the Mādhyamika school, which in India at this period gained influence over the Yogācāra system." But this speculation is groundless. Apart from the questionable assumption that the ethics of inaction follows more from the Yogācāra standpoint, the fact is that Śāntarakṣita and Kamalaśīla themselves represented in their extant writings some form of Yogācāra philosophy. Richardson,[87] on the other hand, is inclined to see the influence of the Taoist outlook in the ethics of inaction defended by the Chinese priests. The *ho-shang*, says he, "perhaps influenced by Taoist quietism, preached that enlightenment could be attained instantaneously by complete inactivity." The Indian teachers, on the other hand, "holding the traditional view, argued that it was a gradual process requiring activity extending over a long series of lives." But the exact ethical implication of the Taoist standpoint is itself a difficult question[88] and the controversy, as described by Bu-ston, gives us the impression that it was more of the nature of a clash between two rival interpretations of the Mahāyāna standpoint itself.

Be that what it may, according to the Tibetan historians this philosophical debate leading to Kamalaśīla's victory was an important landmark in the religious history of Tibet. But this was not the end of the whole episode. Bu-ston[89] adds that after the king finally declared victory of the followers of Śāntarakṣita and proclaimed that in Tibet only this interpretation was to be followed, "four Chinese butchers, sent by the *ho-shang*, killed the teacher Kamalaśīla by squeezing his kidneys." Shortly after this, Khri-sroṅ-lde-btsan died.

87. Richardson 31. 88. Needham ii. 34ff. 89. Bu-ston ii. 196.

26. *Ral-pa-can*

After Khri-sroṅ-lde-btsan, says 'Gos lo-tsā-ba,[1] the "Tibetan kings, till king Ral-pa-can, continued to maintain the deeds of their ancestors." This means that they continued to work for the Doctrine.

Ral-pa-can, a grandson of Khri-sroṅ-lde-btsan, was the last Buddhist king of central Tibet. After his assassination came the great disaster to Buddhism. His younger brother gLaṅ Dar-ma assumed power and, as the Tibetans put it, destroyed the Doctrine. With the death of gLaṅ Dar-ma, the history of Tibetan monarchy came to its end.

Between Khri-sroṅ-lde-btsan and Ral-pa-can Tibet witnessed an enlightened period of its history. But this period is most difficult to follow. Its chronology is uncertain and even the names of the kings confusing. Roerich[2] rightly suggests, we "shall have to await a thorough investigation of the Tibetan chronicles" for a fuller knowledge of this period. With the present state of Tibetan researches, it is perhaps desirable to state the problems concerning the period rather than to try to reach any hasty solution.

'Gos lo-tsā-ba[3] gives us the following chronology :

Khri-sroṅ-lde-btsan,	AD 755-780
Mu-ne-btsan-po,	780-797
Ju-tse-btsan-po,	797-804
Khri-lde-sroṅ-btsan,	804-814
Ral-pa-can,	814-835
gLaṅ Dar-ma,	836-841.

But there are many difficulties about it. First, it is not easy to accept 780 as the date of Khri-sroṅ-lde-btsan's death. It contradicts 'Gos lo-tsā-ba's own dating of the bSam-yas monastery[4] and also the evidence of the Chinese annals,

1. BA i. 44. 2. *Ib.* i. Intro. p. xx. 3. *Ib.* i. 51ff.
4. See Section 25, Notes 58-62.

according to which the king died in 797. Secondly, the name Ju-tse-btsan-po is puzzling. It occurs in no other Tibetan history and Petech[5] argues that it is only the product of a wrong re-transliteration of the name of Mu-ne-btsan-po : the *T'ang-shu* gives the name of Mu-ne-btsan-po as Tsu-chih-tsien and 'Gos lo-tsâ-ba wrongly reconstructs it as Ju-tse-btsan-po.

This, says Petech, creates for 'Gos lo-tsā-ba the unhappy situation of recognising an extra king. Therefore, eliminating Ju-tse-btsan-po from the list and following more closely the Chinese dating, Petech[6] gives a revised chronology :

Khri-sroṅ-lde-btsan,	AD 755-797
Mu-ne-btsan-po,	797-804
Khri-lde-sroṅ-btsan,	804-817
Ral-pa-can,	817-836
gLaṅ Dar-ma	836-842.

Khri-sroṅ-lde-btsan, says Petech,[7] had three sons called Mu-ne-btsan-po, Mu-rug-btsan-po and Mu-tig-btsan-po.[8] Of these, the eldest Mu-ne-btsan-po ascended the throne after his father's death only to be assassinated shortly afterwards. The second son predeceased his father, also by assassination. Mu-tig-btsan-po ascended the throne after the assassination of Mu-ne-btsan-po. Mu-tig-btsan-po, also called Khri-lde-sroṅ-btsan, *alias* Sad-na-legs, had five sons ; of these Ral-pa-can was the second and gLaṅ Dar-ma the third. The first son called gTsaṅ-ma[9] became a Buddhist monk and was later murdered by the order of gLaṅ Dar-ma.

Such a reconstruction of the history of this period is not without its own difficulties. First, it is too much to admit that 'Gos lo-tsā-ba failed to understand the Chinese transliterations of Tibetan names. He is perfectly aware, e.g., that K'a-li-k'a-tsu in Chinese is equivalent to Ral-pa-can,[10] or, as Petech himself admiringly observes, he "did know how to reconstruct the form K'a-li-k'a-tsu of his source into the original Tibetan

5. Petech 74 f. 6. *Ib*. 77-82. 7. *Ib*. 71ff. 8. Petech 74 is aware of the uncertainty about these names : "not one source agreeing with the others on this point." 9. *Ib*. 79. 10. BA. i. 52.

Khri-gtsug(-lde-btsan Ral-pa-can)."[11] 'Gos lo-tsā-ba freely uses also the Chinese transcription of the name of gLaṅ Darma, namely Ta-mo.[12] Secondly, the Chinese annals do not really give any equivalent of the name of Mu-ne-btsan-po and Petech himself admits that the name Tsu-chih-tsien of the Chinese annals, alleged to be the Chinese transcription of Mu-ne-btsan-po and wrongly retranscribed by 'Gos lo-tsā-ba as Ju-tse-btsan-po, cannot be really reduced to any Tibetan original. "Probably", says Petech,[13] "the text is corrupt, because it is impossible to find a Tibetan equivalent for this name." This is one of the instances of how the Chinese annals fail us for the period immediately after Khri-sroṅ-lde-btsan. Thirdly, the period of reign attributed by Petech to Mu-ne-btsan-po is much longer than would find acceptance by any Tibetan authority. The usual account is that he ruled for about a year and a half,[14] though according to the *rGyal-rabs-bon-gyi-'byuṅ-gnas*, it was for three years.[15] Fourthly, there is much confusion about the name of Khri-lde-sroṅ-btsan, whom Petech identifies with Mu-tig-btsan-po or Sad-na-legs and, following 'Gos lo-tsā-ba, makes the immediate predecessor of Ral-pa-can. Lastly, Petech totally ignores Bu-ston's version of the history of this period, which, in brief, is as follows[16] :

Khri-sroṅ-lde-btsan died 69 years of age.

Mu-ne-btsan-po assumed the reign in the Water-Male-Tiger year [A.D. 822].

Having reigned for a year and 7 month, he died 17 years of age.

After that, his younger brother Khri-lde-btsan-po, then 4 years of age, was made king, and was (later on) known by his *alias* Sad-na-legs.

Five sons were born to him : Khri-lde-sroṅ-btsan, Ral-pa-can-gtsaṅ-ma, Khri-dar-ma-u-dum-btsan, Lha-rje-lhun-grub, Khri-chen-po.

11. Petech 46. 12. BA i. 53. See Roerich Intro. p. xiv.
13. Petech 74. 14. Bu-ston ii. 196. This agrees with *Chin T'ang-shu* –See Roerich BA i. Intro. p. xx n. 15. See Roerich BA i. Intro p.xx
16. Bu-ston ii. 196-7. The dates given by Bu-ston of Mu-ne-btsan-po's accession (A.D. 822) and of Ral-pa-can's assassination (A.D 841) do not agree with those given by either 'Gos lo-tsā-ba or the Chinese annals.

Ral-pa-can became king at 18 and at 36, in the Female-Iron-Bird year [i.e. A.D. 841], was assassinated.

Thereafter, the bTsan-po gLaṅ-dar-ma-u-dum-btsan took possession of the kingdom.

The period of Mu-ne-btsan-po's reign apart, Bu-ston's account differs from the version proposed by Petech in many important points. The younger brother of Mu-ne-btsan-po, who succeeded him and was better known as Sad-na-legs, was really called, according to Bu-ston, Khri-lde-btsan-po, and he had for his eldest son Khri-lde-sroṅ-btsan, a name equated by Petech to that of Sad-na-legs, the younger brother and successor of Mu-ne-btsan-po. Who, then, according to Petech, was the eldest son of Sad-na-legs ? Petech answers that his name was gTsaṅ-ma. In Bu-ston's account, however, gTsaṅ-ma was but the last part of Ral-pa-can's name. Are we, then, to assume that Petech is here in confusion ? Even assuming this, however, the question of the real name and fate of the eldest son of Sad-na-legs, who should have normally been the successor to the throne, remains unanswered. But the modern scholar alone is not to be accused of the confusion. The Tibetan historians themselves appear to be confused about the genealogy of the Tibetan kings after Khri-sroṅ-lde-btsan. This will be evident from a comparison of the two lists of the five sons of Sad-na-legs given by Bu-ston and Sum-pa. Thus :

Bu-ston	*Sum-pa*[17]
1. Khri-lde-sroṅ-btsan	1. gTsaṅ-ma
2. Ral-pa-can-gtsaṅ-ma	2. Lha-rje
3. Khri-dar-ma-u-dum-btsan	3. Lhun-grub
4. Lha-rje-lhun-grub	4. Dar-ma
5. Khri-chen-po.	5. Ral-can.

Thus, the end part of Ral-pa-can's name in the former, viz. gTsaṅ-ma, becomes the full name of the first in the latter list and this tallies with Petech's view that gTsaṅ-ma[18] was the

17. Sum-pa 151n. S. C. Das in JASB 1881 224ff evidently depends on this account.

18. Interestingly, Bu-ston ii. 197 says that gTsaṅ-ma was also the name of Ral-pa-can's eldest son.

name of the first son of Sad-na-legs. Secondly, the fourth name in the former list is split up into two in the latter. To accommodate these two additions, Sum-pa's list eliminates two names from the list given by Bu-ston, namely the first and the last ones. The omission particularly of the name Khri-lde-sroṅ-btsan from Sum-pa's list cannot be lightly treated. 'Gos lo-tsā-ba mentions it as the name of the king who immediately preceded Ral-pa-can. However, it is interesting to note that though Sum-pa eliminates the name of Khri-lde-sroṅ-btsan from the list of the five sons of Sad-na-legs, he combines it with that of Ral-pa-can and says, "Khri-lde-sroṅ-btsan Ral-pa-can of the Fire-Dog year (i.e. born in the Fire-Dog year) nourished the kingdom"—*me-khyi-lo-pa-khri-lde-sroṅ-btsan-ral-pa-can-gyis-rgyal-srid-bskyaṅs.*[19] This Fire-Dog year mentioned by Sum-pa as the date of the birth of Ral-pa-can is presumably A.D. 806, for it cannot be either 746 or 866. Since Bu-ston says that the king was 36 years old in the Iron-Hen year (presumably A.D. 841), the Fire-Dog year was the date of the birth of Ral-pa-can according to Bu-ston also. Further, as we shall presently see, Sum-pa's proposed identification of Ral-pa-can with Khri-lde-sroṅ-btsan appears to be supported by other important Tibetan evidences.

In spite of all the confusion about Tibetan history after Khri-sroṅ-lde-btsan, however, the following can perhaps be broadly assumed : Khri-sroṅ-lde-btsan was succeeded by his eldest son Mu-ne-btsan-po, who was murdered shorty afterwards and was succeeded by his youngest brother better known as Sad-na-legs. This king had five sons, among whom Ral-pa-can succeeded him. After some time, Ral-pa-can was murdered and was succeeded by his brother gLaṅ Dar-ma, who, after having ruled for a brief period, was himself murdered. With this murder, the history of Tibetan monarchy came to its end.

Of the successors of Khri-sroṅ-lde-btsan, the names of Mu-ne-btsan-po, Ral-pa-can and gLaṅ Dar-ma interest us most. The reasons, however, are quite different. Ral-pa-can

19. Sum-pa 151.

was by far the most pious follower of Buddhism among the Tibetan monarchs while gLaṅ Dar-ma was most intensely opposed to it. But Mu-ne-btsan-po's name is remembered by the Tibetan historians primarily because of some reason which has at least apparently nothing to do with the support or suppression of Buddhism. The strange thing persistently told about him is that, though a monarch, he tried his best to enforce some kind of economic equality among his Tibetan subjects.

Mu-ne-btsan-po, says Bu-ston,[20] "thrice established equality between the rich and the poor of his Tibetan subjects." Sum-pa[21] repeapts this : Mu-ne-btsan-po established equality among his Tibetan subjects, the rich and the poor. "Three times," says the *Chronicle of Ladakh*,[22] "he equalised the rich and hungry of Tibet." S. C. Das[23] compiles the following account about him : "During the infancy of Mu-ne-btsan-po the state affairs were conducted in his name by his pious ministers. He commenced his independent reign with a generous determination of raising all his subjects to the same level. He ruled that there should be no distinction between poor and reach, humble and great. He compelled the wealthy to share their riches with the indigent and helpless, and to make them their equal in all the comforts and conditions of life. Thrice he tried this experiment, but every time he found that the poor returned to their former condition ; the rich becoming richer still, and the poor, by growing more indolent and wretched, turning poorer still. The Paṇḍits and lo-tsā-ba-s attributed this curious phenomenon to the consequence of the good and evil acts of their former births."

The philosophical explanation suggested above of the failure of Mu-ne-btsan-po's socialism is to be found in the *Chronicle of the Fifth Dalai Lama*[24] and Petech[25] argues that such an attempted explanation itself indicates that the king's repeated

20. Bu-ston ii. 196. 21. Sum-pa 151. 22. Francke AIT ii. 88, though this chronicle confuses Mu-ne-btsan-po with Mu-khri-btsan-po.
23. S. C. Das in JASB 1881. 226. 24. See Petech 71n. 25. *Ib.* 71.

efforts to enforce economic equality in Tibet appeared extremely strange even to the Tibetan historians themselves. But it does not follow that the account is fictitious. Petech[26] observes, "This story may at first sight appear an absurdity. But it seems to me that such stories are difficult to invent root and branch (besides, to what purpose ?). There must have been some sort of a foundation for the growth of such a legend."

How, then, are we to look back at the strange socialistic tendency of the Tibetan monarch ? Could it be because of his pious zeal for Buddhism ? That he was personally a pious and enlightened Buddhist need not be doubted. We have already discussed[27] the possibility of his participation in the translation of a Buddhist text under an Indian *paṇḍita* called Dīpaṃkara-candra or Dīpaṃkara-rāja. Bu-ston[28] says, he "caused four great religious services to be celebrated at bSam-yas." According to Sum-pa,[29] the copy of the *Sūtra-piṭaka* of the *Tri-piṭaka* he presented to this monastery is still existing in its collection.

Mu-ne-btsan-po's devotion to Buddhism is unquestioned. But do we have in this a full explanation of his effort to enforce economic equality among his subjects ? His father Khri-sroṅ-lde-btsan was a great patron of Buddhism. But we have nowhere even any vague suggestion of his socialistic tendency. The same is true of his nephew Ral-pa-can, who, of all the Tibetan monarchs, was personally the most pious and devout Buddhist. The later ruler of western Tibet, Ye-śes-'od, who, according to the Tibetan historians sacrificed even his life to the cause of Buddhism,[30] is never mentioned as showing any tendency to equalise the rich and the poor. In short, Tibetan history contains no hint that the message of the Buddha as the Tibetan rulers understood it had anything to inspire a socialistic tendency in them. Apparently, therefore, we have to seek elsewhere a possible explanation of Mu-ne-btsan-po's

26. *Ib.* 27. See Section 5, pp. 49f. 28. Bu-ston ii. 196.
29. Sum-pa 151. 30. See Section 29.

"far-reaching reform, which might almost be called a revolution."[31]

Petech[32] has an interesting explanation of this, though he modestly calls it "a simple hypothesis, based on very uncertain foundations." He suggests that though Khri-sroṅ-lde-btsan was the most powerful of the Tibetan kings who kept the Tibetan aristocracy under strong control and who, in order to destroy one important source of the political and economic power of this aristocracy, took the programme of an aggressive suppression of the Bon religion, the aristocracy nevertheless remained powerful. In one of the songs sung at the foundation ceremony of the bSam-yas monastery, "the noble singers display a strong sense of pride and a clear consciousness of their power and wealth."[33] The power of the Tibetan nobility always remained a threat to Tibetan monarchy and Mu-ne-btsan-po's economic reform could have been designed to destroy this power. "The power of the nobility," says Petech,[34] "reflected itself in that of the ministers ; only a few of the more energetic kings succeeded in getting rid of their regents-ministers, who acted, though nominally on behalf of the king, in reality according to their own convenience. Mu-ne-btsan-po as heir-apparent had occasion to feel the influence of the aristocracy, and had before him the example of his father's vigorous action. He decided to free the monarchy from the power of the nobility, destroying the very foundation of its strength. Accordingly, he gradually confiscated in three successive steps the estates of landed proprietors (that were nothing but the old tribal chiefships of the 5th and 6th century subdued by gNam-ri-sroṅ-btsan), either joining them with the private possessions of the crown, or parcelling them among the commoners."

This hypothesis easily explains the murder of Mu-ne-btsan-po after a brief reign—in fact the briefest in Tibetan history

31. Petech 76. 32. *Ib.* 71f. 33. *Ib.* 71-2. The song is preserved in the *Pad-ma'i-bka'-thaṅ.* 34. *Ib.* 72.

—though the Tibetan historians generally give a private reason for the murder. He was poisoned by his mother, according to the usual account,[35] because he married one of the widows of his father. But S. C. Das[36] does not attach much importance to this account and says, "that promising king was poisoned by his mother, who perpetrated this foul act to place her youngest son on the throne." Petech[37] adds that Mu-ne-btsan-po's mother herself came from one of the Tibetan aristocratic families, in the interest of which she might have poisoned her son : "It may well be that his death was due to personal reasons, but I am inclined to believe that the queen, who profoundly felt the duty of solidarity with her clan, rendered herself the interpreter of the wishes of the entire aristocracy, removing her son who threatened to do away with the nobility."

After the death of Mu-ne-btsan-po, his younger brother—possibly the youngest of the three—better known in Tibetan history as Sad-na-legs, ascended the throne. His reign, though considerably longer than that of Mu-ne-btsan-po, was on the whole uneventful. We do not hear much about him either from the Chinese or from the Tibetan sources. But the Tibetan historians have to say a lot about his son and successor, who, again, is better known by the name Ral-pa-can.

The honorific name Ral-pa-can itself speaks eloquently about the Buddhist piety of the king. *Ral-pa* is the Tibetan equivalent of the Sanskrit word *jaṭā* or matted hair. "His devotion to the priestly congregation," says S. C. Das,[38] "was so great that he offered his own *ral-pa* or flowing locks to be turned into carpet-seats for the use of the Lamas." 'The nick-name Ral-pa-can," says Petech,[39] "is explained by the *rGyal-rabs-gsal-ba'i-me-loṅ* thus : the king, in order to show his veneration for the monks and the lo-tsā-ba-s, wrapped his hair with long pieces of cloth, on which the holy men sat."

35. See Francke AIT ii. 89n ; Petech 72. 36. S. C. Das in JASB 1881. 227. 37. Petech 72. 38. S. C. Das in JASB 1881. 228. 39. Petech 79.

Ral-pa-can was about the only Tibetan king who, inspired by the message of the Buddha, took active steps to bring a halt to the military campaigns of the Tibetans and establish a peaceful relation particularly with the Chinese. Though Bu-ston[40] says, "he made war with China, was victorious, and the numerous reports of his generals were written down in the Long Stone (rDo-riṅs) in Lhasa," the actual edict on the famous Lhasa Pillar embodying the peace-treaty between Tibet and China effected on the initiative of Ral-pa-can, speaks of the pacifist mentality of the Tibetan king. "The Great king of Tibet," reads this treaty,[41] "the Miraculous Divine Lord, and the Great King of China, the Chinese Ruler Hwang-ti, being in the relationship of 'nephew and uncle,' have conferred together for the alliance of their kingdoms. They have made and ratified a great agreement...With the single desire of acting for the peace and benefit of all their subjects they have agreed on the high purpose of ensuring lasting good...Between the two countries no smoke nor dust shall be seen. There shall be no sudden alarms and the very word 'enemy' shall not be spoken... This solemn agreement has established a great epoch when Tibetans shall be happy in the land of Tibet, and Chinese in the land of China. So that it may never be changed, the Three Precious Jewels of Religion, the Assembly of Saints, the Sun and Moon, Planets and Stars have been invoked as witnesses."

Petech suggests that the peace thus effected was largely due to the fact that both Tibet and China had, by the time of Ral-pa-can, already exhausted themselves by the military excesses of the preceding centuries : "The empire of the T'angs was nearly on its last legs and was not in a position to busy itself with what happened outside the frontiers of China proper. Tibet was now exhausted by the long and unequal struggle on three fronts. Peace was called for by the force of circumstances."[42] At the same time Petech does not at all doubt the basically pacifist policy of Ral-pa-can : "The pacific mentality of the king manifested itself in a lull in military activity...

40. Bu-ston ii. 197. 41. Richardson 244-5. 42. Petech 80.

As we have seen, the treaty between Tibet and the Caliphate was concluded round about 810. Little later on, in 822, the famous treaty was signed which finally closed Tibet's long-lasting fight with its great neighbour... Unlike the treaty of 783, the 822 peace was not broken...and lasted until the fall of the monarchy."[43]

But the religious zeal of the monarch found its highest expression in his patronage of Buddhist learning. "Immediately after his accession he sent offerings to the different temples built by his ancestors. He built a new nine-storeyed temple, of which the three lower storeys were of stone, the three middle of brick, and the topmost three of wood. In the upper floors he kept Buddhist scriptures, images, and model shrines. In the middle floors he accommodated the Paṇḍits and translators of the holy writs, and the ground floors he reserved for the use of his court and state affairs... Thinking that the propagation of religion depended much upon the predominance of the clergy, he organised many classes of priesthood. To each monk he assigned a small revenue derived from five tenants."[44]

This enthusiasm for Buddhist learning led the king to adopt new measures for the proper translation of Indian works. "Ral-pa-can," says Bu-ston,[45] "who was considered to be the incarnation of Vajrapāṇi, began to reign 18 years of age and built the palace of 'On-caṅ-rdo with nine storeys. Before, in the time of his forefathers, the teacher Bodhisattva (Śānta-rakṣita), Jñānendra, Shaṅ-rgyal-ñen-ña-bzaṅ, bLon-khri-bshir-saṅ-śi, the translators Jñānadevakoṣa, Khyi-'brug of lCe, the *brāhmaṇa* Ananta and others created a literary language that contained many words unintelligible to the Tibetans. Besides, different translations were made from the Chinese, from the language of Li and Sahor, etc. Owing to this there were many different renderings of words and the study of the Doctrine became very difficult. Seeing this, the king issued the following order : The Aparāntaka teachers Jinamitra, Surendrabodhi,

43. *Ib*. 79-80. 44. S. C. Das in JASB 1881. 227-8.
45. Bu-ston ii. 196-7.

Śīlendrabodhi and Bodhimitra, the Tibetan teachers Ratnarakṣita and Dharmatāśīla, the skilful translators Jñānasena, Jayarakṣita, Mañjuśrīvarman, Ratnendraśīla and others are to translate the Hīnayānistic and Mahāyānistic Scriptures into Tibetan directly from the Sanskrit. The titles are to be registered and written down so as to form an index. In no case are the rules of translation to be violated, and one must make the translations so that it could be possible for everyone to study. —Moreover, the texts translated before were re-edited in the new language, 3 different forms of instructions were made, and it was prescribed that the Hīnayānistic Scripture other than that acknowledged by the Sarvāstivādins, and the secret charms were not to be translated."

Rockhill[46] estimates that at least half of the existing collections of the bKa'-'gyur and bsTan-'gyur were done by these *paṇḍita*-s and translators. Bu-ston was one of the redactors of these two great Tibetan collections in their present form. It is impossible to treat lightly his statement concerning the history of the Tibetan translation of the Buddhist works. At the same time, what he says about this translation activity under the patronage of Ral-pa-can raises an interesting question.

According to him, the Indian scholars specially commissioned by Ral-pa-can were Jinamitra, Surendrabodhi, Śīlendrabodhi and Bodhimitra. The Tibetan translators who worked under them were Jñānasena, Jayarakṣita, Mañjuśrīvarman, Ratnendraśīla and others. Further, the centre of this translation activity was the newly built nine-storeyed palace called 'On-caṅ-rdo. All these names occur in the colophon of the famous Sanskrit-Tibetan dictionary usually referred to as the *Mahāvyutpatti.*[47] In this was first laid down rigid rules for the use of Tibetan equivalents of Sanskrit words to be used in the translation of Buddhist works. But this colophon mentions king Khri-lde-sroṅ-btsan[48] rather than Ral-pa-can under

46. Rockhill LB 224-5. 47. mDo cxxiii. 44.

48. N. Dutt in *Prajñā* Foreword pp. vi-vii mentions this royal patron as Khri-sroṅ-lde-btsan !

whose patronage the dictionary was prepared. This dictionary "comprising about 9,500 expressions", says the colophon,[49] contains "vocabulary prepared under the order of king Khri-lde-sroṅ-btsan, by the Masters *upādhyāya ācārya* Jinamitra, Surendrabodhi, Śīlendrabodhi, Dānaśīla and Bodhimitra of Mi-'og (Aparānta), *upādhyāya* Ratnarakṣita and Dharmatāśīla of Tibet, the lo-tsā-ba-s Jñānasena, Jayarakṣita, Manjuśrī-varman, Ratnendraśīla, (and so on) of Tibet, in pursuit of the Mahāyāna and Hīnayāna texts." The place of the execution of the work is mentioned as 'On-caṅ-rdo, i.e. the nine-storeyed palace built by Ral-pa-can as mentioned by Bu-ston. Further, according to the colophon of the *Mahāvyutpatti,* the work was presented to the king by Ban-de-chen-po dPal-gyi-yon-tan, the great Buddhist monk mentioned by Bu-ston[50] as belonging to the reign of Ral-pa-can. All these details of the colophon clearly agree with those given by Bu-ston, only with this difference that while Bu-ston gives the name of the king under whose patronage the great literary activity was carried on as Ral-pa-can, the colophon of the *Mahāvyutpatti* mentions him as Khri-lde-sroṅ-btsan. The *sGra-sbyor-bam-po-gñis-pa* or the *Nighaṇṭu: Mahāvyutpatti*[51] also mentions Lha-btsan-po Khri-lde-sroṅ-btsan, under whose order the work received its final form.

How, then, are we to account for the discrepancy between Bu-ston and the bsTan-'gyur colophons regarding the name of this king? One way of doing it is to identify Ral-pa-can of Bu-ston's account with Khri-lde-sroṅ-btsan of the colophons. Lalou[52] does this and this seems to be the suggestion of Sum-pa's mention of the name as Khri-lde-sroṅ-btsan-ral-pa-can.

Professor Lama Chimpa[53] tells me, "Most of the sources agree that Khri-lde-sroṅ-btsan was no one else but Ral-pa-can. Ral-pa-can was in fact only an epithet used for this king because of his famous *ral-pa* or matted hair, the equivalent of Sanskrit *jaṭā*. The Tibetan history *Pad-dkar-chos-'byuṅ*[54]

49. See Cordier ii. 487. 50. Bu-ston ii. 197. 51. mDo cxxiv.1. See colophon of the Peking edition No. 5833. 52. Lalou 176.
53. Personal communication.
54. Xylograph copy in the Visvabharati University.

clearly says that Khri-lde sroṅ-btsan was none but Khri-ral-pa-can."

Assuming this tradition to be valid, Petech's theory concerning the identity of Khri-lde-sroṅ-btsan with Sad-na-legs (Ral-pa-can's father) cannot be accepted. Petech argues that the youngest son of Khri-sroṅ-lde-btsan and the successor of Mu-ne-btsan-po was known by various names : "in his intercourse with his teacher (Padmasambhava), he was called Mu-tig-btsan-po ('Pearl King', probably an initiatic name) ; with his father he was called Khri-lde-sroṅ-btsan (probably the true personal name...) ; with the ministers he was called Sad-na-legs (a nick-name which in the chronicles normally substitutes all the others, and was probably the popular name of the king) ; in his relations with China the name Mu-ru-btsan-po was used."[55]

The evidence offered by Petech himself[56] in support of this theory is not a very strong one. Besides, Bu-ston's version flatly contradicts the view that Sad-na-legs was but the nickname of Khri-lde-sroṅ-btsan. According to him, it was rather the nickname of the younger brother of Mu-ne-btsan-po, whose real name was Khri-lde-btsan-po and the name of whose eldest son was Khri-lde-sroṅ-btsan. At the same time the difficulty in identifying Ral-pa-can with Khri-lde-sroṅ-btsan must not be overlooked. 'Gos lo-tsā-ba[57] gives the full name of Ral-pa-can as Khri-gtsug-lde-btsan Ral-pa-can. In the Lhasa Pillar[58] edict also his name occurs as Khri-gtsug-lde-btsan. These indicate that the real name of Ral-pa-can could have been Khri-gtsug-lde-btsan rather than Khri-lde-sroṅ-btsan. Besides, both Bu-ston and 'Gos lo-tsā-ba mention Ral-pa-can as different from Khri-lde-sroṅ-btsan. According to Bu-ston,[59] Khri-lde-sroṅ-btsan was the name of the eldest brother of Ral-pa-can who never ascended the Tibetan throne. In the account given

55. Petech 74-5.

56. Petech mentions the evidence of the *Pad-ma'i-bka'-thaṅ*.

57. BA i. 52. D-TED 361 gives the name as The Powerful Khri-ral-pa.

58. Richardson 244. 59. i.e. assuming the accuracy of Obermiller's translation.

by 'Gos lo-tsā-ba, however, Khri-lde-sroṅ-btsan did ascend the Tibetan throne, though his relation to the successors of Khri--sroṅ-lde-btsan is somewhat confused. In one place[60] he mentions the name of Khri-lde-sroṅ-btsan as immediately succeeding Mu-ne-btsan-po while in another place[61] he mentions the peculiar name of Ju-tse-btsan-po as intervening between Mu-ne-btsan-po and Khri-lde-sroṅ-btsan. In both cases, however, 'Gos lo-tsā-ba mentions Khri-lde-sroṅ-btsan as immediately preceding Ral-pa-can to the Tibetan throne.

In view of all these confusions it is unsafe to try to have any definite theory about the identity of Khri-lde-sroṅ-btsan or even about the real name of Ral-pa-can. The real solution of these problems perhaps awaits a more thorough investigation into Tibetan history. One point, however, appears to be clear. With Ral-pa-can the history of Tibetan Buddhism reached the crest before its fall and the next wave of regeneration reached its peak again when Atīśa came to Tibet.

There are clear indications in the Tibetan sources that the intense piety of Ral-pa-can resulted in his eventual murder. Bu-ston[62] says, "Now, as the government of the city was entrusted to a monk, the ministers who rejoiced in sinful deeds were enraged and made secret machinations in order to violate the precepts of the Doctrine. The king's son gTsaṅ-ma who had taken orders was expelled to T'omo. Scandalous talk was spread about that the queen Ṅaṅ-tshul-ma and the great Ban-de Yon-tan-dpal had secret intercourse with each other. Finally, the great Ban-de was murdered and the queen committed suicide. The king himself, 36 years of age, in the Female-Iron-Bird year [A.D. 841] was assassinated by dPas-rgyal-to-re and Co-re-legs-smra who turned round his neck."

Petech[63] argues that this murder was engineered by the Tibetan aristocracy that saw in Ral-pa-can's zeal for Buddhism real threat to its own interest : "The Buddhistic zeal of the dynasty was responsible for gradual replacement of the aristo-

60. BA i. 37. 61. *Ib*. i. 52. 62. Bu-ston ii. 197.
63. Petech 81.

cracy by Buddhist monks in the most influential charges of the court. The *Bodhimor* speaks plainly about this...In 836 a conspiracy was formed and the king was assassinated by two noble men." That this conspiracy was the work of the aristocracy, argues Petech, is evident from the names of the noble men who murdered the king : "Among the conspirators and the chief supporters of the new regime occur a few of the most famous names of the old families that once formed the backbone of the state."

After the murder of Ral-pa-can his brother gLaṅ Dar-ma was installed on the throne, under whose violent persecution Buddhism was 'destroyed' in Tibet.

27. gLan Dar-ma

Waddell[1] says that after ascending the throne gLaṅ Dar-ma "at once commenced to persecute the Lamas and did his utmost to uproot the religion." Bu-ston, however, gives us the clear impression that, only some years after being installed on the throne, gLaṅ Dar-ma actively associated himself with the offensive against the Buddhists already launched by the powerful ministers including the murderers of Ral-pa-can. After the murder of Ral-pa-can, says Bu-ston,[2] the "devil-like dPas-rgyal-to-re who was appointed minister for inward affairs, the minister sNa-nam-rgyal-tsha-khri-gsum and others did much that was contrary to the precepts of the Doctrine. The school-house where the lo-tsā-ba-s and *paṇḍita*-s had translated the kanonical works was destroyed, the translations remained in-achived, and the consecration of the 'On-caṅ-rdo was not performed. Thereafter, *when the king grew older*, devil took possession of his mind, and he ordered that all the monks were to renounce the religious life." From 'Gos lo-tsā-ba's[3] account also we have the same impression of some time lag between the accession of gLaṅ Dar-ma and his persecution of Buddhism. According to him, gLaṅ Dar-ma ascended the throne in the Fire-Male-Dragon year, i.e. A.D. 836. After this, "unrest took place in the kingdom of Tibet," and, in the following Iron-Male-Ape year (A.D. 840) till the year Iron-Female-Hen (A.D. 841) Dar-ma again ruled. In this Iron-Hen year the Doctrine ceased to exist." From this Roerich[4] infers, "It seems the king was deposed in 839 A.D. and again reinstated in the following year (A.D. 840)." After being thus reinstated, the king launched his offensive against the Buddhists.

1. Waddell L 34.
2. Bu-ston ii. 197-8 ; emphasis added.
3. BA i. 53.
4. Roerich BA i. Intro. p. xiv.

Historically, however, the more important question is: What could have been the actual motive of gLaṅ Dar-ma's persecution? From the Tibetan historians themselves, we do not have any clear analysis of it. 'Gos lo-tsā-ba[5] simply says that the king was of wicked character. This, as an explanation of the persecution, is hardly more illuminating than Bu-ston's statement that a devil took possession of him. The *Chronicle of Ladakh*[6] has a weird tale intended to explain the cause of the persecution. According to it, four heretical Brahmins, "unable to tolerate either the many *paṇḍita*-s who had been invited to Tibet by the ruler Ral-pa-can, or the offerings of golden writings, or the spread of Buddha's teaching over Tibet," killed themselves in order to be reborn as four demons to bring ruin to Tibet; these four demons were gLaṅ Dar-ma and his associates.

Francke[7] suggests that gLaṅ Dar-ma's persecution was because of a private grudge. Though older than Ral-pa-can, he was excluded from the succession to the throne by the Buddhist ministers on the ground that he was inimical to Buddhism. He got his chance when Ral-pa-can was murdered by the enemies of the Buddhists, with whom he naturally joined hands in persecuting the latter. These enemies of the Buddhists were in favour of reviving the Bon religion, whose hope, again, centered in gLaṅ Dar-ma.

But it is difficult to determine who, between Ral-pa-can and gLaṅ Dar-ma, was actually older. The Tibetan sources are not agreed on this, neither are the modern scholars. Francke's view seems to be based on the *Chronicle of the Fifth Dalai Lama*, according to which gLaṅ Dar-ma was older than Ral-pa-can; "he should have ascended the throne after the death of his father, but was excluded from it on account of his Bon-po faith."[8] Sum-pa[9] also takes gLaṅ Dar-ma as older than Ral-pa-can and S. C. Das[10] accepts this view. According to

5. BA i. 53. 6. Francke AIT ii. 90-1. 7. Francke HWT 59. 8. See Petech 79n. 9. Sum-pa 151n. 10. S. C. Das in JASB 1881. 227 & 229.

Bu-ston,[11] however, Ral-pa-can was actually older of the two brothers and Petech[12] relies on this account.

In view of these differences among the Tibetan authorities themselves it would be unsafe to subscribe to the view that an unjust exclusion from the throne explains gLaṅ Darma's grudge against the Buddhists. Besides, the magnitude of his persecution would call for a more adeqate explanation than is provided by a mere private grudge. Tibetan historians simply tell us that it was primarily a clash of creeds—gLaṅ Dar-ma was as enthusiastic a supporter of the Bon Religion as Ral-pa-can was of Buddhism. Even assuming this, however, it is necessary to try to trace the political and economic undercurrents of this clash of creeds and a clue to this is perhaps to be sought in the old conflict between Tibetan monarchy and Tibetan aristocracy.

The main internal problem which Tibetan monarchy had to face throughout the period of its existence in history was caused by the extremely powerful aristocratic families, which were originally the Tibetan clans first unified by gNam-ri-sroṅ-btsan and from which the Tibetan court subsequently drew its influential ministers. Sroṅ-btsan-sgam-po succeeded in fully establishing his own authority on these aristocratic families, which nevertheless remained alert to utilise every opportunity to capture the state power. Immediately after the death of Sroṅ-btsan-sgam-po, the power was usurped by the minister 'Gar. who represented an influential family of Tibetan aristocracy. The regency of 'Gar and his son was overthrown by Sroṅ-btsan's energetic great-grandson Khri-'du-sroṅ-btsan, *alias*, 'Dus-sroṅ-maṅ-po-rje, who, unfortunately for the monarchy, died early. The ministerial intrigues started in full swing, again, when Khri-sroṅ-lde-btsan ascended the throne as a helpless minor. On growing up, however, he succeeded in bringing the Tibetan nobility under the control of his iron grip, and presumably with the design of destroying their power, aggressively suppressed the Bon religion in favour of Buddhism.

11. Bu-ston ii. 196. 12. Petech 79 & 81.

This was really the first clash of creeds that Tibet witnessed. At its basis, however, was the clash between the political and economic interests of aristocracy and monarchy in Tibet. The former frequently enjoyed hereditary Bon priesthood, from which was derived considerable economic and political power. In the interest of the monarchy, therefore, Khri-sroṅ-lde-btsan had to suppress Bon and patronise Buddhism as a substitute religion. Śāntarakṣita and Padmasambhava were brought to Tibet, the first full-fledged monastery was established and Khri-sroṅ-lde-btsan, the most war-like of the Tibetan kings after Sroṅ-btsan-sgam-po, became also one of the greatest patrons of Buddhism. This was how the Tibetan aristocracy was ideologically disarmed. His son and successor, the young Mu-ne-btsan-po, appears to have tried further measures to curb the economic power of the aristocracy. He made an experiment with the most radical form of land-reform in Tibet. But he was murdered by his own mother, who came from one of the famous families of Tibetan aristocracy and evidently acted in the interest of the threatened nobility. This was followed by some kind of a lull in the conflict between aristocracy and monarchy, which characterised the reign of Sad-na-legs. But the conflict became sharp, again, during the reign of Ral-pa-can who, perhaps inspired mainly by his personal piety, became an ardent supporter of the Buddhists. In him, therefore, Tibetan aristocracy saw new threats to its own existence and, as a result Ral-pa-can was eventually murdered. The assassins of Ral-pa-can installed gLaṅ Dar-ma on the throne. gLaṅ Dar-ma might have had strong personal grudge against the Buddhist officials and this might have contributed to the zeal with which he joined the persecution of the Buddhists. But the more important point seems to be that the offensive was already launched by the representatives of the Tibetan aristocracy, Ral-pa-can's murder itself being an expression of this. gLaṅ Dar-ma's succession to the throne was manoeuvered by the aristocracy in whose hands, therefore, he had to be largely a puppet. His personal perference for the Bon religion need not be doubted. The aristocracy would not have chosen him for the throne if he were himself in favour of the Buddhists. But his personal covictions might have after all been secondary in importance. The circumstances that made him the king also demanded of him measures directly opposed to those that were adopted by Khri-sroṅ-lde-btsan. Acting in the interest of the monarchy, Khri-sroṅ-lde-btsan found it necessary to suppress the Bon religion, while, being but a tool of aristocracy gLaṅ Dar-ma found it equally necessary to suppress Buddhism and reinstate Bon, the ideological weapon of Tibetan aristocracy.

As is only to be expected of the Tibetan historians, the picture they usually give of gLaṅ Dar-ma is that of evil incarnate. "This king became the target of all Lamaist historians who painted him with the foulest colours as a combination of Nero and Julian the Apostate ; the *T'ang-shu,* under Buddhist influence, increases the dose."[13]

'Gos lo-tsā-ba[14] says, "He was addicted to wine and of a wicked character. Unrest took place in the kingdom of Tibet. At Si-ha-ci'u an artificial hill, demarcating the boundary in Tibetan controlled territory, tumbled down. For three days the river Klu-chu flowed upstream. Evil omens appeared, and the kingdom was disintegrating." According to the account compiled by S. C. Das,[15] "He reviled the first Chinese Princess Wen-ch'eng-kung-chu (wife of king Sroṅ-btsan-sgam-po) as an evil goblin who had brought the image of Śākyamuni into Tibet. 'It was for that inauspicious image', said he, 'that the Tibetan kings were short-lived, the country infested with maladies, subjected to unusual hoar-frost and hail-storms, and often visited by famines and wars.' 'When this image,' continued he, 'was being brought from the top of Sumeru mountain, the gods were vanquished in a war with the demons. Śākya's accession to power, first in India and afterwards in China, made the people unhappy and poor, by the demoralising effect of his wicked teachings.' To slander Buddha in such blasphemous language was his great delight, and in no discourse

13. Petech 81. 14. BA i. 53. 15. S. C. Das in JASB 1881. 229.

did he indulge himself so much as in reviling that holiest of holies." The Tibetans even believe[16] that being but a devil, he had actually two horns on his head, which he kept concealed by a peculiar mode of hair-doing. "These horns," says Francke,[17] "proved that gLaṅ Dar-ma was a Devil in his role of 'Julian the Apostate' of Buddhism. But the idea of his having horns may have been suggested by the first part of his name, which means 'ox'."

Bu-ston[18] describes the nature of his persecution : "To all those who did not wish to give up the distinctive marks of monkhood, he ordered to give bows, arrows, drums and tambourins, and sent them to transact the business of hunters. Those who disobeyed were put to death. As the king was not able to remove the statue of Śākyamuni, he ordered to hide it, having buried it in sand, barred the doors of the temple, covered them with plaster and ordered to draw upon them the picture of a monk drinking wine. The doors of bSam-yas and Ra-mo-che were likewise plastered with mould, and the books for the greater part hidden amidst the rocks of Lhasa."

Understandably, the Tibetan historians glorified as an inspired saint the person who finished off such a ruler. His name is given as dPal-gyi-rdo-rje,—a name much more celebrated in the Tibetan histories than those of the great army generals leading the most successful Tibetan campaigns. Even outside the historical works, dPal-gyi-rdo-rje's name is widely popular and his murder of gLaṅ Dar-ma is celebrated in the form of popular masquerades.[19]

The Tibetans describe with ardent zeal how dPal-gyi-rdo-rje was inspired to commit this 'holy' murder and how cleverly he executed it. "The goddess dPal-ldan-lha-mo descending from heaven appeared before him and exhorted him in the following terms : 'O saint, in these days there are none so powerful as thou. Wouldst thou deliver the country from the hands of that sinful tyrant gLaṅ Dar-ma ?' In the morning

16. Francke HWT 60. 17. *Ib.* 18. Bu-ston ii. 198.
19. Waddell L 529.

the saint inquired of his servant the condition of Tibet, upon which he was told the cruelties practised by gLaṅ Dar-ma."[20] "He mounted," continues Bu-ston,[21] "a white horse, having smeared it black with coal, put on a fur-coat with the white side inward and the black one outward, took an iron bow and an iron arrow, came to Lhasa, saw the king as he was reading the inscriptions of the Long Stone, dismounted before him... Having approached him, he lowered his knee and at the same time, bent his bow. The king, in his turn, thought that he was saluting him. At the first salutation he bent the bow. At the second he fitted the arrow, and at the third he loosened the bow-string. The arrow, parting, struck the breast (of the king). (dPal-rdo-rje) said : 'I am the black demon Ya-sh'er. If a sinful king is to be killed, it must be done in such a manner.' With these words he fled. A great clamour arose in Lhasa : 'The king has been murdered ; hasten to the pursuit of the assassin !' (dPal-rdo-rje) then washed the horse in the lake of Mi-nag, put on his coat, having turned it with the white part outward, and, saying : 'Now I am the white demon of the skies', continued his flight. It was thus impossible for the pursuers to get hold of him." An account of the last lamentation of gLaṅ Dar-ma is given by S. C. Das[22] : "The king pulled the reeking arrow out with both his hands, and in the agonies of death, when his proud heart was subdued with anguish, exclaimed : 'Why was I not killed three years back that I might not have committed so much sin and mischief, or three years hence, to enable me to root out Buddhism from the country', and died."

But the Tibetan historians say that gLaṅ Dar-ma's desire to destroy the Doctrine was at least temporarily fulfilled. "Now", according to Bu-ston,[23] "of the *paṇḍita*-s, some were banished and some driven out of the country. The greater part of the lo-tsā-ba-s had fled, and Tiṅ-ṅe-'dzin-bzaṅ-po of Ñaṅ, Rin-chen-mchog of Ma, and others were killed by

20. S. C. Das in JASB 1881. 230.
21. Bu-ston ii. 199.
22. S. C. Das in JASB 1881. 230.
23. Bu-ston ii. 199.

murderers who were sent to them. In such a manner the Doctrine was rooted out." 'Gos lo-tsā-ba also says, "The Doctrine ceased to exist."[24]

With the death of gLaṅ Dar-ma came also the end of Tibetn monarchy proper. Some of his successors "continued however to disguise their ambitions under the name of rightful princes of the ancient royal house. These princes succeeded in founding strong states in the west where the Tibetan immigration was more recent and the immigrants were freer from the bonds of the clans. The monarchic tradition, extinct in Tibet proper, took refuge in territories originally non-Tibetan, in the western states."[25]

The story of this will be taken up by us particularly in connection with Ye-śes-'od, the ruler of western Tibet, whose tremendous zeal for Buddhist renaissance eventually culminated in the coming of Atīśa to Tibet. Before, however, we leave the account of gLaṅ Dar-ma, it is necessary to have a few words on the possible date of his persecution of Buddhism.

This date is crucial for Tibetan history, both in its religious and secular aspect. It is not only the date of the greatest setback for Tibetan Buddhism but also of the fall of Tibetan monarchy. But the question of this date presents baffling problems. The Tibetan historians themselves seem to depend upon two distinct traditions, which lead them to two different sets of calculations, ultimately resulting in a difference of sixty years or a complete cycle of the sexagenary system. Of these two traditions, one is clearly based on the Chinese annals. It is difficult to be exact about the source of the other, though it appears that when the Tibetan historians try to relate the date of the persecution with later events of Tibetan history they rely on it. This is best illustrated by the writings of 'Gos lo-tsā-ba.

When giving the dates of Tibetan history on the basis of Chinese tradition, 'Gos lo-tsā-ba[26] says, "It is stated that till

24. BA i. 53. 25. Petech 85. 26. BA i. 53.

this Earth-Female-Sheep year 208 years had elapsed (since the founding of the T'ang dynasty). If one calculates properly, the T'ang empire must have lasted for 222 years. This Earth-Female-Sheep year is the fourth year since the accession of gLaṅ Dar-ma. In the following Iron-Male-Ape year till the year Iron-Female-Hen, Dar-ma again ruled. In this Iron-Hen year the Doctrine ceased to exist. Immediately after that, the king was murdered by dPal-gyi-rdo-rje. Therefore, scholars consider this year Iron-Hen to be the first year of the period which began after the setting of the Doctrine."

First, what is meant by the Earth-Female-Sheep year above? According to the Tibetan sexagenary cycle, we have three successive Earth-Female-Sheep years as A.D. 779, 839 and 899. But since 'Gos lo-tsā-ba says that the T'ang empire must have lasted for 222 years during the Earth-Female-Sheep year he speaks of, it can be taken only as A.D. 839, the year of the establishment of the T'ang empire (according to 'Gos lo-tsā-ba) being A.D. 618, an Iron-Male-Tiger year of the Tibetan calendar.[27] Thus, according to the passage quoted, A.D. 839—an Earth-Female-Sheep year—was the fourth year since the accession of gLaṅ Dar-ma. In the Tibetan calendar an Earth-Sheep year is followed by an Iron-Ape year, which, again, is followed by an Iron-Hen year. As there is no ground to believe that gLaṅ Dar-ma ruled for more than sixty years, the Iron-Ape year and the Iron-Hen year of the passage are to be taken as A.D. 840 and 841 respectively. In short, according to the above passage, the persecution of the Doctrine took place in A.D. 841.

But this contradicts the other calculations of 'Gos lo-tsā-ba himself when he tries to correlate the date of the persecution with some later events of Tibetan history.

"Bu-ston Rin-po-che," says 'Gos lo-tsā-ba,[28] "basing himself on the words of an old woman, has stated that the Doctrine had disappeared in the Iron-Female-Hen year, and was re-established after the lapse of 73 years,[29] in the year

27. *Ib.* i. 48. 28. *Ib.* i. 60-1. 29. 'Gos lo-tsā-ba actually misquotes Bu-ston, who speaks of 70 years. See Bu-ston ii. 211.

Water-Female-Hen. But 'Brom-ston-pa, who was very learned in the history of the Doctrine, said : 'In the 78th year, which was an Earth-Male-Tiger year, (the Doctrine) reappeared. Atiśa came to Tibet in the year Water-Male-Horse, which was the 65th year after the Earth-Male-Tiger year."

What is meant here by the Earth-Male-Tiger year of the reappearance of the Doctrine ? According to the Tibetan calendar, we have three successive Earth-Male-Tiger years as A.D. 918,978 and 1038. In the present context, however, it can be taken only as A.D. 978. The reasons are clear. 'Gos lo-tsā-ba says that the Water-Male-Horse year of the coming of Atīśa to Tibet was the sixty-fifth year after this Earth-Male-Tiger year and the Water-Male-Horse year of Atīśa's coming to Tibet was A.D. 1042, it being preposterous to conceive it either as A.D. 982 (the preceding Water-Horse year) or as A.D. 1102 (the succeeding Water-Horse year). On the authority of 'Brom-ston-pa, 'Gos lo-tsā-ba further argues that the Earth-Male-Tiger year of the reappearance of the Doctrine was the 78th year of the destruction of the Doctrine. Therefore, assuming that the Earth-Male-Tiger year of the reappearance of the Doctrine was A.D. 978, we are led to conclude that 'Gos lo-tsā-ba takes here A.D. 901 as the date of the destruction of the Doctrine. In the Tibetan calendar, A.D. 901 is also an Iron-Hen year, but not the Iron-Hen year of the preceding *rab-byuṅ* or A.D. 841, which 'Gos lo-tsā-ba previously mentions as the date of the persecution depending on the Chinese tradition.

We have already noted the same discrepancy of 60 years in 'Gos lo-tsā-ba's calculations in connection with his date of the birth of Sroṅ-btsan-sgam-po. Roerich[30] further shows that, after taking A.D. 901 as the date of the persecution *in relation to the date of Atīśa's coming to Tibet*, all the subsequent calculations of 'Gos lo-tsā-ba are based on the assumption that the date of persecution was A.D. 901 rather than A.D. 841. Here is only one example.

30. Roerich BA i. Intro. p. ix ff; 61n.

According to 'Gos lo-tsâ-ba, the famous Tibetan scholar Rin-chen-bzaṅ-po was born in an Earth-Male-Horse year[31] and he was 85 when Jo-bo Atīśa came to Tibet.[32] Thus the Earth-Male-Horse year of his birth is to be taken as A.D. 958. "At the age of thirteen," adds 'Gos lo-tsā-ba,[33] "he (Rin-chen-bzaṅ-po) was ordained... Thus the year of the lo-tsā-ba's ordination is the 70th year from the year Iron-Hen of the suppression of the Doctrine." Assuming A.D. 958 as the year of Rin-chen-bzaṅ-po's birth, he was, according to the Tibetan mode of calculation, 13 years old in A.D. 970, an Iron-Horse year. This Iron-Horse year was the 70th year from the Iron-Hen year of the suppression of the Doctrine, i.e. 69 years passed between the Iron-Hen year of the persecution and the Iron-Horse year of the lo-tsâ-ba's ordination. In other words, the Iron-Hen year of the suppression of the Doctrine is assumed here to be A.D. 901.

To sum up : 'Gos lo-tsā-ba depends on two distinct traditions for dating the year of the persecution of the Doctrine. According to the first—which is based on the Chinese annals—it happened in A.D. 841, while according to the second—the source of which is not yet clear to us—it happened in A.D. 901. Roerich[34] comments, "The discrepancy of sixty years between the date of the Chinese annals and the Tibetan chronicles is difficult to explain." The explanation perhaps awaits further researches into Tibrtan chronology.

31. BA i. 68. 32. *Ib.* 33. *Ib.* 34. Roerich BA i. Intro. p. xv.

PART III

ATĪŚA IN TIBET

28. *The Subsequent Propagation of the Doctrine*

To the Tibetan Buddhists, the story of Atīśa in Tibet is that of the final reassertion of Buddhism in the Land of Snow after it went to pieces under the persecution of gLaṅ Dar-ma. Though the beginning of this process is to be traced to a period earlier than Atīśa and though in the initial stages the initiative for Buddhist revival was taken by a handful of surviving Tibetan Buddhists, their efforts were nebulous, sporadic and often misguided. From Jo-bo Atīśa came not only the greatest impetus for Buddhist renaissance but also the right direction for purifying the Doctrine then surviving in Tibet, i.e. for removing from it certain theories and practices which a section of the Tibetans wrongly mistook as the essence of Buddhism. That is why, the story of Atīśa in Tibet is usually told by the Tibetans beginning with what they call the period of the subsequent propagation of the Doctrine.

"The period which followed the year of the persecution of the Doctrine," says Roerich,[1] "is one of the darkest in the whole history of Tibet." The Tibetan historians tell us that, thanks to the original initiative of three fugitive hermits, the continuity of the Doctrine was somehow maintained, though outside central Tibet (dBus and gTsaṅ) and without any royal support. The first Tibetan king to have taken up the cause of Buddhism after gLaṅ Dar-ma was a ruler of upper mÑa'-ris, better known in Tibetan history by his ordained name Ye-śe-'od, meaning Jñānaprabha. The history of Tibetan Buddhism after him is clear and the most important event in it is the coming of Atīśa to Tibet. However, the history of Buddhism between gLaṅ Dar-ma and Ye-śes-'od is obscure and frag-

1. BA i. Intro. p. xiv.

mentary and the Tibetan authorities themselves are sharply divided over it. This is evident from the writings of Bu-ston and 'Gos lo-tsā-ba, both of whom give their own accounts of the period after dismissing[2] various rival accounts. Depending mainly on these two authorities[3] we may have a rough idea of some of the leading events of this period.

Three monks of the meditative monastery of dPal-chu-bo-ri, on coming to know that gLaṅ Dar-ma had rooted out the Doctrine, loaded some mules with Buddhist scriptures and fled to western Tibet. They reached mṄa'-ris, from there proceeded to 'Or and from 'Or went to Amdo (mDo-smad). The names of these three monks are given as dMar-ban (i.e. the monk belonging to the dMar Lineage) Śākyamuni of gYor-btsod, gYo-dge-'byuṅ of Draṅ-chuṅ-mdo, and gTsaṅ-rab-gsal of rGya. At Amdo they met a person who was to play a leading role in the subsequent propagation of the Doctrine and was to receive the ordained name dGe-ba-rab-gsal, but was more famed as dGoṅs-pa-rab-gsal. According to 'Gos lo-tsā-ba he was ordained under the three fugitive monks. But Bu-ston says that under them he was first made a novice. Later, wanting to be fully ordained, he had to search for two more monks, because the minimum number of monks that could confer full ordination was five. He approached dPal-gyi-rdo-rje, the inspired saint who killed gLaṅ Dar-ma. But dPal-gyi-rdo-rje could not agree to it, because of his recent record of killing the king. Eventually, two Chinese priests (*ho-shang*) called Ke-vaṅ and Gyi-vaṅ were found and, along with the three fugitive monks, they conferred full ordination on dGe-ba-rab-gsal. Thus it appears that even after the defeat of the Chinese priests by Kamalaśīla, some of them remained in Tibet and at least two played a significant role in the subsequent propagation of the Doctrine.

According to 'Gos lo-tsā-ba, dGe-ba-rab-gsal was born in the Water-Male-Mouse year,[4] i.e. A.D. 892, and he died at the age of 84 in the Wood-Female-Hog year,[5] i.e. 975. These dates

2. Bu-ston ii. 201ff; BA i. 67. 3. Bu-ston ii. 201ff; BA i. 63ff.
4. BA i. 64. 5. *Ib.* i. 67.

have an important bearing on the date of the persecutien of the Doctrine by gLaṅ Dar-ma. Assuming the minimum age for ordination to be eighteen, the earliest date of dGe-ba-rab-gsal's ordination was A.D. 909-10. Thus the assumption that the Doctrine was destroyed by gLaṅ Dar-ma in A.D. 841 will lead us to imagine that it took over seventy years for the three fugitive monks to come to Amdo and ordain dGe-ba-rab-gsal. The possibility of this being remote, it is more logical to accept the other date of the persecution, namely A.D. 901.

In his 49th year,[6] dGe-ba-rab-gsal proceeded towards mount Dan-tig, where he "himself" built temples and *stūpa*-s[7] and resided for thirty-five years.[8] He made this "fiendless and peaceful forest" the centre of his activities and, according to 'Gos lo-tsā-ba, ordained ten persons to whom the Buddhist revival owed a great deal. Bu-ston[9] gives the names of these ten men as : "five men of dBus, namely kLag-pa-lam-pa kLu-mes-tshul-khrims, Śes-rab-'briṅ Ye-śes-yon-tan, Ragśi-tshul-khrims-'byuṅ-gnas, rBa Tshul-khrims-blo-gros and Ye-śes-blo of Sum-pa, and five men of gTsaṅ, namely from Gurmo Rab-kha-pa-lo-ston and rDo-rje-dbaṅ-phyug, Śes-rab-seṅ-ge of Śab-sgo-lṅa'i-tshoṅ-btsun, the two brothers 'Od-brgyad of mÑa'-ris U-pa-de-dkar-pa of Pho-thoṅ,—altogether ten men,"—evidently counting the two brothers as one. But he gives a somewhat different account of their ordination, according to which, along with dGe-ba-rab-gsal, the three fugitive monks and the two Chinese priests took part in conferring it. In Tibetan history these ten men are famous as the Ten Men of dBus and gTsaṅ, though, because some of them left no spiritual lineage, the Tibetan authorities sometimes mention Six Men instead of Ten.

The activities of these Ten or Six Men, though meagre, could not have been much earlier than the coming of Atīśa to

6. *Ib.* i. 67. 7. *Ib.* i. 65. 8. *Ib.* i. 67. 9. Bu-ston ii. 202.

Tibet. 'Gos lo-tsā-ba[10] says, "When Atīśa came to Tibet, the disciples of these 'Six'—Khu, rṄog and many others were still alive." We shall come to them again while discussing Atīśa's Tibetan career. 'Gos lo-tsā-ba[11] further says, "Atīśa came to Tibet in the year Water-Male-Horse (A.D. 1042), which was the 65th year after the Earth-Male-Tiger year. At that time Sum-pa Ye-śes-blo-gros (Ye-śes-blo of Sum-pa) one of the 'Six Men of dBus and gTsaṅ', was still living, for in the letter, which had been sent by 'Brom-ston to the great scholars of dBus, conveying an invitation to come to welcome Atīśa, stood the following sentence: 'The leader, who had first established the monastic vow, the great *bhadanta* Ye-śes-blo-gros...'." Thus, if one of the leaders of Buddhist renaissance after gLaṅ Dar-ma was alive in A.D. 1042, A.D. 901 rather than A.D. 841 is to be accepted as a more plausible date of the persecution.

10. *Ib.* i. 72. 11. *Ib.* i. 61.

29. *The Pious King Ye-ses-'od*

The story of Tibetan Buddhism becomes clearer again from 'Khor-lde *alias* Ye-śes-'od and his successors. From the Buddhist point of view, Ye-śes-'od was one of the most pious kings of Tibet. He renounced the kingdom and accepted the monk's life. Further, according to the usual Tibetan accounts, he even sacrificed his life to the cause of Buddhism. It is, therefore, interesting to note that this Tibetan ruler, to whom Buddhist renaissance in Tibet owed so much, was a direct descendant of gLaṅ Dar-ma, who did his best to annihilate Buddhism in Tibet.

We may follow Bu-ston[1] to see the descent of Ye-śes-'od from gLaṅ Dar-ma : "Now, the eldest wife of gLaṅ Dar-ma declared that she was pregnant with a child, and then, after she had sought and found a little child, she showed it saying :—It has been born to me yesterday. The ministers said to this :—A child born a day before cannot have teeth. Let him carefully preserve the instructions of his mother[2] ! Accordingly the boy was known by the surname of Yum-brtan (preserving his mother's word)... The younger queen (of gLaṅ Dar-ma) had a son born in the year of the Wooden-Cow.[3] As she feared that the elder queen would kill the boy or carry him away, she held watch over him, keeping him constantly in the light, of the sun at day-time and of that of a lamp by night. Owing to this he was called 'Od-sruṅs—'guarded by light'."

Yum-brtan and 'Od-sruṅs fought with each other and divided the kingdom into two parts, the former taking possession of the eastern provinces and the latter of western Tibet.

1. Bu-ston ii. 199–200. 2. As Obermiller says in his note, the meaning of this is not quite clear. 3. A.D. 857. Evidently, therefore, Bu-ston assumes a date of gLaṅ Dar-ma's death later than the date given by 'Gos lo-tsā-ba. See also Section 26, note 16.

"This unfortunate position," says S. C. Das,[4] "gave rise to incessant quarrels and disturbances, both the brothers constantly engaging in wars against each other. Thus, after the partition of the kingdom of Tibet the descendants of gÑa'-khri-btsan-po ceased to exercise universal sway over the county. They became weak and imbecile in consequence of which they fell in the opinion and esteem of their subjects."

Bu-ston[5] says that 'Od-sruṅs died at the age of 63. S. C. Das[6] gives the date of his death as A.D. 980. His son was dPal-'khor-btsan, who, according to 'Gos lo-tsā-ba[7] and Sum-pa,[8] was killed by the subjects. He had two sons,[9] bKra-śis-brtsegs-pa-dpal and Ñi-ma-mgon. The former remained in upper gTsaṅ and the latter moved to mṄa'-ris to the west of Tibet. From this time onwards mṄa'-ris came to political prominence.

Ñi-ma-mgon had three sons, —dPal-gyi-mgon, bKra-śis-mgon and lDe-gtsug-mgon. The eldest son ruled Maṅ-yul,[10] the second son ruled sPu-raṅs and the youngest son ruled Shaṅ-shuṅ, which was the older name of Gu-ge. These three districts comprising the province of mṄa'-ris were poetically described as "sPu-raṅs surrounded by snowy mountains, Gu-ge surrounded by rocky cliffs and Maṅ-yul filled with lakes."[11]

According to 'Gos lo-tsā-ba,[12] bKra-śis-mgon had two sons : 'Khor-re ('Khor-lde) and Sroṅ-ne (Sroṅ-lde), while according to Bu-ston,[13] 'Khor-lde and Sroṅ-lde were the sons of lDe-gtsug-mgon. Sum-pa[14] follows Bu-ston, whose account is accepted also by S. C. Das.[15] Francke[16] suggests that bKra-śis-mgon died without issue and his kingdom was inherited by the descendants of lDe-gtsug-mgon. This is, therefore, a point about which it is difficult to be exact.

4. Das in JASB 1881. 236. 5. Bu-ston ii 200. 6. Das in JASB 1881. 236. 7. BA i. 37. 8. Sum-pa 152. 9. Bu-ston ii. 200 ; BA i. 37. 10. Bu-ston ii. 200 says it was the country of Mar ; 'Gos lo-tsā-ba, BA i. 37, says it was Mar-yul ; following Sum-pa 152, S. C. Das gives the name as Maṅ-yul : D-TED 362. For Mar-yul and Maṅ-yul, see Francke AIT ii 93ff. 11. D-TED 362. 12. BA i. 37. 13. Bu-ston ii. 200. 14. Sum-pa 152. 15. Das in JASB 1881. 236. 16. Francke AIT ii. 94n.

'Gos lo-tsā-ba[17] and Sum-pa[18] say that 'Khor-lde had two sons, called Nāgarāja and Devarāja. The father and the two sons were ordained and the government was handed over to Sroṅ-lde.[19] The ordained name of 'Khor-lde was Ye-śes-'od or Jñānaprabha, though he is generally referred to by the highly respected epithets like Lha-bla-ma[20] (*devaguru*) or Lo-chen (*paṇḍita*) and mKhan-slob-gcig-pa (the only *guru*).[21]

According to Bu-ston, 'Gos-lo-tsā-ba and Sum-pa, Sroṅ-lde

GENEALOGICAL TABLE : RULERS OF WESTERN TIBET

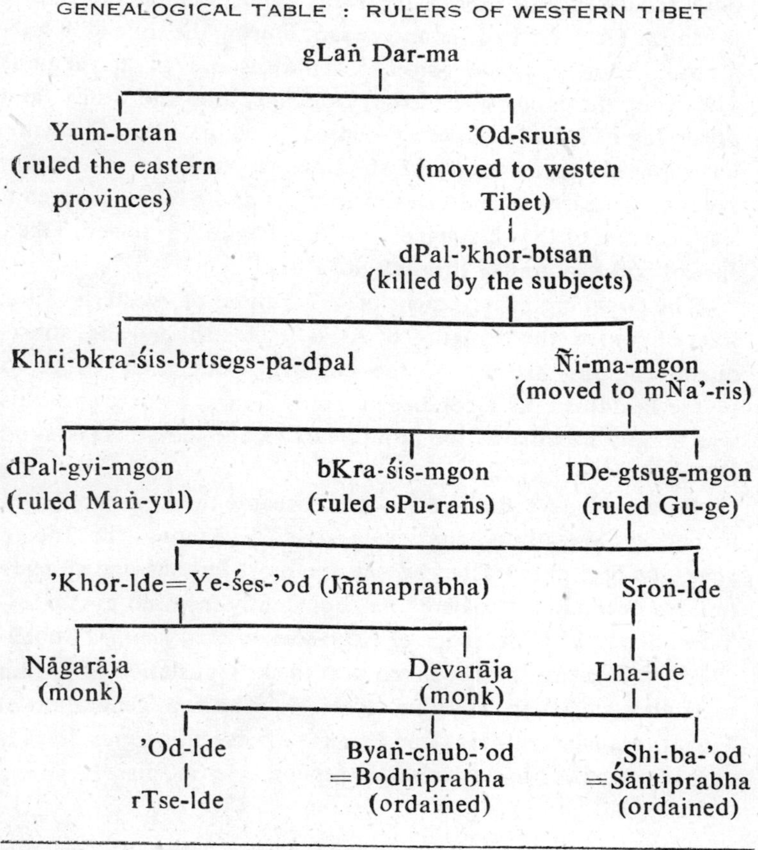

17. BA i. 37. 18. Sum-pa 152. 19. BA i. 37; Bu-ston i. 212.
20. BA i. 84. 21. Francke AIT ii. 169.

was succeeded by his son Lha-lde,[22] who had three sons, called 'Od-lde, Byaṅ-chub-'od (Bodhiprabha) and Shi-ba-'od (Śāntiprabha). Both Byaṅ-chub'-od and Shi-ba-'od took up ordination and 'Od-lde succeeded his father. 'Od-lde was succeeded by his son rTse-lde.[23]

Whatever might have been the political importance of these rulers of western Tibet, they enjoy great prestige in Tibetan history because they—particularly 'Khor-lde and the successors of his younger brothers—played very important role in the Buddhist renaissance in Tibet after it was almost completely extinct in central Tibet, i.e. in dBus and gTsaṅ. During the time of 'Khor-lde and Sroṅ-lde, says Bu-ston,[24] "in dBus and gTsaṅ religious discipline, the exposition of the Doctrine, and the study and preaching of it had altogether ceased." Again, "the Doctrine, having been rooted out by gLaṅ Dar-ma, had, for a certain number of years, ceased to exist in dBus and gTsaṅ...In such a way the fire of the Doctrine, having begun in lower Tibet, spread and expounded through mÑa'-ris."

The crowning achievement of the rulers of western Tibet was, of course, the bringing of Atīśa. This shaped the subsequent religious history of the country. But their effort to revive Buddhism in Tibet began some years before and this was mainly because of the intiative of 'Khor-lde or Ye-śes-'od (Jñānaprabha).

Bu-ston[25] says that Ye-śes-'od "became the householder of numerous lo-tsā-ba-s and *paṇḍita*-s." Among the Indian *paṇḍita*-s brought to Tibet by him the most famous one appears to have been Dharmapāla.[26] And, evidently inspired by Ye-śes-'od's efforts, Lha-lde, son of Sroṅ-lde, invited *paṇḍita* Subhāṣita,[27] who seems to have taken part in the translation of Indian texts though not in any big scale.[28] The new generation of Tibetan translators after gLaṅ Dar-ma's persecution grew largely as a result of the initiative of Ye-śes-'od. He Selected 21 young

22. Bu-ston ii. 213 ; BA i. 37 ; Sum-pa 152. 23. BA. i. 37.
24. Bu-ston ii. 200 & 212. 25. *Ib*. ii. 213. 26. See *supra* Section 1, p. 10f. 27. Bu-ston ii. 213. 28. rG.xxxiii. 3 ; mDo vi.

men of Tibet for study in India,[29] among whom Rin-chen-bzaṅ-po (Ratnabhadra) shaped into the greatest and most respected of the Tibetan lo-tsā-ba-s.

Ye-śes-'od built[30] "the incomparable and miraculous monastery" (*anupama nirābhoga vihāra*) of Tho-liṅ (mTho-gliṅ or Tho'lding) at Shaṅ-shuṅ (Gu-ge), probably with the help of Rin-chen-bzaṅ-po.[31] This monastery, described as "a cultural link between greater India, Pāla Bengal and Tibet,"[32] is still held in "high esteem by Hindu *sanyāsī*-s, who call it Ādi-badri."[33] It is situated on the upper Sutlej and, in the map of Turkistan, is called Totlingmat—*mat* (*smad*) meaning 'lower,' i.e. the lower part of the city.[34] "To visit Tho-liṅ by the shortest route from India one must reach Badrināth and then cross the main Himalayas by Mana Pass...It is situated in the deep gorge of the Sutlej river before it has crossed the Himalayas on its way to the Punjab."[35] Sum-pa[36] calls it Tho-liṅ-gser-khaṅ, the Golden Temple of Tho-liṅ, and compares it with bSam-yas. "It has a celebrated temple in three storeys, said by some to be modelled afrer that of Buddha Gayā,"[37] and contains frescoes and images reminiscent of Indian art at its best.[38] It became an important centre of learning, as is evidenced by the works in the bsTan-'gyur translated in this monastery,[39] including the translation of one of the largest work on Indian logic done by Dīpaṃkara himself, viz. the *Pramāṇa-vārttika-alaṃkāra-ṭīkā* by Jaya (Jina).[40] It was in this monastery that Dīpaṃkara also wrote his *Bodhi-patha-pradīpa*.

29. Bu-ston ii. 212 : according to Sum-pa 181, of these 21 men 15 were scholars and 6 attendants. 30. BA i. 84; Bu-ston ii. 213.
31. Francke AIT i. 28; Waddell L 283. 32. Chatterjee in JUPHS xiii. 30 33. *Ib.* 34. Waddell L 283: Francke AIT ii. 100.
35. Chatterjee in JUPHS xiii. 30-1. Incidentally, though Atīśa's first Tibetan destination was the Tho-liṅ *vihāra*, he followed a different route to it : See Section 32. 36. Sum-pa 182. 37. Waddell L 283.
38. Chatterjee in JUPHS xiii. 31. 39. mDo xxiv. 5; xxxi. 9 (xxxiii. 1); xliv. 3; lxxiv. 2; xc. 5; xcix-c; c.l; c.2; cxvi. 11; rG. xxxiv. 9; xl. 15, lvi.1, lxix. 141, 170; lxxiii. 30, lxxxii. 77, 81, 89. 40. See Sec. 6, Appendix B.

The Tibetan historians further tell us that the zeal of spreading the true form of the Doctrine in Tibet led king Ye-śes-'od even to sacrifice his own life. "Lha-bla-ma Ye-śes-'od," says 'Gos lo-tsā-ba,[41] "though he had given up his kingdom, continued to act as commander of the troops. While fighting the Gar-log[42] (Quarluq), he suffered defeat, and was thrown into prison (by them). The Gar-log said to Ye-śes-'od : 'If you renounce the refuge to the Three Jewels, we shall let you out of prison. Otherwise, produce gold equal in weight to your body, and we shall then free you.' For a long time he remained in captivity. The officials (of the kingdom) secured most of the required gold by collecting gold from mÑa'-ris itself, and by levying tax on monks in dBus and gTsaṅ. However they failed in collecting gold equal in weight to Ye-śes-'od's head. Then his 'nephew' Byaṅ-chub-'od proceeded to see him in the Gar-log territory, and said to him : 'We have now obtained gold equal in weight to your body ; when we shall find (the remaining) gold equal in weight to your head, we shall come to invite you.' Ye-śes-'od replied : 'I have now become old, and am of no use to any one. Spend the gold collected by you, to invite *paṇḍita*-s in order to establish the Doctrine.' They followed his words and invited many scholars (from India), and thus established the teaching of the Doctrine."

In the life of Atīśa translated by S. C. Das we have a lengthy and highly emotional version of this story : the king was captured by the Gar-logs when he was collecting enough gold for the purpose of inviting some eminent Indian *paṇḍita* and this was the parting message of Ye-śes-'od to his "nephew" Byaṅ-chub-'od—"My son, you should preserve the tradition and the religion of our ancestors, that is of the utmost importance to us all. In my opinion in our country the laws based on Buddhism should be maintained. My *karma* will not permit me to see the wished-for reformation. I am now grown old,

41. BA i. 244-5.

42. Rahula in *2500 Years* 233 conjectures that this "probably refers to a place named Gartog, which was situated to the north of the Manasasarovara lake and had a gold mine."

and verge on death's door. Even if you succeed in releasing me, my life may not extend to more than ten years. In none of my former births, I believe, did I die for the sake of Buddhism. This time let me, therefore, be a martyr to the cause of my religion. Do not give a grain of gold to this cruel *rājā*. Take back the entire quantity of it that you may conduct religious services in the great monasteries and spend in bringing an Indian *paṇḍita* to Tibet. If ever you send any messenger to the great Indian *paṇḍita* Dīpaṃkara Śrī-jñāna, let this message of mine be conveyed to him: 'Lha-bla-ma, the king of Tibet, has fallen into the hands of the *rājā* of Gar-log while endeavouring to collect gold for diffusing the religion of Buddha and for the *paṇḍita* himself. The *paṇḍita* should therefore vouchsafe his blessings and mercy unto him in all his transformed existences. The chief aim of the king's life has been to take him to Tibet to reform Buddhism, but, alas that did not come to pass! With a longing look to the time when he could behold the *paṇḍita*'s saintly face, he resigned himself absolutely to the mercy of the Three Holies."[43]

Such an emotionally surcharged account of the entire episode, evidently intended to provide a dramatic background to the story of Atīśa's invitation to Tibet, is likely to appear somewhat unreal to the fact-finding mind of the modern historian. Was there really any Tibetan king called Ye-śes-'od, whose great enthusiasm to reform Buddhism in Tibet eventually resulted in the bringing of Atīśa there? Francke, during his expedition to the Tibetan border, frankly wondered. The whole thing was perhaps only a fable! This scepticism explains his tremendous excitement when he first came across an inscription in the village of dKor below sPu, a plain on the right bank of the Sutlej, containing the name of Ye-śes-'od and belonging to his time. "I was told," says he,[44] "that there was an inscribed stone in the village of dKor, below sPu, and went

43. JBTS I. i. 14. 44. Francke AIT i. 19.

to examine it...On the reverse of the stone is a Tibetan inscription of eleven lines... While we were examining the stone, a Christian Tibetan, who was with us, began to read the first lines : *dPal-lha-btsan-po Lha-bla-ma Ye-śes*... When he had got so far, I suddenly remembered that I had heard of a person whose name began *Lha-bla-ma Ye-śes.* But what is the syllable following after *Ye-śes ?* It suddenly flashed on me that it was *'od*, and that *Lha-bla-ma Ye-śes-'od* was the name of the royal priest, the early king of Gu-ge, who had tried in vain to draw the famous Buddhist monk Atiśa to his kingdom. Did the inscription really contain his name—a name which has not yet been traced anywhere ? We all went close to the stone, and looked at it from all sides, even from below. And lo, it was so. The stone contained the full name of this famous personage of Tibetan history and the words following the name were *sku-ring-la*, meaning 'in his lifetime.' I was so overjoyed at the discovery of this important record that I could not help jumping about in the field, and then embraced the Lama, who was just on the point of becoming displeased with my treatment of his crop."

Francke himself explains the cause of this great excitement : "The story of king Ye-śes-'od is found in the second part of the Tibetan historical work *dPag-bsam-ljon-bzaṅ*... Up to the present, nobody had known whether the story containd in those works was really true and whether the persons mentioned in it had actually lived or not. This inscription of king Ye-śes-'od is the first record which can be brought forward to confirm the statements of the Tibetan historians."[45] Francke comes across in other inscriptions[46] the names of Rin-chen-bzaṅ-po, Byaṅ-chub-'od and of Atiśa himself (Phul-byuṅ) and becomes fully convinced of the historicity of Atiśa's invitation to Tibet.

45. *Ib.* 46. *Ib.* i. 37, 40, 41 etc.

30. Tibet on the Eve of Inviting Atiśa

For understanding the nature of Atiśa's reforms in Tibet, it is useful to begin with some idea of the religious setting of the country on the eve of his coming there.

The learned Tibetan scholar Chos-kyi-ñi-ma[1] says that after the destruction of the Doctrine by gLaṅ Dar-ma "bLa-chen dGons-pa-rab-gsal collected the remains of Buddhism from mDo (Amdo) and Lower Ḳhams and Lo-chen Rin-bzaṅ (Rin-chen-bzaṅ-po) fostered (the remains of the Doctrine recovered from) Upper mÑa'-ris and increased the *saṅgha*-s of dBus and gTsaṅ. But some of them (monks) followed the Tantra and turned away from the Vinaya. Some others followed the Vinaya and turned away from the Tantra. In this way, the Doctrine was divided. Most of them had allegiance to the *siddhānta* only in words, and the full understanding of the Doctrine was, of course, far away. Even the semblance of the Doctrine was very rare. Specially during the destruction of the Doctrine by gLaṅ Dar-ma some of the Tāntrikas wrote whatever fragments of the Tantras remained in their memory, adding to these whatever occurred to their mind and claimed these to have been true Tantras, which omitted the essence of the Tantra. Some others wrote purely fanciful things and called these the true Tantras. Some others even said to their wives : 'Prepare good wine for me ; I am going to write a full treatise on Tantra today.' Then from India came one called the Red Ācārya, another with Blue Robe, and others. And they taught the false doctrine in the name of *sbyor* and *sgrol*. They said *sbyor* (*yoga*) meant the union with women and *sgrol* (*mokṣa*) meant the killing of the living beings

1. See Section 5, Appendix A.

like the enemies. In this way, many false doctrines were spread in the name of Tantra. Because of all these there remained very few people with pure theory (*dṛṣṭi*) and practice (*caryā*)."

To the Tibetan historians, the Red-robed Indian Tāntrika—primarily responsible for popularising the corrupt practices in Tibet sometimes before the coming of Dīpaṃkara— was more than a mere myth. He is usually mentioned as an *a-tsa-ra*,[2] which, in Tibetan, signifies a corrupt *ācārya* : in the religious dances of Tibet, an *a-tsa-ra* appears as a clown and as a caricature of the Indian *brāhmaṇa*. His name is given as Prajñāgupta (Śes-rab-gsaṅ-ba) and is said to have been "a *paṇḍita* of Oḍḍiyāna, who had become the disciple of Ratnavajra, the Kashmirian." His eighteen important Tibetan disciples are mentioned as the Robber-monks (Ar-tsho-ban-de-s) kidnapping Tibetan peoples for offering human sacrifices to the *ḍākiṇī*-s. Though some of the later Tibetan Tāntrikas[3] would not denouce this *a-tsa-ra* and his followers, according to the usual account, in "the Xth century A.D. an Indian *paṇḍita* Prajñāgupta, who was also known by the name of *ācārya* (*a-tsa-ra*) Śam-thabs-dmar-po ('the Red-robed') translated the *Phyag-chen-thig-le-rgyud*. The eighteen Ar-tsho-ban-de-s were his disciples, according to some authors. The doctrine of the eighteen Ar-tsho-ban-de-s consisted of a corrupt form of Tantric practices ; they kidnapped women and men, and used to perform human sacrifices during Tantric feasts (*gaṇacakra-pūjā*). It is said that their practices caused the Tibetan kings of Gu-ge to invite dPal Atīśa."[4]

If Ye-śes-'od was really as ardent a Buddhist as the Tibetan historians want us to believe, it was but natural for him to feel greatly worried over such a situation. Buddhism, in its philosophical aspect, did inspire him. But he was at a loss to understand how far the Tāntrika practices alleged to be Buddhistic did really represent the true spirit of the Doctrine.

2. BA. ii. 697f and 1049f. For *a-tsa-ra*, see D-TED 1345.
3. BA ii. 1050. 4. *Ib*. ii. 697-8.

Wherefrom could he expect proper light to be thrown on this doubt ? It could only be India, though he had hardly any realistic idea of how fast Indian Buddhism itself was then getting transformed into various brands of later Tantrism.

We are thus told that Ye-śes-'od, deeply disturbed by the practices of the Tibetan Buddhists of his time, selected a team of young and talented Tibetans and sent them to India specially to find out how far the Tāntrika practices were to be accepted as genuinely Buddhistic. Ye-śes-'od, says Bu-ston,[5] "acknowledged the Vehicle of Philosophy (*mtshan-ñid-theg-pa*) to be the Word of the Buddha, but as concerns the Tantras, he was in doubt as to their being the true teaching, since the Tantric exorcists indulged in perverse acts, as that of deliverance through sexual ecstasy, etc. Accordingly, he selected 21 young men, Rin-chen-bzań-po and others, and sent them to India in order to study the Doctrine. But, with the exception of Rin-chen-bzań-po and Legs-pa'i-śes-rab, they died without having achieved their study. Rin-chen-bzań-po became profoundly versed in all the branches of Tantra and philosophy and, having invited the *paṇḍita*-s Śradhākaravarman, Padmākaragupta, Buddhaśrīśānta, Buddhapāla, Kamalagupta, and others, achieved the translation of the philosophical part of the kanon and of the 4 divisions of Tantra. In particular, many texts of the Yoga-tantra, the Guhya-samāja, etc. were translated and the Tantric parts of Scripture revised." Sum-pa's[6] version of this is summed up by S. C. Das as follows :

"Lha-bla-ma Ye-śes-'od felt disgusted with the Tantric Buddhism which then prevailed in Tibet in an alarming extent. He doubted if that debased mysticism was at all Buddhism. With a view to reform the degenerate and corrupt Buddhism, the king selected fourteen intelligent and assiduous young men headed by Rin-chen-bzań-po of mŃa'-ris to proceed to India with six attendants for studying Buddhism. They carried with them a large quantity of gold for presenting to the *paṇḍita*-s under whom they would study there. The king commanded them

5. Bu-ston ii. 212-3. 6. Sum-Pa 181. Contents p. xv-xvi

to bring with them, if possible, any of the eminent *paṇḍita*-s such as the learned Ratnavajra of Kashmir, Dharmapāla of Eastern India, *paṇḍita* Karuṇa of Ratnadvīpa from the West, Prajñābala of Magadha, besides some very eminent scholar from among one hundred learned *paṇḍita*-s of Vikramaśīla. They were also told that among them there were two very able to do good to others. There were also at Vikramaśīla thirty-seven *paṇḍita*-s who were without equals in learning and moral virtues. There was only one among them whom all regarded as the crown-gem of the religious men of India. There were ten other *paṇḍita*-s out of whom eight were regarded as the ornaments of Jambudvīpa and two as her eyes. In the first place, from among all these learned men the king commanded : 'Bring the best one, secondly bring the sacred precepts, and, lastly, bring images and rare books of value.' Accordingly, a party of twenty-one men proceeded to their destination, to give effect to their respective missions...Out of the twenty-one men, only three, (*lo-chen* Rin-chen-bzaṅ-po, *lo-chuṅ* Grags-'byor-śes-rab and rÑog Legs-śes) returned to Tibet crowned with success. The rest did not came back. They all died in India and elsewhere. Though these three learned Lamas greatly improved the condition of the Buddhist Church by their example and exertions to the satisfaction of the king and his royal uncle the Lha-bla-ma, yet the necessity for bringing to Tibet a great *paṇḍita* reformer and holy man for the good of the general public was keenly felt."

Two points in particular are to be noted about the accounts just quoted.

First, though Ye-śes-'od's scepticism of the Tāntrika practices led him to send Rin-chen-bzaṅ-po and others to India, Rin-chen-bzaṅ--po himself returned to Tibet as an enthusiastic follower of some form of Tantrism itself. It is true that he grew into a critic of the "Tantras of the Older Believers" (the rÑiṅ-ma'i-rgyud-'bum[7]), refused to accept them as representing "pure" Tantra,[8] and that his name is specially associated[9]

7. These Tantras are not included in the bKa'-'gyur.

8. BA i. 102n.

9. Sum-pa 182 ; BA i. 204ff

with what the Tibetans call "the New Tantras" (gSaṅ-sṅags-gsar-ma,[10] the Later School of Mystical Incantations). But whatever might have been the nature of reformed Tantrism introduced by Rin-chen-bzaṅ-po into Tibet, the Tibetan historians tell us that only at the age of eighty-five, as a consequence of his coming in touch with Atīśa in Tibet, his approach to Buddhist religion had to be fundamentally altered.[11] From this we are led to infer that the Tāntrika reforms he is reputed to have introduced into Tibet were in need of more basic reformations.

Secondly, though the Tibetan authorities mention several names of eminent Indian Buddhists in the two accounts we have quoted, these names, is so far as they are traceable in the history of Indian Buddhism, are but names of later Tāntrikas. Śraddhākaravarman, Padmākaragupta and Buddhaśrīśānta were famous representatives of the Guhya-samāja Tantra[12] belonging to the Lineage of Buddhajñānapāda or Jñānapāda—a Lineage that was introduced into Tibet by Rin-chen-bzaṅ-po himself.[13] Ratnavajra of Kashmir, referred to by Sum-pa, was also a famous Tāntrika, probably a disciple of Maitri-pā[14] and mentioned as one of the six gatekeeper *paṇḍita*-s of Vikramaśīla : "at the eastern (gate) Śānti-pā ; at the southern gate Vāgīśvarakīrti ; at the western gate Prajñākaramati ; at the northern gate Nā-ro-pan-chen (the *mahā-paṇḍita* Nā-ro) ; in the centre—Ratnavajra and Jñānaśrī."[15]

We have some rough idea of the time when these famous Tāntrikas enjoyed prominence at the Vikramaśīla *vihāra*. "When lo-tsā-ba Rin-chen-bzaṅ-po was nearing the age of fifty" two Tibetan scholars sent to India met them.[16] Since Rin-chen-bzaṅ-po was born in A.D. 958,[17] it was in the first decade of the eleventh century that these great Tāntrikas were gate-keeper scholars at Vikramaśīla. But Rin-chen-bzaṅ-po himself was sent to India by Ye-śes-'od earlier than this. He was ordained at the age of thirteen,[18] i.e. in A.D. 970, and

10. BA i. 204ff. 11. See Section 33. 12. BA i. 372f
13. *Ib.* 14. BA i. 729. 15. BA i. 206. 16. *Ib.* i. 205.
17. *Ib.* i. 68 ; 328. 18. *Ib.* i. 68.

was presumably sent to India shortly afterwards, because it is said that he was sent to India while very young.

But how little did Ye-śes-'od know that Indian Buddhism, towards the end of the tenth century, was merging imperceptibly into Tantrism! The study of the classical works of Buddhism which Śāntarakṣita introduced into Tibet was fast deteriorating in India and Atīśa himself, at the age of thirty-one—i.e. roughly forty years after Rin-chen-bzaṅ-po's coming to India—had to leave India and proceed abroad (Suvarṇadvīpa) for advanced studies in classical Buddhism.[19]

Therefore, though the Tibetan scholars tell us that Rin-chen-bzaṅ-po came thrice to Kashmir[20] and "attended on seventy-five *paṇḍita*-s,"[21] we do not expect him to have acquired a thorough grounding in classical or pre-Tāntrika Buddhism. He acquired instead a proficiency in the Tantras. As a result, Ye-śes-'od's efforts to reform Buddhism in Tibet could not be fully successful by the measures he himself took. If Rin-chen-bzaṅ-po propagated a renewed veneration for the Tantras in Tibet, it is futile to expect the less learned Tibetans to remain aloof from the sexual and other practices which were deeply embedded in Tantrism and which had moreover possible affinity with the age-old practices of the Bon religion. Chos-kyi-ñi-ma says that "in general" the Bon-po-s are "great drinkers of wine and eaters of meat. They are not careful to refrain from female company."[22]

In any case the Tibetan historians tell us that in spite of all that Ye-śes-'od did for Buddhism, his "nephew" Byaṅ-chub-'od, who inherited his pious sentiments for Buddhism, continued to worry over the "corrupt" practices of the Tibetan Buddhists. This led him to invite Atīśa to Tibet. As 'Gos lo-tsā-ba[23] puts it, "Byaṅ-chub-'od thought: 'Though many monks are found in the country of Tibet, there exist many wrong practices in respect of *sbyor* (sexual practices) and *sgrol* (ritual murder) in the study of Tantra. Some, who had

19. See *supra* Section 10. 20. BA i. 352. 21. *Ib.* i. 68.
22. JASB 1881. 205. 23. BA i. 245.

practised these rites, preached extensively that one could obtain Enlightenment through (the mere acceptance) of the principle of Relativity (*śūnyatā*, *stoṅ-pa-ñid*) without practising meritorious works. Though the doctrine of the Pratimokṣa had spread (in Tibet), those who practised the precepts of the Path of the Bodhisattva had deteriorated. Now we desire to invite scholars who would remove these moral faults. *Paṇḍita*-s, invited previously, did excellent work in some parts of the country, but their work did not benefit the whole of Tibet. But if we were to invite the Venerable Master (Jo-bo-rje), he would be able to refute these heresies and thus benefit for the Doctrine would arise'."

Such, then, were the conditions of Tibetan Buddhism in the background of which Atīśa was invited to Tibet. The Tibetan historians, as we shall presently see,[24] specially emphasise Atīśa's reform of those Tāntrika practices that so much worried Ye-śes-'od and Byaṅ-chub-'od.

Bu-ston tells the story of his invitation very briefly : Byaṅ-chub-'od "gave gold to five men, Nag-tsho Tshul-rgyal etc. and ordered them to select the translator rGya-brtson-'grus-seṅ-ge as their chief, and to invite a good *paṇḍita*. Accordingly they invited Dīpaṃkara-śrī-jñāna." For further details of this, we have to begin with the career of the two Tibetan scholars named by Bu-ston.

24. Section 33. 25. Bu-ston ii. 213.

31. *Jayasila and Viryasimha*

The Sanskrit equivalent of the name of Tshul-khrims-rgyal-ba is Jayaśīla. He is more commonly referred to as Nag-tsho lo-tsā-ba or simply Nag-tsho. Vīryasiṃha is the Sanskrit equivalent of the Tibetan name brTson-'grus-seṅ-ge of rGya. These two Tibetan scholars played the most important role in inviting Atīśa to Tibet, though Vīryasiṃha died in Nepal while accompanying the Master to Tibet. That is why Nag-tsho alone is frequently mentioned as the Tibetan scholar who brought Atīśa to Tibet.

"Nag-tsho lo-tsā-ba was born in the year Iron-Female-Hog," i.e. A.D. 1011.[1] In the same year was born another eminent Tibetan scholar called Khu-ston brTson-'grus-gyuṅ-druṅ, often mentioned simply as Khu-ston.[2] Nag-tsho was a native of Guṅ-thaṅ of mṄa'-ris.[3] It is said that after reaching Tibet and before proceeding to the Tho-liṅ *vihāra* Atīśa spent about a month at the residence of Nag-tsho.[4]

It appears that Nag-tsho came twice to India[5] and only his second visit was with the assignment of inviting Atīśa to Tibet. "While he (Byaṅ-chub-'od) was thinking thus," says 'Gos lo-tsā-ba,[6] "Nag-tsho Tshul-khrims-rgyal-ba, a native of Guṅ-thaṅ, who lived as a monk, proceeded for study to India. rGya brTson-'grus-seṅ-ge acted as his guide, and he studied many

1. BA i. 247. 2. *Ib.* i. 88 ; 93. 3. D-TED 221. Rahula in *2500 Years* 234 makes an unfortunate confusion and gives the absurd impression that Guṅ-thaṅ-pa and Tshul-khrims-rgyal-ba were two separate persons : "The *upāsaka* Guṅ-thaṅ-pa had been to India and lived there for two years. Devaguru (Lha-bla-ma) secured his services for this work. Guṅ-thaṅ persuaded *bhikṣu* Tshul-khrims-rgyal-ba (Śīlajaya or Jayaśīla) an inhabitant of Nag-tsho, and some other people to accompany him." Incidentally, Nag-tsho literally means 'one with black face' and was presumably a tribal name. 4. Das in JBTS I. i. 27. The place is mentioned as Zo-gna Chen-po. 5. D-TED 731. 6. BA i. 245.

doctrines with the Master and several other scholars. On his return to Guṅ-thaṅ, Lha-btsun-pa (Byaṅ-chub-'od) called him into his presence and said to him : 'You must go and invite the Venerable Master (Atīśa). Should you succeed in pleasing me by inviting him, later I shall make you pleased. You should not transgress the command of me, known as the king.' Nag-tsho after receiving the king's command" proceeded to India.

'Gos lo-tsā-ba's assertion that already during his first visit to India Nag-tsho "studied many doctrines with the Master" does not agree with the life of Atīśa translated by Das in which a passage quoted from Nag-tsho's "own narrative" describes the great thrill he experienced when he had the first sight of Atīśa at the Vikramaśīla *vihāra*[7] and this during his second visit to India. Evidently Nag-tsho did not meet Atīśa during his first visit to India, though the account of his first visit itself need not be doubted because Byaṅ-chub-'od was likely to entrust the task of inviting Atīśa only to a Tibetan who had already some knowledge of Indian conditions and Indian language. In the life of Atīśa translated by S. C. Das, Byaṅ-chub-'od tells Nag-tsho, "Now Vinayadhara, that you are accustomed to hot climate and are acquainted with the way to India and can talk and interpret the Indian language, you should go as our envoy to bring him to Tibet."[8]

In this biography we have some more details of Nag-tsho's first visit to India. When Byaṅ-chub-'od felt the need of "the services of a worthy envoy" to bring an eminent Indian *paṇḍita*, "he was told that there was a certain Buddhist scholar, a native of Guṅ-thaṅ, belonging to the family of Nag-tsho who was versed in Sanskrit. His name was Tshul-khrims-rgyal-ba, and though a young man of twentyseven years, he was well-versed in the Vinaya of Buddhist monachism and was therefore well-known under the epithet of Vinayadhara. As he had been to India for studying Sanskrit, the king's selection fell upon him... At this time Tshul-khrims having studied the

7. See *supra* Section 15, pp. 138f.

8. Das in JBTS I. i. 15.

Abhidharma and other Buddhist works, during a residence of two years in India, was on his way back to Tibet. He had become an accomplished lo-tsā-ba and Buddhist scholar, having translated several Sanskrit works such as the *Ārya-satya-dvaya* (Two Great Truths), its commentary, the *Sārasaṃgraha* by Atīśa, its commentary by Bhūmigarbha, *Ratnamālā*, *Yogacaryā* and its synopsis. At the monastery of Kusumapurī, he had translated the hymns called *Vajradharmagīta*."

The translation activity attributed here to Nag-tsho is not corroborated by the bsTan-'gyur. Dīpaṃkara's treatise on the Two Truths called the *Satya-dvaya-avatāra*[9] in this collection is found to have been translated by Vīryasiṃha. Bhūmigarbha or Kṣitigarbha is not found in the bsTan-'gyur as the author of any treatise.[10] However, it appears from the above account that Nag-tsho, after his first visit to India, returned to Tibet at the age of twenty-seven and that during this first visit he spent some time at the Kusumapurī *vihāra*, which, according to Sum-pa,[11] was situated at Vaiśālī and was the reputed centre of the second Buddhist council.

'Gos lo-tsā-ba does not provide us with the date of Vīryasiṃha's birth. The year of his death seems to be A.D. 1041—the Iron-Female-Serpent year that Atīśa spent in Nepal *en route* to Tibet.[12]

According to 'Gos lo-tsā-ba, Nag-tsho was accompanied by Vīryasiṃha during his first visit to India. The biography of Atīśa translated by Das does not say this in so many words, though according to it when Nag-tsho reached Vikramaśīla during his second visit to India and met Vīryasiṃha there, the latter recognised him and said, "Are you not my pupil Nag-tsho[13] ?" The two Tibetans knew each other before their reunion at the Vikramaśīla *vihāra*.

According to 'Gos lo-tsā-ba's account also Vīryasiṃha was residing at the Vikramaśīla *vihāra* when Nag-tsho reached it.

9. mDo xxix. 9 ; xxxiii. 3. No work called *Sārasaṃgraha* by Atīśa is found in the bsTan-'gyur.
10. Kṣitigarbha is mentioned as the translator only of rG. xv. 2.
11. Sum-pa 42.
12. BA i. 247.
13. Das in JBTS I. i. 17.

Nag-tsho and his party, says 'Gos lo-tsā-ba,[14] "reached Vikramaśīla during the night. While they were reciting prayers in Tibetan, rGya brTson-'grus-seṅ-ge, who was sitting on the roof of the entrance hall, overheard them, and shouted : 'Are you Tibetans ? Tomorrow we shall meet surely.' On the next day rGya brTson-'grus-seṅ-ge led Nag-tsho into the presence of the Master." It thus appears that though Nag-tsho went back to Tibet after spending about two years in India during his first visit, his companion Vīryasiṃha stayed back and continued his studies at the Vikramaśīla *vihāra*. But S. C. Das says that Vīryasiṃha also visited Vikramaśīla twice,[15] without telling us anything about his first visit.

'Gos lo-tsā-ba has nothing more to say about Vīryasiṃha. This is somewhat strange, for it is clear from the evidences of the bsTan-'gyur that presumably during the period he spent at the Vikramaśīla *vihāra* Vīryasiṃha became a skilled lo-tsā-ba and he was perhaps the earliest of the Tibetan translators who worked directly under Dīpaṃkara.

The bsTan-'gyur contains a considerable number of works translated by Vīryasiṃha under Dīpaṃkara.[16] Interestingly, Dīpaṃkara is not the only Indian *paṇḍita* under whom Vīryasiṃha worked as a lo-tsā-ba. The *Śrī-cakra-samvara-stotra-sarvārtha-siddhi-viśuddha-cūḍāmaṇi-nāma*[17] of Siddhācārya Dvārika-pā was translated by *upādhyāya* Dharmavajra of Kashmir and lo-tsā-ba brTson-'grus-seṅ-ge (Vīryasiṃha) of rGya. Though mentioned as a translator of four other works included in the bsTan-'gyur,[18] we have hardly any more knowledge of this Dharmavajra. The *Dohākoṣa-pañjikā-nāma*[19] was translated by *upādhyāya* Jayadeva of India and lo-tsā-ba of rGya ; the latter was possibly the same as Vīryasiṃha, though the Indian *paṇḍita* Jayadeva was by no means a very prominent one.[20] Another work in the bsTan-'gyur[21] appears

14. BA i. 245-6. 15. D-TED 306. 16. See Appendix B.
17. rG. xii. 11. 18. rG. xii. 11; xxvi. 1; xxxv. 3; lxxxii. 65.
19. rG. xlvi. 44. 20. Jayadeva is mentioned as a translator of rG. lxvi. 18; rGyal-ba'i-lha is mentioned as a translator of rG. xlvi. 44 and xlviii. 145. 21. rG. xxvi. 7.

to have been translated by Vīryasiṃha, though we have no knowledge of the Indian *paṇḍita* under whom this translation was done. Though these translations are minor in importance, Vīryasiṃha's work directly under Dīpaṃkara shows that he became one of the most promising lo-tsā-ba-s trained in India.

During the journey to Tibet, Atīśa originally chose Vīryasiṃha as his interpreter, though he could not reach Tibet in Atīśa's party. "On the way", says Bu-ston,[22] "rGya brTson-'grus-seṅ-ge died and they arrived, having appointed Nag-tsho to be interprete." The life of Atīśa translated by S. C. Das gives us a more detailed account of Vīryasiṃha's death. He was already sick before Atīśa's party started for Tibet—"laid up with fever at Śrī Nālandā, in consequence of which he had to be carried in a *dooly* to Vikramaśīla."[23] After Atīśa's party reached Nepal, he "had a relapse of fever. At the time of proceeding to Palpa, his illness took a serious turn."[24] Tibetans—including 'Brom-ston-pa[25]—view Vīryasiṃha's grave illness as the consequence of his learning some secret charm under a Tīrthika Tāntrika. But they also give us a realistic account of the measures taken by Atīśa's party to evade the difficulties that were likely to result from Vīryasiṃha's death in Nepal. "rGya-brtson lay in his death-bed. On this side of Palpa, according to the custom of the country, when a stranger dies in the house of the host, the latter gets his property. rGya-brtson was carried to the riverside where the party halted for the night. rGya-brtson breathed his last that night in consequence of which his property was saved. Some of his books were left in the host's place which he himself had left in the host's charge. Along with them the commentary of the work called the *Principal Sins*,[26] which was translated by Atīśa and rGya-brtson happened to be left. It was afterwards recovered

22. Bu-ston ii. 213. 23. JBTS I. i. 23. 24. *Ib*. 26.
25. *Ib*. 26n. 26. It is difficult to identify the work referred to. Atīśa's work on the ten principal sins, namely, the *Daśa-akuśala-karma-patha-(deśanā)*, mDo xxxi 21 & xxxiii. 19, as preserved in the bsTan-'gyur, was translated by Jayaśīla under Atīśa.

and esteemed as one of the best translations among the translated sacred texts."[27] 'Brom-ston-pa's account of Vīryasiṃha's death, as quoted by S. C. Das,[28] is as follows: "All means to cure him having failed, rGya-brtson died at midnight. They disposed of his dead body secretly by taking it to the riverside. In the morning his clothes and beddings were carried in a *dooly* to show as if he was still alive and medicines were being administered to the sick man. This was done with a view to avoid the government investigation about the cause of his death which would in consequence cause unnecessary delay and trouble."

It was only natural for Atīśa to be greatly moved by the death of such a faithful and talented Tibetan disciple. "The death of so good and accomplished a lo-tsā-ba like rGya-brtson made Atīśa very much distressed at heart. He said: 'My going to Tibet, it appears, will not be of much value. Now that my tongue has dropped off, I shall not be of service to the Tibetans. It is a pity that amongst the moral merits of the people of Tibet, there was not one by which rGya-brtson could be saved from an untimely death."[29] Nag-tsho tried to console the Master by offering his own services and by adding that there were many accomplished Sanskritists in Tibet eager to serve him. Atīśa had no other alternative than to depend on Nag-tsho as the Tibetan interpreter. "However, as you are the best among all the lo-tsā-ba-s," said he to Nag-tsho, "I shall also be able to learn to speak Tibetan from you."[30]

There is no doubt that of all the Tibetans Nag-tsho had the longest association with Atīśa. It is repeatedly asserted that he attended for 19 years on the Master.[31] How are these nineteen years to be accounted for?

After reviewing the controversy over the date of Atīśa's death, 'Gos lo-tsā-ba comes to the definite conclusion that it must have been the Wood-Male-Horse year, i.e. A.D. 1054.[32]

27. JBTS I. i. 26. 28. *Ib.* 26n. 29. *Ib.* 26. 30. *Ib.*
31. BA i. 261; 321. JBTS I. i. 7n.
32. BA i. 216.

According to the same historian, Atīśa left India for Tibet in A.D. 1040.[33] Though Nag-tsho was not actually present by the death-bed of Atīśa,[34] we may perhaps assume that the calculation of the 19 years overlooks the brief period he was absent from Atīśa just before the Master's death. Thus, from A.D. 1040 to A.D. 1054, we have an account of [14 or] 15 years during which Nag-tsho attended on Atīśa. How are the remaining [5 or] 4 years to be accounted for ? Evidently, these were the years that Nag-tsho spent in India under Atīśa, during his second visit to India when he came with the mission of inviting Atīśa and stayed mainly at the Vikramaśīla *vihāra.* In the life of Atīśa translated by Das, however, is said, "From the time that Nag-tsho had arrived at Vikramaśīla till his departure, full three years had elapsed."[35] The discrepancy between this statement and that of 'Gos lo-tsā-ba, therefore, amounts to a difference of about one year [in Tibetan calculation] of Nag-tsho's stay at the Vikramaśīla *vihāra.*

The story of how he invited Atīśa to Tibet is told in detail in Atīśa's biography translated by S. C. Das, which claims to be based on Nag-tsho's own communication. But there is one peculiarity about the story of this communication itself. When Phyag-sor-pa approached him for learning this account, Nag-tsho said, "I am well-versed in that for I know how we brought him here. I served him for a period of nineteen years. *Till now nobody except you has ever inquired of Atīśa's life and doings.*"[36] This, to say the least, is peculiar and it is inconceivable that the alleged indifference was due to any want of veneration for Atīśa, for already during Phyag-sor-pa's time the bKa'-gdams-pa sect was well-organised, to the followers of which Atīśa was practically deified. Could it be that the indifference of which Nag-tsho complained was really due to some loss of prestige that Nag-tsho himself suffered ? 'Gos lo-tsā-ba mentions how, because of his absence from the Master's death-bed, Nag-tsho was discredited among the

33. *Ib.* i. 247. 34. *Ib.* i. 260. 35. JBTS I. i. 23.
36. JBTS I. i. 7n ; emphasis added.

followers of the bKa'-gdams-pa sect. From Atiśa himself, according to 'Gos lo-tsā-ba,[37] Nag-tsho came to know the great fame of the Kashmirian *paṇḍita* Jñānākara. When Atiśa was nearing his death, Nag-tsho "received at sÑe-thaṅ a message saying that Jñānākara had come to Nepal. Nag-tsho seeing that the health of the Master was deteriorating, did not wish to separate from him, but feeling that he would be unable to meet the *paṇḍita* (Jñānākara), he felt sad. Afflicted by sorrow, his body became emaciated. Then the Master himself ordered him : 'It is difficult to meet *kalyāṇa-mitra*-s of the Mahāyāna. You, lo-tsā-ba, should go yourself ! I also shall not remain for long, and we shall meet in Tuṣita.' Then Nag-tsho made the following two requests : that he might be given at the time of his death permission to be reborn in Tuṣita in the Master's presence, and that the Master should appear at the time of the consecration ceremony of the image of the Master which will be unveiled in his native place. The Master promised him. With reference to this story, the bKa'-gdams-pa-s of later times imputed that the lo-tsā-ba, who had left the Master at the time of the Master's passing into *nirvāṇa*, did not keep (his) vows. Śar-ba-pa expressed his disapproval of this in the account written by him : 'The present day's lack of felicity is due (to the action) of this lo-tsā-ba. But our bKa'-gdams-pa-s are often addicted to slander.' In connection with this (it must be added) that in general, when the Master came to Tibet, 'Brom-ston acted as supporter (*bdag-gñer*) and helper, and the Master used to open his Mind to him only."[38]

Nag-tsho's ambition of translating more and more texts under famous Indian *paṇḍita*-s was apparently satisfied. After Dīpaṃkara's death, says 'Gos lo-tsā-ba,[39] "Nag-tsho translated many texts, assisted by Jñānākara, the Nepalese Śāntibhadra, Kṛṣṇa-samaya-vajra and others." He did, in fact, become one of the greatest of the Tibetan translators, as is obvious from

37. BA i. 260 38. *Ib.* i. 260-1. 39. *Ib.* i. 261.

the large number of works in the bsTan-'gyur translated by him.[40] Still, with his long association with Dīpaṃkara he failed to be a leader of the religious sect founded by the Master in Tibet. But more of this later.

40. The bsTan-'gyur contains over one hundred and twentyfive works translated by Jayaśīla of Nag-tsho.

32. Journey to Tibet

There is considerable controversy among the modern scholars concerning the exact date of Dīpaṃkara's departure for Tibet. Even the real problem of this date is sometimes wrongly posed. Thus, e.g., R. C. Majumdar[1] says, "the date of his departure has been fixed by various authorities at 1038, 1039, 1040, 1041 and 1042 A.D." What is overlooked, however, is that the authorities referred to express themselves on the possible dates of two different events altogether. These are : i) Dīpaṃkara's departure from India and ii) his arrival in Tibet, or, more specifically, at mÑa'-ris. From the point of view of precise dating, the difference between the two events is material. Apart from the time taken for the journey, Atīśa spent about a year in Nepal *en route* to Tibet, and he also halted, though for brief periods, at different places, like the shores of the Manasasarovara lake, which he admired much. Between the date of his departure from India and his arrival at mÑa'-ris, therefore, it is reasonable to assume a gap of about two years. Yet R. C. Majumdar, in his above statement, lumps together different views expressed by different scholars on the possible dates of these two events. This is clear from the references on which the statement is based. Thus :

1038 : *JASB*. 1891. p. 51.
1039 : S. C. Das, *Indian Pandits*, pp. 50, 70.
1040 : Levi, *Nepal*, ii. p. 189 ; *dPag-bsam-ljon-bzaṅ*, index, p. liv.
1041 : *IHQ*. vi. p. 159.
1042 : *JASB*. 1881. p. 237.

Of these, A.D. 1038 is suggested by S. C. Das (in *JASB* 1891. 51) as the year in which Atīśa "visited" Tibet, the presumption of this being that he left India earlier. Again, A.D. 1041 is suggested by D. C. Bhattacharyya (in *IHQ* vi. 158) as

1. R. C. Majumdar in HB i. 145. S. K. Chatterjee in HB i. 387 even says that Dīpaṃkara "went to Tibet about 1035 A.D."

the year in which "Atīśa left for Tibet", which means that he reached Tibet later. Interestingly in *JASB* 1881. p. 237, S. C. Das himself says, "he (Atīśa) quitted his monastery Vikrama Śīlā for Tibet in the year 1042 A.D.," assuming thereby that he could not have reached Tibet before A.D. 1044 !

This bewildering variety of dates suggested by the modern scholars is at least partly because of a somewhat casual attitude to the Tibetan evidences, on the basis of which alone the dates can be correctly ascertained. This is apparent from how S. C. Das, in his different contributions, expresses different views on the date, though, curiously enough, the source on which he ultimately depends is not necessarily different. Thus, e.g., on the basis of the *Re'u-mig*,[2] he says, "Prabhu Śrīmat Atīśa (Jo-bo dPal-ldan Atīśa) arrived at mṄa'-ris in A.D. 1038." Though Francke[3] and Waddell[4] accept this date and though this is perhaps also the basis of the assertion of S. C. Das himself in *JASB* 1891 p. 51 that Atīśa "visited" Tibet in A.D. 1038, it is necessary to remember that the *Re'u-mig* is the chronological table of important events, etc., contained in Sum-pa's *dPag-bsam-ljon-bzaṅ* and, therefore, contains the view of Sum-pa himself.[5] Though the printed Tibetan version of this work does not contain the *Re'u-mig*, S. C. Das, while editing this version, adds an English Index to it and the Index (p. liv.) mentions : "Naya Pāla,... one of the celebrated kings of the Pāla dynasty, during whose reign (about A.D. 1040) Dīpaṃkara Śrījñāna (Atīśa) visited Tibet."

Yet Sum-pa himself leaves nothing vague about the dates of Atīśa's departure from India and of his arrival at mṄa'-ris. "At the age of 59", says he,[6] "by the end of the Iron-Dragon year, along with the two lo-tsā-ba-s, he reached Nepal from India and stayed one year in the country of Anantakīrti at the Samatha *vihāra*... Then in the Water-Horse (year), he reached Guṅ-thaṅ mTho-ldiṅ (Tho-liṅ) of mṄa'-ris province of Tibet."

2. S. C. Das in JASB 1889. 40.
3. Francke AIT ii. 177n.
4. Waddell L 34n ; in ERE ii. 194.
5. S. C. Das, Intro. to Sum-pa, p. iii ; in JASB 1889. 37f.
6. Sum-pa 185. See Sec. 3, Appendix A.

What, then, does Sum-pa mean here by the Iron-Dragon and Water-Horse years ? In the Tibetan calendar, three successive Iron-Dragon years are A.D. 980, 1040 and 1100 while three successive Water-Horse years are A.D. 982,1042 and 1102. Since Atiśa was indisputably a contemporary of Nayapāla of Bengal, it would be as preposterous to accept the Iron-Dragon year of the above passage as A.D. 980 or A.D. 1100 as it will be to take the Water-Horse year as A.D. 982 or A.D. 1102. In other words, Sum-pa's statement is to be taken only in the sense that towards the end of A.D. 1040, Atiśa reached Nepal from India, and, after spending a year there, he reached mṄa'-ris in A.D. 1042. Moreover, in the Tibetan calendar, between an Iron-Dragon year and a Water-Horse year there intervenes an Iron-Serpent year. Therefore, Sum-pa's statement contains the additional suggestion that Atiśa spent the Iron-Serpent year or A.D. 1041 in Nepal.

All these fully agree with the dates given by 'Gos lo-tsā-ba. "The master," says he,[7] "who was born in the Water-Male-Horse year (A.D. 982), in his 57th year [evidently a misprint for 59th year], in the year Iron-Male-Dragon (A.D. 1040) left India. The Iron-Female-Serpent year (A.D. 1041) the Master spent in Nepal. In the year Water-Male-Horse (A.D. 1042), the Master proceeded to mṄa'-ris." Elsewhere also 'Gos lo-tsā-ba says[8] that the year immediately preceding that of Atiśa's arrival at mṄa'-ris was an Iron-Female-Serpent year or A.D. 1041.

The way in which 'Gos lo-tsā-ba seeks to be absolutely certain about a date is by linking it with A.D. 1476, a Fire-Ape year, which is the year of the composition of his own work. The date of Atiśa's arrival in Tibet being for him a crucial one, he makes two statements in which he establishes this date according to this method. "In general," runs one of these,[9] "from the coming of the Master to Tibet till the present Fire-Male-Ape (year : A.D. 1476) —435 years have passed." The other[10] is : "495 years have passed from the birth of the

7. BA i. 247. 8. *Ib.* i. 71. 9. *Ib.* i. 283. 10. *Ib.* i. 267.

Venerable Master (A.D. 982) to the Fire-Female-Ape year [evidently a mis-translation of *me-pho-spre'u* meaning the Fire-Male-Ape year]. Since the Master's coming to mÑa'-ris, this year is the 435th year." It needs only to be remembered that according to the Tibetan mode of reckoning years, 435 years elapse between A.D. 1042 and 1476.

We have already seen[11] some examples of how the Water-Horse year or A.D. 1042, as the year of Atīśa's coming to Tibet, is taken by 'Gos lo-tsā-ba as a cardinal date for Tibetan chronology. We may have a few more examples of how he connects the same date with the dates of certain other important personalities of the religious history of Tibet.

The great Tibetan translator Rin-chen-bzaṅ-po was born in A.D. 958,[12] an Earth-Male-Horse year. "When the lo-tsā-ba Rin-chen-bzaṅ-po was eighty-five, Atīśa (Jo-bo-rje) came to Tibet and met him."[13] In the Tibetan view, Rin-chen-bzaṅ-po was 85 in A.D. 1042. "In the eightyfifth year of the lo-tsā-ba Rin-chen-bzaṅ-po," repeats 'Gos lo-tsā-ba,[14] "in the year Water-Male-Horse (A.D. 1042), Atīśa reached mÑa'-ris."

'Brom-ston-pa, the foremost of the Tibetan disciples of Atīśa, died in the year Wood-Male-Dragon, i.e. A.D. 1064,[15] and this was "twentythree years after the coming of Atīśa to Tibet."[16] Here, again, the date of Atīśa's coming to Tibet is assumed to be A.D. 1042.

Rin-chen-sñin-po was born in the Water-Male-Ape year,[17] i.e. A.D. 1032. "When he was eleven, the Master came to Tibet."[18]

Chad-kha-pa died in A.D. 1175, because it was followed by the Fire-Male-Ape year or A.D. 1176.[19] "From the arrival of the Master in Tibet till the death of Chad-kha-pa—134 years (elapsed)."[20]

More examples are not necessary. 'Gos lo-tsā-ba seeks to

11. See Sections 21 & 27. 12. BA i. 68. 13. *Ib.*
14. *Ib.* i. 123; cf. i. 250. 15. *Ib.* i. 186 ; cf i. 264.
16. *Ib.* i. 72. 17. *Ib.* i. 286. 18. *Ib.*
19. *Ib.* i. 282. 20. *Ib.*

establish beyond any doubt that Atīśa arrived in Tibet (mṄa'-ris) in A.D. 1042. Therefore, allowing a reasonable time for the journey and admitting that he spent a year in Nepal before proceeding to mṄa'-ris, we may depend on the following dates :

A. D. 1040 — Atīśa left India for Tibet.

A. D. 1041 — he spent in Nepal.

A. D. 1042 — he reached mṄa'-ris.

Our main source for a descriptive account of Atīśa's departure from India and of his journey to Tibet is the biography translated by S. C. Das, which, as we have noted, claims some special importance from the tradition of being based on the personal communication of Jayaśīla (Nag-tsho) to Phag-sor-pa. It is true that some of the incidents recorded in it are for us without much of historical value, while those that appear to be historically significant are not necessarily corroborated by collateral evidences. Still our starting point is this biography and our main effort should be to seek for corroborative evidences, as far as possible, for the narration it contains.

Atīśa's decision to accept the Tibetan invitation appears to have originally been a secret one.[21] He apprehended in particular the possibility of the required permission being refused by the *sthavira* of the Vikramaśīla monastery. Accordingly, the preparations for the journey were secretly carried out, though, when the *sthavira* came to discover Atīśa's real intention, he granted him the permission somewhat grudgingly.

A question is sometimes raised as to how far the disturbed conditions in eastern India caused in particular by the Muhammadan invasion influenced Atīśa's decision in favour of the Tibetan invitation. Bell thinks that it largely did so : Atīśa, in his view,[22] was one of the "Pandits who flocked to Tibet" when the "Muhammadan invaders were establishing their power in the plains of India and were attacking Hindus and Buddhists alike." But this looks like an anachronism.

21. See Sec. 15, pp. 130ff.   22. Bell RT 53.

That on the eve of Atīśa's departure for Tibet parts of India were actually disturbed by Muhammadan invasion need not be doubted. In life of Atīśa translated by Das, the *sthavira* of Vikramaśīla, while granting Jayaśīla the permission to take Atīśa to Tibet, said, 'The looming signs prognosticate evil for India. Numerous Turuskas are invading India, and I am much concerned at heart. May you proceed to your country with your companions and with Atīśa to work for the good of all living beings there."[23] But this must not be construed to mean that the Muhammadan invasion elsewhere in India caused in the Pāla territory in A.D. 1040 such a state of panic as to tempt Atīśa an escape in the Tibetan invitation. Muhammad Bakhtyār's invasion of eastern India and the devastation by him of a Buddhist monastery, usually mentioned as the final blow to Indian Buddhism, actually took place about a century and half after Atīśa left for Tibet.[24] The invasion of Mahmud of Ghazni did not directly affect the territory under Mahīpāla's rule[25] and his raid on the Somanāth temple (A.D. 1024/25) took place while Atīśa was perhaps in Suvarṇadvīpa studying under Dharmakīrti.[26] Thus, there is no evidence of any alarming condition caused by Muhammadan invasion in eastern India on the eve of Atīśa's departure for Tibet, though the *sthavira* of the Vikramaśīla *vihāra* might have felt uneasy about the Muhammadan invasion then taking place in other parts of India. Further, as against Bell's view, it needs to be remembered that Atīśa's original plan was to visit Tibet for a period of three years only, after which he was to return to his Indian monastery. The *sthavira* of Vikramaśīla told Jayaśīla, "I lend his services to your country for three years and after that you must bring him back here."[27] From 'Gos lo-tsā-ba's account also it is clear that after spending three years in Tibet, Atīśa "was preparing to return to India"[28] and, in A.D. 1045, the Master along with his retinue journeyed back as far as sKyi-roṅ,[29] the town of western Tibet bordering

23. JBTS I.i. 24. 24. HB i. 223 ; 242. 25. *Ib*. i. 141. Smith OHI 190ff. 26. Rahula in *2500 Years* 230. 27. JBTS I. i. 23 ; cf BA i. 247. 28. BA i. 251. 29. *Ib*. i. 254.

on Nepal.[30] What prevented him from actually coming back to India is a different story altogether. This will be discussed in our next section. For the moment the point is that if Atīśa fled in panic of the Muhammadan invasion he could not possibly have planned to return to India after spending only three years in Tibet.

What, then, could have influenced him in favour of his acceptance of the Tibetan invitation ? Any answer to the question not based on the Tibetan sources would be at best conjectural, while, apart from certain stories of miraculous inspiration,[31] the only thing that the Tibetan sources have to say about Atīśa's decision is that he was moved by compassion for the Tibetan people and the accounts of ups and downs in the history of Buddhism in Tibet, was annoyed with the corrupt practices which he was told were passing for the true form of Buddhism in Tibet and that he was deeply touched by the report of how Ye-śes-'od sacrificed his life for the Doctrine.[32] Dīpaṃkara must have felt that his journey to Tibet at such an advanced age was going to have an adverse effect on his health. But he was not perturbed by this thought. The typical Tibetan way of putting this is that "the Master consulted his tutelary deity and a *yoginī* at Vajrāsana, and these unanimously told him : 'By all means go to Tibet ! In general benefit will arise for the Doctrine, and in particular, great benefit will arise from your association with the *upāsaka* ('Brom-ston-pa). But your life will be shortened by twenty years !' The Master then thought for himself : 'If benefit for the Doctrine and living beings were to arise, then the shortening of one's own life did not matter.' He proceeded with the preparations for his departure."[33] In other words, disregarding the possible consequences to his health Dīpaṃkara decided to go to Tibet and this, as the Tibetans believe, dictated by the consideration for the propagation of the Doctrine.

30. D-TED 101.
31. JBTS I. i. 19f ; Bu-ston ii. 213.
32. JBTS I. i. 19ff.
33. BA i. 246 ; cf JBTS I. i. 20.

Leaving the Vikramaśīla *vihāra*, Dīpaṃkara first made a pilgrimage to Buddhagayā. "Then," says Rahula,[34] "he sent some of the Tibetans with his own men to Nepal, and with the interpreter Vikrama of rGya (Vīryasiṃha of rGya) and some other men, altogether twelve people, Atīśa set out for Bodh Gayā. Before leaving India, Atīśa felt the need to see once more the places where Siddhārtha Gautama had become the Buddha. Atīśa visited Vajrāsana and many other holy places. Then, along with the scholars, Kṣitigarbha and 19 others, he reached a small *vihāra* on the frontier of India."

In the biography translated by S. C. Das, we have more details of the party with which Dīpaṃkara started for Tibet : "Atīśa, accompanied by *paṇḍita* Bhūmigarbha, Nag-tsho, rGya-brtson, Bhūmisaṅgha, Vīryacandra and a large retinue set out for Mitra *vihāra*. The monks of that monastery received him with veneration and demonstration of joy. rGya-brtson with two servants, Nag-tsho with six and Atīśa with twenty attendants set out from here to Tibet."[35]

Thus, apart from the two Tibetan disciples, we have in this list the names of three others who accompanied Atīśa to Tibet. They were Kṣitigarbha (or Bhūmigarbha), Bhūmisaṅgha and Vīryacandra. Elsewhere[36] the same biography mentions another companion as *paṇḍita* Parahitabhadra.

Of these, *paṇḍita* Kṣitigarbha (or Bhūmigarbha), as we learn from 'Gos lo-tsā-ba,[37] was "one of the five special disciples" of the Master. He was the elder brother[38] of the famous Vajrapāṇi (Phyag-na), the renowned preacher of the Mahāmudrā Tantra in Nepal and Tibet.[39] Since Vajrapāṇi was born in A.D. 1017, Kṣitigarbha must have been somewhat older.

Bhūmisaṅgha is described in the biography as "*mahārājā* Bhūmisaṅgha, the royal monk, the principal disciple of Atīśa,"[40] and though it is said that he was "the king of western India"[41] —or even "king of the whole of western India, who is majestic and bright in learning, who is mighty to

34. Rahula in *2500 Years* 236 35. JBTS I. i. 24. 36. *Ib.* 29.
37. BA i. 262. 38. *Ib.* ii. 842. 39. *Ib.* ii. 855ff.
40. JBTS I. i. 25. 41. HB i. 676.

be able to overpower the world"[42] —we have hardly any positive historical knowledge about him. Nevertheless, to Atīśa's biographer he was a great king : "To him the king of kings also bow down his head. For the sake of the exalted dignity of this royal personage, the king of Nepal sent a large escort (about 425) up to the lake Ma-pham (Manasa-sarovara)."[43]

About *paṇḍita* Parahitabhadra, we learn practically nothing definite from the Tibetan sources.

Most interesting, however, in the list of Dīpaṃkara's Indian companions is the name of Vīryacandra. The biography mentions him as a brother of Dīpaṃkara.[44] This agrees with Nag-tsho's *stotra* to Atīśa, according to which, the younger brother of Dīpaṃkara, who was originally called Śrīgarbha, "became the monk Vīryacandra."[45] We have thus the interesting information that Dīpaṃkara's younger brother accompanied him to Tibet as one of his monk-followers. But we hear no more of him.

Another interesting thing mentioned in the biography is the gift of an elephant by Atīśa to the king of Nepal.[46] The name of the elephant is given as Dṛṣta-uṣadhi[47] and it is added that, while making the gift, Atīśa advised the king not to use the animal for any war purpose ; the elephant was rather to be used for "carrying sacred objects, scriptures, symbols and images."[48] Granting factual basis for this, we may presume that up to Nepal, Atīśa made the journey on elephant-back though the route he followed from Nepal to mÑa'-ris precluded the possibility of taking the elephant any further.

Atīśa's biographer does not give us much detail of the route he followed up to Nepal. But it is not difficult to infer. From the Vikramaśila *vihāra* he went to Buddhagayā and from Buddhagayā he proceeded to the Svayambhū *caitya* of Nepal. Buddhagayā is situated within six miles of the modern town of Gayā and the Svayambhū *caitya* within two miles of the modern town of Kathmandu. Roughly

42. JBTS I. i. 30. 43. *Ib.* 44. *Ib.* 25. 45. BA i. 242n. : Quoted by Roerich. 46. JBTS I. i. 27. 47. *Ib.* 48. *Ib.*

speaking, therefore, Atīśa proceeded from Gayā to Kathmandu. It is perhaps reasonable to presume further that he went *via* modern Patna, for there is no reason to think that he followed any route other than the one traditionally followed by the traders and pilgrims, i.e. the old route connecting Patna with Kathmandu through Champaran. "The principal route (to Nepal) for through traffic is that which runs through the British district of Champaran, with Kathmandu and Patna for its two points of terminus."[49]

One of the details given in the biography about Atīśa's journey up to Nepal is concerning a small monastery where the Master was warmly received: "Near the frontier, within the Indian territory, there was a small *vihāra*. When Atīśa and his party reached the place the priestly community (*saṅgha*) of the monastery gave him a very warm reception."[50] To this S. C. Das adds the following note,[51] without unfortunately mentioning his source: "Atīśa said to his companions and followers: 'A Buddhist high official residing in the frontier town C'indilla Krama had asked me to consecrate the site of a temple which he intended to erect. For the last one or two years I have not been able to attend to his request. Now I must go there.' Accordingly, he went to C'indilla. Having consecrated the site he said to his followers: 'Now that I shall go to conduct a religious service at Svayambhū (in Nepal) you may return to Vikrama(śila)'."

The other information given by the biographer about the Master's journey up to the Svayambhū *caitya* are mainly for the purpose of glorifying his spiritual powers with which he could easily overcome dangers and adversaries. Thus, after crossing the Indian frontier, Atīśa and his party "arrived at a place sacred to the Tīrthikas" and the Tīrthika teachers there were greatly impressed by Atīśa's exposition of the Tīrthika Doctrine itself, so great was the Master's knowledge even of the Tīrthika religion. However, a section of the Tīrthikas felt jealous of the Buddhists. "It is said that attempts were made by them

49. W. W. Hunter in IGI vii. 109. 50. JBTS I. i. 24. 51. *Ib.* 24n.

to assassinate Atīśa by sending after him eighteen robbers." But the robbers became like dumb statues as soon as they saw his venerable face and Atīśa himself restored sense to the stupefied, saying, "I pity the robbers."[52]

The Master next arrived at "a deserted camping ground of a herdsman." Then "proceeding northward he entered the country of Nepal and halted there for the night." The local chiefs of this place were extremely rude and conspired another robbery, which, again, was foiled by the Master with his miraculous power.[53]

"Then the party reached the sacred place of Ārya Svayambhū. The beasts of burden were unloaded and all the packings were deposited at the place of their encampment, and a temporary wall was raised round the baggages."[54] This description appears to be realistic and the place-name is identifiable. The biographer mentions "the *rājā* of Svayambhū" who "made grand preparations for the reception of Atīśa and collected a large quantity of provisions and other necessaries for the use of his followers. He sent his officers to escort the sage from a place called Krishong-bro, which was a long way off from his palace." This *rājā* received Atīśa in his palace and "a religious service on a grand scale was conducted by Atīśa for furthering the prosperity of the *rājā* and of his people."[55]

Who exactly was meant by the *rājā* of Svayambhū is not clear. The biographer does not mention any name, though from his subsequent narration it is clear that by this *rājā* he does not mean the king of Nepal, whose name is given as Anantakīrti and whom Atīśa met after proceeding to Palpa from the Svayambhū *caitya* of Kathmandu. In any case, the biographer gives us the impression that in spite of the gorgeous reception received at the Svayambhū *caitya*, Atīśa did not stay there for a long time.

After that he proceeded to Palpa, when Vīryasiṃha's illness took a serious turn, eventually resulting in his death.[56]

52. *Ib.* 24-5. 53. *Ib.* 25. 54. *Ib.* 55. *Ib.* 25-6.
56. See Section 31.

Apart from the loss of this faithful interpreter, the biographer tells us of three things in particular relating to Dīpaṃkara's stay in Nepal. These are : 1) a letter written by him to king Nayapāla, 2) his composition of the work called *Caryā-saṃgraha-pradīpa* and 3) the rousing reception received by him from king Anantakīrti of Nepal, who was at that time in Palpa and who was inspired by Atīśa to build the Tham (sThaṃ) *vihāra*.

The historicity of the letter written by Dīpaṃkara to Nayapāla is unquestioned. The actual letter, though in its Tibetan translation, is preserved in the bsTan-'gyur and is called the *Vimala-ratna-lekha*.[57] In the Peking edition, its colophon reads, "Here ends the *Vimala-ratna-lekha-nāma*, sent by *sthavira mahāpaṇḍita* Dīpaṃkara-śrī-jñāna to *rājā* Nirapāla (Nayapāla)." Its opening verse is, "Naryapāla (Nayapāla), who was born in Magadha, had spread the Doctrine and has ruled the kingdom according to *dharma*,—may he be prosperous."

This letter is often mentioned by the historians of eastern India. But the possible significance of the occasion of writing it is not generally discussed. The contents of the letter are likely to throw some light on this question. Significantly, nowhere in this letter Atīśa mentions the fact of his leaving India or of his intended visit to Tibet. It is, therefore, baseless to conjecture that the letter contained some kind of apology for leaving India without the king's consent. The letter mentions nothing about his journey, nothing about his reaching Nepal. Neither does it contain any query about anything or anybody in India—nothing, in fact, about the Vikramaśīla *vihāra* or about any person including Nayapāla himself. On the contrary, it is only a collection of religious and moral precepts, which the sixty years old monk thought fit to convey to a beloved and young ruler. But why did he want to convey all these *from Nepal*, when there was apparently nothing to prevent him from doing it while in India or even after reaching

57. See Sec. 5, Appendix C.

his destination in Tibet? The presumption is that when Atīśa was in Nepal something happened in the career of Nayapāla himself and Atīśa considered it fit to send some form of special message to him to suit the occasion. What could such an occasion possibly be? Could it be the formal coronation ceremony of the young king? Assuming such a possibility, we are led to infer that the formal coronation of Nayapāla took place in A. D. 1041, the year Atīśa spent in Nepal. The possibility seems to agree with the statements of both Sum-pa and Tāranātha, according to whom Nayapāla ascended the throne at the time of Atīśa's departure for Tibet. "Thereafter," says Sum-pa,[58] "Bheyapāla's son Neyapāla (Nayapāla) became king just at the time Jo-bo (Atīśa) proceeded for Bod (Tibet)." Tāranātha[59] repeats this: "King Bheyapāla's son was Neyapāla. At the time of Jo-bo-rje's departure for Tibet, he (Nayapāla) was just placed in the kingdom (i.e. became king). This is said in the authentic biographies. Also a letter sent to him from Nepal is seen."

Both D. C. Bhattacharyya[60] and S. C. Sarkar[61] draw our attention to these statements, though how far these statements, along with the internal evidence of the *Vimala-ratna-lekha*, call for a correction of the usually accepted date of Nayapāla's accession (A.D. 1038) is a question into the intricacies of which we do not have the scope here to enter.

The second important thing the biographer says about Atīśa's stay in Nepal is his composition of the *Caryā-saṃgraha-pradīpa*: "Then the party proceeded to a place called Holka of Palpa to avail themselves of the hospitality of a friend of Atīśa, a Buddhist sage, who, owing to his deafness, was called the deaf *sthavira*. Here Atīśa spent one month. The deaf *sthavira* heard (!) from Atīśa a complete discourse on the *pāramitā*-s, which are different from the *mantra* portion of the sacred books, for full six days. The *sthavira* having had no faith in the *mantra*-s, Atīśa explained to him that the way to

58. Sum-pa 119.
59. Tāranātha (Benares ed.) 224.
60. D. C. Bhattacharyya in IHQ vi. 159.
61. S. C. Sircar in JBORS xxvi. 387.

the attainment of Bodhihood lay both in the *mantra*-s and the *pāramitā*-s. Accordingly, he wrote the work called *Caryā-saṃgraha-pradīpa.* The lo-tsā-ba [Jayaśīla] translated it into Tibetan with Atīśa's assistance."[62]

The work called *Caryā-saṃgraha-pradīpa*[63] written by Dīpaṃkara and translated by lo-tsā-ba Jayaśīla under him is preserved in the bsTan-'gyur. Its analysis reveals some interesting points.

First, it contains the statement : "I have done (written) this in Nepal on my friend's request. O *sthavira* ! do like this, since you are not devoted to the *guhya-mantra*."[64] This shows that the work was actually composed by Dīpaṃkara while he was in Nepal with the special intention of being communicated to a *sthavira* who had no faith in the *guhya-mantra* (Tantra). Thus the internal evidence of the work fully corroborates the statement of the biographer and confirms the authenticity of the biography. The claim of its being based on the personal communication of Jayaśīla does not, therefore, appear to be fictitious.

But the internal evidence of the work needs to be analysed further, particularly because it has important light to throw on the difficult question of Atīśa's attitude to Tantra (*mantra*). Composed with the special objective of addressing one who lacked faith in the *mantra*, the text opens with the declaration that the *guhya-mantra* is as scriptural as the *pāramitā*-s :

"Salutation to Lokeśvara.

And we bow down to the Highest Being, whose sayings open our ignorant hearts as light opens the lotus.

The teacher Buddha said, 'Enlightenment (*bodhi*) can be attained with the help of the secret spells (*guhya-mantra*) as well as *prajñāpāramitā*. I shall, accordingly, explain it."

After an introduction like this, what Atīśa passes on to discuss in the same work may, apparently at least, look most peculiar. If the work is designed to restore in the *sthavira* faith

62. JBTS I. i. 27.

63. mDo xxxi. 23 : xxxiii. 2.

64. Free translations of this, as well as of the other passages of this work quoted below, are by courtesy of Professor Lama Chimpa.

in the *guhya-mantra*, we normally expect Atīśa to pass on to discuss in the work mainly the theme of the *guhya-mantra*. However, in the very next sentences Atīśa says :

"But I shall not mention the *guhya-mantra* here. (Instead of that), I shall briefly discuss here the *bodhisattvacaryā*-s, which are the *caryā*-s of *prajñāpāramitā*. Work first for *cittotpāda* and then take up the *bodhisattva-saṃvara*. Study the *sūtra*-s in their entirety and listen to all the *śāstra*-s. Guard the purity of your vow (*saṃvara*) with body-word-mind (*kāya-vāc-citta*) as prescribed by these (i.e. the *sūtra*-s and *śāstra*-s). Never allow it (the *saṃvara*) to be defiled.

Keep your conduct (*śīla*) pure. Take measured food. Keep the openings of your sense organs closed. Do not sleep during the first and the last quarter of the night. Practise *yoga*. Beware even of the slightest sin.

Divide the night into three parts and wake up during the last part. (You) may wash the face, but that is not essential. Sit on a comfortable seat and meditate on the elements (*dharma*-s). Failing to overcome the disturbances caused by imagination, you may get up (from the meditation) and think of everything as but appearance, like a magical show. During this time, devote yourself to devotional acts and perform the seven-fold worship (*saptāṅgapūjā*) and pray in various ways. After this, try to continue the meditation...

In short, observe the ten *caryā*-s prescribed by Maitreya-nātha. Do not allow your mind to agitate. When you do anything, think as if it were a magical show. If you have wealth, offer it to the *saṅgha*-s, arrange for a feast for the children and give it to the helpless ones. This is virtue for a *yogin*...."

And so on. There is, in short, nothing in this work to suggest a recommendation of the *guhya-mantra* beyond the bare and formal acceptance of its scriptural validity. Practically the same attitude to *guhya-mantra* was expressed by Atīśa in some of his other writings as well. In the *Caryā-gīti* and its auto-commentary,[65] he retained the form of the Tantra but infused it with the content of classical Mahāyāna, both in its philosophical and ethical aspects. In the *Bodhi-patha-pradīpa*[66] he boldly declared the incompatibility of *guhya-abhiṣeka* with the ascetic ideal of the monk, without at the same time formally rejecting *guhya-abhiṣeka* as such. This attitude was for him perhaps inevitable. He lived and preached in an age in which Mahāyāna Buddhism became so much transformed into Mantrayāna and the latter acquired such a tremendous spiritual prestige that it would have been almost a heresy for a Mahāyāna Buddhist to deny its scriptural authority. At the same time, Dīpaṃkara had his basic moorings in classical Mahāyāna or Mahāyāna in its pre-Tāntrika phase. Therefore, in spite of his formal recognition of Tantrayāna, he was anxious above all to explain and emphasise the classical form of the Mahāyāna. The *Caryā-saṃgraha-pradīpa* is an interesting document of how he tried to do this.

The third important thing told in the biography about Atiśa's stay in Nepal relates to the king called Anantakīrti : "They then reached the plain of Palpa called Palpoi-than. At this time the king named Anantakīrti who ruled over Nepal held his court there. He received Atiśa with much cordiality and reverence."[67] Atiśa persuaded the king to build a monastery which was to be called the Tham (sTham) *vihāra* and the king even allowed "his son prince Padmaprabha to be ordained as a monk-pupil of Atiśa." It is added that Atiśa left Nepal for Tibet after the work on the Tham *vihāra* was commenced and the prince Padmaprabha had lessons in Tibetan and Sanskrit and eventually became an adept in Buddhism.[68]

It is difficult to have corroborative evidences from the Nepalese sources for all these. Any king bearing the name Anantakīrti and ruling Nepal during the middle of the eleventh century hardly figures in the Nepalese annals. Rahula

65. See Sections 1-3, Appendix C. 66. *śloka*-s 63-5. See Section 6, Appendix C. 67. JBTS I. i. 27; 68. *Ib.*

Sankrityayan, without doubting the royal patronage received by Atīśa in Nepal, suggests the possibility of the real name of the king being different. "At this time," says he,[69] "king Jayakāmadeva of the Ṭhākurī dynasty was probably the ruler of the country. He showed them the utmost respect and asked them to stay in Nepal. Atīśa could not refuse his request, and lived there for one year. During this period he initiated one of the princes of the royal blood into the order." Regmi,[70] however, allows the following conjecture about Anantakīrti: "Could this king be an immediate successor of Lakṣhmīkāmadeva, whom Bhāṣkara had expelled? There is no identity between the two names, Anantakīrti and Jayadeva, as apparently considered. But Anantakīrti's existence may be established by identifying him with Yaśodeva, the father of Vanadeva of Bendall's *Ins. V*. S. Lévi considers that Yaśodeva was not in any way connected with the throne of Nepal."

At the same time, regarding the Nepalese evidences Regmi points out, "Atīśa's visit is noted neither in the chronicles nor in the *ms.* and inscription records of Nepal. There is not even a legend about this visit."[71] This, to say the least, is strange, it being difficult to believe that the entire account of the Tibetan historians and biographers concerning Atīśa's stay in Nepal *en route* to Tibet was drawn from mere imagination. Moreover, the recorded evidences in the bsTan-'gyur, particularly of the *Vimala-ratna-lekha* and the *Caryā-saṃgraha-pradīpa* which were written by Dīpaṃkara during his stay in Nepal, are too solid to make the account of his visit to Nepal a fictitious one. In spite of the strange silence of the Nepalese sources concerning Dīpaṃkara's visit to Nepal, Regmi[72] himself proposes to accept as authentic the account of the great Tibetan scholar Chag-chos-rje-dpal, commonly mentioned as Chag lo-tsā-ba and said to have "studied the Doctrine (at the feet) of twelve *paṇḍita*-s, four Tibetan lo-tsā-ba-s, twentyone learned monks and others"[73] and also praised "as the most

69. Rahula in *2500 Years* 236-7 70. Regmi 122. 71. *Ib.* 129.
72. *Ib.* 559ff. 73. BA ii. 1058

learned of the translators after Rin-chen-bzaṅ-po."[74] Born in A.D. 1197,[75] he came to Nepal in c. A.D. 1226[76] and spent there "eight full years"[77] after which he came to India and left for us a well-known description of Mahābodhi. "While in Nepal the monk resided in the monastery of Svayambhū," but has mentioned two more monasteries in Nepal, one of which was called Tham, "also known as First *vihāra* or Upper *vihāra*."[78] "The Tibetan monk," says Regmi,[79] "saw in the Tham monastery a golden image of Śākyamuni in front of the *stūpa*."

We have, thus, in the writings of an eminent Tibetan scholar, who spent a considerable number of years in Nepal within two centuries of Atīśa's stay there, positive evidence of the existence of the Tham *vihāra*, with the foundation of which Atīśa's name is closely associated. Further, as we have already seen,[80] 'Brom-ston-pa, the foremost of the Tibetan disciples of Atīśa himself, gives us a highly realistic account of the death of Vīryasiṃha in Nepal. Therefore, even in default of any direct Nepalese source to corroborate the account of Atīśa's stay in Nepal, the Tibetan evidences in favour of it cannot be brushed aside.

What is likely to interest the modern readers most about Dīpaṃkara's journey to Tibet is the question of the route that he possibly followed. It is not difficult to have a rough idea of it, if we bear in mind certain points of fundamental importance.

First, Dīpaṃkara could have no reason to follow any route other than the one usually followed by traders and pilgrims, and the routes followed by traders and pilgrims particularly in the highly mountaneous regions do not change even in the course of many centuries because of reasons obvious to

74. *Ib.* 75. *Ib.* ii. 1047n. 76. Regmi 559. 77. BA ii. 1057.
78. Regmi 560. 79. *Ib.* 561. Chag lo-tsā-ba's work is edited by Altekar and translated into English by Roerich, Patna 1959. According to Chag lo-tsā-ba, the sThaṃ *vihāra* was called the Dharma-Dhātu *vihāra* by the Indians. Regmi 561 proposes to identify it with the Lham *vihāra* mentioned in the colophon of the *Aṣṭasāhasrikā-prajñāpāramitā*.
80. See Sec. 31.

students of physical geography. Secondly, we have in the Tibetan sources not only a clear indication of the general direction of Dīpaṃkara's journey but also the distinct mention of certain important landmarks of the route he followed. Hence the problem of reconstructing Atīśa's route to Tibet is mainly the problem of tracing the traditional route in this Himalayan region in accordance with the Tibetan evidences concerning the general direction of his journey as well as the important landmarks in it.

To begin with, Atīśa's original destination was not central Tibet. He was invited by the rulers of mṄa'-ris and the most important monastery sponsored by them was Tho-liṅ, where the first official reception of Dīpaṃkara took place. Further, he proceeded to mṄa'-ris *via* Nepal. Thus, in short, from Vajrāsana or Buddhagayā he went to Nepal and from Nepal he proceeded to Tho-liṅ. This is quite clear even from the brief reference to his journey given by 'Gos lo-tsā-ba[81]: "(The Master) made extensive offerings to Vajrāsana. Then when they had reached Nepal, the Master had an auspicious dream. They spent one year (in Nepal), and built the great temple of sThaṃ *vihāra*, and deposited there provisions (in support) of a numerous clergy. Many were ordained...When they arrived in mṄa'-ris, Lha-bla-ma made extensive preparations to welcome (them) and proceeded to the monastery of mTho-ldiṅ (Tho-liṅ), where Lha-bla-ma made a discourse on the attainment of his cherished object."

The biography of Atīśa translated by S. C. Das gives more details of this journey. The main points of this are : Dīpaṃkara went to Palpa from the Svayambhū *caitya*, from Palpa he proceeded to Manasasarovara and from there to Tho-liṅ. After leaving Palpa, says the biographer,[82] "the party entered Tibet...Then the party proceeded to Maṅ-yul Guṅ-thaṅ. When they arrived at a place called Zo-gna Chen-po, Atīśa was received at the residence of Nag-tsho, where he spent one month. Then travelling on from sPu-raṅs, the party came to

81. BA i. 247.

82. JBTS I. i. 27-30.

a place called Dok Mamolin near the shore of the lake Ma-pham (Manasasarovara)...This place appeared so very holy and delightful, that Atiśa halted there for seven days...The report of Atiśa's arrival at the bank of the lake Ma-pham now spread all over the three provinces of mÑa'-ris-bskor-gsum...Then the party arrived at Tho-liṅ called gLiṅ-gser-gyi-lha-khaṅ," i.e. the Golden Temple.

Thus, the main direction followed by Dīpaṃkara was from Palpa to Manasasarovara and from Manasasarovara to Tho-liṅ.

The first question that interests us, therefore, is the question of the route he possibly followed from Palpa to Manasasarovara. The lake being a famous place of pilgrimage for the Indians, a number of traditional routes to it are known.[83] But most of these being from Almora, Simla, Joshimath, Badrinath, etc. do not interest us for the moment. The only route that interests us is the one from Nepal to Manasasarovara. Svami Pranavananda, who has travelled extensively in this area, speaks of only one route from Nepal to Manasasarovara : "From Kathmandu *via* Muktinath, Khocharnath and Taklakot."[84] Palpa is west of Kathmandu and almost directly south of Muktinath and, therefore, is situated very near the route shown by Pranavananda[85] from Nepal to Manasasarovara *via* Taklakot.

The presumption that Dīpaṃkara followed this route up to the shore of Manasasarovara becomes strong when we note that some of the places in this route still cherish the memory of Atiśa's association. Thus, in Khocharnath, which the Tibetans call Khochar, there is a famous monastery called Khocharnath Gumpha or simply Khochar Gumpha. One of the reasons of this monastery being considered particularly holy by the Tibetans is that "Dīpaṃkara Śrījñāna had spent a rainy season here."[86] This was evidently on his way to Manasasarovara. Some other places in the same route also cherish the holy memory of the Master. Thus, there is a village

83. Pranavananda 89. 84. *Ib.* 85. *Ib.* Map No. 1. 86. *Ib.* 64.

in this route, called Gejin[87] (dGe-byin), literally meaning "Gift of Piety" (*puṇya-datta*). Within a hundred yards of this, according to the Tibetan belief, there "are the footprints of Atiśa or Śrījñāna."[88] Within five miles of the village, there is a place called Kangje (rKan-rjes), meaning Foot-print, and this name was presumably based on the tradition of Dīpaṃkara travelling by it. The spring called Dup-chhu (Grub-chu), literally The Water of Bliss, derives its name from the belief that it was "said to have been dug by Dīpaṃkara Śrījñāna."[89]

Such traditions do not grow out of nothing and are explained by the circumstance that the route *via* Taklakot with which these traditions are connected is the most important of the traditional routes from Nepal to Manasasarovara along which Dīpaṃkara must have proceeded.

Pending further researches in the traditions associated with various place-names of western Tibet, the route Dīpaṃkara followed from Manasasarovara to Tho-liṅ remains somewhat conjectural. There seems to be two traditional ways[90] of covering the distance. Of these, one is the route that proceeds to the Chiu Gompha with the two lakes Rakkastal (Langak Tso) and Manasasarovara on two sides, i.e. part of the route usually followed by the pilgrims for circumambulating Manasasarovara, and from the Chiu monastery to proceed to Tho-liṅ after a somewhat long detour in the northern regions of the lake. The other route is from the western shore of Manasasarovara to Chhakra and from there to Tho-liṅ *via* Gyanina Mandi, Gomba Chiu, Mani Thanga, Sibchibim and Dapazong. The second of these two routes is shorter and since the Tibetan sources do not mention Dīpaṃkara's party moving towards Tho-liṅ with the two lakes on two sides, it is perhaps safer to assume that he followed the second route. But our exact knowledge of Atiśa's route from Manasasarovara to Tho-liṅ awaits a fuller investigation of the local traditions of this region.

87. *Ib.* 135-6. 88. *Ib.* 135n. 89. *Ib.* 136.
90. *Ib.* Map No. 1. Pranavananda gives the Tibetan names as pronounced.

We may end the account of Atiśa's journey to Tibet with two more points.

First, the biography translated by S. C. Das contains a descriptive account of Atīśa during this journey, which, whatever may be its authenticity, is the only description we have of its kind : "Atīśa surrounded by his companions...altogether 35 in number, rode towards Tho-liṅ. The horse, on which the great sage rode, ambled gently like the walking of the golden swan. ...His demeanour, personal beauty, though sixty years old, and his pleasant appearance made him worthy of divine honour. A smile was ever present on his face, and Sanskrit *mantra*-s were always on his lips. His voice was distinct, loud and impressive. His expressions were happy, oh, how sweetly he talked, and how noble he looked ! At the end of a sentence, he often said *Ati Bhāla* ! *Ati Bhāla*, *Ati Maṅgal*(*a*), *Ati Bhāla Haé*. The names Ārya Tārā, Ārya Acala, Mahā Kāruṇika, Śākya Muni dekha (?), etc. were always present on his lips."[91]

Specially significant in this are the words put into the lips of Dīpaṃkara : *ati bhāla* ! *ati bhāla*, *ati maṅgal*(*a*), *ati bhāla haé*. These are the only recorded Indian words supposed to have been actually spoken by Atīśa outside his academic discourses. No Tibetan could have manufactured the words, i.e., to the Tibetan biographer the words could only come down from someone who actually heard these as spoken by an Indian. Since the biography is said to be based on the personal communication of Jayaśīla, the possibility of these words being actually pronounced by Atīśa cannot be uncritically rejected. Such a possibility has some light to throw on the question whether Atiśa was a Bengalee or not. P. C. Majumdar[92] says, "the word *bhāla*, delivered by Dīpaṃkara himself, is, to my best contention, a genuine Bengali word. From a linguistic point of view, the word *bhāla* or *bhālā* seems to be an old Bengali word prevalent in the period not earlier than eleventh century A.D."

Another point of interest in this biography is the peculiar

91. JBTS I. i. 29.

92. P. C. Majumdar in ISPP vii. 439f.

importance it attaches to Atīśa's appreciation of the first cup of tea he tasted in the Tibetan soil.[93] The representative of the king, on coming to receive Atīśa on the Tibetan border, offered the Master "tea prepared in Tibetan manner poured in a cup decorated with figures of the Chinese dragon" and described as "celestial drink which contains the essence of the wishing tree." Atīśa asked the name of the drink, which was praised so much. "The lo-tsā-ba (Jayaśīla) said, 'Venerable Sir, it is called *cha* (tea). The monks of Tibet also drink it.' Atīśa observed, 'So excellent a beverage as tea must have originated from the moral merits of the monks of Tibet." Such a long account of the Master's appreciation of tea in a somewhat brief biography appears to us to be curious and disproportionate. But the Tibetans believe that Atīśa actually wrote a poem in praise of tea after he had his first cup of it in Tibet; the poem is popular among the Tibetans and is frequently to be found in the notebooks they carry.[94] How far this praise of tea attributed to Atīśa is authentic may be difficult for us to determine. But the fact is that tea occupies an extremely important part in the daily life of the Tibetans: After being introduced from China by the grandson of Sroṅ-btsan-sgam-po, tea remains the national beverage of Tibet. "The well-to-do Tibetan of modern times drinks thirty to seventy cups of tea in a day."[95] Could it be that the Tibetans project their own appreciation of the drink on the Master to whom they feel their culture owe so much?

93. JBTS I. i. 27.

94. Personal communication from Professor Lama Chimpa.

95. Bell TPP 25.

33. 'Thirteen Years' in Tibet

In A.D. 1042, a Water-Horse year, Atiśa reached mÑa'-ris. 'Gos lo-tsā-ba claims to be categorical about this date : "all bKa'-gdams-pa-s agree that the year of Atiśa's coming was a Horse year, but there exists a disagreement as to the element of the year. After thoroughly examining the biographies of rGya-ma-pa, uncle and nephew, sNe'u-zur-pa, sPyan-sña and sPu-to-pa, one can state that Atiśa came (to Tibet) in the year Water-Male-Horse (A.D. 1042). This was the sixty-first year of Atiśa. After a minute examination of ancient chronicles, I consider the above account...to be reliable...In short, I consider the date of the religious king Sroṅ-btsan-sgam-po, and the dates of Atiśa, 'Brom and others...to be correct.[1]"

'Gos lo-tsā-ba adds that the Master died in A.D. 1054, a Wood-Horse year, and claims to be equally categorical about it : "On the twentieth day of the middle autumn month of the year Wood-Male-Horse (A.D.1054) the Master proceeded to Tuṣita. In the writings of ancient bKa'-gdams-pa-s there is much disagreement as to the elements of this Horse year, but I have given (the date) after a thorough examination of the different dates mentioned in the *Lives* of (contemporary) teachers. *This year Wood-Male-Horse is certain.*"[2]

Accordingly, Jayaśīla of Nag-tsho, who was born in A.D. 1011, was fortyfour at the time of the Master's death.[3] Śes-rab-'od died at the age of seventy-five in the Iron-Female-Hog year, i.e. A.D. 1131.[4] This means that he was born in A.D. 1057, a Fire-Hen year. "The Fire-Hen year of his birth is the Fire-Hen year which followed the Wood-Horse year of the death of the Master."[5] These are some of the ways in which 'Gos lo-tsā-ba connects the date of Atiśa's death with other

1. BA ii. 1086.
2. *Ib.* i. 261 ; emphasis added
3. *Ib.* i. 88 ; 261 ; 328.
4. *Ib.* i. 311.
5. *Ib.*

events of Tibetan history. However, his mere statement that he is certain of the date of Atīśa's death, because this is arrived at on the basis of a thorough examination of the lives of contemporary teachers, is perhaps enough to convince us of the accuracy of this date, because, among the Tibetan historians, 'Gos lo-tsā-ba shows the keenest sense of reckoning of dates.

Assuming these dates to be correct, therefore, we are to admit that Atīśa lived in Tibet from A.D. 1042 to 1054, i.e. for 'thirteen years,' according to the Tibetan mode of calculation. Assuming, again, A. D. 982, another Water-Horse year, as the date of his birth, he died at the age of seventy-three, i.e. according to the Tibetan calculation.

Sum-pa[6] reviews the different opinions expressed by Tibetan authorities concerning the number of years Atīśa spent in Tibet and he himself subscribed to the view that it must have been for 'thirteen years.' In view of 'Gos lo-tsā-ba's datings, however, it would be useless for us to enter into the question over again. What interests us rather is his career of these 'thirteen years' in Tibet.

Of these years, the first three were spent by him in mṄa'-ris. As Sum-pa puts it, "he saw the third year at mṄa'-ris."[7] Invited as he was by the rulers of Western Tibet, it was only natural for him to spend the first few years of his stay in Tibet in mṄa-'ris-bskor-gsum, which was then detached from central Tibet, both from the religious and political points of view. It appears further that his original plan was to stay in Tibet only for these three years, after which he was preparing to return to India. "The Master," says 'Gos lo-tsā-ba, "spent three years (in mṄa'-ris), and the religious practice based on the method of the Master received wide acceptance. When he was preparing to return to India, he was met by 'Brom, while residing at a place called rGyal-shiṅ of sPu-raṅs."[8] One of the *Sayings of Atīśa* opens with the introduction: "After spending two (? three) years in mṄa'-ris, during which time Jo-bo-rje delivered many *upadeśa*-s to *devaguru* Bodhiprabha

6. See Section 3, Note 2. 7. Sum-pa 186. 8. BA i. 251.

(Lha-bla-ma Byaṅ-chub-'od) and to others, he once thought of returning to India and was about to enter the way back to India. At that time Bodhiprabha requested him saying, 'Please give me one more *upadeśa*."[9]

Both 'Gos lo-tsā-ba and Sum-pa refer, though vaguely, to the troubled conditions on the route back to India, which might have partially influenced his decision not to return. "After three days," says 'Gos lo-tsā-ba, "the Master and his retinue resumed their journey and went towards sKyi-roṅ (sKyid-groṅ). They spent the Hen year there. They intended proceeding towards Bal-po-rdzoṅ, but the road was closed because of internal feuds, and they were unable to proceed there."[10] sKyid-groṅ[11] (Kirong) is the Tibetan town on the border of Nepal and Bal-po[12] in Tibetan means Nepal. The Hen year of the passage is to be taken as the Wood-Hen year or A.D. 1045, and from the mention of the year by mere animal name, which is so unusual for 'Gos lo-tsā-ba, we are led to presume that he is quoting here some earlier source. Thus, in A.D. 1045 Atīśa came as far as sKyid-groṅ and wanted to proceed to Nepal, but he could not return because "the road was closed." Sum-pa[13] also says, "Though Nag-tsho had promised to Ratnākara to bring back (Dīpaṃkara) to India within three years, because of the fighting among the three *ban-sde*-s (? Nepalese nobles. See J-TED 365.), it was not necessary (*ma-dgos*) for him to return. This meant a great fortune for Tibet and this was because of the grace of Tārādevī."

But such troubles vaguely referred to might have reasonably postponed Atīśa's plan of returning and are hardly adequate to explain the fact that he did not return to India at all. 'Gos lo-tsā-ba clearly hints that the Master's decision not to return to India after three years was due to considerations additional to the troubles on the route back. After 'Brom-ston-pa sent messages to the scholars of central Tibet requesting them to

9. See Appendix C, Section 7. 10. BA i. 254. 11. D-TED 101.
12. *Ib*. 868. 13. Sum-pa 185.

invite Atīśa there, says 'Gos lo-tsā-ba, "Nag-tsho understood that the Master was intending to proceed to dBus, and by grasping the Master's robe, he cried : 'I had promised the *sthavira* (of Vikramaśīla) to bring you back within three years. I am not brave enough to go to hell ! You had better return to India !' The Master said to him : 'O lo-tsā-ba ! no fault will arise, should one be unable to carry out (the promise)', and he comforted him."[14] This suggests that after coming in touch with 'Brom-ston-pa Atīśa revised his dicision of returning to India from mÑa'-ris, evidently because he was impressed by 'Brom-ston-pa regarding the necessity of extending his missionary activities in central Tibet.

The first three years of his stay in mÑa'-ris proved crucial for his eventual success in Tibet. During these three years he earned a tremendous religious and academic prestige which, like a snow-ball rolling down a mountain, augmented itself during the subsequent years of his stay in the Land of Snow. The events of outstanding importance that took place during these three years were :

a) the grand reception organised for him by the rulers of western Tibet, who were then culturally much more advanced than the rulers of central Tibet and the great devotion to Dīpaṃkara particularly of the monk-prince Byaṅ-chub-'od (Bodhiprabha),

b) the submission earned by Atīśa from Rin-chen-bzaṅ-po (Ratnabhadra), the greatest Tibetan scholar of the time,

c) his literary activities, inclusive of the composition of the *Bodhi-patha-pradīpa*, and

d) his meeting with 'Brom-ston-pa, who became the foremost of the Tibetan disciples of Dīpaṃkara and to whose organisational activities was largely due the eventual success of Dīpaṃkara's religious reforms in Tibet.

We may briefly review these four major events.

"When they (i.e. Atīśa and his party) arrived in mÑa'-ris," says 'Gos lo-tsā-ba,[15] "Lha-bla-ma made extensive preparations

14. BA i 254-5.

15. *Ib.* i. 247.

to welcome (them) and proceeded to the monastery of Tho-liṅ, where Lha-bla-ma made a discourse on the attainment of his cherished object." *Lha-bla-ma*, meaning *deva-guru* or Divine Preceptor, is usually used as an honorific for the monk-rulers of western Tibet, particularly for Ye-śes-'od and Byaṅ-chub-'od, though in this passage it refers to the latter. For 'Gos lo-tsā-ba adds that in response to the request of Lha-bla-ma, Atīśa wrote his *Bodhi-patha-pradīpa*, while, from the colophon of the work we know that it was written because of the special request of Byaṅ-chub-'od.

Atīśa's biography translated by S. C. Das gives us a more detailed and gorgeous account of his arrival in Tibet and of his reception there. In this occurs the following : "The Tibetan escort, consisting of 300 horsemen, under four generals, marched along keeping Atīśa's party, who were all dressed in white, in the middle. At this time, the generals sang the song of welcome like those wise ministers of king Khri-sroṅ-lde-btsan, who, three centuries ago, had escorted *ācārya* Śānta-rakṣita from the confines of India to Tibet."[16] Comparing this with the sober accounts[17] of Śāntarakṣita's coming to Tibet given by Bu-ston and 'Gos lo-tsā-ba, we may be easily led to suspect exaggeration in the biographer's account of the grand reception also of Atīśa. But such a suspicion is unfounded. There was a qualitative difference between the situations under which Śāntarakṣita and Dīpaṃkara came to Tibet. In spite of all that the Tibetan historians are fond of saying about the glorious things done for Buddhism from the time of Sroṅ-btsan-sgam-po, the fact is that before the activities of Śāntarakṣita and the founding of the bSam-yas monastery, the Tibetans had at best only a confused and rudimentary idea of Buddhism. Therefore, in spite of the great intrinsic stature of Śāntarakṣita as a Buddhist scholar, the Tibetans then knew too little about Buddhism to organise any rousing reception for him. By contrast, already on the eve of Dīpaṃkara's arrival in Tibet, the movement for Buddhist renaissance gained momentum

16. JBTS I. i. 28.

17. See Section 25.

particularly because of the initiative of Ye-śes-'od; and the entire ruling family of western Tibet which welcomed Atiśa was not only devoted to Buddhism but also highly enlightened. Indian *paṇḍita*-s like Dharmapāla and Subhāṣita were brought to Tibet and Tibetan scholars like Rin-chen-bzaṅ-po were sent to India for studying Buddhism. Apparently, these measures were not enough to restore the purity of the Doctrine, at least not to the satisfaction of Ye-śes-'od. Hence was his persistence in the effort of bringing an *ācārya* of greater eminence, an effort which, after his death, was continued by Byaṅ-chub-'od in particular. Therefore, when all these efforts actually culminated in the coming to Tibet of no less a Buddhist than the *mkhan-po* (*upādhyāya*) of Vikramaśīla, it was but natural for the rulers of western Tibet to organise a grand reception for him. In other words, though the story of the grand reception organised for Śāntarakṣita during the reign of Khri-sroṅ-lde-btsan is apparently unreal, the account of Atīśa's reception is quite convincing.

In the biography of Atīśa translated by S. C. Das is to be found a long speech of welcome supposed to have been delivered by the 'senior general' of the Tibetan escort of 300 horsemen sent to receive the Master. In this speech occur the following interesting sentences: "... Though Lha-chen (the old king) has gone to the land of rest like the moon in her 29th lunation, yet Lha-btsun-pa the present king has risen like the luminous disc of the day in the cloudless firmament of Tibet. ...Lha-btsun-pa Byaṅ-chub-'od is rich and powerfull like Indra."[18]

Lha-chen[19] literally means the great god, *mahā-deva*, and is generally used as an address for kings, while *lha-btsun-pa*[20] means the noble god and is an honorific for members of the royal families. In the passage above, the former refers to Ye-śes-'od and the latter to Byaṅ-chub-'od. In other words, these two are referred to as the former king and the present king respectively. This may appear to be somewhat peculiar.

18. JBTS I. i. 28-9. 19. D-TED 1333. 20. *Ib.* 1004.

Neither Ye-śes-'od nor Byaṅ-chub-'od was an actual ruler, both living the lives of monks. At the same time, the importance still maintained by both in the administration of western Tibet seems to have been considerable enough to justify the 'senior general' in characterising the two as the old and present kings respectively. Beginning with Ye-śes-'od, the ruling family of western Tibet showed a peculiar solidarity effected through their Buddhism-oriented state-policy, as a result of which even those members of the family who lived the lives of monks remained also the policy-makers of the state.

Atīśa came to mṄa'-ris during the reign of 'Od-lde.[21] But Byaṅ-chub-'od, the younger brother of 'Od-lde, was already a favourite of Ye-śes-'od, which is clear from the story of the latter's last days. It was specially because of the initiative of Byaṅ-chub-'od, taken after the death of Ye-śes-'od, that Jaya-śīla of Nag-tsho was sent to India to bring Atīśa to Tibet. In the Buddhist chronicles of Tibet 'Od-lde, though actually the ruler, remained somewhat in the background, overshadowed as it were by the eminence of Byaṅ-chub-'od primarily because of the latter's devotion to the Master. We have, however, definite evidence in the same chronicles that neither 'Od-lde nor his father Lha-sde remained indifferent to the cause of Buddhist renaissance. 'Gos lo-tsā-ba[22] says, "in the time of Lha-sde —Subhūti Śrīśānti, known as the Great *paṇḍita* of Kashmira, was invited. He translated many *sūtra*-s and *śāstra*-s belonging to the Prajñāpāramitā class, including the *Aṣṭasāhasrikā-prajñāpāramitā*, its commentary, the *Abhisamayālaṃkāra-ṭīkā* and other works." From the bsTan-'gyur[23] it is clear that this Indian *paṇḍita* considerably helped the Tibetans to translate the Buddhist works. 'Od-lde also invited Indian *paṇḍita*-s to work for the Buddhist renaissance in western Tibet. Bu-ston[24] says, "The king 'Od-lde invited Śūnyaśrī," though there is nothing in the bsTan-'gyur to indicate Śūnyaśrī's academic contribution and the only thing 'Gos lo-tsā-ba has to say about

21. BA i. 70. 22. *Ib.* i. 69. 23. mDo ix. 2; x. 1; xcv. 10; xcvi; xcvii; xcviii; rG. xiii. 50; xv. 1. 24. Bu-ston ii. 2.5.

him is that he played some role in the propagation of the Guhyasamāja, known as the 'system of Jñānapāda or Buddhajñāna': "In the meantime, the *paṇḍita* Śūnyaśrī and gÑaṅ lo-tsā-ba also taught much the system of Buddhajñāna in Tibet."[25] Nevertheless, the mention of 'Od-lde inviting Śūnyaśrī to Tibet is indicative of his earnestness for the Buddhist renaissance.

Of the three sons of 'Od-lde, Shi-ba-'od was most scholarly. "The youngest (brother) named monk Shi-ba-'od was a scholar in all the sciences of Buddhist and heretical doctrines, and a very learned translator."[26] Bu-ston[27] says, "The prince Shi-ba-'od in his turn translated the *Śrī-paramādi-ṭīkā*, the logical work of Śāntirakṣita, etc." The internal evidences of the bsTan-'gyur fully testify to the academic contributions of Shi--ba-'od, which includes the translation of the stupendous *Tattva-saṃgraha-kārikā* by Śāntarakṣita. Its colophon mentions the translators as "*mahā-paṇḍita* Guṇākara-śrī-bhadra of the Anupamapura monastery of Kashmir, which was founded by *mahārājā* Lalitāditya, and the grand lo-tsā-ba dPal-lha-btsan-po *śākya-bhikṣu* Shi-ba-'od."[28] Further, from the mention of Shi-ba-'od alone as the translator of some of the works in the bsTan-'gyur[29] we may easily infer that his knowledge of Sanskrit must have been sound.

rTse-lde, the son and successor of 'Od-lde, was no less a supporter of Buddhism, though his most important contribution to the cause of Buddhism came a few years after the death of Atīśa and presupposed the work of Atīśa in Tibet. This was the Great Religious Council (*chos-'khor*) convened by him in A.D. 1076, famed in Tibetan history as the Council of the Fire-Dragon year. We may have here a few words on the importance of the Council for the Buddhist revival in Tibet.

Though the Tibetan historians say that after the destruction

25. BA i. 372. 26. *Ib*. i. 244. 27. Bu-ston ii. 214.
28. mDo cxiii. 1. 29. rG. xiv. 20; mDo cxvi. 11.

of the Doctrine by gLaṅ Dar-ma a handful of fugitive monks somehow or other maintained the continuity of the Doctrine under the most adverse conditions, historically the fact is that Buddhist renaissance in its real sense received the first significant form in western Tibet under the direct patronage of the rulers there. Atīśa's own activities, to begin with, remained localised in western Tibet. After a few years, however, he started an extensive tour of Tibet—including central Tibet—propagating the Doctrine everywhere he went. "From the west," as Richardson[30] rightly says, "Atīśa's activities extended into central Tibet and, under his inspiration, ruling nobles all over the country fostered a revival of Buddhism." As a result, there were Buddhist revivals in different parts of Tibet. In the Great Religious Council of the Fire-Dragon year (A.D. 1076) convened by rTse-lde, the Buddhist activities hitherto somewhat localised in the different parts of the country, first received a pan-Tibetan form. In this Council assembled "most of the great Tripiṭakadhara-s of dBus, gTsaṅ and Khams," each setting "in motion the wheel of the Doctrine."[31]

The Tibetan chronicles contain further accounts of how rTse-lde—and even his son dBaṅ-phyug-lde—worked for Buddhism in Tibet.[32] Interesting also are the information we have about rTse-lde from the colophons of some of the works in the bsTan-'gyur. From these we learn that along with his uncles Shi-ba-'od and Byaṅ-chub-'od, rTse-lde took the initiative to get difficult texts of Buddhist logic[33] translated into Tibetan. Thus, the *Vādanyāya-prakaraṇa*[34] of Dharmakīrti was translated by *mahā-upādhyāya* Jñānaśrībhadra of India and lo-tsā-ba *bhikṣu* Śubhamati under the request of *śrī-deva-bhaṭṭāraka* Śāntiprabha (Shi-ba-'od) and dPal-lha-btsan-po Khri-bkra-śis-mṅa'-bdag rTse-lde-btsan (i.e. rTse-lde, son of 'Od-lde). The *Pramāṇa-vārttika-alaṃkāra*[35] by *mahācārya*

30. Richardson 39.
31. BA i. 70; 325; 328, etc.; cf Sum-pa 152.
32. Bu-ston ii. 215; BA i. 325.
33. For the standpoints represented by these works on Buddhist logic, see Stcherbatsky BL i. 46-7.
34. mDo xcv. 16.
35. mDo xcix & c.

Prajñākaragupta, again, was translated under the joint patronage of Shi-ba-'od, Byaṅ-chub-'od and rTse-lde ; the correction of the translation of the colossal work was carried out by a number of scholars—Indian, Tibetan and Chinese. The *Pramāṇa-vārttika-alaṃkāra-ṭikā*[36] of Jaya (or Jina) was translated by Dīpaṃkara and lo-tsā-ba Byaṅ-chub-śes-rab (Bodhiprajña) under the request of Shi-ba-'od, Byaṅ-chub-'od and rTse-lde.

All these give us some idea of how deeply Buddhism-oriented and at the same time highly enlightened was the ruling family of western Tibet, in response to whose invitation Dīpaṃkara went there. The great veneration shown by the members of the family to the Master must have contributed to the spread of his fame in Tibet. At the same time, it is idle to expect full explanation of his success in Tibet from this patronage. The great fame Dīpaṃkara acquired in Tibet within a short time of his arrival there was due above all to his own scholarly abilities and the extremely bold stand he took for the religious reform in Tibet. These are well-illustrated by two significant events of the first three years of his Tibetan career, namely the way in which he humbled the pride of Rin-chen-bzaṅ-po and the composition of the *Bodhi-patha-pradīpa* by him.

Rin-chen-bzaṅ-po was undoubtedly the first Tibetan scholar of Buddhism in the real sense of the term after the persecution of the Doctrine by gLaṅ Dar-ma. We may quote 'Gos lo-tsā-ba for a brief account of him : "in the year Earth-Male-Horse (A.D. 958) the lo-tsā-ba Rin-chen-bzaṅ-po was born. At the age of thirteen, he was ordained by the *upādhyāya* Ye-śes-bzaṅ-po... When the great translator was a young man, he journeyed to Kashmira, and there studied numerous treatises on the Mantrayāna and (works) belonging to the *sūtra* class. A prominent scholar, he translated many texts and *sūtras*-s as well as *mantra*-s, composed extensive explanations on the Prajñāpāramitā and the Tantras, and taught the rite of initiation

36. mDo ci & cii.

and (the performance) of propitiations... He attended on seventy-five *paṇḍita*-s, and heard from them the exposition of numerous treatises on the Doctrine. Lha-chen-po Lha-lde-btsan bestowed on him the dignity of Chief Priest and of Vajrācārya. He was presented with the estate of Sher in sPu-raṅs, and built temples. He erected many temples and shrines at Khra-tsa, Roṅ and other localities, as well as numerous *stūpa*-s. He had many learned disciples, such as Gur-śiṅ-brtson-'grus-rgyal-mtshan others, as well as more than ten translators who were able to correct translations. Others could not compete with him in his daily work, such as the erection of images and translation (of sacred texts), etc."[37]

It is no wonder, therefore, that such a scholar-priest should figure prominently in the inscriptions and other records of western Tibet. Francke draws our attention to these. The oldest of the existing temples of sPu, says Francke,[38] "is asserted to have been built by lo-tsā-ba Rin-chen-bzaṅ-po, the spiritual adviser of king Ye-śes-'od." An inscription of Tsoṅ-kha-pa's time, adds he, mentions "besides the names of the reformer (Tsoṅ-kha-pa) and one or two of the contemporaries, those of an eminent Lama king of Gu-ge, Byaṅ-chub-'od, of the famous Lama Rin-chen-bzaṅ-po."[39] Another inscription "speaks of the foundation of the Tabo monastery... and the people who were connected with that event. ...It tells of a renovation of the Tabo monastery by Byaṅ-chub-'od... The inscription contains also (the names) of the two most important Lamas of the period, namely Rin-chen-bzaṅ-po and Atīśa."[40]

It needs to be remembered further that Rin-chen-bzaṅ-po's great fame as a scholar rested primarily on his knowledge of the Tantras. "The *later* spread of the Tantras in Tibet was greater than the *early* spread (of the Tantras), and this was chiefly due to this translator (Rin-chen-bzaṅ-po)."[41] We have

37. BA i. 68-9. 38. Francke AIT i. 20. 39. *Ib*. i. 37.
40. *Ib*. i. 41. For other historical records relating to Rin-chen-bzaṅ-po, see Francke AIT i. 16, 27, 28, 32, 33, 35, 82, 87, 88, 89. 41. BA i. 68.

already discussed[42] the possible reasons of his specialisation in the Tantras and we have seen that the religious reform he introduced under the patronage of king Ye-śes-'od was after all some kind of reform of Tantrism itself, his reformed Tantra being known in Tibet as gSaṅ-sṅags-gsar-ma or New Tantra.

There was thus in Tibet none to equal at that time Rin-chen-bzaṅ-po as a scholar with a specialised knowledge of the Tantras. He was moreover about twenty-four years older than Atīśa. When Atīśa arrived at mÑa'-ris, Rin-chen-bzaṅ-po was in his eighty-fifth year. To earn the humble submission of such an elderly and eminent scholar with a superior knowledge of Tantrism evidently meant the academic conquest of contemporary Tibet. 'Gos lo-tsā-ba describes how easily Atīśa earned this :

"At that time the lo-tsā-ba Rin-chen-bzaṅ-po thought : 'His knowledge as a scholar is hardly greater than mine, but since he has been invited by Lha-bla-ma, it will be necessary (for me) to attend on him.' He accordingly invited him to his own residence at the *vihāra* of Tho-liṅ. (In the *vihāra*) the deities of the higher and lower Tantras were represented according to their respective degrees and for each of them the Master composed a laudatory verse. When the Master sat down on the mat, the lo-tsā-ba (Rin-chen-bzaṅ-po) inquired from him : 'Who composed these verses ?' —'These verses were composed by myself this very instant,' replied the Master, and the lo-tsā-ba was filled with awe and amazement. The Master then said to the lo-tsā-ba : 'What sort of doctrine do you know ?' The lo-tsā-ba told him in brief about his knowledge and the Master said : 'If there are men such as you in Tibet, then there was no need of my coming to Tibet !' Saying so, he joined the palms of his hands in front of his chest in devotion. Again the Master asked the lo-tsā-ba : 'O great lo-tsā-ba ! when an individual is to practise all the teachings of Tantras sitting on a single mat, how is he to act ?' The lo-tsā-ba replied : 'Indeed, one should practise according to

42. See Section 30.

each (Tantra) separately.' The Master exclaimed : 'Rotten is the lo-tsā-ba ! Indeed there was need of my coming to Tibet ! All these Tantras should be practised together.' The Master taught him the Magic Mirror of the Vajrayāna, and a great faith was born in the lo-tsā-ba, and he thought : This Master is the greatest among the great scholars !"[43]

It is difficult for us to be clear about the exact point of the controversy. From 'Gos lo-tsā-ba's account one may be inclined to think that Atīśa proved Rin-chen-bzaṅ-po's ignorance of a somewhat minor point of Tāntrika practice. But that could not have been a real fact. Rin-chen-bzaṅ-po was indeed too great a scholar in Tantrism to be easily rebuffed by anybody with any flimsy details of it. Apparently, he saw in Atīśa such a tremendous proficiency in Tantrism—or, what is more plausible, such a new insight into the essence of Tantrism—that the old lo-tsā-ba, with all his pride of having learnt Tantrism under a great number of *paṇḍita*-s, bowed down before Dīpaṃkara. This is evident from the fact that his meeting with Atīśa became a decisive turning point for his spiritual and academic career. 'Gos lo-tsā-ba describes this at some length : "It is said that the great lo-tsā-ba had sixty learned teachers, besides the Master, but these others failed to make the lo-tsā-ba meditate. The Master said, 'O great lo-tsā-ba ! The sufferings of this Phenomenal World are difficult to bear. One should labour for the benefit of all living beings. Now, pray practise meditation.' The lo-tsā-ba listened attentively to these words, and erected a house with three doors, over the outer door he wrote the following words : 'Within this door, should a thought of attachment to this Phenomenal World arise even for one single moment only, may the Guardians of the Doctrine split (my) head !' Over the middle door (he wrote) : 'Should a thought of self-interest arise even for one single moment only, may the Guardians of the Doctrine split (my) head.' Over the inner door (he wrote) : 'Should an ordinary thought arise even for one single moment only, may the Guardians of the Doctrine split (my) head.' After the

43. BA i. 249 ; cf. Bu-ston ii. 213-4.

departure of the Master [from mÑa'-ris], he practised one-pointed meditation for ten years."[44] Elsewhere, 'Gos lo-tsā-ba repeats this: "At last he (Rin-chen-bzaṅ-po) was initiated by Atīśa into the method of propitiations (*sādhana*). On the three successive gates outside of his meditative cell, he wrote the following inscriptions: 'Should thoughts of property, selfishness, etc. be born in me even for one moment, then may the Religious Protectors split my head'."[45]

Francke points to an interesting inscription of western Tibet from which it is clear that the account of Rin-chen-bzaṅ-po's submission to Atīśa was more than merely imaginary: "The inscription says that Rin-chen-bzaṅ-po was made a 'light of wisdom' by the agency of Atīśa. This is apparently a reference to the controversy between the two Lamas which ended with Rin-chen-bzaṅ-po's acknowledgement of Atīśa's superiority."[46] To this are to be added the internal evidences of the bKa'-'gyur and bsTan-'gyur which clearly indicate that the great Tibetan scholar fully submitted to Atīśa from the academic point of view also.[47] Though already famed as the greatest translator of the age, he felt the need of getting his translations revised by Atīśa. "He (Rin-chen-bzaṅ-po)," says 'Gos lo-tsā-ba,[48] "requested the Master to correct (his previous translations of the *Aṣṭasāhasrikā*, the *Viṃśati-ālokā* and the great commentary on the *Aṣṭasāhasrikā-prajñāpāramitā*." Such revisions apart, Rin-chen-bzaṅ-po sat under Dīpaṃkara for the translation of a considerable number of Buddhist works.

Among the achievements of Dīpaṃkara during the first three years of his stay at mÑa'-ris, special mention needs to be made of the composition of the *Bodhi-patha-pradīpa*, because it proved crucial not only for the success of his entire Tibetan career but moreover, in an important sense, for the subsequent history of Tibetan Buddhism.

The colophon of the work[49] mentions the Tho-liṅ monas-

44. BA i. 250. 45. *Ib*. i. 69. 46. Francke AIT i. 41.
47. See Appendix B. 48. BA i. 249.
49. mDo xxxi. 9; xxxiii. 1. See Section 6, Appendix C.

tery of Shaṅ-shuṅ (Gu-ge) where it was composed and the introductory verses clearly mention that it was composed in response to the special request of Byaṅ-chub-'od : "On the request of my good disciple Byaṅ-chub-'od, I shall, after worshipping with profound respect all the Jinas of the three times, along with their *dharma* and *saṅgha*, expound the *Bodhi-patha-pradīpa*. The work also concludes with the words : "The explanation of *Bodhi-patha*, based on *sūtra*-s etc., is here presented in a condensed form by *ācārya* Dīpaṃkara-śrī to Byaṅ-chub-'od at his request." 'Gos lo-tsā-ba explains the special reason why Byaṅ-chub-'od requested Dīpaṃkara to compose a work like this : "Lha-bla-ma (Byaṅ-chub-'od) made the request that since there was disagreement on points of Doctrine between various scholars in Tibet, the Master should compose a treatise which would serve as an antidote for it. The Master composed the *Bodhi-patha-pradīpa*."[50]

The work consists of only sixty-six verses. Though extremely brief, its impact on Tibetan Buddhism was nevertheless stupendous. Chos-kyi-ñi-ma[51] quotes Tsoṅ-kha-pa as saying, "When he came to upper mÑa'-ris, he was requested to reform Buddhism. In response to this, he wrote the *śāstra Bodhi-patha-pradīpa*, which contains in brief the essence of the whole *sūtra*-s and *tantra*-s and through which Buddhism was widely spread." Sum-pa[52] says, "By writing the *Bodhi-patha-pradīpa*, which is respected by both the old and new bKa'-gdams-pa (new bKa'-gdams-pa means the dGe-lugs-pa) and which contains the essence of both *sūtra*-s and *tantra*-s, he showed the path to Lha-bla-ma Byaṅ-chub-'od and others." But it is difficult to form an adequate idea of the main contents of the work and their importance in the religious history of Tibet from the almost stereotyped statements like these. At the same time, a full elucidation of the work is beyond the scope of our present discussion. Requested to do so by Byaṅ-chub-'od and Jayaśīla, Dīpaṃkara himself had to write an enormous work called the *Bodhi-mārga-pradīpa-pañjikā*,[53]

50. BA i. 248. 51. See Section 5, Appendix A. 52. Sum-pa 185.
49. mDo xxxi. 9 ; xxxiii. 1. See Section 6, Appendix C.
53. mDo xxxi. 10. See its colophon in Appendix B.

the auto-commentary on the *Bodhi-patha-pradīpa*. Moreover, the great work of Tsoṅ-kha-pa is by intention an elucidation of the main ideas of the *Bodhi-patha-pradīpa*.

Nevertheless, it is necessary to have here some idea of a few leading features of the text, particularly for understanding the nature of the religious reforms for which Atīśa is so famous in Tibet. What, then, are these leading features ?

As a Mahāyāna Buddhist, Dīpaṃkara could not have possibly believed in any ideal other than that of universal emancipation. As a Mādhyamika philosopher, again, he could not have preached any doctrine other than that of universal nothingness, i.e. the *śūnya-vāda* specially associated with the names of Nāgārjuna and Candrakīrti. These two, taken together, form the fundamental theme of the *Bodhi-patha-pradīpa*.

"Then," said he, "the first thing to do is to establish empathy (*maitrī-citta*) with all living beings, inclusive of the three kinds of beings with degraded births (*tri-durgati-jātāni*) suffering from birth and death, etc. Look at all living beings suffering from miseries and arrive at the firmest determination (*citta-utpādana*) to work with the resolution of never turning back (*anivṛtta-pratijñā*) for the liberation of all living beings from the miseries that are born of miseries."[54] "Do not be anxious," he repeated, "to attain quick enlightenment for yourself. Live up to the end of the *saṃsāra* for the sake of even a single living being. Purify the boundless and unthinkable (number of) *kṣetra*-s and live for (the emancipation of) each individual by name that exists in all the ten directions."[55]

Such precepts apart, Dīpaṃkara followed another method of ennobling the Mahāyāna ideal of universal emancipation. It is to be found in his famous theory of *tri-puruṣa*, or three personality types, with which he opens the work. "Persons (*puruṣa*)," he says, "are to be known as (belonging to either of

54. *śloka*-s 9-10. 55. *śloka*-s 28-9

the) three (types) : inferior (*adhama*), mediocre (*madhyama*) and superior (*uttama*). The characteristics of each are very clear. Therefore, I shall write the distinguishing features of each. By the *adhama puruṣa* is to be known one who, in one's own interests, acts in every way for the worldly pleasures only (*saṃsāra-sukha-mātra*). One who, indifferent to the pleasures of birth (*bhava-sukha*) and by nature opposed to sinful acts, works for oneself alone, is to be known as the *madhyama-puruṣa*. One who always wishes to remove all the sufferings of others by his own sufferings is the *uttama-puruṣa*."[56] Clearly enough, the superior person is the Mahāyānist while the mediocre one, with the ideal of the individual emancipation, is the Hīnayânist so-called. From the plain meaning of the passage it appears that by the inferior persons Dīpaṃkara meant those that were without any concern for the religious ideal, though the Tibetan scholars, who have written so much on this doctrine of *tri-puruṣa*, usually take the *adhama-puruṣa* to mean only the lay Buddhist devotee.[57] Be that what it may, and however much profound may be the significance the Tibetan Buddhists read in this doctrine of personality types, one of its clear implications is the declaration in favour of the Mahāyāna ideal of universal emancipation.

Equally unambiguous is the philosophical doctrine of universal nothingness or *śūnya-vāda* emphasised by his work. "That which exists by nature cannot come into being. Again, that which by nature is non-existing is like the sky-flower. Both (alternatives) implying fallacy (*doṣa*), both are unreal (literally, belong to the category of non-being). Things can be born neither of themselves, nor of others, nor of both. These cannot be without cause either. Hence, they are by nature natureless (*svabhāvena niḥ-svabhāva*). Again, the nature of things, examined either as units or compounds, cannot be determined. Therefore, it is certain that they are void."[58] "This world, arising out of delusional thought (*vikalpa*) is itself delusional (*vikalpātmaka*). Therefore, *nirvāṇa* is best because

56. *śloka*-s 1-4. 57. JBTS I. i. 41. 58. *śloka*-s 47-9.

it is completely free from *vikalpa.*"[59] "With the help of the scriptural instructions and logical thinking know it for certain that everything is non-born (*ajāta*) and nature-less (*a-svabhāva*). Then meditate on the *nirvikalpa.*"[60]

Such then were the religious ideal and the philosophical view that Dīpaṃkara wanted to emphasise most in his *Bodhi-patha-pradīpa.* At the same time he had to be realistic enough to see that his effort did not go unresponded. He was not writing just a scholarly treatise on Buddhist religion and philosophy , he was commissioned instead to prepare a manual on Buddhism specifically to serve the spiritual needs of the Tibetans of the time. The *Bodhi-patha-pradīpa,* in other words, was intended above all to be a manifesto of Buddhist reform in Tibet. There is no doubt that in Tibet there were then advanced students of Buddhist philosophy like Shi-ba-'od. But they were clear exceptions. At that time even among those that formally accepted Buddhism in Tibet, the large majority had all sorts of queer notions about the creed itself. Particularly annoying were the theories and practices then enjoying religious sanction under the name of Tantra. These included drunkenness, debauchery and bloody sacrifices including the sacrifice of the human beings. Philosophical subtleties in defence of *śūnya-vāda* were destined to be largely wasted on such people and Dīpaṃkara did not go into these. "In the *Śūnyatā-saptati-vidyā, Mūla-madhyamaka,* etc.," he simply said, "the nature (*svabhāva*) of everything is emphatically asserted to be void (*śūnya*). This text (if all these are explained here in details) would be voluminous. Therefore, (all these details) are not explained here. Only the doctrine (*siddhānta*) already proved (*siddha*) is clearly stated here for contemplation."[61]

Without ignoring the importance of philosophical wisdom, Dīpaṃkara evidently felt that the most urgent task at that time in Tibet was the task of moral reform. Without it, philosophical wisdom, by itself, could serve no purpose.

59. *śloka* 54. 60. *śloka* 57. 61. *śloka*-s 50-1

Hence was the great emphasis on the need of moral reform in the *Bodhi-patha-pradīpa*. *Prajñā* or the highest wisdom, said he, "is that knowledge which is the realisation of the intrinsic nature of the void (*svabhāva-śūnyatā*)" of everything[62] ; but he insisted on establishing it on the secure basis of right conduct or *upāya*. "*Prajñā* without *upāya* and *upāya* without *prajñā* are said to be unfree. Therefore, do not ignore any (of them). For removing doubts as to what is *prajñā* and what is *upāya*, it is necessary to distinguish clearly between *prajñā* and *upāya*-s. As said by the Jinas, except the *prajñāpāramitā*-s, all the *kuśala-dharma*-s like the *dāna-pāramitā* etc. are the *upāya*-s. One quickly attains enlightenment (*bodhi*) not by mere meditation on the void (*nairātmya*) but by (first) acquiring in oneself the mastery of the *upāya*-s (*upāya-abhyāsa*) and (then) meditation on *prajñā*."[63] Incidentally, the six *pāramitā*-s recognised by the Buddhists are : 1) charity (*dāna-pāramitā*), 2) morality (*śīla-pāramitā*), 3) forgiveness (*kṣānti-pāramitā*), 4) assiduity (*vīrya-pāramitā*), 5) meditation (*dhyāna-pāramitā*) and 6) wisdom (*prajñā-pāramitā*). Therefore, according to Dīpaṃkara, the first five of these constitute the *upāya*-s, upon the secure basis of which alone wisdom could be established. In other words the precondition for philosophical wisdom was the practice of charity, morality, forgiveness, assiduity and meditation.

More quotations are not necessary here to see how in the same text Dīpaṃkara returned again and again to the supreme importance of moral conduct for a true Buddhist. He also took care to explain in it the correct form of worship and meditation, into the theosophical subtleties of which we do not have the scope here to enter. However, it is necessary to have here a few words on Dīpaṃkara's attitude to Tantrism expressed in the *Bodhi-patha-pradīpa*.

"The *brahmacārī*," said Dīpaṃkara, "cannot receive *guhya-jñāna-abhiṣeka*, for it is strongly prohibited in the *Ādi-buddha-mahā-tantra*. For the *brahmacārī* receiving this initiation means violation of the prohibitions and hence a fall from the

62. *śloka* 46.

63. *śloka-s* 42-5.

tapas-saṃvara (vow of asceticism). Such a *vratī* will suffer great sin (*mahā-pātaka*) and will certainly fall among the low-born. He will never attain *siddhi.* But there is nothing wrong about that *abhiṣeka* for him who has learnt and can explain the Tantras, offer the right kind of fire-offerings, has received the proper initiation from his *guru* and has the real understanding of all these."[64]

S. C. Das[65] says that Atīśa "inserted" into the text these lines when, later in central Tibet, he was pointedly questioned about Tantrism by six leading Tibetan intellectuals of the time, namely Khu, rŇog and four others. According to the biography of Atīśa compiled by Nagwang Nima and Lama Chimpa, however, when these Tibetan scholars in gTasṅ asked Atīśa questions concerning the Tantras, the Master replied, "Answers to all these are to be found in my *Bodhi-patha-pradīpa*... I wrote the book in response to king Bodhhiprabha's request to explain the same and similar questions."[66] Admitting any of the two alternatives, we are led to believe that during his later Tibetan career Atīśa had to face certain categorical questions concerning his real attitude to the Tantras put forth by the leading Tibetan intellectuals of his time. The possibility of this is itself interesting. These Tibetan scholars, themselves brought up in an atmosphere in which supreme importance was laid on the Tantras, evidently felt puzzled by the Master's attitude to the Tantras and this, again, could only be because they failed to find the expected emphasis on the Tantras in the Master's teachings.

For Dīpaṃkara himself. the question concerning the Tantras must have been a complex one. He lived and preached in an age in which any outright rejection of the Tantras was inconceivable. At the same time, he was too well-versed in classical Buddhism to stand any nonsense in the name of the Tantras. He, therefore, bluntly declared that the beliefs and practices which enjoyed the sanction of the Tantras in the popular mind were imcompatible with the ascetic ideal of the

64. *śloka*-s 63-6.

65. S. C. Das in JBTS I. iii 25.

66. See Appendix A. Section 6 (sub-section 60).

true monk. Nevertheless, the Tantras were not to be rejected as such because of their association with these beliefs and practices. Therefore, he prescribed as preconditions of the Tantric initiation a correct insight into the real teachings of the Tantras, an extreme purity of moral conduct and a right guidance by the ideal *guru*, i.e. by one who had already attained full insight into the real meaning of the Tantras. "When the *guru*," said Dīpaṃkara, "being fully pleased confers the initiation that purifies all sins, he (the initiate) becomes a fit receptacle for the *siddhi*-s"[67] Interestingly, we have in Tibetan history a concrete example of what Dīpaṃkara really meant by the right guidance of the ideal *guru*. Before coming in contact with the Master, Rin-chen-bzaṅ-po had not only great theoretical knowledge of the Tāntrika literature but also the instructions from a large number of *guru*-s—sixty or seventy-five in all. Apparently, the guidance he received from these *guru*-s was not adequate. At the age of eightyfive, when the learned Tāntrika came in touch with Dīpaṃkara, the latter, as his true *guru*, showed him the correct path and Rin-chen-bzaṅ-po realised for the first time in his life the supreme importance of meditation. This meditation, to which the scholar devoted the rest of his life, had nothing reminiscent of Tantrism popularly understood.

From certain passages of the Tibetan histories, it further appears that Dīpaṃkara concentrated primarily on the reform of Tantrika practices in Tibet. "Nothwithstanding the fact," says 'Gos lo-tsā-ba,[68] "that some of the Tantric precepts were to be found in dBus, gTsaṅ and mṄa'-ris, Tantric practices became defiled. Meditation on the ultimate reality was abandoned, and many coarse practices made their appearance, such as sexual practices, ritual killing (*sbyor-sgrol*), the *gtad-ser* (*gtad-pa* means the ritual burial of magic spells with the intention of harming one's enemy ; *ser-ba*, production of hail-storms), and others. (This situation) was noticed by the kings of mṄa'-ris, and though they did not voice their objection openly, they sent

67. *śloka* 62.

68. BA i. 204.

invitations to numerous learned *paṇḍita*-s (in India), who were able to remove these obstacles by placing living beings on the Path of Purity." Lord Atīśa, adds the historian, "also prohibited indirectly the coarse practices of lay Trantics." "The Master," repeats 'Gos lo-tsā-ba, "composed the *Bodhi-patha-pradīpa* which expounded the stages of the paths of the three classes of men. ...Thus the Master emitted the Lion's roar saying that *sbyor-ba* and *sgrol-ba* were unsuitable for practice by one who followed the word of Tantras only. Because of his holding in high esteem the fruits of deeds, the Master was known as '*paṇḍita* of *karma* and its effects.' When he heard that he was known so, he said : 'This mere name was of benefit,' and was pleased."[69]

But all these should not lead us to believe that Dīpaṃkara, or any religious reformer in Tibet, succeeded in fully eradicating from the Tibetan mind the fascination for Tantrism. There remained in Tibet staunch followers of Tantra who did not react favourably to the preachers against it. Before the coming of Dīpaṃkara, king Ye-śes-'od himself preached against Tantrism for which the later Tibetan Tāntrikas did not forgive him. As Rahula[70] says, "Jñānaprabha (Ye-śes-'od) himself was not attached to Tantrism. On the contrary he wrote a book against it. The Tibetan Tāntrikas believe that the royal ascetic went to hell for writing this book."

However, in spite of Dīpaṃkara's denunciation of popular Tantrism even the later Tibetan Tantrikas did not denounce him so summarily. One reason for this was perhaps the great stature of the Master in Tibetan history. But the other reason could have been that Dīpaṃkara did not flout Tantrism openly. Thus, in the *Caryā-saṃgraha-pradīpa*[71] he expounded his ascetic ideal only after a formal pledge to the scriptural authority of *guhya-mantra*, while in the *Caryā-gīti*[72] he fully retained the form of the Tantra though infusing it with the content of classical Buddhism. Besides, his own knowledge of the Tantras was too imposing to be questioned even by the

69. *Ib.* i. 248-9.
70. Rahula in *2500 Years* 232.
71. See Section 32.
72. See Appendix C.

staunchest supporter of Tantrism. After all, he began his own career as a full-fledged Tāntrika and could easily humble the pride of the greatest Tāntrika scholar of Tibet with a decisively superior knowledge of Tantrism itself. Thus, in short, he left little scope to be branded as a heretic from the Tāntrika point of view itself, however much eager he might have been to preach in Tibet the Mahāyāna ideal of universal emancipation and the Mādhyamika philosophy called *śūnya-vāda*.

At the same time there are clear indications of a suppressed grudge against him expressed by some of the later Tāntrikas on the ground that he did not properly emphasise the importance of esoteric Tantrism while preaching in Tibet. But the mode of expressing this grudge is interesting. Finding it difficult to denounce Dīpaṃkara directly, the later Tāntrikas make 'Brom-ston-pa somehow or other responsible for the Master's indifference to esoteric Tantrism. In other words, they complain that though Dīpaṃkara himself was as a matter of fact eager to preach the Tantras, he was actually prevented from doing it by 'Brom-ston-pa. Not that even 'Brom-ston-pa was unaware of the importance of the Tantras ; he had full knowledge of these and was himself initiated into Tantrism. But he apprehended that the propagation of it in any extensive scale was going to have adverse effect on the moral conduct of the Tibetans. This led him to prevent the Master from preaching the Tantras.

"'Brom was very learned in both Tantras and Sūtras. He kept secret the Vajrayānic doctrine, and did not teach it extensively."[73] "While staying at bSam-yas, the Master bestowed on 'Brom at 'Chims-phu numerous methods (*thabs*) concerning Tantric ceremonies, the Dohā (Saraha's) and many other hidden precepts. 'Brom's chief purpose was to expel persons of immoral conduct, who were conducting themselves according to the word of the Tantra, from the class held by the Master. Therefore, he pretended not to have studied secret texts. In this connection rJe-btsun Mid-la, when he met Dags-po Lha-rje expressed his disapproval (of 'Brom's attitude)."[74]

73. BA i. 265. 74. *Ib.* i. 261.

Specially interesting is the last sentence of this statement. The famous Tibetan poet Mid-la or Mid-la-ras-pa (born A.D. 1040[75]) was one of the foremost disciples of Mar-pa (born A.D. 1012[76]), the founder of the bKa'-brgyud-pa sect in Tibet. Mar-pa himself was reputed to have secret Tantric initiations under a number of eminent Indian Siddhācāryas, inclusive of Naro-pā, Maitri-pā and Kukkuri-pā.[77] The Tantra on which special emphasis is laid by his followers is known as the Mahāmudrā. The Tibetan exponents of the Mahāmudrā adopt a peculiarly dual attitude to Atīśa. On the one hand they cannot perhaps afford to deny all connections of Atīśa with this Tantra, while, on the other hand, they cannot forgive 'Brom-ston-pa for not allowing Atīśa to preach it properly.

Thus in one of the passages[78] of 'Gos lo-tsā-ba we find the later followers of the Mahāmudrā trying their best to show that Atīśa—and even 'Brom-ston-pa himself—took part in the translation and propagation of this Tantra, though " 'Brom suspected that these (teachings) might have a bad influence on the morals of Tibetan (monks), and abstained from preaching them much." From another passage[79] in the same work, however, it is clear that Mid-la-ras-pa was extremely annoyed with 'Brom-ston-pa for not allowing Dīpaṃkara to preach the Tantra in Tibet. bLo-gros-grags-lha-rje sGam-po-pa (born in A.D. 1079) "heard numerous rites of initiation at Lower Dags-po" , but "on hearing the name of Mid-la being pronounced" by a beggar, he "was filled with strong faith" and went to him. "The teacher (Mid-la) then gave him a skull-cup full of wine. sGam-po-pa thought that being a monk it was improper to drink it. The Teacher having perceived (his thought), insisted that he should drink it. After he had drunk it all, the Teacher inquired about his name. sGam-po-pa said that his name was bSod-mams-rin-chen (Puṇyaratna, 'Gem of Merit'). The Teacher then repeated three times : 'Merit, merit, merit', and sang : 'Come

75. *Ib*. ii. 405. 76. *Ib*. ii. 404. 77. *Ib* ii. 400-1.
78. BA ii. 843-4. 79. *Ib*. ii. 455-6, emphasis added.

out of the Accumulation of Merit (*puṇyavarga*), Gem of Living Beings', and then added : 'This will be your welcome !' sGam-po-pa then made his request : 'Pray bestow on me the hidden precepts.' (Mid-la) said to him : 'Were you initiated ?' sGam-po-pa replied : 'I received many initiations into the Rin-chen-rgyan-drug, the Cycle of Saṃvara, etc. from Mar-yul-blo-ldan. I also listened to many expositions of the hidden precepts of the bKa'-gdams-pa-s in Northern dBu-ru. I have experienced for thirteen days a mystic trance characterised by the absence of sensations.' (The Teacher) emitted a loud laugh : 'Ha, ha', and said : 'Better than this trance, is the trance of the gods of the *rūpa* and *arūpa dhātu*-s who are able to meditate throughout an entire cosmic period (*kalpa*). But it is of no benefit for enlightenment. It is similar to (the saying) : Sand, when pressed, will not become liquid butter. The 'bKa-gdams-pa-s possess hidden precepts, but they have no secret instructions. *Because a demon had penetrated the heart of Tibet, the Venerable Master* (*Atīśa*) *was not allowed to preach the Vajrayāna* (*by 'Brom-ston,* who objected to it, when the Master was about to begin the preaching of the Dohā), *but if he were allowed to do it, by now Tibet would have been filled by Saints* ! The bKa'-gdams-pa's *utpannakrama* degree consists only of meditations on tutelary deities in the *widower aspect* (i.e. without their *śakti*-s), and their *sampannakrama* degree consists only of meditations on the merging of the World and its inhabitants into the sphere of *ābhāsvara* (here *śūnyatā* is meant)'."

Accusing the bKa'-gdams-pa-s of meditating on tutelary deities in their widower aspect is interesting. It is technically called *ekavīra-sādhana*, for *ekavīra* (*dpa'-bo-gcig-pa*) means tutelary deity without its *śākti* or female counterpart.[80] Though annoying for the Tāntrikas, Dīpaṃkara did in fact write a special treatise on it called the *Ekavīra-sādhana-nāma.*[81] This, again, has some light to throw on his attitude to the followers of popular Tantrism or, as the Tibetans put it, to those who followed only the words of the Tantras.

80. *Ib*. ii. 440.

81. rG. xiii. 41.

The assertion of the Tibetan Tāntrikas that Dīpaṃkara was prevented by 'Brom from laying proper emphasis on Tantrism in his teachings can hardly be convincing. The possibility of 'Brom imposing his own judgment on Dīpaṃkara particularly in matters of the Master's teachings appears to be quite remote. The picture of 'Brom we usually have is that he had complete devotion to Dīpaṃkara. Therefore, his distaste for popular Tantrism could have as well been because of Atīśa's influence upon him. However, even admitting the story of 'Brom preventing Dīpaṃkara from preaching Tantrism, the only conclusion we are led to is that Dīpaṃkara did not preach Tantrism in Tibet, at least not to the satisfaction of the later Tāntrikas.

We may thus sum up Atīśa's attitude to the Tantras : Without ever formally denying their scriptural authority and even taking an active part in the composition and translation of some of the Tāntrika treatises, he concentrated in his own teachings on the fundamentals of Mahāyāna Buddhism in its classical or pre-Tāntrika form and he insisted that an insight into the real significance of the Tāntrika practices meant the recommendation of some form of intense meditation on the phenomenal world being unreal, any attachment to which, therefore, meaning only misery for the living beings. Rather than making any allowance to the coarse practices then enjoying the sanction of the Tantras, Dīpaṃkara himself put the strongest emphasis on moral purity, asceticism and the method of meditation.

However, the grudge of the later Tibetan Tāntrikas against 'Brom was not without its own logic. Without subscribing to the view that he prevented Atīśa from preaching Tantrism in Tibet, it is necessary to note that Atīśa's religious reform in Tibet *in its organisational aspect* was largely due to 'Brom-ston-pa. As a matter of fact, Atīśa's meeting with 'Brom proved to be a turning point in his Tibetan career. While he was preparing to return to India after spending three years in mṄa'-ris, he first met 'Brom and the latter somehow or other persuaded the Master to cancel his programme in favour of a tour of central Tibet, which, from the point of view of the

Buddhist religion, had a glorious past but which, after the persecution of the Doctrine by gLaṅ Dar-ma, was passing through a grave crisis. " 'Brom told the Master about the many *vihāra*-s and the many thousands of monks in Lhasa, bSam-yas, and other monasteries of central Tibet. The Master said : 'Such a great number of *brahmacārin*-s does not exist even in India ! There must be many *arhat*-s also,' and saying so the Master saluted several times in the direction of central Tibet (dBus), This encouraged 'Brom and he requested the Master to visit dBus. The Master said, 'If the monastic community were to invite me, I could not refuse the order of the community, and would proceed there.' Then 'Brom sent a message through dBaṅ-phyug-mgon of Shaṅ" which begins and ends as follows : "Of the Jambudvipa, which has the shape of a chariot......you should reach here before autumn."[82] Unfortunately, the historian does not give the full text of the letter.

Though 'Brom spoke of many *vihāra*-s and many thousands of monks in central Tibet, it is quite evident that he felt that the monks there were in need of being properly guided and he saw in Atīśa the required qualities of a teacher who alone could rightly guide the Tibetan Buddhists of the time. Hence was his eagerness to take Atīśa to central Tibet. Evidently, again, Atīśa also felt that there was much for him to do in central Tibet. He revised the decision of returning to India and allowed 'Brom to organise the tour of central Tibet, which 'Brom did with great enthusiasm and ability. The result was that Atīśa's religious reforms did not remain confined to western Tibet ; central Tibet also witnessed a resurgence of Buddhism. Here, again, it is necessary to remember that this was largely due to the continuation of Atīśa's work by 'Brom-ston-pa even after the Master's death, though 'Brom himself always maintained an attitude of extreme humility : he called himself only an *upāsaka* or lay-devotee and claimed to do everything in the mere capacity of a faithful follower of Dīpaṃkara.

82. BA i. 254.

Since Dīpaṃkara's religious reforms in Tibet owed so much to the organisational work of 'Brom-ston-pa, the Tibetan Buddhists look back at his meeting with the Master as nothing short of a miracle. It was miraculously predicted even before Atīśa left India and it was engineered by the divine grace of Tārādevī. When, at Vikramaśīla, Atīśa consulted his tutelary deity about the desirability of his going to Tibet, the latter "directed him in a dream to go to the great Tīrthika city called Mukhena in the neighbourhood of Vikramaśīla, at the centre of which there stood on a hillock a small Buddhist temple. He was told that there he would meet with a female ascetic who could tell him all that he wished to know. Then in the following morning Atīśa carrying a handful of *cowries* went there. While he was seated in a prayerful mood with the offerings placed on a *maṇḍala*, before the image of Tārā, there suddenly appeared, from what quarter none could tell, a *yoginī* with locks flowing to her feet and reaching the ground. To her Atīśa presenting the *cowries* asked : 'If I go to Tibet in compliance with the invitation of the king, shall I be of service to the living beings of Tibet ?' To this she replied : 'Yes, if you go to Tibet you will be of great service to them and particularly to an *upāsaka* (i.e. 'Brom-ston-pa) and through him to the whole country'."[83] To this is added the following account of his first meeting with 'Brom : "When he (i.e. 'Brom) reached mÑa'-ris, the venerable Tārā said to the Master : 'Within three days and half, your *upāsaka* will reach here in comfort. Prepare to receive him !' The Master then placed a vase for initiation at his pillow and blessed it with *mantra*-s. On the midday of the fourth day, when the Master, his retinue and a lay-supporter were invited to partake of food, while going there, the Master (watched the road for 'Brom) saying : 'The Venerable Lady (Tārā) did she say an untruth ?' Then (passing) through the street, he met face to face with 'Brom. The latter without speaking to the retinue, followed the Master, as if he had associated with him before."[84]

83. JBTS I. i. 20.

84. BA i. 253-4

In the history of Tibetan Buddhism, there was something qualitatively new about the organisational activity of 'Brom-ston-pa for the propagation of the Doctrine. Before him, the Tibetans that took the initiative for the spread of Buddhism in Tibet were either actual rulers like Khri-sroṅ-lde-btsan, Ral-pa-can and Ye-śes-'od or Tibetan ministers like those of Khri-sroṅ-lde-btsan. Buddhism, in other words, was presented to the people with a stamp of aristocratic sanction as it were. The first team of genuinely Tibetan monk-scholars which Śāntarakṣita tried to build up would have perhaps substantially altered the situation but for the persecution of gLaṅ Dar-ma, which followed the activities of Śāntarakṣita. By contrast, 'Brom-ston-pa himself began life as a humble person and had to work his way towards being a scholar through most adverse circumstances. From the nature of his organisational activities it appears moreover that he concentrated mainly on the creation of a real mass-basis for Buddhism in Tibet by mobilising the Tibetan scholars themselves to follow the path shown by the Master. The result was the first emergence in Tibet of a genuinely Tibetan sect of Buddhism, based of course above all on the interpretation of Buddhism given by Dīpaṃkara. This was the bKa'-gdams-pa sect, actually founded by 'Brom, though eventually reformed by the great Tsoṅ-kha-pa into what is called the "new bKa'-gdams-pa" or the dGe-lugs-pa sect, which became the most dominant sect of Tibetan Buddhism. Thus, as the leading Tibetan disciple of Dīpaṃkara and as the founder of the bKa'-gdams-pa sect the role of 'Brom-ston-pa in the religious history of Tibet is immensely important.

His full name is given as 'Brom-ston-pa rGyal-ba'i-'byuṅ-gnas,[85] the Sanskrit equivalent of the latter part of this being Jayākara. S. C. Das[86] says that 'Brom was the name of an ancient Tibetan family in which he was born. 'Gos lo-tsā-ba gives the year of his birth as A.D. 1005, a Wood-Female-Serpent year,[87] and that of his death as A. D. 1064, a

85. BA i. 262. 86. D-TED 935. 87. BA i. 251.

Wood-Dragon year.[88] He was born in sTod-luṅ,[89] a district north-west of Lhasa.[90] S. C. Das gives the name of the village of his birth as Phu-rtsa-gye-mo.[91]

"His mother died early. From his childhood he had a penetrating mind, and decided that it was better for him to go to some other place than to quarrel with his step-mother. So he went to gShu and studied reading and writing. While living there, he met Jo-bo Se-btsun who was journeying from Khams to Nepal and India. Faith (in him) was born."[92] One of the interesting things said about his educational career is that when he "attended on Jo-bo Se-btsun, he learnt the work of a translator from Smṛti."[93] Smṛti was a *paṇḍita* who for some years got stranded in Tibet: "At the time of the princely teacher Ye-śes-'od, two *paṇḍita*-s, Smṛti and Sūkṣma-dīrgha came, having been invited by the Nepalese Padmaruci. But as the translator had died in Nepal of cholera, the two *paṇḍita*-s who did not know the Tibetan language, roamed about in dBus and gTsaṅ, and Smṛti was forced to become a shepherd in rTa-nag."[94] Subsequently, however, Smṛti was invited to Maṅ-yul, became proficient in the Tibetan language and translated some of his own works into Tibetan.

The other things said about 'Brom's educational career only show under what difficulties he pursued it. He requested Se-btsun to be accepted as an attendant and went to the latter's place. "In the house he performed various works, even that of grinding barley grains, and outside of the house he looked after the herd of horses and cattle. Armed with the three kinds of arms (arrow, lance and sword) and riding on a good horse, he used to watch (the herd) against brigands. While he was grinding flour, he used to keep his books nearby, and study them. In this manner he pursued his studies with great diligence. In the neighbourhood there lived a scholar called Grammar Thorn (*sgra'i-tsher-ma*), and with him he studied much the Lañtsa and the Vartula scripts."[95]

88. BA i. 72 ; 186 ; 264. 89. *Ib.* i. 251. 90. D-TED 553.
91. *Ib.* 823. 92. BA i. 251. 93. *Ib.* i. 205. 94. Bu-ston ii. 214.
95. BA i. 252.

In spite of all these odds, however, 'Brom became very learned and an extremely competent translator. Both as a scholar and translator, he seems to have maintained an attitude of staunch puritanism. As the true inheritor of the Mādhyamika philosophy preached by Dīpaṃkara, " 'Brom said to sPyan-sṅa : 'All say that it is impossible to read the 84,000 sections of the Doctrine, therefore meditate well on the *śūnyatā* only'. "[96] "He used to say : 'The main point of my understanding of the Mādhamika is Nothingness.' By this he meant the Absolute Negation (*med-dgag*) of existence, for Dharmakīrti had said : 'The Absolute Negation of existence is Nothingness' (*med-par-dgag-pa-ni-ci-yaṅ-ma-yin-pa'i-phyir-ro*) in his Autocommentary on the first chapter of the *Pramāṇavārttika*."[97] As a translator, again, he showed the unmistakable attitute of reaching perfection. Thus, unlike Jayaśīla, e.g., who cared most for the quantity of translations, 'Brom was above all concerned with the purity of the rendering. The number of works in the bsTan-'gyur of which he is mentioned as the translator is not considernble and in spite of his close association with Dīpaṃkara only two works in the bsTan-'gyur are found as translated by 'Brom under the Master.[98] Yet, from the colophon of the *Ārya-aṣṭa-sāhasrikā prajñāpāramitā* in the bKa'-'gyur, we can easily see how much care and conscientiousness he showed in rendering Buddhist scriptures. It is a fundamental work for the Māhāyana Buddhists and is enormous in bulk. It was not easy to reach perfection in the Tibetan translation. Accordingly, a number of Tibetan lo-tsā-ba-s sat under Indian *paṇḍita*-s for rendering it. What is specially relevant for our present purpose is to note how much care 'Brom-ston-pa himself devoted to its right rendering. We quote the colophon in full : "Translated, revised and edited by Indian *upādhyāya*-s Śākyasena and Jñānasiddhi and the great reviser lo-tsā-ba *ban-de* Dharmatāśīla and others. Again, by

96. *Ib*. i. 264. 97. *Ib*. i. 265. 98. The bsTan-'gyur contains the following as translated by 'Brom, only the last two of which were done under Dīpaṃkara : mDo lxxxix. 1; rG. xxvi. 82; xlv 8, 9; xlviii. 40; lxxiv. 8; lxxxiii. 37, 51; lxxi. 345 and lxxii. 64.

the request of the great king and lord of Tibet dPal-lha-btsan-po bKra-shis-lha-lde-btsan, translated by the Indian *upādhyāya* Subhāṣita and the grammarian *bhikṣu* Ratnabhadra in accordance with the commentary. Again, revised and edited by the Indian *upādhyāya mahā-paṇḍita* Dīpaṃkara-śrī-jñāna and the great reviser lo-tsā-ba *bhikṣu* Ratnabhadra, comparing it with the commentary from the Central Land (*yul-dbus*, evidently Magadha). Again, at sÑe-thaṅ Na-mo-che of sKyi-smad, the major part finalised by both *mahā-paṇḍita* Dīpaṃkara-śrī-jñāna and lo-tsā-ba 'Brom rGyal-ba'i-'byuṅ-gnas ('Brom Jayākara) at the time of expounding the *Aṣṭa-sāhasrikā*. Again, edited for the second time at the Rwa-sgreṅ *vihāra* by lo-tsā-ba 'Brom Jayākara, on the basis of a comparison of three manuscripts (*mdo-gsum*, literally three *sūtra*-s). And again, the same lo-tsā-ba prepared an explanation (*bśad-pa*) and finalised in parts. In later time, the great lo-tsā-ba *śākya-bhikṣu* bLo-ldan-śes-rab (Matiprajña) finalised it by collecting many original manuscripts from Kashmir and Magadha."[99]

But 'Brom is remembered by the Tibetan Buddhists not primarily as a translator but as a religious organiser. His organisational activity, again, is divited into two periods, namely, 1) the period covering the last nine or ten years of Atīśa's life and 2) the period of about ten years that 'Brom lived after the death of Atīśa.

The chief purpose of 'Brom during the first of these two periods was to organise for Dīpaṃkara an extensive tour of central Tibet and to mobilise the Tibetan teachers behind the Master. It appears that 'Brom had made up a plan of all these even before he met Dīpaṃkara. While proceeding to mÑa'-ris to meet the Master for the first time, he met Ka-ba Śākya-dbaṅ-phyug and told him, "This time I am going to meet the *paṇḍita*. If he is to be invited to dBus, I shall send you a letter. You should then confer with the important men of the locality and come to welcome him."[100] Ka-ba agreed to this.

99. See Section 8, Appendix B. 100. BA i. 253.

After 'Brom met Atīśa and persuaded him to proceed to central Tibet, " 'Brom's letter was transmitted to Ka-ba by Shaṅ-dbaṅ-phyug-mgon, and Ka-ba paid great attention to the matter. He informed Shaṅ-chen-po of rGyal and others... When the great men (notables) of dBus had reached dPal-thaṅ, they found that the Master and his retinue had already reached upper dPal-thaṅ, for the Master had received the message when still at sKyi-roṅ."[101]

The accounts of Atīśa's tour of central Tibet that come down to us are inevitably overgrown with extensive legends. Most of the typical legends are to be found in the new biography[102] of Dīpaṃkara compiled by Nagwang Nima and Lama Chimpa. Instead of repeating these, we may try to sum up here the account of Atīśa in central Tibet as given by 'Gos lo-tsā-ba[103] :

From mÑa-'-ris, Atīśa and his party proceeded to dPal-thaṅ, where the Master was received by eminent Tibetan teachers. Then they reached rGyaṅ, where the monks held a reception for the Master, which pleased him. "On the road to gTsaṅ, the Master did not receive a great reception and therefore he went towards Ñan-tsho. There the people held an excellent reception in honour of the Master, and there also he received excellent disciples... When they were proceeding to Roṅ, the Master and his retinue happened to run short of provisions. At Lha, a nun... presented the Master with the image of a horse made of gold on which a small boy made of turquoise was riding... Then at 'Chiṅ-ru a girl who was going to be married, offered the Master her head-ornaments, and when the parents scolded her, she jumped into the river gTsaṅ-po... On reaching sNa-bo-la, they hoisted banners and blew large brass trumpets invented by Lha-btsun-pa. The crowd (of villagers) ran away, shouting : 'War has come !' On arrival in Dol, (the inhabitants) did not prepare a general reception for the Master and his retinue, but instead invited each of them in turn to each house... There in order to benefit living

101. *Ib.* i. 255. 102. See Section 6, Appendix A. 103. BA i. 255ff.

beings, the Master built a dyke (*rags*). Now the place is known as Lha-rje-rags. At Gra-phyi-tshoṅ-'dus, a small household prepared a good reception and the Master asked: 'Where is the monastery (i.e. bSam-yas)?' and they replied: 'It is seen from the mountain spur over there.' The Master became pleased. Having reached the ferry of sPel-dmar, they proceeded towards Chos-'khor bSam-yas. Lha-btsun Bodhi-rāja (a descendant of the royal line of Sroṅ-btsan) arranged a good reception for them, and numerous Tibetan teachers and notables assembled. Khu-ston praised his country to the Master and the Master promised to visit it, and journeyed to Thaṅ-po-che. There the Master resided for one month at Rags-rtsigs-khaṅ-pa. ...Since Khu did not arrange a proper reception, the Master and his retinue fled from the place, and entered the ferry-boat of Myaṅ-po... Then the Master and his retinue spent a month at 'On-lha-khaṅ Ke-ru... After that the Master proceeded to bSam-yas and took up residence at dPe-dkar-gliṅ. (Residing) there he prepared with the assistance of the lo-tsā-ba (Nag-tsho) many translations... On the whole the Master was very pleased with the monastery and intended to stay there for a considerable time. The Master heard that one named the Lady 'Chims-mo (Jo-mo 'Chims-mo) was teaching children many wicked words (about him), and decided to go to another place. 'Brom then sent a letter to Baṅ-ston, and the latter came to bSam-yas to welcome the Master with about 200 horsemen. The Master and his retinue proceeded to rGod-dkar-la. For half a month the Master resided at rGya-phibs of Sri. Then he proceeded to sÑe-thaṅ, where many students had gathered... He read on one occasion the *Abhisamayā-laṃkāra* to an assembly of numerous hearers at sÑe-thaṅ... After that the Master was invited by rÑog Legs-pa'i-śes-rab to Lhasa. Avalokiteśvara assuming the form of a white man welcomed the Master." Atīśa recovered from inside a beam the history of Lhasa and along with his disciples prepared copies of it. "After that he spent (some time) at sÑe-thaṅ... The wealth which the Master had amassed while preaching to others, was despatched on three occasions through Chag-khri-mchog and other disciples to India for offering to the teaches and the monastic community (of Vikramaśīla)... After that the Master proceeded to Yer-pa, and rṄog Byaṅ-chub-'byuṅ-gnas entertained him... While the Master was in residence there, 'Brom went to see his relatives in order to ask them for gold. Having obtained many requisites, he came back. At Yer-pa he offered the Master many presents which became known as the Great Offering of 'Brom. After the Master had been invited by Ka-ba Śākya-dbaṅ-phyug, he preached extensively at Lan-pa-spyil-bu of 'Phan-yul... Thus sÑe-thaṅ, Lhasa, Yer-pa and Lan-pa are the places where the Master preached extensively the Doctrine. Then again he proceeded to sÑe-thaṅ."

From this time onwards, his physical strength began to decline fast. He spent the last part of his life at sÑe-thaṅ and "proceeded toTuṣita" in A.D. 1054.

One of the last things attributed to Dīpaṃkara was a request to 'Brom to built a monastery that could serve as a centre for the continuation of the religious reforms to which Dīpaṃkara himself dedicated the last part of his life. Apparently, he saw in 'Brom the required qualities for this task, though 'Brom himself in his characteristically modest way said that he was not equal to it. "The Master said to 'Brom : 'You should build a small monastery, and I shall entrust my teaching to you. Keep it.' 'Brom replied : 'In general, I am unfit to do it, and in particular, I am only an *upāsaka* unable to perform great works.' The Master replied : 'Do the work according to my instructions ! I shall bless you. Do not despair'."[104]

After the death of Atīśa, 'Brom was for sometime stunned with grief. But he quickly recovered and dedicated himself to the Master's instructions : "While 'Brom-ston-pa afflicted by great sorrow was pondering as to what he should do, Ka-ba Śākya-dbaṅ-phyug arrived there and divided the ashes of the Master equally between Khu, rṄog and others. Images and objects of meditation he gave to 'Brom. Khu, rṄog and 'Gar-dga'-ba

104. BA i. 261.

erected silver shrines to preserve the relics given to them. Then having gathered the offerings, presented by Ka-ba and others, they held a great memorial ceremony in the Sheep year (A.D. 1055). 'Should there happen to be any one belonging to Bha-rag, they should assist me', saying so 'Brom built a *vihāra* at sÑe-thaṅ. During the life-time of the Master, those whom he used to support, were called the *sa-dra* of the Master [*sa-dra* meaning 'class or crowd' in Tibetan]. 'Brom took into his service all those whom the Master used to support, and proceeded to sTod-luṅs. He spent some time in the sandy valley of gNam. About that time the chiefs of 'Dam held a council and resolved to invitie 'Brom to Rwa-sgreṅ. He also received an invitation from 'Phaṅ-kha-ber-chuṅ. In the New Year of the Fire-Male-Ape year (A.D. 1056) he proceeded to Rwa-sgreṅ. There he built the main shrine with the two columns [at present this shrine built by 'Brom is preserved inside the temple of Rwa-sgreṅ] and the upper court-yard. After that, he never again participated in worldly matters, saying: 'I shall now give up the world' and only preached the Doctrine."[105]

With this monastery of Rwa-sgreṅ as its centre, 'Brom formed the first nucleus of a sect of Tibetan Buddhism, which came to be known as the bKa'-gdams-pa sect. The bKa'-gdams-pa-s "were called so because they believed and preached that an individual should practise the entire teaching of the Jina (the *sūtra* and *tantra*/Theravāda and Mahāyāna),"[106] though from a survey of the Six Basic Texts of this sect[107] it is clear that the followers of this put decisive emphasis on the Mahāyāna doctrine in its classical or pre-Tāntrika phase.

'Brom himself "lived for nine years more at Rwa-sgreṅ"[108] and it appears that during his lifetime the number of the followers of the bKa'-gdams-pa sect was not very large: "During the life-time of 'Brom there were not more than 60 meditative ascetics, residing permanently (at Rwa-sgreṅ)."[109]

105 *Ib*. i. 262-3. 106. *Ib*. i. 264. See also Section 5, Appendix A.
107. See Sec. 2, Note 14. 108. BA i. 264. 109. *Ib*.

However, the movement started by him went on gathering momentum and the bKa'-gdams-pa sect (eventually reformed by Tsoṅ-kha-pa and called the dGe-lugs-pa sect) became the strongest religious force in Tibet.

It is beyond our scope to review here the history of the development of the bKa'-gdams-pa sect.[110] But it is necessary to note that the Tibetan historians attribute its great success to the organisational work of 'Brom-ston-pa in particular. As 'Gos lo-tsā-ba puts it, " 'Brom's labours have been very extensive and lasted for a long period of time."[111] But 'Brom himself, with his characteristic modesty, never claimed to be anything more than a humble follower of Atīśa :

> In this Himalayan country there are many that follow thee with a still greater reverence (than I can have). (Nevertheless), please remain as my *guru* and guide me with the same kindness that the mother has for her child. ...O thou Great One, please remain as my *nātha* everywhere and for all time. Kindly give me the first sermon for attaining full enlightenment... Thus prays 'Brom-ston-pa.[112]

110. See Sec. 5, Appendix A. 111. BA i. 327.
112. *stotra* to Dīpaṃkara, *śloka*-s 28 & 30.

APPENDICES

APPENDIX A

Biographical Materials

Tibetan Sources Rendered into English under
Professor Lama Chimpa

Section 1. Introductory Note.
Section 2. 'Brom-ston-pa's *stotra* to Dīpaṃkara.
Section 3. Extracts from *dPag-bsam-ljon-bzaṅ* of Sum-pa.
Section 4. Extracts from *dGos-'dod-kun-'byuṅ* of Tāranātha.
Section 5. General History and Philosophy of the bKa'-gdams-pa sect.
Extract from *Grub-mtha'-thams-cad-kyi-khuṅs-daṅ-'dod-tshul-ston-pa* of Thu-bkan bLo-bzaṅ Chos-kyi-ñi-ma.
Section 6. A New Biography of Dīpaṃkara compiled in Tibetan from Tibetan sources by Nagwang Nima and edited by Lama Chimpa.

Section 1

Introductory Note

Certain important Tibetan source-materials relating to the life and teachings of Dīpaṃkara are given in this *Appendix* in English translation.

It begins with the famous *stotra* in thirty *śloka*-s (*sum-cu-pa*) to Dīpaṃkara by 'Brom-ston-pa.

The next section contains a literal translation of an extract from the *dPag-bsam-ljon-bzaṅ* by Sum-pa-khan-po-ye-śes-dpal-'byor, the famous historian of Buddhism of the eighteenth century (born A.D. 1702, died at the age of 73). He is better known by the abbreviated name Sum-pa, meaning "one from the country of Sum, a province of western Tibet." As edited by S. C. Das, the Tibetan original of this history was published from Calcutta in 1908.

Tāranātha's history of Buddhism, in its Indian portion, does not contain much about Atīśa. Only a few scrappy statements of the historian are given in Section 4 of the present *Appendix*.

The next section of the *Appendix* contains a literal translation of the history and doctrine of the bKa'-gdams-pa sect from the work of the learned Tibetan scholar Chos-kyi-ñi-ma, a short account of whose life is given by S. C. Das in JASB, Vol. 50, 1881, pp. 187ff. The translation is based on the edition of the work published in 1963, Saranatha, Varanasi, edited by Chos-rje-bla-ma.

The *Appendix* ends with the translation of a new biography of Dīpaṃkara compiled in Tibetan from the Tibetan sources by Nagwang Nima and edited by Lama Chimpa. In his own Preface to this work, the author mentions his sources. Both the author and the editor of this biography are now in India, —the former in the Benares Hindu University and the latter in the Visvabharati University.

Section 2

'Brom-ston-pa's *stotra* to Dīpaṃkara

This *stotra* of thirty *śloka*-s is addressed to *mahā* Jo-bo (*mahā-prabhu*), the one-god (*eka-deva*) of Tibet. *Oṃ svasti.*

I offer prayer to the feet of Dīpaṃkara-śrī, who was born in the noble *Jīva*-family of the kings of *sa-hor* of *tri-sampanna*[1] Bengal in the same line to which Śāntijīva (Śāntarakṣita) belonged. //1//

I offer prayer to the feet of Dīpaṃkara-śrī, who excelled in serving his parents, was modest, beautiful and charming, possessed *prajñā* and *karuṇā*, had a humble and tender heart, and was (also) skilful and had great mental strength. //2//

I offer prayer to the feet of Dīpaṃkara-śrī, who was a master of various worldly subjects, like the arts and medicine, and also of all the branches of knowledge (*sarva-veda*). //3//

I offer prayer to the feet of Dīpaṃkara-śrī, who was not attracted by *kāma* and who, by renouncing his right to the kingdom, was ordained a *bhikṣu* by the *Mahāsaṅghika.* //4//

I offer prayer to the feet of Śrī Atīśa, the pure, who was well-versed in Tathāgata as explained in the fourth part (*varga*) of the *Vinaya-Piṭaka* and who was above any sin. //5//

I offer prayer to the feet of Śrī Atīśa, who under the guidance of many *guru*-s and scholars, mastered the three Piṭaka-s, grammar, logic and all the *upadeśa*-s and who had a vast knowledge. //6//

I offer prayer to Śrī Atīśa, who receiving the nectar of *bodhicitta* from the *guru* of Suvarṇadvīpa—himself of royal descent—worked for the welfare of the living beings. //7//

I offer prayer to Atīśa, the only father, who, with his hearty love for the needy and the distressed, earned the gratitude of

1. *phun-sum-tshogs* - possessed of the three, [grace, glory and wealth]; perfect; complete. D-TED 825 ; J-TED 344.

all this *saṃsāra,* whether the *sura*-s, the *asura*-s or the human beings. //8//

I offer prayer to his feet, who by his clear comprehension and concentrated meditation on the sayings of the *siddha-sad-guru*-s and of the tutelar deity, himself earned *siddhi* and the power to foretell the future. //9//

I offer prayer to thy feet—thou who art the object of worship and love and who, in spite of coming to the Himalayas for the sake of the devotees in Tibet, remained the *guru* of the great men of thy country and race. //10//

Though Buddhism could exist in Tibet even without the arrival there of a great scholar like thee, yet many people (in Tibet) were mistaken about its deeper significance and thou gave them the right teaching ; to thy feet I offer prayer. //11//

I offer prayer to his feet, who, by translating the *śāstra*-s, by correcting the previous translations, by commenting on *śāstra*-s and composing *śāstra*-s himself—led the disciples along the correct path and helped the Doctrine to flourish. //12//

With his own great knowledge, he refuted the wrong views of the Tīrthikas and brought back to the path of liberation those that praised and followed the evil path of Māra and Mahādeva,—to the feet of that excellent guide to the seekers of liberation, I offer my prayer. //13//

I offer prayer to his feet, who, by repeated practice through the cycle of births, of the six *pāramitā*-s, viz., *dāna*, *śīla*, *kṣamā*, *vīrya*, *dhyāna* and *prajñā*, attained perfection in both the *varga*-s (viz. *jñāna-varga* and *puṇya-varga*, the two pursuits of life). //14//

I offer prayer to thy feet—thou who accomplished the four essentials of the assembly, viz., fulfilling others' requirements according to their needs, using kind words in speech, working for the welfare of the devotees according to the rules of common interest and winning the goals of others by one's own strength. //15//

I offer prayer to thy feet,—thou, who art the mine of virtues and art rich in the seven riches, viz., *śraddhā*, *śīla*, *śravaṇa*, *dāna*, *prajñā*, *vinaya* and *lajjā*. //16//

I offer prayer to thy feet—thou who possessed *deva-cakṣuḥ-abhijñāna*[2] (as evidenced by the following): when the good disciple 'Brom-ston-pa, related to thee by his devotion of past lives, was coming to thee from a great distance, thou said, "The *upāsaka* is going to turn up today." //17//

I offer prayer to thy feet,—thou who possessed *śravaṇa-abhijñāna* (as evidenced by the following): when thy devoted disciple prayed to thee by playing the cymbal at Magadha, thou told 'Brom that thou heard the sound, even from Tibet. //18//

I offer prayer to thy feet—thou who possessed *ṛddhi-abhijñāna* (as evidenced by the following): while in Lhasa, on hearing the sound of cymbal played by the gods, thou went up to the sky, bowed down to the gods, prayed to them and circumambulated in the sky. //19//

I offer prayer to thy feet, oh thou kind-hearted Master, by whose kindness was recovered the royal testament[3] that was

2. mṅon-par-śes-pa : *abhijñāna*, "pre-science, certain gifts or supernatural perception of which six kinds are enumerated : 1) *divya-cakṣurvijñāna* (*deva-cakṣuḥ-abhijñāna*), seeing anything clearly as if with divine sight. By the exercise of this power one can see (realize) the sufferings of all kinds of living beings. 2) *divya-śrotram* (*śravaṇa-abhijñāna*), divine hearing in a perfect manner. By the exercise of this knowledge one can hear the sound of the smallest insect and understand the different languages, articulate and inarticulate, of all living beings. 3) *para-citta-jñānam*, knowledge of another's heart ; knowing of another's thought. 4) *ṛddhi-vidhi-jñānam*, knowledge of the four forms of miracle. By the exercise of this knowledge one knows the events of his former and future states of existence, and also the circumstances of his death and birth. By the exercise of one's miraculous knowledge, it is possible to move one's body without being seen. 5) *pūrva-nivāsa-anusmṛti-jñānam*, the power of remembering the acts of one's former existence or life. 6) *āsravakṣaya-jñānam*, knowledge of the destruction of the passions. By the exercise of the knowledge of decay and destruction one can quickly attain to the state of the omniscient (*sarvajña*) by purifying himself of all impurities of the heart. By the exercise of the power of knowing all living beings one can perceive as well the stages of their moral perfection or culture." (D-TED, 365-6)

In the present *stotra*, out of the six *abhijñāna*-s mentioned above, 'Brom-ston-pa attributes three to Dīpaṃkara in *śloka*-s 17-9.

3. *bka'-chems* - see p. 204, note 25.

lying hidden in the treasury ; the Dākinī opened its door for thee and thou had (already) the permission of Śākyamuni (to see it). //20//

I offer prayer to thy feet—thou who art the eternal life-saviour and renowned as Nāgārjuna the second, for, the means of saving the lives of people suffering from Nāga-roga[4] were introduced by thee and people were healed by them. //21//

I offer prayer to the feet of the *guru* of the *deva*-s on whom, while he was sitting on the sand at 'Or in sÑe-thaṅ, Indra and the other gods showered, as flowers, the *pañca-ratna* from heaven. //22//

I offer prayer to thy feet—thou, who, on hearing that the girl from gYor-po-'chiṅ-ru met death (because of being rebuked) for offering the head-ornament, performed the last rites for her and said that the *kulaputrī* was going to be reborn in heaven ; thus did thou offer leadership to all the living beings. //23//

I offer prayer to his feet who foresaw the future and said, "From here I shall proceed to the Tuṣita ; I shall meet in the Tuṣita those that will have reverence and love for me." //24//

I offer prayer to his feet who is honoured everywhere—in Tuṣita by the name, Vimala Ākāśa, in the Aryan country (*ārya-deśa*) by the name, Dīpaṃkara, and in this Himalayan country by the name, Śrīmat Atiśa. //25//.

I offer prayer to thy feet,—thou who blessed us directly by showering the *pratisṭhāna-puṣpa* from the Tuṣita when I, 'Brom-ston, built the Rwa-sgreṅ monastery and prayed for thy blessings for the living beings. //26//.

From the heaven thou lookest with merciful eyes at those that, perceiving thy greatness, pray to thee with a clear mind and in a distinct manner ; I pray to thee that thou bless those that are devoted to thee. //27//.

In this Himalayan country there are many that follow thee with a still greater reverence (than I can have). (Nevertheless), please remain as my *guru* and guide me with the same kindness that the mother has for her child. //28//.

4. *klu-nad* : probably leprosy. D-TED 45.

Being blind, men in the *kali-yuga* follow as *kalyāṇamitra*-s those that are really not so and thus they fail to be free from the prison of this *saṃsāra* ; kindly pull them out soon with the hook of your *karuṇā*.[5] //29//.

Oh thou Great One, please remain as my *guru* (*nātha*) everywhere and for all time. Kindly give me the first sermon for attaining full enlightenment... Thus prays 'Brom-ston-pa. //30//.

5. For "hook of mercy" see Rockhill LB 207.

Section 3

Literal translation of extracts from *dPag-bsam-ljon-bzaṅ* by Sum-pa mKhan-po Ye-śes-dpal-'byor (Edited by S. C. Das, Calcutta 1908)

---

[183] Specially during time of the three sons of Lha-lde, Atīśa, the great scholar of (all the) five branches of knowledge, was invited to Tibet and the Buddha's teachings spread very widely.

At the time the Buddha came to the world, he (Atīśa) was born as a householder called Jinaputra-bhadracaryā in Rājagṛha.

One thousand eight hundred fifteen years after the Fire-Hare year of the Buddha's *nirvāṇa*, towards the end of the Fire-Sky-Ocean (*me-mkha'-rgya-tsho'i*) [period], he (Atīśa) acted as if being reborn in the Water-Horse year [A.D. 982] in *za-hor* in Bengal in Eastern India in the central palace with golden banners of the city of Vikramapura in the noble family which had the greatest *paṇḍita* Śāntijīva in its line of descent, having for his father king Kalyāṇaśrī and mother Padmaprabhā and as the middle of the three sons with the name Candragarbha. It is said that in his youth he had five queens and nine princes called Puṇyaśrī etc. were born of him.

Then about how he attained academic and spiritual abilities :

From his early childhood he accepted Tārādevī as his tutelar deity, who was the tutelar deity of his previous births.

By the age of 29, he acquired full mastery of all the branches of general science, like grammar, logic, fine arts and therapeutics, etc. Already, when he was only fifteen he defeated a learned non-Buddhist logician.

Then, without caring for the kingdom and in search of *dharma* he went to the temple of the Black Mountain (Ri-nag-po), received the *abhiṣeka* from *guru* Rāhulagupta, acquired the esoteric name Jñāna-guhya-vajra and became a profound adept in *mantra* (*sṅags*).

At (the age of) 29, by the instruction of his *guru* and tutelar deity, he received the *pravrajyā* ordination in Odantapurī under Śīlarakṣita, a Mahāsāṅghika *ācārya*. Thus he became a *bhikṣu* and received the name Dīpaṃkara-śrī-jñāna.

By (the age of 31) he learnt under Dharmarakṣita and others the *Mahāvibhāṣā*, etc., and acquired proficiency in "external" knowledge like philosophy and *lakṣaṇa-śāstra* and also became a scholar of both "lower" and "higher" (? Hīnayāna and Mahāyāna) Piṭakas.

Then he went to Suvarṇadvīpa and thoroughly studied for twelve years the practice of *bodhicitta*, both *praṇidhāna* and *avatāra*. In short **[p. 184]** he cared for the *tri-saṃvara*-s as one cares for one's eye-balls.

And he either personally met or had visions of twelve *guru*-s, like Śānti-pā, Naro-pā, the junior Kuśalī-pā, the junior Avadhūti-pā, Dombi-pā, etc.

For twelve years he practised both the *yāna*-s—both Hīnayāna and Mahāyāna – acquired profound knowledge of Sūtra and Tantra, and after being fully established in meditational practices [Sum-pa mentions the details thereof] he attained *abhijñāna*-s and *ṛddhi*-s and had the visions of Tārā, Avalokiteśvara, Trisaṃvaravyūha (?) and Hevajra.

What he did for Buddhism in India and Tibet :

He served the cause of Buddhism by all the four (*śakti*-s), namely the *yoga*-(*śakti*), *kula*-(*śakti*), *aiśvarya*-(*śakti*) and *vidyā*-(*śakti*), and specially by defeating the *tīrthika*-s with five umbrellas and eight (umbrellas) and thirteen (umbrellas). Thus he became the *śiromaṇi* of the five hundred.

His main students in India were four, namely, *paṇḍita* Piṭo-pā, Dharmākaramati, Madhyasiṃha and Bhūgarbha. If Mitragupta is added, they were five. And many. Also many in Kashmir, Suvarṇadīvpa, etc.

He became the *upādhyāya* (*mkhan-po*) of Vikramaśīla, etc. And when he left, *sthavira* (*gnas-brtan*) Ratnākara and others were there.

It was the time of the "Later Spread of the Doctrine." Many *paṇḍita*-s came to Tibet, but could not succeed in removing the dirt from Buddhism in Tibet. So Ye-śes-'od and others, attracted by the fame of Jo-bo Atīśa, *alias* Dīpaṃkara-śrī-jñāna, were very eager to invite him to Tibet. So they sent lo-tsā-ba gTsaṅ-stag-tshal-pa dGe-bsñen rGya brTson-seṅ-ge (Vīryasiṃha of rGya) with gold (to India for inviting Dīpaṃkara to Tibet). But this time he could not succeed. (He) came back, returned the gold and narrated what had happened. Again, he went to India with Nag-tsho Tshul-khrims-rgyal-ba (Jayaśīla) of Guṅ-thaṅ.

At that time, the Tibetans and Gar-log-pa-s were fighting each other. Ye-śes-'od was leading the Tibetan army. The Tibetans were defeated and the king of Gar-log captured and imprisoned him (Ye-śes-'od) and (said), "Either you renounce Buddhism or pay gold equal in size to your body. Otherwise we will not set you free."

Lha-bla-ma said that he would not renounce his faith (*śaraṇa-gamana*) and remained in their prison for a very long time.

Then the officers of mÑa'-ris (for the purpose of collecting the ransom) imposed taxes even on the monks and collected gold equal in size to his body only (i.e. without the head). When the gold of only the size of his head remained to be collected, they sent a message to Ye-śes-'od saying, "We are going to get your release very soon."

Then the bLa-ma replied, "No. I am old. Even if I am released I cannot be of much service to Buddhism. Instead of purchasing my release, it is better to spend the gold for inviting the *paṇḍita*. And make offerings at Tho-liṅ. Also, get the repairs done to the grandfather's temple at bSam-yas."

After this, he died very soon.

Then the nephew Byaṅ-chub-'od, for carrying out his wish, gave the gold to Nag-tsho lo-tsā-ba, who was then 27 years old and had just returned from India, and said to him, "In our country Buddhism is having its ups and downs. Specially some are being misled by the Red Ācārya (*ācārya* dMar-po) [Note of the text : Some people called him Guhya-prajña and received many *abhiṣeka*-s of the *tīrthika*-s from him.] Since the Red Ācārya's arrival, the Tāntrika studies have become much polluted. Some people follow the system of the 18 *aramo-bandhe* (?). The monks are claiming to be the followers of *mantra* (*sṅags*) and, abandoing their *dhyāna*-s and *śuddha-siddhānta*, they are running after wine and women. Moreover, the one with Blue Robe, in the name of *yoga* (*sbyor*) and *mokṣa* (*sgrol*), is corrupting many in various ways and is leading them to act according to their own desires. This is doing great damage to the cause of the Doctrine. So we should search for some *paṇḍita*, who can remove the darkness of these wrong views."

He (Byaṅ-chub-'od) sent him (Nag-tsho), along with five others, [Note of the text : gDan, A-ston, Kan-ston, rGya-ston and one local interpretor] to India. They stayed as students after reaching Vikramalaśīla (Vikramaśīla).

Later on, with rGya-brtson-seṅ, who was already residing there, they went with a *maṇḍala* of gold, offered it to Jo-bo and said that he must come to Tibet.

Then Jo-bo also consulted Tārādevī, who told him, "If (you) go there, your life will be shorter. But you will be very helpful for the Doctrine and for many people led by the **[p. 185]** *upāsaka*."

So he agreed (to go to Tibet).

At the age of 59, by the end of the Iron-Dragon year, [AD. 1040] along with the two lo-tsā-ba-s, he reached Nepal from India and stayed one year in the country of Anantakīrti at the Samatha *vihāra*. rGya-brtson-seṅ-blo-gros passed away there.

Then in the Water-Horse (year) [A.D. 1042], he reached Guṅ-thaṅ Tho-liṅ of mÑa'-ris province of Tibet. 'Od-lde, along with his people, gave him a grand reception. By writing the *Bodhi-patha-pradīpa*, which is respected by both the old and new bKa'-gdams-pa-s and which contains the essence of both Sūtra and Tantra, he showed the path to Lha-bla-ma Byaṅ-chub-'od and others.

Though Nag-tsho had promised to Ratnākara to bring back (Dīpaṃkara) to India within three years, because of the fighting among the three Ban-sde-s (? Nepales nobles : J-TED 365), it was not necessary (*ma-dgos*) for him to return. This meant a great fortune for Tibet and this was because of the grace of Tārādevī.

In sPu-raṅs-rgyal he met *upāsaka* 'Brom, as was foretold by Tārādevī. He ('Brom) and rṄog-lo invited him to dBus and gTsaṅ. (Atīśa) gradually reached gTsaṅ and bSam-yas [Note of the text : In the Fire-Pig(year) : AD. 1047] of dBus. Then Khu-ston invited him to Yar-kluṅs-thaṅ-po-che. But the circumstances were not favourable and (he) escaped to 'On and came again to bSam-yas and Goṅ-gar.

At the end of his 66th year, Bod-ston sent 200 horsemen to receive him at sÑe-thaṅ. There in his meditation he had the visions of Maitreyanātha and Mañjughoṣa and completed *dharma-sādhana.*

He was invited to Lhasa by rṄog-lo-legs-śes, was invited to Yer-bu-pu-raṅs by rṄog-byams-'byuṅ. He ('Brom) offered him the "Great Offering" (*'bul-chen*).

Then he was invited to Lan-pa by sKa-ba Śākya-dbaṅ-phyug.

It is said that in Tibet the Buddhist centres (of Atīśa) are Ke-ru of Maṅ-yul and Tsha-na of Byaṅ. The Rwa-sgreṅ *vihāra* of dBus also is the result of his influence.

About his works :

On general science, the *Cikitsā-jīva-sāra* and the *Vimala-sandeśa* [Note of the Text : Sent to Rājā Nemapāla] etc.

On *sādhāraṇa-yāna*, the *Daśa-akuśala-deśanā*, the *Karma-vibhaṅga*, etc.

On *sādhāraṇa-mahāyāna*, the *Mārga-dīpa* along with its *ṭīkā*, the *Madhyamaka-upadeśa*, etc. as *madhyamaka-śāstra.*

On *a-sādhāraṇa-(mahāyāna)*, the *Lokeśvara-sādhana*, the *Saṃvara-sādhana-ṭīkā* on Lui-pa's *vidhi*, etc.

Again, when he was staying at Yer-pa-lha-ri, in response to the request of Pha (Father 'Brom), Jo-bo wrote on *Manaḥ-abhyāsa-maṇimālā*, the *Pitṛ-dharma* (*pha-chos*) containing 26 chapters. At (the request of) Bu (son), Khu and rṄog, Jo-bo wrote the *Rasāyana-dāna-vyākhyāna*, having 22 chapters and the *pariśiṣṭa*, the total coming to 49 chapters.

These are mainly the works of Jo-bo and his disciples. Therefore, these are being respected by all the sects—the old bKa'-gdams-pa, the Sa-(skya) and the dGe-(lugs-pa), etc. But biographies by dKon-mchog-'baṅs, etc. express some doubt. And the *Chos-'byuṅ-brgya-rtsa* are written on Jo-bo's wish, though all of them are not his own work. But *Maṇimālā* (name of one of the hundred writings), etc. are his own works.

These works along with many other *upadeśa*-s, specially the *upadeśa* on the three *puruṣa*-s, which is like the junction of the three rivers, and on the *guhya-tantra* (were of great value) for Tibet. (It happened) as if the Buddha himself came to Tibet.

Specially, before Jo-bo's arrival in Tibet, some of the monks liked the *sbyor* and *grol* and the others said that the *grol* (*mokṣa*) could be obtained only by *śūnyatā-siddhānta*, but they abandoned the practices (*caryā*) and others followed only the *vinaya* without at all believing in the teachings and practice of *bodhicitta* and **[p.186]** the *guhya-tantra*. Still others claimed to be the followers of the *tantra* (*sṅags*) without believing in *pratimokṣa*. Thus religion in Tibet was either abandoned or became one-sided. At that time Jo-bo taught in his *Patha-pradīpa* that these paths were not in conflict with each other... These were meant to be practised by "the three types of persons" (*tri-puruṣa*-s). Thus, (said Jo-bo), "The *Ādibuddha-mahā-tantra* vigorously prohibits the *guhya-abhiṣeka* for one who has taken (the vow of) *brahmacaryā*."

In this way, for the ordinary *bhikṣu*, the practices of *guhya* and *jñāna abhiṣeka*-s are prohibited, though he should have respect for these.

Thus by implication he rejected all the older and coarser religions of Tibet. In this way, he removed all the false religions, wrong imaginations and doubts of the Tibetans, and established Buddhism in its original purity. He repaired what was already damaged and built the new. Thus he removed the dirt from the Doctrine here.

He saw the third year at mṄa'-ris, the fifth year at (dBus) and gTsaṅ and other places, the eighth year at sÑe-thaṅ. (His) total (stay in) Nepal and Tibet (was for) fifteen years. In Tibet itself, (his stay was for) thirteen years. At last (he) handed over (the charge of) Buddhism to 'Brom and at sÑe-thaṅ 'Or, on the 18th of the middle month of autumn, he departed for the Tuṣita to be reborn as Vimala-ākāśa. Gro-luṅ-pa and others said, "From human life he became a Buddha of the *bhadra-kalpa.*"

What is said above about the number of years he spent in Tibet is just according to the general account. But the *Mārga-krama* says that he was in mṄa'-ris for 3 years, in sÑe-thaṅ for 9 years, in dBus, gTsaṅ and other places, for 5 years,—which means 17 years (in all). This is said according to the *rNam-thar-chen-mo*, etc., which counted the first and the last years of the middle period twice and counted 2 years more for his travels between sÑe-thaṅ, dBus, and to other places. Thus it is a rough account.

Nag-tsho said, "I had been under him for 19 years." (Further), "(He said), in Vikramaśīla at the time of his departure for Tibet, 'I shall leave my mortal body after 18 years'." The *Lam-yig-gsaṅ-'khor-ma* says, "Born in India in the Fire-Male-Horse year [AD 946 !], till the age of 60, he protected India by the Doctrine." The *rNam-thar-yi-ge* says, "Jo-bo was born in the Iron-Horse year [AD 970 !] after 3047 years of the Buddha's *nirvāṇa* ; in the Fire-Tiger year [AD 1026 !] he left India for Tibet, in the Wood-Pig year [AD 1035 !] he was at bSam-yas, in the Fire-Hare year [AD 1027 or 1087] he reached sÑe-thaṅ, on the 18th day of dBo-zla of the Water-Horse year [AD 1042 or 1102 !], he passed away at sÑe-thaṅ."

Such calculations are very difficult. But most of the scholars agree that he was born in the Water-Horse year [AD 982]. So the Fire-Horse year [AD 946], as mentioned in the *Lam-yig*, seems to be a verbal error.

The following lo-tsā-ba-s translated many Buddhist works sitting at the feet of Jo-bo : Lo-chen and Lo-chuṅ Grags-'byor-śes-rab, Nag-tsho, Śākya-'od, Yol-lcags-rdo-rje-dbaṅ-phyug, dGe-blo and others.

Jo-bo's *rNam-thar-rgyas-pa*, like the *Lam-yig-chen-mo*, is not very reliable. Some of these (mistakes) are pointed out in the *rNam-thar-brgya-rtsa-brgyad*. But what is said in the *Mārga-krama* of rJe (Tsoṅ-kha-pa) is very good. Also, what is described in Nag-tsho lo-tsā-ba's *bsTod-pa-brgyad-cu-pa* and Gro-luṅ-pa's *bsTod-pa-sum-cu-pa* is mostly correct. Hence these are followed here.

Section 4

Extracts from *dGos-'dod-kun-'byuṅ* of Tāranātha. Tibetan Edition edited by Mongolian Lama Gurudeva, Tibetan Printing Press, Saranath, Benares 1964.

---

[224] Just after the six *dvāra-pāla*-s (Gate-keepers) Dīpaṃkara-śrī-jñāna, known as Jo-bo-rje dPal-ldan Atīśa, was invited as an *upādhyāya* (to Vikramaśīla). He also looked after Odantapurī...

King Bheyapāla's son was Neyapāla (Nayapāla). At the time of Jo-bo-rje's departure for Tibet, he (Nayapāla) was just placed in the kingdom (became king). It is said in the authentic biographies. A letter sent to him (Nayapāla) from Nepal (written by Dīpaṃkara) is also seen.

Section 5

The General History and Philosophy of the bKa'-gdams-pa sect

Translated from *Grub-mtha'-thams-cad-kyi-khuṅs-daṅ-'dod-tshul-ston-pa*—lit. "Explanation of the Origin and General View of all Schools," Etc. by

Thu-bkan-blo-bzaṅ Chos-kyi-ñi-ma
(Edited and printed by Chos-rje Lama. Saranath, Varanasi 1963).
About the author and the work, see S. C. Das, JASB Vol. 50, Part i, 1881, pp 187ff.

[p. 54]. The bKa'-gdams-pa sect is going to be discussed under three heads. First, how it had its origin in the kindness of *mahā* Jo-bo. Secondly, how the other sects are related to it. Thirdly, what in general are the doctrines of the bKa'-gdams-pa sect.

The previous teachers have explained the meaning of the word "bKa'-gdams" in various ways. rJe-rin-po-che (Tsoṅ-kha-pa) once asked sPyan-Iṅa-rin-chen-'phel, "What is the meaning of bKa'-gdams ?" sPyan-Iṅa replied, "It is called bKa'-gdams, because it conveys the preachings of the Buddha word for word, without omitting any word." He (Tson-kha-pa) was delighted and said, "That is (right). That is (right)". And he went to the monastery class and said, "The teacher Rin-chen-'phel has taught me a very important point about the Holy Religion. What he said is perfectly right. That is why Atīśa's preaching (gdams) is received by us in the brief form as *tri-puruṣa-mārga-krama.* Therefore it is bKa'-gdams-pa." And 'Brom said, "The wonderful words (bka') are the Tripiṭaka ; its *upadeśa* (gdams-pa) is decorated by (the doctrine of) *tri-puruṣa* ; even the mere turning of the gold-and-jewel rosary of the bKa'-gdams is inevitably efficacious."

Now about the origin of the specially excellent system of bKa'-gdams doctrine. It was initiated by Jo-bo-rje-dpal-ldan Atīśa (*prabhu śrīmat* Atīśa), expanded by sTon-pa-rin-po-che ('Brom) and widely spread by the three brothers. gLaṅ, Śar and Bya-yul-pa and others made it even more extensive.

The elaborate biography of Jo-bo-rje can be known from other sources. It will be mentioned here only briefly.

In the *Chos-'byuṅ-gsal-ba'i-sgron-me* it is said, "(Jo-bo was) born as the son of the king of *za-hor* in East (Eastern India). He became a complete master of the inner and outer (i.e. Buddhist and non-Buddhist) doctrines. With pure *tri-saṃvara*-s, he became *sthavira vinayadhara*. **[p. 55]** He studied the philosophies of the eighteen schools of the four fundamental sects (of Buddhism) separately without mixing and fully retained these in his mind. He was respected by all and accepted as an authority. He became the head of all the big monasteries of Magadha,—rNam-gnon-ṅaṅ-tshul (Vikramaśila), etc. He had visions of numerous tutelar deities and there was no Piṭaka unknown to him. He fully drank the necter of *bodhicitta* flowing from the *bhadra-kalaśa* of gSer-gliṅ (Suvarṇadvīpi Dharmakīrti). With his art of demonstrations and polemics he could madden the elephants of opposition and he satisfied the fortunate ones by true doctrine according to their own understanding. He was called the Bodhisattva of the Bhadrakalpa and he was appointed by Naro-pā as the head of the Doctrine. That was *śrī-yukta* Dīpaṃkara-śrī".

How Jo-bo-rje came to Tibet.

Thus : in the Land of Snow Buddhism had many ups and downs. The teachers, the students and the subjects taught—those three on which the Doctrine depends were corrupted by Hva-śaṅ (Ho-shang). (He was) defeated by Kamalaśila. Then were spread the *siddhānta* and *caryā*. The bad king gLaṅ Dar-ma destroyed (the Doctrine) and Tibet remained under darkness for about seventy years. Then bLa-chen-dgoṅs-pa-rab-gsal collected the remains of Buddhism from mDo (Amdo) and lower Khams and Lo-chen-rin-bzaṅ (Rin-chen-bzaṅ-po) fostered (the remains of the Doctrine recovered from) western Tibet (mṄa'-ris) and increased the *saṅgha-s* of dBus and gTsaṅ. But some of them (monks) followed Tantra and turned away from Vinaya, some others followed Vinaya and turned away from Tantra. In this way, the Doctrine was divided. Most of them had allegiance to the *siddhānta* only in words and the full understanding of the Doctrine was, of course, far away. Even the semblance of the Doctrine was very rare.

Specially during (after ?) the destruction of the Doctrine by gLaṅ Dar-ma, some of the Tāntrikas wrote whatever fragments of the Tantras remained in their memory, adding to these whatever occurred to their minds and claimed these to have been true Tantras, which omitted of course the essence of the Tantras. Some others wrote purely fanciful things and called these true Tantras. **[p. 56].** Some others said to their wives, "Prepare good wine for me; I am going to write a full treatise on Tantra today."

Then from India came one called the Red Ācārya, another with Blue Robe and others. And they taught the false doctrine in the name of sByor and sGrol. They said sByor (*yoga*) meant the union with women and sGrol (*mokṣa*) meant the killing of the living beings like the enemies. In this way, many false doctrines were spread in the name of Tantra. Because of all these there remained very few people with pure theory (*dṛṣṭi*) and practice (*caryā*). And most of the people followed the wrong religion.

Then Lha-bla-ma Ye-śes-'od, Pho-braṅ Shi-ba-'od and Lo-chen Rin-bzaṅ and others wrote many things refuting the errors of the false doctrines spread over the whole country. But these were not of much help. At that time Lha-bla-ma Ye-śes-'od, the king of mṄa-ris, could not bear to see such a condition of Buddhism in Tibet and wanted to invite a good *paṇḍita* from India who could be a real authority. The only way he could try this was to send rGya brTson-'grus-seṅ (Vīryasiṃha of rGya) with lots of gold to invite Atīśa. But (he) failed to invite. He (Ye-śes-'od) decided to collect more gold for the purpose of this invitation. He went to collect more gold and was captured by the king of Gar-Log and kept imprisoned. Byaṅ-chub-'od, the nephew (*dbon-po*) of Ye-śes-'od, collected lots of gold to get the release of his uncle (*khu-bo*). But (his uncle) did not agree and Ye-śes-'od was killed by the Gar-logs.

As his (i. e. of Ye-śes-'od) representative, Byaṅ-chub-'od sent Nag-tsho lo-tsā-ba Tshul-khrims-rgyal-ba with lots of gold to India to invite the *paṇḍita* from there. Nag-tsho and rGya-brtson-seṅ jointly explained to Atīśa the situation of Buddhism in Tibet and they told him what Ye-śes-'od suffered in the cause of inviting him. Though there were many predictions of Jo-bo's going to Tibet, that night Dīpaṃkara prayed to his tutelar deity Tārādevī again. She said that there was somewhere a *ḍākini* and he was to go and ask her. He did it and was told : "Yes, you will greatly help the Doctrine if you go to Tibet ; specially with the help of an *upāsaka* **[p.57]** you will spread the Docrine there."

He (Atīśa) realised how the lo-tsā-ba-s, both Lha-bla-ma, uncle and nephew, suffered in the cause of Buddhism, which had many ups and downs there, and he decided. There are so many things to say in this connection for understanding how one should suffer for the pure and rare religion. It is necessary to write everything for explaining the minute points. But I have to omit some of these to avoid the discussion being too elaborate.

What he did for Buddhism after reaching Tibet : The *Mahāmārga-krama*, while describing the greatness of Jo-bo-rje, said, "When (he) came to mṄa'-ris, he was requested to reform Buddhism ; in response to this he wrote the *śāstra Bodhi-patha-pradīpa,* which contains in brief the essence of the whole of *sūtra*-s and *tantra*-s and through which Buddhism was spread widely. Also, three years at mṄa'-ris, nine years at sÑe-thaṅ, five years at dBus and gTsaṅ and at other places he taught to the fortunate people the complete *upadeśa* of both *sūtra* and *tantra*. He salvaged the doctrine that was already sunk and nourished the fragments of it that were surviving. And he washed away the filth of distorted views and made the Doctrine pure." Thus it is said. To careful thought this reveals very deep and varied significances. After spending 17 years in Tibet, he attained *nirvāṇa* at the age of seventythree at sÑe-thaṅ in the Male-Water-Horse year on the 18th day of the month of dByu-gu [i.e. the 9th month of the Tibetan calander—D-TED 915] and went to Tuṣita near Maitreyanātha and became a Bodhisattva called Vimala-ākāśa.

Jo-bo-chen-po had many learned and spiritually accomplished disciples, both in India and Tibet. Among them, however, (the foremost was) 'Brom Rin-po-che rGyal-ba'i-'byuṅ-gnas, who received his *upadeśa* (directly) in the way in which something is poured from one pot to another, who was blessed as the head of the Doctrine (bKa'-gdams-pa) and as an incarnation of Ārya Avalokiteśvara, about whom Atīśa himself was foretold by his tutelar deity Tārādevī and who was described as *upāsaka dharma-vardhaka* in the **[p.58]** *Buddha-avataṃśaka* and *Karuṇā-puṇḍarīka sūtra*-s, who initiated the bKa'-gdams Doctrine which was later widely spread by the three brothers. All these, if mentioned in details, would make the (present) work voluminous. These can be learnt from the bKa'-gdams *chos-'byuṅ*-s. Here these are going to be stated only briefly.

As the *Chos-'byuṅ-gsal-ba'i-sgron-me* said, "For ten years dGe-bśes-ston-pa ('Brom) was the leader of the Saṅgha. He built Jo-bo's monastery Śrī Rwa-sgreṅ and collected many learned students and teachers. Then for about more than 20 years, by the influence of the Three Brothers, the sun of the Doctrine reached its zenith in dBu-ru and Byaṅ (central and northern Tibet) and the whole of Tibet was filled with light. *Mahā-ṛṣi* Po-to-ba had students with pure *dṛṣṭi* (theory) and *caryā* (practice) and their number sometimes reached up to 2,000. sPyan-lṅa-pa had collected about eight to nine hundred students. Phu-chuṅ-ba also had many (students) and (he) helped numberless in indirect ways. In the *Thun-brgyad-ma* of Kham is said that he had collected about 800 famous students. gLaṅ-thaṅ-Pa, the beloved disciple of the Three Brothers, had about 1,000 disciples and the great *kalyāṇamitra* Śar-ba-pa had about 3,000 notable disciples. *Kalyāṇamitra* Ya-gad-pa had about 1,000 and Bya-yul-pa 2,700 disciples. In general, there were numerous scholars and it was during this time that Buddhism was most widely spread."

The kings of mÑa'-ris, the uncle and nephew Lha-bla-ma, cared only for Buddhism and they never cared for their body, life and wealth. Under great risk they succeeded in inviting Jo-bo-rje Śrīmat Atiśa to Tibet, who made the false Tantra disappear and removed as darkness is removed by the rising sun the wrong *siddhānta* that *tantra* and *sūtra* were opposed like heat and cold. Even the much later descendants of bLa-chen (Ye-śes-'od), who held pure *dṛṣṭi* and *caryā*, were followers of Jo-bo. **[p. 59]** dBus and gTsaṅ were filled with eminent scholars of Buddhism, the followers of bKa'-gdams-pa of Jo-bo, and they were like the lotus, pure both inside and outside. Then the whole of dBus and gTsaṅ was full of monasteries of the bKa'-gdams-pa sect.

Even now some of these, like the Rwa-sgreṅ in the north and the sNar-thaṅ of gTsaṅ called the Mahā-bodhi-nirjana-sthāna etc., are existing. These are frequently mentioned in the works of the bKa'-gdams-pa-s. Among these, the Rwa-sgreṅ, which was built by the superior knowledge of 'Brom-rje-rgyal-ba'i-'byuṅ-gnas is the source of the bKa'-gdams river. The sNar-thaṅ was built by gTum-ston-blo-gros-grags-pa, the disciple of Śar-ba-pa. The succeeding head abbots of sNar-thaṅ come down as a chain of golden mountains.

Under the influence of time, the other monasteries of the bKa'-gdams-pa sect are now almost deserted. Some of these are even seen being occupied by the nuns. The bKa'-gdams-pa-s had great contempt for women. Once a woman, who was in fact a *ḍākinī*, came to a bKa'-gdams-pa monastery and was driven away by force. She said, "You dislike women now ; but your monasteries will some day be occupied by women."

Thus did she curse. That is why, it has happened like this. This is said by several authoritative persons.

Secondly, the sects known as bKa'-rgyud-pa, Sa-skya-pa and dGe-ldan-pa,—all came to being under the blessings of Jo-bo-rje.

The grand founder of the bKa'-rgyud-pa was Mes-po-lho-brag Mar-pa lo-tsā-ba, who, when he went to India for the second time, met Jo-bo-rje and received *upadeśa* from him. Specially, the incomparable Dwags-po-lha-rje received the *upadeśa* of the bKa'-gdams-pa from rGya-yon-bdag, a student of Jo-bo's personal disciple rNal-'byor-pa-chen-po. After that he received the *mahāmudrā* from rJe-btsun-mid-la. And he wrote the *Lam-rim-thar-rgyan* (*Mārga-karmānta-alaṃkāra*), which is like the confluence of the bKa' and the Phyag (i.e. of the bKa'-gdam-pa and the Mahāmudrā). His disciple Gro-mgon-phag-mo-gru-pa received the *upadeśa* of the bKa'-gdams-pa from dGe-bśes-dol-pa and wrote the *śāstra* called *bsTan-rim* (*Śāsana-krama*). 'Bri-guṅ-'jig-rten-mgon-po received it (the bKa'-gdams-pa *upadeśa*) from gLaṅ-luṅ-pa ; and sTag-luṅ-thaṅ-pa-chen-po received it from Chad-kha-pa ; [p, 60] Karma-dus-gsum-mkhyen-pa received it from rNal-'byor-pa-śes-rab-rdo-rje, a disciple of Śar-ba-pa. They preached the practical aspect (*caryā*) of the bKa'-gdams-pa doctrine.

Therefore, the *mahāmudrā* and the *Saṭ-dharma* contain the essence of the bKa'-rgyud-pa doctrine. The *upadeśa*-s of *bodhicitta*, all coming from the tradition of the bKa'-gdams religion, went to the making of the Mahāyāna religion (in Tibet), like yeast for wine.

Mañjughoṣa Sa-skya Paṇḍita ('Jam-dbyaṅs-sa-paṅ) received the bKa'-gdams-pa *upadeśa* from sPyi-bo-lhas-pa, a student of sNe'u-zur-pa. His works were mainly on the *sādhāraṇa* Mahāyāna of the bKa'-gdams-pa system. The later Sa-skya-pa-s also follow the same way.

The great rGyal-ba Tsoṅ-kha-pa was in fact (spiritually) the same as the incarnation of Jo-bo-rje. This is proved by reliable treatises. Only in the eyes of the common people he appeared to receive the *upadeśa* of *mārga-krama* (i.e. Jo-bo's

Bodhi-patha-pradīpa) of the bKa'-gdams-pa-s from *mahā-upādhyāya* Nam-mkha'-rgyal-mtshan (Ākāśadhvaja) and Chos-skyabs-bzań-po (Dharma-śaraṇa-bhadra). He removed the dirt of doubt and distortions and whatever other changes occurred in Jo-bo's *upadeśa* in the course of time. And he wrote the incomparably well-said *śāstra Lam-rim* (*Mārga-krama*), both the elaborate (*chen*) and the condensed (*chuń*) one, and other works. Thus, according to the bKa'-gdams-pa histories, the Ri-bo-dge-ldan-pa (dGe-lugs-pa) system is fully based on the bKa'-gdams-pa doctrines, only with the slight addition in appearance of the Mādhyamika *siddhānta*-s and the *guhya-tantra*-s. So it is nothing but the bKa'-gdams-pa doctrine. Some of the Chos-'byuńs even call the dGe-ldan-pa as but the new bKa'-gdams-pa. Now about the bKa'-gdams-pa *śāstra*-s. Among the bKa'-gdams-pa *śāstra*-s, Pha-chos (*pitṛ-dharma*) contains 26 chapters, one of which foretells the furure : "The place where Kīrtināma (Sumatikīrti or Tsoń-kha-pa) will at last nourish the survivals of the Doctrine will be the best place and it will be helpful for many." Also, lo-tsā-ba said, "The name of a branch often stands for the trunk of the tree." The implications of this are two-fold. First, the dGa'-ldan monastery (is like branch which stands for its founder) rJe-bla-ma (Tsoń-kha-pa). Secondly, the **[p. 61]** bKa'-gdams-pa is like the main trunk, while the bKa'-gdams-gsar-pa (i.e. new bKa'-gdams-pa or the dGe-ldan-pa, i.e. the dGe-lugs-pa) and the dGa'-ldan-pa (i.e. the monks of the dGa'-ldan monastery) are like its branch. Again, Zul-phu-ba compiled a great biography of Jo-bo and received the bKa'-gdams-pa *upadeśa* from sTod-luń-pa. His (Zul-phu-ba's) disciples succeeding one another were all good *vinayadhara*-s and without exception the followers of the bKa'-gdams-pa.

Not merely this. Even the line of the teachings of the *lakṣaṇa-śāstra*-s, too, comes from Jo-bo's kindness. If asked "Why ?", (the answer is) : Here in Tibet the Madhyamaka, the Pramāṇa-s and the Prajñāpāramitā,—all these are taught by rŇog Lo-chen-po (the great lo-tsā-ba of rŇog or Legs-pa'i-śes-rab), his disciples and the disciples of their disciples. And rṄog lo-tsā-ba Legs-pai-śes-rab was not only a personal disciple of Jo-bo-chen-po but moreover he alone was the son to have received at Yer-pa-lha-ri the secret teachings of the bKa'-gdams-pa *śāstra*-s. Jo-bo once foretold that he (rṄog) was to build a great monastery called gSaṅ-phu and he (rṄog) did build it. His (rṄog's) both disciple and nephew bLo-ldan-śes-rab received Jo-bo's teachings from his uncle. And he helped to maintain the continuation of the spread of the Doctrine. His disciples : bLo-gros-'byuṅ-gnas of Gro-luṅ, the profoundly learned scholar of the whole *śāstra*-s ; 'Bre-chen-po-śes-rab-'bar, the specialist in Prajñāpāramitā ; Gaṅs-pa-śe'u, the specialist in Pramāṇa ; Khyuṅ Rin-chen-grags, the specialist in Madhyamaka ; Shaṅ, Tsho, sPoṅ, etc. etc., were all great authorities. Gro-luṅ-pa was from his boyhood a student of both Jo-bo-rje and 'Brom and he learnt the bKa'-gdams-pa doctrine. He wrote an exposition of the smaller writings of Jo-bo, called Chos-chuṅ-brgya-rtsa (literally, One Hundred Writings) and the bsTan-rim, both elaborate (*che*) and brief (*chuṅ*) and the Don-khyogs-chuṅ-ba'i. The former (bsTan-rim-che) contains the whole essence of the *Bodhi-patha-pradīpa* and this has no equal. That is why, rGyal-ba Tsoṅ-kha-pa read it and received it with great respect. He modelled his *Mahā-mārga-krama* on it. The disciples of Gro-luṅ-pa : 'Bre , Gaṅs-pa ; Khyuṅ ; Shaṅ and others. Their learned students came like the sky covering the world (i.e. came in great numbers and filled the world) and the tradition of their teachings and writings is still existing.

To put it briefly, as 'Gos-lo-gshon-nu-dpal says in the *Deb-sṅon*, "In the life-stories [p. 62] of the *kalyāṇa-mitra*-s who had appeared in Tibet in later times, and of the *yogin*-s who had been Saints, statements are found that they had met the *kalyāṇa-mitra*-s of the bKa'-gdams-pa-s. 'Brom's labours have been very extensive and lasted for a long period of time. Above I have briefly described the results of the settings into motion of the Wheel of Law by Dīpaṃkara-śrī-jñāna." So one should know that whatever happened to the pure Doctrine and *siddhānta* in the Land of Snow is the result of Jo-bo-chen-po's arrival and teachings in Tibet. Thirdly, two things in particular need to be discussed about the bKa'-gdams-pa-s. These are their works and their personal character. About the first, 'Brom said, "My *guru* says that every religion is drawn by the square-way (? *gru-bshi-lam*)." rNal-'byor-pa-chen-po (Mahāyogī) says about *upadeśa*, "One who merely quotes from the Be'u-bum does not possess the real *upadeśa* ; one should have a complete understanding of *śāstra*-s as the *upadeśa*." sGom-pa-rin-chen-bla-ma says, "To know that Vinaya goes with Tantra and Tantra goes with Vinaya is the essence of the traditional sayings of my *guru* (Jo-bo)." In general, the differentia of the bKa'-gdams consists in viewing at the totality of the words of the Buddha, without rejecting or accepting any part of it, as the cause leading every living being to Buddhahood. That is why, there is no *dharma* which is not contained in the (teachings of the) bKa'-gdams. However, in the common understanding, (the bKa'-gdams have) two, viz. *śāstra* and *upadeśa*, or, if gDams-nag and Man-ṅag are treated separately (they have) three. As for their *śāstra*-s, some are mainly on *siddhānta*, some mainly on *caryā* and some jointly on the two. Jo-bo's *Satya-dvaya-avatāra* and *Mādhyamika-upadeśa*, etc. are of the first type. The examples of the second type are *Caryā-saṃgraha-pradīpa* and *Citta-utpāda-saṃvara-vidhi*, etc. The (example of the) third (type) is the *Bodhi-patha-pradīpa*, which contains the essence of the Tripiṭaka of the Buddha and the Four forms of Tantra, along with their commentaries without overlooking even a single word. It shows every man the successive stages of spiritual practice and is wonderfully well-written.

rJe-bla-ma (Tsoṅ-kha-pa), in his *Bodhi-mārga-krama*, said, "Though there are many *śāstra*-s composed by Jo-bo, **[p. 63]** yet the most complete and fundamental of all these is the (*Bodhi*)-*patha-pradīpa*. It contains the essence of both *sūtra* and *tantra*. So it is all-comprehensive in character. By placing the main emphasis on the process of controlling the mind it has become very important from the practical point of view and (it is) also very easy. It is (also) decorated by the teachings of the two great exponents of Mahāyāna. So it is more important than all other (*śāstra*-s)."

The following are known as the Six Basic Śāstras-s of the bKa'-gdams-pa : Bhūmi, Alaṃkāra, Śikṣā, Caryā, Jātaka and Udāna. Among these, Śikṣā and Caryā expound the *darśana* and *caryā* jointly. The others mainly show the character of the *bodhisattva* (*bodhisattva-caryā*). And the works known as Jo-bo's Chos-chuṅ-brgya-rtsa ("The Hundred Items") are also bKa'-gdams-pa *śāstra*-s. The *Mūla-prajñā*, *Śūnyatā-saptati* and *Ratnamālā* are also so. The *upadeśa*-s that are mainly philosophical are (as follows) : Jo-bo's *upadeśa* coming through sPyan-lṅa-ba as "The Explanation of the Four Truths" (bDen-bshi'i-khrid) ; (Jo-bo's *upadeśa* coming through) Phu-chuṅ-ba as "The Explanation of the Pratītya-samutpāda" (rTen-'Brel-Gyi-'Khrid : Pratītya-samutpāda-vyākhyāna) and (Jo-bo's *upadeśa* coming through) Yogī as "The explanation of the Two-fold Truth" (bDen-pa-gñis-kyi-'khrid). By the explanation of the four truths and *pratītya-samutpāda* are shown the *sādhāraṇa pudgala-nairātmya* (gaṅ-zag-gi-bdag-med) and by the explanation of the two-fold truth very minute *dharma-nairātmya* (chos-kyi-dag-med) (are shown). Among Jo-bo's students the Mahā-yogī was the foremost exponent of *satya-dvaya* (the two-fold truth) and he taught both Gro-luṅ-pa and sPyan-lṅa-ba. Again, sPyan-lṅa-ba taught the secret religion to sTod-luṅ-pa and Bya-yul-pa. sTod-luṅ-pa wrote many things on *Guhya-dharma* (*lkog-chos*), *Saṅgha-dharma* (*tshogs-chos*) and also on *Racanā-dharma* (*brtsams-chos*). The students Khyuṅ-khams also wrote many things which were widely spread. Saṅs-rgyas-dpon, too, wrote many documents both brief and elaborate. 'Chad-kha-pa wrote on the *siddhānta-śāstra*, commented on by Lha-luṅ-dbaṅ-phyug, containing elaborate discussions on the Buddhist and non-Buddhist doctrines.

Jo-bo-chen-po himself held the theory (*dṛṣṭi*) of the Mādhyamika-Prāsaṅgika-s (dBu-ma-thal-'gyur-pa) and could explain to the bKa'-gdams-pa-s all that Nāgārjuna said in the Mahā-mādhyamika works. And it is proved by *Bodhi-patha-*

pradīpa-mūla-ṭīkā and [p. 64] the *Madhyamaka-upadeśa-mūla-ṭīkā*. 'Brom once asked Jo-bo about the *siddhānta* of Candrakīrti. He (Jo-bo) was much pleased, folded his hands and said, "That is wonderful. In eastern India we now follow this philosophy."

While explaining the doctrine of graduated path to Master Po-to-ba and the Three Brothers, he showed his philosophical conclusion just like those of Madhyamaka philosophy of Candrakīrti. Both the teacher and student rŇog-lo (i.e. Legs-pa'i-śes-rab and bLo-ldan-śes-rab) often referred to the *śāstra*-s of Bhavya and Candra (Candrakīrti) as authority, but they themselves subscribed mainly to the doctrines of Śāntarakṣita (Sāntijīva) and his disciples. Some theories of mental purification (bLo-sbyoṅ), which come down from gSer-gliṅ-pa (Dharmakīrti of Suvarṇadvīpa) agree mainly with the rŇan-brdsun-pa sect of the Yogâcāra school. But even then the later bKa'-gdams-pa-s were mostly unable to explain these Indian *śāstra*-s. This is said by my *guru* Sarvajña (Thams-cad-mkhyen-pa). The *caryā-pradhāna-upadeśa*-s are the *upadeśa*-s of *mahāyāna-citta-śodhana* and these *caryā*-s are to love others more than one's self, to increase the *bodhicitta* which is already generated and to produce the *bodhicitta* yet to be generated...

[p. 71]... There are many wonderful works. If I try to mention all these the (present) work would be voluminous. One wanting to know these extensively should consult the *Chos-'byuṅ-gsal-sgron*...

Section 6

A New Biography of Atīśa compiled in Tibetan from the Tibetan sources by
Nagwang Nima.
Revised, edited and condensed by Lama Chimpa.

AUTHOR'S PREFACE

This work was originally started by my friend Lama Chimpa of the Visvabharati University. He intended it to be a short article on the life of Dīpaṃkara Śrījñāna. After working it out, however, he thought that it was a better idea to develop it into a comparatively bigger biography of the great *ācārya*. Accordingly, he requested me to take up the work, which I was very happy to do.

For the purpose of working on the present biography, I had to re-examine and re-read the relevant Tibetan sources, among which the following are in need of special mention : the *chos-'byuṅ*-s by Pan-chen-ye-śes-rtse-mo, bSod-nam-grags-pa, Las-chen-kun-rgyal (called the *Chos-'byuṅ-gsal-ba'i-sgron-me*) and the *bKa'-gdams-chos-'byuṅ*. Apart from the *chos-'byuṅ*-s, I have particularly relied on the following : the *bsTod-pa-brgyad-cu* by lo-tsā-ba Nag-tsho Tshul-khrims-rgyal-ba or Jayaśīla, who was for nineteen years a student of Dīpaṃkara, the *Jo-bo-rje'i rNam-thar-rgyas-pa* by 'Brom-ston-pa, who was the direct successor of Dīpaṃkara in Tibet, and the *Jo-bo-rje'i rNam-thar* by Ye-śes-rgya-mtsho, who was a student of the Fifth Dalai Lama. Of these works, the last appears to me to be most authentic and I have generally depended on it in cases of there being conflicting accounts about some incident in Dīpaṃkara's life or about some cf his activities.

Apart from the vast body of written literature on the life of Dīpaṃkara, Tibet has a rich oral tradition about the Master. I have incorporated some of these into the present biography.

I hope that this biography, though brief, will be of some use to the historians of India and Tibet.[1]

—*Nagwang Nima*

1. This preface is prepared on the basis of a personal letter of Reverend Nagwang Nima to Professor Lama Chimpa.

1. *Benedictory Verses*

We bow down to all the Tathāgatas of the ten directions and three times (past, present and future), the honoured sources of body, speech and mind, of all the 84,000 *dharmaskandha*-s and of all the kind teachers and traditional lords. May we be led by them through the cycle of births.

2. *The Early Kings*

The Vinaya declares that the king is the noblest of all, just as the words of the Lord Buddha are the noblest of all words of all the worlds including the world of the gods, or, as the ocean is greatest of all the waters, the moon is brightest in the night sky and the sun most prominent of all the luminaries.

Accordingly, we begin with some account of the kings of India and Tibet from the earliest times.

The first king of the world was Mahāsammata. It is generally believed that between him and Śuddhodana, our Buddha's father, there were 155,149 kings. But there are other opinions expressed on this point. According to Sa-skya rJe-btsun-grags-pa-rgyal-mtshan,[1] the number of these intervening kings is 1,074,548. In his *Deb-ther-sṅon-po* (*The Blue Annals*), 'Gos lo-tsā-ba says that this number is 1, 121, 514; the *Vaidūrya-dkar-po*,[2] however, declares the number to be 937,500.

3. *Our Buddha, the Incomparable King of the Śākyas*

Our aeon is known as the *sahasra-bhadra-kalpa*.[3] In this aeon, man's life-span was once 80,000 years. In the next age of this aeon, when Krakucchanda appeared as the Buddha, man lived for 40,000 years. In the next age when Kanakamuni appeared as the Buddha, man's life-span was 30,000 years. The Buddha of the next age was Kāśyapa and in this age man lived for 20,000 years. In the present age of the *sahasra-bhadra-kalpa*, of which the Buddha is Śākyamuni, man's life-span came down to 100 years. His father, Śuddhodana, had three other

1. Born in A.D. 1147. See BA i. 306.
2. A historical and chronological work of great repute, composed in the 17th century. See S. C. Das in JASB, 1881. 195n.
3. Bu-ston i. 90f ; S. C. Das in JBTS 1895. 13ff; ERE i. 187f ; Sum-pa 14f.

brothers, called Sita-odana, Droṇa-odana and Amṛta-odana. Sita-odana, the eldest brother, had two sons, called Jina and Bhadra, and a daughter called Sītā. Droṇa-odana had two sons, called Śākya-nāma and Ārya-odana, and a daughter called Droṇā. Amṛta-odana had two sons, called Ānanda and Devadatta, and a daughter called Amṛtā. Śuddhodana married the two daughters of Śākya-suprabuddha, the king of Devadarśita. The elder queen Mahāprajāvatī gave birth to the *śrāvaka* Śubhānanda. From the left arm-pit of the younger queen Māyādevī was born our Buddha, the Incomparable King of the Śākyas. At the time of his birth were also born 500 horses, 500 elephants and 500 children of the Śākyas and the king's treasure increased 500 times.[4] Four great sons of four other kings were also born at that time. They were Bimbisāra of Magadha, Prasenajit of Kośala, Pracaṇḍaprabha of Ujjayinī and Udayana of Kauśāmbī.

4. *The First King of Tibet*

At the time of the birth of the fifth descendant of Udayana's grandson there occurred a terrible evil omen, the like of which never occurred before. Hence the baby was put into a box and thrown into the river. On the bank of the river some Indian farmers found the box. They opened it and saw the baby inside. The baby was reared up by them. On growing into a young man he came to know all about these. He felt bitter and left the country. After wandering for several years he reached a small hill in a place called rTse-thaṅ in Tibet. The local cowherds found him there and, drawn by his extraordinary beauty, people started collecting round him. They prepared a neck-chair (*gña'-khri*), placed him on it and carried it on their shoulders. There was none to equal him and he was honoured as the king. This was the first king of Tibet and his Tibetan name was gÑa'-khri-btsan-po, literally, "the Neck-chaired Mighty One." The religion then most wide-spread in Tibet was Bon. In accordance with this religious belief, there grew all sorts of wild rumours about this king falling from heaven.

4. cf. Bu-ston ii. 12.

But the fact is as just narrated. The first Dalai Lama is believed to have been the 38th incarnation of this first king, who is considered to be Avalokiteśvara himself. This is mentioned in the well-known Chronicle of the Fifth Dalai Lama.

5. *The Beginning of Literary Tradition in Tibet*

There was a long succession of kings between gÑa'-khri-btsan-po and Lha-tho-tho-ri-gñan-btsan, during whose reign the first religious materials came to Tibet. These were in the form of a golden *caitya* and the *śāstra*-s entitled the *Kāraṇḍa-vyūha-sūtra* and the *100 Precepts Concerning Worship.* But at that time none in Tibet could read. The *śāstra*-s were carefully preserved. The fifth descendant of Lha-tho-tho-ri-gñan-btsan was king Sroṅ-btsan-sgam-po, under whose great patronage Tibet was to receive the first initiation in the literary tradition. He sent Thon-mi Sambhoṭa and a party to India for the purpose of learning the Indian language. They learnt the Indian language and the Indian script under Devavidyāsiṃha and a Brāhmaṇa called Lipidatta. He also acquired the knowledge of grammar and literature and became profoundly learned. Thon-mi devised suitable scripts for the Tibetan language. These were modelled on the Indian scripts known as Lan-tsha and Vartula. Eight Tibetan grammars, modelled on Indian grammar, were also prepared by him. Further, the *Ratnamegha-sūtra* was translated into the Tibetan language. He presented all these to the king.

6. *The Early Monasteries in Tibet*

When Thon-mi returned to Tibet, the king was residing in the Śilāprāsāda (Pho-braṅ-pha-boṅ-kha, literally—The Stone Palace). The palace owed its name to the circumstance of being built on a huge rock. The materials of new learning were preserved in a place called the Golden Cave (gSer phug). The rumour is that the Tibetans once quarried gold in this cave and hence it was thus called. In this cave were also placed the images of Avalokiteśvara, Mañjughoṣa and Vajrapāṇi. Thus the cave became the first religious centre of Tibet. In this cave were translated twenty-one Sūtra and Tantra works.

From then on, Buddhism gradually gained grouud in Tibet. Under the king's initiative the Tibetans next built thirteen monasteries, including the famous shrines of Lhasa. In these shrines were placed the various images of gods and goddesses, including those of Akṣobhyavajra and of Śākyamuni. Of these two images, one was brought from Nepal by the Nepalese princess and the other from China by the Chinese princess. Both the princesses were married to king Sroṅ-btsan-sgam-po and both were devout Buddhists. They helped the rapid spread of Buddhism in Tibet.

7. *Ma-shaṅ's Hostility*

After more than a hundred years Khri-sroṅ-lde-btsaṅ became the king. When he was very young, Tibet was virtually under the rule of the minister Ma-shaṅ. This minister was intensely hostile to Buddhism. He wanted to destroy even the two famous images of Akṣobhyavajra and Śākyamuni. But he was prevented from doing this because of the influence of others. Instead of destroying these, he got these buried under the earth, converted the shrine of Lhasa into a butcher's shop and murdered many influential Buddhists. On growing up, the young king realised how gravely wrong all these had been. He was himself in favour of Buddhism and worked for the re-establishment of the Doctrine in Tibet. With this purpose he invited the famous Indian *ācārya* Śāntarakṣita to Tibet.

8. *Śāntarakṣita and Padmasambhava in Tibet*

Śāntarakṣita came to Tibet and started preaching the Doctrine. This enraged the local demons. They caused a terrible thunder to strike the Red Rock and got the temple of 'Phaṅ washed away by flood and a devastating famine to visit Tibet. Those of the ministers that were already opposed to Buddhism urged that the Indian *ācārya* was to be sent away. The king told everything to Śāntarakṣita. Instead of being angry, the *ācārya* simply said, "Your local demons are so angry because they know that they cannot survive the spread of Buddhism. However, I will bring *ācārya* Padmasambhava, who is now in

Nepal and who, with his great magical power, will easily subdue them all." The king agreed to this and requested some of his trusted ministers to accompany Śāntarakṣita to Nepal. Because of his supernatural knowledge (*abhijñāna*), Padmasambhava came to know that Śāntarakṣita and his party were on their way to Nepal with the purpose of inviting him to Tibet. Instead of waiting for them to reach Nepal, Padmasambhava came down to Maṅ-yul to meet them and accompanied them back to Tibet. With his magical power, he subdued all the local demons of Tibet. This helped the reassertion of Buddhism in Tibet and the bSam-yas monastery was built. Śāntarakṣita delivered many sermons to the Tibetans and their king. He wrote books on Buddhism and conferred the *bhikṣu*-initiation on seven monks in accordance with the Sarvāstivāda system. After this, many Indian *ācārya*-s came to Tibet and many Tibetan lo-tsā-ba-s sat under the Indian *paṇḍita*-s like Vimalamitra, Buddhaguhya, Viśuddhisiṃha and others for the translation of many *sūtra*-s and *tantra*-s into Tibetan.

9. gLaṅ Dar-ma and the persecution of Buddhism

Tibet witnessed the most terrible persecution of the Doctrine after king gLaṅ Dar-ma came to power. By his men was murdered the Buddhist king Ral-pa-can (Jaṭānika). They also killed many lo-tsā-ba-s and *paṇḍita*-s, ransacked all the monasteries and shrines, forced the monks to renounce Buddhism and threw into the river all the Buddhist *śāstra*-s they could manage to get. Because of this terrible persecution, Buddhism was virtually wiped out in Tibet. Only the two famous images of Śākyamuni, being hidden underground by some of the ministers, survived his ravages. The king arrested these ministers and asked for the information of these images. But they refused to part with any. Accordingly, some of them were sentenced to death, others to life-imprisonment. The king also employed many artists to paint on the walls of bSam-yas monastery and the Lhasa shrine the caricature of the Buddhist *bhikṣu*-s indulging in wine and women. These being exhibited to the public helped to destroy their veneration.

10. *"The Second Beginning" of the Doctrine*

This terrible persecution of Buddhism went on for some time, after which a person called Lha-luṅ dPal-rdo-rje killed the devilish king gLaṅ Dar-ma with an iron arrow. After the death of gLaṅ Dar-ma, the king 'Od-sruṅs and his son dPal-'khor-btsan devoted themselves to the cause of rebuilding Buddhism in Tibet and tried to get the tradition of *bhikṣu-dīkṣā* reintroduced. With this purpose in view, real *bhikṣu*-s in Tibet were searched for. By this time, however, the whole of Tibet was left with only a few *bhikṣu*-s who escaped the persecution. By them, under very difficult conditions, was eventually reintroduced the system of *bhikṣu-dīkṣā*. Thus began "the second beginning" of Buddhism in Tibet.

11. *The Great Teacher Dīpaṃkara Śrījñāna*

There had thus been many ups and downs in the history of Buddhism in Tibet. Many Indian teachers were invited to teach there. Among them the contributions of Dīpaṃkara Śrījñāna, also called Jo-bo-rje (literally, *prabhu*) Śrī Atīśa, were the most outstanding. The Tibetans are most grateful to him because of the purity of the doctrine he preached. As the *guru* Tsoṅ-kha-pa (Sumatikīrti), in his *Bodhi-mārga-krama*, said, "The teaching of Maitreyanātha's Prajñāpāramitā was gift of Dīpaṃkara to us ; these teachings he explained in his *Bodhi-patha-pradīpa.*" Under Dīpaṃkara's influence Buddhism in Tibet flourished more and more. This was the result of his great piety. "Every act of mine", as he himself once said, "follows *dharma*. It is because of this that I never face any great odd. I am never in want, because I can offer everything to others and to the gods. You should also practise the same thing. Practise it at least occasionally. Listen. Do not do anything for your own sake. Do not keep with yourself even the *puṇya* that you will thus accumulate. Deposit it in the treasury of the gods." Dīpaṃkara having been so exceedingly noble and kind to us, it will be an act of piety on our part to try to remember him and some of his deeds—however humble may be our own effort. But let us try to remember his *guru* first.

12. Suvarṇadvīpī, the Great Guru of Dīpaṃkara

Dīpaṃkara had many *guru*-s from whom he received wisdom in various forms. Among them, he was specially indebted to gSer-gliṅ-pa (i.e. Suvarṇadvīpī), because it was from him that he received the *upadeśa* of *bodhicitta*. This *guru* is generally known as Suvarṇadvīpī, because he was the son of the king of Suvarṇadvīpa. His real name, however, was Dharmakīrti. In Suvarṇadvīpa, only few were Buddhists, others hostile to Buddhism. The latter did not like him, but they could do no harm to the prince after all. Since his early childhood, Dharmakīrti became a devotee of the Buddha. When he was only seven, he came across, while wandering in a forest, an image of the Buddha about six inches high. He began to worship the image and, as he grew up, his devotion to the Buddha grew too. So his father sent him to India to learn the Buddhist doctrines. He learnt all the *śāstra*-s and became a world-famous scholar. He then went back to Suvarṇadvīpa and preached the Doctrine. To the other *guru*-s of Dīpaṃkara we shall presently return.

13. Greatness of Dīpaṃkara

About Dīpaṃkara's greatness, three things in particular are in need of being specially remembered. First, though born in the royal family he renounced the world and became a *bhikṣu* to follow the path of the Buddha. Secondly, he acquired all the wisdom during his lifetime. Thirdly, after acquiring this wisdom, he employed it wholly to the cause of the living beings.

14. Birth of The Master

In Vikramapura of Gauḍa (Bengal), there was a very powerful king called Kalyāṇaśrī. He was as wealthy as Kuvera himself. His palace was called "The Palace of Nine Hundred and Ninety-nine Golden Flags", because these were flying on top of it. His chief queen Śrīmati Prabhāvatī gave him three sons, called Padmagarbha, Candragarbha and Śrīgarbha. Dīpaṃkara was none but the second son Candragarbha. He was born in the Water-Male-Horse year (A.D. 982). When the new-born baby was lying in a top-floor room of the palace, there came from outside the loud sound of music and of the beating of the drum. The king looked out and wondered. The queen saw that something resembling a freshly bloomed lotus was falling in front of the baby and the baby's face looked like that of Tārādevī. Accordingly, it was believed that Tārādevī was his tutelar deity and her favour followed him through the cycle of his births. He was reared up with special care. On growing up, however, he realised how full of evils the world was. So he renounced the kingdom in the way in which one only spits and took to the yellow robe.

15. *Extraordinary Beauty*

The accumulated *puṇya* resulting from his practice of universal compassion (*karuṇā*) and forgiveness (*kṣamā*) during his previous births gave him the most extraordinary physical charm. A mere look at him was enough to inspire in people a reverence for and a confidence in him. As lo-tsā-ba Nag-tsho Tshul-khrims-rgyal-ba (Jayaśīla) said in the *stotra* to Dīpaṃkara : "You look so beautiful, soft and bright. The moment one looks at you one is filled with a belief in and love for you. Any eye, ever set on you, being dissatisfied with everything else, is lost for ever." Dīpaṃkara was never ill, for he harmed no one. As the same lo-tsā-ba said in the *stotra*: "You are never ill, for you have renounced violence. Your accumulated *puṇya* makes you look so charming and so confidence-inspiring." Dīpaṃkara himself once said, "I was loved by all my teachers even because of my mere look."

16. *Early Education*

Up to the age of ten, Dīpaṃkara learnt reading and writing, the healing art and the fine arts. By the age of ten he completed all these. When he was only fifteen, he finished studying the whole of the *Nyāya-bindu* and could defeat in philosophical debate even the foremost non-Buddhist logicians of his time.

By the age of twenty-one, he acquired complete mastery over all the 64 arts and over grammar and logic of both the Buddhists and non-Buddhists. His fame was widespread already in his early youth.

17. How he Defeated the Tīrthikas

Before the days of Dīpaṃkara, the Buddhists in Bengal were often defeated by the *tīrthika*-s and had to embrace their faith. Under Dīpaṃkara's influence, things changed. The *tīrthika*-s, defeated by the Buddhists, had to embrace Buddhism and the Buddhists that were formerly converted by the *tīrthika*-s came back to the Buddhist faith. Here are some incidents showing how Dīpaṃkara defeated the *tīrthika*-s. The daughter of a *tīrthika* once fell in love with Dīpaṃkara. With the hope of winning him over, she went on telling her father, "Why do you not convert the *bhikṣu* into the *tīrthika*-way ?" So the father challenged Dīpaṃkara and asked for a philosophical debate. But he was easily defeated by Dīpaṃkara and had to embrace Buddhism. A *tīrthika paṇḍita* from South India—one with five umbrellas—once challenged Dīpaṃkara saying, "You are considered to be the foremost *paṇḍita* among the Buddhists while I happen to be the foremost one among the non-Buddhists. Let us have a debate. One who gets defeated will have to be the follower of the other." The debate started with the king of Magadha as the judge. After a little while, however, the *tīrthika* scholar was fully vanquished and had to fall on Dīpaṃkara's feet. With the group of his own students, he embraced Buddhism and became Dīpaṃkara's follower. On hearing this, another *tīrthika guru*—one with eight umbrellas—challenged Dīpaṃkara. But he also was easily defeated and had to embrace Buddhism. After this, another *tīrthika*—one with thirteen umbrellas and highly renowned as an expert in the *pramāṇa-śāstra*—challenged Dīpaṃkara and asked for a debate. It was organised with great pomp and grandeur. A large number of scholars gathered to listen to the debate and special seats of honour were allotted to them. As the debate progressed, its subject became increasingly abstruse, leaving few and fewer scholars with the ability to follow it. At one stage, only fifteen scholars could understand what the two were arguing about. Still later their number dwindled to five and eventually only the two participants knew the point of their debate. At this stage the *tīrthika paṇḍita* put forth his final question, which baffled Dīpaṃkara for a moment. He meditated on Tārādevī, under whose grace the answer came to him immediately. With this answer, the *tīrthika* was fully vanquished. Along with his students, he had to become Dīpaṃkara's follower. All these were told by Kṛṣṇa *paṇḍita* to lo-tsā-ba Jayaśīla.

18. Tāntrika Initiation

At the age of twenty-two, Dīpaṃkara sat in meditation in the temple of the Black Mountain and had the direct vision of Hevajra. After this he met his *guru* Rāhulagupta, who initiated him in the *vajra-ḍākinī-tantra.* His name was accordingly changed into Jñāna-guhya-vajra. He had again a vision of Hevajra and this meant the fulfilment of his meditations. He next met many teachers of Vajrayāna and learnt from them a great deal about the Vajra Tantra, both its scriptural literature and esoteric rituals. At this stage, he met in the dream the famous *paṇḍita* Vagīśvarakīrti and received from him one lac four hundred and fifty-one *tantra*-s. This made him feel : "I have understood the Vajra Tantra fully and I am the only one to do it." The same night, however, he had another dream in which many *ḍākinī*-s brought before him many *śāstra*-s of the Tantra, about the existence of which he had no previous knowledge whatsoever. This dispelled the vanity that took possession of him for the moment.

19. The Incident of the Vajraḍākinī

In Vikramapura, he once met a nude woman wearing a necklace of bones and skulls. She herself looked like a skeleton, laughing at one moment and weeping at the next. Dīpaṃkara thought that this was quite strange and he felt that she had perhaps some esoteric instructions to impart. So he mentally bowed down to her and asked if he could receive any *upadeśa* from her. "If you care for the *upadeśa* you will have to go to eastern Bengal," she said and went away. Dīpaṃkara followed her until she reached a *mahā-śmaśāna*. There she suddenly turned back and asked Dīpaṃkara, "How did you guess that I had some special *upadeśa* to impart ? Do I look like having any ?" "Yes", replied Dīpaṃkara, "you certainly do." Pleased with him, she got him initiated into the *adhiṣṭhāna vidhi*. Though brief, this was profound in spiritual significance. Immediately after this, he looked at her, and lo, there was a beautiful Vajraḍākinī before him ! She made him feel that his body was that of a male deity ready to be united with that of a female deity and thereby obtain the unique esoteric bliss (*atulya-guhya-samādhi*). For several years more, Dīpaṃkara received instructions in the *tantra*-s from *guru* Avadhūti-pā. During these years he practised the *vrata*-s and learnt the songs of the *ḍākinī*-s.

20. *The Ordination*

After all these, he was told by his tutelar deity Tārādevī as well as by his *guru* Rāhulagupta that it was time for him to work for the living beings and this according to the *pravrajyā* rules. He had also a dream' in which Hevajra told him, "Oh, thou noble-born one, move no further along the path of the Avadhūti-caryā. Thousands await your following when you take the *pravrajyā* ordination." In another dream, he saw Śākyamuni, along with his *saṅgha*, was proceeding to have the midday meal. Dīpaṃkara saw himself among the monks. Śākyamuni looked at him and said, "Why does not this person go in for the *pravrajyā* ordination ?" All these led him to decide in favour of the *bhikṣu-dīkṣā*. At the age of 29 he received the ordination under Śīlarakṣita the Mahāsāṅghika. With this initiation, he received the name Dīpaṃkara Śrījñāna.

21. *Study of the Mahāyāna śāstra*-s

After receiving the *bhikṣu-dīkṣā*, Dīpaṃkara devoted himself fully to the study of the Mahāyāna scriptures. He specially studied the *Mahāvibhāṣā* under *guru* Dharmarakṣita in the Odantapurī *vihāra*. It took him a long time to study this great work. From Vidyā-kokila the elder, *guru* Bodhibhadra of Nālandā, Avadhūti-pā the younger and *guru* Prajñābhadra he received special instructions in the difficult doctrines of Nāgārjuna. Under his *guru*-s Śānti-pā and Suvarṇadvīpī, he learnt the teachings of Viśiṣta-mārga-krama, which comes down from Maitreyanātha and Asaṅga. In this way, he acquired full mastery of the Mahāyāna *śāstra*-s.

22. Great Wisdom

While in Tibet, Dīpaṃkara once said, "Apart from my *guru*-s Śānti-pā and Suvarṇadvīpī, the real difference between what is truly Buddhist and what is not was known only to me. My *guru*-s are no longer in this world and I am now in Tibet. What happens to my India today ?" Great indeed was his wisdom. Apart from what are said above, he received the wisdom of internal realisation from Avadhūti-pā and Yogī Dombi and of philosophical profundities from Nāro-pā. He received the *upadeśa* of *karma-sañcaya-adhiṣṭhāna* from Ballācārya, of *ṛddhi-adhiṣṭhāna* from *paṇḍita* Mahāmānava, of *vajra-varāhī-adhiṣṭhāna* from Bhūtakoṭi-pā and of *ādya-anukaraṇa* from *guru* Jetāri and Ratnakīrti.

23. Wisdom not Easy to Acquire

And he willingly faced any hazard in striving after wisdom. After receiving from his *guru* Dharmakīrti of Suvarṇadvīpa the *upadeśa* of *karuṇā, maitrī* and *bodhicitta*, he made a voyage along with the sea-going merchants to get precious jewels with which to honour the preceptor properly. There was a fearful storm and the ship drifted away to a strange place. In this place, he came across an enormous sea-monster swallowing up a huge whale. But Dīpaṃkara remained undaunted as ever. Wisdom, he knew, was not easy to acquire. While in Tibet, he once referred to this incident and told his pupils, "I have myself faced great dangers and difficulties for the sake of receiving the *upadeśa*. You seek the *upadeśa* and yet you want to follow the easy way. How can that be possible ?"

24. Meticulous Care for Minor Details

You can imagine how great he was ! At the same time he

never overlooked or ignored any trivial detail of the daily conduct. He had the wisdom of philosophical profundities; he was also extremely careful of observing all the rules of daily life, inclusive of what may appear to others as but minor detail of conduct. Dīpaṃkara was not like a petty *bhikṣu*, who is proud of his three vows (*tri-saṃvara*-s) in the way in which a yak is proud of its beautiful tail and mane and who would repeatedly atone for the violation of the vows by re-purification (*punaḥśodhana*) according to injunctions (*vidhi*). Dīpaṃkara never needed any *punaḥśodhana* for he never violated any minute detail of any vow.

25. *Abilities for Scriptural Writings*

He was specially qualified for scriptural writings because of three outstading reasons. First, he was instructed to do it by his tutelar deity. Secondly, he had the profoundest knowledge of the scriptures. Thirdly, he had the complete mastery over the art of writing. Thus he could clearly explain the real teachings of the Buddha. With the grace of the Tathāgata's *śata-akṣara-upadeśa* he had the visions of many Buddhas and Bodhisattvas and because of his *karuṇā*, *maitrī* and *bodhicitta*, the tutelar deities appeared before him personally. Hence there cannot be any doubt about the truth of his writings. To his writings we shall return later.

26. *The Ideal of Universal Emancipation*

Along with a group of merchants of Jambudvīpa, Dīpaṃkara once went on pilgrimage to Magadha and offered *khasarpaṇa*-s at the Buddhagayā temple. At that time there lived an old man with his wife in Buddhagayā. He had a dream in which he was told by a *devatā* that *bhikṣu* Dīpaṃkara Śrījñāna was then personally present in Buddhagayā and that the old man could obtain great *puṇya* by making offerings to Dīpaṃkara. So the old man went in search of Dīpaṃkara and at last found him making the offerings in the Buddhagayā temple. The old man made his own offerings to Dīpaṃkara. Though Dīpaṃkara then accepted the offerings, he later thought that this was not quite proper. Rather than enjoying the glamour of being a great *bhikṣu,* he thought, it was better for him to retire into the solitude and devote himself exclusively to meditations. Accordingly, he went to the Kṛṣṇa-giri and sat in meditation. Paṇḍita Rāhulagupta, by virtue of his own *abhijñāna,* came to know all about this. He appeared before Dīpaṃkara and said, "You have already the visions of many *kuladevatā*-s and *maṇḍaladevatā*-s and are in possession of the ordinary *siddhi*-s (*sādhāraṇa-siddhi*-s). Therefore, rather than wasting your time in the solitude of the mountains, you should now practise *karuṇā, maitrī* and strive after the *bodhicitta.* Avalokiteśvara is the presiding deity of *bodhicitta.* It is time for you to accept him as your *kuladevatā* and to dedicate all your pious acts to the cause of the living beings and this until the end of the *saṃsāra.*" Dīpaṃkara remembered that he had already received a similar advice from his *guru* Dharmakīrti of Suvarṇadvīpa. He also remembered the following conversation he once overheard between two potters and two girls :

—What is the best way to reach the state of the Buddha ?

—Meditation on *bodhicitta.*

Moreover, there was a temple built by Nāgārjuna with an ivory image of the Buddha. The image spoke to Dīpaṃkara and said, "Oh Yogi, it is time for you to be a *buddha.* Move along the path of *bodhicitta.*" All these led Dīpaṃkara to move along the path of *bodhicitta.* And the enlightenment entered him as smoothly as a thing is removed from one place to another.

27. *In the Vikramaśila vihāra*

During the reign of king Mahīpāla, Dīpaṃkara was invited to join the Vikramaśila *vihāra* as the principal *ācārya.* Under his care, the monastery greatly prospered : larger accommodations for the *bhikṣu*-s were built and new subjects introduced for study and teaching. He drew a large number of new *bhikṣu*-s to the monastery and started for them a new system of teaching. Apart from what he did for the Vikramaśila *vihāra*, Dīpaṃkara was invited to many other *vihāra*-s and a large number of scholars there regarded him as their *guru.* There are two outstanding statues in the Vikramaśila *vihāra.* One of these in that of Nāgārjuna and the other is that of Dīpaṃkara. The two are placed on two sides of the entrance to the monastery and it is said that the statues were made by the students of the *vihāra* during the lifetime of Dīpaṃkara.

28. Leadership of the Buddhist Order

Because of his outstanding abilities, the very leadership of the Buddhist order was eventually conferred on Dīpaṃkara. There are, generally speaking, four means of protecting religion. These are : 1) *yoga-śakti* or the power of *yoga*, 2) *aiśvarya-śakti*, or the power of wealth, 3) *kula-śakti* or the power of birth and 4) *vidyā-śakti* or the power of learning. Any one of these protects religion ; but Dīpaṃkara had all the four in him. As it is said in a *stotra* to him : "You are the best *paṇḍita* with all the four abilities. You have proved your supremacy over all others, both Buddhists and the *tīrthika*-s." So it was only natural that the leadership of the Buddhist Order was to be conferred on him.

29. Leadership Conferred by Nāro-pā

Shortly before Dīpaṃkara's departure for Tibet, *mahā-paṇḍita* Nāro-pā paid a visit to the Vikramaśīla *vihāra*. All the *bhikṣu*-s of the *vihāra* came out to extend a reverential welcome to him. Dīpaṃkara took his left arm and led him to the Central Hall of the monastery. There, in the assembly of all the *bhikṣu*-s, Nāro-pā said to Dīpaṃkara, "From this day on, the responsibility of the Buddhist Order and Faith will rest on you." Dīpaṃkara humbly protested and said, "When you are there how can such a great responsibility be shouldered by me ? It will be like a mere firefly trying to illumine the world in spite of there being the sun and the moon." But Nāro-pā did not listen to any protest. "No", he said, "it is time you realise your real abilities. You alone are fit for such a responsibility. I am old and am not going to stay in the world very long. So you have got to accept the responsibility." After saying this, Nāro-pā left the *vihāra* and went southwards. Twenty days later he received his *nirvāṇa*. When Dīpaṃkara came to Tibet, he carried with him Nāro-pā's relics. This was placed in a golden *caitya* in the sÑe-thaṅ monastery.

30. *The First Invitation to Tibet*

After the terrible persecution by gLaṅ Dar-ma, Buddhism was being gradually revived in Tibet. The pious king who gave the greatest impetus to the revival of Buddhism after this period was Lha-bla-ma Ye-śes-'od (Devaguru Jñānaprabha). He had three nephews, —'Od-lde (Senaprabha), Lha-bla-ma Byaṅ-chub-'od (Devaguru Bodhiprabha) and Shi-ba-'od (Śānti-prabha). The king and his nephews were devout Buddhists and were famous scholars of their time. As Dīpaṃkara's fame reached them, the king thought that it would prove a great blessing for Tibet if Dīpaṃkara could be invited there. He discussed this with his nephews, ministers and nobles, who agreed with him fully. So it was decided that an invitation was to be sent to Dīpaṃkara for coming to Tibet. rGya-brtson-'grus-seṅ-ge (Vīryasiṃha), who later became a lo-tsā-ba, was deputed to carry this invitation. His party left for India with 16 *droṇa*-s of gold. After a difficult journey, Vīryasiṃha reached the Vikramaśila *vihāra*, offered the gold to Dīpaṃkara and conveyed to him the king's invitation. But Dīpaṃkara refused it, saying, "There are only two reasons for which one may go to Tibet. The first is to get gold, which I do not need. The second is *karuṇā*, which, again, I do not sufficiently have." Saying this, he returned the gold to Vīryasiṃha. Vīryasiṃha burst into tears and, clinging to a corner of Dīpaṃkara's robes, earnestly said, "Have mercy on us, please." Dīpaṃkara, however, remained unmoved. Vīryasiṃha went back to Tibet and returned the gold to the king. After this, he himself came back to India for studying in the Vikramaśīla *vihāra*.

31. *The Testament of Devaguru Jñānaprabha*

The king Devaguru Jñānaprabha decided to collect more gold for the purpose of inviting Dīpaṃkara. However, while trying to do it he fell in the hands of the Gar-logs and became a prisoner. The Gar-logs declared that the king could be released only on the following condition : either he was to renounce his Buddhist faith or a ransom was to be paid in gold equalling the king's body. As it was impossible for the king to renounce the Buddhist faith, his ministers started collecting the gold from all parts of Tibet and for this purpose taxes were imposed even on the monks. A lot of gold was collected ; only the amount to equal the king's head was wanting. His nephew Bodhiprabha sent this information to the king, expressing the hope that his release was to be soon obtained. In reply, however, the king sent the following message to Bodhiprabha : "You have, indeed, done a great deal for me. But the gold you have collected should better be spent for the purpose of inviting Dīpaṃkara to Tibet. That is immensely more important for Tibet than obtaining my personal release. In case Dīpaṃkara refuses the invitation again he should be persuaded at least to send some other *paṇḍita* of his own selection. And get the repairs done to the temples of Lhasa and bSam-yas." And the king died by the time this message reached his people. Bodhiprabha decided to work according to the king's last wishes.

32. The Mission of Jayaśīla.

At that time, Nag-tsho Tshul-khrims-rgyal-ba (Jayaśīla) was staying in India. He had already spent two years there and had learnt the Indian languages. The Tibetan court sent the following message to him : "This is the time for you to serve Tibet. In Tibet today, Buddhism is going down and down specially because, as you are well aware, thirteen *paṇḍita*-s of less eminence that were previously invited, rather than serving the cause of Buddhism, are in fact doing great damage to the Faith. Two of them in particular, one with the red robe and the other with blue robe are propagating all sorts of false doctrines in the names of true *tantra* and the real path to *mokṣa*. Tibetan Buddhists in large number are renouncing their yellow robes in favour of their red and blue ones. We tried to invite Dīpaṃkara Śrījñāna of the Vikramaśīla *vihāra* for defending Buddhism in Tibet. But we failed to persuade him. You are a successful Tibetan, used to the Indian climate and with knowledge of the Indian language. You are, therefore, hereby appointed as the messanger of Tibet to the *upādhyāya* of the Vikramaśīla *vihāra.* Try to persuade him to come personally. Failing this, try your best to persuade him to send at least another *paṇḍita* of his own choice." Jayaśīla, however, refused the assignment, saying, "I am now pursuing my own studies, which are likely to be upset if I try to carry out this task. Besides, inviting the *upādhyāya* is too heavy a responsibility to be undertaken by me." King Bodhiprabha sent him a second message : "The king's order is final. The refusal to carry it out means death. On the other hand, if you carry out the order properly, you will be amply rewarded. You can continue your studies in India or Tibet as you please, but only after you obey this order. In any case, you have got to obey it". Jayaśīla, therefore, could no longer refuse the order. He was then 27 years old. The Tibetan court asked him if one hundred persons sent from Tibet would be enough to help him. But he said that only five men would be enough ; instead of more men the court should send more money to help him to carry out the order. Five men were accordingly sent to help him. They carried 16 *droṇa*-s of gold for the *upādhyāya,* 7 *pala*-s of gold for the *sthavira* of the Vikramaśīla *vihāra,* 7 *pala*-s of gold towards the travelling expenses, five *pala*-s of gold for the local interpreters and one *pala* of gold for the Tibetan envoys themselves.

33. *Jayaśīla Reached the Vikramaśīla vihāra.*

With them Jayaśīla started for Vikramaśīla. On the way they had a narrow escape from a group of robbers. They had to spend a night in a bamboo cottage and the robbers knew that they were carrying gold with them. So the robbers plotted to kill them for the gold. But they discovered the plot in time and escaped by the back door. They next met a *rājā* of Nepal going with his party to Buddhagayā. They joined this party and reached Buddhagayā. From Buddhagayā, they started for Vikramaśīla. Jayaśīla was greatly thrilled to have the first distant glimpse of the golden top of the Vikramaśīla temple shinning in the sun. He felt that this glorious sight meant an assurance for him that his mission was going to succeed. Yet Vikramaśīla was still far off and the party had to walk for three more days to reach the bank of the Ganges. As Jayaśīla and his party were planning to rest and spend the night there, the sound of the bell of the Vikramaśīla *vihāra* reached them. They thought it would be improper to spend the night outside the *vihāra* even after being so near it. So they gave up the idea of resting and, marching through the darkness of the night, moved forward to the *vihāra* and reached its gate.

34. *Jayaśīla met Vīryasiṃha*

At that time, Vīryasiṃha was residing in Vikramaśīla as a student. He was staying in a room on top of the gate of the *vihāra*. Jayaśīla with his party, after reaching the gate, asked "Who is in, please ?" Vīryasiṃha came out with a lamp in his hand and said, "It is me. Vīryasiṃha. A Tibetan." They recognised each other and were greatly thrilled. "I can easily guess", said Vīryasiṃha "that you have come to invite Dīpaṃkara to Tibet. But it is no use trying to see him at this late hour of night. Better wait and try to meet him tomorrow morning." "Yes", said Jayaśīla, "I have been ordered by the Tibetan court to try my very best to invite Dīpaṃkara to Tibet. If he refuses to go, I am to try my best to persuade him to send at least another *paṇḍita* of his own selection to Tibet." Vīryasiṃha said, "There are of course many great *paṇḍita*-s under him like Tathāgatarakṣita and Sumatikīrti. But there is none to equal him anywhere in the world. What is most important, moreover, is that he has the *karuṇā* so badly needed for Tibet. Better meet *sthavira* Ratnākara first and tell him that you have come here for the purpose of studying." Jayaśīla agreed to this suggestion.

35. *Dīpaṃkara Accepted the Invitation*

One day Dīpaṃkara was alone in his quarter, resting.

Jayaśīla and others went to him with a *maṇḍala* about a cubit high and placed it before him along with a written petition. Vīryasiṃha translated the petition for Dīpaṃkara. It mentioned how the Tibetan king was a *bodhisattva,* how the three generations of Tibetan kings worked for the cause of Buddhism in Tibet, how the devil gLaṅ Dar-ma tried to destroy Buddhism in Tibet, how the king Devaguru Jñānaprabha sacrificed his life for inviting Dīpaṃkara to Tibet, how his nephews were staking everything for it, how in Tibet the false religion was being propagated by the false *paṇḍita*-s—and so on. The petition, in short, mentioned everything, and added, "The young king of Tibet, a *bodhisattva,* is now appealing to you once again with all his earnestness to come to Tibet and give the Tibetans the true Doctrine. The young king feels that this appeal cannot be ignored by you, whose heart is so full of *karuṇā.*" This time Dīpaṃkara realised that the Tibetan king was a real *bodhisattva.* And he thought: "The request of a *bodhisattva* cannot be refused. Besides, Tibet has suffered so much for me. It is time for me to accept the invitation." To the Tibetans he said, "My sympathy is with you. Though I am old, have a heavy duty here and many an unfinished work to complete, yet I shall try to go. But in any case I do not need the gold." And he returned the gold to them.

36. Divine Predictions and Inspirations

There were already divine predictions about Dīpaṃkara's going to Tibet. These inspired him in favour of the decision. Dīpaṃkara once went to the temple of Amitābha in Buddhagayā. In this temple, the image of Avalokiteśvara suddenly spoke to him thus, "In the north there is a *kṣetra* of mine and your tutelar deity Tārādevī is already residing there in the cause of the living beings. A large number of people there awaits your guidance. You have got to go there and work for the living beings." Thus it was foretold by Avalokiteśvara himself that the Tibetans were to be the followers of Dīpaṃkara. Another inspiration came from Tārādevī herself. Dīpaṃkara had once to expel a *bhikṣu* from Vikramaśīla. Immediately after this he had a dream in which Tārādevī told him, "The *bhikṣu* that you have expelled is a *bodhisattva.* One should not act against a *bodhisattva* even unconsciously. One who does nothing even after being told about it will have the body as huge as the Sumeru mountain with thousands and crores of birds and insects feasting on it." "But how am I to avoid such a consequence ?", asked Dīpaṃkara. Tārādevī told him, "You have to go to the north and devote yourself to the cause of spreading the Mahāyāna Doctrine there. You will also have to print there seven *sa-tsha* (*sañcā*—clay model of *caitya*) every day."

37. *What the Yoginī-s said*

In a dream, Tārādevī once told Dīpaṃkara, "There is a small Buddhist shrine nearby. Go there and you will meet a *yoginī*. She has something extremely important to tell you." Next morning Dīpaṃkara went to the shrine with a bunch of flowers in his hands. In the shrine he saw a woman with matted hair. He offered the flowers to her and asked, "I have been invited to Tibet. Am I going to be a success ?" The *yoginī* replied, "Yes, great success awaits you there. You will meet an *upāsaka* ('Brom-ston-pa) in Tibet and he will work for the further success of your mission."

38. *Sacrifice of Twenty Years of Life.*

After making up his mind to go to Tibet, Dīpaṃkara went on a pilgrimage to Buddhagayā. On the eve of this pilgrimage, *upādhyāya* Jñānaśrī Mitra gave him a handful of *kaḍi*-s and said, "There is an old *jaṭādhāriṇī* woman in a cave of Buddhagayā. Give these *kaḍi*-s to her." Dīpaṃkara went to Buddhagayā, made his usual offerings, but forgot about the woman and the *kaḍi*-s. As he was about to leave Buddhagayā, a woman with matted hair appeared before him and asked, "Where are my *kaḍi*-s ?" Dīpaṃkara immediately realised that this was no ordinary woman. He begged pardon of her, gave her the *kaḍi*-s and asked, "I have been invited to Tibet. Am I going to be a success there ?" She replied, "If you go to Tibet you will be a great success, but your life will be shortened." "Shortened by how many years ?", asked Dīpaṃkara. "If you do not go to Tibet," she replied, "you will live up to the age of ninety-two. If, however, you go there you will not reach an age beyond seventy-three." Dīpaṃkara thought, "Twenty years of life do not matter at all, if by sacrificing this I can work for the Doctrine and for the living beings." How he loved others more than he loved himself!

39. Prediction of his Leaving the Mortal Body in Tibet

Guru Halāhala once told Dīpaṃkara, "In the future you will have to go to the north, build monasteries there and you will have a large following. It will be an arduous task for you, for the country is a jungle without proper facilities. And you will not come back from that country." In Somapurī, while he was expounding the *Tarkajvālā*, Dīpaṃkara himself said, "After twenty years from now on I shall cast my mortal body in Tibet and shall proceed to Tuṣita." In a *stotra* to him is said : "When you were at Somapurī, expounding (*gsuṅ*) the *Tarkajvālā*, you said that twenty years from then on you will leave your mortal body in Tibet." In the same *stotra* it is added, "Two years after that, when you were about to leave Vikramaśīla for Tibet, you repeated that eighteen years hence you would leave your mortal body in Tibet."

40. Preparations and Departure

When Dīpaṃkara decided to go to Tibet, he had so many unfinished works at hand. He wanted to complete these before his departure. So he said to Jayaśīla and Vīryasiṃha, "I shall need about eighteen months to complete the unfinished works here. Would you agree to wait for these months ?" They answered, "Eighteen months do not matter at all. We are prepared to wait even for years to accomany you to Tibet." Dīpaṃkara advised them to go to Ratnākara, the *sthavira*, and request him to make necessary arrangements for their stay and further studies in Vikramaśīla during these eighteen months. And they did so. On the eve of Dīpaṃkara's departure for Tibet, Jayaśīla completed his stay of three years and five months in India and was already an accomplished scholar.

Ratnākara, the *sthavira*, told him, "You are a successful student of the *vihāra*. My great scholar is being taken by the Tibetan ruler and for the sake of the Tibetans themselves I cannot stop him. But do bring him back after three years." Though Jayaśīla promised to do so, it, as we shall see, could not be fulfilled.

41. Journey to Tibet and the Death of Vīryasiṃha

By the end of the Iron-Male-Dragon year (A. D. 1040), Dīpaṃkara started for Tibet. It was the year of Nāro-pā's *nirvāṇa*. The next year Dīpaṃkara reached Nepal and stayed there for one year. In this year Vīryasiṃha died in Nepal. Vīryasiṃha was a noble soul. He studied under Dīpaṃkara for a long time and became a very skilled lo-tsā-ba. His contribution to inviting Dīpaṃkara to Tibet is unforgettable. His untimely death made Dīpaṃkara most sad, who said, "We have no luck. You Tibetans have no luck. You will no more have Vīryasiṃha with you." At the time of his death, Vīryasiṃha is said to have uttered the following: "I, an *upāsaka*, am going to the natural place. Human nature being what it is, nobody will have any mercy for my body. I am going to be one with the sky. I worked for Tibet. I worked in India. I am now departing. Only one would be enough for the Himavat."

42. Reception at Tibet

In the Water-Male-Horse year (A.D. 1042) Dīpaṃkara reached mÑa'-ris. Jayaśīla was then thirtyone. He next proceeded to Maṅ-yul. There he went to the shrine of mTho-ldiṅ (Tho-liṅ). The reception party, headed by king Bodhi-prabha, was already at the shrine. Dīpaṃkara was given a grand reception. The following *stotra* of welcome was recited by the reception party: "O Great Teacher, you had such a long journey to Tibet through Nepal. It must have been extremely tiring. You are of course super-human and the physical strain cannot touch you. Nevertheless our mortal eyes cannot help seeing fatigue in you. It is so kind of you to come to guide this teacherless country without guidance and ravaged by the *mleccha*-s. Please pardon us for the poor ceremony we could at best manage for such a great occasion. Please pardon Tibet for the want of proper religious arrangements, which are already destroyed and devastated." This *stotra* was collectively recited. Then Jayaśīla moved forward and recited the following special *stotra* of welcome: "With the greatest hope in my heart, I, Jayaśīla, approach your feet. Oh Lord, pardon me for all my follies. Pardon us all for the trouble you had to take for our sake by way of coming to Tibet *via* Nepal. It is indeed our greatest joy to have you amongst ourselves." King Bodhiprabha next moved forward and recited the following *stotra*: "I, *bhikṣu* Bodhiprabha, am here to invite my long-cherished *guru* to the land of Tibet. The real *śāstra-nīti* is going to be propagated in Tibet by this great *guru*." Then, on behalf of the assembled Tibetans, he added, "What we deserve is not profound philosophy. We are rather greatly in need of the knowledge of true conduct—the knowledge of the causes and results of actions." Another eminent member of the welcoming delegation, rMog-cog-rdo-rje-'chaṅ, said, "Teach us please the religion that is neither too high nor too low. Teach us the religion that can help us, the Tibetans." To all these, Dīpaṃkara replied, "Your way of requesting for precepts shows indeed your wisdom." He felt very happy and delivered his first sermon there.

43. *Instructions to Ratnabhadra*

Ratnabhadra or lo-tsā-ba Rin-chen-bzaṅ-po was proud of his own scholarship. He thought, "This *paṇḍita* cannot after all be wiser than myself. But since the king himself has invited him to Tibet, I shall have to offer my formal services to him." Thus thinking, he took Dīpaṃkra round the temple of Tho-liṅ. On the walls of the shrine there, Dīpaṃkara saw the pictures of the Tantric deities. He recited a *stotra* for each and then took the seat offered to him. The lo-tsā-ba wondered at Dīpaṃkara's feat and asked, "From which text you have been quoting all these *stotra*-s ?" Dīpaṃkara said, "These *stotra*-s are not quoted from any text. I was inspired to compose these by the images of the *devatā*-s." This smashed the pride of Ratnabhadra. Dīpaṃkara next asked him, "In which subject do you feel weak ?" Ratnabhadra gave an account of his own knowledge. On listening to this, Dīpaṃkara said with folded hands, "Ah, you are such a great *paṇḍita* ! Since you are here, what could be the need of bringing me to Tibet ?" Then he asked him a difficult question concerning *dhyāna*. The lo-tsā-ba said, "This is to be practised separately according to the Tantras and the Sūtras." Dīpaṃkara wondered at the answer and said, "I can now see the need of myself being invited to Tibet." Everybody present burst into a laughter. Ratnabhadra was completely humbled and begged of Dīpaṃkara the real *upadeśa*. Dīpaṃkara imparted this to him.

44. Meditations of Ratnabhadra

Ratnabhadra offered everything he had to Dīpaṃkara as the preceptor's fee. But Dīpaṃkara said, "Instead of all these, you better offer your services to me and accompany me as my interpreter." Ratnabhadra said, "I am an old man with grey hair; I would like to do some meditation, if you please. And I want some magical power from you." This made Dīpaṃkara very indignant and he said, "My dear Ratnabhadra, because of the accumulated *puṇya* of your previous births, you have already received the message of the Buddha and you had also good teachers to teach you the real meaning of the message. That is the nectar (*amṛta-ouṣadha*) that alone can cure the sickness, which is this world. You have already got the lamp of True Dharma which alone can remove the darkness of *moha*. Have a grip on your own mind. Do not run after the futile magical powers and do not waste your wonderful possession. This is my final *upadeśa* to you. Go and meditate on this." Ratnabhadra went to a cave, sealed its entrance with iron nails and sat in meditation. Outside the cave he wrote, "If within this cave I think of any ordinary thing even for a moment, may the keepers of *dharma* make my head fall immediately on the ground." For twelve years he sat in meditation and had ultimately the direct vision of the Cakra Saṃvara Maṇḍala. And he said, "Before I came in touch with Dīpaṃkara, I had sixty other teachers. But Dīpaṃkara alone could show me the path to true *siddhi*."

45. Monasteries and Shrines Visited by Dīpaṃkara

From the temple of Tho-liṅ, Dīpaṃkara went to the shrine of sPu-raṅs-rgyal in Maṅ-yul. The learned men of Tibet, including 'Brom-ston-pa, received him there. In this shrine Dīpaṃkara distributed some gifts to the monks. He next proceeded towards central Tibet with a big party. When he left Maṅ-yul, the whole people there gathered to give him a farewell. Among them, those that had any gift to offer offered it to him; others offered him only their reverential bows. When he reached Tsha-sna, a large number of people greeted him. He delivered many sermons to the common people. From Tsha-sna he proceeded by a somewhat lonely path to Ñan-mtsho. He was received there in a big way and he delivered many sermons. 'Gos-lhas-btsan[5] met Dīpaṃkara fiirst at this place. He next went to Roṅ. A large gathering of students and teachers received him there. A nun came to him and offered him a golden horse with a turquoise-horseman on it. He liked it very much and gave her the following *upadeśa* : "Serve those that are sick and those that are tired. Serve the parents and the old. This is true religion. By thus serving, you will acquire all the *puṇya* that one acquires by meditating on the *bodhicitta* and *śūnyatā*." When he reached gNam-byaṅ-thaṅ, he pointed his fingers to a mountain and asked, "What is there ?" Everybody in the party looked at that direction and saw three rows of rainbow above the mountain. It was a glorious sight indeed ! "The Lhasa temple is there", they said. Dīpaṃkara exclaimed, "Ah, what a noble place it is ! I see the sons and daughters of heaven worshipping there." Dīpaṃkara next gradually proceeded to sNa-bo-la. After reaching the

5. A Tibetan scholar who, already during the time of Ye-śes-'od, acquired eminence and who eventually became an important follower of Atīśa : BA i. 102 ; 326-7 ; 360.

place, the members in the party blew the Rag-duṅ (the large brass trumpet). Scared by its sound, people started rushing to their homes and the animals ran wild. Dīpaṃkara laughed and said, "The same thing happened in the valley of Nepal and in the Maṅ-yul village." He was invited there to perform the *pratiṣṭhāna* ceremony in the newly built temple of Gra-phyi in the market place. He performed the solemn ceremony.

46. *Visit to bSam-yas and other places*

Dīpaṃkara next asked, "Where is the bSam-yas *vihāra* ?" His attention was drawn to a hill and he was told that the monastery was at its foot. He felt excited to be so near the *vihāra* and, wanting to reach it quickly, crossed a river by boat. In the Chos-'khor-bsam-yas he was received by Lha-btsun Bodhirāja[6] and many eminent persons gathered there to pay their respects to Dīpaṃkara. He was next invited by Khu-ston to Yar-kluṅs.[7] On his way to Yar-kluṅs he stayed in a house built by Khri-bzaṅ with horns at Thaṅ-po-che. He delivered many sermons there and 'Brom-ston-pa came to meet him again in Yar-kluṅs. He had the opportunity of listening to Dīpaṃkara on various subjects. Then came Khu-ston to meet Dīpaṃkara and, at the sight of the Master, shouted with excitement, "Ah, Atīśa is here !". He rushed to place his cap on Dīpaṃkara's feet and took him to Yar-kluṅs. Dīpaṃkara next went to the Ke-ru temple at 'On in Yar-kluṅs and spent a month there. He particularly admired a painting on the front wall of the temple, which is still being worshipped as sacred and holy. From there he went to bSam-yas and stayed at dPe-dkar-gliṅ. He examined many Indian manuscripts in the bSam-yas *vihāra* and was highly impressed with these. "These are", he said, "evidences of how strong Buddhism had once been in Tibet. These works are difficult to be found even in India." When he was in bSam-yas, Baṅ-ston sent a party of 200 horsemen to invite him. But he proceeded instead to rGod-dkar-la and spent a fortnight in rGya-phibs of Sri. Then came rÑog

6. BA i. 257 : said to be a descendant of the royal line of Sroṅ-btsan.
7. D-TED 1130.

Legs-pa'i-śes-rab to invite him to Lhasa proper. A ceremony on a grand scale was organised to receive him there. After the reception ceremony, he was invited to the famous shrine of Lhasa. In this shrine, while looking at the image of Avalokiteśvara, he exclaimed, "How wonderful it is ! Why ! It is more than an image. I see there Avalokiteśvara himself." He was equally thrilled to look at the famous image of the Śākyamuni and he exclaimed, "Ah ! To me, he seems to be alive !" He spent the winter in Lhasa. People of Lhasa said that this winter was particularly fortunate for them and they had so many auspicious omens. Next summer, he was invited to Yer-pa-ba-reṅ by rÑog Byaṅ-chub-'byuṅ-gnas, where he delivered many sermons. He was next invited to 'Phan-yul by sKa-ba Śākya-dbaṅ-phyug. He stayed there in Lan-pa-spyil-bu. Here, too, he delivered many sermons. He then proceeded to Yer-pa, where he again received an invitation from Baṅ-ston ; but he directed his way to Lhasa again. He stopped at sÑe-thaṅ.

47. *In Lhasa*

When Dīpaṃkara, being invited by rÑog Legs-pa'i-śes-rab, went to the Lhasa temple, a tall man with long beards appeared at the temple door and said, "Welcome, Oh great *paṇḍita*, may thou achieve the highest success." Dīpaṃkara rushed at him, but he went inside the temple and melted into the image of Avalokiteśvara. With a deep sigh Dīpaṃkara said, "Ah, I missed Avalokiteśvara." After entering the temple, Dīpaṃkara wondered : How could the Tibetans build a temple like this ! As he was thus wondering, a mad woman came near him and asked, "Do you want to know the history of the temple ?" Dīpaṃkara realised that she was not really a mad woman ; she was a *yoginī* instead. So he bowed down to her in his mind and said, "Ah yes. I am most interested." "The history", she said, "lies buried two and a half *vyama*-s[8] from the *kalaśa-stambha* of the temple. But never mention this to anybody else." Dīpaṃkara dug up the place and found the

8. The measure of the two extended arms : Monier-Williams SED 1038.

history written in the form of a book. But the watch-god of the treasure told him, "Y oucan read and copy out the history, but only as much as you can in a single day." So Dīpaṃkara, along with his four disciples including 'Brom-ston-pa, started to copy it out. In the course of the day, they finished copying it, except that part of it which dealt with the Lhag-bag corner of the temple. This copy is still preserved in Tibet. Thus he found the treasure of Tibet. In the *Sum-cu-pa* is said, "The *ḍākinī* opened its door for thee and thou had (already) the permission of Śākyamuni (to see it)" In Lhasa, Dīpaṃkara saw another *yoginī* staying in the guise of a mad woman. But he knew that the *devatā*-s went to her. She lived in the *śmaśāna.* After Dīpaṃkara visited this place, it became a holy one.

48. *The Monasteries and Shrines built by Dīpaṃkara*

Dīpaṃkara built monasteries and shrines not only in Tibet but also in India and Nepal. In Nepal he built the sThaṃ *vihāra.* In Maṅ-yul he built the Ke-ru monastery and in Byaṅ he built the Tsha-sna temple. He spent one month in Ke-ru and the people of 'On were prosperous and happy. The Rwa-sgreṅ monastery of dBus was built by 'Brom-ston-pa ; but as it was built under the blessings of the Master, scholars consider it to have been built by Dīpaṃkara himself. That is why, when Kha-che-pan-chen[9] went to this monastery, he said that he was going to see Atīśa's monastery. Also Khro-lo, in his *stotra* to Dīpaṃkara, said, "You have built many centres of Buddhism in India, Nepal and Tibet. The Rwa-sgreṅ *vihāra* is your creation. Under your inspiration the number of Buddhists in the world increased in lacs. Make a gift to us, please, of a tiny bit of your abilities." Wherever Dīpaṃkara spent a single night became a holy place. Some of these grew into big monasteries. Whatever he did in Tibet was for the good of the common people. The Tibetans are above all greatful to him because of the purity of the Doctrine he preached.

9. The Kashmirian *paṇḍita* Śākyaśrībhadra (A.D. 1127-1225): BA ii. 1062-4.

His exposition of the Doctrine remains strongest in Tibet even today. It was under the blessings of Dīpaṃkara that the sÑe-thaṅ monastery once became foremost in Tibet. The special study of the *lakṣaṇa-śāstra* was introduced there. The Yer-pa-sgrub-sde is the second of the biggest monasteries built by Dīpaṃkara. Next to this is the monastery of Thaṅ-po-che. Even the Dol-dars-ma, where Dīpaṃkara spent only one night, became a fine monastery. It eventually became a centre of the bKa'-gdams-pa sect and is specially renowned for the study of *sūtra*-s and *tantra*-s. The Ñan-mtsho-gnas-rñiṅ, where Dipaṃ-was invited by Yol-chos-dbaṅ and spent three months, became, under his blessings, a great monastery and it remains so even today. He stayed for only a fortnight in rGya-phibs of Sri. It became a renowned centre for the study of the Vinaya and it produced many distinguished scholars. It is because of the kindness of Dīpaṃkara that practically every Tibetan has a religious faith and a belief in the life after death. Nothing was left undone by Dīpaṃkara for Tibet.

49. Dīpaṃkara Dispelled the False Knowledge of Tantra

Said Dīpaṃkara, "The *brahmacārī* cannot receive the *guhya-jñāna-abhiṣeka*... For a *brahmacārī* receiving that initiation means the violation of the prohibitions and hence the fall from his *tapas-saṃvara*. Such a *vratī* (*brahmacārī*) will suffer the *mahāpātaka* and will certainly fall into the low-born (*durgati*). He will never attain the *siddhi*." The implication of this is clear. The practices of Tantra are incompatible with *brahma-carya*, and therefore also with the life of the *bhikṣu* Jayaśīla, in the *stotra* to him, said, "The practice of the Tantra without the right *guru* or without the knowledge of the Mahāyāna *śāstra*-s leads to the loss of *bodhicitta* and *karuṇā*. One who does this is born as a *yakṣa*, *rākṣasa* and *piśāca*. The so-called Tāntrikas, who follow only the words of the Tantras without awareness of their secret essence, move along the wrong path. To them you have shown the right path. You are great indeed." gZus-rdo-rje-mtshan[10] once told Dīpaṃkara, "I am a follower

10. One of the Tibetan disciples of Atīśa from upper gTsaṅ : BA i. 262.

of the Vinaya and at the same time I am a Tāntrika." Dīpaṃkara sarcastically answered, "You have done no good. Being not an omniscient you can hardly have the knowledge of both." When Dīpaṃkara was in sÑe-thaṅ, an Indian *paṇḍita* came to see him. The two sat for the whole night and talked. While talking, they were bursting into laughter, as if enjoying a great joke. Next morning, 'Brom-ston-pa said to him, "You must have been very happy to receive somebody from your country. We heard you laughing so much. What is the news that he has brought for you ?" Dīpaṃkara said, "Yes. The funniest thing has happened there. A Hevajra Yogī claims to have entered the *srotāpatti-phala*.[11] We were so tickled by this !" This incident is related by rMog-cog. dGe-bśes-brag-rgyab-pa said, "Before Atīśa's arrival, Buddhism in Tibet became something quite strange. Even the monks' robes were of three different colours. By Dīpaṃkara's kindness, we could learn something of the *vinaya* and the Vinaya-system. It is for us now to continue it."

50. Debunking a Pretentious Guru

In Yer-pa, Khu-ston said to Dīpaṃkara, "Here is a man called Dar-yul-pa. He claims to be a *guru* and to possess *abhijñāna*-s. But he is in fact only a bluffer possessed by Devaputra Māra. Please defeat him so that he can no longer harm the cause of Buddhism." Dīpaṃkara laughed and said, "Yes. It seems that I need to send a huge army to defeat him." Then he told the simple way to discredit this man. Acting according to Dīpaṃkara's instructions, Khu-ston put a small pea into his own mouth and asked this man. "Please tell us something about Dīpaṃkara's previous and future births." The man said a lot of things without the least hesitation. Khu-ston next asked him, "Please tell me what is there within my own mouth." The man could not answer and proved himself to be a fool. With the defeat of this man were also defeated so many other pretending teachers who were resisting the cause of Buddhism in Tibet.

11. D-TED 929 : "one of the four graded results of progressive perfection."

51. Evil Plots and Bitter Comments

Jo-mo-'chims-mo, a female leader of a hostile sect, wanted to drive away Dīpaṃkara from Tibet. When he was staying in bSam-yas, she employed two parties of street urchins, got them to memorize certain filthy *śloka*-s and arranged that these were to be recited near Dīpaṃkara separately. One of them came to Dīpaṃkara and said, "This *paṇḍita* is teaching nothing and his lo-tsā-ba-s are translating nothing. The *paṇḍita* has no time to preach and the king has no sense." The other party said, "Dīpaṃkara has no time to worship the gods. The young king is kept engaged to external ceremonials only and has no time to think." Another poet called gTsaṅ-pa-smon-te wrote a poem saying, "Since the arrival of this Indian *paṇḍita*, diseases rather than religion is spreading in Tibet. Every valley and every place is being converted into *śmaśāna*." Dīpaṃkara noticed all these and simply said, "One should stay away a hundred *yojana*-s from such filthy challenges." When Dīpaṃkara was on his way to 'Chiṅ-ru, a newly-married girl, as a mark of her own devotion to the Master, offered all her ornaments to him. This made the members of her family furious. They said, "You have given away all the valuables to the greedy Indian, who always runs after rich presents." The abuses became too heavy for her to bear and she threw herself into the gTsaṅ-po (the Brahmaputra). Dīpaṃkara felt very sad and performed for her the rites of *durgati-śodhana*. Incidents like these provoked some bitter comments in Dīpaṃkara. In bSam-yas he was requested by some Tibetan teachers to say something about his own future birth. He replied, "What shall I say about it ? This-much, however, is sure that my next incarnation will not be in Tibet." When they asked "Why ?", Dīpaṃkara said, "You Tibetans do not know how to respect the *upadeśa*-s and you do not know how to do the real offerings to gods." On another occasion he told 'Brom-ston-pa, "You Tibetans do not know how to respect your *guru*, for you think that the *guru* is just an ordinary person." At sÑe-thaṅ, two *a-tsa-ra*-s, with small bundles on their backs, came near the Master. Atīśa said to rNal-'byor-pa, "Take away their bundles." When rNal-'byor-pa did it and searched the bundles, he found a small box within. As soon as the box was opened, there sprang out from within it a sharp knife which stuck to the wall and remained grafted on it. Dīpaṃkara said, "This is how the *tīrthika*-s wanted to kill me. The knife was designed to murder me. The *tīrthika*-s want me to stop the spread of the Doctrine in Tibet."

52. His Personal Piety

How much Dīpaṃkara himself cared for the objects of worship is evident from the words of Jayaśīla, who said, "For ninteen years I served him as his student and I never saw him being careless of *kāya-vāc-citta*, the objects of worship." This he repeated in his *stotra* to Dīpaṃkara : "Oh *guru*, Oh *kalyāṇamitra*, I never saw you being careless of *kāya-vāc-citta*." Whoever saw him, heard him or came in touch with him in any form found blessings for himself. In the Vikramaśīla Vihāra, a dog used to sleep under the stairs on which he walked. After death, it was reborn as a man and eventually became *bhikṣu* Praṇidhānajñāna, a painter and follower of Dīpaṃkara. This *bhikṣu* once requested Vajrapāṇi, "Please tell me somthing about my own future." The *mahācārya* replied, "You are in close touch with Dīpaṃkara. Devote yourself fully to him. Paint as many portraits of Dīpaṃkara as you can." He painted about 70 pictures and obtained great blessings.

53. His Supernatural Powers

When Dīpaṃkara was coming to Tibet, a gang of robbers tried to attack his party. The Master used his magic spell and threw a pinch of dust at them. The robbers immediately froze to stones. After his party passed them all, he threw another pinch of dust at the robbers. This enabled them to move again, but they could see nothing. "I cannot see !", "I cannot see !", said the robbers and they groped. The Master addressed them and said, "There are many ways of earning the livelihood properly. Why, then, should you commit robbery ?" He then threw another pinch of dust at them. This enabled them to see again. They bowed down before him and silently went away.

On another occasion, a *bhikṣuṇī* saw Dīpaṃkara circumambulating the shrine of bSam-yas, walking in air about a man's height above the ground. She requested a monk to ask Dīpaṃkara about its mystery. But Dīpaṃkara evaded the question and said, "Perhaps she has made some mistake." In Lhasa, however, the monk himself saw Dīpaṃkara circumambulating the temple in the same way. He said to Dīpaṃkara, "So the nun has made no mistake after all !" Dīpaṃkara laughed and said, "I was quite famous for this even in India." And he gave the monk the *upadeśa* of this *pradakṣiṇa*. 'Brom-ston-pa also saw him walking in the air. He saw him, moreover, entering the small hole of a bamboo, though wearing the *mukuṭa* and *trivastra* and holding the *bhikṣā-pātra* and *daṇḍa* in his hands. And 'Brom-ston-pa thought : The Master has the magic power of *ṛddhi-samādhi*.

In dPe-dkar-gliṅ at bSam-yas, Dīpaṃkara and 'Brom-ston-pa were once sleeping, separated only by a curtain. The Master suddenly woke up and asked 'Brom-ston-pa, "Do you hear any sound ?". 'Brom-ston-pa could hear nothing. Dīpaṃkara said, "I heard the sound of a cymbal being played by a student of mine in India remembering me." In the *Sum-cu-pa*, this incident is recorded as follows : "His faithful follower in Magadha remembered him and played the cymbal. He heard the sound in Tibet and told 'Brom-ston-pa about it. This is the sign of his *śravaṇa-abhijñāna*. We bow down to him." In Maṅ-yul, he was once teaching *sādhanā* to 'Brom-ston-pa and others. His listeners, including even 'Brom-ston-pa, thought that the Master was perhaps using a word wrongly. When they were thus thinking, he waved his hand and said to them, "No. I am not making any mistake. The mistake, rather, is yours." This is a sign of his *paracitta-abhijñāna*. As 'Brom-ston-pa said, "Yes. We realised that the mistake was ours. He had the power of knowing the mind of anybody within a journey of three days." He was once going from Yer-pa to 'Phan-yul. But he suddenly changed the route and proceeded towards sÑe-thaṅ instead. He explained this by saying, "An old female devotee of mine is dying in sÑe-thaṅ. I have, therefore, to go there for her funeral rites." When he reached sÑe-thaṅ, the old woman was already dead. He performed the funeral rites for her. This is a sign of his *sāmānya-abhijñāna.* Once, while he was going from sÑe-thaṅ to gTsaṅ, he pointed his finger to the mountains of Sa-skya and said, "In that mountain dwells a great man, who is an incarnation of Mañjughoṣa." On another occasion while proceeding to gTsaṅ-roṅ, he saw a child and said, "Though he cannot talk to me, he is in fact my friend Kṛṣṇācārya reborn thus." He reminded his pupils of this child again in Lan-pa and said, "This child is going to be very important for the destiny of Tibet." These are signs of his *ṛddhi-vidhi-abhijñāna.*

54. Protector of Meditations

When Dīpaṃkara was in sÑe-thaṅ, dGe-bśes-dgon-pa-pa once sat in meditation. His meditation was one night disturbed by a terrible sound. As he turned he saw a big black scorpion coming out of the ground. But he could not move away, because that meant leaving the seat of meditation. The only thing he could do was to remember Dīpaṃkara. This made the scorpion turn and go away. Next morning Dīpaṃkara came to him and asked, "Why did you call me in the night ?" He felt amazed and told Dīpaṃkara everything. Dīpaṃkara gave him the *upadeśa* of *yoga-rakṣā.* To 'Brom-ston-pa and many others the Master gave many *upadeśa*-s for helping their meditations. He had, accordingly, the reputation of being the *dhyānarakṣaka.* It is said that a disciple of Dīpaṃkara once sat in meditation in India and was facing a great disturbance. Dīpaṃkara removed the causes of the disturbance from Tibet. When he was in Yer-pa, Shaṅ-btsun-'ol-rgod asked some *upadeśa* from him. The Master said, "Man's life is short and his tasks are numerous. One never knows when one is going to die. Therefore meditation is the best thing to do. It prolongs your life, makes the burden on you lighter and leads you along the path to enlightenment (*bodhipatha*)." There are many other things said about how he protected the meditators and the way in which he removed the obstacles to meditations. He always laid the greatest emphasis on meditation.

55. *Karuṇā for the Lower Animals*

When Dīpaṃkara was coming to Tibet he once saw three pups and became fond of these. He brought them to Tibet. It is believed that their descendants are still in Tibet. Whenever he saw the calves and young goats, he used to address them, "Ah ! I hope you are alright." Someone asked him, "Why do you speak to the animals in this manner ?" He simply answered, "I have as much *karuṇā* for the animals as for the human beings." Wherever he went, he used to touch and caress the animals and said, "How I wish you would be next born in better lives." This way of touching and talking to the animals was considered undignified in the standard of the Tibetan nobles. Khu-ston, therefore, once told him, "Please behave like a noble man. Touching the animals and speaking to them is not approved of by our nobles." Dīpaṃkara replied, "My greatest love is for these animals. The claim to my love by your Tibetan lords come next to theirs. The *karuṇā* and *maitrī* in me is stronger for the weak."

56. *Loved and Respected by All*

Dīpaṃkara was loved and respected not only by the common people but also by the kings and the nobles, including the Indian kings Mahīpāla and Nayapāla, the south-Indian king Kṛṣṇa, and various other kings of Nepal and Tibet. As it is said in a *stotra* to him, "Magadhapati..." etc. Generally speaking, the Tibetans respected him, bowed down before him and placed before him their gifts and offerings. But we shall mention here the more outstanding of these. Lha-bla-ma Byaṅ-chub-'od (Bodhiprabha), the king of western Tibet, made an offering of one hundred *pala*-s of gold to him. On behalf of the Tibetan people, the Tibetan king placed before him the offering of *saptaratna*,[12] all made of gold and studded with precious

12. Seven (really six) different precious articles believed to be the extra-

jewels. A life-size golden image of *strī-ratna*, studded with jewels, was separately offered to him at sÑe-thaṅ. In a *stotra* to him it is said : "None that ever saw you, heard from you or touched you, is left without reverence for you. In this world there is none that can be compared to you." Dīpaṃkara was loved and honoured not only by the human beings but also by the gods and others. In bSam-yas, he once looked at the sky and said, "O, the *devatā*-s come worshipping me." In sÑe-thaṅ everyone saw *pañcaratna-puṣpa* showering on him from the sky and he said, "Ah, these are being showered by Indra, the king of the *devatā*-s." As it is recorded in the *Sum-cu-pa*, while he was sitting on the sand at 'Or of sÑe-thaṅ, Indra and the other gods showered the *pañcaratna-puṣpa* from heaven." Lo-chen Rin-chen-bzaṅ-po said, "Oh, *paṇḍita*, *guru* of the *devatā*-s, your *viśuddhakāya* is decorated with the *śīla*-s." He was once seen with a horse-headed man sitting with folded hands before him. When asked by rNal-'byor-pa about this man, he simply said, "Oh, he is the king of the *kinnara*-s." He was asked, "Were you not afraid of him ?" He simply said, "Why should I be afraid ? He is just like any other man, though a little different in appearance." As is said in the *Be'u-bum*, "You were not afraid to look at the man with horse-head"...etc.

57. *The Inspired Exponent of the Mādhyamika View*

Dīpaṃkara once said, "Meditating only on *śūnyatā* without the *upāya* cannot lead to Buddhahood. It is necessary to meditate on both and to be careful. You Tibetan scholars often claim that you are Mādhyamikas. On examination, however, I find you to have reached not even the stage of the Yogācāras." His kindness to the Tibetans led him to explain to them, in the form of many *upadeśa*-s and many treatises, the Mādhyamika view. His exposition of the Mādhyamika view was directly inspired by Maitreyanātha through Nāgārjuna. When he was in sÑe-thaṅ, a famous *yogī* came to see him.

ordinary treasures of a Cakravartī Rāja ; the precious wheel, the precious elephant, the precious gem, the precious wife, the precious minister and the precious general—D-TED 1183.

After some discussions with him the *yogī* went away. When asked about him, Dīpaṃkara replied, "He is my old friend Maitrī Bhṛkholi." Immediately after the *yogī* left, he looked at the sky and kept looking for the whole night. In the morning he said, "Maitreyanātha and Mañjuśrī appeared in the sky. I was looking and listening to them." Then he rushed to write something, saying, "The whole night Maitreyanātha and Mañjuśrī were discussing the Mahāyāna view. How glorious was the scene! Vajrapāṇi himself was acting as their guard and surrounding them were many *deva-putra*-s. I must hurry to record their discussion."

Dīpaṃkara had the habit of bowing down in empty temples. People asked him, "Whom do you offer your salutations in the empty temples?" "The empty temples", he replied, "remind me of *śūnyatā*." In his teachings he always laid the greatest emphasis on the views of Nāgārjuna and Asaṅga, the great Mahāyānists.

He also reminded his pupils of the supreme importance of *karuṇā* for the right realisation of their views.

When he was in sÑe-thaṅ, four *paṇḍita*-s of Tibet came to him with the hope of learning from him the main *siddhānta*-s of the Mahāyāna handed down from Nāgārjuna and Asaṅga. Dīpaṃkara was then sitting on meditation. After he got up from his seat, he looked at the *paṇḍita*-s and exclaimed, "Ah, it seems I have before me the gathering of all the great scholars of Tibet." "We have come to you," they said, "with the hope of learning the *siddhānta*-s." Dīpaṃkara explained to them the essential difference between Buddhism and non-Buddhism and added, "Generally speaking, the *siddhānta*-s are numerous. You should have a proper knowledge of the main *siddhānta*. As for the other *siddhānta*-s, only a brief knowledge of their essence would do for you." "Tell us please," said they, "what is the main *siddhānta*? How, moreover, are we to learn the other *siddhānta*-s in brief?" Dīpaṃkara said, "The main *siddhānta* is *karuṇā*. There is no limit to the need for it by the living beings and only the *bodhicitta* can satisfy it. The main thing for you to try, therefore, is *bodhicitta-utpādana*. This leads to the realisation that everything, both internal and external, are unreal, though appearing to be real. Keep all the *puṇya*-s that you earn deposited for the living beings. That is the main thing for you to do." On another occasion, somebody wanted to have Dīpaṃkara's *upadeśa* and requested Shaṅ-sṅa-chuṅ-ston-pa to take him to the Master. But Shaṅ-sṅa-chuṅ-ston-pa said, "What is the use of that ? He will only tell you to practise meditation and strive after the *bodhicitta*, or some other useless thing like this." Dīpaṃkara came to know of this and sarcastically remarked, "Yes. Shaṅ-sṅa-chuṅ-ston-pa appears to be quite right. Not only you Tibetans but some of my Indian students also seem to be eager to have the *upadeśa* but do not like to practise it. You do not believe in the greatness of the *bodhicitta*." Dīpaṃkara himself always laid the greatest emphasis on the *bodhicitta*. As he said in one of his books, "I bow down to *bodhicitta*, which alone destroys all the miseries (*sarva-durgati*) and leads all the living beings to *mokṣa*. *Bodhicitta* raises one to the status of the *sambuddha*." Somebody once approached him for an *upadeśa* on alchemy. He simply said, "The *rasāyana* of the *bodhicitta* is the highest *rasāyana*."

The young king Bodhiprabha, after showing the proper reverence to him, made the following request : "There are many scholars in Tibet and many a one is claiming to be the real *guru*. They are fighting each other, each trying to establish the supremacy of some doctrine or other. As a result, various doctrines are passing today in Tibet as the true doctrine of the Buddha. Please, therefore, write a book explaining the True Doctrine. The book should preferably be brief so that it can serve a very wide purpose. Such a work will remove all the confusions and misrepresentations of the Buddhist doctrine." There was also a request from Khaṅ-gsar-ba-rmog-cog for a book neither too profound nor too superficial, because only a book like that could truly help the people of Tibet. In response to requests like these, Dīpaṃkara wrote the *Bodhi-patha-pradīpa*. It contains the essence of the *Tripiṭaka*-s and shows the true path for three types of persons. As the sun illumines the world, the book showed the people of Tibet the real way of approaching the Sūtra and the Tantra systems. As it is said in a *stotra* to Dīpaṃkara: "Before the arrival of our *guru*, all understandings of the *śāstra*-s were going wrong. The coming of the *mahājñānī* was like sun-rise on Tibet."

Six famous scholars of Tibet,—gYuṅ-druṅ, 'Gar-dge-ba, Shaṅ-chen-po, Śākya-dbaṅ-phyug, Khu-ston and Legs-pa'i-śes-rab,—once had a long discussion among themselves. On the basis of this, they decided to put forth some questions to Dīpaṃkara, who was then proceeding to gTsaṅ. The questions were: 1) Can *prajñā* by itself or *upāya* by itself lead one to Buddhahood? 2) Does one who has already received the *bodhicitta saṃvara* require the *pratimokṣa saṃvara?* 3) Can one be a *vajrācārya* without being himself initiated? 4) Is it proper for a *brahmacārī* to receive the three *abhiṣeka*-s*?* 5) Can one practise the *guhya-tantra* without proper initiation? After listening to these questions, Dīpaṃkara said, "Answers to all these are to be found in my *Bodhi-patha-pradīpa*. Apparently, you have not read the book carefully. I wrote the book in response to king Bodhiprabha's request to explain the same and similar questions." The six scholars read the book carefully and found clear answers to their questions.

There is no subject that Dīpaṃkara did not teach in Tibet and he left no good work undone there. He taught all the Buddhist *śāstra*-s and made people understand all these. He taught the householders how to observe the *upavāsa* and *tri-śaraṇa-gamana*. The monks learnt from him how to protect the *śīla*-s. To the Tāntrikas he gave instructions of solemn vows and to the performers of virtuous deeds (*puṇya-karmin*-s) he taught the method of depositing the *puṇya*. He taught the people how to perform the last rites for the dead, how to serve the living and nurse the sick. He loved all the people, the lower and the higher. But his special teaching was that of the three ways, as explained in his *Bodhi-patha-pradīpa.*

58. 'Brom-ston-pa Appointed as Successor

Dīpaṃkara said to 'Brom-ston-pa, "I hereby entrust on you the responsibility of preserving all the Mahāyāna *śāstra*-s as interpreted by Nāgārjuna and Asaṅga and the *mahāpuruṣa-dharma and siddhānta-nīti* which come down to us from Trikāla Buddha and Bodhisattva through the unbroken chain of *ācārya*-s." 'Brom-ston-pa said, "Oh Master, with the little knowledge that I have, how can I at all accept such an enormous responsibility! Please appoint somebody more able to be your successor." Dīpaṃkara said, "There is none like that. This is my order to you. You have got to accept the responsibility." Following was the last message of Dīpaṃkara to 'Brom-ston-pa : "As you have not yet acquired all the *abhijñāna*-s, it will be difficult for you to work by yourself for all the living beings. But always remember one thing : *dharma* depends on the *saṅgha* and the *saṅgha* depends on the *vinaya.* So you have got to be careful of the *vinaya* above all. Teach your students the *vinaya* most carefully. And build a good *vihāra* for the special study of the *vinaya.*"

59. Nirvāṇa

In sÑe-thaṅ, Dīpaṃkara fell ill. He performed many *pujā*-s and said, "Most of my teachers are in the Tuṣita. I must go to them." At that time, *paṇḍita* Jñānākara of Kashmir, a student of Naḍo-pā, came to Nepal. Jayaśīla wanted to go to him and bring him to Tibet. But he was unable to leave Dīpaṃkara, who was then very ill and was not going to live long. Dīpaṃkara told him, "It is a rare fortune to meet a Mahāyāna *guru.* I am myself going to meet my *guru* Maitreya-nātha in Tuṣita. After I depart, make a life-size image of mine and send it to India. Do not worry. We shall meet again in Tuṣita." Jayaśīla said, "This will of course be done by us. Please confer the *pratiṣṭhāna* on this image. And keep your eyes on us, please, from the Tuṣita." His last message to his disciples was : "I am leaving 'Brom-ston-pa to succeed me. Have the same respect for him as you had for me. Do not get distracted by worldly affairs. My blessings shall be with you." Dīpaṃkara cannot die, of course. In the eyes of the common people, however, he breathed his last at the age of seventy-three in the Wood-Male-Horse year (A.D. 1054) in sÑe-thaṅ on the 20th day of the middle of autumn. Says the *stotra* : "You lived for the living beings and you left your mortal body to assume the *praṇidhāna-kāya* near Maitreyanātha in the Tuṣita heaven." Along with the three years that he spent in western Tibet and four years in gTsaṅ and dBus, six years in sÑe-thaṅ, the total period of his stay in Tibet seems to have been thirteen years. But some mention this as seventeen years. This point remains controversial.

'Brom-ston-pa mixed the remains of his ashes with medicines and sandal wood and gave the greater part of it to the Rwa-sgreṅ monastery in a silver *stūpa*. Khu-ston-pa, rÑog-ston-pa and others received small parts of it and they placed these in *caitya*-s built in different holy places. The last rites were organised in a big way. The lo-tsā-ba-s received his collection of Indian manuscripts and rNal-'byor-pa received his Tāntrika collection. Khu-ston-pa took the golden idol of Śākyamuni, which Dharmakīrti of Suvarṇadvīpa gave to Dīpaṃkara. This made Khu-ston very happy. Another gold-gilted image of the Buddha along with those of Sāriputra and Maudgalyāyana, the chief disciples of Śākyamuni, were placed in the 'Or temple. In the same temple were placed eight *caitya*-s containing Dīpaṃkara's relics. His wealth was spent, according to his own wish, for the purpose of building new monasteries and later particularly for the development of the Rwa-sgreṅ *vihāra*. His precious golden idol of Tārādevī was placed in gSaṅ-phu and eight *caitya*-s were built there to contain his relics. The relic of Naḍo-pā, which Dīpaṃkara carried with him to Tibet, was placed in another *caitya* in 'Or. His other images of gods and goddesses were also placed in the shrine of 'Or.

60. *Epilogue*

According to the Buddhist scriptures, four *kāla*-s or periods are specially important. These are the periods of learning, of practising, of reading and of the "mere symbol". We are now passing through the period of reading. How can we describe his greatness, which was as vast as the sky and as deep as the ocean ? We could say just something and this according to our own humble abilities.

APPENDIX B

The works of Dipamkara

Section 1 : Introductory Note.

Section 2 : Works in the bsTan-'gyur of which Dīpaṃkara is both author and translator.

Section 3 : Works in the bsTan-'gyur of which Dīpaṃkara is author only.

Section 4 : Works in the bsTan-'gyur of which Dīpaṃkara is translator only.

Section 5 : Works in the bsTan-'gyur connected in other ways with Dīpaṃkara.

Section 6 : Works in th the bsTan-'gyur, though with some variation in the name of the author or translator, are to be attributed to the same Dīpaṃkara.

Section 7 : Works in the bKa'-'gyur of which Dīpaṃkara is translator or reviser.

Section 1

Introductory Note

The general principles of identifying Dīpaṃkara and his works in the bKa'-'gyur and bsTan-'gyur are discussed in Section 5, pp. 37-55. An effort is made here to prepare a complete list of the works in the two great Tibetan collections that mention Dīpaṃkara as the author, translator, corrector or reviser. For obvious reasons, the list is divided under a number of sections.

Generally speaking, only the Sanskrit titles of the works, arranged alphabetically, are mentioned in each section. Occasionally, however, are also given their Tibetan sub-titles, particularly when these show any interesting variation.

Except in the last section, after the name of each text is first given its position and number in the bsTan-'gyur according to Cordier's *Catalogue*. In the last section, however, instead of this is mentioned the number of the text according to the Sendai *Catalogue*. Where two such numbers occur, the latter is generally a literal reproduction of the former.

Next is given the reference to the same text in the Peking edition of the bKa'-'gyur and bsTan-'gyur published by the Tibetan Tripiṭaka Research Institute, Tokyo-Kyoto, under the supervision of the Otani University, Kyoto. In this reference is first given the number of the volume of the *Tibetan Tripiṭaka* in which the text occurs, and then, after a stroke-sign, the serial number of the text itself, followed by a stroke-sign again, the page-number, the folio-number and the line-number where the text begins. Thus, e.g., K 52/2205/15-3-8 means that in the Tokyo-Kyoto edition, the text is to be found in Volume Number 52, its Serial Number is 2205 and that in this volume the text begins in page 15, folio 3 and line 8.

For a realistic idea of Dīpaṃkara's works, it is not enough

to have a mere list of the titles of which he was the author or translator or both. It is necessary, moreover, to have some idea of the actual length of each work. Some of these works are extremely short, being nothing more than a few sentences of *upadeśa* or only a short *stotra*, while the lengths of some others are staggering. Here is an example of such variation in length : in the *Tibetan Tripiṭaka* (Tokyo-Kyoto), the shortest work of which Dīpaṃkara is the author occupy only three lines, and this as inclusive of the Indian title, Tibetan sub-title and the colophon ; by contrast, the longest work (of which Dīpaṃkara is a translator) occupy 13,016 lines in the same edition.

It is, therefore, considered worthwhile to give some idea of the actual length of each work. This is done by mentioning the number of lines it occupies in the Tokyo-Kyoto edition of the *Tibetan Tripiṭaka*. But these lines do not correspond to our idea of printed lines in modern publications. Nevertheless, we may have some idea of the actual length of each work from the mention of the number of lines it occupies in the Tibetan original. The *Bodhi-patha-pradīpa*, the *Caryā-gīti* and the *Vimala-ratna-lekha*, English translations of which are given in Appendix C, occupy 53, 25 and 27 lines respectively in the *Tibetan Tripiṭaka*. Calculating on the basis of this, it should be possibe to have some idea of the length of the other works.

In the present Bibliography, after thus mentioning the length of each work, are given the names of its author and translators, along with epithets like *paṇḍita*, *mahā-paṇḍita*, etc., the significance sometimes attributed to which being already discussed in section 5. These names are given on the basis of Cordier's *Catalogue*. For the purpose of identifying the author or translator of a text more fully, the equivalents of his name as occurring in what Cordier calls *Index Tibetan* and *Index Mongolian* are often added within brackets. In cases, however, in which the name of the author or translator is found only in these indices, the index is mentioned before the name and no bracket-sign is used.

Since the colophons of the texts as understood by Cordier

do not always agree with those as actually found in the Peking edition and since, moreover, the colophons of the Peking edition—in spite of their intrinsic importance—have not so far been made available in English translation, it has been considered worthwhile to add to each text its colophon of the Peking edition in English translation. These translations are intended to be literal.

All these colophons are translated under Professor Lama Chimpa.

The following abbreviations are used—

a.	Author
IM	*Index Mongolian*
IT	*Index Tibetan*
K	Tokyo-Kyoto edition of the Tibetan Tripiṭaka
mDo	mDo-'grel
rG	rGyud-'grel
t.	Translator

SECTION 2

Works in the bsTan-'gyur of which Dīpaṃkara is both author and translator

1. *Abhisamaya-vibhaṅga-nāma*

rG xiii 38. K 52/2205-15-3-8. About 293 lines.

a. mahā-yogīśvara Lui-pāda and mahā-paṇḍita Dīpaṃkara-śrī-jñāna (IT Jo-bo-rje ; IM Atīśa). t. paṇḍita Dīpaṃkara-śrī-jñāna and lo-tsā-ba bhikṣu Jayaśīla.

Colophon K : written by mahā-paṇḍita Dīpaṃkara-śrī-jñāna by commenting (or interpreting) in the tāntrika way the Ṣaṭ-kula-heruka-upāya-mūla-mahā-maṇḍala of yogīśvara Lui-pā ; translated and revised by the same Indian paṇḍita and lo-tsā-ba bhikṣu Jayaśīla.

Note : Depending on Cordier's understanding of the colophon, modern scholars argue that its joint author Lui-pā must have been a senior contemporary of Dīpaṃkara. [S. K. Chatterjee ODBL i. 118 ; S. K. De in HB i. 341 ; S. B. Dasgupta ORC 6 ; H. P. Sastri BGD (Bengali) intro. 15]. But the colophon K translated above gives us the impression that the work of Lui-pā was a different one.

2. *Amṛtodaya-nāma-bali-vidhi..*

rG lxxii 70. K 81/4596/280-1-1. About 144 lines.

a. IT Jo-bo-rje ; IM Atīśa. t. upādhyāya Dīpaṃkara-śrī-jñāna of India and lo-tsā-ba Siddha of Khu (Śākya-bhikṣu, probably Sanātanavīrya of Yar-kluṅs monastery).

Colophon K : translated by Indian upādhyāya Dīpaṃkara-srī-jñāna and finalised by Siddha of Khu.

3. *Akṣobhya-sādhana-nāma*

rG lxiii 26. K 77/3477/61-1-3. About 27 lines.

a. ācārya Dīpaṃkara-śrī-jñāna (IT Jo-bo-rje ; IM Atīśa) t. author and lo-tsā-ba bhikṣu Jayaśīla of Nag-tsho.

Colophon K : written by ācārya Dīpaṃkara-śrī-jñāna ; translated and revised by the same paṇḍita and Tibetan lo-tsā-ba Jayaśīla.

4. *Aṣṭa-bhaya-trāṇa*

rG lxxi 386. K 81/4510/94-4-2. About 11 lines.

a. ācārya paṇḍita Śrī-dīpaṃkara-jñāna (IT Jo-bo-rje ; IM Atīśa). t. IT author, the upādhyāya of India and lo-tsā-ba Jayaśīla.

Colophon K : written by ācārya paṇḍita Śrī-dīpaṃkara-jñāna.

5. *Āpatti-deśanā-vidhi*

mDo xxxii 12. K 103/5369/177-1-4. About 11½ ines.

a. ācārya Śrī-dīpaṃkara-jñāna (IT Jo-bo-rje ; IM Atīśa). t. author, the upādhyāya of India, and lo-tsā-ba bhikṣu Jayaśīla.

Colophon K : written by ācārya Śrī-dīpaṃkara-jñāna ; translated and revised by the ācārya himself and the Tibetan lo-tsā-ba bhikṣu Jayaśīla.

6. *Ārya-acala-krodha-rāja-stotra*

rG lxix 121 ; lxix 122. K 79/3884/265-4-3 ; 79/3885. About 13½ lines.

a. lxix 121 : paṇḍita Dīpaṃkara-jñāna (IT Jo-bo-rje ; IM Atīśa) ; lxix 122 : mahā-ācārya Śrī-dīpaṃkara-jñāna (IT Jo-bo-rje ; IM Atīśa). t. author and lo-tsā-ba bhikṣu Jayaśīla.

Colophon K (79/3884) : written by paṇḍita Dīpaṃkara-jñāna; translated and revised by the same paṇḍita and lo-tsā-ba bhikṣu Jayaśīla.

7. *Ārya-avalokita-lokeśvara-sādhana*

rG xl 21. K 66/2757/30-1-4. About 27½ lines.

a. mahā-ācārya Śrī-dīpaṃkara-jñāna (IT Jo-bo-rje ; IM Atīśa). t. IT upādhyāya Dīpaṃkara-śrī-jñāna of India and reviser lo-tsā-ba bhikṣu Ratnabhadra.

Colophon K : I, Dīpaṃkara-śrī-jñāna, have written it on the basis of the collection of upadeśa-s (upadeśa-saṃgraha). Written by mahā-ācārya Śrī-dīpaṃkara-jñāna.

8. *Ārya-gaṇapati-rāga-vajra-samaya-stotra-nāma*

rG lxxii 34. K 81/4561/224-1-4. About 9 lines.

a. paṇḍita Dīpaṃkara-śrī-jñāna (IT Jo-bo-rje ; IM Atīśa) t. author and lo-tsā-ba Jayaśīla of Nag-tsho.

Colophon K : written by paṇḍita Dīpaṃkara-śrī-jñāna, translated by the same mahā-paṇḍita and lo-tsā-ba Jayaśīla.

9. *Ārya-tārā-stotra*

rG lxxi 387. K 81/4511/94-5-5. About 11½ lines.

a. Dīpaṃkara-śrī-jñāna (IT Jo-bo-rje ; IM Atīśa) t. author, the upādhyāya of India, and lo-tsā-ba Jayaśīla.

Colophon K : written by Dīpaṃkara-śrī-jñāna ; translated by the same Indian ācārya and Tibetan lo-tsā-ba Jayaśīla.

10. *Āyuḥ-sādhana*

rG lxxxii 34. K 86/4863/121-2-2. About 15 lines.

a. IT mahā-paṇḍita Dīpaṃkara-jñāna. t. IT author and lo-tsā-ba Candraprabha of Gyi-jo.

Colophon K does not mention author or translator.

11. *Eka-smṛti-upadeśa*

mDo xxx 22 ; xxxiii 12. K 102/5323/53-5-7 ; 103/5389. About 17½ lines.

a. paṇḍita Dīpaṃkara-śrī-jñāna (IT Jo-bo-rje ; IM Atīśa). t. author and lo-tsā-ba Jayaśīla.

Colophon K : written by paṇḍita Dīpaṃkara-śrī-jñāna ; translated by the same paṇḍita and lo-tsā-ba Jayaśīla.

12. *Karma-vibhaṅga-nāma*

mDo xxxi 22 ; xxxiii 20. K 103/5356/54-1-5 ; 103/5397. About 93 lines.

a. ācārya mahā-paṇḍita Śrī-dīpaṃkara-jñāna (IT Jo-bo-rje ; IM Atīśa). t. author, the mahā-upādhyāya of India and reviser lo-tsā-ba bhikṣu Jayaśīla.

Colophon K 103/5356 : written by ācārya mahā-paṇḍita Śrī-dīpaṃkara-jñāna ; translated and revised by the same Indian ācārya mahā-paṇḍita and lo-tsā-ba bhikṣu Jayaśīla.

13. *Karma-āvaraṇa-viśodhana-vidhi-bhāṣya-nāma*

mDo xxxvii 10. K 105/5508/150-4-3. About 108 lines.

a. ācārya Dīpaṃkara-śrī-jñāna (IT Jo-bo-rje ; IM Atīśa). t. author and lo-tsā-ba bhikṣu Jayaśīla of Nag-tsho.

Colophon K : written by ācārya Dīpaṃkara-śrī-jñāna ; translated by the same paṇḍita and lo-tsā-ba Jayaśīla.

14. *Kāya-vāk-citta-supratiṣṭhā-nāma*

rG xlviii 154. K 70/3322/29-3-1. About 97 lines.

a. Śrī-dīpaṃkara-jñāna (IT Jo-bo-rje ; IM Atiśa). t. upādhyāya Dīpaṃkara of India and lo-tsā-ba Vīryasiṃha of rGya. Place of translation : the Vikramaśīla vihāra.

Colophon K : written by Śrī-dīpaṃkara-jñāna ; translated and revised very nicely by Indian upādhyāya Dīpaṃkara and lo-tsā-ba Vīryasiṃha of rGya at Vikramaśīla.

15. *Khasarpaṇa-avalokita-sādhana*

rG lxxxii 13.

a. mahā-ārya Dīpaṃkara-śrī-jñāna. t. author and lo-tsā-ba bhikṣu Śākyamati

Note : Evidently the text is not traced. K 86/4843 mentions one as Śrī-khasarpaṇa-lokanātha-sādhana-nāma with the name of Padmākarapāda as the author.

16. *Garbha-saṃgraha-nāma*

mDo xxxi 11 ; xxxiii 5. K 103/5345/46-4-2 ; 103/5382. About 12 lines.

a. mahā-ācārya Śrī-dīpaṃkara-jñāna (IT Jo-bo-rje ; IM Atiśa). t. author and lo-tsā-ba bhikṣu Śīlākara (Tshul-khrims-'byuṅ-gnas).

Colophon K : written by mahā-ācārya Śrī-dīpaṃkara-jñāna; translated and revised by the same paṇḍita and lo-tsā-ba bhikṣu Śīlākara-śānti. (Title in K : Saṃgraha-garbha-nāma).

17. *Caryā-gīti-vṛtti.*

rG xiii 45. K 52/2212/29-3-1. About 43 lines.

a. paṇḍita Dīpaṃkara (IT Jo-bo-rje ; IM Atiśa). t. author and lo-tsā-ba Jayaśīla.

Colophon K : translated by paṇḍita Dīpaṃkara and lo-tsā-ba Jayaśīla.

18. *Caryā-saṃgraha-pradīpa*

mDo xxxi 23 ; xxxiii 2. K 103/5357/56-3-2 ; 103/5379. About 21 lines.

a. ācārya mahā-paṇḍita Śrī-dīpaṃkara-jñāna (IT Jo-bo-rje; IM Atiśa). t. author, the upādhyāya paṇḍita Dīpaṃkara-śrī-jñāna of India and lo-tsā-ba bhikṣu Jayaśīla.

Colophon K: written by ācārya, the Indian upādhyāya paṇḍita Dīpaṃkara-śrī-jñāna ; translated and corrected by lo-tsā-ba bhikṣu Jayaśīla.

19. *Citā-vidhi*

rG lxxxii 39. K 86/4868/123-2-4. About 18 lines.

a. mahā-ācārya Śrī-dīpaṃkara-jñāna (IT mahā-paṇḍita Dīpaṃ-mar-me). t. upādhyāya Dīpaṃkara-śrī-jñāna of India and lo-tsā-ba Candraprabha of Gyi-jo.

Colophon K : written by mahā-ācārya Dīpaṃkara-śrī-jñāna. It is new. Translated by Indian upādhyāya Dīpaṃkara-śrī-jñāna and Tibetan lo-tsā-ba Candraprabha of Gyi-jo.

20. *Cittotpāda-saṃvara-vidhi-krama*

mDo xxxii 7 ; xxxiii 26. K 103/5364/171-5-1 ; 103/5403. About 70 lines.

a. mahā-ācārya Śrī-dīpaṃkara-jñāna (IT Jo-bo-rje ; IM Atīśa). t. author, the upādhyāya of India, and reviser lo-tsā-ba bhikṣu Śubhamati (dGe-ba'i-blo-gros). The same work was translated later by the author and lo-tsā-ba bhikṣu Jayaśīla, though IT mentions Jayaśīla as the corrector only.

Colophon K : written by mahā-ācārya Śrī-dīpaṃkara-jñāna; translated by the same Indian paṇḍita and lo-tsā-ba bhikṣu Śubhamati. And again, revised by the same paṇḍita and lo-tsā-ba Jayaśīla.

21. *Jala-bali-Vimala-grantha*

rG Ixxii 71. K 8I/4597/283-3-8. About 17 lines.

a. ācārya Śrī-dīpaṃkara-jñāna (IT Jo-bo-rje ; IM Atīśa). t. author and lo-tsā-ba Jayaśīla. Copyist : Legs-pa'i-śes-rab, of the tribe rÑog of sPu-raṅs. Place of translation : sKyi-groṅ in Maṅ-yul. Copyist : Suprajña (Legs-pa'i-śes-rab).

Colophon K : written by ācārya Śrī-dīpaṃkara-jñāna at sKyi-groṅ in Maṅ-yul by the request of Legs-pa'i-śes-rab ; translated by the same paṇḍita and lo-tsā-ba Jayaśīla.

22. *Tārā-bhaṭṭārikā-sādhana*

rG lxxi 384. K 81/4508/90-4-5. About 51 lines.

a. mahā-ācārya Śrī-dīpaṃkara-jñāna (IT Jo-bo-rje ; IM

Atiśa). t. upādhyāya Dīpaṃkara-śri-jñāna of India (IT author) and lo-tsā-ba bhikṣu Śubhamati.

Colophon K : written by mahā-ācārya Śrī-dīpaṃkara-jñāna; translated and revised by the Indian upādhyāya Dīpaṃkara-śrī-jñāna and Tibetan lo-tsā-ba bhikṣu Śubhamati.

23. *Daśa-akuśala-karma-patha(-deśanā)*

mDo xxxi 21 ; xxxiii 19. K 103/5355/53-3-8 ; 103/5396. About 20 lines.

a. mahā-ācārya Śrī-dīpaṃkara-jñāna (IT Jo-bo-rje ; IM Atiśa). t. author, the upādhyāya of India and reviser lo-tsā-ba bhikṣu Jayaśīla.

Colophon K: written by mahā-ācārya Śrī-dīpaṃkara-jñāna ; translated and revised by the same Indian paṇḍita and the great lo-tsā-ba bhikṣu Jayaśīla. (Title in K 103/5355 : Daśa-akuśala-karma-mārga-deśanā ; 103/5396 : Daśa-akuśala-karma-pada-deśanā).

24. *Dīpaṃkara-śrī-jñāna-dharma-gītikā*

rG xlviii 34. K 69/3202/195-2-2. About 4½ lines.

a. and t. not separately mentioned either in Cordier's *Catalogue* or in Colophon K.

25. *Deva-pūjā-krama*

rG lxxxii 33. K 86/4862/120-4-6. About 19 lines.

a. IT mahā-paṇḍita Dīpaṃkara-jñāna. t. IT author and lo-tsā-ba Candraprabha of Gyi-jo.

Colophon K : mentions neither author nor translator.

26. *Dharma-dhātu-darśana-gīti*

rG xlvii 47 ; mDo xxxiii 11. K 69/3153/179-5-8 ; 103/5388/191-3-5. About 108 lines

a. rG xlvii 47 : mahā-ācārya Dīpaṃkara (IT Jo-bo-rje ; IM Atiśa) ; mDo xxxiii 11 : mahā-ācārya Dīpaṃkara-śrī-jñāna (IT Jo-bo-rje ; IM Atiśa). t. rG xlvii 47 : author and lo-tsā-ba bhikṣu Jayaśīla of Nag-tsho ; mDo xxxiii 11 : author, the upādhyāya of India, and lo-tsā-ba bhikṣu Jayaśīla.

Colophon K (both) : written by mahā-ācārya Dīpaṃkara-śrī-jñāna and translated by the same Indian upādhyāya and Tibetan lo-tsā-ba Jayaśīla.

27. *Nāga-bali-vidhi*

rG lxxii 72. K 81/4598/284-1-1. About 13 lines.

a. mahā-paṇḍita Śrī-dīpaṃkara-jñāna (IT Jo-bo-rje ; IM Atīśa). t. author and lo-tsā-ba Ratnabhadra.

Colophon K : written by mahā-paṇḍita Śrī-dīpaṃkara-jñāna who touched the dust of the feet of Tārādevī ; translated by lo-tsā-ba Ratnabhadra.

28. *Pañca-caitya-nirvapaṇa-vidhi*

rG lxix 136. K 79/3899/288-3-3, About 8 lines.

a. upādhyāya Dīpaṃkara-śrī-jñāna of India (IT Jo-bo-rje ; IM Atīśa). t. IT author and lo-tsā-ba Jayaśīla.

Colophon K : written by Dīpaṃkara-śrī-jñāna.

29. *Peyotkṣepa-vidhi*

rG lxxxii 31. K 86/4860/119-5-7. About 13½ lines.

a. IT mahā-paṇḍita Dīpaṃkara-jñāna. t. IT author and lo-tsā-ba Candraprabha of Gyi-jo.

Colophon K : mentions neither author nor translator, but simply gives the tile *Peyabalividhi*.

30. *Prajñā-pāramitā-piṇḍārtha-pradīpa*

mDo x 2 ; cxxviii 10. K 92/5201/103-3-5 ; 146/5873. About 148 lines.

a. mDo x 2 : Śrī-dīpaṃkara-jñāna (IT Jo-bo-rje ; IM Atīśa ; IT & IM—disciple of Śānti-pā ; Śāntipāda ; śākya-bhikṣu Ratnākaraśānti) ; mDo cxxviii 10—Śrī-dīpaṃkara-jñāna. Variant : bhikṣu Dīpaṃkara-śrī-jñāna of Bengal. t. mDo x 2 : author and lo-tsā-ba mahā-mahā-paṇḍita Jayaśīla. mDo cxxviii 10 : Place of translation—the nirābhoga vihāra of bSam-yas.

Colophon K (92/5201) : This alone contains the Buddha's doctrines ; the Bengal-born bhikṣu Dīpaṃkara-śrī-jñāna wrote it according to the *śāstra*-s and *guru-vacana*-s. Written by Śri-dīpaṃkara-jñāna and translated by the same paṇḍita and lo-tsā-ba mahā-mahā-paṇḍita Jayaśīla. Again at bSam-yas, the *nirābhoga-vidyāgārasthāna*, Dīpaṃkara produced (?) it while he was explaining the *Viṃśati-sāhasrikā*. Later on, the proper book was formed (?) by both the paṇḍita and lo-tsā-ba from the Vivarta.

[Note : Vivarta evidently means the Vartula script. See BA i.162]. Here is the latest version. The Vivarta (i.e. the text in the Vartula script), the Indian original (and this)—all three are in 'Chims-phu. It is said that this work is included in Śata-sāhasrikā, translated by Vairocana.

31. *Prajñā-hṛdaya-vyākhyā*

mDo xvi 14. K 94/5222/297-3-6. About 86 lines.

a. Dīpaṃkara-śrī-jñāna (IT Jo-bo-rje ; IM Atīśa). t. upādhyāya Dīpaṃkara-śrī-jñāna of India and lo-tsā-ba bhikṣu Jayaśīla.

Colophon K : On the request of bhikṣu Suprajña to Dīpaṃkara-śrī-jñāna was written the meaning of that *śāstra* by me. Now, in Tibet there are still the bad manners of the ancient tradition. So I do not know if this *upadeśa* would be useful or not. But I hope it will be useful at least for the wise men, (who) must understand the śāstra thoroughly and must not talk with anger. Translated and revised by the Indian upādhyāya Dīpaṃkara-śrī-jñāna and lo-tsā-ba Jayaśīla.

32. *Bodhi-citta-mahāsukha-āmnāya*

rG xxvi 67. K 59/2619/103-3-7. About 11½ lines.

a. upādhyāya Dīpaṃkara-śrī-jñāna (IT Jo-bo-rje ; IM Atīśa). t. upādhyāya Dīpaṃkara-śrī-jñāna of India and reviser lo-tsā-ba Śubhamati.

Colophon K : (does not mention the author but says) translated by the same Indian upādhyāya Dīpaṃkara-śrī-jñāna and lo-tsā-ba Śubhamati on the request of the royal Bodhiprabha.

33. *Bodhi-patha-pradīpa*

mDo xxxi 9 ; xxxiii 1. K 103/5343/20-4-1 ; 103/5378. About 53 lines.

a. mahā-ācārya Śrī-dīpaṃkara-jñāna (IT Jo-bo-rje ; IM Atīśa). t. author, the upādhyāya of India and reviser lo-tsā-ba bhikṣu Śubhamati. Place of translation—the Tho-liṅ vihāra in Shaṅ-shuṅ in the province of mṄa'-ris.

Colophon K : written by mahā-ācārya Śrī-dīpaṃkara-jñāna ; translated by the same Indian paṇḍita and the great lo-tsā-ba Śubhamati. This book is written in the Tho-liṅ temple of Shaṅ-shuṅ.

34. *Bodhi-mārga-pradīpa-pañjikā-nāma*

mDo xxxi 10. K 103/5344/21-5-6. About 989 lines.

Tibetan sub-title (K 103/5344) : auto-commentary of the *Bodhi-patha-pradīpa* done by Jo-bo-rje and it's Indian title is *Bodhi-mārga-pradīpa-pañjikā-nāma.*

a. śākya-bhikṣu mahā-paṇḍita Dīpaṃkara-śri-jñāna of the royal family of Bengal (IT Jo-bo-rje ; IM Atīśa). t. mahā-upādhyāya guru bodhisattva Śrī-dīpaṃkara-jñāna-pāda of Bengal and lo-tsā-ba bhikṣu Jayaśīla of Nag-tsho. The colophon mentions lo-tsā-ba Byaṅ-chub-'od of mÑa'-ris-bskor-gsum, disciple of the author.

Colophon K : *Bodhi-mārga-pradīpa-pañjikā-nāma.* Written by śākya-bhikṣu mahā-paṇḍita bodhi-sattvacārī Dīpaṃkara-śrī-jñāna, a descendant of the Bengalee king. This is the best tree of bodhisattva ; (grown) on the soil of śraddhā from the seed of śīla, the sapling of kindness is watered by samādhi ; having karuṇā and bodhicitta as its roots, the prajñāpāramitā as its branches and the sapta-ratna-s its flowers, from which spreads the fragrance of daśa-kuśala-s to disciples. Representing the Buddha this time, Dīpaṃkara-śrī-pāda was born in Bengal ; he is very famous, well-versed in the dharma-nīti-s, beautifully ornamented with the saṃvara-s, learned, powerful and eminently qualified to be the guru of the living beings. He is the only son of the Buddha whose teachings are (more) precious than gold and musk and who teaches according to the inclinations and nature (of the three kinds of) men. He never thinks of avoiding like poison the unfaithful, but he never follows them and indulges in evil. He never violates his own codes of action. He has always the power of crushing evil adversaries. He is very fortunate and took his birth at the centre of the noblest place, in the royal race. By "natural birth", (however), he belongs to the Mahāyāna race, born as a son of Praṇidhāna Bhadra Buddha. Thus this guru Dīpaṃkara-śrī-jñāna is bodhisattva, adorned with

karuṇā. Śākya-bhikṣu Jayaśīla, a very loyal disciple of this mahā-puruṣa guru, with high respect and unfailing services (for the guru) thinks (that this work is) "nothing but the Cakra-saṃvara-yoga-tantra-rāja and the essence of the essence of the 84,000 dharma-skandha-s. Therefore, follow this day and night. We may fail to follow all the upadeśa-s of this ; but not only I, Nag-tsho, all the Tibetan disciples should remember and respect this guru with body-speech-mind and should always bow down before him." Translated and revised by the Indian mahā-paṇḍita guru bodhisattva, the Bengalee Śrī-dīpaṃkara-jñāna-pāda and lo-tsā-ba bhikṣu Jayaśīla. This mahā-puruṣa who is very famous and well-versed in dharma-nīti and who, like the sun works always for the sake of others, brings the whole of Tibet to the religious path. Being requested by Bodhiprabha and Jayaśīla for a commentary on the *Bodhi-patha-pradīpa*, he produced this work with great kindness and profound knowledge. But he said, "Do not show it to all. Keep it secret."

Note : The last sentence of the above colophon perhaps indicates the Tibetan way of attributing great importance to the work : a work of great importance is often expected to be kept secret. Sometimes such works are physically kept under sealed lock.

35. *Bodhisattvādikarmika-mārgāvatāra-deśanā.* (Sanskrit title in K : *Bodhisattva-karma-ādi-mārga-avatāra-deśanā.*)

mDo xxxi 15 ; xxxiii 13. K 103/5349/48-4-1 ; 103/5390. About 35½ lines.

a. ācārya Śrī-dīpaṃkara-jñāna (IT Jo-bo-rje ; IM Atīśa). t. author and lo-tsā-ba Jayaśīla. Translation executed by the request of bhikṣu Bodhiprabha, the disciple of Dīpaṃkara.

Colophon K : (At the end of the text Dīpaṃkara says, "This is the bhadra-mārga of the uttama-puruṣa-s, explained to the disciples like Bodhiprabha and others...''). On bhikṣu Bodhi-prabha's request to the great guru bodhisattva, bhikṣu Jayaśīla revised and translated it. The Mahāyānists should read it. Written by ācārya Dīpaṃkara-jñāna ; translated by the same paṇḍita and lo-tsā-ba Jayaśīla.

36. *Bhagavad-akṣobhya-sādhana*

rG lxiii 27. K 77/3478/61-4-6. About 8½ lines

a. Śrī-dīpaṃkara-jñāna (IT Jo-bo-rje ; IM Atīśa) t. author and lo-tsā-ba bhikṣu Jayaśīla of Nag-tsho.

Colophon K : written by Śrī-dīpaṃkara-jñāna ; translated by the same Indian upādhyāya and Tibetan lo-tsā-ba Jayaśīla.

37. *Madhyamaka-upadeśa-nāma*

mDo xxx 23 ; xxx 25 ; xxxiii 4. K 102/5324/54-2-8 ; 102/5326; 103/5381/187-3-8. About 17 lines (in K 103/5381). (Because of the longish colophon of the K 102/5324 version, it is about 21½ lines).

a. mDo xxx 23 mahā-ācārya Śrī-dīpaṃkara-jñāna (IT Jo-bo-rje ; IM Atīśa) ; mDo xxx 25 : ācārya Śrī-dīpaṃkara-jñāna. t. author, the upādhyāya of India and lo-tsā-ba bhikṣu Jayaśīla of Nag-tsho. Place of translation—the grand vihāra of 'Phrul-snaṅ at Lhasa.

Colophon K 102/5324 : written by mahā-ācārya Śrī-dīpaṃkara-jñāna ; translated and revised by the same Indian paṇḍita and lo-tsā-ba bhikṣu Jayaśīla at the Lhasa Temple. "Being requested at the Lhasa temple by bhaṭṭāraka Legs-pa'i-śes-rab of rṄog, the paṇḍita Dīpaṃkara-śrī and I have translated it. The śāstra-s of sthavira Dīpaṃkara-śrī preach the system of the three puruṣa-s. So, no one can enter the way of challenging it",—this is said by Jayaśīla of Nag-tsho. K 103/5381 : written by ācārya Śrī-dīpaṃkara-jñāna ; translated and revised by the same Indian ācārya and lo-tsā-ba Jayaśīla at the Lhasa temple.

38. *Mantra-artha-avatāra*

rG lxxxii 27. K 86/4856/118-1-6. About 25 lines.

a. ācārya Dīpaṃkara-śrī-jñāna (IT mahā-paṇḍita Dīpaṃkara-jñāna). t. IT author and lo-tsā-ba Candraprabha of Gyi-jo.

Colophon K : written by ācārya Dīpaṃkara-śri-jñāna. Tibetan sub-title K : A king called Candra (?) said that the Tantra-yāna did not represent the words of the Buddha. To remove his doubts was written Dīpaṃkara's *Mantra-artha-*

avatāra. (Next is quoted the following *śloka*) : "Jambudvīpa (is best of the four dvīpa-s and thus is better than) the three other dvīpa-s. The human being is best of the six kinds of living beings. The best siddhi is (obtained) in the Yāna of the Buddha, not among the Tīrthikas. Among the yāna-s of the Buddha, the ārya-mahāyāna (is best, and therefore superior to) the śrāvaka-yāna, the pratyeka-buddha-yāna. Among the mahāyāna-s, the tantra-yāna is best. It is like this. So one must try to enter the mantra-yāna."

39. *Mahā-yakṣa-senāpati-nīlāmbara-dhara - vajrapāṇi - sādhana-nāma*

rG lxxxii 19. K 86/4848/109-1-5. About 60 lines.

a. mahā-ācārya Śrī-dīpaṃkara-jñāna (IT Dīpaṃkara). t. upādhyāya Dīpaṃkara-śrī-jñāna of India (IT author) and reviser lo-tsā-ba bhikṣu Ratnabhadra.

Colophon K : written by mahā-ācārya Śrī-dīpaṃkara-jñāna; translated by Indian upādhyāya Dīpaṃkara-śrī-jñāna and lo-tsā-ba bhikṣu Ratnabhadra.

40. *Mahāyāna-patha-sādhana-varṇa-saṃgraha*

mDo xxxi 17; xxxiii 15. K 103/5351/50-1-6; 103/5392. About 67 lines.

a. mahā-ācārya Śrī-dīpaṃkara-jñāna (IT Jo-bo-rje ; IM Atīśa). t. author, the upādhyāya of India, and lo-tsā-ba bhikṣu Śubhamati.

Colophon K : written by mahā-ācārya Śrī-dīpaṃkara-jñāna; translated and revised by the same Indian ācārya and lo-tsā-ba bhikṣu Śubhamati.

41. *Mahāyāna-patha-sādhana-saṃgraha*

mDo xxxi 18 ; xxxiii 16. K 103/5352/51-4-8 ; 103/5393. About 8 lines.

a. mahā-ācārya Śrī-dīpaṃkara-jñāna (IT Jo-bo-rje ; IM Atīśa). t. author, the upādhyāya of India and lo-tsā-ba bhīkṣu Śubhamati.

Colophon K : written by mahā-ācārya Śrī-dīpaṃkara-jñāna; translated and revised by the same paṇḍita, the Indian ācārya and lo-tsā-ba bhikṣu Śubhamati.

42. *Mumūrṣu-śāstra*

rG lxxxii 36. K 86/4865/121-5-7. About 17½ lines.

a. IT mahā-paṇḍita Dīpaṃkara-jñāna. t. IT author and lo-tsā-ba Candraprabha of Gyi-jo.

Colophon K : does not mention author or translator, but simply says, "Here ends Mumūrṣu-śāstra, the bodhicitta-viśodhana-upadeśa."

43. *Mūlāpatti-ṭīkā*

rG xlviii 145. K 69/3313/285-4-2. About 103 lines.

a. mahā-paṇḍita Dīpaṃkara-śrī-jñāna. t. author (IT Jo-bo-rje ; IM Atīśa) and lo-tsā-ba bhikṣu Jayaśīla of Nag-tsho.

Colophon K : written by mahā-paṇḍita Dīpaṃkara-śrī-jñāna ; translated by the same paṇḍita and lo-tsā-ba Jayaśīla.

44. *Mṛtyu-vañcana*

rG lxxxii 35. K 86/4864/121-4-1. About 29½ lines.

a. IT mahā-paṇḍita Dīpaṃkara-jñāna. t. IT author and lo-tsā-ba Candraprabha of Gyi-jo.

Colophon K : does not mention either author or translator.

45. *Ratna-karaṇḍodghāṭa-nāma-madhyamaka-upadeśa*

mDo xxx 24. K 102/5325/54-5-6. About 414 lines.

a. Śrī-dīpaṃkara-jñāna (IT Jo-bo-rje; IM Atīśa). t. author, upādhyāya Dīpaṃkara-śrī-jñāna of India, and mahā-upāsaka Vīryasiṃha and bhikṣu Jayaśīla. The text was exposed by Dīpaṃkara-śrī-jñāna to his disciple the śākya-bhikṣu Jayaśīla at the mahā-vihāra of Vikramaśīla founded by Devapāla.

Colophon K : written by Dīpaṃkara-śrī-jñāna on the request of śākya-bhikṣu Jayaśīla, the good disciple, at the Vikramaśīla temple connected with the solemn vow (*thugs-dam* See D-TED 579) of Devapāla. Dīpaṃkara has done it according to his guru's sayings, not for financial purpose. It should not be given to those who are without strict observances. One who does not devote oneself to ārya Nāgārjuna's śāstra has abandoned the real Doctrine. So such an one will go to hell. Thus ends the Precious Jewel of Mahāyāna's Madhyamaka-upadeśa, called the *Karaṇḍodghāṭa,* written by mahā-paṇḍita Śrī-dīpaṃkara-jñāna. Translated and revised by the same Indian upādhyāya Dīpaṃkara-śrī-jñāna and lo-tsā-ba mahā-upāsaka Vīryasiṃha of rGya and bhikṣu Jayaśīla.

46. *Lokātīta-saptāṅga-vidhi*

rG xlviii 121 (Literally reproduced mDo xxxiii 22, with the variation of the Sanskrit title as *Lokottarāṅga-saptaka-vidhi*). K 69/3289/258-1-5. About 11 lines.

a. ācārya mahā-paṇḍita Śrī-dīpaṃkara-jñāna of India (IT Jo-bo-rje ; IM Atiśa). t. author and reviser lo-tsā-ba bhikṣu Śākyamati. Work composed at the grand vihāra of Śrī-nirābhoga at bSam-yas, south of Lhasa.

Colophon K : written by ācārya mahā-paṇḍita Śrī-dīpaṃkara-jñāna at the bSam-yas nirābhoga temple ; translated by the same paṇḍita and lo-tsā-ba Śākyamati.

47. *Vajrayoginī-sādhana*

rG lxxiv 5. K 82/4671/111-3-7. About 3 lines.

a. paṇḍita Dīpaṃkara-śrī-jñāna (IT mahā-ārya Śrī-jñāna-dīpaṃkara). t. author and lo-tsā-ba Ratnabhadra.

Colophon K : written by paṇḍita Dīpaṃkara-śrī- jñāna ; translated by the same paṇḍita and lo-tsā-ba Ratnabhadra.

48. *Vajra-yoginī-stotra*

rG xiv 68. K 52/2298/278-3-3. About 13 lines.

a. paṇḍita Dīpaṃkara (IT Jo-bo-rje ; IM Atiśa). t. paṇḍita Dīpaṃkara and lo-tsā-ba Ratnabhadra.

Colophon K : written by paṇḍita Dīpaṃkara ; translated by the same paṇḍita and lo-tsā-ba Ratnabhadra.

49. *Vajra-yoginī-stotra*

rG xiv 75. K 52/2305/283-2-5. About 14 lines.

a. mahā-paṇḍita Dīpaṃkara-śrī-jñāna. t. author and lo-tsā-ba Śuka of Khu.

Colophon K : written by mahā-paṇḍita Dīpaṃkara-śrī jñāna ; translated by the same paṇḍita and lo-tsā-ba Śuka of Khu.

Note : This text is different from the above.

50. *Vajrāsana-vajragīti*

rG. xiii 42. K 52/2209/25-3-3. About 26 lines.

a. mahā-paṇḍita Śrī-dīpaṃkara-jñāna (IT Jo-bo-rje ; IM Atiśa). t. IT Dīpaṃkara-śrī-jñāna and lo-tsā-ba bhikṣu Jayaśīla.

Colophon K : For showing the real truth to others which he himself realised, this vajra-gīta was sung by Dīpaṃkara-śrī-jñana at...sÑe-thaṅ at the time of his departure to Vajra-dhara-sthāna.

Note : The Colophon is obscure and could not be fully understood.

51. *Vajrāsana-vajragīti-vṛtti.*

rG xiii 43. K 52/2210/26-1-5. About 106½ lines.

a. mahā-paṇḍita Dīpaṃkara-śrī-jñāna. t. Dīpaṃkara-śrī-jñāna and lo-tsā-ba bhikṣu Jayaśīla.

Colophon K : written by mahā-paṇḍita Dīpaṃkara-śrī jñāna ; translated by the same paṇḍita and bhikṣu Jayaśīla.

52. *Vasupati-upādhi-pañcaka-stotra-vasumeghāveśa-nāma*

rG lxxxiii 65. K 86/5000/219-1-2. About 11 lines.

a. Dīpaṃkara-jñāna. t. the author, mahā-paṇḍita of India, and the grand lo-tsā-ba Vīryasiṃha.

Colophon K : Composed by Dīpaṃkara-śrī-jñāna at the time of his vision of the five, namely Vasupati along with his four followers. Translated by the paṇḍita of India and the great lo-tsā-ba Vīryasiṃha.

53. *Vimala-ratna-lekha-nāma*

mDo xxxiii 103 ; xciv 33. K 103/5480/282-3-6 ; 129/5688. About 27 lines.

a. Sthavira mahā-paṇḍita Dīpaṃkara-śrī-jñāna (IT Jo-bo-rje ; IM Atīśa). t. author and lo-tsā-ba bhikṣu Jayaśīla. Called *Vimala-ratna-lekha-nāma*, sent by sthavira mahā-paṇḍita Dīpaṃkara-śrī-jñāna to king Nayapāla.

Colophon K : sent by sthavira mahā-paṇḍita Dīpaṃkara-śrī-jñāna to king Naryapāla, this Vimala-ratna-lekha, containing 40 ślokas, ends here. Translated this time by the same guru and lo-tsā-ba Jayaśīla. Revised once.

54. *Vimaloṣṇīṣa-dhāraṇī-vidhi*

rG lxix 137. K 79/3900/288-4-3. About 15 lines.

a. IT Jo-bo-rje. IT (author and ?) Tshul-rgyal (Jayaśīla).

Colophon K : mentions neither author nor translator.

55. *Vimaloṣṇīṣa-dhāraṇī-vidhi*

rG lxix 138. K 79/3901/289-1-2. About 9 lines.

a. ācārya Śrī-dīpaṃkara-jñāna (IT Jo-bo-rje ; IM Atīśa). t. IT (author and ?) Tshul-rgyal.

Colophon K : written by ācārya Śrī-dīpaṃkara-jñāna.

Note : This text is different from the above.

56. *Śmahoma*

rG lxxxii 37. K 86/4866.

a. IT mahā-paṇḍita Dīpaṃkara-jñāna. t. IT author and lo-tsā-ba Candraprabha of Gyi-jo.

57. *Śrī-guhya-samāja-lokeśvara-sādhana-nāma*

rG xl 20. K 66/2756/24-2-6. About 230 lines.

a. mahā-paṇḍita Dīpaṃkara-śrī-jñāna (IT Jo-bo-rje ; IM Atīśa). t. upādhyāya Dīpaṃkara-śrī-jñāna of India and reviser bhikṣu Ratnabhadra.

Colophon K : written by mahā-ācārya Śrī-dīpaṃkara-jñāna ; translated and revised by Indian upādhyāya Dīpaṃkara-śrī-jñāna and lo-tsā-ba Ratnabhadra.

58. *Śrī-guhya-samāja-stotra*

rG xl 22. K 66/2758/30-4-8. About 17 lines.

a. mahā-paṇḍita Dīpaṃkara-śrī-jñāna (IT Jo-bo-rje ; IM Atīśa). t. upādhyāya Dīpaṃkara-śrī-jñāna of India and reviser lo-tsā-ba bhikṣu Ratnabhadra.

Colophon K : written by mahā-ācārya Śrī-dīpaṃkara-jñāna ; translated by the same paṇḍita and lo-tsā-ba bhikṣu Ratnabhadra.

59. *Śrī-cakra-saṃvara-sādhana*

rG xiii 39. K 52/2206/22-5-5. About 40 lines.

a. mahā-upādhyāya Dīpaṃkara-śrī-jñāna of India (IT Jo-bo-rje ; IM Atīśa). t. upādhyāya Dīpaṃkara-śrī-jñāna and lo-tsā-ba bhikṣu Ratnabhadra.

Colophon K : written by Indian mahā-upādhyāya Śrī-dīpaṃkara-jñāna ; translated by the same Indian upādhyāya and lo-tsā-ba bhikṣu Ratnabhadra.

60. *Śrī-bhagavat-abhisamaya-nāma*

rG xiii 40. K 52/2207/23-5-5. About 44½ lines.

a. upādhyāya Śrī-dīpaṃkara-jñāna of India. t. IT Dīpaṃkara-jñāna and lo-tsā-ba Ratnabhadra.

Colophon K : written by Indian ācārya Śrī-dīpaṃkara-jñāna ; translated and revised by Tibetan lo-tsā-ba Ratnabhadra.

61. *Śrī-vajrapāṇi-stotra*

rG lxviii 200. K 79/3714/161-5-5. About 22 lines.

a. ācārya Dīpaṃkara-śrī-jñāna (IT Jo-bo-rje ; IM Atīśa). t. author and lo-tsā-ba Vīryasiṃha of rGya.

Colophon K : written by ācārya Dīpaṃkara-śrī-jñāna ; translated by the same paṇḍita and lo-tsā-ba Vīryasiṃha.

62. *Śrī-vajra-yoginī-sādhana-nāma*

rG xiv 74. K 52/2304/282-5-6. About 15 lines.

a. paṇḍita Dīpaṃkara-śrī jñāna. t. author and lo-tsā-ba Vīryasiṃha of rGya.

Colophon K : written by prabhu Dīpaṃkara-śrī-jñāna ; translated by the same paṇḍita and lo-tsā-ba Vīryasiṃha.

63. *Satyadvaya-avatāra*

mDo xxix 9 ; xxxiii 3. K 102/5298/146-2-5 ; 103/5380. About 21½ lines.

a. ācārya mahā-paṇḍita Śrī-dīpaṃkara-jñāna (IT Jo-bo-rje ; IM Atīśa). t. author and lo-tsā-ba Vīryasiṃha of rGya.

Colophon K : written by ācārya mahā-paṇḍita Śrī-dīpaṃkara-jñāna ; translated and revised by the same paṇḍita and lo-tsā-ba Vīryasiṃha.

64. *Sapta-parva-vidhi*

rG lxxxii 38. K 86/4867/122-5-3. About 17½ lines.

a. IT mahā-paṇḍita Dīpaṃkara-jñāna. t. IT author and lo-tsā-ba Candraprabha of Gyi-jo.

Colophon K : does not mention author or translator.

65. *Samaya-gupti*

rG lxxxii 29. K 86/4858/119-1-6. About 17 lines.

a. Tīpaṃkara (Dīpaṃkara) (IT mahā-paṇḍita Dīpaṃkara-jñāna. t. IT author and lo-tsā-ba Candraprabha of Gyi-jo.

Colophon K : written by Dīpaṃkara.

66. *Samādhi-sambhāra-parivarta.*

rG xlviii 120 ; mDo xxxiii 21. K 69/3288/257-5-2 ; 103/ 5398/202-5-8. About 11 lines.

a. ācārya mahā-paṇḍita Śrī-dīpaṃkara-jñāna. t. author and lo-tsā-ba bhikṣu Śākyamati.

Colophon K (103/5398) : written by ācārya mahā-paṇḍita Śrī-dīpaṃkara-jñāna ; translated and revised by the same Indian ācārya and lo-tsā-ba bhikṣu Śākyamati.

67. *Sarva-karmāvaraṇa-viśuddhi-kara-vidhi.*

mDo cxxviii 11. K 146/5874/192-2-8. About 16 lines.

a. mahā-ācārya Śrī-dīpaṃkara-jñāna (IT paṇḍita Dīpaṃkara-śrī-jñāna). t. author and lo-tsā-ba Jayaśīla of Nag-tsho.

Colophon K : written by mahā-ācārya Śrī-dīpaṃkara-jñāna; translated by the same paṇḍita and lo-tsā-ba Jayaśīla of Nag-tsho.

68. *Sarva-karma-āvaraṇa-viśodhana-nāma-maṇḍala-vidhi*

rG xliii 28. K 77/3479/61-5-7. About 25 lines.

a. ācārya Dīpaṃkara (IT Jo-bo-rje ; IM Atiśa). t. author and lo-tsā-ba Ratnabhadra.

Colophon K : written by ācārya Dīpaṃkara ; translated by the same paṇḍita and lo-tsā-ba Ratnabhadra.

69. *Sarva-tathāgata-samaya-rakṣā-sādhana*

rG lxix 135. K 79/3898/288-1-8. About 12 lines.

a. upādhyāya Dīpaṃkara- śrī-jñāna of India (IT Jo-bo-rje ; IM Atiśa). t. author and lo-tsā-ba Jayaśīla of Nag-tsho.

Colophon K : written by Indian paṇḍita Dīpaṃkara-śrī-jñāna ; translated by the same paṇḍita and lo-tsā-ba Jayaśīla of Nag-tsho.

70. *Sarva-samaya-saṃgraha-nāma*

rG lxxii 20. K 81/4547/209-4-6. About 98 lines.

a. mahā-paṇḍita Dīpaṃkara-śrī-jñāna (IT Jo-bo-rje : IM Atiśa). t. author, the bhaṭṭāraka mahā-guru and lo-tsā-ba bhikṣu Jayaśīla.

Colophon K : Summing up the śāstra-s and the upadeśa-s

of the guru-s (this work was) written by Dīpaṃkara-śrī-jñāna, the bhikṣu born in Bengal ; translated and revised by the same bhaṭṭāraka mahā-guru and lo-tsā-ba bhikṣu Jayaśīla.

71. *Siddha-eka-vīra-mañjughoṣa-sādhana*

rG lxviii 11. K 79/3527/81-4-8. About 31½ lines.

a. mahā-ācārya Śrī-dīpaṃkara-jñāna. t. upādhyāya Dīpaṃkara-śrī-jñāna of India (IT author) and lo-tsā-ba bhikṣu Śubhamati.

Colophon K : written by mahā-ācārya Śrī-dīpaṃkara-jñāna; translated and revised by Indian ācārya Dīpaṃkara-śrī-jñāna and Tibetan lo-tsā-ba Śubhamati.

72. *Sūtra-samuccaya-sañcayārtha*

mDo xxx 32. K 102/5333/170-2-4. About 42 lines.

a. ācārya Dīpaṃkara-śrī-jñāna (IT Jo-bo-rje ; IM Atīśa). t. author and lo-tsā-ba Vīryasiṃha of rGya.

Colophon K : Tibetan bhikṣu Jayaśīla, offering 14 pala-s of gold with flowers to ācārya Dīpaṃkara-śrī-jñāna, requested him to come to Tibet. For completing his meditational practice he could enter his way (to Tibet) after 16 months. At the time of his departure for Tibet, the beloved students requested him for the final *upadeśa* (bka'-chems—literally, "testament"). He delivered this, which is the essence of the *sūtras*, as his *upadeśa* to them. At that time, Vīryasiṃha asked for his permission to translate it ; he received the permission and did the translation. Wanting to propagate this, bhikṣu Jayaśīla said, "The Tibetan masters are very proud and jealous. Let their ahaṃkāra be washed away by this precious water." Being requested by the pupils (ban-de-s) of the Ke-ru temple in the same way, he (Dīpaṃkara) gave this to them along with other upadeśa-s. Jo-bo's guru Avadhūti-pā gave him three upadeśa-s together, viz. apratiṣṭhita siddhānta, karmānta-cittotpādana-vidhi and sūtra-samuccaya-artha-upadeśa.

73. *Sūtra-artha-samuccaya-upadeśa*

mDo xxxi 20 ; xxxiii 18. K 103/5354/52-3-3 ; 103/5395. About 45 lines.

a. ācārya mahā-paṇḍita Śrī-dīpaṃkara-jñāna (IT Jo-bo-rje ;

IM Atiśa). t. author, the mahā-upādhyāya of India, and lo-tsā-ba bhikṣu Jayaśīla.

Colophon K : written by ācārya mahā-paṇḍita Śrī-dīpaṃkara-jñāna ; translated and revised by the same Indian ācārya and lo-tsā-ba bhikṣu Jayaśīla.

74. *Sekopadeśa*

rG lxxxii 28. K 86/4857/118-4-7. About 15 lines.

a. ācārya Dīpaṃkara-śrī-jñāna (IT mahā-paṇḍita Dīpaṃkara-jñāna). t. IT author and lo-tsā-ba Candraprabha of Gyi-jo.

Colophon K : the Sekopadeśa of Dīpaṃkara-śrī-jñāna ends here.

75. *Saudha-dāna*

rG lxxxii 30. K 86/4859/119-3-8. About 15½ lines.

a. IT mahā-paṇḍita Dīpaṃkara-jñāna. t. IT author and lo-tsā-ba Candraprabha of Gyi-jo.

Colophon K : does not mention author or translator.

76. *Saṃcodana-sahita-svakṛtya-krama-varṇa-saṃgraha*

mDo xxxi 19 ; xxxiii 17. K 103/5353/52-1-1 ; 103/5394. About 18 lines

a. ācārya mahā-paṇḍita Śrī-dīpaṃkara-jñāna (IT Jo-bo-rje ; IM Atiśa). t. author, the mahā-upādhyāya of India and lo-tsā-ba bhikṣu Śubhamati.

Colophon K : written by ācārya mahā-paṇḍita Śrī-dīpaṃkara-jñāna; translated and revised by the same Indian mahā-ācārya and lo-tsā-ba bhikṣu Śubhamati.

77. *Saṃsāra-manoniryāṇī-kāra-nāma-saṃgīti*

rG xlvii 46 ; mDo xxxiii. 9. K 69/3152/179-2-1 ; 103/5386. About 31½ lines.

a. mahā-ācārya Śrī-dīpaṃkara-jñāna (IT Jo-bo-rje ; IM Atiśa). t. author and lo-tsā-ba Vīryasiṃha of rGya. Later on, author and lo-tsā-ba Jayaśīla of Nag-tsho. Place—Vikramaśīla vihāra.

Colophon K : written by mahā-ācārya Srī-dīpaṃkara-jñāna; translated by the same Indian upādhyāya and lo-tsā-ba Vīryasiṃha at the Vikramaśīla temple. And, again, revised by the same guru and lo-tsā-ba Jayaśīla.

78. *Homa-vidhi*

rG lxxxii 32. K 86/4861/120-2-4. About 16 lines.

a. IT mahā-paṇḍita Dīpaṃkara-jñāna. t. IT author and lo-tsā-ba Candraprabha of Gyi-jo.

Colophon K : no colophon.

79. *Hṛdaya-nikṣepa-nāma*

mDo xxxi 12 ; xxxiii 6. K 103/5346/46-5-7 ; 103/5383. About 21 lines.

a. ācārya mahā-paṇḍita Śrī-dīpaṃkara-jñāna (IT Jo-bo-rje ; IM Atiśa). t. author, the mahā-upādhyāya of India and lo-tsā-ba bhikṣu Jayaśīla of Nag-tsho.

Colophon K : written by ācārya mahā-paṇḍita Śrī-dīpaṃkara-jñāna at sÑe-thaṅ temple in dBus ; translated and revised by the same Indian mahā-ācārya and lo-tsā-ba Jayaśīla.

Note on Section 2

At the end of *Citā-vidhi* (No. 19 above—rG lxxxii 39), Cordier quotes from the Colophon saying that the above thirteen works (viz. rG lxxxii 27-39 (No.s 38, 73, 64, 74, 29, 77, 25, 10, 44, 42, 55, 63 and 9 in our list) are collectively called 'the thirteen mantra-s of Dīpaṃkara' (*dīpaṃkara-mantra-krama-trayodaśaḥ*) or 'the thirteen mantra-mahādharma-s of Atīśa' (*atīśa-mantra-mahā-dharma-trayodaśaḥ*). In K Vol. 86, p. 123, folio 4, line 3, too, these works are collectively called the thirteen mantra-vidhi-s of Dīpaṃkara or the thirteen works on mantra by Atīśa.

Section 3

Works in the bsTan-'gyur of which Dīpaṃkara is Author Only

1. *Adhyayana-pustaka-paṭhana-puraskriyā-vidhi*
mDo xxxii 19 ; xxxiii 23. K 103/5376/180-1-6 ; 103/5400. About 10 lines.
a. ācārya mahā-paṇḍita Śrī-dīpaṃkara-jñāna (IT Jo-bo-rje; IM Atiśa) t. not mentioned.
Colophon K : written by ācārya mahā-paṇḍita Śrī-dīpaṃkara-jñāna.

2. *Amitābha-hṛdaya-rāga-yamāri-sādhana-nāma*
rG xliii 19. K 67/2804/70-4-6. About 15 lines
a. upādhyāya paṇḍita Śrī-dīpaṃkara of India (IT Dīpaṃkara-jñāna). t. IT yogī Prajñāśrījñānakīrti.
Colophon K : written by ācārya Dīpaṃkara.

3. *Ārya-gaṇapati-cintā-ratna-(sādhana)*
rG lxxxiii 52. K 86/4987/211-5-1. About 12 lines.
a. yogīśvara vratacārī Kṛṣṇa. Sub-title : text coming from (Jo-bo-rje). t. not mentioned.
Colophon K : written by yogīśvara vratacārī Kṛṣṇa. This is very important. For yogī sPyan-sṅa said, "I have many gods for dhana-sādhana, including Nātha ; but none is as quick as this."
Note : Tibetan sub-title in the K : upadeśa of Kṛṣṇa-gaṇapati-sādhana coming from Jo-bo-rje.

4. *Ārya-ṣaḍakṣarī-sādhana*
rG lxxxii 9. K 86/4839/101-2-2. About 13 lines.
a. mahā-ācārya Śrī-dīpaṃkara (IT mahā-ārya-śrī ; Colophon Jo-bo-rje ; IM Aiśa). t. not mentioned.
Colophon K : written by mahā-ācārya Śrī-dīpaṃkara-jñāna. Ekadeva Jo-bo-rje wrote it at Yer-pa. Tibetan sub-title K ; śāstra of Jo-bo-rje.

5. *Ārya-hayagrīva-sādhana-nāma*

rG lxix 118. K. 79/3881/262-3-7. About 54 lines.

a. ācārya Śrī-dīpaṃkara-jñāna (IT Jo-bo-rje ; IM Atiśa) t. not mentioned.

Colophon K : written by ācārya Śrī-dīpaṃkara-jñāna.

6. *Ekavīra-sādhana-nāma*

rG xiii 41. K 52/2208/25-1-1. About 18 lines.

a. ācārya paiṇḍapātika Śrī-dīpaṃkara-jñāna of Bengal (IT Jo-bo-rje ; IM Atiśa). t. lo-tsā-ba Jayaśīla of Nag-tsho.

Colophon K : ācārya bhikṣu Śrī-dīpaṃkara-jñāna of Bengal ; translated by Tibetan lo-tsā-ba Jayaśīla.

7. *Kartaridhara-jñānanātha-ātma-utpādana-japa-stotra*

rG lxxxiii 8. K 86/4943/178-1-7. About 22½ lines.

a. Jo-bo-rje (IM Atiśa). t. not mentioned.

Colophon K : This also is written by Jo-bo-rje.

8. *Karma-vajra-gaurī-sādhana-nāma*

rG xliii 24. K 67/2809/72-2-8. About 13 lines.

a. IT Dīpaṃkara-jñāna of India. t. Yogī Prajñāśrījñānakīrti.

Colophon K : does not mention author or translator.

9. *Kula-praṇidhāna-nāma*

mDo cxxxvi 35. K 150/5933/242-5-5. About 9 lines.

a. ācārya mahā-paṇḍita Śrī-dīpaṃkara-jñāna (IT Jo-bo-rje; IM Atiśa) t. not mentioned.

Colophon K : written by ācārya mahā-paṇḍita Śrī-dīpaṃkara-jñāna (Next is quoted a śloka from Aśvaghoṣa). Translated by paṇḍita Dānaśīla.

10. *Gaṇapati-gūhya-sādhana-nāma*

rG lxxxiii 55. K 86 4990/212-3-5. About 24 lines.

a. ācārya Dīpaṃkara-jñāna (IT Jo-bo-rje ; IM Atiśa) t. not mentioned.

Colophon K : written by ācārya Dīpaṃkara-śrī-jñāna.

11. *Guru-kriyā-krama*

mDo xxxii 17 ; xxxiii 25. K 103/5374/179-1-5 ; 103/5402. About 15 lines.

a. ācārya mahā-paṇḍita Śrī-dīpaṃkara-jñāna (IT Jo-bo-rje; IM Atiśa) t. not mentioned.

Colophon K : written by ācārya mahā-paṇḍita Śrī-dīpaṃkara-jñāna.

12. *Caṇḍa-khaḍga-yamāri-sādhana-nāma*

rG xliii 30. K 67/2815/75-1-8. About 11½ lines.

a. IT Dīpaṃkara-jñāna. t. IT yogī Prajñāśrījñānakīrti.

Colophon K : does not mention author or translator.

13. *Caṇḍa-mahāroṣaṇa-sādhana-paramārtha-nāma*

rG lxxxii 68. K 86/4896/151-4-8. About 26½ lines.

a. mahā-ācārya Dīpaṃkara-śrī-jñāna (IT and Original—Dīpaṃkara paṇḍita of Bengal). t. paṇḍita Nirvāṇaśrī of India and lo-tsā-ba Tāranātha.

Colophon K : written by Dīpaṃkara-śrī-jñāna, the mahā-ācārya paṇḍita of Bengal ; translated by the Indian paṇḍita Nirvāṇaśrī and the foolish (*mūrkha*) Tāranātha at gYar-khral.

Note : The word *mūrkha* in the colophon indicates Tāranātha's own way of showing modesty.

14. *Caryā-gīti*

rG xiii 44 ; mDo xxxiii 10. K 52/2211/28-4-8 ; 103/5387. About 25 lines.

a. mahā-ācārya Śrī-dīpaṃkara-jñāna (IT Jo-bo-rje ; IM Atīśa). t. rG xiii 44 : Jayaśīla. Corrector paṇḍita Vajrapāṇi and lo-tsā-ba bhikṣu Dharmaprajña ; mDo xxxiii 10 : paṇḍita Vajrapāṇi and lo-tsā-ba bhikṣu Dharmaprajña.

Colophon K : 103/5387—Here ends the song of śīla-caryā (*tshul-khrims-kyi-spyod-pa*) by mahā-ācārya Śrī-dīpaṃkara-jñāna. Translated and propagated by paṇḍita Vajrapāṇi and lo-tsā-ba bhikṣu Dharmaprajña. 52/2211—Composed and sung by mahā-ācārya Śrī-dīpaṃkara-jñāna in the form of śīla-caryā. Translated, corrected and propagated by paṇḍita Vajrapāṇi and bhikṣu Dharmaprajña.

Note : The anomaly in the way in which Cordier puts the name of the translators is obvious. Though he calls the second (i.e. mDo xxxiii 10) a "literal reproduction" of the first (i.e. rG xiii 44), and though according to him Vajrapāṇi and Dharmaprajña are the translators of the latter, yet he mentions Jayaśīla as the translator of the former ; Vajrapāni and

Dharmaprajña, according to Cordier, being only its corrector. An examination of the colophon of the Peking edition of the work, as occurring in both versions, reveals nothing to support Cordier's assertion that Jayaśīla was connected with the translation of this work, though it gives us some indication of the possible source of Cordier's confusion. The colophon of the first version begins with the words, "Here ends the song of khrims-kyi-spyod-pa" etc. Khrims-kyi-spyod-pa means śīla-caryā and is evidently used in the colophon to stand for the Caryā-gīti itself, the main theme of it being *śīla* or conduct. Cordier, it appears, mistakes this Tibetan rendering of the text-name as meaning the famous lo-tsā-ba Jayaśīla: this, once done, the only way in which he can connect the names of Vajrapāṇi and Dharmaprajña (in the case of rG xiii 44) is with the words "corrected by" in the colophon. However, the source of this confusion being absent in the case of mDo xxxiii 10, he gives only the names of Vajrapāṇi and Dharmaprajña as the translators of the text. To sum up, therefore, there is no reason to think that Jayaśīla was the translator of this work.

15. *Daṇḍa-dhṛk-vidāra-yamāri-nāma-sādhana*

rG xliii 29. K 67/2814/74-5-5. About 12 lines.

a. mahā-ācārya Dīpaṃkara (IT Dīpaṃkara-jñāna). t. yogī Prajñāśrījñānakīrti.

Colophon K: written by mahā-ācārya Dīpaṃkara; translated by yogī Prajñāśrījñānakīrti by himself.

16. *Pratītya-samutpāda-hṛdaya-mantra-patrikā-sūkṣma-vyūha-nāma*

rG lxxxiv 13. K 87/5025/86-2-4. About 7½ lines.

a. Atīśa (IT Jo-bo). t. lo-tsā-ba śākya-bhikṣu Jayaśīla of Nag-tsho.

Colophon K: Nag-tsho translated (this) from Atīśa. If it is more than that then it is wrong writing. So the scholars should follow this. But the fools do not see in spite of their eyes. Please excuse me if there is any error or mistake. By the puṇya of this the power of omniscience should be quickly obtained. Translated and revised by Jayaśīla.

17. *Prajñā-sukha-padma-yamāri-sādhana-nāma*

rG xliii 31. K 67/2816/75-3-4. About 11½ lines.

a. upādhyāya Dīpaṃkara of India (IT Dīpaṃkara-jñāna). t. yogī Prajñāśrījñānakīrti

Colophon K : written by Indian upādhyāya Dīpaṃkara and translated by yogī Prajñāśrījñānakīrti himself.

18. *Pāramitā-yāna-sañca(ka)-nirvapaṇa-vidhi*

mDo xxxii 16 ; xxxiii 24. K 103/5373/178-5-2 ; 103/5401. About 11 lines.

a. ācārya mahā-paṇḍita Śrī-dīpaṃkara-jñāna (IT Jo-bo-rje ; IM Atīśa). t. not mentioned.

Colophon K : written by ācārya mahā-paṇḍita Śrī-dīpaṃkara-jñāna.

19. *Bali-vidhi*

rG xxi 71. K 56/2418/316-2-5. About 36 lines.

a. mahā-ācārya bhikṣu Dīpaṃkara-śrī-jñāna of Bengal (IT Jo-bo-rje ; IM Atīśa). t. not mentioned.

Colophon K : bhikṣu Dīpaṃkara-śrī-jñāna, born in Bengal, wrote this *Bali-vidhi* under the blessings of his guru.. done by mahā-ācārya Śrī-dīpaṃkara-jñāna.

20. *Bodhisattva-caryāvatāra-bhāṣya*

mDo cxxviii 9. K 146/5872/172-5-2. About 587 lines.

a. Dīpaṃkara-śrī-jñāna (IT mahā-ārya Dīpaṃkara). At the end of the third section is mentioned that the commentary is written according to the views of bla-ma gSer-gliṅ-pa (guru Suvarṇadvīpī). t. not mentioned.

Colophon K : written by Dīpaṃkara-śrī-jñāna. There are many to ride this mighty horse of bodhisattva..., but there are few to reach its goal. Some people talk about it just for the pleasure of the ear. Some others comment on this śāstra, though wrongly. Some people comment even on its mere title. Thus was disturbed Śāntideva's mind. Numerous comments without importance are of little use to the living beings. (Therefore) Śāntideva explained the views of Maitreyanātha very extensively. It came down traditionally thus: bhikṣu Eladhārī (?), Vīryavajra, āyuḥ-siddha Mahāratna, the guru Pāla of Suvarṇadvīpa (Dharmapāla or Dharmakīrti), the great Dīpaṃkara-śrī, lo-tsā-ba Nag-tsho of Guṅ-thaṅ and ṛṣi mahā-prajña Śānti. Now I, too, have reverence for this viśuddha siddhānta and caryā.

21. *Bodhisattva-caryā-sūtrīkṛtāvavāda*

mDo xxxi 8 ; xxxi 14 ; xxxiii 8. K 103/5342/20-1-3 ; 103/5348 ; 103/5385. About 22 lines.

a, mahā-ācārya Śrī-dīpaṃkara-jñāna (IT Jo-bo-rje, IM Atīśa). t. not mentioned.

Colophon K : written by mahā-ācārya Śrī-dīpaṃkara-jñāna.

22. *Bodhisattva-maṇyāvalī*

mDo xxxi 13 ; xxxiii 7. K 103/5347/47-3-4 ; 103/5384. About 22 lines.

a. upādhyāya Śrī-dīpaṃkara-jñāna of India (IT Jo-bo-rje ; IM Atīśa). t. not mentioned.

Colophon K : written by Śrī-dīpaṃkara-jñāna.

23. *Mahā-sūtra-samuccaya-nāma*

mDo xxxii 1. K 103/5358/57-1-1. About 3665 lines.

a. śākya-sthavira mahā-paṇḍita Śrī-dīpaṃkara-jñāna (IT Jo-bo-rje ; IM Atīśa). t. Jayānanda, Sūryakīrti, etc.

Colophon K: This *dharma* (work) is of śākya-sthavira mahā-paṇḍita Śrī-dīpaṃkara-jñāna, follower of the best Mahāyāna. It is written down (copied ?) by the hands of Jīvadhārī. This Indian book changed (transcribed) into Tibetan script is the great gift of śākya-sthavira mahā-paṇḍita Guṇakīrti (Yon-ton-grags-pa), the follower of the best Mahāyāna. And for the living beings it is written down (copied again ?) by the hands of bhikṣu Kumāraprajña. Then śākya-bhikṣu Sūryakīrti (Ñi-ma-ston-grags-pa)...and Ban-de of Khu translated it... then revised by the request of Guṇakīrti by the brāhmaṇa paṇḍita Jayānanda of Kashmir and the profound translators Pa-tshab and Khu in the Yaṅ-gaṅ temple.

24. *Mudgara-krodha-yamāri-sādhana-nāma*

rG xliii 28. K 67/2813/74-4-1. About 11½ lines.

a. upādhyāya Dīpaṃkara of India (IT Dīpaṃkara-jñāna) t. IT yogī Prajñāśrījñānakīrti.

Colophon K : written by Indian upādhyāya Dīpaṃkara.

25. *Ratna-sambhava-yamāri-sādhana-nāma*

rG xliii 18. K 67/2803/70-2-8. About 14 lines.

a. upādhyāya paṇḍita Śrī-dīpaṃkara of India (IT Dīpaṃkara-jñāna) t. yogī Prajñāśrījñānakīrti.

Colophon K : written by mahā-ācārya Śrī-dīpaṃkara ; translated by yogī Prajñāśrījñānakīrti himself.

26. *Ratnālaṃkāra-siddhi*

rG xiv 72. K 52/2302/281-4-5. About 28 lines.

a. mahā-paṇḍita Dīpaṃkara-śrī-jñāna (IT Jo-bo-rje ; IM Atiśa). t. not mentioned.

Colophon K : written by mahā-paṇḍita Dīpaṃkara-śrījñāna.

27. *Vajra-gīti-sukhārddha-sādhana-nāma*

rG xliii 23. K 67/2808/72-1-4. About 12 lines.

a. IT Dīpaṃkara-jñāna. t. IT yogī Prajñāśrījñānakīrti.

Colophon K : mentions neither author nor translator.

28. *Vajra-carcikā-sādhana-nāma*

rG xliii 21. K 67/2806/71-3-2. About 13 lines.

a. upādhyāya paṇḍita Śrī-dīpaṃkara of India (IT Dīpaṃkara-jñāna). t. yogī Prajñāśrījñānakīrti.

Colophon K : written by ācārya mahā-paṇḍita Dīpaṃkara and yogī Prajñāśrījñānakīrti himself.

29. *Vajra-tīkṣṇa-yamāri-sādhana-nāma*

rG xliii 20. K 67/2805/71-1-4. About 13 lines.

a. upādhyāya paṇḍita Śrī-dīpaṃkara of India (IT Dīpaṃkara-jñāna). t. yogī Prajñāśrījñānakīrti).

Colophon K : written by mahā-ācārya Dīpaṃkara ; translated by yogī Prajñāśrījñānakīrti himself.

30. *Vajra-ḍāka-yoginī-sādhana-nāma*

rG xliii 22. K 67/2807/71-4-7 (Sanskrit title : Vajraḍākinī...). About 13 lines.

a. ācārya Dīpaṃkara (IT Dīpaṃkara-jñāna). t. IT yogī Prajñāśrījñānakīrti.

Colophon K : written by ācārya Dīpaṃkara.

31. *Vajra-vārāhī-sādhana*

rG xiv 73. K 52/2303/282-3-1. About 21½ lines.

a. mahā-paṇḍita Śrī-dīpaṃkara-jñāna (IT Jo-bo-rje ; IM Atiśa) t. not mentioned.

Colophon K : written by mahā-paṇḍita Śrī-dīpaṃkara-jñāna.

32. *Vairocana-yamāri-upāyikā-nāma*

rG xliii 17. K 67/2802/70-1-2. Tibetan sub-title : *Vairocana-yamāri-abhisamaya-nāma.* About 14 lines.

a. upādhyāya paṇḍita Śrī-dīpaṃkara of India (IT Dīpaṃkara-jñāna). t. yogī Prajñāśrījñānakīrti.

Colophon K : written by Indian upādhyāya famed as paṇḍita (mkhas-par-grags-pa) Dīpaṃkara ; translated by yogī Prajñāśrījñānakīrti himself.

33. *Śaraṇa-gamana-deśanā*

mDo xxxi 16 ; xxxiii 14. K 103/5350/49-3-4 ; 103/5391. About 25½ lines.

a. guru bodhisattva Dīpaṃkara-śrī-jñāna (IT Jo-bo-rje ; IM Atiśa). t. not mentioned.

Colophon K : written by guru bodhisattva Dīpaṃkara-śrī-jñāna.

34. *Śrī-gaṇapati-śānti-sādhana*

rG lxxxiii 51. K 86/4986/211-2-5. About 20 lines.

a. Jo-bo (IT Jo-bo-rje ; IM Atiśa, śākya-bhikṣu Dīpaṃkara-śrī-jñāna). t. not mentioned ; upadeśa to 'Brom-ston-pa.

Colophon K : written by Jo-bo according to *siddhi-sādhana* (rG lxix 148 ?). He gave it to 'Brom-ston and 'Brom-ston gave it to sPyan-sṅa.

35. *Śrī-sahaja-saṃvara...* (Title incomplete)

rG xiii 21. not found in K.

a. Dīpaṃkara. t. lo-tsā-ba of Nag-tsho, śākya-bhikṣu Jayaśīla.

36. *Śrī-hayagrīva-sādhana*

rG lxix 119. K 79/3882/263-5-4. About 15 lines.

a. ācārya Śrī-dīpaṃkara-jñāna (IT Jo-bo-rje ; IM Atiśa. t. not mentioned.

Colophon K : written by mahā-ācārya Śrī-dīpaṃkara-jñāna.

37. *Sunipuṇa-mahādeva-vighna-rāja-sādhana-nāma*

rG lxxxiii 46. K 86/4981/209-3-1. About 9 lines.

a. Dīpaṃkara. t. not mentioned.

Colophon K : written by ācārya Dīpaṃkara.

38. *Homa-vidhi*

rG lxiii 32. K 77/3483/63-3-4. About 11½ lines.

a. Dīpaṃkara-śrī-jñāna (IT Jo-bo-rje ; IM Atiśa). t. not mentioned.

Colophon K : written by Dīpaṃkara-śrī-jñāna.

Note : This text is different from the one bearing the same title and mentioned in the previous section.

Section 4

Works in the bsTan-'gyur of which Dīpaṃkara is translator only.

1. *Abhisamaya-alaṃkāra-nāma-prajñāpāramitā-upadeśa - śāstra-vṛtti-durbodha-āloka-nāma-ṭīkā.*

mDo vii 3. K 91/5192/1-1-7. About 2044 lines.

a. ācārya Dharmakīrti-śrī of Suvarṇadvīpa. The work was composed during the reign of Deva-śrī-varma-rāja, Cūḍāmaṇi, *alias*, Cūḍāmaṇimaṇḍapa, in Malayagiri in Vijayanagara of Suvarṇadvīpa. t. upādhyāya paṇḍita Dīpaṃkara-śrī-jñāna of India and the grand lo-tsā-ba bhikṣu Ratnabhadra.

Colophon K : written by Dharmakīrti on the request of king Śrī-cūḍāmaṇivarma during the tenth year of the reign of Srī-cūḍāmaṇivarma at Vijayanagara of Suvarṇadvīpa. The work was completed on the second day of middle-spring month. *Durbodha-āloka-nāma* ends. Translated and revised by Indian upādhyāya Dīpaṃkara-śrī-jñāna and the translator the great lo-tsā-ba bhikṣu Ratnabhadra. (Tibetan sub-title : by ācārya Dharmakīrti of Suvarṇadvīpa).

2. *Aṣṭa-śata-sādhana*

rG lxxi 362. K 81/4488/65-2-3. About 237 lines.

a. mahā-ācārya Candragomin. t. upādhyāya Dīpaṃkara-śrī-jñāna of India and lo-tsā-ba bhikṣu Jayaśīla.

Colophon K : written by mahā-ācārya Candragomin ; translated by Indian ācārya Dīpaṃkara-śrī-jñāna and lo-tsā-ba Jayaśīla. And again revised by Indian paṇḍita Dānaśrī and Tibetan lo-tsā-ba Matikīrti.

3. *Āpatti-deśanā-vidhi*

mDo xxxii 11. K 103/5368/176-3-4. About 24½ lines.

a. sarvāstivādī paṇḍita Devaśānti. t. upādhyāya Dīpaṃkara-śrī-jñāna of India (IT Jo-bo-rje ; 1M Atīśa) and lo-tsā-ba bhikṣu Jayaśīla.

Colophon K : written by paṇḍita Devaśānti ; translated and revised by Indian ācārya Dīpaṃkara-śrī-jñāna and Tibetan lo-tsā-ba bhikṣu Jayaśīla.

4. *Ārya-tārā-devī-stotra-muktikā-mālā-nāma*

rG lxxxii 40. K 86/4869/123-4-6. About 43 lines.

a. mahā-ācārya Candragomin. t. upādhyāya Dīpaṃkara-śrī-jñāna of India (lT Jo-bo-rje ; lM Atīśa) and lo-tsā-ba bhikṣu Jayaśīla of Nag-tsho. Place of translation : Vikramaśīla vihāra.

Colophon K : This necklace of *maṇi* (meant to enlighten) those poets who are ignorant of the Tārā-pañca-vidyā. Written by mahā-ācārya Candragomin or "Immortal Moon" ('Chi-med-zla-ba). Translated and revised by Dīpaṃkara-śrī-jñāna and the Tibetan lo-tsā-ba Jayaśīla of Nag-tsho at the temple of Vikramaśīla.

5. [*Ārya*]-*nīlāmbara-dhara-vajrapāṇi-kalpa-nāma-dhāraṇī-ṭīkā*

rG lxvi 6. K78/3500/124-5-7. About 108 lines.

a. ācārya Nāgārjuna. t. upādhyāya Dīpaṃkara-śrī-jñāna of India (lT Jo-bo-rje ; lM Atīśa) and lo-tsā-ba Vīryasiṃha of rGya. (lT Jayaśīla of Nag-tsho.). Place of translation : Nālandā.

Colophon K : written by ācārya Nāgārjuna and translated by Indian paṇḍita Dīpaṃkara-śrī-jñāna and Tibetan lo-tsā-ba Vīryasiṃha of rGya at the corridor of Śrī Nālandā.

6. *Ārya-prajñā-pāramitā-upadeśa-nāma*

rG lxiii 15. K 77/3466/31-2-4. About 7 lines.

a. Śrī Kampala. t. upādhyāya Dīpaṃkara-śrī-jñāna of India (lT Jo-bo-rje ; lM Atīśa) and lo-tsā-ba bhikṣu Śubhamati.

Colophon K : written by Śrī Kambala ; (translated and) revised by Indian upādhyāya Dīpaṃkara-śrī-jñāna and Tibetan lo-tsā-ba bhikṣu Śubhamati.

7. *Ārya-maitreya-sādhana*

rG lxxi 345. K 81/4471/61-1-2. About 18 lines.

a. ācārya Asaṅga. t. the grand ārya bhikṣu Atīśa and probably 'Brom-ston-pa or Jayākara.

Colophon K : written by ācārya Asaṅga ; translated by mahā Jo-bo and dGe-bśes-ston-pa ; later revised by mahā-paṇḍita Buddhaśrī and gNubs lo-tsā-ba.

8. *Ārya-ṣaḍakṣara-sādhana*

rG lxviii 160. K 79/3674/137-1-2. About 15 lines.

a. mahā-ācārya Pūjāvajra. t. mahā-upādhyāya Dīpaṃkara-śrī-jñāna of India (IT Jo-bo-rje ; IM Atiśa) and lo-tsā-ba bhikṣu Śākyamati.

Colophon K : written by mahā-ācārya Pūjāvajra; translated by mahā-upādhāya Dīpaṃkara-śrī-jñāna of India and lo-tsā-ba bhikṣu Śākyamati.

9. *Ārya-sahasrabhuja-avalokiteśvara-sādhana*

rG lxviii 40. K 79/3555/97-4-8. About 148 lines.

a. ācārya ārya Nāgārjuna. t. upādhyāya mahā-paṇḍita Dīpaṃkara-śrī-jñāna of India and lo-tsā-ba bhikṣu Ratnabhadra.

Colophon K : written by ārya ācārya mahātmā Nāgārjuna... translated by Indian ācārya mahā-paṇḍita Dīpaṃkara-śri-jñāna and lo-tsā-ba bhikṣu Ratnabhadra. The mahā-puruṣa Atiśa gave this to deva-guru Bodhiprabha, 'Brom-ston-pa and yogī Prajñāvajra ; 'Brom-ston-pa gave it to Bya-yul-pa. It is said that this is the deepest *sādhana* of (all) the *sādhana*-s of the Jambudvīpa. Jo-bo stayed in Tibet for 14 years and he died at the age of seventy-seven(?). sTon-pa ('Brom) was his student for 13 years ; Yogī and Āraṇyaka were for nine years. Yogī Prajñāvajra, Phyag-pa-khri-mchog and Phyag-dar-ston-pa were his students for 5 years each. dGe-bśes-gsaṅ-phu-ba was his student for 10 years.

10. *Ārya-acala-sādhana-nāma*

rG lxix 120. K 79/3883/264-2-4. About 56 lines.

a. maitra-pāda Dharmakīrti, the guru of Suvarṇadvīpa. t. ācārya Dīpaṃkara-śri-jñāna (IT Jo-bo-rje ; IM Atiśa).

Colophon K : written by guru Suvarṇadvīpī ; ācārya Dīpaṃkara-śrī-jñāna translated it himself and gave it to bhikṣu Īśvaradhvaja.

11. *Ārya-avalokiteśvara-khasarpaṇa-sādhana*

rG lxviii 159. K 79/3673/136-3-8. About 17½ lines.

a. not mentioned. t. upādhyāya Dīpaṃkara-śrī-jñāna of India and lo-tsā-ba bhikṣu Śākyamati.

Colophon K : translated by Indian upādhyāya Dīpaṃkara-śrī-jñāna and lo-tsā-ba bhikṣu Śākyamati.

12. *Ārya-aṣṭabhaya-trāta-nāma-tārā-sādhana*

rG lxxi 370. K 81/4494/74-1-1 (under the title *Ārya-tārā-aṣṭa-bhaya-trāta-nāma-sādhana*) .About 35 lines.

a. mahā-ācārya Candragomin. t. upādhyāya Dīpaṃkara-śrī-jñāna of India (lT Jo-bo-rje ; lM Atiśa) and lo-tsā-ba Jayaśīla of Nag-tsho.

Colophon K : written by mahā-ācārya Candragomin ; translated by Indian ācārya Dīpaṃkara-śrī-jñāna and Tibetan lo-tsā-ba Jayaśīla. Again, revised by Indian ācārya bodhisattva Dānaśrī and Tibetan lo-tsā-ba Matikīrti of Mala.

13. *Ārya-aṣṭa-sāhasrikā-prajñāpāramitā-vyākhyāna-abhisamaya-alaṃkāra-āloka-nāma*

mDo vi. K 90/5189/63-1-1. About 6,736 lines.

a. mahā-paṇḍita ācārya Haribhadra. t. originally translated by upādhyāya Subhāṣita of India and grand lo-tsā-ba bhikṣu Ratnabhadra (958-1055 A.D.) by order of the Tibetan king śākya bhikṣu Senaprabha ('Od-lde), the brother of Bodhiprabha and Śāntiprabha. Later translated by upādhyāya paṇḍita Dīpaṃkara-śrī-jñāna (981-1054 A.D.) of India and lo-tsā-ba bhikṣu Ratnabhadra. The correction was done on the basis of the original that came from Magadha. (Others also translated it still later). [Cordier's date of Atiśa's birth is untenable.]

Colophon K : written by mahā-paṇḍita ācārya Haribhadra. Translated by the Indian upādhyāya Subhāṣita and the great lo-tsā-ba bhikṣu Ratnabhadra. Again, translated and revised by Indian upādhyāya mahā-paṇḍita Dīpaṃkara-śrī-jñāna and the great lo-tsā-ba bhikṣu Ratnabhadra, comparing with the book of Magadha. Later on (translated by) mahā-paṇḍita Dhīrapāla, who was decorated with two lacs of śāstra-s and bhikṣu Dhīmatprajña.

14, *Eka-vīra-sādhana-nāma*

rG xiii 11. K 51/2181/254-5-1. About 15 lines.

a. mahā-ācārya Dombi Heruka. t. ārya Dīpaṃkara (IT Jo-bo-rje ; IM Atīśa) and lo-tsā-ba Jayaśīla of Nag-tsho.

Colophon K : written by ācārya Dombi Heruka ; translated by prabhu Dīpaṃkara and Jayaśīla of Nag-tsho.

15. *Kalaśa-sādhana-nāma*

rG lxviii 187. K 79/3701/151-3-6. About 6 lines.

a. ācārya Suvāgīśvarakīrti t. IT paṇḍita Dīpaṃkara- śrī-jñāna of India (Jo-bo-rje) (IM Atīśa) and lo-tsā-bā Vīryasiṃha of rGya.

Colophon K : written by ācārya Suvāgīśvarakīrti.

16. *Kulika-mata-tattva-nirṇaya-nāma*

rG xiv 35. K 52/2265/207-4-6. About 106 lines.

a. Oḍḍiyānasiddha (probably śākya bhikṣu Indrabhūti). t. mahā-upādhyāya Dīpaṃkara of India (IT Dīpaṃkara-śrī-jñāna).

Colophon K : written by Siddha of Oḍḍiyāna ; translated by Indian mahā-ācārya Dīpaṃkara-śrī-jñāna.

17. *Kṛṣṇa-yamāri-cakra-nāma*

rG lxxxi 11. K 86/4798/2-2-4. About 58 lines.

a. ācārya Lalitavajra. t. paṇḍita Dīpaṃkara and lo-tsā-ba Vajrakīrti.

Colophon K : does not mention author or translator.

18. *Kṛṣṇa-yamāri-cakroddyota*

rG lxxxi 10. K 86/4797/1-1-8. About 44½ lines.

a. paiṇḍapātika Buddha-śrī-jñāna. t. paṇḍita Dīpaṃkara-śrī-jñāna of India and lo-tsā-ba Jayaśīla.

Colophon K : author bhikṣu Buddhaśrījñāna, translated by Indian paṇḍita Dīpaṃkara-śrī-jñāna and lo-tsā-ba Jayaśīla. Later on revised by bhikṣu Vajrakīrti.

19. *Kṛṣṇa-yamāri-sādhana*

rG xliii 10. K 67/2795/62-4-8. About 140 lines.

a. paiṇḍapātika bhikṣu Kamalarakṣita. t. upādhyāya mahā-paṇḍita Dīpaṃkara-śrī-jñāna of India (IT Jo-bo-rje; IM Atīśa) and lo-tsā-ba bhikṣu Jayaśīla of Nag-tsho.

Colophon K : collected by bhikṣu Kamalarakṣita ; translated and revised by Indian upādhyāya mahā-paṇḍita Dīpaṃkara-śrī-jñāna and lo-tsā-ba bhikṣu Jayaśīla.

20. *Gaṇapati-guhya-sādhana-nāma*

rG lxxii 33. K 81/4560/223-3-4. About 23½ lines.

a. Amoghavajra. t. upādhyāya Dīpaṃkara-śrī-jñāna (IT Jo-bo-rje ; IM Atīśa) and lo-tsā-ba Jayaśīla of Nag-tsho.

Colophon K : written by śrī siddha Amoghavajra ; translated by paṇḍita Dīpaṃkara-śrī-jñāna and lo-tsā-ba Jayaśīla of Nag-tsho. This, along with *Gaṇapati-vāhya-sādhana*...etc. are received by me (?) from guru Dharmaśrī-bhadra.

21. *Cakra-nāma*

rG lxxxi 13. K 86/4800/4-1-5. About 25 lines.

a. mahā-ācārya Lalitavajra. t. paṇḍita upādhyāya Dīpaṃkara of India and lo-tsā-ba Vajrakīrti.

Colophon K : It is from the Śata-sāhasrika-tantra of mahā-ācārya Lalitavajra ; translated by Indian paṇḍita upādhyāya Dīpaṃkara and Tibetan lo-tsā-ba Vajrakīrti.

22. *Cakra-upadeśa-nāma*

rG lxviii 182. K 79/3696/150-1-1. About 12 lines.

a. mahā-ācārya Suvāgīśvarakīrti. t. paṇḍita Dīpaṃkara-śrī-jñāna of India (IT Jo-bo-rje ; IM Atīśa) and lo-tsā-ba Vīryasiṃha of rGya.

Colophon K : Here ends the *Cakra-upadeśa* by ācārya Suvāgīśvarakīrti. Dīpaṃkara, the profound paṇḍita of sūtra and tantra was invited by lo-tsā-ba Vīryasiṃha of rGya, the learned among the grammarians of Tibet, with great effort and by spending a lot of gold and jewels.

23. *Catuḥ-mahārāja-bali-nāma*

rG lxxii 64. K 81/4590/262-5-1. About 14½ lines.

a. not mentioned. t. paṇḍita Dīpaṃkara-śrī-jñāna (IT Jo-bo-rje ; IM Atīśa) and probably lo-tsā-ba 'Brom-ston-pa or Jayākara.

Colophon K : translated by paṇḍita Dīpaṃkara-śrī-jñāna and lo-tsā-ba dGe-bśes-ston-pa

24. *Citta-ratna-viśodhana-nāma*

rG lxxxiv 16. K 87/5028/88-4-2. About 105 lines.

a. rājā Indraputi (Indrabhūti). t. upādhyāya Dīpaṃkara-śrī-jñāna of India and lo-tsā-ba Master of Khu (Khu-ston) dÑos-grub (Siddha).

Colophon K : written by rājā Indrabhūti ; translated by Indian upādhyāya Dīpaṃkara-śrī-jñāna and Tibetan lo-tsā-ba Siddha, sTon of Khu.

25. *Tattva-pradīpa-nāma*

rG lxviii 188. K 79/3702/151-4-4. About 10 lines.

a. ācārya Suvāgīśvarakīrti. t. IT Jo-bo-rje (IM Atīśa) and lo-tsā-ba Vīryasiṃha of rGya.

Colophon K : written by ācārya Suvāgīśvarakīrti.

26. *Tattva-siddhi-nāma-prakaraṇa*

rG lxxii 4. K 81/4531/119-3-5. About 228 lines.

a. ācārya Śāntirakṣita. t. upādhyāya Dīpaṃkara-śrī-jñāna of India (IT Jo-bo-rje ; IM Atīśa) and lo-tsā-ba bhikṣu Ratnabhadra.

Colophon K : written by ācārya Śāntirakṣita, translated and revised by Indian ācārya Dīpaṃkara-śrī-jñāna and lo-tsā-ba bhikṣu Ratnabhadra.

27. *Tri-ratna-tārā-stotra*

rG xxvi 14. K 59/2567/72-5-8. About 4 lines.

a. not mentioned. t. upādhyāya Dīpaṃkara-śrī-jñāna of India and lo-tsā-ba Jayaśīla of Nag-tsho. Place of translation : Vikramaśīla vihāra.

Colophon K : translated and revised by Indian upādhyāya Dīpaṃkara-śrī-jñāna and Tibetan lo-tsā-ba Jayaśīla of Nag-tsho at the Vikramaśīla temple.

28. *Tri-śaraṇa-(gamana)-saptati*

mDo xxxii 9 ; xxxiii 101. K 103/5366/174-4-7 ; 103/5478. About 16 lines.

a. ācārya Candrakīrti. t. upādhyāya mahā-paṇḍita Dīpaṃkara-śrī-jñāna of India (IT Jo-bo-rje ; IM Atīśa) and lo-tsā-ba bhikṣu Ratnabhadra.

Colophon K : written by ācārya Candrakīrti ; translated

and revised by Indian ācārya mahā-paṇḍita Dīpaṃkara-śrī-jñāna and lo-tsā-ba bhikṣu Ratnabhadra.

29. *Tri-samaya-vyūha-rāja-śatākṣara-sādhana*

rG lxxxvi 14. K 87/5104/229-1-7. About 30 lines.

a. mahā-ācārya Keladharanandī. t. upādhyāya Dīpaṃkara-śrī-jñāna of India (IT Śrī-jñāna) and lo-tsā-ba Śubhamati.

Colophon K : written by mahā-ācārya Keladharanandī ; translated by Indian ācārya Dīpaṃkara-śrī-jñāna and Tibetan lo-tsā-ba Śubhamati. Revised and compared with the old translation and also with the text in Indian script.

30. *Tri-skandha-sādhana-nāma*

mDo xxxvii 11. K 105/5509/153-2-7. About 18 lines.

a. ācārya Kṛṣṇapāda (IT Kṛṣṇa ; IM Kāla). t. mahā-upādhyāya Dīpaṃkara-śrī-jñāna of India (IT Jo-bo-rje ; IM Atīśa) and lo-tsā-ba bhikṣu Jayaśīla.

Colophon K : written by Indian ācārya Kṛṣṇa-pā; translated by Indian mahā-upādhyāya Dīpaṃkara-śrī-jñāna and lo-tsā-ba Jayaśīla.

31. *Daśa-tattva*

rG xxi 11. K 56/2358/98-5-6. About 77 lines.

a. ācārya Dombi-pāda (IT Dombi Heruka). t. upādhyāya Śrī-dīpaṃkara-jñāna of India (IT Jo-bo-rje ; IM Atīśa) and lo-tsā-ba bhikṣu Śubhamati.

Colophon K : written by ācārya Dombi-pā ; translated and revised by Indian upādhyāya Śrī-dīpaṃkara-jñāna and lo-tsā-ba bhikṣu Śubhamati.

32. *Nava-Kuṃkuma-stava*

rG lxviii 17. K 79/3533/83-5-6. About 7½ lines.

a. ācārya Siṃhācala. t. upādhyāya Dīpaṃkara-śrī-jñāna of India (IT Jo-bo-rje ; IM Atīśa) and lo-tsā-ba bhikṣu Jayaśīla of Nag-tsho.

Colophon K : written by ācārya Acalasiṃha ; translated by Indian upādhyāya Dīpaṃkara-śrī-jñāna and lo-tsā-ba bhikṣu Jayaśīla.

33. *Nāgeśvara-rāja-sādhana*

rG lxxi 341. K 81/4467/58-5-6. About 40 lines.

a. ācārya mahātmā Nāgārjuna. t. upādhyāya Dīpaṃkara-śrī-jñāna of India lo-tsā-ba bhikṣu Ratnabhadra.

Colophon K : written by ācārya mahātmā Nāgārjuna ; translated and revised by Indian ācārya Dīpaṃkara-śrī-jñāna and Tibetan lo-tsā-ba bhikṣu Ratnabhadra.

34. *Nikāya-bheda-vibhaṅga-vyākhyāna*

mDo xc 12. K 127/5640/253-1-1. About 170 lines.

a. ācārya Bhavya. t. mahā-paṇḍita Dīpaṃkara-śrī-jñāna of Bengal of Eastern India (IT Jo-bo-rje ; IM Atīśa) and lo-tsā-ba bhikṣu Jayaśīla. Place of translation : vihāra of Lhasa.

Colophon K : written by ācārya Bhavya ; translated and revised by ācārya paṇḍita called mahā-paṇḍita Dīpaṃkara-śrī-jñāna of Bengal (Baṃgal) and Tibetan lo-tsā-ba bhikṣu Jayaśīla at Lhasa temple on the request of bhikṣu Legs-pa'i-śes-rab.

Note : unlike Bhamgal, which is the most frequently found Tibetan transliteration of the word for Bengal, we have in this colophon the clearly written word Baṃgal.

35. *Nidāna-pudgala-saṃgraha-kārikā*

mDo xc 5. K 127/5633/210-2-4. About 126 lines.

a. paṇḍita vinayadhara śākya-bhikṣu Balaśrībhadra. t. upādhyāya Dīpaṃkara-śrī-jñāna of India and lo-tsā-ba śākya-bhikṣu Kumāraśīla. Place of translation : Tho-liṅ vihāra.

Colophon K : written by paṇḍita vinayadhara śākya-bhikṣu Balaśrībhadra of north Kashmir ; translated and revised by Indian upādhyāya Dīpaṃkara-śrī-jñāna and lo-tsā-ba śākya-bhikṣu Kumāravara (gShon-nu-mchog) at Tho-liṅ temple.

36. *Nīlāmbara-dhara-vajrapāṇi-sādhana-nāma*

rG. lxviii 181. K 79/3695/149-2-5. About 28 lines.

a. mahā-ācārya Suvāgīśvarakīrti. t. paṇḍita Dīpaṃkara-śrī-jñāna of India (IT Jo-bo-rje ; IM Atīśa) and lo-tsā-ba Vīryasiṃha of rGya.

Colophon K : written by ācārya Suvāgīśvarakīrti.

37. *Nīlāmbara-upasiddhi-nāma*

rG lxviii 174. K 79/3688/144-3-1. About 14 lines.

a. ācārya Nāgārjuna. t. paṇḍita Dīpaṃkara-śrī-jñāna of India (IT Jo-bo-rje ; IM Atiśa) and lo-tsā-ba Vīryasiṃha of rGya.

Colophon K : written by ācārya Nāgārjuna and translated by Indian paṇḍita Dīpaṃkara-śrī-jñāna and Tibetan lo-tsā-ba Vīryasiṃha of rGya.

38. *Pañca-skandha-prakaraṇa*

mDo xxiv 3. K 99/5267/1-1-6. About 511 lines.

a. mahā-ācārya Candrakīrti. t. upādhyāya Dīpaṃkara-śrī-jñāna of India (IT Jo-bo-rje ; IM Atiśa) and lo-tsā-ba bhikṣu Jayaśīla of Nag-tsho. Place of translation : Tshaṅs-pa-'byuṅ-gnas.

Colophon K : written by ācārya Candrakīrti; translated and revised by Indian upādhyāya Dīpaṃkara-śrī-jñāna and lo-tsā-ba bhikṣu Jayaśīla at Brahmākara temple on the request of śrī-deva-bhaṭṭāraka Bodhirāja (Dhīrāja ?) and the Saṅgha in the Pig year.

39. *Pratītya-samutpāda-dravya-rakṣā*

rG lxviii 195. K 79/3709/155-3-8. About 8 lines.

a. not mentioned. t. IT Jo-bo-rje (IM Atiśa) and Vīryasiṃha of rGya.

No Colophon in K.

40. *Prāyaścitta-amṛta*

rG lxviii 175. K 79/3689/144-4-7. About 7 lines.

a. ārya Nāgārjuna. t. IT Jo-bo-rje (IM Atiśa) and lo-tsā-ba Vīryasiṃha of rGya.

Colophon K : written by ācārya Nāgārjuna.

41. *Bodhisattva-caryāvatāra-piṇḍārtha*

mDo xxvii 7. K 100/5281/235-2-5. About 26½ lines.

a. Dharmapāla, the guru of Suvarṇadvīpa. Text expounded at the request of his disciples Kamalarakṣita and Dīpaṃkara-śrī-jñāna. t. upādhyāya Dīpaṃkara of India (IT Jo-bo-rje ; IM Atiśa) and lo-tsā-ba Jayaśīla.

Colophon K : written by guru Dharmapāla of Suvarṇadvīpa on the request of the respectful students Kamalarakṣita and Dīpaṃkara-śrī--jñāna ; translated by Indian upādhyāya

Dīpaṃkara and Tibetan lo-tsā-ba Jayaśīla. (Tibetan sub-title : *Badhisattva-caryāvatāra-piṇḍārtha* of Dharmapāla on the request of Jo-bo).

42. *Bodhisattva-caryāvatāra-ṣaṭtriṃśat-piṇḍārtha*

mDo xxvii 6. K 100/5280/233-4-2. About 67 lines.

a. Dharmapāla, the guru of Suvarṇadvīpa. t. paṇḍita Dīpaṃkara (IT Jo-bo-rje ; IM Atiśa) and lo-tsā-ba Jayaśīla of Nag-tsho.

Colophon K : written by guru Dharmapāla of Suvarṇadvīpa by the request of the respectful disciples Kamalarakṣita and Dīpaṃkara. Translated and revised by paṇḍita Dīpaṃkara and lo-tsā-ba Jayaśīla.

43. *Bodhisattva-bhūmi-vṛtti*

mDo liv 5. K 112/5545/1-1-3. About 851 lines.

a. ācārya Guṇaprabha, the guru of rājā Harṣavardhana Śīlāditya of Thāneśvara. t. upādhyāya Dīpaṃkara-śrī-jñāna of India (IT Jo-bo-rje ; IM Atiśa) and lo-tsā-ba bhikṣu Jayaśīla of Nag-tsho.

Colophon K : written by ācārya Guṇaprabha ; translated and revised by Indian upādhyāya Dīpaṃkara-śrī-jñāna and lo-tsā-ba bhikṣu Jayaśīla. The Indian original (work) was not legible. So the translation is incomplete. There are still about 7 *bam-po*-s.

Note : bam-po : "that which has been gathered together, what is put or grouped into one ; and, hence, frequently a section or subdivision of a book, a number of chapters taken together ; a series of pages ; a set of śloka-s." D-TED 866. "...in metrical compositions it is said to comprize a number of 300 verses." J-TED 366.

44. *Bhaṭṭāraka-ārya-ekādaśa-mukha-avalokiteśvarasya-sādhana*

rG lxviii 42. K 79/3557/102-1-6. About 30 lines.

a. bhikṣuṇī Lakṣmī (IM Lakṣmīṅkarā). t. upādhyāya Dīpaṃkara-śrī-jñāna of India and lo-tsā-ba Ratnabhadra.

Colophon K : written by bhikṣuṇī Lakṣmī ; translated by

Indian upādhyāya Dīpaṃkara-śrī-jñāna and lo-tsā-ba Ratnabhadra.

45. *Bhikṣu-varṣāgra-pṛcchā*

mDo xc. 21. K 127/5649/309-1-1. About 104 lines.

a. not mentioned. t. upādhyāya Dīpaṃkara-śrī-jñāna of India lo-tsā-ba bhikṣu Jayaśīla.

Colophon K : translated and revised by Indian upādhyāya Dīpaṃkara-śrī-jñāna and lo-tsā-ba bhikṣu Jayaśīla at the Lhasa temple.

Note : Obermiller (Bu-ston Intro. 4) attributes the work to Padmākaraghoṣa. But 'Gos lo-tsā-ba (BA i. 30) : "the *Bhikṣu-varṣāgra-pṛcchā*, composed by the ācārya Padmasambhava and translated (into Tibetan) by Dīpaṃkara-śrī-jñāna and Nag-tsho..." Cf. Roerich BA i. 30n : "According to Tibetan scholars the author of the above text (i. e. *Bhikṣu-varṣāgra-pṛcchā*) has been the founder of Buddhism in Tibet, according to others he was another person bearing the same name. In the old indexes of the bsTan-'gyur this text and the *Śrāmaṇera-varṣāgra-pṛcchā* are the only two texts in the Sūtra class ascribed to Padmasambhava."

46. *Madhyamaka-bhramaghāta-nāma*

mDo xviii 5. K 95/5250/142-5-4. About 42 lines.

a. mahā-ācārya Āryadeva. t. upādhyāya Dīpaṃkara-śrī-jñāna of India (IT Jo-bo-rje ; IM Atīśa) and lo-tsā-ba bhikṣu Jayaśīla of Nag-tsho.

Colophon K : written by mahā-ācārya Āryadeva ; translated and revised by Indian upādhyāya Dīpaṃkara-śrī-jñāna and lo-tsā-ba bhikṣu Jayaśīla on the request of king Sukhācārya of Jambudvīpa at Nālandā temple. I have heard like this.

47. *Madhyamaka-ratna-pradīpa-nāma*

mDo xviii 9. K 95/5254/262-4-6. About 627 lines.

a. ācārya mahā-paṇḍita Bhavya (Bhāvaviveka). t. mahā-paṇḍita Dīpaṃkara-śrī-jñāna (IT Jo-bo-rje ; IM Atīśa) and lo-tsā-ba Vīryasiṃha of rGya, Jayaśīla of Nag-tsho, etc. Place of translation : Somapurī vihāra.

Colophon K : written by mahā-paṇḍita Bhavya according to the words (work ?) of ācārya ārya Nāgārjuna. Later on Vīryasiṃha and Jayaśīla of Nag-tsho translated it by revising again and again at the Somapurī temple under the oral communication (?) of mahā-paṇḍita Dīpaṃkara-śrī-jñāna to guru bhaṭṭāraka Tāmradvīpī upāsaka Nātha.

Note : some of the words in Colophon K are of doubtful meaning.

48. *Madhyamaka-hṛdaya-kārikā*

mDo xix 1. K 96/5255/1-1-1. About 670 lines.

a. mahā-ācārya Bhavya. t. upādhyāya Dīpaṃkara-śrī-jñāna of India (IT Jo-bo-rje; IM Atīśa) and lo-tsā-ba bhikṣu Jayaśīla.

Colophon K : written by mahā-ācārya Bhavya ; translated and revised by Indian upādhyāya Dīpaṃkara-śrī-jñāna and lo-tsā-ba bhikṣu Jayaśīla at Lhasa temple.

49. *Madhyamaka-hṛdaya-vṛtti-tarkajvālā*

mDo xix 2. K 96/5256/19-4-7. About 5,385 lines.

a. ācārya Bhavya (Bhāvaviveka). t. upādhyāya Dīpaṃkara-śrī-jñāna of India (IT Jo-bo-rje ; IM Atīśa) and lo-tsā-ba Jayaśīla.

Colophon K : written by ācārya Bhavya ; translated by both (?) paṇḍita bhaṭṭāraka Prajñāprabhāsa. Indian upādhyāya Dīpaṃkara-śrī-jñāna and lo-tsā-ba bhikṣu Jayaśīla translated and revised it at Rasa (ancient name of Lhasa) temple.

Note : BA i. 311 : "In the *Tarkajvālā*, translated by Nag-tsho, it is stated that the text has been translated by the two—Nag-tsho and mkhas-btsun Śes-rab-'od who revised the yoga-caryā-tathatā." BA. i. 324 : "He (rṄog-legs-pa'i-śes-rab) then requested the Master and the lo-tsā-ba (Nag-tsho) to translate the *Tarkajvālā*. The Master agreed and Nag-tsho prepared a complete translation at Lhasa."

50. *Madhyamaka-artha-saṃgraha*

mDo xix 4. K. 96/5258/154-3-5. About 19 lines.

a. Bhāvaviveka. t. Jayaśīla. IT Jo-bo-rje and lo-tsā-ba Jayaśīla ; IM Atīśa and lo-tsā-ba Jayaśīla.

Colophon K : written by ācārya Bhavya ; translated by bhikṣu Jayaśīla.

51. *Mahā-yakṣa-senāpati-vajrapāṇi-nāma-sādhana*

rG lxviii 178 ; lxviii 180. K 79/3692/145-2-6 ; 79/3694. About 59 lines.

a. mahā-ācārya Suvāgīśvarakīrti. t. paṇḍita Dīpaṃkara-śrī-jñāna of India (IT Jo-bo-rje ; IM Atiśa) and lo-tsā-ba Vīryasiṃha of rGya.

Colophon K : written by mahā-ācārya Suvāgīśvarakīrti ; translated and revised by Indian paṇḍita Dīpaṃkara-śrī-jñāna and lo-tsā-ba Vīryasiṃha of rGya.

52. *Mahāyāna-saṃgraha-bhāṣya*

mDo lvi 3. K 112/5551/272-5-2. About 1,458 lines.

a. ācārya Vasubandhu. t. upādhyāya Dīpaṃkara-śrī-jñāna of India (IT Jo-bo-rje ; IM Atiśa) and lo-tsā-ba bhikṣu Jayaśīla.

Colophon K : written by ācārya Vasuvandhu ; translated and revised by Indian upādhyāya Dīpaṃkara-śrī-jñāna and lo-tsā-ba bhikṣu Jayaśīla in the temple of dPe-dkar-gliṅ at bSam-yas, the nirābhoga-sthāna. Its length is 2,180 śloka-s and 8 bam-po-s.

53. *Mṛtyu-vañcana-upadeśa*

rG xxvi 68. K 59/2620/103-5-2. About 270 lines.

a. ācārya Vāgīśvarakīrti. t. upādhyāya Dīpaṃkara-śrī-jñāna of India and lo-tsā-ba bhikṣu Ratnabhadra.

54. *Mṛtyu-vañcana-upadeśa*

rG lxxxi 21. K 86/4808/21-2-1. About 352 lines and 3 folios of charts.

a. ācārya mahā-paṇḍita Vāgīśvarakīrti, under the inspiration of Tārādevī. t. upādhyāya Dīpaṃkara-śrī-jñāna of India and lo-tsā-ba bhikṣu Ratnabhadra.

Colophon K : written by ācārya mahā-paṇḍita Vāgīśvarakīrti, who received the blessings of Tārādevī ; translated and revised by upādhyāya Srī-dīpaṃkara-jñāna and lo-tsā-ba bhikṣu Ratnabhadra.

Note : This text is different from the previous one bearing the same title.

55. *Mṛtyu-vañcana-piṇḍārtha*

rG lxxxi 19. K 86/4806/19-2-2. About 29 lines.

a. ācārya Vāgīśvarakīrti. t. paṇḍita Dīpaṃkara-śrī-jñāna and lo-tsā-ba bhikṣu Ratnabhadra.

Colophon K : written by ācārya Vāgīsvarakīrti.

56. *Mṛtyu-vañcana-piṇḍārtha*

rG lxxxi 20. K 86/4807/19-5-7. About 50 lines.

a. IT same as above. t. IM same as above.

Colophon K : no colophon.

57. *Meghāloka-gaṇapati-sādhana-nāma*

rG lxxii 35. K 81/4562/224-2-5. About 15 lines.

a. ācārya brāhmaṇa Ratnavajra. t. paṇḍita Dīpaṃkara-śrī-jñāna and lo-tsā-ba Jayaśīla of Nag-tsho.

Colophon K : written by ācārya brāhmaṇa Ratnavajra ; translated by Indian paṇḍita Dīpaṃkara-śrī-jñāna and lo-tsā-ba Jayaśīla of Nag-tsho.

58. *Yamāri-sādhana*

rG xliii 40 ; lxxxvi 56. K 67/2824/85-5-5 ; 87/5146. About 22 lines.

a. ācārya Sugatigarbha. t. upādhyāya Dīpaṃkara-śrī-jñāna of India and lo-tsā-ba bhikṣu Ratnabhadra.

Colophon K : written by ācārya Sugatigarbha and translated by Indian upādhyāya Dīpaṃkara-śrī-jñāna and lo-tsā-ba bhikṣu Ratnabhadra.

59. *Yamāri-sādhana*

rG lxix 113. K 79/3876/260-2-5. About 15½ lines.

a. not mentioned. t. upādhyāya Dīpaṃkara-śrī-jñāna (IT Jo-bo-rje ; IM Atīśa) and lo-tsā-ba bhikṣu Jayaśīla of Nag-tsho.

Colophon K : Thus ends *Saṃgraha-sādhana-upāya* as said in *Ārya-kṛṣṇa-yamāri-tantra*... Translated and revised by Indian upādhyāya Dīpaṃkara-śrī-jñāna and lo-tsā-ba bhikṣu Jayaśīla.

Note : This text is different from the above.

60. *Vajradhara-vajrapāṇi-karma-sādhana-nāma*

rG lxxxii 20. K 86/4849/110-4-1. About 29 lines.

a. yogī Vīryaśrī. t. upādhyāya Dīpaṃkara-śrī-jñāna of India and lo-tsā-ba bhikṣu Ratnabhadra.

Colophon K : written by yogī Vīryaśrī ; translated and

revised by Indian upādhyāya paṇḍita Dīpaṃkara-śrī-jñāna and lo-tsā-ba bhikṣu Ratnabhadra. Copied out by Jo-bo's disciple Siddhārtha (Don-grub).

61. *Vajra-pavitra-karma-sambhāra*

rG lxviii 176. K 79/3690/144-5-6. About 5 lines.

a. bhaṭṭāraka Nāgārjuna. t. lT Jo-bo-rje (lM Atiśa) and lo-tsā-ba Vīryasiṃha of rGya.

Colophon K : written by bhaṭṭāraka Nāgārjuna.

62. *Vajrapāṇi-sādhana-nāma*

rG lxviii 194. K 79/3708/155-1-5. About 19 lines.

a. mahācārya Śraddhākaravarman. t. lT Jo-bo-rje (lM Atiśa) and lo-tsā-ba Vīryasiṃha of rGya.

Colophon K : written by mahā-ācārya Śraddhākaravarman.

63. *Vajrapāṇi-sādhanopāyikā-nāma*

rG lxviii 179; 184. K 79/3693/146-4-8; 79/3698. About 41½ lines.

a. mahā-ācārya Suvāgīśvarakīrti. t. paṇḍita Dīpaṃkara-śrī-jñāna of India (lT Jo-bo-rje ; lM Atiśa) and lo-tsā-ba Vīryasiṃha of rGya.

Colophon K : written by ācārya Suvāgīśvarakīrti according to the *Dhāraṇī-ṭīkā*. Here ends *Dhāraṇī-sādhana-upāya...* Translated by Indian paṇḍita Dīpaṃkara-śrī-jñāna and lo-tsā-ba Vīryasiṃha of rGya.

64. *Viveka-kathā*

mDo xxxiii 50 ; xciv 16. K 103/5427/242-4-7 ; 129/5671. About 51 lines.

a. mahā-ācārya Gopadatta. t. upādhyāya Dīpaṃkara-śrī-jñāna of India and lo-tsā-ba bhikṣu Śubhamati. [xciv 16 mentions translator as upādhyāya Dīpaṃkara of India (lT Jo-bo-rje ; lM Atiśa) and lo-tsā-ba bhikṣu Śubhamati].

Colophon K (103/5427) : Written by Bhūpāladatta (Bhūjībadatta ; Sa-'tsho). Translated and revised by Indian ācārya Dīpaṃkara-śrī-jñāna and lo-tsā-ba bhikṣu Śubhamati. 129/5671 : Translated by Indian ācārya Dīpaṃkara and lo-tsā-ba bhikṣu Śubhamati.

65. *Vyākhyā-pradīpa*

rG lxviii 185. K 79/3699/151-1-8. About 8½ lines.

a. ācārya Vāgīśvarakīrti. t. IT Jo-bo-rje and lo-tsā-ba Vīryasiṃha of rGya.

Colophon K : written by ācārya Vāgīśvarakīrti. (The Colophon does not mention the name of the text, though it is given in the index of K as *Jñāpakārtha-vṛtti-pradīpa*).

66. *Śikṣā-samuccaya-abhisamaya-nāma*

mDo xxxi 4 ; xxxiii 87. K 103/5338/1-3-1. 103/5464. About 13 lines.

a. Suvarṇadvīpa-rāja śrīmat Dharmapāla (expounded this text to Kamala or Kamalarakṣita and Dīpaṃkara or Dīpaṃkara-śrī-jñāna). t. Śrī-dīpaṃkara-jñāna (IT Jo-bo-rje ; IM Atīśa) and bhikṣu Jayaśīla.

Colophon K : translated by Śrī-dīpaṃkara-jñāna and bhikṣu Jayaśīla. The text was expounded by Suvarṇadvīpa rāja śrīmat Dharmapāla to Kamala and Dīpaṃkara.

67. *Śrī-ājñā-vinivarta-gaṇapati-sādhana-nāma*

rG lxxii 36. K 81/4563/224-4-4. About 15 lines.

a. mahā-acārya Indrabhūti. t. mahā-paṇḍita Dīpaṃkara-śrī-jñāna (IT Jo-bo-rje ; IM Atīśa) and lo-tsā-ba Vīryasiṃha of rGya. Place of translation : Svayambhūgartagiri (?)

Colophon K : written by mahā-ācārya Indrabodhi and nicely translated by mahā-paṇḍita Dīpaṃkara-śrī-jñāna and lo-tsā-ba Vīryasiṃha at Yambukartari(?).

68. *Śrī-cakra-saṃvara-vistara-prabandha*

rG xiv 14. K 52/2244/153-1-6. About 39 lines.

a. ācārya Bhūripāda. t. Jo-bo-rje (IM Atīśa) and lo-tsā-ba bhikṣu Ratnabhadra.

Colophon K : written by ācārya Bhūri-pā and translated by Jo-bo-rje and lo-tsā-ba Ratnabhadra.

69. *Śrī-nīlāmbara-dhara-vajrapāṇi-kalpa-bali-vidhi-nāma*

rG lxviii 183. K 79/3697/105-2-5. About 26 lines.

a. mahā-ācārya Suvāgīśvarakīrti. t. IT Jo-bo-rje and lo-tsā-ba Vīryasiṃha of rGya.

Colophon K : written by mahā-ācārya Suvāgīśvarakīrti.

70. *Śrī-vajrapāṇi-māraṇa-karma-sambhāra-saṃgraha-nāma*

rG lxviii 189. K 79/3703/151-5-6. About 25 lines.

a. ācārya Suvāgīśvarakīrti. t. IT Jo-bo-rje and lo-tsā-ba Vīryasiṃha of rGya.

Colophon K : written by ācārya Suvāgīśvarakīrti.

71. *Śrī-vajrapāṇi-stotra*

rG lxviii 199. K 79/3713/161-4-3. About 10 lines.

a. ācārya Vīryacandra. t. Jo-bo-rje (IM Atiśa śākya-bhikṣu Dīpaṃkara-śrī-jñāna) and lo-tsā-ba Vīryasiṃha of rGya.

Colophon K : written by ācārya Vīryacandra ; translated by Jo-bo-rje and Vīryasiṃha of rGya.

72. *Sattvārādhana-stava*

bsTod 17. K 46/2017/36-4-8. About 17½ lines.

a. ācārya Nāgārjuna. t. upādhyāya mahā-paṇḍita Dīpaṃkara-śrī-jñāna of India. (IT Jo-bo-rje ; IM Atiśa) and lo-tsā-ba bhikṣu Jayaśīla (IM Śīlajaya) of Nag-tsho.

Colophon K : Compiled by ācārya Nāgārjuna in chanda. Translated and revised by Indian upādhyāya mahā-paṇḍita Dīpaṃkara-śrī-jñāna and lo-tsā-ba bhikṣu Jayaśīla.

73. *Saptāṅga-sādhana*

rG lxviii 177. K 79/3691/145-1-3. About 10½ lines.

a. ācārya ārya Nāgārjuua. t. IT Jo-bo-rje and lo-tsā-ba Vīryasiṃha of rGya.

Colophon K : written by ācārya ārya Nāgārjuna.

74. *Samayāmṛta-khāda-nāma*

rG lxxxi 12. K 86/4799/3-4-6. About 14½ lines.

a. IT ācārya Lalitavajra. t. IT paṇḍita Dīpaṃkara and lo-tsā-ba Vajrakīrti.

Colophon K mentions neither author nor translator.

75. *Siddhikrama*

rG lxviii 186. K 79/3700/151-3-1. About 5½ lines.

a. ācārya Suvāgīśvarakīrti. t. IT Jo-bo-rje and lo-tsā-ba Vīryasiṃha of rGya.

Colophon K : written by ācārya Suvāgīśvarakīrti.

76. *Supatha-deśana-parikathā*

mDo xciv 20. K 129/5675/217-5-6. About 479 lines.

a. ācārya Sura. t. mahā-upādhyāya Dīpaṃkara-śrī-jñāna of India (IT Jo-bo-rje ; IM Atiśa) and the grand lo-tsā-ba bhikṣu Ratnabhadra.

Colophon K : written by ācārya Sura ; translated and revised by Indian mahā-ācārya Dīpaṃkara-śrī-jñāna and mahā lo-tsā-ba bhikṣu Ratnabhadra.

77. *Seka-prakriyā*

rG xl 15. K 66/2750/1-1-1. About 211 lines.

a. ācārya mahā-paṇḍita Śrī Nandivajra. t. mahā-paṇḍita Śrī-dīpaṃkara (IT Jo-bo-rje ; IM Atiśa) and Ratnakīrti, lo-tsā-ba of Ba-ri. Place of translation : Tho-liṅ vihāra.

Colophon K : In length the text is 300 chanda-s and 1 bam-po. Written by ācārya mahā-paṇḍita Nandavajra ; translated by Indian upādhyāya mahā-paṇḍita Dīpaṃkara-śrī-jñāna and Tibetan lo-tsā-ba Ba-ri at the Tho-liṅ temple under the instructions of King lDe-btsan.

Section 5

Works in the bsTan-'gyur connected with Dīpaṃkara in other ways

1. *Catuḥ-tattva*

rG lxxiv 39. K 82/4705/186-5-7. About 56 lines.

a. Dombi-pā. t. Tāranātha, after comparison of the text with the commentary of Dīpaṃkara ; executed by the request of ācārya Buddhagupta of India and paṇḍita Nīrvāṇaśrī. Colophon mentions Naro-pā and Maitrī-pā.

Colophon K : written by Dombi-pā. Translated on the upadeśa of Indian ācārya Buddhagupta under paṇḍita Nirvāṇaśrī according to the commentary of Dīpaṃkara-śrī. Previously it was called *Alpa-vajra-vāhya-saṃgraha* and the descendant of Naro-pā commented on it. Vajrapāṇi Caturbhuja called it *Mahā-vajra-vāhya-saṃgraha*. It was studied by the students of Maitrī-pā also.

2. *Tyādyantasya-prakriyā-padārohaṇa-nāma*

mDo cxxxiii 1. K 149/5897/19-1-1. About 1,222 lines.

a. IM upādhyāya Nandakīrti. t. śākya Dharmaśrībhadra and others. The translation was executed at the grand religious centre Ri-phug under the blessings of paṇḍita Dīpaṃkara-śrī-jñāna.

Colophon K : written by upādhyāya Nandakīrti. Translated by śākya-bhikṣu Dharmaśrībhadra on the request of mahā-upādhyāya and mahā lo-tsā-ba Bu-ston into Tibetan language from the Indian book of Śrī Dharmabhadra, which is in his own handwriting. The translation was executed at the dharma-sthāna cave (Ri-phug) blessed by paṇḍita Dīpaṃkara-śrī-jñāna.

3. *Vāda-nyāya-prakaraṇa-nāma*

mDo xcv 16. K 130/5715/148-1-8. About 567 lines.

a. mahā-ācārya Dharmakīrti. t. mahā-upādhyāya Jñāna-śrībhadra of India and lo-tsā-ba bhikṣu Śubhamati. Version executed by the order of śrī deva-bhaṭṭāraka Śāntiprabha and the king of Tibet dPal-lha-btsan-po Khri-bkra-śis-mṅa'-bdag-rtse-lde-btsan, the son of 'Od-lde-btsan (c. 1050-1075 A.D.). Corrected by mahā-paṇḍita Dīpaṃkara and lo-tsā-ba bhikṣu Dharmakīrti.

Colophon K : Tarkavidyā-nāma-adhyāya. Written by mahā-ācārya Dharmakīrti ; translated and revised by Indian mahā-upādhyāya Jñānaśrībhadra and bhikṣu Śubhamati on the request of dPal-lha-btsun-po Shi-ba-'od (śrī-devaguru Śāntiprabha) and dPal-lha-btsan-po Khri-bkra-śis-mṅa'-bdag rTse-lde-btsan (i.e. rTse-lde, son of 'Od-lde). Again corrected by mahā-paṇḍita Dīpaṃkara and lo-tsā-ba bhikṣu Dharmakīrti also.

4. *Vajrayāna-mūlāpatti-ṭīkā*

rG lxviii 146. K 70/3314/1-1-1. About 687 lines.

a. ācārya Mañjuśrīkīrti. t. Upadhaśrīvajraśrīla and lo-tsā-ba bhikṣu Vīryasiṃha of rGya. The translation was done at the city of Purisa (?) at the time of the arrival of Dīpaṃkara at the Tiger Park at Myaṅ-ro (Ñaṅ-ro).

Colophon K : written by ācārya Mañjuśrīkīrti : translated by Dīpaṃkara at Myaṅ-ro sTag-tshal, on his way to Tibet. In the city of Purisa, ācārya Upadhaśrīvajraśrīla and lo-tsā-ba Vīryasiṃha translated with great careful thinking and respect. Then I, lo-tsā-ba Ratnakīrti, went to many Nepalese houses and compared it with many old commentaries and made it perfectly correct.

5. *Vajrasattva-sādhana-nāma*

rG xxxiii 18. K 62/2678/19-5-2. About 152 lines.

a. ācārya Candrakīrti. t. mahā-paṇḍita Tathāgatarakṣita and lo-tsā-ba Kumārajvālā. Place of translation : Vikramaśīla vihāra. Corrected : upādhyāya mahā-paṇḍita Dīpaṃkara-rakṣita of India and lo-tsā-ba (Ratnakīrti) of Ba-ri of Khams origin. Correction executed at the śrī-anupama-nirābhoga vihāra.

Colophon K : written by ācārya Candrakīrti. In length it is 102 pada-s. Translated by mahā-paṇḍita Tathāgata-rakṣita and lo-tsā-ba Kumārajvālā of gLog-kya at śrī Vikramaśīla temple. And again, Indian upādhyāya Dīpaṃkara-rakṣita and the Kham-pa bhikṣu lo-tsā-ba Ba-ri revised it and commented on it at the śrī anupama-nirābhoga temple.

Note : See *supra* p. 52f on Dīpaṃkara-rakṣita.

6. *Śrī-mahā-kāla-sādhana-nāma*

rG lxxxii 69. K 86/4897/152-3-2. About 54 lines.

a. ācārya brāhmaṇa Vararuci t. among others, Dīpaṃkara and Ratnabhadra. (But Cordier's understanding is doubtful. The colophon mentions a list of "descent from one to another," which evidently implies the transmission of the text from one ācārya to another but which Cordier took as a list of successive translators).

Colophon K : written by ācārya brāhmaṇa Vararuci. translated by ācārya Rāhula, "the red" and Tibetan lo-tsā-ba Gyi-ljaṅ. Its tradition is : Vajradhara, brāhmaṇa Vararuci Kuśalavajra, Śraddhākara, Dīpaṃkara, Ratnabhadra, śrāvaka Pūrṇa,...... (a long list of names ending with) Ratnakīrti.

7. *Śrī-mahākāla-abhiṣeka-vidhi*

rG xxvi 80. K 59/2632/159-4-3. About 39 lines.

a. brāhmaṇa Vararuci-pāda. t. colophon mentions Dīpaṃkara and Ratnabhadra among many others. (But Cordier's understanding appears to be doubtful : the colophon mentions a long list of "descent from one to another" (brgyud), which Cordier takes as a list of successive translators).

Colophon K : written by brāhmaṇa Vararuci-pāda ; translated by Mahākāla-jīvadhara and lo-tsā-ba Sitamuṇḍa of Gyi-ljaṅ. Its tradition is : brāhmaṇa Vararuci, Sukha-vajra, then Śraddhākara, then Dīpaṃkara, then Ratnabhadra and śrāvaka Pūrṇa,... (a long list of names).

Section 6

Works in the bsTan-'gyur, though with some variation in the name of author or translator, are to be attributed to the same Dīpaṃkara

1. *Pramāṇa-vārttika-alaṃkāra-ṭīkā*

mDo ci & cii (cii is continuation of ci; ci contains part I and cii parts II-IV). K 133/5720/1-1-1. About 13,016 lines.

a. IM Jaya (Jina). t. paṇḍita Dīpaṃkara-rakṣita of śrī Vikramaśīla of India and the grand lo-tsā-ba ban-de Bodhiprajña (Byaṅ-chub-śes-rab) of Shaṅ-shuṅ of Maṅ-'or. Translation executed by the order of deva-samrāṭa śākya-bhikṣu deva-guru Śāntiprabha (Shi-ba-'od)... Place of translation : Śrī-anupama-nirābhoga vihāra of Tho-liṅ.

Colophon K : written by ācārya Jaya ; translated very carefully by mahā-paṇḍita Śrī-dīpaṃkara-rakṣita, the Indian upādhyāya of Śrī-vikramaśīla and the great lo-tsā-ba 'Or-ban-de Byaṅ-chub-śes-rab (Bodhiprajña) of Shaṅ-shuṅ at the anupama-nirābhoga temple of Tho-liṅ, under the request of Tibet's bodhisattva-vaṃśadhara-narottama, created by the gods, Lha-btsan-po śākya-bhikṣu Lha-bla-ma Shi-ba-'od (deva-guru Śāntiprabha) and Lha-btsan-po dBaṅ-phyug-btsan-po'i mÑa'-bdag-chen-po Khri-bkra-śis rTse-lde-btsan (i.e. rTse-lde, son of 'Od-lde).

Note : See *supra* p. 52f on Dīpaṃkara-rakṣita.

2. *Vajra-bhairava-gaṇacakra-nāma*

rG xliii 67. K 67/2848/121-5-4. About 37 lines.

a. ācārya Ratnākaraśānti. t. upādhyāya Dīpaṃkara-rakṣita of India and lo-tsā-ba bhikṣu Vajrakīrti of Rva.

Colophon K : written by ācārya Ratnākaraśānti ; translated by Indian ācārya Dīpaṃkara-rakṣita and lo-tsā-ba bhikṣu Vajrakīrti.

3. *Vajra-sattva-sādhana-bhāṣya*

rG xxxiv 9. K 62/2704/302-3-7. About 103 lines.

a. ācārya Tathāgatarakṣita. t. upādhyāya mahā-paṇḍita Dīpaṃkara-rakṣita of India and lo-tsā-ba Ratnakīrti of Ba-ri. Place of translation : śrī-anupama-nirābhoga vihāra of Tho-liṅ.

Colophon K : written by ācārya Tathāgatarakṣita ; translated by Indian upādhyāya mahā-paṇḍita Dīpaṃkara-rakṣita and lo-tsā-ba Ba-ri of Khams at the anupama-nirābhoga temple of Tho-liṅ.

4. *Śrī-cakra-saṃvara-sahaja-tattva-āloka*

rG xiii 53. K 52/2219/56-1-5. About 17 lines.

a. mahā-ācārya Amitavajra. t. paṇḍita Dīpaṃkara-rakṣita of India and lo-tsā-ba Dharmeśvara (Chos-kyi-dbaṅ-phyug) of Mar-pa.

Colophon K : written by mahā-ācārya Amitavajra : translated by Indian paṇḍita Śrī-dīpaṃkara-rakṣita and ācārya Dharmeśvara of Mar-pa.

5. *Samaya-tārā-stava*

rG lxxxii 48. K 86/4876/127-1-3. About 33 lines.

a. not mentioned. Text revealed by ācārya Vāgīśvara during his stay at Ratnagiri in Kośala. t. upādhyāya Dīpaṃkara-kīrti (IT mahā-ārya Dīpaṃkara-jñāna of India) and lo-tsā-ba Prabhākara of mTshur.

Colophon K : written by Vāgīśvarakīrti the immortal and the resident of Ratnagiri of Kośala ; translated by Indian upādhyāya Dīpaṃkara-kīrti and lo-tsā-ba Prabhākara of mTshur.

Note : See *supra* 51f on Dīpaṃkara-kīrti.

Section 7

Works in the bKa'-'gyur of which Dīpaṃkara is translator or reviser

1. *Abhidhāna-uttara-tantra-nāma*

Sendai 369. K 2/17/40-5-3. About 2,100 lines.

t. (Sendai) : Dīpaṃkara-śrī-jñāna and Rin-chen-bzaṅ-po.

Colophon K : Translated, revised and edited by Indian upādhyāya mahā-paṇḍita Dīpaṃkara-śrī-jñāna and great Tibetan lo-tsā-ba bhikṣu Ratnabhadra. Later also revised by mahā-paṇḍita Jñānaśrī and lo-tsā-ba Khyuṅ-po Chos-kyi-brtson-'grus (Dharmavīrya of Khyuṅ-po). Later revised by removing the irrelevances and by filling up the gaps by paṇḍita Ananta and Lo-chuṅ. Thus it was brought to perfection and finalised. There is nothing of deeper significance than this.

2. *Ārya-avalokiteśvara-paripṛcchā-sapta-dharmaka-nāma-mahā-yāna-sūtra*

Sendai 150. K 33/817/36-4-6. About 11 lines.

t. (Sendai) : Dīpaṃkara-śrī-jñāna and dGe-ba'i-blo-gros.

Colophon K : Translated and revised by Indian upādhyāya Dīpaṃkara (Dipam-*dkar* : evidently a corruption in copying)-śrī-jñāna and lo-tsā-ba bhikṣu Śubhamati (dGe-ba'i-blo-gros).

3. *Ārya-aṣṭa-sāhasrikā-prajñā-pāramitā*

Sendai 12. K 21/734/57-1-1. About 4,904 lines.

t. (Sendai) : Śākyasena, Jñānasiddhi and Dharmatāśīla. Revised by Subhāṣita and Rin-chen-bzaṅ-po. Then revised by Dīpaṃkara-śrī-jñāna and Rin-chen-bzaṅ-po. Then revised by Dīpaṃkara-śrī-jñāna and 'Brom-rgyal-ba'i-'byuṅ-gnas. Then revised by 'Brom-rgyal-ba'i-'byuṅ-gnas. Then revised by 'Brom. Then revised by bLo-ldan-śes-rab.

Colophpn K : Translated, revised and edited by Indian upādhyāya Śākyasena and Jñānasiddhi and the great reviser lo-tsā-ba *ban-de* Dharmatāśīla and others. Again by request of the great king and lord of Tibet dPal-lha-btsan-po bKra-śis-lha-lde-btsan, translated by the Indian upādhyāya Subhāṣita and the grammarian (*sgra-bsgyur*—literally, 'word-changer') bhikṣu Ratnabhadra in accordance with the commentary. Again revised and edited by Indian upādhyāya mahā-paṇḍita Dīpaṃkara-śrī-jñāna and the great reviser lo-tsā-ba bhikṣu Ratnabhadra, comparing it with the commentary from the Central Land (*yul-dbus*, evidently Magadha). Again, at gÑe-thaṅ (sÑe-thaṅ) Na-mo-che of sKyi-smad, the major part finalised by both mahā-paṇḍita Dīpaṃkara-śrī-jñāna and lo-tsā-ba 'Brom-rgyal-ba'i-'byuṅ-gnas ('Brom Jayākara) at the time of expounding the *Aṣṭa-sāhasrikā.* Again, edited for the second time at the Rwa-sgreṅ vihāra by lo-tsā-ba 'Brom Jayākara, on the basis of a comparison of three manuscripts (*mdo-gsum*, literally 'three *sūtra*-s'). And again, the same lo-tsā-ba prepared an explanation (*bśad-pa*) and finalised in parts. In later time, the great lo-tsā-ba śākya-bhikṣu bLo-ldan-śes-ab (Matiprajña) finalised it by collecting many original manuscripts from Kashmir and Magadha (*yul-dbus*).

4. *Ārya-tathāgata-vaidūrya-prabhā-nāma-balādhāna-*(*baladhana*)-*samādhi-dhāraṇī*

Sendai 505. K 6/137/139-3-1. About 37 lines.

t. (Sendai) Jinamitra, Dānaśīla, Śīlendrabodhi, Ye-śes-sde. Reviser Dīpaṃkara-śrī-jñāna and Tshul-khrims-rgyal-ba (Jayaśīla).

Colophon K : Translated, revised and edited by Indian upādhyāya Jinamitra, Dānaśīla and Śīlendrabodhi and the great reviser lo-tsā-ba ban-de Ye-śes. Again, Indian upādhyāya Dīpaṃkara-śrī-jñāna and bhikṣu Jayaśīla edited it into the new language at the golden temple of Tho-liṅ.

5. *Ārya-nīlāmbara-dhara-vajrapāṇi-kalpa-nāma-dhāraṇī*

Sendai 748 & 948. K 6/132/98-5-1. About 17 lines.

Colophon K : Translated by Indian upādhyāya Dīpaṃkara-śrī-jñāna and the Tibetan lo-tsā-ba Vīryasiṃha of rGya at the corridor of Śrī Nālandā.

6. *Ārya-vajrapāṇi-nīlāmbara-dhara-tri-loka-vinaya-nāma-tantra*
Sendai 501. K 6/133/99-1-8. About 62 lines.
t. (Sendai) Dīpaṃkara and Rin-chen-bzaṅ-po.
Colophon K : Translated by Indian upādhyāya Dīpaṃkara and the great reviser lo-tsā-ba bhikṣu Ratnabhadra.

7. *Ārya-vajrapāṇi-nīlāmbara-dhara-vajra-pātāla-nāma-tantra*
Sendai 499. K 6/129/30-2-5. About 93 lines.
t. (Sendai) Dīpaṃkara-śrī-jñāna and Bya'i-gloṅ-pa-can.
Colophon K : translated by Indian upādhyāya Dīpaṃkara and the grammarian lo-tsā-ba bhikṣu Byạ'i-gdoṅ-pa-can.

8. *Ārya-raśmi-vimala-viśuddha-prabhā-nāma-dhāraṇī*
Sendai 510 & 982. K 7/218/188-4-8 ; 11/607. About 171 lines.
t. (Sendai) Vidyākarasiṃha and dPal-gyi-lhun-po'i-sde. Reviser Atīśa and 'Brom-ston-pa.
Colophon K : Translated, revised and edited by Indian upādhyāya Vidyākarasiṃha and the great reviser lo-tsā-ba dPal-lhun-po'i-sde. Translated with correct transliteration by Jo-bo Atīśa (Adhiśa) and kalyāṇamitra 'Brom-ston-pa.

9. *Gaṇḍī-samaya-sūtra* (Ghaṇṭī ?)
Sendai 299. K 38/965/301-3-2. About 18 lines.
t. (Sendai) Dīpaṃkara-śrī-jñāna and dGe-ba'i-blo-gros.
Colophon K : Translated by Indian upādhyāya Dīpaṃkara-śrī-jñāna and lo-tsā-ba bhikṣu Śubhamati.

10. *Bodhisattva-pratimokṣa-catuṣka-nirhāra-nāma-mahāyāna-sūtra*
Sendai 248. K 36/914/155-5-7. About 224 lines.
t. (Sendai) Dīpaṃkara-śrī-jñāna and Śākya-blo-gros and dGe-ba'i-blo-gros.
Colophon K : Translated, revised and edited by Indian upādhyāya Dīpaṃkara-śrī-jñāna, the great reviser lo-tsā-ba bhikṣu Śākyamati and bhikṣu Śubhamati.

11. *Mahā-gaṇapati-tantra-nāma*

Sendai 666. K 7/337/284-2-6. About 90 lines.

t. (Sendai) Dīpaṃkara-śrī-jñāna and rGyal-ba'i-'byuṅ-gnas.

Colophon K : Brought for the welfare of the world by the Indian upādhyāya Dīpaṃkara-śrī-jñāna and gifted to rGyal-ba'i-'byuṅ-gnas ('Brom). This tantra fulfils one's wishes.

12. *Sarva-tathāgata-kāya-vāc-citta-kṛṣṇa-yamāri-nāma-tantra*

Sendai 467. K 4/103/155-3-4. About 312 lines.

t. (Sendai) Dīpaṃkara-śrī-jñāna and Tshul-khrims-rgyal-ba.

Colophon K : Translated, revised and edited by the great Indian upādhyāya paṇḍita Dīpaṃkara-śrī-jñāna and Tibetan lo-tsā-ba bhikṣu Jayaśīla. Again, bhikṣu Dar-ma-grags revised. From that bhikṣu rDo-rje-grags revised.

13. *Siddhi-ekavīra-mahā-tantrarāja-nāma*

Sendai 544. K 6/163/271-1-1. About 200 lines.

t. (Sendai) Dīpaṃkara-śrī-jñāna and dGe-ba'i-blo-gros. Reviser Tshul-khrims-rgyal-ba.

Colophon K : Translated by the great Indian upādhyāya Dīpaṃkara-śrī-jñāna and lo-tsā-ba bhikṣu Śubhamati ; revised by bhikṣu Jayaśīla.

APPENDIX C

Selected Writings of Dipamkara

Translated by
Lama Chimpa *and* Alaka Chattopadhyaya

Section 1. Introductory Note
Section 2. *Caryā-gīti*
Section 3. *Caryā-gīti-vṛtti*
Section 4. *Dīpaṃkara-śrījñāna-dharma-gītikā*
Section 5. *Vimala-ratna-lekha*
Section 6. *Bodhi-patha-pradīpa*
Section 7. *Sayings of Atīśa* : *A*
Section 8. *Sayings of Atīśa* : *B*
Section 9. Sanskrit restoration of the *Bodhi-patha-pradīpa* by Mrinalkanti Gangopadhyaya
Section 10. Photostat reproduction of the manuscript containing the *Sayings of Atīśa*.

Section 1

Introductory Note

Of the large number of works of Dīpaṃkara preserved in Tibetan translation in the bsTan-'gyur, the Tibetan authorities consider the *Bodhi-patha-pradīpa* to be most important. It occurs twice in the bsTan-'gyur (mDo xxxi 9; xxxiii 1). The present translation generally follows the text as edited by S. C. Das (JBTS I. i. 57-74). Where, however, it differs significantly from the text of the Peking edition and the latter appears to give clearer meaning, the translation follows the latter. The Sanskrit original of the work, even if not lost, cannot be easily traced today. Professor Mrinalkanti Gangopadhyaya attempts a restoration of it, which is also reproduced here.

The *Vimala-ratna-lekha* (mDo xxxiii 103 & xciv 33) is the famous letter written by Dīpaṃkara to Nayapāla from Nepal *en route* to Tibet. The present translation follows the Peking edition of the text (*The Tibetan Tripiṭaka*, vol. 103, No. 5480).

The *Caryā-gīti* (rG xiii 44; mDo xxxiii 10), *Caryā-gīti-vṛtti* (rG xiii 45) and the *Dīpaṃkara-śrī-jñāna-dharma-gītikā* (rG xlviii 34) are translated from their Peking editions (*The Tibetan Tripiṭaka*, 103. 5387 ; 52.2212 and 69.3203 respectively).

To these are added the *Sayings of Atīśa* taken from a manuscript copy now in possession of Professor Lama Chimpa. Portions of the manuscript translated are given also in photostat reproduction.

The translations are intended to be literal and annotated.

Section 2

Caryā-gīti

In Indian language it is called the *Caryā-gīti*, in Tibetan *sPyod-pa'i-glu.*

Salutation to Ārya Mañjuśrī Kumārabhūta.[1] Salutation to Vajrāsana.[2]

This world is as reflection (*prativimva*). When examined, the nature of its self is found to be nature-less (*svabhāva-hīna*). The self (also) is a reflection. Oh, my silly mind, do not

1. "Mañjuśrī Kumārabhūta is the first of the eight spiritual sons (*upa-putra*) of the Buddha : (a) Mañjuśrī, (b) Vajrapāṇi, (c) Avalokiteśvara, (d) Kṣitigarbha, (e) Sarvanivāraṇa Viṣkambhi, (f) Ākāśa-garbha, (g) Maitreya, (h) Samantabhadra. He is ordinarily called 'Jam-dpal dByaṅs (Mañjuṣrī Ghoṣa), the noble one with sweet voice. He is the Bodhisattva who presides over science and learning. The Mahāyāna scriptures were chiefly delivered to him by the Buddha. The work called *Yum-rnam-'grel* explains the reason why he is called Kumārabhūta or 'grown youthful' : 'The Bodhisattva who observes only *brahmacarya* from the time he has imbibed faith in Buddha until he attains to the state of *bodhi* (enlightenment) is called Kumāra or the youthful ; for then all his faculties, moral and psychic etc. are fully developed and his wisdom perfect.' His state then may be compared with that of a youthful person. Mañjuśrī being the divine Bodhisattva, who presides over learning and *prajñā* and all kind of arts and sciences, is believed to be a youth at all times and in all ages. He never grows old. Among the Tīrthikas etc. the goddess Sarasvatī is believed to be always youthful... Like Gaṇeśa, Mañjuśrī is first invoked in all literary undertakings." JBTS I. i. 39n.
2. An epithet of the Buddha. Also "the navel of India, namely Gayā, considered the holiest of all places in the Buddhist world." D-TED 705.

(be deluded) by ignorance. You are under darkness so long as this knowledge does not dawn on you. //1

The self as well as all the living beings are clearly seen (as reflections are seen) in a vast mirror (*maṇi-darpaṇa*) on a day with clear sky. Why do you have the delusion about the difference between yourself and others, in the way in which the child is deluded by its own reflection ? //2

One who sees permanence in reflections is like the animal fighting (its own) shadow (reflected image). Firmly meditate on the *maṇḍala-cakra*.[3] With the knowledge of this, the *yogī* does not stay there (i.e. at the stage of mistaking reflections as real). //3

The great bliss (*mahāsukha*),[4] precious and noble (*priya* and *uttama*), is already included in the *maṇḍala*. How do you think that what you imagine and create in your mind is by nature (*svabhāva*) like that ? //4

How can one attain the best enlightenment (*anuttara bodhi*) so long as the nature of all these is not realised ? The complete (*aśeṣa*) negation (*abhāva*) of delusional actions (*vikalpa-karma*)[5] is of the nature of the perfect beatitude (*uttama mahāsukha*). //5

---

3. See D-TED 56 for the Tāntrika significance of *maṇḍala-cakra*. However, as Dīpaṃkara himself explains in the *Caryā-gīti-vṛtti* (See Section 3), by the meditation on the *maṇḍala-cakra*, here, he means the meditation on the *pratītya-samutpāda* and its implication, as claimed by the Mādhyamikas, viz. *śunyatā*. In other words, he retains here the Tāntrika form but makes the meditation *śunya-vādī* in content.

4. "In Buddhism there are two kinds of happiness : the happiness of bliss that terminates or becomes exhausted and the happiness that is eternal and cannot be exhausted; the first being mixed up with the miseries of transmigratory existence, the latter remaining unaffected by any cause." D-TED 668. For the conception of *mahāsukha* in Buddhist Tantrism, see S.B. Dasgupta, ITB 128-44.

5. *rnam-rtog* : *vikalpa* : unreal conclusions, imagination,

Keep your mind aloof from the *loka-aṣṭa-dharma.*[6] Be firm on your *puṇya-samādhi*-s.[7] Thus you will remain pure and completely free from all unnecessary actions. //6

Whatever is the product of the various *vikalpa*-s is devoid of good and pure nature. That *tattva* alone is pure which is absolutely free from *karma* and *vikalpa.* //7

The absorption in the highest meditation on truth (*mahā-agni* of *tattva-samādhi*) will, as the flame of the great fire, burn like oblations the dirt (*mala*) of *kleśa*-s.[8] When the world is known, the whole world will be like the void (*ākāśa*—emptiness). //8

---

aberrations of the mind. In philosophy—obscuration namely of the clear and direct knowledge of truth by reasonings in the mind of the individual ; error. D-TED 759.

6. "Eight worldly doctrines or principles: 1) gain, profit: *lābha,* 2) loss : *a-lābha,* 3) fame, reputation : *yaśaḥ* 4) bad-name, notoriety : *a-yaśaḥ,* 5) scandal, slander : *nindā,* 6) praise : *praśaṃsā,* 7) happiness : *sukha,* 8) misery or unhappiness : *duḥkha.* D-TED 428.

7. *tiṅ-ṅe-'dsin, samādhi.* Intense contemplation, profound meditation, perfect absorption of thought into object of meditation. The following nine *samādhi*-s of a Bodhisattva are mentioned : 1) *ratnasamudgata,* complete coming forth of jewels, 2) *su-pratiṣṭha,* well-established, 3) *akampa,* unagitated, 4) *a-vinivartanīya,* not liable to return, 5) *ratnākara,* abode or mine of jewels, 6) *sūrya-prabhātejaḥ,* brilliance like sun-shine, 7) *sarvārthasiddha,* successful in effecting all objects, 8) *jñānā-loka,* light of knowledge and 9) *pratyutpanna-buddha-sammukhā-vasthita-samādhi,* meditation attained in presence of the future Buddha. D-TED 516.

8. *ñon-moṅs-pa.* The word has often "the technical meaning of *misery* as the result of ignorant clinging to existence and the world, and therefore in the Buddhist sense the misery of sin." According to Buddhism, the ten smaller causes of moral misery are : wrath, spite, ostentation or, show, adherence to what is contrary to Buddhism, illusion, deception, jealousy, covetousness,

Have no illusion about the nature of the world, which is like emptiness (*ākāśa*). Do not remain blind under the darkness of the *vikalpa*-s. The world remains the same before and after. Past, future and the present do not differ. //9

Just as one suffering from [the disease called] *timira*[9] sees the hair in the sky, so does one afflicted with the disease (*timira*) of *vikalpa*, sees the world. Therefore, meditate on and examine the numerous *vikalpa*-s, which by nature are restless (*capala svabhāva*) and empty [lit. like *ākāśa*]. //10

Guard your *śīla*, the great treasure, so that it is not stolen by the dangerous thieves of *pāpa-vipāka*. Do not, oh mind, make the long night of the worldly existence an endless one under the sleep of delusion (*moha-nidrā*). Be alert ! //11

There can be no day without the sun. Similarly, how can there be *samādhi* without the treasure of *śīla* ? The thief has entered the chamber of your sleep. Oh you, your great treasure of *śīla* is running the risk of being stolen. //12

Do not allow your mind to desire unbecoming actions (*abhadra kārya*) even for a single moment. Keep close watch on it till the sun of *tattva* rises. Till this sun-rise, remain firmly attached to the principles of duty as one remains attached to the jewel (*maṇi*)[10] //13

---

pride, arrogance. The ten greater causes of moral or mental misery are : want of faith, repentance or regret, bartering, also vacillating, inattention or changing the mind, confusion or mental derangement, practising actions in accordant with custom, irreverence, laughing aloud, ignorance, immodesty. D-TED 489-90.

9. *timira*—"darkness of the eyes, partial blindness (a class of morbid affections of the coats,—*paṭala*,—of the eye)"—Monier-Williams SED 447. This seems to be a favourite example of the perception of illusory objects used by the Mahāyāna Buddhists. Cf. Vasubandhu : *yathā taimirikasya-asat-keśacandr-ādi-darśanam, Viṃśatikā*, verse 1. Cf. also *Sarva-darśana-saṃgraha* (Anand. Ed.) p. 13 : *timira-ādi-upahata-akṣṇām-keśa-uṇḍūka-nāḍī-jñāna-bhedavat*.

10. The exact meaning of the last sentence is not clear.

Your self and the living beings are identical. Do not allow the inner evil (*doṣa*) to differentiate between the self and others. This inner evil is *vikalpa*. Subdue it like a poisonous snake ; charm it with *amṛta-rasa*. //14

The inner evil is like the hydra-headed poisonous snake. The [right] understanding of all the living beings is the great *amṛta-rasa*. It brings tranquillity to the mind of the *mahā-yogī*. //15

That *mahā-sukha* of *nirvāṇa* is to be known as best which comes from the continuous drinking of this great *amṛta-rasa*. By nakedness and performance of sacrifice one does not become a *brāhmaṇa*. Nor does one become a *brāhmaṇa* by wearing matted hair (*jaṭā-dhāraṇa*), nor by the nature of birth (*kulasvabhāva*). //16

He who has purity of body-speech-mind (*kāya-vāk-citta*) is a [true] *brāhmaṇa*. This is said by the Buddha. One [i.e. a true *brāhmaṇa*] must renounce all the ten vices (*daśa-pāpa*) and must strengthen the ten virtues (*daśa-puṇya*)[11] //17

Even though born low, one should, throughout one's life, avoid immoral action (*adharma ācaraṇa*), conquer anger by forgiveness (*kṣamā dharma*) and renounce the desire for worldly pleasures. //18

We have given here the tentative meaning that appears to us to be appropriate for the context.

11. The ten sins or vices (*pāpa*-s or *a-kuśala-karma*-s) are the exact opposite of the ten virtues (*daśa-puṇya*-s), namely 1) not to kill anything living, 2) not to take what has not been given (those who closely stick to the precept go even so far that they will not touch or accept an alms unless it be put into their hands), 3) not to fornicate, 4) not to tell a lie, 5) not to abuse or revile, 6) not to talk foolishness, 7) not to calumniate, 8) not to be avaricious or covetous, 9) not to think upon doing harm or mischief, 10) not to entertain heretic notions, or positively, to be orthodox. J-TED 85.

Always bathe in the ocean of *kuśala-dharma.* Avoid the evil (*doṣa*) of lust, fear and delusion (*moha*). It is because of stupidity that you do not understand [the futility of] riding again and again the skeleton that drops dirt [i.e. woman]. //19

Avoid *kāma* and *moha,* the paths to miseries. Oh, my mind, clean your own dirt. Take refuge with reverence, to the *sad-guru,* [who is] like the fountain. Wash the linen that is dirty with the filth of the Great Delusion (*mahā-moha*). //20

The precepts of the *guru* are like clear water. Accept these and learn to wash yourself. Oh, my mind, understand and see yourself well. Clean the great filth of delusion. //21

One that does not listen to the preachings (*dharma-vacana*) of the Śākyamuni is like one that enters the forest fire or flood. You have certainly to go to the other world in the future. Therefore, listen to the words of the Buddha. //22

Never be an agent of *adharma* after listening to the precepts of Śākyamuni. There is none [else] to hold you back from the Avīci hell.[12] He alone who, after listening to *dharma* meditates on the meaning of *dharma*, will gain heaven with ease and attain *mokṣa.* //23

Dharma is the lamp [that guides through] the darkness of ignorance and it is the ship in which one crosses the ocean of existence. //24

Here ends the song of *śīla-caryā* by *mahā-ācārya* Dīpaṃ-kara-śrī-jñāna ; translated, revised and finalised by the Indian *paṇḍita* Vajrapāṇi and lo-tsā-ba *bhikṣu* Dharmaprajña (Chos-kyi-śes-rab).

---

12. One of the eight hells the torments of which are excruciating.

Section 3

Caryā-gīti-vṛtti

In Indian language it is called *Caryā-gīti-vṛtti,* in Tibetan *sPyod-pa'i-glu'i-'grel-pa.*

Salutation to Mañjuśrī Kumārabhūta. Salutation to Yuganaddha,[1] the all-perfect.

For the welfare of others I am explaining this *Caryā-gīti.*

The pure philosophy (*samyak-siddhānta*) is explained here in a two-fold way. It is a *vajra-gīti* in form and in it are primarily shown the *nirodha satya.*[2]

The *caryā-gīti* is *ātma-pratiṣṭha* [i.e. has its own blessings] and it shows the *mārga-satya*[3] and the *saṃvṛti satya.*[4]

The words "as reflection (*prativimva*)" etc. (*Caryā-gīti,* 1) have two objects (*viṣaya*-s) to be seen with the eyes of knowledge (*jñāna-cakṣu*), viz. the *nāsti-svabhāva*[5] and the *asti-svabhāva.*[6] [In short, in the *Caryā-gīti* the words "as reflection" etc. are used to indicate what is unreal and what is real).

The *nāsti-svabhāva* is that which, though not existing, is seen. For example, [things] seen by diseased vision [i.e. by a person suffering from the eye-disease called *timira*].

---

1. For *yuganaddha*, see J-TED 488; D-TED 1095; S. B. Dasgupta ITB 113ff. In the present context it appears to have been used as an epithet of the Buddha.
2. The Third Noble Truth (*ārya-satya*) namely concerning the cessation (*nirodha*) of suffering.
3. The Fourth Noble Truth, namely concerning the path (*mārga*) that leads to the state free from suffering.
4. Truth from the phenomenal point of view, as contrasted with the *pāramārthika satya* or the ultimate truth.
5. *med-pa,* literally "to be not, not to be, to be non-existent" ; the opposite of "to be" ; in short the unreal.
6. *yod-pa,* literally "to be, to exist", i.e. the real.

"As reflection" etc. In it [i.e., in the example of the reflected-image of the face in the mirror] there are three [factors] : the clear mirror, the proximity of the face and the sky being without cover. Similarly, because of the distortions of the *citta* and *vāyu*,[7] caused specially by ignorance (*avidyā*),[8] the living beings of the three worlds[9] are seen. Still, [their] truth does not follow because of their being seen. That is why, it is said, "When examined the nature [of the self is found to be] nature-less." (*Caryā-gīti*, 1)

By what examination (*parīkṣaṇa*) is this non-existence known ? Know the *svabhāva* of *ātman* and the living beings of

---

7. *rluṅ*, literally air. The word has, however, technical meaning in physiology and mysticism, which is more relevant in the present context. "In physiology : one of the three humours of the body, supposed to exist in nearly all the parts and organs of the body, circulating in veins of its own, producing the arbitrary and the involuntary motions and causing various other physiological phenomena. When deranged, it is the cause of many diseases, especially of such complaints the origin and seat of which is not known, as rheumatism, nervous affections, etc... In mysticism : *rluṅ-dzin-pa* seems to be equal to *dbugs-bsgyaṅ-ba* and to denote the drawing in and holding one's breath during the procedure called *gtum-mo* which is as much as to prepare one's self for contemplation, or enter into a state of ecstasy." J-TED 537-8.

8. *ma-rig-pa*, *avidyā*, ignorance. "Mostly used in the specific Buddhist sense, namely for the innate principal and *fundamental error* of considering perishable things as permanent and of looking upon the external world as one really existing, with Buddhists in a certain manner the original sin from which every evil is proceeding." J-TED 527.

9. According to Buddhistic speculation, the three worlds are : 1) the earth with the six heavens of the gods, as the "region of desire"(*kāmaloka*), 2) above this is the "region of form" (*rūpaloka*) and 3) ultimately the "region of formlessness" (*a-rūpa-loka*).

the three worlds as but reflections, which are merely seen. Know these as non-born [*ajāta*, i.e. never came to exist]. This is shown by addressing "Oh," etc. (*Caryā-gīti*, 1)

Make no mistake about the reflection (*prativimva*). Make no error about the nature (*svabhāva*) of the reflection.

To explain more fully the example and its implications cryptically mentioned as "with clear sky" etc. (*Caryā-gīti*, 2).

The reflection is the joint product of the three, viz., 1) the clear sky, 2) the *maṇi-darpaṇa* [mirror] and 3) the face. Similarly, *ātman* and the three worlds which are [but] reflections, are seen because of *citta*, *vāyu* and *karma*, working under [the influence of] ignorance (*avidyā*). To misunderstand these and to think these to be permanent and real (*samyak*) is [to behave] as foolishly as the lion does when it dies in the sea[10] by seeing [and jumping to fight] its own shadow, or as foolishly as the ignorant child who tries to scratch its own reflection.

Similarly, looking at the *ātman* and the three worlds, which are but reflections, why do you make the mistake of *ātma* and *para*? Hence it is said, "Why do you have the delusion" etc. (*Caryā-gīti*, 2).

As it is said in the *sūtra*, too, "In spite of beeing seen it is not there in the mirror. The *svabhāva* of everything is like that."

Again, "There is nothing real. It is only the mind, under the turmoil caused by habit, that see the real", thus it is said.

Thus *ātman* and the three worlds, the objects of the layman's knowledge, are unreal like the sky-flower [i.e. as unreal as a flower growing in the sky].

Now, as to seeing [knowing] the *asti-svabhāva* [the real].

For this it is said, "Firmly meditating on the *maṇḍala-cakra*" etc. (*Caryā-gīti*, 3). There are five [marks] of this [meditation on the *maṇḍala-cakra*], viz. the power of *pratītya-*

---

10. *rgya-mtsho*, literally the sea. But according to the current parable, the lion killed itself by jumping into "the well" to fight its own shadow.

samutpāda[11] being always there, to be it, to know as it, to meditate as it, to obtain blessings (*adhiṣṭhāna*).[12] In this way, for purifying the *citta* and *vāyu* [i.e. making *citta* and *vāyu* free from *āsrava* or impurity, the influence of *avidyā*] concentrate on the *āśraya-āśrita* [i.e. *pratītya-samutpāda*] *devatā*[13] and know it as the cause of cause.

When the three—viz. *citta*, which is the co-operating cause, *vāyu*, which is the general cause and the quality of being pure (*anāsrava*)—are combined, [all the] creations of the mind [literally, body of the mind, i.e. things that owe their thinghood to the mind, the mental] will appear as *māyā*.[14]

---

11. The doctrine of dependent origination or conditional existence of things, i.e., the view that the existence of everything is conditional or dependent on a cause. Nāgārjuna used this as the central argument of his *Śunyavāda*: "The Law of Dependent Origination (*pratītya bhāva*)", said Nāgārjuna, "is equivalent to and proof of the intrinsic unreality (*śunyatā*) of things. A thing which is found to come into existence in dependence upon an antecedent fact must forfeit its claim to intrinsic reality." (*Vigrahavyāvartanī*, verse 22. Tr. S. Mookerjee in NNMVRP, i. 17). As Stcherbatsky (CBN 41) explains, "a dependent existence is no real existence, just as borrowed money is no real wealth."

12. From the literal meanings of the words, the details of all the implications are not clear. Broadly speaking, however, it is clear that the "meditation on the *maṇḍala-cakra*" is here intended to mean the "meditation on the *pratītya-samutpāda*."

13. The Tāntrika meditation on *maṇḍala-cakra* is the meditation on a *devatā*, there being a *devatā* corresponding to each *maṇḍala*, whose house the *maṇḍala* is supposed to be. The meditation on the *maṇḍala-cakra*, here, is intended to mean the meditation on *pratītya-samutpāda*. Hence, *pratītya-samutpāda* itself is conceived as the *devatā* of this meditation, which leads to the knowledge of the *asti-svabhāva* or the realisation of the truth, which is of course nothing but *śunyatā*.

14. The sense seems to be as follows: since *citta* and *vāyu*,

When this knowledge, viz. that the quality of the *anāsrava-svabhāva* is the *svabhāva* of everything, dawns, then it [the creation of the mind] is not there [i.e. there is no longer the delusion of things being real].

Therefore, relying on the *kalyāṇa-mitra*(*guru*) of *samyak-buddhi*, one should reach the firm knowledge of the self with the help of the three and twelve examples. [The significance of "the three and twelve examples" is not clear].

The abiding blessing (*adhiṣṭhāna*) resulting from the meditation that subdues the five senses is the certain knowledge that everything is *māyā*.

All these are further to be known from the words of Devapāla and other Ārya-s.

"The *yogī* with the knowledge of truth will never behave like that" (*Caryā-gīti*, 3). This is said [because it is not enough to know that everything is *māyā*], for in spite of knowing that the *māyā*-woman is created by *māyā* there grows the lust for her.[15] Therefore, that [knowledge] will have to be [further purified by] *prabhā* (*'od-gsal*).[16]

The two words "*mahā-sukha*" (*Caryā-gīti*, 4) are easy to understand.

"How do you know that what your reasonings create in your mind", etc. (*Caryā-gīti*, 4)—This is in refutation of the *yogī* who has no [knowledge] of the marks (*lakṣaṇa*) of *satya-dvaya*. And this is easy to understand.

"How can one attain the best enlightenment without

---

under the influence of *avidyā* (which is *āsrava* or defilement) cause the delusive idea of the reality of self and the three worlds, when the influence of the *avidyā* (*āsrava*) is removed, i.e., when *citta* and *vāyu* become defilement-free, (i.e., are combined with the quality of *anāsrava*), it will be realised that everything is the illusory creation of the mind.

15. That an example like this was current among the Mahāyāna Buddhists is evident from Nāgārjuna's *Vigrahavyāvartanī*, verse 27.

16. The supernatural enlightening of the saints. J-TED 502.

realising the nature" etc. (*Caryā-gīti*, 5) refers to the *prabhā* (*'od-gsal*) and *yuganaddha*.

"The complete negation of all delusional action" etc. (*Caryā-gīti*, 5) refers to the 160 *loka-citta*-s (*'jig-rten-pa'i-sems*). These will be purified by the *prabhā*.

If one asks, "How to realise the *uttama-mahā-sukha* ?", [the answer is], "Keep your mind aloof from the *loka-aṣṭa-dharma*" and "Be firm on *uttama samādhi*" (*Caryā-gīti*, 6).

There are two ways to achieve it [the *uttama samādhi*. These are]

1) The ordinary path (*sādhāraṇa-varga*), which means to be possessed of the *śīla*-s (*śīla-yukta*), to be detached from enjoyments, to be forgiving, to have firm determination, to be repelled by noise, to be careful, to be continually conscious of the *satya-dvaya*, to be possessed of the knowledge of what should be done and what should not be done, to be divorced from the five *āvaraṇa*-s,[17] to be aware of the right measure of food, to be impartial in the treatment of friends and foes.

2) The extra-ordinary (*a-sādhāraṇa-varga*), which means the attainment of the four powers (? due to the four *abhiṣeka*-s or *dbaṅ-skur-ba*), to have firm *bodhicitta* and to have reverence for the *guru*.

When you are in this *varga*, your body-speech-mind (*kāya-vāk-citta*), the three coverings (*tri-āvaraṇa*), will be purified.

"Completely free from all unnecessary actions" (*Caryā-gīti* 6) and "*vikalpa*-s" etc. (*Caryā-gīti* 7)—these two are in refutation of the *yogī*-s who are engaged to such unnecessary actions. And that is easy to understand. This is clear, because [in that stage] the *tri-bhava*, the *loka-citta* and the endless *vikalpa*-s will have no efficacy. Thus is attained a stage of pristine purity. In that state the five senses will be under

17. "The five kinds of moral obscurations are the following : 1) defilements or sins of passionate desires, 2) sins of an evil heart, i. e. of the wish to do evil to others, 3) sins of laziness and indolence, 4) sins of sleep and 5) sins of doubt." D-TED 333.

control and the *loka-citta*,—the dirt of *kleśa*—will be burnt in the fire of *samādhi*. (*Caryā-gīti* 8). The *tri-loka* and the *loka-citta* will then be like the centre of the sky (*Caryā-gīti*, 8). The knowledge of all living beings will be dissolved into nothingness [lit, will be like the sky. *Caryā-gīti*, 8].

The knowledge of everything as it appears is in the nature of a dirt and it is necessary to cleanse it, of the knowledge of everything as seen. This is implied by the words, "Do not remain blind under the darkness of the *vikalpa*-s" (*Caryā-gīti*, 9). If asked, "Why ?", [the answer is] : there is no difference between the *tri-prāṇī*-s if viewed from the point of view of their natural purity. The difference is due to *kalpanā* (*rtog-pa*).

"Under the darkness" etc. (*Caryā-gīti*, 10) is easy to understand.

Now is being shown the necessity of avoiding, till the purification of all *karma*-s, all the minute *karma-phala*-s, the sources of misery.

"The thief of *pāpa*" etc. (*Caryā-gīti*, 11) is easy to understand.

Sārthavāha[18] (?) became merciful by renouncing his own *karma*-s through the *sūrya-prabha-samādhi*.[19] Thus it (? *karma*) is unnecessary when the *kalyāṇa-citta* within oneself is fulfilled. Hence are used the words, "principles of duty" etc. (*Caryā-gīti*, 13). And it is easy to understand.

A *brāhmaṇa* is to be known by a man's views (*dṛṣṭi*) and behaviour (*ācaraṇa*), not by his descent (*kula*) etc. Thus is said, "nakedness" etc. (*Caryā-gīti*, 16). This is easy to understand.

Attach no importance to one's *kula*; consider rather whether one follows the right path. This is indicated by the words, "One with low birth" etc. (*Caryā-gīti*, 18).

18. In the Peking edition, which is followed here, this word is not clearly printed. Our reading of the word is tentative.
19. One of the nine meditations of a Bodhisattva. D-TED 516.

"Again and again" (*Caryā-gīti,* 19) is said to bring him back to the right path who, under delusion, continually moves in the vicious circle.

The implications of addressing as "Oh," and of saying, "Oh my mind, clean your dirt yourself" etc. (*Caryā-gīti,* 21) are [as follows] : It is like cleaning the dirt of the face with the help of the mirror. The *guru* is like the mirror, his *upadeśa* is like water, which cleans *avidyā,* the dirt in need of being removed. That is why it is said, wash the dirt of *kalpanā* by the water of the *guru's* precepts (*Caryā-gīti*, 21).

Everything is the delusional product of *citta* and *vāyu.* You should understand yourself like that. Realise the *svabhāva* of *citta* and *vāyu* as but *ākāśa.*

One who does not listen to the words of Śākyamuni and who is not fortunate enough to have heard it, looks like [one in] fire (cf. *Caryā-gīti* 22). Remember, one has certainly to go beyond this world. Therefore, it is necessary to practise *bodhicitta* etc. after listening to the words of Śākyamuni (*Caryā-gīti*, 22). After listening to that, never act contrarywise.

Except that (*muni-vacana*), nothing can stop one from going to the Avīci hell. Listen to it and practise the precepts : the temporary result of that will be the attainment of heaven (*svarga*) and the ultimate result of that will be the attainment of the final illumination. (*Cayrā-gīti,* 23).

The lamp for the darkness of *avidyā* is *dharma, śaraṇa-gamana, bodhicitta* etc. and, finally, the supreme absorption in the great bliss (the *samādhi* or *mahā-sukha*). This lamp will certainly be illumined. Therefore, you must depend upon it [the *muni-vacana*] for crossing the *saṃsāra* (*bhava*) as one depends on the boat or the ship for crossing the sea.

Here ends the *Caryā-gīti-vṛtti* translated by *paṇḍita* Dīpaṃkara and lo-tsā-ba Jayaśīla.

Section 4

Dīpaṃkara-śrī-jñāna-dharma-gītikā

Salutation to the Buddha.

If you know *vikalpa*, the dangerous thief, to be a danger, then guard against it the great treasure of *śīla* and keep it safe.

Oh, do not be a fool and remain sunk in a sleep of delusion (*moha*) throughout the long night which is *saṃsāra*. Keep close watch on your mind. If you remain asleep the thief will enter your room and your treasure of *śīla* will be stolen. Without the wealth of *śīla*, there will be no *samādhi*. And without *samādhi* there will be no sunrise. Therefore, save your *samādhi*.

Even for a single moment do not imagine that the wealth of *śīla* is an ordinary wealth. Then will emerge absolute knowledge (*tattva-jñāna*) like the rising sun. Thus there will be the dawn and the end of *saṃsāra*.

Oh, do not be fool. Guard your *citta*.

Thus ends *Dīpaṃkara-śrī-jñāna-dharma-gītikā* (*Dīpaṃkara-śrī-jñāna'i-chos-kyi-glu*).

Section 5

Vimala-ratna-lekha-nāma

In Indian language it is called *Vimala-ratna-lekha-nāma*, in Tibetan *Dri-ma-med-pa'i-rin-po-che'i-phrin-yig*.

Salutation to the *guru*-s. Salutation to Bhaṭṭārikā Tārādevī.

Naryapāla, who was born in Magadha, has spread Buddhism and has ruled the kingdom according to *dharma*, may he be prosperous. //1

You have made gifts in the past, have observed the 'ten virtues' (*daśa-puṇya*), have practised forgiveness (*kṣamā*) and courage (*vīrya*). That is why you, *deva*, are perfect with the three.[1] //2

Place with reverence on your head the instructions of the *guru*-s and the obedience to the *sūtra* and *tantra-śāstra*-s. This will bring blessings for yourself and for others. //3

Avoid all doubts and vacillations. Be particularly active for attaining *siddhi.* Avoiding sleep, folly, and laziness, remain assiduous and ever careful. //4

Always guard the doors of the senses with remembrance, continuous knowledge and care. Examine repeatedly the movement of the mind day and night. //5

Behave like [one with] eyes with regard to your own fault but as the blind with regard to the faults of the others. Avoid arrogance and egoism and always meditate on the *śunyatā* //6

Give publicity to your own faults ; do not find faults of others. Give publicity to the virtues of others ; keep your own virtues hidden. //7

Do not accept gain and gifts. Always avoid profit and fame. Meditate on *maitrī* and *karuṇā*. Strengthen the *bodhicitta*. //8

---

1. Possessed of the three, viz. grace, glory and wealth. D-TED 825.

The ten *akuśala-karma*-s are to be avoided. Reverence is to be always strengthened. Remember to curb the desires, to remain self-content and to act in the virtuous way. //9

Give up anger and egoism. Have a humble mind. Avoid the wrong way of living and live the life of *dharma*. //10

Renouncing all worldly objects get enriched by the *ārya-dhana*.[2] Always avoid noisy places and live in solitude.//11

Do not be garrulous ; keep the tongue under control. When you come across the *guru* and the *ācārya*, serve them with reverence. //12

Whosoever acts for the *dharma*—be he a distinguished person, a beginner or just an ordinary person, should be regarded as the *guru*. //13

While looking at the living beings pining under miseries, raise the *bodhicitta* in you. Assume towards them the same attitude that the parents have to the child. // 14

Renouncing all worldly occupations meditate always on *samādhi*. Avoiding the sinful friend, follow the *kalyāṇa-mitra*. //15

Do not be indifferent to the *bhikṣu*-s that transgress the *śīla*, those that are wanting in *dharma* and those that are observed to commit the sins. //16

Do not spend more than three days with unholy companions or companions of sin, those that have no reverence for the *ācārya*-s etc., those that are ungrateful, those that think only of this life and those that are wanting in reverence. //17 & 18

Avoid the places of anger and discontent. Go there where there is bliss. Renouncing those to whom you are attached, be without attachment. //19

Attachment will not lead to welfare. It destroys the very essence of *mokṣa*. Remain always with the *kalyāṇamitra*. //20

Complete first the work that you begin first and this by

---

2. Riches of a Buddhist saint. Seven of these are mentioned, viz. the wealth of faith, of pure morals, of modesty, of sensibility to *dharma*, of attentiveness, of charity, of wisdom. D-TED 846.

following the *guru* and studying the *sūtra*-s. Or else, both will be spoiled. //21

Again, atone for the sin. Care for the good *puṇya*. Even while following the worldly affairs, keep the mind detached. //22

Suppress egoism when the mind gets swelled. Remember the precepts of the *guru* whenever the mind becomes careless. //23

Encourage the mind when it gets depressed. Remember *prajñā-pāramitā* and make the actions tranquil. //24

Look at the objects that attract or repel as but the creations of *māyā*. Consider the undesirable sounds as but mere echoes. //25

Look at the sufferings of the body as but the [results of the] past actions. //26

After completing the work retire into solitude and remain there like the corpse of the animal that is not found by any. Your self should keep itself hidden. //27

Be always on the alert. Go on counting your own defects and remember the essence of the *vrata*-s when desire, ill-will, sleep, folly, laziness and weariness etc. crop up in your mind. Meditate on impermanence and death. //28

Speak carefully in the presence of others. Avoid browbeating and sneering. Always remain with a smiling face. //29

Be ever generous to others. Do not be miserly. Always avoid jealousy. Act as the protector of the others' minds. //30

Always avoid clash with others. Do not show artificial grace and do not make new friends. Always maintain alertness. Be always forgiveful and remain content with the minimum of desire. //31

Consider yourself to be but a humble servant. Learn to be ashamed and remain humble. Be careful to make others happy. Abide by your *saṃvara*-s.[3] //32

---

3. Obligation, engagement, duty. These are mainly three, viz. the vow of an ordinary Buddhist for self-emancipation, the vow of a Bodhisattva for universal liberation and the

Avoid insulting others. Be modest. While advising others, have love for them and concern for their welfare. //33

Have reverence for the Buddhist religion. Never get distracted from the religion of truth. Always have reverence for God and keep the *tri-cakra*[4] pure. //34

Get yourself sprinkled all over first by universal love (*karuṇā*). Be famed as the performer of the seven forms of worship[5] thrice during the day and the night. Have a direct realisation of *tri-skandha*.[6] //35.

Work for removing the sufferings of the living beings. Make your prayer (*praṇidhāna*) extensive and pray for the attainment of enlightenment. Have the Great Enlightenment (*mahā-bodhi*) as the object of all your actions.' //36

Tāntrika or mystical vow. We find also priestly vows, the vows of a *dāna-pati* (alms-giver) and the vows of a physician. D-TED 722.

4. *'khor-gsum*, literally three circles, Sanskrit *tri-maṇḍala*. Schmidt—"everything that belongs to archery." More correctly, arrow, knife and spear. J-TED. 58. The precept 'to keep these pure' perhaps refers to the practice of *ahiṃsā*—i.e. not to allow these to be tainted by blood.

5. "The seven kinds of offerings : flowers, incense, scent, light from butter-lamp, edibles such as cakes, fruits, etc., and other acceptable objects with which he may worship. In the work called *Kun-bzaṅ-spyod-pa'i-smon-lam*, seven methods of making worship are mentioned : 1) salutation, 2) making offerings, 3) confession of sins, 4) rejoicing, 5) invocation or exhortation, 6) making of prayers for blessings or favour irrespective of what can be claimed owing to one's moral merits, with or without deserving it, 7) prayers for a blessing based on moral merits. These all belong to the Mahāyāna school. In the Hīnayāna, only three kinds of prayers are observed : 1) salutation, 2) recitation of *sūtra*-s etc., 3) asking for benediction."—S. C. Das in JBTS I. i. 45n.

6. The three aggregates, probably, referring to the aggregates of the mental, moral and material substances.

Always take vows and remain careful of their fulfilment. You will thus fulfil the two *varga*-s[7] and will remove the two *āvaraṇa*-s. //37

Make your human life worth-while and lead your sight towards *nirvāṇa*. Work for the welfare of yourself and of others. Attain nobility. //38

Perhaps my words are not like the sweet notes of the cuckoo of the early summer or that of the young peacock. [Moreover, all these] are already said by many a learned men. Nevertheless, I am writing in order to remove the king's distress. //39

Give careful consideration to these words inspired by the thought of your welfare. Why accuse others of being sceptical ? Always meditate on the six deities (*ṣaṭ-deva*) and keep the vows (*saṃvara*) pure. Rule the kingdom according to the principles of *dharma* and remain yourself full of forgiveness.//40

Here ends *Vimala-ratna-lekha-nāma*, sent by *sthavira mahā-paṇḍita* Dīpaṃkara-śrī-jñāna to *rājā* Nirapāla.

7. viz. the *jñāna-varga* and the *puṇya-varga*.

Section 6

Bodhi-patha-pradīpa

In Indian language it is called *Bodhi-patha-pradīpa*, in Tibetan *Byaṅ-chub-lam-gyi-sgron ma.*

Salutation to Bodhisattva Mañjuśrī Kumārabhūta. On the request of my good disciple Byaṅ-chub-'od (Bodhiprabha), I shall, after worshipping with profound respect all the *Jinas* of the three times[1] along with their *dharma* and *saṅgha*,[2] expound the *Bodhi-patha-pradīpa.*

---

1. "*jina* (victor). In the *Sūtra* it is mentioned : 'I am victorious over all *pāpa-dharma* (sinful things). Having overcome them all, I have become Conqueror—*jina*.' Hence, this title is applicable to Buddhas, Bodhisattvas, Arhats, etc., whoever has overcome the *hetu* (cause), that is sin itself, and its legions represented by Māra, the result of fruit of all sin." "The three times—past, present and future. The Buddhas of all these times are to be reverenced and adored conjointly, for they form the commonwealth of the Buddhas." S. C. Das, J B T S, I. i. 39 n.

2. "*saṅgha*—literally meaning one devoted to virtue, but religiously signifies the entire body of the Bodhisattvas, Arhats and Pratyeka Buddhas, together with those who have attained the eight saintly conditions or stages and have fully understood and comprehended the value of taking refuge in the *tri-ratna* and know what is really good, have imbibed true faith in *dharma* and lastly are entirely devoted to it so as *never to turn away from it.* The eight conditions evidently apply to the life of genuine and earnest *bhikṣu*-s and *bhikṣuṇī*-s." *Ib.*

Puruṣa[3] is to be known as [belonging to either of the] three [types, viz.] : *adhama* (inferior), *madhyama* (mediocre) and *uttama* (superior). The characteristics of each are very clear. Therefore, I shall write the distinguishing features of each. //1

By the *adhama puruṣa*[4] is to be known one who, in one's own interests, acts in every way for the worldly pleasures only (*saṃsāra-sukha-mātra*). //2

One who, indifferent to the pleasures of birth (*bhava-sukha*) and by nature opposed to sinful acts, works for oneself alone, is to be known as the *madhyama puruṣa*.[5] //3

---

3. The word *skyes-bu* literally means *jana* (? *jāta*) or anything born. However, it is taken here in the following special sense : "*puruṣa* that does or works having certain ends, or has the ability to do a thing. Hence *puruṣa* is one who is possessed of the ability of working in the cause of humanity or the world, the effect of which will be carried to a future existence." *Ib.* 40n.

4. In dealing with the three *puruṣa*-s, the Tibetan writers speak only of the followers of the Buddha and the *adhama puruṣa* is generally taken to mean the lay devotee or *upāsaka*, who is moreover a follower of the Mahāyāna. "The chief act in the religious career of an *upāsaka*, the model 'Inferior Puruṣa', is to find out his own *guru* or spiritual instructor, who will implant in him the primary Buddhist ideas, and then lead him to higher conceptions of Buddha's doctrines." *Ib.* 41n.

5. The *madhyama puruṣa* is generally taken to mean the follower of the Hīnayāna school. "The chief points of difference wherewith to distinguish the *madhyama puruṣa* from the other two lie in the means he adopts for attaining to his own emancipation, by having regard to his personal interests only. He, therefore, properly belongs to the Hīnayāna school...... The followers of the Mahāyāna school seem to be divided in their opinion regarding the question whether the *madhyama puruṣa*, belonging as he does generally to the Hīnayāna, at all gets final emancipation from the miseries of *bhava*. i.e....to

One who always wishes to remove all the sufferings of others by his own sufferings is the *uttama puruṣa*.[6] //4

To the noble being (*parama-prāṇī*), who is desirous of the highest enlightenment (*uttama-bodhi*),[7] I shall explain the best means[8] as preached by the teachers.[9] //5

Offer flowers, incense, etc., whatever you may obtain to

---

reach the state of *nirvāṇa*. Some dogmatically hold that he does not, while others more liberal in their views say that he does reach to *nirvāṇa*." *Ib*. 42n.

6. The *uttama* (or *parama*) *puruṣa* means an absolute believer of the Mahāyāna doctrines. "He who becomes sincerely compassionate to all living beings that have been roving in the wide ocean of worldliness and who are being tormented in the intolerable fire of the world by sufferings, as if he himself had been afflicted like them with the miseries of recurring existence, who, earnestly concerned in the well-being and miseries of others, works for their deliverance, eradicating the causes and consequences of their sufferings in such a manner so that they may not take root again—who acquires the precious mind of a Bodhisattva and thereby practises all kinds of duties which belong to Jinaputra is the *parama puruṣa*." *Ib*. 43n.

7. By "the *parama prāṇī* desirous of *uttama bodhi*" Atīśa perhaps referred to king Bodhiprabha, in response to whose request he wrote the *Bodhi-patha-pradīpa*.

8. *samyak-upāya*—"the perfect and entire means for attaining to supreme enlightenment. They are of two kinds : perfected moral and psychic development and acquisition of occult powers and concentration."— *Ib*. 44n.

9. *bla-ma-rnams*, literally *gurujana*-s or the elders. Po-to-ba reads the following significance in the use of this word : "In this manner Atīśa has set forth the importance of a spiritual instructor, that is one should bear in mind that the extent of his spiritual progress and prosperity depends a good deal on the kindness of his spiritual instructor." *Ib*. 44n.

the picture[10] of the Samyak-sambuddha [Buddha, the all-perfect], the *caitya*[11] and the scriptures.[12] //6

Kneeling down and with folded hands, first repeat the *śaraṇa-gamana*-s thrice. Until the final attainment of the essence of *bodhi* (*bodhi-sāra*), revere the *tri-ratna*-s with a mind that never turns back. Also perform the seven forms of worship as mentioned in the *Samanta-bhadra-caryā*. //7 & 8

Then the first thing to do is to establish empathy (*maitrī-citta*) with all living beings, inclusive of the three kinds of beings with degraded births (*tri-durgati-jātāni*),[13] suffering from both birth and death, etc. Look at all living beings as suffering from miseries and arrive at the firmest determination (*citta-utpādana*) to work with the resolution of never turning back (*anivṛtta-pratijñā*) for liberating all living beings from the miseries that are born of miseries. //9 & 10

The qualities of *praṇidhāna-citta-utpādana* are explained by Maitreyanātha in the *sDoṅ-po-bkod-pa'i-mdo*. Read it or listen to it from the *guru*. Thus it should be known that the qualities of *sambodhi-citta* are unlimited. Therefore, practise this repeatedly. // 11 & 12

The *puṇya* of that (*bodhicitta*) is well-explained in the *Vīra-datta-paripṛcchita-sūtra* etc... I shall write (about it) only in three brief verses. //13

---

10. "Representations of Buddha, in drawing, in relief or molten and clay images of the same called 'representative symbol' to represent him as in life." *Ib.*

11. "Tombs or tomb-like structures wherein relics or images and scriptural writings are deposited, these are called the 'commemorative symbols'." *Ib.*

12. "The sacred Buddhist Scriptures, together with their twelve expositions, come under the name of 'symbol of the precepts'." *Ib.*

13. The three kinds of beings with degraded birth are: 1) beasts, birds, insects, worms, reptiles, etc., 2) the *preta*-s or those in the tantalus, the manes of the dead, and 3) those in hell.

If the *puṇya* of *bodhicitta* had visible form (*rūpa*), it would have filled the whole firmament (*antarīkṣa*) and yet remain unexhausted. // 14

The offerings of one, who, with folded hands bows down in mind to the *bodhicitta*, being boundless, are far greater than those of one who fills the *buddha-kṣetra*-s,[14] numbering as many as the grains of sand on the bank of the Ganges, with jewels offered to Lokanātha (the Buddha). //15 & 16

After the *praṇidhāna-citta-utpādana* for *bodhi*, try always to increase it with great care. Preserve for remembrance even in the next life the *śikṣā*[15] as explained (*yathā-ukta*). //17

The perfect *praṇidhāna-citta-utpādana* cannot be increased without having within oneself the vow (*saṃvara*) of *avatāra-citta-utpādana*. Desirous of increasing the vow of perfect enlightenment (*sambodhi saṃvara*), one must acquire it [i.e. the vow of *avatāra-citta-utpādana*] with great care. //18

One can always have the seven kinds of *pratimokṣa saṃvara*. However, without being [specially] fortunate one cannot have the vow of *bodhisattva*. //19

As preached by the Tathāgata, the glory (*śrī*) of *brahmacarya* is the noblest of the seven kinds of *pratimokṣa* vows. That is intended to be the vow of the *bhikṣu*. //20

According to the principles (*vidhi*) regarding 'the [ten] stages of saintly perfection of a Bodhisattva' (*bodhisattva-bhūmi*),[16] as explained in the *śīla-adhyāya*, one should receive

---

14. "The fancied sphere of a particular Buddha or Bodhisattva ; e.g. Sukhāvatī is the sphere of Amitābha Buddha, Tibet the chosen land of Avalokiteśvara Bodhisattva." D-TED 1265.

15. The three *śikṣā*-s are enumerated as : a) *adhi-śīla-śikṣā*, i.e. training in higher conduct, b) *adhi-samādhi-śikṣā*, i.e. training in higher meditation and c) *adhi-prajñā-śikṣā*, i.e. training in higher wisdom. D-TED 1323.

16. The ten stages or degrees of saintly perfection, called *daśa-bhūmi*, are : 1) beatitude (*pramuditā*), 2) spotless purity (*vimalā*), 3) enlightenment (*prabhākara*), 4) illumination (*arciṣmatī*),

the saṃvara-s from a sad-guru with appropriate accomplishments (samyak-lakṣaṇayukta). //21

One is to be known as the right guru who is with pure saṃvara [in oneself], has full mastery over the rules of saṃvara (saṃvara-vidhi) and has kind forgiveness for those that are fallen from saṃvara (saṃvara-patita). //22

To those that have failed to find such a guru in spite of various efforts, I shall explain the principles of 'taking the pure vow.' //23

As explained in the *Mañjuśrī-buddha-kṣetrālaṃkāra-sūtra*, when, in the past, he was born as Amba Rāja,[17] Mañjuśrī got initiated into the *bodhicitta*. This will be clearly noted down.[18] //24

He [Mañjuśrī] attained the supreme enlightenment (*samyak sambodhi citta*) in the presence of the Nāthas and invited all the living beings to the freedom from the cycle of births (*bhava-cakra*). //25

From then on until the attainment of the final enlightenment (*uttama-bodhi*), never allow the mind to be polluted by ill-will, anger, miserliness and envy. //26

By the adherence to *brahmacarya* and the avoidance of sin

---

5) unconquerable (*sudurjayā*), 6) salvation (*abhimukti*), 7) far-reaching (*duraṅgamā*), 8) immovable (*acalā*), 9) righteousness (*sādhumati*) and 10) spiritual cloud (*dharma-meghā*). D-TED 1257.

17. "Anciently, when there was no measure of time, Mañjuśrī was born as the Cakravartī Rājā called Amba Rāja (Heaven King) ; how in the presence of the Tathāgata called Meghanāda Rāja he took the vow of (becoming) a Bodhisattva has been described in the work *Mañjuśrī-buddha-kṣetrālaṅkāra-sūtra*. The devotee should observe the ceremonies mentioned therein." S. C. Das in JBTS I. i. 48n.

18. As S. C. Das (in JBTS I. i. 48n) points out, the next six *śloka*-s, i.e. *śloka*-s number 25 to 30, are quoted from the *Mañjuśrī-kṣetrālaṅkāra-sūtra*.

and lust and by remaining content with the *śīla-saṃvara*, one follows the precepts of the Buddha. //27

Do not be anxious to attain quick enlightenment (*bodhi*) for yourself. Live up to the end [of the *saṃsāra*] for the sake of even a single living being. //28

Purify the boundless and unthinkable [number of] *kṣetra*-s and live for [the emancipation of] each individual by name that exists in all the ten directions. //29

Purify all your actions,—physical, oral and mental,—and never indulge in any sinful act (*akuśala-karma*). //30

By your own purified body-speech-mind, you will place yourself in the *saṃvara* of *avatāra-citta*·; you will thus have high reverence for the three *śikṣāpada*-s of *śīla* [moral courses] that you have acquired. //31

By that [viz. purification, etc. mentioned above] and by being careful of the pure *sambodhi-sattva*-vow[19] among [all] vows, one's enlightenments (*sambodhi-saṅgha*) will be attained. //32

As shown by all the Buddhas, the acquirement [*utpādana*, literally, production] of *abhijñāna* alone is the cause of the fulfilment of the essence (*svabhāva*) of all the *puṇya*-s and all the *jñāna*-s. //33

One without the power of *abhijñāna* cannot work for the sake of the living beings, just as a bird with unfledged wings cannot fly in the sky. //34

The *puṇya* that can be acquired by one with *abhijñāna* in only a day-and-night, cannot be acquired by one without *abhijñāna* even in one hundred lives. //35

One who wants to attain quickly the full perfection of supreme enlightenment can succeed not by idleness but by working hard with the help of *abhijñāna*. //36

Abhijñāna cannot be attained without tranquillity (*śamatha*)[20]; therefore, one should work again and again to reach *śamatha*. //37

---

19. the vow for perfect enlightenment.

20. *shi-gnas* or *śamatha* "implies an absolute inexcitability of

One who loses even a single component of the state of tranquillity (*śamatha*) cannot, even by hard meditation for thousands of years, reach *samādhi*. //38

Therefore, firmly adhere to the components [of *śamatha*] as explained in the chapter on the *samādhi-varga*. Whatever may be the object of your meditations, direct the mind always to *puṇya*. //39

Abhijñāna cannot be attained without the *yoga-śamatha* state being accomplished. Without *prajñāpāramitā*, *āvaraṇa*[21] cannot be dispelled. //40

Therefore, for fully abandoning the *kleśa-vṛti* and *jñeya-vṛti*, the *yogī* should constantly meditate on *prajñā-pāramitā* along with the *upāya*-s. //41

Prajñā without *upāya* and *upāya* without *prajñā* are said to be unfree [lit. "tied", i.e. one by itself cannot act]. Therefore, do not ignore any [of them]. //42

---

mind, and a deadening of it against any impressions from without, combined with an absorption in the idea of Buddha, or which in the end amounts to the same thing, in the idea of emptiness and nothingness. This is the aim to which the contemplating Buddhist aspires, when, placing an image of Buddha as *rten* (a statue or figure of Buddha or of other divine beings, which the pious may take hold of and to which their devotions are more immediately directed) before him, he looks at it immovably, until every other thought is lost, and no sensual impressions from the outer world any longer reach or affect his mind. By continued practice he acquires the ability of putting himself also without *rten* merely by his own effort, into this state of perfect apathy and of attaining afterwards even to 'the supernatural powers of a saint'." J-TED 474.

21. "The two kinds of moral and mental obscurations are : 1) defilement of misery that caused by habits, etc. (*kleśa-vṛti*) and 2) the sin produced from the objects of cognition (*jñeya-vṛti*). According to the Mahāyāna doctrine, these two sins vanish as soon as one has attained to the eight stages of Bodhisattva perfection." D-TED 333.

For removing doubts as to what is *prajñā* and what is *upāya*, it is necessary to distinguish clearly between *prajñā* and *upāya*-s. //43

As said by the Jinas, except the *prajñā-pāramitā*-s all the *kuśala-dharma*-s like the *dāna-pāramitā*-s etc. are the *upāya*-s.[22] //44

One quickly attains enlightenment (*bodhi*) not by mere meditation on the void (*nairātmya*) but by [first] acquiring in oneself the mastery of the *upāya*-s (*upāya-abhyāsa*) and [then] by meditation on *prajñā*. //45

As it is well-explained [in the scriptures], *prajñā* is that knowledge which is the realisation of the intrinsic nature of the void (*svabhāva-śunyatā*),—of the *skandha-dhātu*-s[23] and of the *āyatana*-s[24] being unborn (*ajāta*). //46

That which exists by nature cannot come into being. Again that which is by nature non-existing is like the sky-flower. Both [alternatives], implying fallacy (*doṣa*), both are unreal [literally, belong to the category of non-being]. //47

Things (*bhava*) can be born neither of themselves, nor of others, nor of both. These cannot be without cause either. Hence, they are by nature natureless (*svabhāvena niḥ-svabhāva*). //48.

Again, the nature of all things (*dharma*-s), examined either

---

22. Six *pāramitā*-s are generally enumerated. These are: 1) *dāna-pāramitā* (charity), 2) *śila-pāramitā* (morality), 3) *kṣānti-pāramitā* (forgiveness), 4) *vīrya-pāramitā* (assiduity), 5) *dhyāna-pāramitā* (meditation) and 6) *prajñā-pāramitā* (wisdom). According to Atīśa, therefore, the first five *pāramitā*-s constitute the *upāya*-s.

23. i.e. the aggregates of the elements.

24. "The five (or six) seats, i.e. organs, of the senses (the sixth is *manas*, the inner sense); the senses themselves; this conception, however, has been greatly altered and varied by the fanciful theories of medical and philosophical authors." J-TED 28.

as unities or as compounds, cannot be determined. Therefore, it is certain that they are void. //49

In the *Śunyatā-saptati-vidyā*, *Mūla-madhyamaka*, etc. the nature (*svabhāva*) of things is emphatically asserted to be void (*śunyatā*). //50

This text [if all these are explained here in details] will be voluminous. Therefore, [all these details] are not explained here. Only the doctrine (*siddhānta*) already proved (*siddha*) is clearly stated here for contemplation. //51

Therefore, the nature (*svabhāva*) of everything is unsupported [*anālambana*, lit. not proved by any *pramāṇa*]. So to meditate on the void (*nairātmya*) is to meditate on *prajñā*. //52

The nature (*svabhāva*) of everything, as seen by *prajñā*, is invisible [i.e. *prajñā* sees no *svabhāva* in anything]. This *prajñā* is demonstrated by logic. Therefore, meditate on *prajñā* without any doubt [*vikalpa*, delusional thought]. //53

This world (*bhava*), arising out of delusional thought (*vikalpa*) is itself delusional (*vikalpātmaka*). Therefore, *nirvāṇa* is best because it is completely free from *vikalpa*. //54

As said by the Tathāgata, *vikalpa* is the Great Ignorance (*mahā-moha*). It causes one to fall in the ocean of *saṃsāra*. (Therefore), be firm on the *a-vikalpa samādhi* [contemplation without any disturbing reflection], (which is) as pure as the *ākāśa*. //55

As said in the *Nirvikalpa-avatāra-dhāraṇī* also, if the Jina-putra (Bodhisattva) takes his stand on the Real Doctrine (*satya-dharma*) by meditating on the *nirvikalpa*, he will, by overcoming the difficult *vikalpa*-s, gradually attain the *nirvikalpa*. //56

With the help of the scriptural instructions and logical thinking know it for certain that everything is non-born (*ajāta*) and nature-less (*a-svabhāva*). Then meditate on the (*nirvikalpa*). //57

Then, meditating thus, one can gradually reach the stage of *uṣṇa* etc. and then move on to the stage of *pramuditā* etc. . After that, the Buddhahood would be quite near. //58

If one wants easily (*sukhena*) to complete the *bodhi* by the rites[25] like *śanti* and *vistara* with the power of spells (*mantra*) and also with the power of *aṣṭa-siddhi* resulting from the rites of Bhadra-kumbha etc., or, if one wants to follow the path of the Guhya-tantra by performing the practices (*kriyā*) and rites (*caryā*) prescribed in the Tantras, then, for the sake of being properly initiated by the *ācārya*, offer jewels etc. to him by way of serving him and please him by obeying him in every way. //59-61

When the *guru*, being fully pleased, confers the initiation that purifies all sins, he [the initiate] becomes a fit receptacle for the *siddhi*-s. //62

The *brahmacārī* cannot receive *guhya-jñāna-abhiṣeka*, for it is strongly prohibited in the *Ādi-buddha-mahātantra*. //63

For the *brahmacārī* receiving this initiation means the violation of the prohibitions and hence a fall from the *tapas saṃvara*. Such a *vratī* will suffer great sin (*mahā-pātaka*) and will certainly fall among the low-born. He will never attain *siddhi*. //64 & 65

But there is nothing wrong about that *abhiṣeka* for him who has learnt and can explain the Tantras, offers the right kind of fire offerings, has received the proper initiation from his *guru* and has the real understanding of all these. //66

The explanation of *bodhi-patha*, based on *sūtra*-s etc., is here presented in a condensed form by *ācārya* Dīpaṃkara-śrī to Bodhiprabha at his request. Here ends the *Bodhi-patha-pradīpa* by mahā-ācārya Śrī-dīpaṃkara-jñāna. Translated, revised, and established by the Indian ācārya Dīpaṃkara-śrī-jñāna and the Tibetan lo-tsā-ba bhikṣu Śubhamati. *maṅgalam*.

Written by *māhā-ācārya* Śrī-dīpaṃkara-jñāna. Translated by the same Indian *paṇḍita* and the great lo-tsā-ba Śubhamati. This book is written in the Tho-liṅ temple of Shaṅ-shuṅ.

---

25. Certain Tāntrika rites, like *śānti*, *vistara*, *aṣṭa-siddhi*, *bhadra-kumbha*, etc.—supposed to lead to enlightenment quickly—are referred to here ; Atiśa's main point, however, is that these rites can be performed only after being properly initiated by a *sad-guru*.

Section 7

Sayings of Atīśa : A

[Fol. 6. a]...After spending two years in mÑa'-ris, during which time Jo-bo-rje delivered many *upadeśa*-s to Devaguru Bodhiprabha (Byaṅ-chub'-od) and to others, he once thought of returning to India and was about to enter the way back to India. At that time, Bodhiprabha requested him saying, "Please give me one more *upadeśa*." Jo-bo said that he had already delivered many *upadeśa*-s on previous occasions. Bodhiprabha insisted on having another *upadeśa*. So the following was delivered [by Jo-bo-rje].

[Fol. 6. b] Oh! Being unreliable because of my [own] inferior knowledge, it is improper for me to deliver sermons to you, already in possession of high knowledge and extremely clear thinking. Nevertheless, being inspired by you, my dearest friend—dearer than my heart—I am leaving this advice for you. //1

Friends, till the attainment of enlightenment the *guru* is indispensable. Therefore, rely on the *sad-guru*. It is necessary to listen to the teachings of the *guru* till you reach the final understanding. Listen, therefore, to the *guru*'s teachings. Mere knowledge of the Doctrine is not enough for attaining the Buddhahood. It is necessary, moreover, to practise virtue. Therefore, keep away from the place that may cause harm to your mind and stay where virtue increases. //2

[Fol. 7. a] Noise is harmful until the attainment of firmness. Therefore, take shelter in the silence of the forest life. Avoid those friends that add to your *kleśa* and stick to those that increase your *puṇya*. Keep your mind under control. The worldly affairs have no end. So leave these and keep yourself free. Accumulate *puṇya* day and night and always keep watch on your own mind. //3

Meditation on the mere basis of advice is not possible. Whenever you act and whatever you do, do according to and with reverence for the words of the *guru*. This is the way of attaining fulfilment swiftly and certainly. The law is that one who acts with whole-hearted *dharma* is not bothered by the problems of livelihood. Friends, desire cannot be satisfied as thirst cannot be quenched with salt water. It is vain to try to satisfy the desire. //4

[Fol. 7. b] Crush the mind inflated with arrogance and pride. Be peaceful and disciplined. Even that which is [vulgarly] called *puṇya*[1] is no more than [mere] noise and as such an obstacle to *dharma*. Therefore, renounce [even] that. Gain and honour are like the devil's snare [lit, the *pāśa*-s of Māra]. Remove these as you remove the boulders from the road. The words of praise and fame are but deceptions. So throw these out in the way you spit. //5

Happiness, prosperity and friendship of the present are but momentary. Discard these in the way you throw out the spittle. The future lives longer than the present one. Save that wealth [viz. *puṇya*] ; that alone will provide you when you make the journey to the next world. One will eventually have to abandon everything and depart. Nothing will go with one. Therefore, have no craving. Love the lower people. Do not injure or insult them. //6

[Fol. 8. a] Love the enemy and the friend equally ; have no partiality. Have no jealousy for those with good qualities but have respect for them and cultivate their qualities in you. Do not examine the faults of others ; examine those of your own and leave those in the way in which you shed off your

---

1. *bsod-nams*, *puṇya* belonging to the world of desires and is subject to decay. This is contrasted with *dge-ba*, i.e. *puṇya* or *kuśala* which is undestructible, consisting of the enduring works of piety performed by saints belonging to the superior states of existence. D-TED 269.

poisonous blood. Do not think of your own *puṇya* ; think of the *puṇya* of the others. Respect others and serve them. //7

Have the same feeling for the living beings as the parents have for their son. Have always a smiling face. Avoid anger and speak softly with a loving heart. Be careful of your words and speak simply, for too much of unnecessary words are bound to contain errors. Too much of unnecessary action spoils **[Fol. 8. b]** the *puṇya* ; let not be your actions tainted by *adharma*. //8

There is no sense in getting tired with useless actions. Everything being determined by past actions, nothing happens by mere wish. Therefore, keep yourself free and be happy. Listen ! For a noble person death is better than shameful acts. So, be straight and steady. The pleasures and pain of this life are but the results of the actions of the past lives. Therefore, do not blame anybody for these. //9

[Fol. 9. a] All happiness comes from the blessings of the *guru*. One must, [therefore], be grateful to him. You cannot control others unless you can control yourself. Therefore, control yourself first. You cannot help others to be successful without [yourself] attaining *abhijñāna*. Therefore, work hard for the *siddhi*. One will have to leave the savings behind. This is sure. Therefore, do not accumulate sin in the name of wealth. //10

Enjoyment and distraction have no substance. Therefore, enrich yourself with *dāna*, the (only) wealth. You will thereby become beautiful in this life and happy in the next. Always uphold *viśuddha-śīla*. Anger is specially powerful in the *kali-yuga*. Therefore, protect yourself with the armour (*varma*) of forgiveness, Do not lag behind under the influence of laziness. Kindle the fire of courage for attaining *siddhi*.//11

Human life is being wasted by distractions. Therefore, care for meditation. Truth is not realised under the spell of ignorance. Therefore, be careful of the meaning of truth. Friends ! Do not sink into the mire of *saṃsāra*. **[Fol. 9. b]** Reach the dry land of *mokṣa*. Try to understand properly the precepts of the *guru*. Meditate on *saṃsāra* as but the river of misery. //12

These are not empty words. You should lisen to these with care and place these in the depth of your heart. If you act thus then you will make yourself as well as others happy. This is my humble precept. And I pray that you listen to it. Devaguru Bodhiprabha was thus advised by the only god (*eka-deva*) Jo-bo-rje. //13

Section 8

Sayings of Atīśa : B

[Fol. 9. b] Jo-bo, when he was staying at Yer-pa-brag, gave this *upadeśa* to Ye-śes-'bar-ba of 'Ol-rgod.

Salutation to *bhagavatī ārya Tārādevī*. Salutation to the good *guru*-s.

[Fol. 10. a] Oh *kulaputra*, consider carefully these words of mine. Man's life in this *kali-yuga* is generally short while the objects of knowledge are numerous. One is uncertain about how long one is going to live. Hasten to curb your desires with care. Do not say : "I am a *bhikṣu*", so long as you care for material wealth and livelihood, with which the householder is concerned. You may be living in a monastery, but do not say, "I am a *bhikṣu*, I live in the monastery", etc., so long as you are affected by worldly affairs. Do not say, "I am a *bhikṣu*, I live in the monastery" etc., so long as you harbour worldly wishes or any thought of injuring others.

You may be living in the monastery, but do not say, "I am a *bhikṣu*, I live in the monastery", etc., so long as you **[Fol. 10. b]** do not renounce the company of the householders and you continue to stay with them and waste your time by indulging in romantic and worldly gossips. Do not say, "I am a *bhikṣu*, a *bodhisattva*", etc., if you cannot bear even a little injury by others or help others even a little. If you say anything like that, you will thereby tell a great lie to the householders. The *gṛhastha* may be deceived by you, But, first of all, it is impossible to deceive those whose eyes see everything, Secondly, you cannot prevent the effects of such deceptions from recoiling back on you.

[Fol. 11. a] Thirdly, you cannot deceive men that are related to and united with *dharma*. Again, remember now what you promised before the gods and the *guru*-s at the time of the *bodhicitta-utpādana*. When you come across those that deserve to be forgiven, never say that it is difficult to forgive. Remember [that at the time of taking the vow you promised] not to refuse even that which is difficult. At the time of taking the vow you should have already ascertained if it was easy or difficult. It will be deceiving god and *guru* if, after taking the vow, you fall from it. Therefore, remember that you cannot refuse even that which is difficult.

Again, the purpose of living in the monastery is to stop **[Fol. 11. b]** having intercourse with the householders, to renounce partiality for the relatives and to avoid the causes of distractions provoked by the sexual and other desires. Watch the great treasure of your *bodhicitta*. Do not allow the mind to get troubled by worldly worries even for a moment.

The *vikalpa* of *saṃsāra* becomes particularly powerful because of being repeatedly provoked by the non-attachment to *dharma* in the past and because of the feebleness of the intellect due to habit. Therefore it is meaningless to live in the monastery if strong measure is not taken against these. Otherwise, [you will be] like the birds and beasts that live there.

[Fol. 12.a] Never say, "It is difficult to do it now, so I will do it later." If there is a hole [of some weakness] in what you think, then the Māra of *kleśa*-s[1] will enter through it. If it thus enters then there will be obstacle to *bodhicitta*. If there is this obstacle, not to speak of helping others, there will be nothing but *durgati* for yourself. Remember this. Even though you claim that you are performing *dharma*, your words would thus be empty and meaningless.

Oh, *kulaputra*, when at the end you die, do not be the cause of sorrow and suffering for the *guru*-s and the *deva*-s. Again, do not be the cause of regret and doubt to the pious householders.

---

1. D-TED 666 : one of the four devils.

Even if you say, "I am acting according to *dharma*", **[Fol. 12. b]** [in fact] *dharma* and the person [yourself] will remain separate if you do not repeatedly correct your own mind by comparing it with the scriptures and, at the time of death, rather than there being the slightest mark of the practice of *bodhicitta*, there will [only] be the mark of *durgati*. The only thing that it will lead to is what brings sorrow and sufferings for others.

Therefore, at the time of death do not remain empty-handed by destroying *dharma* with the arrogant claim, "I have spent a pious life." In short, there is no need for *dharma*, if in spite of living in the monastery you do not renounce *karma* in this life and turn your intellect and mind against the desires (*kāma*).

Your *dharma* will be miscarried if in spite of claiming to be aloof from *karma* you remain involved in it and, moreover, if you do not guard against fall in both the lives [i.e, in this life and in the next]. Such miscarried *dharma* will be *dharma* only in name. **[Fol. 13. a]** Therefore, friend, do not think in that way. Jewels once lost by the blind are not recovered.

While meditating, do not count the number of years and months [devoted to it]; rather, try to find out how much or how little self-knowledge you have acquired in your mind and how much or how little control you have acquired over your habits.

Look at the heaviness or lightness of *kleśa*. Always guard your own mind. Do not make yourself miserable, do not deceive yourself, do not deceive the god and the *guru*, do not allow yourself to fall or cause the fall of others. Whatever fall from *karma* has happened in this life has afterall happened [i.e. no use worrying over that].

Take this example. If there be a heap of dirt before you, you need quickly to clean it. Why get annoyed if it is cleared with the help of others? In the same way, **[Fol. 13. b]** all the *vikalpa*-s of this life—inclusive of one's own relatives—are to be directly abandoned. Why get annoyed if your *guru* and [good] friends help you to abandon these ?

After promising before the gods and the *guru*-s to work for the welfare of every living being, do not discriminate between the objects of your charity. There may be differences among the objects of charity ; but you cannot differentiate [among these] from your end. Because there are no differences among them from the point of view of one who practises the *bodhicitta*. Do not be angry with one even if one harms you. How can you meditate on forgiveness if you get angry with one who harms ? When there occurs any *kleśa* [anger, etc,] it is necessary to remember its antidote. What is the use of that *dharma* which is contaminated by *kleśa* ?

Therefore, while assuming the standpoint of the *bodhicitta*, which is most precious, if there be any gap in the form of the failure of meditation, then you should take refuge to the **[Fol. 14. a]** excellent words [i.e. the words of the *guru*]. Do not cultivate friendship with an evil companion. Live in unknown places. Do not allow defilement (*āsrava*) to accumulate [by living] in one place. Whatever you do, do according to *dharma*. Whenever you act, act for the suppression of *kleśa*. This is *viśuddha-dharma*. Strive after that. Have no egoism if you acquire good quality in one out of a hundred actions. If you do, you will be under the grip of Māra. Remain in a solitary place. Be peaceful and self-controlled. Curb the *kāma*-s and be self-content. Overlook your own virtues and do not find the faults of others. Avoid actions that bring fear and shame.

[Fol. 14. b] Do not multiply the *vikalpa*-s. Keep the mind clean. Keep your mind aloof from sexual pleasure. Think always of *dharma*. Accept defeat and avoid bragging. If you have any desire at all, have the desire for kindness. Be moderate about everything. Respect and serve others with ease. Run away from the *saṃsārī* persons as from wild beasts [? as wild beasts do]. One is not a *dhārmika* if one does not renounce the worldly affairs.

There is no *prabrajyā* without the renunciation of the four forms of *gṛhasthakarma*-s.[2]

---

2. *so-nams*, comprises husbandry, trading, tending and rearing up cattle, etc. D-TED 1282.

One who does not renounce *kāma* is not a *bhikṣu.* One who is without *maitrī* and *karuṇā* is not a *bodhisattva.* One who has not renounced *karma* is not a *mahā-dhyānī.* Do not get burnt[3] in *kāma.*

[Fol. 15. a] In short, living in the monastery and meditating on *dharma* one should not allow one's *karma* to increase. Thus there will be no regret (*anutāpa*) at the time of death.

Thus said Dīpaṃkara himself. And he added,

This *kali-yuga* is not the time for smiling ; it is time to have courage. It is not the time for holding high positions ; it is time to hold humble positions.

It is not the time to live in the crowd. It is time to take shelter in solitude. It is not the time to guide the students ; it is time to guide oneself. It is not the time to follow mere words [of *śāstra*-s] ; it is time to meditate on their true significance. It is not the time to be drifted ; it is time to remain firm at one place.

Thus said.

3. *khol-pa*, lit. boiled. D-TED 155.

Section 9

Sanskrit restoration by Professor Mrinalkanti Gangopadhyaya
of the
Bodhi-patha-pradīpa

namo Mañjuśrīkumārabhūtāya Bodhisattvāya. kālatrayasya jinebhyaḥ sarvebhyo dharmasaṅghābhyāṃ ca teṣāṃ mahatā sambhramena namaskṛtya śiṣyottamena Bodhiprabheṇa prārthito Bodhipathapradīpaṃ prakarṣeṇa vivṛṇomi.

puruṣāstrividhā jñeyā uttamādhamamdhyamāḥ /
vyaktaṃ tallakṣaṇaṃ bhedaḥ pratyekantu vilikhyate // 1
yenopāyena sarveṇa sāṃsārikasukhāni vai /
svamarthameva kāmyante so'dhamaḥ puruṣaḥ smṛtaḥ // 2
bhavasukhādudāsīnaḥ svārthamātrārthikāstathā /
pāpakarmaviruddhātmā sa vai madhyama ucyate // 3
ātmaduḥkhena duḥkhānāmanyeṣāmapi sarvathā /
icchati saṃkṣayaṃ yo vā uttamaḥ puruṣo mataḥ // 4
jīveṣu paramo yo hi vāñchati bodhimuttamām /
upāyaṃ sampravakṣyāmi tasmai sadgurudarśitam // 5
sambuddhacitracaityānāṃ saddharmāṇāṃ tathā puraḥ /
puṣpadhūpādivastūni yathāprāptaṃ nivedayet // 6
kṛtvā jānudvayaṃ bhūmau trirādau kuru sāñjaliḥ /
śaraṇagamanaṃ śraddhāṃ triratnāya samācara //
ālābhād bodhisārasya nivṛttiśūnyacetasā /
samantabhadracaryoktāḥ saptapūjāstathaiva ca // 7-8
sarvajīve tataścādau mṛtyujanmādipīḍite /
durgatitrayajāte ca maitrīcittaṃ samānayet //
duḥkhahetoḥ parikliṣṭān dṛṣṭvā jīvānaśeṣataḥ /
duḥkhebhyo duḥkhahetubhyaḥ prāṇināṃ mokṣalipsayā /
bodhicittasamutpādaḥ kāryo'nivṛttasamvidā // 9-10

tathā ye ye praṇidhānacittotpāde guṇāḥ kila /
proktāḥ sūtre drumavyūhe Maitreyena ta eva ca /
sūtrasya tasya pāṭhena śravaṇenāthavā guroḥ /
guṇān sambodhicittasyānantān vijñāya kṛtsnaśaḥ /
tadbhāvena tataḥ kuryāccittotpādaṃ punaḥ punaḥ // 11-12
proktaṃ sūtre tu tatpuṇyaṃ Vīradattasya pṛcchite /
tribhireva tataḥ pādaiḥ samāseneha likhyate // 13
puṇyaṃ ca bodhicittasya yadi rūpānvitaṃ bhavet /
ākāśaṃ pūrayitvāpi na hi niḥśeṣatāṃ vrajet // 14
manasā bodhicittāya praṇato yaḥ kṛtāñjaliḥ /
anantāstasya pūjāḥ syuriti ślāghyatarāḥ punaḥ /
gaṅgāyāḥ siktāsaṃkhyairlokanāthasamarpitaiḥ /
buddhakṣetraṃ mahāratnaiḥ kurvāṇasyāpi saṃkulam //15-16
praṇihitaṃ samutpādya cittaṃ vahuprayatnataḥ /
sadā varddhaya saṃrakṣa śikṣāṃ yathoktameva ca /
yena syāt smaraṇaṃ tasyāḥ parasminnapi janmani // 17
nātmani viṣayīkṛtyāvatāracittasamvaram /
yathārthato bhavennaiva praṇidhānapravardhanam /
sambodhisamvaravṛddhikāmastasmai yated dhruvam // 18
sapta ca pratimokṣādisamvarāḥ sulabhāḥ sadā /
samvaro bodhisattvasya bhāgyenaiva hi labhyate //19
uttamā brahmacaryasya śrīḥ proktā ca tathāgataiḥ /
saptasu protimokṣesu mato'sau bhikṣusamvaraḥ // 20
śīlādhyāyoktavidhinā bodhisattvasya bhūmiṣu /
samyaglakṣaṇayuktāt sadgurorgṛhṇīta samvaram // 21
samvarasya vidhau prājñaḥ samvare ca svayaṃ sthitaḥ /
kṣamākāruṇyayuktaśca samvarāt patiteṣvatha /
asāveva ca vijñeyo gururnāma yathārthataḥ // 22
yenāprapto gurustādṛk prayatnairvividhairapi /
parasamvaralābhārthaṃ tasmai vyākhyāmyahaṃ vidhim //23
Mañjuśrībuddhakṣetrālaṃkārasūtre yathā punaḥ /
prokto Mañjuśriyā pūrvam amvarājo yadābhavat /
bodhicittasamutpādo likhyate vyaktam atra tat // 24
sambodhicittamutpādya nāthānāmeva sammukham /
āhūtāḥ prāṇinaḥ sarve bhavacakrād vimuktaye // 25
kāluṣyaṃ krodhakārpaṇye īrṣyā vātaḥ paraṃ punaḥ /
uttamabodhilābhādā citte kuryāt kadāpi na // 26

brahmacaryāṃ samācarya pāpaṃ kāmaṃ tāthā tyajan /
buddhaśikṣānuvṛttaḥ syāt santuṣṭaḥ śīlasamvare // 27
svayaṃ ca satvaraṃ prāptuṃ bodhiṃ mā bhūt samutsukaḥ /
hetoḥ prāṇina ekasyāpyāsaṃsāraṃ tathā vaset // 28
kṣetrāṇyaparimeyānyacintyāni ca viśodhaya /
daśasu saṃsthitānāṃ ca nāmagrāhaṃ diśāṃ vasa // 29
vācikaṃ kāyikaṃ karma caittikaṃ ca viśodhaya /
akuśalāni karmāṇi mā kadāpi samācara // 30
vākkāyacittena viśodhitenāvatāracittasya nijasya samvare /
saṃsthāpayannarjitaśīlaśikṣāpadatraye śraddhitamānoso bhavet //31
tena yatnena viśuddhasambodhisattvasamvare /
samvareṣu samādhīnāṃ paripūrṇo gaṇo bhavet //32
tattvasampūraṇe heturgaṇasya jñānapuṇyayoḥ /
abhijñānotpāda eva sarvabuddhābhisammataḥ //33
apūrṇapakṣapakṣī khe yathā noḍḍayate tathā /
abhijñānavalāyuktaḥ prāṇino' rthaṃ na sādhayet //34
divārātramabhijñānayuktaḥ puṇyaṃ yadarjayet /
abhijñānaviyuktastu janmāśatair labheta na //35
sīghraṃ sambodhisaṃghaṃ yaḥ sampūrayitum icchati /
abhijñānena yatnena nālasyena tu sidhyati //36
asādhayitvā śamathamabhijñānaṃ na sambhavet /
śamathasya tataḥ siddhyai yatnaṃ kuryāt punaḥ punaḥ //37
śamathāṅgavināśe ca dhyānenāpi prayatnataḥ /
sahasrairapi varṣāṇāṃ samādhirna hi sidhyati //38
samādhivargādhyāokte tadaṅge bhava susthitaḥ /
ekatame'pi lambānāṃ puṇyasaṃsthaṃ manaḥ kuru //39
yogaśamathasiddhau cābhijñānamapi sidhyati /
prajñāpāramitāyogaṃ vinā naśyati nāvṛtiḥ //40
kleśajñānavṛtiṃ tasmād yogī tyaktumaśeṣataḥ /
upāyasahitāṃ dhyāyet prjñāpāramitāṃ sadā //41
upāyarahitā prajñopāyaḥ prajñāṃ vināthavā /
anubaddhamiti proktaṃ tadekamapi na tyajet //42
kā prajñā ka upāyo vā śaṃkāmetāṃ nirāsitum /
upāyānāṃ prajñāyāśca pravibhedaṃ sphutaṃ kuru //43
prajñāpāramitāvarjaṃ dānapāramitādayaḥ /
sarve kuśaladharmāṇāmupāyāḥ kathitā jinaiḥ //44

upāyābhyāsavaśena prajñādhyānena cātmani /
śīghraṃ bodhiṃ prāpnuyānna nairātmyadhyānamātrataḥ //45
skandhadhātoḥ samūhānāmajātāyatanasya ca /
svabhāvaśunyatājñānaṃ prajñeti hi prakīrtitam //46
anucitaṃ sadutpādo' sadapyākāśapuṣpavat /
ubhaye doṣaprasaṅgādabhūtamubhayaṃ punaḥ //47
svato na parato nāpi jāta ubhayato'pi na /
aheturnāpi bhāvastat prakṛtyā niḥsvabhāvatā //48
ekānekatayā vātha sarvadharmaparīkṣaṇe /
svabhāvo labhyate neti niḥsvabhāvo' vadhāryate //49
śunyatāsaptatividyāmūlamadhyamakādiṣu /
svabhāvaḥ sarvabhāvānāṃ proktaṃ śunyatvameva hi //50
tenārthenādhikaṃ śāstraṃ bhavennehokta eva tat /
siddhasiddhāntmātraṃ ca bhāvanārthaṃ pravakṣyate //51
svabhāvo' śeṣadharmāṇāmanālambanameva tat /
nairātmyabhāvamāmātraṃ prajñāyā bhāvanā bhavet //52
prajñayā sarvadharmāṇāṃ svabhāvaḥ kvāpyadṛṣṭavat /
bhāvanīyāvikalpaṃ sā prajñā vidyāparīkṣitā //53
vikalpātmaka evāyaṃ bhavo vikalpasambhavaḥ /
vikalpāśeṣanirmukto nirvāṇaścottamo mataḥ //54
mahāmohaśca saṃkalpaḥ proktamiti tathāgataiḥ /
saṃsārasāgare pātahetustāvat tato bhava /
avikalpasamādhistho' kalpavyaktaṃ yathā nabhaḥ //55
Nirvikalpāvatāradhāraṇyāmapi—
saddharmaṃ jinaputraścāvikalpaṃ cintayan bhavet /
nirvikalpaṃ prāptastīrtvā vikalpān durgamān kramāt //
iti proktam //56
ajātā niḥsvabhāvāśca dharmā iti viniścitaḥ /
śāstreṇa vidyayā caivāvikalpaṃ bhāvayet sadā //57
tadbhāvena dhyānāt prāpta uṣmādikaṃ kramād bhavet /
Pramuditādikaṃ cāpi syād buddhatvamathācirāt //58
mantraprabhāvasiddhasya śāntivistarakarmaṇaḥ /
kumbhabhadrādisiddhāṣṭasiddhyādervā valena ca //
bodhisamūhasampūrṇakāmaḥ sukhena yo bhavet /
guhyatantracaryāmicchet kriyācaryādināthavā //
tantroktenābhiṣekārthaṃ sarvathā sadguroḥ sukham /
sevayā ratnadānenotpādayecca nirantaram //59-61

siddhyai siddhaṃ bhavet pātraṃ guroḥ prītāttu pūrṇataḥ /
abhiṣekaṃ yadi prāptaḥ sarvapāpaviśodhakam // 62
guhyaprajñābhiṣekaṃ na gṛhṇīyurbrahmacāriṇaḥ /
ādibuddhamahātantre yanniṣiddhaṃ viśeṣataḥ // 63
grahe tadabhiṣekasya niṣiddhācaraṇaṃ punaḥ /
tapaḥsamvarapatanaṃ bhaveddhi brahmacāriṇaḥ //
mahāpātakapatanaṃ tasya ca vratino bhaved /
durgatipatanaṃ nūnaṃ nāsti siddhiḥ kadācana // 64-65
tantraṃ sarvaṃ śrutaṃ yena vyākhyātumapi śakyate /
arcanāyajñadānādyācaryate vā yathāyatham //
abhiṣekaṃ guroḥ prāpto vetti sarvaṃ tadeva ca /
tadarthamabhiṣeko'sau nirdoṣa eva sammataḥ // 66
Bodhiprabhānunītenācāryadīpaṃkaraśriyā /
sūtrādidharmasamproktaṃ samālocay yathāsthitam /
Bodhipathasya vyākhyānaṃ kṛtamatra samāsataḥ // 67

Mahācāryaśrīdīpaṃkarajñānakṛtabodhipathapradīpaḥ samāptaḥ

maṅgalam

Section 10

Photostat Reproduction of the Manuscript Containing The Sayings of Atīśa

The portion of the manuscript translated as "Sayings of Atīśa : A" begins with the words *Jo-bo-rje-ñid-daṅ-po-mṅa'-risu* ...occurring in line 2, Folio 6a.

The portion of the manuscript translated as "Sayings of Atīśa : B" begins with the words *bcom-ldan-'das-'phags-ma*..., line 5, Folio 9b. In the manuscript, the sub-title "*Jo-bo yer-pa'i-brag-la*..." of this passage occurs at the bottom of the folio.

Folio 6a.

6 ༄༅། །ཐམས་ཅད་ཀྱི་རང་བཞིན་སྟོང་པ་མཚན་ཉིད་སྐྱེ་ལམ་སྒྱུ་མ་ལྟ་བུར་རྟོགས

པར་གྱིས་གསུང་། རྗོ་བོ་རྗེ་ཉིད་དང་པོ་མངའ་རིས་ཕྱིན་པའི་དུས་ནམ་མངའ་རིས་སུ་ལོ་གཉིས་བཞུགས

ནས༔ ལྷ་བྱང་ཆུབ་འོད་ཀྱིས་དབུ་མཛད་པ་རྣམས་ལ་གདམས་པ་མང་པོའི་གནང་ནས་རྒྱ་གར་དུ་གཤེགས

པར་དགོངས་ཞལ་ལམ་དུ་བཞུད་ལྷ་བྱང་ཆུབ་འོད་ཀྱིས་ད་རུང་ཞལ་གདམས་ཅིག་ཞུ་བྱས་པས་རྗོ་བོའི

ཞལ་ནས་སྔར་གྱི་ཆོས་ཚོགས་ལགས་གསུང་བ་ལ། ལྷས་ཆེན་སྐྱིད་པས་གདམས་པ་འདི་གནང

བའོ།། ཨེ་མ་ཧོ་མཁྱེན་པ་མཐོ་ཞིང་ཐུགས་དགོངས་ཞིན་ཏུ་གསལ་བའི་གྲོགས་དག་ལ། དང

Folio 6b.

འཁོར་མེད་པའི་བློ་དམན་བདག་གིས་མཆིད་ཕྲིན་གསོལ་བར་མི་རིགས་ཀྱང་སྙིང་ནས་གཅེས་པའི

གྲོགས་པོ་དམ་པ་ཁྱེད་ལ་བདག་གིས་བསྐུལ། བྱིས་པ་བློ་ཆུང་བདག་གིས་གྲོགས་ཀྱི་ཐུགས་ལ

མཆིད་ཕྲིན་འདི་འབུལ་ལོ། གྲོགས་དག་བྱང་ཆུབ་མ་ཐོབ་པར་དུ་བླ་མ་དགོས་པས་བླ་མ་གཉེན

དམ་པ་བསྟེན། གནས་ལུགས་མ་རྟོགས་བར་དུ་ཐོས་པ་དགོས་པས་བླ་མའི་གདམས་ངག

ཉོན༔ ཆོས་ཙམ་ཤེས་པ་ཙམ་གྱིས་སངས་མི་རྒྱ་བས་ཤེས་པས་མི་ཆོག་ཉམས་སུ་ལོང་། སེམས

ལ་གནོད་པའི་ཡུལ་དང་ཐག་བསྲིངས་རྟག་ཏུ་དགེ་བ་འཕེལ་བར་སྡོད། བརྟན་པ་མ་ཐོབ་བར་དུ་འདུ

༄༅། །འཇིགས་གཅོད་པས་དབེན་པའི་ནགས་ཁྲོད་བསྟེན། ཉེ་མ་ངེས་སྐྱེ་བའི་གྲོང་
སྟེན་ད་སེམས་བཟུང་། ནམས་ཀུང་བྱ་བའི་ལས་ལ་ཟིན་པ་མེད་པས་ཚེག་ལ་ལྷན་གྱིས་བསྒྲོད། ཉེ
མཚན་རྣག་ཏུ་དགེ་བ་བསྒོ་ཞིང་རྟག་ཏུ་རང་སེམས་བྱ་ར་གྱིས། མན་ངག་ཡོད་པས་བསྒོམ་པ་མེད
ནམ་ཙི་བྱེད་བླ་མའི་གསུང་བཞིན་བསྒྲུབས། ཀུལ་པ་ཆེན་པོས་བསྒྲུབས་ན་རིང་པོར་མི་ཐོགས་འདུས
བུ་འཕྲུལ་ཏུ་འགྱུར། སྙིང་ནས་ཆོས་བཞིན་བྱས་ན་ལྷ་རྒྱབ་གཞིས་ཀ་ཞེར་ལ་འབྱུང་རྒྱུལ་འདུག །
གྲོགས་དག་འདོད་པ་རྣམས་ལ་ལྷ་ཆུ་འབྲུལ་བཞིན་ངོམས་པ་མེད་པས་ཚིག་ཤེས་མཛོད། དྲོགས

Folio 7b

རྣམ་ང་རྒྱལ་ཁེངས་པའི་སེམས་ཀུན་སློད་ལ་ཞེ་ཞིང་དུལ་བར་གྱིས། བསོད་ནམས་ཟེར་བའི་འདུ་
འཛི་དེ་ཡང་ཆོས་ཀྱི་བར་ཆད་ཡིན་པས་སྤོངས། རྣེ་དང་བཀུར་སྟི་བདུད་ཀྱི་ཞགས་པ་ཡིན་པས་སྤྲད
ཁའི་རྡོ་བཞིན་སོལ། བསྟོད་དང་གྲགས་པའི་ཚིག་རྣམས་སླུ་བྲིད་ཡིན་པས་མཆིལ་སྣབས་བཞིན
ཏུ་དོར། ད་ལྟའི་བདེ་སྐྱིད་གཉེན་གསུམ་འཛོམ་ཡང་ཡུད་ཙམ་ཡིན་པས་རྒྱབ་ཏུ་སྐྱུར། འདི་བས་ཕྱི
མ་རིང་བས་ཕྱི་མའི་རྒྱགས་ཕྱིར་ནོར་རྣམས་གཏེར་དུ་སྦོས། ཐམས་ཅད་བོར་ནས་འགྲོ་བས་ཅིས
ཀྱང་བྱུང་མེད་གང་ལ་འང་ཞེན་མེད་གྱིས། དམན་པ་རྣམས་ལ་སྙིང་རྗེ་སྐྱིད་ལ་ཁྱད་དུ་གསོད་དང་

Folio 8

༨ ༄༅། །བརྐྱལ་བ་སྤྱོངས། ངག་གི་སྡེ་རིས་ཀུན་ལ་ཞེན་ཅིང་ཆགས་པའི་ཕྱོགས་
རིས་མེད་པར་མཛོད། ཡོན་ཏན་ཅན་ལ་ཕྲག་དོག་མི་བྱ་གུས་པར་གྱིས་ལ་ཡོན་ཏན་བླང་། གཞན་སྐྱོན
མི་རྟོག་རང་སྐྱོན་བརྟག་ལ་རང་སྐྱོན་ཕྲག་ངན་བཞིན་དུ་སྤང་། རང་དགེ་མ་བསམ་གཞན་དགེ་བསལ་སྨྲ་
ལ་ཀུན་ལ་བྱམས་བརྩེན་གུས་པར་མཛོད། འགྲོ་བ་ཀུན་ལ་ཕ་མའི་འདུ་ཤེས་བསྐྱེད་ལ་བུ་བཞིན་བྱམས་
པར་གྱིས། རྟག་ཏུ་འཛུམ་པའི་བཞིན་དང་བྱམས་པའི་ཡིད་ཀྱིས་ཁྲོ་མེད་གསོར་པོར་སྨྲོས། འབྲེལ
མེད་སྨྲ་བ་མང་ན་འཁྲུལ་བ་འབྱུང་བ་ཆོད་བཟུང་རན་པར་སྨྲོས། དོན་མེད་བྱ་བ་མང་ལས་ལ་རྒོ་སྤྱོར

Folio 8b.

འཆག་པས་ཚོལ་མེད་བྱ་བ་བཏོག །སྙིང་པོ་མེད་པའི་ལས་ལ་རྩོལ་བ་མ་ཆེ་ངལ་བ་དོན་མེད་ཡིན།
གང་ཡང་འདོད་ཆུང་མི་མཆི་ཕ་རོལ་ལས་ལས་ཀླུབ་པས་ལྷོད་ཀྱིས་སྐྱོང་ཅིག་བདེ། ཀུ་ཡི་དམ་པས
ཁྲེལ་ན་ཤི་དང་འདྲ་བས་གཡོ་མེད་དྲང་པོར་སྤྱོད། ཚེ་འདི་འི་བདེ་སྡུག་སྔ་མའི་ལས་ལས་བྱུང་བས
གཞན་ལ་ཁྲེད་མི་གདའ། བདེ་བ་ཐམས་ཅད་བླ་མའི་བྲིན་རླབས་ལ་གལ་བས་དྲིན་དུ་གཟོ་བར'''
མཛོད༑ རང་རྒྱུད་མ་ཐུལ་བར་དུ་གཞན་རྒྱུད་མི་ཐུལ་བས་ཤ་ཐོག་མར་རང་རྒྱུད་ཐུལ། མཐོང་ཤེས་
མེད་པར་གཞན་དག་སྨིན་པར་མི་ནུས་པས་ན་སྒྲུབ་ལ་བརྩོན་པར་མཛོད། བསགས་པའི་ནོར་རྣམས

Folio 9a.

༄༅། །བཞེངས་ནས་འགྲོ་བར་ངེས་པས་ནོར་ཕྱིར་ལྡོག་མ་སོང་། །ལོངས་སྤྱོད་གཡེངས
བ་འདི་ལ་སྙིང་པོ་མེད་པས་སྦྱིན་པ་ཡོན་གྱིས་བརྒྱན་པ་ཐོང་། ཚེ་འདི་ར་མ་ངེས་ཞིང་ཕྱི་མ་ར་བདེ་བས
རྟག་ཏུ་ཚུལ་ཁྲིམས་རྣམ་དག་བསྲུངས། སྙིགས་མའི་དུས་ན་ཞེ་སྡང་བདོ་བས་ཁྲོ་མེད་བཟོད་པའི་གོ་ཆ
གྱོན༔ ལེ་ལོའི་དབང་གིས་ད་དུང་ལུས་པས་སྒྲུབ་པའི་བརྩོན་འགྲུས་མེ་ལྟར་སྦྱོར། ཡེངས་མ
ལམ་དུ་མི་ཚེ་ཟད་པས་དེ་ནི་བསམ་གཏན་གྱི་བ་རུ་ན། ལོག་ལྟའི་དབང་གིས་གནས་ལུགས་དོན
མི་རྟོགས་པས་ཡང་དག་དོན་ལ་གཞིགས། གྲོགས་དག་འཁོར་བའི་འདམ་རྫབ་འདི་ན་སྐྱིད་མེད༎

Folio 9b.

ཐར་པའི་སྐམ་ལ་ར་གཤེགས། བླ་མའི་གདམས་ངག་ཚུལ་བཞིན་བསྒོམས་ལ་འཁོར་བའི་སྡུག་བསྔལ
རྒྱ་མཚོ་སྐེམས། རང་གི་སེམས་ལ་ཆོས་ལས་དང་ཁ་ཆེག་མིན་གྱིས་གྲོལ་ལ་གསལ་པར་རིགས། དེ་ལྟར་མཛད
ན་བདག་ཀྱང་ངག་འདི་ལ་རང་གཞན་ཀུན་ཡང་སྐྱིད་པ་ར་མཆིས། སྨོངས་པ་བདག་གིས་གདམས་ངག་འདི་ལ
བྱེད་གྱིས་ཅིས་ཀྱང་གསན་པར་ཞུ། ཞེས་ཧེ་བ་ཛྲ་ལྷ་གཅིག་གིས་ལྷ་བཙུན་བྱང་ཆུབ་འོད་ལ་གདམས་པའོ།།
བཅོམ་ལྡན་འདས་འཕགས་མ་སྒྲོལ་མ་ལ་ཕྱག་འཚལ་ལོ། བླ་མ་དམ་པ་རྣམས་ལ་ཕྱག་འཚལ་ལོ། །དེའི
ཀྱི་རྒྱ་གྱེར་གྱིས་ཁོ་བོའི་ཚིག་འདི་དག་ལ་ལེགས་པར་དགོངས་ཤིག །ཕྱི་ནང་སྙིགས་མའི་དུས་ཀྱི་མི་རྣམས

° ཇོ་བོ་ཡེར་པའི་བྲག་ལ་བཞུགས་པའི་ཚེ་ཇོ་ལ་ཆོས་ཞུས་ཤིང་འབར་བས་ གདམས་པ་འདི།།

Folio 10a.

10 ༄༅། །ཀྱེ་ཀེ་ཡེ་ཡུན་ཟླུང་ཞེས་བྱའི་རྣམ་པ་མང་བས། རང་གི་ཚེ་འི་ཚང་ཀྱང་ཟེ་ཙམ་ཟླུབ་པར་
ངེས་པ་མེད་པས་ཀྱང་རྟུ་རང་གི་འདོད་པ་དང་དུ་བླང་བ་ལ་འབད་པར་བྱིས་ཤིག །ཡོ་བྱད་ལ་སོགས་པའི་འཚོ་སྐྱོར་
གི་བྱ་བ་ལ་ཁྲིམ་པ་དང་འདྲ་བར་བྱས་ནས་ངང་ངན་སློང་ངོ་ཞེས་མ་སྨྲ་ཤིག །དགོན་པ་ན་གནས་ཀྱང་འཇིག་
རྟེན་འདི་འི་བྱ་བ་ཉམས་པ་དང་ཉམས་སུ་བོགས་པའི་སྡུག་བསྔལ་དང་ལྡན་པར་བྱས་ནས། ངང་ངན་སློང་དགོན་
པོ་པ་ཡིན་ཞེས་མ་སྨྲ་ཅིག །སེམས་ཚེ་འདི་འི་འདོད་པ་ལ་འདུན་པ་དང་གནོད་སེམས་ལ་སོགས་པ་དང་མ་བྲལ་
བར་བྱས་ནས། ངང་ངན་སློང་དགོན་པ་པ་ཞེས་མ་སྨྲས་ཅིག །དགོན་པ་ན་གནས་ཀྱང་འཇིག་རྟེན་པ་དང་འདྲེས་

Folio 10b.

པ་མི་སྤྱོད་ཅིང་། གང་ཡང་ལྡན་ཅིག་འདུག་པ་དེ་ངག་དང་བྲེ་མོ་འི་གཏམ་དང་། ཁྲིམ་པའི་གཏམ་ལ་སོགས་པས་
དུས་ཡོལ་བར་བྱེད་ཅིང་། ངང་ངན་སློང་དགོན་པ་པ་ཞེས་མ་སྨྲ་ཅིག །ཕ་ལ་ཕ་རོལ་གྱི་གནོད་པ་ཕྲ་མོ་ལ་ཡང་
མི་བཟོད་ཅིང་། གཞན་ལ་ཕན་འདོགས་པ་ཕྲ་མོ་འང་བྱེད་མི་ནུས་པར་ངང་ངན་སློང་བྱང་ཆུབ་སེམས་དཔའ་ཞེས་མ་
སྨྲ་ཅིག །གལ་ཏེ་དེ་ལྟར་སྨྲས་ན་འཇིག་རྟེན་པ་ལ་རྫུན་ཆེན་པོ་སྨྲས་པའོ། །ངོན་ཀྱང་འཇིག་རྟེན་པ་ལ་
དེ་ལྟར་སྨྲ་རུ་བཅུབ་པ་སྲིད་ཀྱང་། གཅིག་ཏུ་ཀུན་དུ་ཟློགས་པ་མེད་པའི་ལྷུན་དང་ལྡན་པ་རྣམས་ལ་མི་
བཅུབ་པོ། གཉིས་སུ་ལས་རྒྱུ་འབྲས་དང་གི་རྗེས་སུ་འབྲང་བས་མི་བཅུབ་པོ། གསུམ་དུ་གང་ཟག

Folio 11a.

༡༡། །ཆོས་ཀྱི་ལྷུན་དང་ལྡན་པ་རྣམས་ལ་མི་འཐུབ་པོ། གཞན་ཡང་འཁོར་གྱིས་བྱང་ཆུབ
ཏུ་སེམས་བསྐྱེད་པའི་དུས་མ། ལྷ་དང་བླ་མའི་སྤྱན་སྔར་ཇི་ལྟར་ཁས་བླངས་པ་ར་ཏན་པར་གྱིས་ཤིག །ཁ་ཟོད
པའི་ཡུལ་ཁྱད་པར་ཅན་དང་ཕྲད་པའི་ཚེ་བཟོད་པར་མི་བྱེད་པར་རོ་ལྟར་དཀའ་ཞེས་མ་སྨྲ་ཅིག །དཀའ་ཡང་
མི་ཐུབ་མི་འཐུབ་པ་ཅན་པར་གྱིས་ཤིག །དཀའ་བ་དང་མི་དཀའ་བའི་རྟོགས་དཔྱོད་ངེས་མེད་པོ་ཁས་མ་བླང་དམ
བཅས་པའི་རྟུལ་ན་ཡིན་གྱིས། ཁས་བླང་དམ་བཅས་ནས་དེ་ནི་ལས་ནམས་ན་ལྷ་དང་བླ་མ་བསླུས་པ་
ཡིན་པས་ཇེལ་ན་དཀའ་ཡང་མི་ཐུབ་མི་ཏུབ་པ་ཏན་པར་གྱིས་ཤིག །གཞན་ཡང་སྒོ་པར་གནས་པའི་སྐྱོན་པ

Folio 11b.

ནི༑ འཇིག་རྟེན་པ་དང་འདྲེས་པ་སྤྱོད་ཞིང་། ནི་ཏུ་ལ་ཞེན་པ་སྤྱོད་བ་ཡིན། དེ་སྤངས་པས་འདོད་པ་ལ་འདུན་པ་ལ་
སོགས་པ་རྟོག་པ་དང་གཡེང་བའི་རྒྱུ་རྐྱེན་ཐམས་ཅད་མེད་པར་ཐུབ་ནས། རང་གི་བྱང་ཆུབ་ཀྱི་སེམས་རིན་པོ
ཆེ་བ་བལྟ་བ་ཡིན་པས། འཇིག་རྟེན་པའི་བྱ་བ་ནམས་ཀྱིས་དགོས་པའི་ལས་ཀྱི་རྗེས་སུ་སྐད་ཅིག་ཀྱང་
མ་འབྲང་ཅིག །ལྷ་ཆོས་ཀུལ་བཞིན་དུ་མ་སྤྱད་བློ་གོམས་སྟོབས་ཆུང་བའི་ཁར་གིས་འཇིག་རྟེན་པའི་རྣམ
པར་རྟོག་པ་ཡང་དང་ཡང་དུ་སྐྱེ་ཞིང་འཕར་ཆེ་བས། དེ་ལ་གཉེན་པོའི་སྟོབས་ཁྱད་པར་ཅན་མ་བསྟེན་ན། །
དགོན་པ་ན་གནས་པ་ལ་དོན་མེད་པ། དེས་ན་གནས་པའི་བྱ་དང་རི་དགས་བཞིན་ནོ།། དེ་དག་ལྟ་དཀའ་བས་ཕྱིས་བུ་

Folio 12a.

72 ༄༅། །ཅིག་ཙམ་ཡང་མེད་པར་གྲོལ་ལ་བསྒོམས་ཅིག །གང་དྲན་པ་ཉམས་པའི་སྣ་ག་དེར་
ན་དེ་ནས་ཉོན་མོངས་པའི་བདུད་འདུག །དེ་ཞུགས་ན་བྱང་ཆུབ་ཀྱི་སེམས་ལ་བར་དུ་གཅོད། དེ་བཅད་ན་གཞན་
དོན་དང་ལ་ཆེ་སྙིང་རྗེ་ཀྱང་རང་སོ་ལས་རོལ་མེད་དོ་སེམས་ཅིག །རང་ཆོས་གྲོལ་སྣམ་ཡང་དོན་མེད་
སྐྱོང་པར་འགྲོ། རིགས་ཀྱི་བུ་ཕ་མ་འཆི་བའི་ཚེ་ན། བླ་མ་དང་ཀྱང་པར་ཅན་རྣམས་ཀྱི་དྲིན་དང་ཡི་སྨུག
སྐྱོ་དུས་མ་གཞུག་ཅིག །གཞན་ཡང་འཇིག་རྟེན་པ་ཆོས་ལ་མོས་པ་རྣམས་ཡི་སྨུག་ཅིང་ཕ་ཆོ་མི་དུས་མ་གཞུག
ཅིག །རང་གི་སེམས་དང་བཀའ་ལུང་གཉིས་བསྟུན་ནས་ཞུ་གྱི་ཡང་དང་ཡང་དུ་མ་གྲོལ་ན་རང་ཆོས་གྲོལ

Folio 12b.

སྣམ་ཡང་ཆོས་དང་གང་ཟག་ཏུ་འཛིན་ནས། འཆི་བའི་ཚེ་ན་བྱང་ཆུབ་ཀྱི་སེམས་འགྱོད་པའི་རྟགས་མེད་
པ་དང་ལོང་གི་རྟགས་བྱུང་ཙམ་གཞན་ཡི་སྨུག་དང་སྐྱ་རེན་སྒྲིབ་ལས་རོལ་མེད་དོ། དེ་བས་ན་རང་མི་ཚེ
ཆོས་ལ་སྐྱུ་སྣམ་པའི་རྒྱལ་དང་ལྡན་པའི་ཆོས་ལ་ཡོ་ལོ་སྤྱོད་དེ་བྱས་ཐལ་འཆི་ཁར་ལག་སྟོང་མ་བྱེད་
ཅིག །མདོར་ན་དགོན་པ་ན་གནས་ཀྱང་ཚེ་འདི་འི་བྱ་བ་མ་སྤངས་འདོད་པའི་འདུན་པ་ལ་བློ་ལོག་ན་ཆོས
ཀྱིས་ཕན་མི་ཐོགས། བྱ་བ་མ་བྱས་ཞེས་བྱ། ཚེ་འདི་ཕྱི་གཉིས་མ་ཉམས་པ་ཅིག་བྱ་སྣམ་ན་ཆོས་
ཞེར་ཕྱིར་དུ་ལོང་བ་པའི་ན། ཞེར་ཕྱིར་དེ་ཡང་ཁ་ཆོས་རྒྱལ་ཆོས་ཅིག་ལུས་མི་འོང་། དེ་བས་ན་གྲོང
ཟླ་ཆོས

Folio 13a.

༄༅། །སྐམ་ཏུམ་སེམས་ཅིག །ལོང་བའི་ལག་ནས་ནོར་བུ་རིན་པོ་ཆེ་ཞིག་ནི་ཤི་ཉིལ་རྡེང་པར་མི

འགྱུར་པོ། །ཉམས་ལེན་བྱེད་དུས་ན་ཡང་ལོ་ངར་བླ་མ་བཀྲང་པར་རྟོགས་པ་ཆེ་ཆུང་རང་གི་སེམས་ལ་རང་གི

སློབ་གཏམས་སྤོབས་ཆེ་ཆུང་ལ་བལྟོས། ཉོན་མོངས་སྤྱི་བྱི་མ་བྱི་ལ་བལྟོས། དག་ཏུ་རང་གི་སེམས་ལ་བྱུང་གྱིས། རང

ལ་རང་ལྷུག་མ་བྱེད། རང་གིས་རང་མ་སླུ། ལྷ་ལ་བླ་མ་མ་སླུ། རང་ཕྱུང་གཞན་ཕྱུང་མ་བྱེད། ཚེ་འདི་ཕྱི་བ་ནམས་ཀྱང

ཉམས་པར་བྱ་རྒྱུ་འདི་ཉམས་ལ་པ་ཡིན། དཔེར་ན་རང་གི་མདུན་ནས་མི་གཅར་བའི་ཕུང་པོ་ཅིག་འདུག་ན་དེ་རང་གིས

རྒྱུར་དུ་ཕྲུགས་ལ་འཐོར་སྒོས་ལ། གཞན་ཞིག་གིས་ཀྱང་གྲོགས་བྱས་ཞལ་འདི་ན་ཅིའི་ཕྱིར་མི་དགའ། དེ་བཞིན

Folio 13b.

ཏུ་ཚེ་འདིའི་རྣམ་པར་རྟོག་པ་ཐམས་ཅད་ནི་རང་གི་གཉེན་པོ་ཡང་ཚོད་ཀྱིས་སྤོང་དགོས་པ་ལ། བླ་མ་དང་གྲོགས

ཁྱད་པར་ཅན་གྱིས་སྤོང་གྲོགས་བྱས་པ་ལ་ཁྱད་ཅིའི་ཕྱིར་མི་དགའ། ལྷ་དང་བླ་མའི་སྤྱན་སྔར་སེམས་ཅན་གྱི་དོན

བྱེད་པར་ཁས་བླངས་ནས་སྨིན་པའི་ཡུལ་ལ་བྱེ་བྲག་མ་འབྱེད། ཡུལ་ལ་བྱེ་བྲག་ཡོད་ཀྱང་རང་གི་བྱང་ཆུབ་ཀྱི་སེམས

སྦྱོང་བ་ལ་བྱེ་བྲག་མེད་དོ། གཏོང་པར་བྱེད་པ་ལ་ལེན་མ་ཐོ། གཏོང་པ་ལ་ལོང་གྲོ་ན་བཟོད་པ་ཧི་ཙམ་ན་བསྒོམ། ཉོན

མོངས་པ་ནམ་བྱུང་ཙ་ན་གཉེན་པོ་དྲན་དགོས་པ་ཡིན། ཉོན་མོངས་པ་ཁ་རྒྱལ་ཏུ་བཏང་བའི་ཆེས་ཀྱིས་དགོས་པ་ཅི

ཡོད༔ དེ་བས་ན་ཀྱོད་ཀྱི་བྱང་ཆུབ་ཀྱི་སེམས་རིན་པོ་ཆེ་ལ་བལྟ་བ་ལ། ཐུན་པ་ནམས་པའི་བུ་གའི་སྐབས་སྐར

Folio 14a.

18 ༄༅། །ཁྱད་པར་ཅན་ལ་བརྟེན། གྲོགས་ངན་པ་དང་མ་འགྲོགས་གནས་ངེས་མེད་དུ་
སྡོད་ཅིང༔ གཞི་གཅིག་ལ་བྲག་པ་སོག་གཤིན་མ་འདུག །ཅི་བྱེད་ཆོས་དང་བསྟུན་ལ་གྱིས། ཅི་བྱས་ཉིན
མཚམས་པའི་གཉེན་པོའི་འགྲོ་བ་གྱིས། དེ་ལྟར་བྱས་ནས་ཡང་དག་པའི་ཆོས་ཡིན་པས་དེ་ལ་བརྩོན་པར་
གྱིས༔ བརྒྱ་ལ་རང་རྒྱུད་ལ་ཡོན་ཏན་སྐྱེས་ན་ང་རྒྱལ་གྱིས་མ་སྨྲ་ཅིག །བདུད་ཀྱི་ངང་དུ་འགྲོའོ། །
པས་མཐའི་གནས་སུ་གནས་ནས་བདག་གིར་ཞི་བ་དང་དུལ་བར་གྱིས། འདོད་པ་ཆུང་བ་དང་ཆོག་ཤེས་པར་
གྱིས༔ རང་གི་ཡོན་ཏན་ལ་མ་ལྟ། གཞན་གྱི་སྐྱོན་ལ་མ་ཆོས། འཛེགས་པ་དང་བག་ཆ་མེད་པར་གྱིས

Folio 14b.

རྣམ་པར་རྟོག་པ་མ་ཆེ། བསམ་པ་བཟང་པོ་གྱིས། ལོག་པ་ལ་མ་ཡེངས་པར་རྒྱུན་དུ་ཆོས་སེམས། །
ངེས་ཤེས་བཟུང་། ཕམ་ལེ་ལོང་། ཡུས་ཁ་སྐྱུངས། ཞེ་འདོད་ཕྱོགས་བརྗོད་སེམས་བསྐྱེད། གང་ལ་ཡང
ཆོ་རིག་པར་གྱིས། མགུ་ལྟ་ཞིང་གསོ་ལྟ་བ་ཅིག་ངོས། ཤེ་ལྕགས་ལྟར་འཇིག་རྟེན་པ་ལ་ཕྲེས་མི་ཆོས
མ་སྤྱོད་ན་ཆོས་པ་མིན་ནོ། ལོ་ནམ་རྣམ་བཞི་མ་སྤྱོད་ན་རབ་ཏུ་བྱུང་བ་མིན་ནོ། འདོད་ན་མ་སྤྱངས་ན
དགེ་སློང་མིན་ནོ། བྱམས་སྙིང་རྗེ་མེད་ན་བྱང་ཆུབ་སེམས་དཔའ་མིན་ནོ། བྱ་བ་མ་སྤངས་ན་སྒོམ་ཆེན
མིན་ནོ། འདོད་པས་མ་ཚེ་ལ་ཅིག །མངོན་ན་སྒོན་པ་ན་གནས་སྐྱ་བྱ་བ་མ་མང་བར་ཆོས། །

Folio 15a

༄༅། །ཧཕའ་ཞིག་བསྒྲིམ་ལ་ནམ་འཆི་བའི་ཚེ་སེམས་ལ་འགྱུར་བ་མེད་པ་ཙིག་གྲིས་ཙིག།
ཅེས་གསུངས་ཡང་ཇོ་བོའི་ཞལ་ནས། ད་ལྡ་སྙིགས་མའི་དུས་སུ་ཡོ་ལོ་གཞོན་པའི་དུས་མ་ཡིན་པ་སྙི་ངུས་འཚོ་
བའི་དུས་ཡིན། ཆོས་བཟུང་བའི་དུས་མ་ཡིན་འཆམས་ལ་བཟུང་བའི་དུས་ཡིན། འཇིགས་གཡུག་བསྟེན་པའི་
དུས་མ་ཡིན་འབེན་པ་བསྟེན་པའི་དུས་ཡིན། སློབ་མ་སྲུལ་བའི་དུས་མ་ཡིན་རང་ཉིད་སྲུལ་བའི་དུས་ཡིན
ཚིག་རྗེས་བཟུང་བའི་དུས་མ་ཡིན་དོན་ལ་ཞལམ་པའི་དུས་ཡིན། ཕན་ཚུན་འགྲོ་བའི་དུས་མ་ཡིན་ས་
གཅིག་ཏུ་སྡོད་པའི་དུས་ཡིན་གསུངས་སོ། ། །དགེ་བཤེས་སྟོན་པ་ལ་སློབ་མ་སྐྱུ་མཆེད་གསུམ་གྱིས་

APPENDIX D

The Tibetan Sexagenary Cycle

R. N. Bhattacharya
&
Alaka Chattopadhyaya

From the second quarter of the eleventh century A.D., the Tibetans adopted the system of reckoning years in terms of cycles of sixty years. In Tibetan, such a cycle is called the *rab-byuṅ*, which is an equivalent of the Sanskrit word *prabhava*.[1] The European scholars usually refer to it as the Sexagenary Cycle. In the Tibetan calendar, after the completion of one such cycle begins another and an identical one.

Each cycle of sixty years is formed by combining the names of five elements with those of twelve animals. The elements, in the order in which they are repeated within each cycle, are : Iron, Water, Wood, Fire, Earth. The 12 animals, in the order in which they are repeated within each cycle, are : Monkey, Hen, Dog, Pig, Mouse, Ox, Tiger, Hare, Dragon, Serpent, Horse, Sheep. Thus, within the cycle, Earth is again followed by Iron and Sheep by monkey. But each of the 5 elements occurs twice in succession and are joined to two successive animals in the list. Thus, e.g., the following will be some of the successive years within a cycle :

Earth-Dragon
Earth-Serpent
Iron-Horse
Iron-Sheep
Water-Monkey
Water-Hen,
etc. etc.

As we shall presently see, a complete cycle begins with a Fire-Hare year and ends in a Fire-Tiger year. The next cycle starts again with a Fire-Hare year.

To the combination of the Element-and-Animal standing for the name of a year are frequently added also the words "Male" and "Female." Thus, e.g., the full designation of an Earth-Dragon year is Earth-Male-Dragon year, that of an Earth-Serpent year is Earth-Female-Serpent year. But these words Male and Female actually stand for what we call

1. *rab=pra* and *byuṅ=bhava*. J-TED 524 : *rab-byuṅ* is also the name of the first year of the cycle of sixty years.

"even" and "odd" numbers expressing the years. Each of the 5 elements, occurring as it does for two successive years, is alternatively termed Male and Female.

P. Pelliot,[2] to whose contribution is largely due a number of clarifications about the Tibetan Sexagenary Cycle, conjectures that it was basically inspired by the ancient Chinese calendar. His main ground is that the names of the animals and elements as occurring in the two calendars are closely similar.[3] But Laufer[4] vigorously rejects the conjecture and draws our attention to the difference between the two calendars. According to the accounts of the Tibetans themselves,[5] the Sexagenary Cycle was originally invented in a country called Śambhala. From there it went to central India (*madhya-deśa*) and the Tibetans received it from the Indians. But modern scholars have not so far been able to arrive at any agreed view as to the identification of the country called Śambhala[6] and Laufer's[7] categorical assertion that it must have meant Turkestan is, in fact, no more than one of the many possible conjectures. In other words, at the present stage of historical researches, the question of the country where the Sexagenary cycle had its origin should preferably be left as an open one.

---

2. P. Pelliot in JA 1913. 633-667.
3. *Ib*. 660.
4. Laufer in *T'oung Pao* 1913. 587f. On the antiquity of the Chinese system, see T. L. Bullock & Louis H. Gray in ERE iii. 82: "The Chinese calendar, which was practically copied by the Japanese,... is scarcely so ancient as is generally supposed. It is true that at an early period the Chinese became acquainted with a twelve-year cycle of Jupiter, depending on that planet's progress through the twelve signs of the zodiac; but this cycle had in China only astrological significance, whereas in India it became part of the calendrical system."
5. BA ii. 753f.
6. Waddell L 306 calls it a mythical country in the north.
7. Laufer in *T'oung Pao* 1913. 591-2.

What is not uncertain, however, is the history of this calendar from its Indian form to its adoption by the Tibetans. In its Indian form the calendar was known as the Kālacakra. Though what is called the Kālacakra Tantra is usually associated with a large overgrowth of esoteric theories and rituals,[8] Laufer[9] seems to be justified in asserting that, in essence, the Kālacakra or "The Wheel of Time" was nothing but a designation of the Sexagenary Cycle and that this system was introduced into Tibet from central India by way of Kashmir.

For the modern student of Tibetan history and literature, the problem concerning the Sexagenary Cycle is above all a practical one. How are we to reduce its dates into those of the modern European (Christian) calendar and how, moreover, can we convert the latter into the former ? The importance as well as the difficulty of the problem can be well appreciated when we remember that even veritable giants among modern European Tibetologists[10] committed absurd mistakes in the matter of such conversions and that the correct conversion of even a single date had in the past been acclaimed[11] as some kind of real academic feat.

In solving this practical problem, however, the determination of a historical point is absolutely essential. What was the exact year of the adoption by the Tibetans of this Kālacakra

---

8. BA ii. 753-839.

9. Laufer *op. cit.* 1907. 403.

10. e.g. Jaschke (J-TED 552) proposes to identify the Wood-Dog, Wood-Pig, Fire-Mouse and Fire-Ox years as A.D. 1834, 1835, 1836 and 1837 respectively. These years of the Christian calendar are in fact Wood-Horse, Wood-Sheep, Fire-Monkey and Fire-Hen years respectively of the Tibetan calendar.

11. e.g. the correct rendering by S. C. Das of A.D. 1901 as an Iron-Ox year in the joint communication of Schlagintweit and Rockhill to the Dalai Lama. See Laufer in *T'oung Pao* 1913. 577n for other examples.

system, which was also the year—according to them—from which their present calculation of the Sexagenary Cycle began. In other words, the year of their adoption of the Sexagenary Cycle is also the first year of their first cycle. Therefore, without a precise determination of this year, our idea of the entire cycle is likely to be wrong. This is well attested to by the fact that a large number of eminent Tibetologists were actually derailed in matters of Tibetan chronology by the erroneous assumption of Alexander Csoma that the year under consideration was A.D. 1026.[12] Thanks, however, to the work of P. Pelliot[13] and others,[14] it is now definitely ascertained that this year was rather A. D. 1027, the year in which the commentary on Kālacakra called the *Vimala-prabhā* was translated into Tibetan.[15] From this year onwards, the Tibetans adopted the Sexagenary Cycle and hence this year is the first year of the first cycle as current among them.

This date, namely A.D. 1027, is crucial for our understanding of Tibetan chronology. Prior to this, the Tibetans calculated their dates only in terms of the twelve animals,[16] as is evidenced by the historical and quasi-historical records of the earlier period.[17] However, from A.D. 1027 onwards, the Tibetans learnt the advantage of using the new system, i.e. the system of dating by prefixing the Animal-name with that of an Element or of dating according to their present Sexagenary Cycle. The advantage of the new system once realised, even

---

12. Csoma de Koros, *Tibetan Grammar*, Calcutta 1834. This wrong date is accepted by Rockhill, Feer, Foucaux and others. See Laufer in *T'oung Pao* 1913. 576ff.

13. P. Pelliot in JA 1913. 633-667.

14. Laufer *op. cit*. 1913. 570 shows that Father A. Desgodins, as far back as 1899, proposed to fix the beginning of the first year of the Tibetan cycle at A.D. 1027.

15. Roerich *A Text-book of Colloquial Tibetan* 44. Cf BA ii. 754, 766.

16. Petech 41.

17. See Roerich *Intro*. to BA i. p. viii-ix.

the later historians began the work of back-calculation in order to re-state or re-construct the date of earlier events in this new form. The most outstanding example of this is the stupendous historical work by 'Gos lo-tsā-ba.

The modern scholars also, after arriving at the definite conclusion that the Sexagenary Cycle was introduced into Tibet in A.D. 1027 and that this year was the first year of the first cycle current among them, found themselves on securer grounds in matters of Tibetan chronology. Important methods are already devised by them for converting Tibetan dates into those of Christian calendar and elaborate charts for the purpose are prepared by Pelliot[18] and Pozdneev.[19] Nevertheless, the existing charts are complicated and are not always easy to handle. Accordingly, efforts are made here to evolve some comparatively simpler methods of converting Tibetan dates into those of the Christian calendar and *vice versa*.

For this purpose, we propose to begin with the first complete cycle of the Tibetans, i.e. the cycle beginning with the year A.D. 1027, which in the Tibetan calendar is a Fire-Hare year, or more specifically, a Fire-Female-Hare year. This cycle is as follows :

Tibetan Year	*Modern Equivalents A D.*	*Tibetan Year*	*Modern Equivalents A D.*
Fire-Hare	1027	Earth-Tiger	1038
Earth-Dragon	1028	Earth-Hare	1039
Earth-Serpent	1029	Iron-Dragon	1040
Iron-Horse	1030	Iron-Serpent	1041
Iron-Sheep	1031	Water-Horse	1042
Water-Monkey	1032	Water-Sheep	1043
Water-Hen	1033	Wood-Monkey	1044
Wood-Dog	1034	Wood-Hen	1045
Wood-Pig	1035	Fire-Dog	1046
Fire-Mouse	1036	Fire-Pig	1047
Fire-Ox	1037	Earth-Mouse	1048

18. P. Pelliot in JA 1913. 664-667.
19. Pozdneev *Erdeni-yin erike*, St Petersburg 1883.

Tibetan Year	Modern Equivalents A.D.	Tibetan Year	Modern Equivalents A.D.
Earth-Ox	1049	Earth-Monkey	1068
Iron-Tiger	1050	Earth-Hen	1069
Iron-Hare	1051	Iron-Dog	1070
Water-Dragon	1052	Iron-Pig	1071
Water-Serpent	1053	Water-Mouse	1072
Wood-Horse	1054	Water-Ox	1073
Wood-Sheep	1055	Wood-Tiger	1074
Fire-Monkey	1056	Wood-Hare	1075
Fire-Hen	1057	Fire-Dragon	1076
Earth-Dog	1058	Fire-Serpent	1077
Earth-Pig	1059	Earth-Horse	1078
Iron-Mouse	1060	Earth-Sheep	1079
Iron-Ox	1061	Iron-Monkey	1080
Water-Tiger	1062	Iron-Hen	1081
Water-Hare	1063	Water-Dog	1082
Wood-Dragon	1064	Water-Pig	1083
Wood-Serpent	1065	Wood-Mouse	1084
Fire-Horse	1066	Wood-Ox	1085
Fire-Sheep	1067	Fire-Tiger	1086

The first year of the next cycle is a Fire-Hare year which is equivalent to A.D. 1087. This is followed by an Earth-Dragon year, which again is followed by an Earth-Serpent year —and so on—the next cycle.

Several facts and some simple rules can be discovered on close examination of the above cycle. Starting with the first year of the cycle as reproduced, we note that $1027=17 \times 60+7$. This shows that 1027 was the seventh year after the completion of 17 previous cycles which we get by back-calculation. The Tibetan name of this year is Fire-Hare. Consequently, the year A.D. 7 was also Fire-Hare and counting from the bottom of the above cycle we find that the Fire-Hare year occupies the 7th place, i.e. if one starts counting from the Iron-Hen year. Thus one finds that *the year A.D. 1 was Iron-Hen.* This is the first important fact discovered on close examination of the cycle.

The name of a year in Tibetan calendar has two parts—the name of an animal and that of an element. There are 12 animals appearing cyclically in the following order : Monkey, Hen, Dog, Pig, Mouse, Ox, Tiger, Hare, Dragon, Serpent, Horse, Sheep. These animals will henceforth be numbered as : 0, 1, 2, 3, 4, 5, 6, 7, 8, 9, 10, 11 respectively.

Next we write down multiples of 12 :

12, 24, 36, 48, 60, 72, 84, 96, 108, 120, 132, 144, 156, 168, 180, 192, 204, 216, 228, 240, 252, 264, 276, 288, 300 ;

312, 324, 336, 348, 360, 372, 384, 396, 408, 420, 432, 444, 456, 468, 480, 492, 504, 516, 528, 540, 552, 564, 576, 588, 600...

That 300 is the first round number (with two zeros at the end) which is the multiple of 12 is the second important fact and leads to the first simple but important rule in this discussion :

All multiples of 12 form a periodic cycle with period 300.

After obtaining this rule, the figures in the second numerical paragraph above (312, 324, etc.) may be dispensed with, for the numbers in this paragraph can be written down from those in the first paragraph by adding 300 to each of them. In fact, all subsequent multiples of 12 can be written in a similar way from the first paragraph by adding 300 or any multiple thereof.

We now turn to the five elements in the nomenclature of the Tibetan calendar. These elements are : Iron, Water, Wood, Fire and Earth, appearing in that order. The Sexagenary Cycle shows that each element is repeated twice before being followed by the next element, so that these form a cycle of ten. Let us take a pair of consecutive Iron years—say A.D. 1030 and 1031. Addition or substraction of 10 or any multiple thereof will always give Iron years. Thus : 1030, 1031 ; 1040, 1041 ; 1050, 1051 ; 1060, 1061 ; 1070, 1071 ; 1080, 1081 etc. are all Iron years. Also, substraction of 1030, which is equal to 103 x 10, shows that the following years of the Christian era are also Iron years : 0, 1 ; 10, 11 ; 20, 21 ; 30, 31 etc.

For mathematical convenience, we have denoted here by

A.D. 0 the year preceding A.D. 1, though it is more conventional to denote that year as 1 B.C.

Inspection reveals the second simple rule in this discussion : *A.D. numbers ending in 0 or 1 correspond to the element Iron of the Tibetan calendar.*

Since in the Sexagenary Cycle, the Iron-pair is followed by Water-pair, Wood-pair, Fire-pair and Earth-pair, in that order, we also get the following corollary to the second rule :

A.D. numbers ending in 2 or 3 correspond to Water ; those ending in 4 or 5 correspond to Wood, those ending in 6 or 7 to Fire, and those in 8 or 9 to Earth.

In the Tibetan calendar, some distinction or anti-thesis is introduced between the two repetitions of each element. As we have already seen, the first appearance of an element is regarded as Element-Male and its repetition as Element-Female. In our system, it will be observed that *even*-A.D. numbers correspond to Elements-Male and *odd*-A.D. numbers to Elements-Female. As already pointed out, the year A.D. I was Iron-Hen or more specifically Iron-Female-Hen.

The correspondence between the last digits of the A.D. numbers and the elements may be set out in the form of a table.

Table I

0	Iron-Male
1	Iron-Female
2	Water-Male
3	Water-Female
4	Wood-Male
5	Wood-Female
6	Fire-Male
7	Fire-Female
8	Earth-Male
9	Earth-Female

Further, if one applies to the Sexagenary Cycle the rule that *even* last digits correspond to Elements-Male and *odd* last digits to Elements-Female, then one finds that the Animals

Monkey, Dog, Mouse, Tiger, Dragon and Horse always go with Elements-Male, whereas Hen, Pig, Ox, Hare, Serpent and Sheep always go with Elements-Female. Referring to the numbers associated with these animals in our scheme, it will be observed that animals numbered *even* go with Elements-Male and those numbered *odd* go with Elements-Female.

We can now prepare the following Table of animals.

Table II

Elements-Male		*Elements-Female*	
0	Monkey	1	Hen
2	Dog	3	Pig
4	Mouse	5	Ox
6	Tiger	7	Hare
8	Dragon	9	Serpent
10	Horse	11	Sheep.

Finally, we prepare the following Table of the multiples of 12 not exceeding 100 :

Table III

12, 24, 36, 48, 60, 72, 84, 96.

How to use the Tables

With the help of Tables I, II and III, we can solve the problem of conversion of the Christian calendar to the Tibetan calendar and *vice versa.*

A) *Conversion of the Christian Calendar to Tibetan Calendar :*

Take a number representing any year of the Christian era. The last digit of the number will, in accordance with Table I, give the name of the Element, indicating also Male or Female. The remainder, after division of this number by 12, will give the name of the Animal from Table II. Thus one gets the names of both Element and Animal of the year in the Tibetan calendar.

Illustrations :

1. Take the year 1043 A.D. The last digit being 3, the

required Element is Water-Female (Table I). Next

1043=12 X 86+11.

The remainder 11 corresponds to Sheep (Table II). Therefore, the required year in the Tibetan calendar is Water-Female-Sheep. If the word Female is dropped, the identification is still unique, for according to Table II, Sheep can go with element Female only.

2. Take, again, the year A.D. 1966. The last digit 6 shows that the required element is Fire-Male (Table I). Now, 1966=12 X 163+10. The remainder 10 corresponds to Horse. The required year is Fire-Male-Horse or simply Fire-Horse.

B) *Conversion of the Tibetan Calendar to Christian Calendar* :

Take any Tibetan year, say Earth-Tiger. Since Tiger can go only with Element-Male (Table II), the fuller name of the year must be Earth-Male-Tiger. By Table I, the element Earth-Male shows that the last digit of the required Christian year must be 8. Now, in Table II, the animal Tiger is numbered 6. Go on adding to this number 6 all multiples of 12 (Table III) until a number ending in 8 is obtained. Thus : 6+12=18. The earliest Earth-Tiger or Earth-Male-Tiger year of the Christian era is A D. 18.

Now, go on adding to 18 the number 60 and its multiples not going beyond 300. Thus : A.D. 18, 78, 138, 198, 258 are all Earth-Tiger years. Other Earth-Tiger years are obtained by adding 300 and its multiples to those. Such are :

A.D. 318, 378, 438, 498, 558,
618, 678, 738, 798, 858,
918, 978, 1038, 1098, 1158, etc.

Take another illustration : Wood-Serpent. In Table II, Serpent is numbered odd (9) and must go with Element-Female. In Table I, Wood-Female corresponds to 5. We are to add to 9 the numbers of Table III until we get a number ending in 5.

9+12=21 ; 9+24=33 ; 9+36=45. So 45 is one of the required numbers. Other required numbers are obtained by adding 60 and its multiples to 45. Thus : 45, 105, 165, 225, 285. Still other required numbers are obtained by adding 300 and its multiples. Thus, Wood-Serpent or Wood-Female-Serpent year of the Tibetan calendar corresponds to any one of the following years of the Christian calendar :

A.D. 45, 105, 165, 225, 285
345, 405, 465, 525, 585
645, 705, 765, 825, 885
945, 1005, 1065, 1125, 1185, etc.

It should be noted that Table III needs be used only in the problem of converting the Tibetan calendar to the Christian calendar and not in the other problem.

Further, the Tibetan equivalents of the Christian years obtained by the above methods are always categorical, whereas when the Tibetan year is mentioned without specifying the cycle (*rab-byuṅ*), we get only a number of possible equivalents in terms of the Christian calendar but not the specific year. When, however, the cycle is specified, it is possible to get the specific equivalent. Thus, the Tibetans say that the present cycle is the sixteenth cycle (i.e. beginning with the cycle starting from A D. 1027). It is possible, therefore, to find the exact equivalents of the years mentioned in this cycle. The Fire-Hare year of this cycle, e.g., is A.D. 1927. The Earth-Dragon year of this cycle, again, is 1928.

Bibliography
&
Abbreviations

ASR - Archaeological Survey of India : Reports.

BA - The Blue Annals. The *Deb-ther-sṅon-po* of 'Gos lo-tsā-ba, tr. Roerich, G.N. 2 vols. Calcutta 1949 & 1953.

Bagchi P. C. - *Bauddha-dharma-o-sāhitya* (Bengali). Calcutta.

Bhāratī - Bengali Monthly.

Bell, C. A. - *Religion of Tibet.* Oxford 1931.

- *Tibet : Past & Present.* Oxford 1927.

Bose, P.N. - *Indian Teachers of Buddhist Universities.* Madras 1923.

Briffault, R. - *Mothers.* 3 vols. London 1952.

Bühler, G. - *Indian Paleography.* Calcutta 1959.

Bu-ston - *A History of Buddhism.* tr. Obermiller, E. 2 Parts. Heidelberg 1931-32.

Chanda, R.P. - *Indo-Aryan Races.* Rajshahi 1916.

Chatterjee, S.K. - *Origin and Development of the Bengali Language.* 2 vols. Calcutta 1926.

Cordier, P. - *Catalogue du fonds tibetain de la bibliotheque Nationale. 2e partie.* Index du bsTan-'gyur. Paris 1909-15.

Csoma de Koros - *Grammar of the Tibetan Language.* Calcutta 1834.

D-TED - Das, S. C. - *A Tibetan-English Dictionary.* Calcutta 1960.

Das, S. C. - *Indian Paṇḍits in the Land of Snow.* Calcutta 1893.

- *Journey to Lhasa and Central Tibet.* London 1902.

Dasgupta, S. B. - *Introduction to Tantric Buddhism.* Calcutta 1958.

- *Obscure Religious Cults.* Calcutta 1946.

Datta, B. N. - *Mystic Tales of Lama Tāranātha.* Calcutta 1957.

Deb-ther-dmar-po. The Red Annals. tr. Tucci. Rome 1959.

Deb-ther-sṅon-po. See BA.

dGe-'dun-chos-'phel - Guide to Buddhist Sacred Places in India (in Tibetan). Calcutta 1939.

Diringer, D. - *Alphabet*. London 1953.

Dikshit, K. N. - *Excavations at Paharpur*. Delhi 1938.

EI - Epigraphica Indica.

Elliot (& Dowson) - *The History of Muhammadan India as told by its own Historians*. London 1867.

ERE - Encyclopaedia of Religion and Ethics. ed. Hastings, 13 vols. Edinburgh. 1908-18.

Francke, A. H. - *Antiquities of Indian Tibet*. Part I Delhi 1914; Part II Delhi 1926.

- *A History of Western Tibet*. London 1907.

'Gos lo-tsā-ba. See BA.

GOS - Gaekwad's Oriental Series.

Guenther, H.V. - *Life and Teachings of Nāro-pā*. Oxford 1963.

HB - *History of Bengal*. Vol. I. ed. R. C. Majumdar. Dacca 1943.

IA - Indian Antiquary.

IC - Indian Culture.

IGI - The Imperial Gazetteer of India. ed. Hunter, W. W. 9 vols. London 1881.

IHQ - Indian Historical Quarterly.

ISPP - Indian Studies : Past & Present.

JA - Journal Asiatique.

James, E. O. - *Cult of the Mother Goddess*. London 1959.

JASB - Journal of the Asiatic Society of Bengal.

JBORS - Journal of Bihar & Orissa Research Society.

JBTS - Journal of the Buddhist Text Society of India.

JRAS - Journal of the Royal Asiatic Society.

JUPHS - Journal of the U. P. Historical Society.

Jīvanī-koṣa (Bengali). ed. Sashibhusan Vidyalamkara.

J-TED. Jaschke, H.A. - *A Tibetan-English Dictionary*. London 1958.

Klaproth, J. - *Description du Tubet etc*. Nouv. Jour. Asiat. iv 80 vi 160.

Koppen, C.F. - *Lamaischie Hierarchie und kirche*. Berlin 1857-9.

La-dvags-rgyal-rabs. See Francke AIT ii.

Lalou, M. - *Répertoire du Tanjur d'aprés le catalogue de P. Cordier*. Paris 1933.

Law, B.C. - *India as Described in Early Texts of Buddhism and Jainism*. London 1941.

Lévi, S. - *Lé Nepal*. 3 vols. Paris 1905-8.

Majumdar, R. C. & others - *Advanced History of India*. London 1950.

Majumdar, R. C. - *Ancient Indian Colonies in the Far East*. Vol. II - Suvarṇadvīpa. Part I Calcutta 1937 ; Part II Calcutta 1938.

Monier-Williams, M. - *A Sanskrit-English Dictionary*. Oxford 1899.

Needham, J. - *Science and Civilization in China*. Vol. II. Cambridge 1966.

Petech, L. - *A Study in the Chronicles of Ladakh*. Supplement to IHQ xiii & xv.

Prajñā. Gangtok 1961.

Pranavananda, Svami - *Kailasa and Manasarovara*. Calcutta 1949.

Regmi, D. R. - *Medieval Nepal*. Part I. Calcutta 1965.

Richardson, H. E. - *Tibet and its History*. London 1962.

Robequain, C. - *Malaya, Indonesia, Borneo and the Philippines*. London 1954.

Rockhill, W. W. - *Diary of a Journey through Mongolia and Tibet*. Washington 1894.

- *Land of the Lamas*. London 1890.
- *Life of Buddha*. London 1907.
- *Notes on the Ethnology of Tibet*. Washington 1895.

Roerich, G. N. - See BA.

Sāhitya - Bengali Monthly.

Samaddar, J. N. - *Glories of Magadha*. Patna 1927.

Sankalia, H. D. - *University of Nālandā*. Madras 1934.

Sastri, H. P. - *Advaya-vajra-saṃgraha* (ed.) GOS xl.

- *Bauddha-gān-o-dohā*. (Bengali). Calcutta.
- *Prācīn-bāṅglār-gaurava*. (Bengali). Calcutta 1963.

Schlagintweit, E. - *Buddhism in Tibet*. London 1863.

Sendai - *A Complete Catalogue of the Tibetan Buddhist Canons.* ed. Hakuju Ui & others. Sendai 1934.

Sircar, D. C. - *Indian Paleography.* (In Press)

Smith, V. - *Oxford History of India.* Oxford 1941.

Sogen, Y. - *Systems of Buddhistic Thought.* Calcutta. 1912.

Stcherbatsky, F. T. - *Conception of Buddhist Nirvāṇa.* Leningrad 1927.

- *Buddhist Logic.* 2 vols. New York 1962.

Sum-pa - *dPag-bsam-ljon-bzaṅ.* ed. S. C. Das. Calcutta 1908.

Tāranātha - *dGos-'dod-kun-'byuṅ.* Benares 1964.

Tibetan Tripiṭaka. Tokyo-Kyoto 1957-58.

T'oung Pao.

2500 Years of Buddhism. ed. Bapat, P.V. New Delhi 1956.

Vidyabhusana, S.C. - *History of the Medieval Schools of Indian Logic.* Calcutta 1909.

Waddell, L.A. - *Lamaism.* Cambridge 1959.

Winternitz, M. - *A History of Indian Literature.* Vol. ii. Calcutta 1933.

Wylie, T.V. - *Place-name Index to G. N. Roerich's translation of the Blue Annals.* Roma 1957.

ZDMG - Zeitschrift der Deutschen Morgenlandischen Gesselschaft.

INDEX

Names of persons, places and texts, only when considered specially significant, are included in the Index. Texts alphabetically arranged in *Appendix B* are not included in the Index excepting when these occur with special significance also outside the Appendix. The following abbreviations are used :

b—biography
g—Dīpaṃkara's *guru*
h—history
i—Indian paṇḍita who went to Tibet
k—Tibetan king
m—Tibetan monk
p—Tibetan place
t—Tibetan translator
v—monastery